W9-BPR-014

0°   20°   0°

Murmansk

Narvik

White Sea

SWEDEN   FINLAND   Archangel

Trondheim

NORWAY

S O V I E T   60°

Bergen   Oslo   Stockholm   Leningrad

ESTONIA

NORTH   DENMARK   LATVIA   Moscow

SEA   *BALTIC SEA*   LITHUANIA   U N I O N

GREAT   NETH.   Berlin   EAST   Warsaw   Tula

EIRE   BRITAIN   GERMANY   PRUSSIA   POLAND

London   BEL.

English Channel   Dunkirk   CZECHOSLOVAKIA

Paris   Maginot   Taganrog

Line   AUSTRIA   HUNGARY

F R A N C E   SWITZ.   RUMANIA

Vichy   ITALY   YUGOSLAVIA   *BLACK SEA*

Rome   BULGARIA   40°

CORSICA   ALBANIA   T U R K E Y

Madrid   SARDINIA   GREECE

GAL   SPAIN   *M E D I T E R R A N E A N*   SICILY   CRETE   SYRIA

Gibraltar   SPAN. MOROCCO   TUNISIA   LEBANON

anca   *S E A*   Benghazi   Alexandria   PALESTINE   JORDAN

MOROCCO   Tobruk   Mersa   Cairo

ALGERIA   Matruh   *Suez*   SAUDI

Canal   ARABIA

LIBYA   EGYPT   *RED*

SEA

20°

FRENCH WEST AFRICA

FRENCH   ANGLO-EGYPTIAN   ERITREA

EQUATORIAL   SUDAN

AFRICA

GOLD   ETHIOPIA

COAST   NIGERIA

Takoradi   0°   20°   40°   H. Faye

ALSO BY JOSEPH P. LASH

• • •

From the Diaries of Felix Frankfurter
Eleanor: The Years Alone
Eleanor and Franklin
Dag Hammarskjöld: Custodian of the Brush-Fire Peace
Eleanor Roosevelt: A Friend's Memoir

JOSEPH P. LASH

Roosevelt

AND

Churchill

1939–1941

The Partnership That Saved the West

W·W·NORTON & COMPANY·INC·

NEW YORK

Grateful acknowledgment is made to Her Britannic Majesty's Stationery Office for permission to reproduce extracts from documents in the Public Records Office; to Cassell & Company and G. P. Putnam's Sons for permission to quote from *The Diaries of Sir Alexander Cadogan,* edited by David Dilks; to Houghton Mifflin Company and Cassell & Company for permission to quote from Winston S. Churchill's *The Second World War: The Gathering Storm,* copyright 1948, *Their Finest Hour,* copyright 1949, *The Grand Alliance,* copyright 1950; to Houghton Mifflin Company and The Times Publishing Company, London, for permission to quote from Anthony Eden's *The Reckoning;* to Atheneum Publishers and William Collins Sons & Co., Ltd., for permission to reprint excerpts from volume II of *The Diaries and Letters of Harold Nicolson: The War Years 1939–1945,* edited by Nigel Nicolson, copyright 1967 by William Collins Sons & Co., Ltd.

Published simultaneously in Canada by George J. McLeod Limited, Toronto. Printed in the United States of America.

FIRST TRADE EDITION

The text of this book is typeset in Linotype Times Roman. Composition, printing, and binding are by the Vail-Ballou Press, Inc.

Library of Congress Cataloging in Publication Data
Lash, Joseph P   1909–
   Roosevelt and Churchill, 1939–1941.
   Bibliography: p.
   Includes index.
   1. World War, 1939–1945—Diplomatic history.
2. Roosevelt, Franklin Delano, Pres. U.S.
1882–1945.   3. Churchill, Winston Leonard Spencer,
Sir, 1874–1965.   4. World War, 1939–1945—United
States.   5. World War, 1939–1945—Great Britain.
I. Title.
D753.L27   940.53'2   76–18276

ISBN 0 393 05594 9

1 2 3 4 5 6 7 8 9 0

TO BENJAMIN V. COHEN

Contents

Photographs follow page 264

Introduction

EVERY GENERATION rewrites history and biography in terms of its own interests, values, and styles. The opening of the Roosevelt-Churchill correspondence, of the war-years files of the British foreign office and war cabinet, of the Roosevelt Map Room papers and other previously sealed materials at Hyde Park, as well as of numerous privately held diaries would alone justify a fresh look at the men and events that were so superbly chronicled by Churchill himself and by Robert Sherwood in *Roosevelt and Hopkins*. But there is, too, the new significance that the decline of empire, America's disastrous involvement in Asia, and Watergate give to the actions and decisions of Roosevelt and Churchill, especially in the critical months between the outbreak of war in September, 1939, and Pearl Harbor, when the survival of democracy itself hung in the balance.

As the tributes flooded in on one of his birthdays toward the end of his life, Churchill remarked to his daughters: "I have achieved a great deal to achieve nothing in the end." My first inclination when I read this remarkable statement was to seek an explanation in his unhappy childhood, in the depressions (he called them his "black dog" moods) that perhaps made it impossible for him ever to savor the joy of accomplishment, or to see in it the response of an old man to limitation and mortality. But there is another, more plausible, explanation. Although Churchill bestrode the war years like a twentieth-century colossus, the tides of history had set against the institution he was most concerned to preserve—the structured world of his Victorian youth headed by a powerful monarch, environed by a gleaming empire. Not all his successes as war leader could salvage that world; indeed, his very successes speeded its transformation. There were, nevertheless, majestic achievements. Without Churchill's leadership and the partnership that he established with Roosevelt, it is doubtful that Britain could have survived as an independent nation and the British as a free people.

American interest in this story has been revived because of Vietnam and Watergate. At the height of America's disenchantment with its involvement in Vietnam, I was asked on a television program what the difference was between the presidential usurpations of power that took the United States into the Vietnam war and Roosevelt's road to Pearl Harbor. Was deception and trickery of Congress and the public not resorted to in both cases? My answer at the time was that history had justified Roosevelt. His analysis of the nature of Hitlerism and the threat that it represented to the United States had been vindicated by what historians subsequently learned.

That was my answer in 1971. But as I examined Roosevelt's conduct before Pearl Harbor more closely, I realized I had done him an injustice—that at no point did he move without having public opinion with him and that a central feature of his greatness was his ability to mobilize public opinion to get from Congress the action that he deemed necessary. Woodrow Wilson once said of the president that "if he rightly interpret the national thought and boldly insist upon it, he is irresistible." Roosevelt's leadership in 1940–1941 illustrates Wilson's point. There is, nevertheless, little doubt that in the autumn of 1941 Roosevelt was seeking to provoke an undeclared war with Germany because he knew that he could not get a declaration of war from Congress. We leave it to the reader to judge whether he was right. I think he was.

Vietnam and Watergate have generated a powerful antipathy to what has been called the "imperial presidency." There is a widespread sense in the United States that a strong executive is dangerous [as "proven" by Watergate] and foreign intervention for any reason is disastrous [as "proven" by Vietnam]. It is prudent, however, before the pendulum swings too far, to look at a critical moment in the history of the English-speaking peoples when, spurred by disenchantment with World War I, a congressional effort to establish its supremacy over foreign policy almost led to disaster. In that period, strong presidential leadership, acting on the Jeffersonian interpretation of the Constitution that "the transaction of business with foreign nations is executive altogether," saved American freedom.

Many of the abuses of power that almost subverted the Republic in recent years had their origins in practices that began in the pre–Pearl Harbor period. Espionage, Fascist and Communist infiltration of the isolationist movement, strikes in the defense plants were facts that Roosevelt, responsible for the nation's safety, could not ignore. But the agencies he created and the methods he authorized to combat them were dangerous, as indeed were the draft, the enlargement of the army and navy, and all the emergency powers that Congress delegated to the president. Roosevelt recognized this. "When the war is won," he said, "the powers under which I act automatically revert to the people—to whom they belong."

We fought a total war with minimum encroachment on civil liberties. The press remained free. Elections were held as usual and fought vigorously. Human rights were enlarged.

If, after that war, secrecy and loyalty checks, abuses of power by the CIA and the FBI, and usurpations of power by a president came close to undermining freedom in the United States, the responsibility is not with the generation that had to fight a total war, but with their successors, who neglected the warning of John Dewey that freedom is a heritage that can be possessed only by rewinning it. Every generation must win it anew.

The period that is covered in this book is one of the great moments in the history of the English-speaking peoples. It bears retelling in light of what we now know about the Roosevelt-Churchill relationship, a unique partnership between two enormously egocentric men whose affection for each other altered the course of history.

...

THE ORIGINAL SUGGESTION for a book based on the Roosevelt-Churchill correspondence came from George Brockway, the president of W. W. Norton & Company, but the day-to-day chore of keeping my spirits from flagging by judiciously administered doses of praise mixed with no-nonsense advice was my editor's, Evan W. Thomas. He is a lovely man without guile, who does not hesitate to pronounce judgment—indeed, feels decidedly uncomfortable until he does—and his appraisals have usually turned out to be sound.

Others who read the manuscript were Trude W. Lash and Jonathan Lash. I have expressed the depth of my gratitude to Trude in *Eleanor and Franklin.* Jonathan brought to his reading of this manuscript not only a lawyer's insistence on exactitude but a stylist's feeling for form and the fresh eye of a generation that was unborn when the events herein described took place. The fact that he found the material worth his careful attention meant a great deal. I am grateful also to Jane Dustan for the careful scrutiny that she gave the galleys.

I worked at many libraries in the course of researching this book. In the first year when I was going through the *Pearl Harbor Attack,* the *Documents on German Foreign Policy,* and similar standard works, I had the use of a desk in the Frederick Lewis Allen Room at the New York Public Library. It was a congenial place to work, and brought me the friendship of several younger writers which has become very precious. There was, of course, my old love, the Franklin D. Roosevelt Library at Hyde Park. In London I found equal helpfulness at the Public Records Office, and in New York the British Information Services were unfailingly cooperative. I made many trips to the Yale University Library, where the late Herman Kahn presided over the Stimson diaries and papers and made his historian's knowledge available to itinerant scholars and writers. I consulted the papers of Harold L. Ickes, Frank Knox, and Felix Frankfurter at the Library of Congress, and those of General Edwin "Pa" Waston at the Alderman Library of the University of Virginia. I made considerable use of the resources of the Oral History Project at Columbia University and was especially benefited by the opening of the marvelous Frances Perkins transcripts. I am obligated to David Kahn, author of *The Codebreakers,* for his helpfulness on some points that came up in connection with Magic and General Bötticher, the German military attaché in Washington before Pearl Harbor.

And I am especially anxious to acknowledge the help and hard work of the copy editor, Carol Flechner, and the designer of the book, Marjorie Flock. Mrs. Freda Weiner typed the manuscript, expertly as always.

A final word—about capitalization. Some have found the copy editor's austere reluctance to use capitals a little disconcerting. It is the standard prescribed by the University of Chicago Press's *Manual of Style,* which is used by W. W. Norton & Company. As a former newspaper reporter I learned that one does not quarrel with an institution's style book. One goes along.

JOSEPH P. LASH

Roosevelt
AND
Churchill

1939–1941

Prologue

I MET Winston Churchill once, but the circumstances were rather special. It was at the White House on New Year's Day, just after Pearl Harbor. I was there at the invitation of Mrs. Roosevelt. The prime minister, with his entourage, had arrived in Washington on December 22 for those meetings with the president code-named Arcadia. He had stayed a week and had then gone up to Canada for a tumultuous reception there that matched the one he had received in Washington. He was due back New Year's Day. On January 1, at breakfast, where Mrs. Roosevelt sat with her house guests in the West Hall, the president sent out word from his bedroom that the prime minister was on his way and that he would like Mrs. Roosevelt to go downstairs and greet him at the door. A few moments later, little Diana Hopkins's sharp ears picked up the chugging of motorcycles, and Mrs. Roosevelt hastened off to do her job as hostess.

At eleven the household climbed into cars to go to church services in Alexandria. George Washington had worshiped there, and there was amused talk among the Americans of the president's roguish pleasure in having the British prime minister lay a wreath at Mount Vernon and pray in Washington's church where the prayer was "George Washington's Prayer for the United States."

At lunch I found myself seated next to the prime minister. I was too awe-struck to open my mouth. There was no necessity. The language cascaded out of him. In my journal I wrote: "He is an exuberant, enormously strong personality, exciting, full of temperament, witty, his phrases resonant with the vigors of the best English stylists, his talk full of imagery."

Bathtubs, he claimed, were a contrivance that America had "foisted" upon the British, but there was nothing like a hot bath before dinner, he conceded, "lying back and kicking one's legs in the air—as at birth."

While he was transferring his hash and poached egg to his plate, the egg slipped from the spoon, but landed safely on the plate. He began to try to set it back on the hash, "to put it on its throne," he explained to Mrs. Roosevelt.

Hitler had sounded awfully anxious in his New Year's Day message, Churchill observed, even invoking Almighty God. "But we have a preemption on the Deity," he added, looking at the president, who was known to be pressing the Russians hard to permit religious freedom. Perhaps it was the prime minister's reference to the Almighty that turned his thoughts to General de Gaulle: "You're being nice to Vichy," he jollied the president, "we're being nice to de Gaulle." He suggested that that was a fair division of labor. The Free French had just occupied Saint Pierre and Miquelon off Newfoundland, much to the distress of the U.S. State Department. The matter should be left to Hull and Halifax, the president indicated. "Hell, Hull, and Halifax," the prime minister muttered.

Shipping was their agenda for the day, the president said, bringing the luncheon to an end. They ought to finish up "those two instruments," Churchill amended, referring to a draft declaration of united purpose and to a directive on unity of command. The president agreed. He would have Secretary Hull and the chiefs of staff at the White House at five. Churchill said he would have his service chiefs and Lord Halifax.

I went into Mrs. Roosevelt's sitting room afterward. She and her secretary "Tommy," Mrs. Malvina Thompson, were comparing impressions of president and prime minister. They asked me mine. The prime minister had the richer temperament, I said, but the president was a more dependable, steadier man in a crisis. Tommy clapped her hands and said she and Mrs. Roosevelt felt the same. The president was more hardheaded, they felt. He was less brilliant, but more likely to do the right thing. The president also gave the impression of being more under control, of never letting himself go.

At dinner the previous evening, before Churchill had returned to the White House from Canada, there had been discussion of the president's realism. Roosevelt had been speaking about his August meeting with Churchill in Argentia. The prime minister had not been able to interest him in intangibles in discussing postwar plans, he said. He was interested in practical arrangements. When he had suggested disarming the aggressors and following it up by progressive disarmament of the victors, Churchill's face had lit up. He had thought it was too advanced an idea for the Americans.

At dinner on New Year's Day, the household reassembled. This time I was seated near the president so that I might talk with him about making a speech to the youth of the world—in a Jefferson setting, perhaps the University of Virginia. He liked the suggestion and told me to take it up with "Pa" Watson, his appointments secretary. He then recalled that the last speech he had given at the University of Virginia was his "stab in the back" thrust at Mussolini. Although il Duce had just brought Italy into the war, the State Department had made the president take the cutting phrase out of the prepared text. On the way to the university, however, Roosevelt had decided to restore it. He asked Mrs. Roosevelt what she thought. If he felt he should, he ought to use it had been her advice. And he did. She did not know at the time whether it was a wise choice, Mrs. Roosevelt took up the story during this recollection, and still did not. But she knew quite well that the president would have always felt unhappy if he had not done so.

He knew that feeling, Churchill chimed in. He was always having to take things out of his speeches.

The president was asked his impression of Stalin. Was he in direct communication with him? Roosevelt said yes, and then went on to note that Stalin had to rule a very backward people, which he thought explained a good deal. He had previously explained in the same way his collaboration with the Brazilian dictator Getulio Vargas. When Hopkins had returned from Moscow in August, the president continued, he had asked him whether the Soviet leader had a sense of humor, and when Hopkins had answered yes, the president also knew that the Russian leader had a sense of proportion.

Russia was much on everyone's mind. The evening before, Hopkins had been quite enthusiastic about the way the Red Army had rebounded. Instead of being finished as a military force, it suddenly seemed as if it might be able to lick Hitler. Some people, Hopkins observed sarcastically, were beginning to fear it might reach Berlin and that if it did all Europe might become Communist. If the Russians had the stuff to lick Hitler, Hopkins was for them. Fears that Europe might go Communist only betrayed insecurity about our own system. He also expressed the belief—perhaps it was more a matter of hope—that Communism would change character: the economics of Communism will be retained but civil liberties will grow once the terrific pressure of capitalist encirclement was lifted.

Another dinner guest, the ruddy and vigorous eighty-four-year-old Dr. Endicott Peabody, headmaster of Groton when Roosevelt had been a pupil there in the 1890s, found Hopkins's enthusiasm for the Red Army a little difficult to take. What about Clarence Streit's plan for "Union Now" based on Anglo-American partnership? It was too insular, Hopkins replied, and asked, What about China and Russia? Moreover, the Streit plan had no chance politically. Despite our common heritage and the cultural and political traditions that the United States shared with England, Dr. Peabody persisted. Hopkins minimized these. Americans would soon start griping about England, he feared.

The president appeared to share Hopkins's views and hopes. Was there any discussion or agreement with Stalin on postwar problems? Roosevelt was asked after his comment that Stalin's sense of humor showed a sense of proportion. Stalin was going to sign the Arcadia declaration, the president replied, and it included freedom of religion. Stalin had also agreed that the aggressor nations should be compulsorily disarmed and that a monopoly of arms should be left in the hands of the United States, Great Britain, and the Soviet Union. The Anglo-American condominium that the president had spoken of after his meeting with Churchill at Argentia had been broadened, some of those at dinner noted to themselves.

The Allied Declaration of Unity and Purpose had been finished, we were told, and Mrs. Roosevelt asked whether it could be read to everyone. The president started to demur, but the prime minister said yes and Hopkins went upstairs to get the document. Churchill was enthusiastic over Roosevelt's suggestion that it should be called "Declaration of the United Nations." He had remembered a line from Byron's *Childe Harold's Pilgrimage,* which he proceeded to recite,* and then he read the declaration.

That evening, after dinner, the declaration was to be signed by representatives of the four great powers. There was discussion about whether to the sentence that stipulated "other nations" could sign, the phrase "and other authorities," meaning de Gaulle, should be added. Roosevelt and Churchill wanted to do so, but would Ambassador Litvinov, who was coming in to sign for the Soviet Union, agree? The president suggested that he and Churchill unite and use their greatest blandishments. Churchill was skeptical. Litvinov would have to refer the matter to Moscow. Why not have two documents with two versions and try the "authorities" one on Litvinov first? Churchill suggested. This was done, Eleanor Roosevelt learned later that evening. Litvinov said he would have to refer it back and that it would take two days, so the matter was dropped.

There was talk, as there had been the night before, about the successes of the Red Army and the Nazi failure to reach Moscow. Churchill recalled that in 1918–1919 he had also gotten as far as Tula, just south of Moscow, in his effort to overthrow the Bolsheviks. Now, however, he forgave "the Russians in proportion to the number of Huns they killed."

"Do they forgive you?" Hopkins asked.

"In proportion to the number of tanks I send," Churchill replied.

Roosevelt thought they did not forgive. He was impatient with the unremitting Soviet pressure to recognize their incorporation of the Baltic republics which they had overrun in the period of the Nazi-Soviet pact. Those seemed to him petty matters compared to the immensity of the issues that now had been joined. There had been "two providential acts," the prime minister said—that Russia had come in on the Allied side rather than on Hitler's, and that Japan had not attacked after the president's "stab in the back" speech on June 10, 1940.

The talk turned to unity of command, of General Wavell's designation as overall commander in the Pacific area. He had liked the prime minister's story, the president said, that in the First World War General Foch had been paid by all the Allied powers, not by France alone, and that in his status of generalissimo he was not a French general. Had the French accepted that as a matter of Gallic frugality? he wanted to know. And had the others agreed to pay as a way of keeping a string on him? The prime minister replied that the others had not wanted him to consider himself a French general.

Was his cabinet not giving him the authority? Roosevelt asked Churchill, in reference to some matter they had discussed that afternoon. That started a discussion about cabinets. At the beginning of his administration, Roosevelt said, he had told his cabinet the story in which Abraham Lincoln had voted aye after his whole cabinet had voted no and had then announced

---

* Here, where the sword United Nations drew,
   Our countrymen were warring on that day
  And this is much—and all—which will not pass away.

that the ayes had it. Three months ago, realizing that the personnel of the cabinet had changed drastically since 1933, he told the story again. But in point of fact, he never took votes. It would probably be unconstitutional to take votes, volunteered Lowell Mellett, at the time the United States government's chief information officer.

Was not Harry Hopkins's position in the cabinet a little anomalous? someone inquired. A good name for Harry, said the president, would be "Minister of Omnium Gatherum"—"and scatterem," Mellett added.

He never took votes, Churchill noted, except on matters of taste—for example, should women be admitted to combat duty? Then he added that he could not abide the title "minister without portfolio." It always conjured up a picture of the king giving a minister his title and then holding back his portfolio. Roosevelt wanted to know what would happen to Lloyd George's slush fund* now that he was dead. That fund had ruined Lloyd George, Churchill thought. He was sixty at the end of World War I. He could have accomplished great things had it not been for the fund.

He hoped Churchill would not run on a ticket of "Hang Hitler" after this war as Lloyd George had run on a "Hang the Kaiser" platform after the first war, commented Roosevelt. Churchill deprecated his political possibilities when that time would come, but he had felt better about the kaiser, he added, than he did about Hitler. The kaiser had been egged on by his advisers. Roosevelt recalled Theodore Roosevelt's visit to the kaiser and the latter's showing off of his 150 uniforms much to TR's disgust. The best thing to do with Hitler, the president then said, would be to put him on a ship from which he would disappear,

Eleanor Roosevelt remarked that there was some feeling that the machinery of the Democratic party was beginning to creak from disuse. "The Republicans creaked more," the president interrupted, and would creak even more when he took Wendell Willkie into the government. There would be loud lamentations from the Republicans then. Churchill thought it was good that Willkie was being brought in. He would probably put him over "the corporations," the president said. Mrs. Roosevelt was troubled lest Willkie be given too much power. He ought to be in charge of "civilian defense," Hopkins teased Mrs. Roosevelt, who was co-director of that much maligned and divided agency. She threw up her hands in mock horror. She preferred Mayor La Guardia of New York, she said.

Hopkins then reported that Ambassador Litvinov had arrived and was upstairs pacing up and down like a caged lion. So Hopkins, the president, and the prime minister went up and the rest of the company went to the West Hall for coffee with Mrs. Roosevelt. A little after ten she was told to come to the president's oval study and to bring her guests with her to witness the signing of the declaration.

The president signed first. Harry Hopkins came over to the door where Mrs. Roosevelt and her guests were standing. Perhaps he should have signed

---

* This was a large fund deriving in part from the sale of honors while Lloyd George was prime minister and controlled by him through hand-picked trustees.

as "Commander in Chief," the president remarked. "President ought to do," Hopkins said dryly. Then the prime minister signed. Roosevelt looked at the signature and called to him, "Hey, ought you not to sign 'Great Britain and Ireland?'" Churchill agreed, corrected his signature, and then stalked around the study with a look of great satisfaction on his face. Litvinov signed next. And finally T. V. Soong signed for China. "Four fifths of the human race," observed Churchill.

In the room there was a sense of Hitler's doom having been sealed.

Chapter One

How the Correspondence Began

B Y SEPTEMBER 11, 1939, the day on which President
Roosevelt sent his first letter to the admiralty's first lord,
Winston Churchill, German panzers, in an awesome display of speed and
power, had effectively split up and outflanked the Polish army and positioned
it for the kill. But the war was only beginning. Between Hitler and mastery
of Europe stood the armor and striking power of Britain and France, both
of which (to Hitler's surprise), after some initial hesitation, had honored
their obligation to Poland by announcing themselves to be at war with
Germany. And behind the Western democracies stood the United States, an
uncertain quantity, whose president, when asked by the press on the day the
war began to comment on the question that was uppermost in the minds of
the American people—"Can we stay out?"—had replied: "Only this, that I
not only sincerely hope so but I believe we can and that every effort will be
made by the Administration so to do."[1]

When Hitler gave the order to execute Case White (as the Polish campaign was known during its planning stages), he had assured his generals that
Britain and France would not go to war for Danzig and the Polish Corridor,
and even if they should, they would not wage war aggressively. His "Directive Number One for the Conduct of the War" called for a holding operation
along the Westwall. "Fuehrer will not take it amiss if England were to wage
a sham war," the German army's chief of staff, General Franz Halder, a man
of some independence of mind, noted in his diary, adding three days later,
"decision against evacuation [in the West] shows that he expects France and
England will not take action." His expectations were fulfilled. The French
strategy of "static defense" while the Polish army was being destroyed seemed
to be "a miracle" to the German high command, which shared Hitler's hope
that Anglo-French passivity was a prelude to another Munich.[2]

There were statesmen in London and Paris who were thinking along
such lines. On that same day (September 11), at 12:32 P.M., a dispatch had

come in to the State Department cable room in Washington from the appease-ment-minded U.S. ambassador in London, Joseph Kennedy. It was marked "Personal for the President and the Secretary of State" and contained Kennedy's account of a talk he had had with the king and queen and with Sir Samuel Hoare, British lord privy seal and confidant of Prime Minister Neville Chamberlain. Hoare felt that after Hitler cleaned up Poland, which he was expected to do in four to six weeks, he would then propose to call this war off and come to some agreement with Britain and France. Having been in the forefront of the appeasement policy, Sir Samuel did not recoil at the prospect. He and the British government realized that to continue the war or even simply to maintain the government on a war footing "means complete eco-nomic, financial and social collapse and nothing will be saved after the war is over."

Kennedy thought it important for the president and Secretary of State Cordell Hull to have this insight into British thinking.

It seems to me that this situation may crystallize to a point where the President can be the savior of the world. The British Government as such certainly cannot accept any agreement with Hitler, but there may be a point when the President himself may work out the plan for world peace. Now this opportunity may never arise, but, as a fairly practical fellow all my life, I believe that it is entirely conceivable that the President can get himself in a spot where he can save the world and I have not thought so up to this moment.[3]

The suggestion that Roosevelt take the lead in a new appeasement move because British opinion would no longer allow Chamberlain to do so was not new to Kennedy. In the tense days after the disclosure of the Nazi-Soviet nonaggression pact, when armies were mobilizing and fleets were steaming to battle stations, Roosevelt had appealed to Italy's King Victor Emmanuel, an ineffectual but mildly pro-Allies monarch, to take some initiative to arrest the crisis. An exasperated Kennedy had telephoned Sumner Welles, the dis-tinguished and fastidious undersecretary of state, to protest that the presi-dent's message to King Victor Emmanuel was "lousy" and had pleased no-body in England. The British wanted one thing of the United States and one thing only, "namely that we put pressure on the Poles. They [the British] felt that they could not, given their obligations, do anything of the sort but that we could." As Jay Pierrepont Moffat, chief of the European division, observed in his diary: "As we saw it here, it merely meant that they wanted us to assume the responsibility of a new Munich and to do their dirty work for them. This idea received short shrift from the President, the Secretary, and Sumner Welles down."[4]

On August 30, a few hours before Hitler's armies swarmed across the Polish borders, Kennedy had again broached the subject of appeasement. He had just seen Chamberlain, who, he reported, "is more worried about getting the Poles to be reasonable than the Germans. He feels there is a great body of public opinion in England headed probably by Eden and Churchill who will suggest to the Poles that they give up nothing and that they have Hitler on the run."[5]

The ambassador notwithstanding, Roosevelt and Hull were interested in stiffening the antiappeasement forces in the British government, not in giving Chamberlain protection for a new and bigger Munich. Four hours after Kennedy's telegram was received, Hull cabled him:

The President desires me to inform you . . . that this Government, so long as present European conditions continue, sees no opportunity or occasion for any peace move to be initiated by the President of the United States. The people of the United States would not support any move for peace initiated by this Government that would consolidate or make possible a survival of a regime of force and of aggression.[6]

That same day, the president reinforced this message to his ambassador by personal letters to Neville Chamberlain and Winston Churchill, a new member of the British cabinet who was the symbol of all-out war against Hitler. "My dear Mr. Chamberlain," Roosevelt wrote the prime minister.

I need not tell you that you have been much in my thoughts during these difficult days and further that I hope you will at all times feel free to write to me personally and outside of diplomatic procedure about any problems as they arise.

I hope and believe that we shall repeal the embargo within the next month and this is definitely a part of the Administration policy.[7]

The message could not have been clearer. In stating that repeal of the embargo was part of his policy, Roosevelt indicated he was prepared to help the Chamberlain government resist and destroy Hitler's regime of force and aggression, not to propitiate it. And to drive home U.S. policy, Roosevelt wrote his second letter to the member of the Chamberlain government most identified with unyielding defiance of Hitler. "My dear Churchill," he began.

It is because you and I occupied similar positions in the World War that I want you to know how glad I am that you are back again at the Admiralty. Your problems are, I realize, complicated by new factors but the essential is not very different. What I want you and the Prime Minister to know is that I shall at all times welcome it if you will keep me in touch personally with anything you want me to know about. You can always send sealed letters through your pouch or my pouch.[8]

Was it "not unusual for the President of the United States to exchange such messages with a member of a foreign government who is not the head of the government or in charge of foreign affairs for that government?" Charles A. Beard, the eminent historian and passionate noninterventionist, demanded to know, when Churchill, on April, 1945, in a memorial tribute to Roosevelt in the House of Commons, disclosed the 1939 invitation to correspond. Of course it was. And Churchill took pains to point out that he had obtained the permission of the prime minister before he accepted Roosevelt's invitation, and that until he himself became prime minister, had limited his communications to naval affairs and "the various actions including especially our action of the Plate River, which lighted the first gloomy winter of the war."[9]

The Roosevelt gesture, even though few knew of it at the time, bolstered Churchill's position. Behind it was lodged a distrust, almost dislike, of Chamberlain as well as appreciation of Churchill's antiappeasement viewpoint. Roosevelt's doubts about Chamberlain had set in a few months after the latter had assumed the prime ministership in January, 1938. Roosevelt, wishing to associate the United States with a major move to halt the drift toward war but in a form that a fiercely noninterventionist American public opinion might accept, was prepared to summon an international peace conference in Washington, but only if the suggestion "met with the cordial approval and wholehearted support of the British Government." Hull, who had violently opposed an earlier version of the plan partly out of temperamental cautiousness and partly because it had been proposed by Sumner Welles, made British and French approval a condition of his agreement to the January initiative. Chamberlain, without consulting his foreign affairs secretary, Anthony Eden, who was out of the country, or his cabinet, rebuffed Roosevelt, saying the president's project risked "cutting across our efforts here" to appease Italy and Germany. When Eden returned, he had insisted on a more affirmative and cordial answer to the president. But Roosevelt, faced by Hull's doubts, by the risks of an isolationist backfire, and by British coolness, had by this time begun to withdraw from the proposal. "So far as we could judge, no feelings of resentment remained after the exchange of telegrams," Samuel Hoare later wrote. Churchill judged differently. He considered the Chamberlain response to Roosevelt as "chilling" and, writing in 1948, said that even at that date he was left "breathless with amazement" that Chamberlain, "with his limited outlook and inexperience of the European scene, should have possessed the self-sufficiency to wave away the proffered hand stretched out across the Atlantic."[10]

Roosevelt disclosed his true feelings about Chamberlain to Sir Arthur Willert in early April, 1939. The Willerts were family friends of the Roosevelts dating back to World War I days when Arthur Willert had served as Washington correspondent of the London *Times* and Roosevelt as assistant secretary of the navy. Willert, while lecturing in America during the spring of 1939, had dined with the president. Felix Frankfurter and Francis Biddle were among the other guests, and Roosevelt, who learned more through his ears than through his eyes, had asked Willert to come back the next afternoon for further discussion. Now the two men sat in Roosevelt's oval study in front of the fireplace talking foreign affairs. Roosevelt kept him there until nearly dinner time. "[Roosevelt's] indignation at Chamberlain's refusal to let him have a hand in trying to settle the troubles the year before still smouldered. The President was bitter about appeasement. He had no use for Chamberlain. He thought Simon and Samuel Hoare about the worst foreign ministers we ever had. . . ."[11]

Roosevelt's displeasure over the January, 1938, repulse had been compounded by Chamberlain's disregard of secret and sensational proposals made by him during the Munich crisis for a heads-of-state conference in the Azores in which he was willing to participate, or, alternatively, if the Western powers found themselves "forced to war," of an offer of U.S. readiness to join a blockade of Germany. Historians have paid little attention to this extraordinary document, yet it is a better guide to Roosevelt's real thoughts during the Munich crisis than the conventional sources of information.

It was Monday, September 19, 1938. Chamberlain had made his first flight to Germany, to Berchtesgaden, where, in return for Hitler's agreement not to settle the Sudeten issue by force, he had agreed to persuade the Czech government to hand over the Sudetenland to Germany. "I formed the opinion that Herr Hitler's objectives are strictly limited," Chamberlain assured his cabinet and the French government on his return. Tremendous pressure was being applied on President Beneš to agree, and London and Paris were waiting for a Czech decision that could mean war.

It was in this setting that Roosevelt summoned the British ambassador Sir Ronald Lindsay for a talk. Lindsay was a rather stiff, unflappable individual, but his dispatch on the meeting with Roosevelt pulsed with excitement. It was dated Washington, September 20, 1938, 2:30 A.M. "The President telephoned to me himself this afternoon to call on him at the White House in the evening, and I had a long conversation," it began. "He emphasized the necessity of absolute secrecy. Nobody must know I had seen him and he himself would tell nobody of the interview. I gathered not even the State Department. He said the Anglo-French note to Czechoslovak Government was the most terrible remorseless sacrifice that had ever been demanded of a State. It would provoke a highly unfavourable reaction in America. . . . Today he would not dare to express approval of the recommendation put to the Czechoslovak Government. He would be afraid to express disapproval of German aggression lest it might encourage Czechoslovakia to vain resistance. . . ." This was an important consideration. "The poor Zchecks! [*sic*]," Eleanor Roosevelt wrote to her husband on September 21. "I don't somehow like the role of England & France, do you? We can say nothing however for we wouldn't go to war for someone else."

But Roosevelt was prepared to go pretty far. He outlined three possibilities to Lindsay: Czechoslovakia, unaided, "would fight and his general staff told him they would be overrun in three weeks." Or, if the Western powers went to war with Hitler, "even if Great Britain, France and Russia were fighting loyally together they would be beaten if they tried to wage war on classical lines of attack. They would suffer terrific casualties and would never get through. He therefore came to the third case. This is the very secret part of his communication and it must not be known to anyone that he has ever breathed a suggestion. If it transpired he would almost be impeached and the suggestion would be hopelessly prejudiced." If the Western powers decided to call a heads-of-states world conference to try to achieve a general settlement, including Herr Hitler, "he himself would be willing to go to it *but not if it was held* in Europe. That he would never do. But he would go half way and attend a conference in the Azores or some other Atlantic Island."

But all of this was preliminary to Roosevelt's stunning disclosure of how far he was prepared to go to help the Western powers in the event they found themselves "forced to war." It was his view that they should wage war

purely by blockade and in a defensive manner. . . . The Powers should close their own frontiers to Germany, stand on an armed defensive and call on all other states adjoining Germany to adopt the same line of non-intercourse. The blockade line should be drawn down the middle of the North Sea, through the Channel to Gibraltar and the Mediterranean should be closed at the Suez Canal.

The word "sanctions" (with its League of Nations connotation) should be avoided. "Blockade must be based on loftiest humanitarian grounds," Roosevelt continued, "and on the desire to wage hostilities with [a] minimum of suffering and the least possible loss of life and property, and yet to bring enemy to his knees." As Roosevelt outlined his scheme, Lindsay thought this was what Roosevelt must have had in mind a year earlier when, in a speech in Chicago in 1937, he had called on peace-loving nations to "quarantine" an aggressor.

The American public, Roosevelt felt, would approve a blockade "if its humanitarian purpose were strongly emphasized." He could not himself initiate such a move, but it was entirely within the constitutional prerogative of a president, on his own authority, to declare that a blockade was of an effective character. He could thus help the blockading powers, and would be willing to do so, in the absence of unfavorable circumstances.

Lindsay asked him, in regard to the Neutrality Act, about the possibility of the U.S. government "turning a blind eye to any evasion of [the] prohibition of export of arms and ammunition in our favour." Roosevelt reacted to this very hesitantly, but then added that if the Western powers did not formally declare war on Germany, he might not have to invoke the arms embargo.

Let them call it defensive measures or anything plausible but avoid actual declaration of war. He had already been able to give himself wide latitude in the interpretation of the Neutrality Law in the Far East and in Ethiopia, and if the law was not changed he would be disposed to do so again. He even indicated that even if Germany declared war on us and we refrained from doing so he might yet be able to find that we were not at war, and that the prohibition of export of arms need not be applied to us.

The president was quite exercised over the effects of successful German aggression on Japan. "He was convinced that the Japanese government was bound by a secret treaty to come to German support in case of war."

Lindsay concluded his report:

Several times in the course of the conversation the President showed himself quite alive to the possibility that somehow or other in indefinable circumstances the United States might again find themselves involved in a European War. In that case he regarded it as almost inconceivable that it would be possible for him to send any American troops across the Atlantic even if his prestige were as high as it had been just after the 1936 elections. But it was just possible that if Germany were able to invade Great Britain with a considerable force, such a wave of emotion might arise, that an American army might be sent overseas.

Although Lindsay's final statement was "I do not think he expects any particular answer," it was quite clear that this disclosure of Roosevelt's innermost thoughts was meant to encourage Chamberlain to stand up to Hitler. There is no evidence that it did.[12]

Lindsay's telegram, which was addressed to Lord Halifax, the foreign secretary, was received in London on September 20 at 10:40 A.M. London time. The British and French were impatiently awaiting the Czech reply to their demand that Czechoslovakia agree to the immediate transfer of the Sudeten-German areas to Germany. Chamberlain's second meeting with Hitler waited on the Czech reply. When the Czech rejection came late in the evening of the twentieth, the British, instead of being emboldened by Roosevelt's offer, ignored it and together with the French redoubled their pressure on President Beneš. Faced with the threat of having to fight Hitler alone, the Czech government yielded. "The partition of Czechoslovakia under pressure from England and France," declared Churchill, who from his back-bench seat in the House of Commons commanded a world audience, "amounts to the complete surrender of the Western Democracies to the Nazi threat of force."

Lindsay, who had rightly regarded his cable as momentous, gently prodded Halifax. "I think it would be useful if you sent me a friendly expression of appreciation of his message which I could convey to him through his Private Secretary." Lindsay's reminder arrived in London on September 22 at 1:20 A.M., a few hours before Chamberlain flew to Godesberg for his second meeting with Hitler. There was no answer to the American president.

The Godesberg talks went badly. Hitler demanded immediate Czech withdrawal from the Sudeten areas followed by an equally immediate German takeover. This was too much, even for Chamberlain. Immediate German occupation "would be condemned as an unnecessary display of force," he wrote Hitler at midnight from his hotel room. Halifax, in London, pressed for more vigorous action; he urged Chamberlain to lift the ban on Czech mobilization. As the situation in Godesberg darkened, Halifax finally replied to Roosevelt. He telegraphed Lindsay at 4:20 P.M. on the twenty-third to convey to the president

my appreciation of his having taken you so far into his confidence, and my assurance that I will observe complete secrecy in that matter. At the present moment it is extremely difficult to forecast events. We have gone as far as we can in an effort to remove what might be considered a German grievance. If our effort fails, there will no longer be any doubt as to Herr Hitler's real intentions.

Should His Majesty's Government be drawn into any conflict, the major role would probably be enforcement of blockade, as [the] President foresees.

However, the position of Italy would complicate the imposition of an effective blockade. "It might be necessary to choose between a neutral Italy with an ineffective blockade and a hostile Italy with an effective blockade," he observed.

Then came another expression of gratitude that in retrospect reads a little patronizingly: "It is of great encouragement to know that the President has been giving thought to these questions and I am most grateful to him for his confidence."[13] Chamberlain, intent on the negotiations with Hitler that eventuated in Munich and "peace for our time," never communicated with Roosevelt at all about the latter's offer to associate the United States with Britain in a world conference in the Azores or in a move to quarantine Germany.

Though Roosevelt's relationship with Chamberlain had been bleak and unsatisfactory, he did not, until September 11, 1939, seek out Churchill; nor, indeed, had Churchill made any serious effort to communicate with Roosevelt. Arthur Willert says that Churchill "was regarded in America as a failed politician. . . . I have no record or memory, for instance, of its [Churchill's name] coming up in the various conversations I had with the President."[14]

Except for a common appraisal of the dangers of Hitlerism, there was little in Churchill's views that would attract Roosevelt. The rupture between Churchill and his Conservative colleagues in the early thirties had originated in his savage opposition to the Government of India Act, whose limited reforms (but reforms nonetheless) were finally approved by Parliament in 1935. The flavor of Churchill's attack is conveyed by his remarks on Gandhi in 1931. It was, he told the West Essex Conservative Association, "alarming and also nauseating to see Mr. Gandhi, a seditious Middle Temple lawyer, now posing as a fakir of a type well-known in the East, striding half naked up the steps of the Vice-regal Palace, while he is still organizing and conducting a defiant campaign of civil disobedience, to parley on equal terms with the representative of the King-Emperor." Sir Samuel Hoare, scarcely a flaming anticolonialist, wrote of Churchill's views on India, that "the India that he had served in the Fourth Hussars was the India of polo and pig sticking; of dashing frontier expeditions, of paternal government freely accepted, and the great white Empress revered as a mysterious goddess. . . . How deeply I sympathized with his nostalgia for a glorious past!"[15]

In 1931, two years before Hitler came to power, Churchill was "the only dissentient voice" in Parliament on disarmament. His views on the New Deal were indistinguishable from those of ex-President Herbert Hoover. At the end of 1937, in a message entitled "What We Ask of the United States," he called on President Roosevelt and the New Dealers, in the interests of the common anti-Hitlerite cause, to abandon their war on "Wealth and Business," their "ruthless war on private enterprise."[16]

Distrusted by British labor, execrated by the liberals, Churchill's rigidly conservative ideology was at opposite poles from the experimentalism and pragmatism of Roosevelt, who was idolized by the American union movement and the acknowledged leader of American liberalism. Despite a fertile

and brilliant mind and a resplendent rhetoric that commanded attention
even when his politics bordered on the eccentric, Churchill, as Arthur Willert
wrote, was widely regarded in America as a has-been. Nevertheless, by the
time of Munich, foreign policy had become dominant in the thinking of
statesmen, and whatever reservations Roosevelt may have had about Churchill's views on colonialism were overshadowed by the British leader's prophetic rightness on the issue of Hitler. While the whole world, even Roosevelt, felt a sense of relief at the escape from war at the time of Munich,
Churchill stood up in the House of Commons and, disregarding a storm of
protest, somberly declared: "We have sustained a total and unmitigated defeat. . . . Do not let us blind ourselves to that. . . . And do not suppose
that this is the end. This is only the beginning of the reckoning." The only
salvation for the democracies was to arm, especially to create an air force
and to bolster Britain's alliances.

Overnight Churchill was no longer speaking as a conservative zealot but
for centrist opinion in the democracies. His views were widely reported in
the American press. They were directly conveyed to Roosevelt by men like
Churchill's old friend Bernard M. Baruch, who had seen a good deal of him
during the Munich crisis. "War is coming very soon," had been Churchill's
gloomy farewell to Baruch. "We will be in it and you will be in it. You will
be running the show over there, but I will be on the sidelines over here."*[17]

Roosevelt was not a Baruch enthusiast. Even though Baruch had been
in London during the Munich crisis, his biographer noted that it was "not
until October 12" that the financier was summoned to the White House for
dinner and to spend the night. However, when Baruch left the next morning,
the press, alerted by Roosevelt's press secretary, was waiting for him. Munich
was not a peace—it was a surrender, Baruch told the reporters. "Mr. Hitler
knew that England and France were not prepared to come to grips at this
time." Then he added, and this was what Roosevelt wanted to get across to
the country, "I hope that we will never be in the humiliating position in
which Chamberlain found himself. . . . We ought to be able to defend ourselves." The tall, white-haired man gestured for emphasis. "I know what I
am talking about. I believe America is unprepared."[18]

A few days later, Churchill broadcasted to the American people. If in
April, May, and June of 1938 Great Britain, France, and Russia had jointly
declared that they would act together against unprovoked Nazi aggression,
said Churchill, Hitler would have been deterred from his purposes and the
moderate forces in Germany would have been strengthened. Had the Western
powers now learned their lesson? he went on to ask. "We are left in no
doubt where American convictions and sympathies lie; but will you wait until
British freedom and independence have succumbed, and then take up the
cause when it is three-quarters ruined, yourselves alone? . . . The pre-

---

* Churchill thought that a Constitution Day address, September 17, 1937, in which
Roosevelt had inveighed against dictatorships, had been "largely influenced" by talks
that Churchill had had with Baruch in London in the summer of 1937.

ponderant world forces are upon our side; they have but to be combined to be obeyed. . . . We must arm. Britain must arm. America must arm."[19]

Roosevelt was at Hyde Park at the time of the broadcast. Had he listened? the press inquired. No, but he had seen the headline, he replied noncommittally. He had to work with the British government, which was led by men who had little love for Churchill. They were in power. They were the ones who had to be stiffened. German air superiority had been a factor leading to the Munich capitulation.

"England and France are far too weak in the air to protect themselves," Ambassador Kennedy had reported a week before Munich, reflecting the findings of Col. Charles Lindbergh. Roosevelt told the British air attaché the day before Chamberlain flew to Munich that he thought the European democracies were giving in to Hitler because of their air inferiority.[20] "Good man," he had cabled Chamberlain when word came that the British leader had accepted Hitler's invitation to participate in the fateful four-power conference in Munich. But the president was determined that the United States should never be put in the position of having to negotiate from weakness. If Germany could turn out 30,000 planes a year, the United States should build 40,000. And though the United States, in the event of war in Europe, would be prohibited by the Neutrality Act from supplying planes to the democracies, Roosevelt thought he could circumvent the arms embargo by exporting the basic components of planes to assembly plants abroad. He suggested that Britain construct such a plant in Canada.

He returned to this idea during a ten-day visit that Col. Arthur Murray and his wife paid him and Eleanor at Hyde Park in mid-October, 1938. Murray, a Scottish aristocrat, the Master of Elibank, was another friend from World War I days when Murray had served as assistant military attaché in Washington. The colonel had been Grey's parliamentary private secretary at the foreign office, and was a pillar of the Liberal establishment.* He did not, incidentally, have an overly worshipful view of Churchill, holding him equally responsible with Lloyd George for the destruction of the Liberal party. During the Murrays' stay at Hyde Park, Roosevelt told him "he wanted to have a 'proper talk' with me about certain important matters which would arise if the 'probable war' took place."

Roosevelt wanted Murray to assure Chamberlain that he "wanted the Prime Minister to feel that he had, insofar as he, the President was able to achieve it, 'the industrial resources of the American nation behind him in the event of war with the dictatorships.' " Roosevelt then repeated the plan that

---

* In the 1906 general election, when the Liberals regained power, Scotland had returned sixty Liberals to nine Conservatives. It did so again in the fateful election of January, 1910, which permanently curbed the power of the House of Lords. Arthur Murray's brother Alick was promoted to chief Liberal whip after that election. Arthur Murray wrote in 1946, and he doubtless must have made this point to Roosevelt in the 1930s, that Churchill as chancellor of the exchequer from 1924 to 1929 had been responsible for cutting the navy and air force "to the very bone."

he had broached to the British air attaché—that in the event Britain found herself at war with the dictators, his purpose would be "to provide partly-finished basic materials, which did not come within the Neutrality Law, for an extra 20,000 to 30,000 planes, to give the necessary overwhelming superiority over Germany and Italy," materials that might be assembled in special plants in Canada and Great Britain.[21]

Murray did not see Chamberlain until the week of December 15, he wrote Roosevelt: "In the course of our conversation Chamberlain said, 'There is no question that in certain circumstances a statement which really brought it home that the vast resources of the United States would be behind Britain might have a deterrent effect, whether on Hitler himself, it is impossible to say. I don't think anybody could say.' "[22] Roosevelt's proposal to help the British and French air programs was referred by Chamberlain to the air minister, Sir Kingsley Wood, where it languished.

The spirit of Munich evaporated. Hitler himself, in a speech at Saarbrücken on October 9, justified strengthening his Westwall fortifications with a reference to the Churchill group. "It only needs that in England instead of Chamberlain, Mr. Duff Cooper or Mr. Eden or Mr. Churchill should come to power, and then we know quite well that it would be the aim of these men immediately to begin a new World War."

As events confirmed his darkest predictions, Churchill's views commanded increasing attention in Washington and elsewhere. Harry Hopkins was recovering from a siege of sickness at Hobcaw, Baruch's baronial plantation in South Carolina. In the course of many talks with his host, Hopkins was familiarized with Churchill's analysis. Henry Wallace at the end of February forwarded to Roosevelt a report that he had received from American businessman William S. Wasserman on a conversation the latter had with Churchill in which Churchill advised that "the very best thing the United States could do was to keep beating the drums and talking back to the dictators. The one thing that might make them hesitate in plunging the world into war was the fear that the United States would soon be in it in a big way."[23] Roosevelt's annual message to Congress in January, 1939, spoke of the "many methods short of war" by which the United States might assist the victims of aggression. And at the top of his "must" list of bills in that session of Congress was repeal of the arms-embargo provisions of the Neutrality Act, an appeal that was rebuffed.

Within the limits and restraints imposed on him by the Neutrality Act and the isolationist mood of the American people, Roosevelt tried to align the United States with the forces resisting aggression. In his long talk with Arthur Willert in early April, 1939, he told the Englishman that

he was giving much thought to ways in which the American navy could help us. He would have to declare certain waters like the eastern Atlantic and the Mediterranean areas of belligerency out of which American shipping must keep, and he did not see why the American navy should not patrol the waters outside those

areas. Then the British navy could concentrate where most needed. Having expatiated upon the efficiency of the American fleet, he exclaimed, "If yours is as
good, and if we stand together we will show the dictators that democracy can still
look after itself."[24]

After German occupation of the remainder of Czechoslovakia and the
Italian smash-and-grab of Albania, Roosevelt confided to Adolf Berle, an
original Brain Truster now serving as assistant secretary of state, that he was
troubled by the dispersal of the British fleet. "He was worried about the proposal of the English to send their fleet to Singapore. He pointed out that if
they lost the Far East they could take it back, but without the Mediterranean
they had nothing. We talked over our own fleet and decided to send the
Pacific fleet back to San Diego."[25] (It was scheduled to put in an appearance
in New York Harbor in connection with the World's Fair.) Roosevelt's worry
over the disposition of the British fleet was another bond with Churchill,
who, on April 13 in the House of Commons and a few days later in a private
letter to Lord Halifax, protested the dispersion of the Mediterranean fleet and
the unpreparedness of the Atlantic fleet.[26]

Both Roosevelt and Churchill, as sea-power enthusiasts, understood
that fleet readiness and concentration at sea constituted the "gleam of
steel" that gave muscle to diplomatic initiative. Roosevelt, on April 14 in
personal messages to Hitler and Mussolini, had appealed to them to give
their neighbors assurances of nonaggression for "ten years at least."

"Keep your fingers crossed!" he told Henry Morgenthau, Jr. "There is
one chance in five. It had to be done."

"And if they turn you down," Morgenthau followed up, "then you will
know where you are at."

"That is the whole point," Roosevelt agreed, and added, "I will have
more news this afternoon about the fleet."

"Their fleet?" Morgenthau, who was no navalist, asked. "No, our fleet.
It is a nice gesture. It is all right."[27]

That afternoon the fleet was ordered back to its normal fleet bases.
"Why five or six weeks ahead of schedule?" reporters asked him. "Because
the Navy is subject to daily changes in orders" was all Roosevelt would say.[28]

"If the President wishes to send a message to the Axis powers which will
be understood," Henry L. Stimson, secretary of state under Hoover, advised
Hull during a stopover in Washington, "he will cancel the visit of the American fleet to the World's Fair without giving any reason and return it at once
to its proper station in the Pacific. He doesn't need to say anything. The
movement of the fleet is a language which the Axis powers well understand."[29]

Whether the message registered in the Axis capitals is unclear. But on
the eve of war, Roosevelt's basic position was understood. Just as it was
said in Berlin that Churchill's return to the cabinet meant an end of appeasement, so there were few illusions about Roosevelt. Hans Thomsen, the
German chargé d'affaires in Washington, cabled home on September 12,
1939:

For the time being, Roosevelt believes himself able to keep the United States out of the war by strengthening the Allies' chance of winning the war through unlimited exportation of arms, military equipment and essential raw materials. But if defeat should threaten the Allies, Roosevelt is determined to go to war against Germany, even in the face of the resistance of his own country.[30]

Chapter Two

An Essentially Similar Problem

FOR THE HEAD of one state to initiate a correspondence with a subordinate minister of another was unorthodox. Roosevelt's letter to Churchill was also remarkable because of its reference to their having occupied "similar positions" in the First World War; and though Churchill's problems at the admiralty in 1939 were complicated by new factors, "the essential is not very different."

Encapsulated in that phrase was the history of sea power in the twentieth century and the Anglo-American partnership that was the central feature of that history. Seeking for the sources and the beginning of the New Deal, chroniclers of the Roosevelt presidency have examined Roosevelt's career as assistant secretary of the navy. But Roosevelt's early years in government are even more instructive in regard to his military-strategic outlook in the months before Pearl Harbor. Thomsen was right when he sought to impress upon his superiors in Berlin his conviction that Roosevelt would not allow the defeat of the Allies even at the risk of war and in the face of the doggedly isolationist mood of a large part of the American people. Behind that determination was a conception of American national interests and what was required for American safety, both rooted in geopolitical notions of the United States' stake in Anglo-American naval supremacy as well as in a balance of power in Europe and Asia. These notions had taken shape during Roosevelt's most impressionable years at Groton and Harvard and in the Wilson administration, a period when foreign policy and naval doctrine merged as a result of the teachings of one of the most remarkable men in American intellectual history, Capt. Alfred T. Mahan.

Mahan's continuing influence is noted in the official navy study, "United States–British Naval Cooperation, 1940–1945," written by Capt. Tracy B. Kittredge. That monograph begins with the emphatic statement:

The cooperation of the United States Navy with the Royal Navy in assuring the supremacy of Anglo-American sea power 1940–1945 was a further expression of the prophetic doctrine defined a half century earlier by the American Naval officer and historian, Captain Alfred T. Mahan. The effective combined American-British partnership, in winning and maintaining command of the sea in World War II, was in conformity with traditions of national policy and naval power repeatedly manifested after 1890.[1]

Mahan's doctrines had a simple grandeur about them. Once stated, they seemed almost self-evident. Sea power was the basis of world power. Throughout most of the nineteenth century, British naval superiority had been unchallenged and had enabled a small island kingdom to dominate an unprecedented world empire. By the beginning of the twentieth century, however, the power of the British fleet, although still superior, had begun to decline in relation to that of other nations. "In explaining this development, Mahan had drawn the conclusion," wrote Kittredge, "that the United States must develop naval power as the basis for its future national defense, but should cooperate with Britain in establishing and maintaining Anglo-American sea power and control of the seas to assure the heritage of the 'Pax Britannica,' which the Royal Navy was no longer able to guarantee alone, as the basis of world peace and of a stable and just world order."[2]

The principles formulated by Mahan were given practical expression on the United States side of the Atlantic by a group of leaders that included Theodore Roosevelt, who read Mahan's first sea-power book through in two days and reviewed the "naval classic" for the *Atlantic;* Henry Cabot Lodge, who reviewed it with equal enthusiasm for the *North American Review;* John Hay, whom Mahan served as "philosophical mentor"; Elihu Root; and Henry Adams, who coined the phrase "the Atlantic System" to characterize the convergence of American and British interests and destiny. Mahan's philosophy of sea power entered the White House with Theodore Roosevelt, who together with Lodge sponsored an unprecedented naval-building program, the purpose of which was to make the United States fighting fleet second only to Great Britain's but which opposed, also in faithfulness to Mahan's teachings, competition between the two navies.[3]

The emphasis on sea power in American military thought coincided with "the rise in Anglo-American friendship," as one writer described British realization that the waning of its power relative to the growth of German and Japanese sea power could be redressed only by an entente with the Americans. In the Spanish-American War, Great Britain had discouraged other European powers from intervening on the side of Spain, and afterward it had consummated this benevolent neutrality by encouraging the United States to annex Hawaii and the Philippine Islands before Germany did. British statesmen, led by Joseph Chamberlain, Lord Salisbury, and Arthur Balfour, henceforth systematically subordinated differences with the Americans to the necessities of a common front with them on the larger issues of world politics.

"When the United States declared war on Spain over the prolonged disturbances in Cuba," Churchill wrote in 1937 in *Great Contemporaries,* "Balfour happened to be temporarily in charge of the Foreign Office. The friendship of Great Britain and Spain was old and valued. No dispute of any kind had separated the two countries which had fought side by side against Napoleon. Balfour's root conviction, perhaps his strongest conviction, was that the English-speaking peoples of the world must stand together. He therefore in a single night reversed the mild Spanish sympathies of the Foreign Office and transformed cold neutrality into a markedly friendly attitude towards the United States. . . . Balfour's decision has stood the test of time."[4]

Senator Lodge wrote to John Hay, ambassador to England and soon-to-be secretary of state:

[England] has expressed her sympathy with us in the Spanish business and down go the dykes and what I have always predicted has come to pass. The heart of America goes out to England at this moment. . . . Race, blood, language, identity of beliefs and aspiration all assert themselves. . . . To me this drawing together of the English-speaking peoples all over the world . . . seems far more momentous, more fraught with meaning to the future of mankind than the freedom of Cuba or the expulsion of Spain from this hemisphere.[5]

And at almost the same time, in a speech in Birmingham, Joseph Chamberlain, father of Neville, spoke in a similar vein: "I go even so far as to say that terrible as war may be, even war itself would be cheaply purchased if, in a great and noble cause, the Stars and Stripes and the Union Jack should wave together over an Anglo-Saxon alliance."[6]

The major barriers to this convergence in the early twentieth century, the Alaskan boundary dispute and U.S. insistence on control of the Panama Canal, were by 1911 settled by British concessions to the American viewpoint so that in 1911 Theodore Roosevelt could write that the Alaskan award represented "the last serious trouble between the British Empire and ourselves. . . . I feel very differently toward England from the way I feel towards Germany."[7]

Largely on the basis of this *rapprochement* with the United States, Lord Fisher, as professional head of the British navy, was able in the first years of the twentieth century "to adopt Mahan's view that the secret of naval warfare is concentration, concentration in defense at home and in offence while attacking." He withdrew British naval vessels from outlying parts of the world to strengthen the home fleet. He ordered the Mediterranean fleet to be based on Malta and created an Atlantic fleet based on Gibraltar. The whole naval strategic situation has undergone a revolution, observed the first sea lord. "That revolution is the birth of the American Navy." As World War I approached, Mahan, the hero of Manila Admiral Dewey, and the U.S. Navy's general board looked to the Royal Navy "to check Germany in home waters as much as the Foreign Office, and the Admiralty . . . seemed to rely on the Monroe Doctrine and Anglo-American understanding" to guarantee the status quo elsewhere. "If, early in the 20th century, Great Britain was informally reinsured in the western hemisphere, the chief naval authorities of the United States counted on British sea power as one of the principal foundations of American world security."[8]

Franklin D. Roosevelt was responsive to these currents and movements.

A sailor from the days of his youth at Campobello, an amateur geographer, in him the doctrines of Mahan found an eager pupil and apprentice. His mother ascribed young Roosevelt's conception of himself as a seafaring man to his Delano heritage—"The Delanos have always been associated with the sea"—and recalled that as a youngster he "used to pore over Admiral Mahan's *History of Sea Power* until he practically memorized the whole book." He had first read it when he was eleven, and had told his future wife Eleanor that it was one of the books that he had found "most illuminating." His interest in naval history was reflected in a large collection of books which his mother said he "began as a boy." At the time of the Spanish-American War, he was so filled with the martial spirit that he wanted to enlist in the navy. But on the fateful morning that he and his Groton classmate were to make their getaway, they came down with the measles. Another of his boyhood wishes was to go to Annapolis, "only my parents objected."[9]

The emergence of the United States as a world power was reflected in the topics that Franklin debated at Groton—"The Increase of Our Navy," "Philippine Independence," and "The Annexation of Hawaii." "We are con," he informed his father and mother in January, 1898, about the latter, and his notes for this debate have survived. "Mr. Peabody has told us that our country cannot be safe without Hawaii. I shall try to disprove this," Franklin said, launching into his argument. At another point in his presentation he noted that "Captain Mahan himself says it is nonsense to think of annexation unless we spend an enormous sum for fortifications. Now is it worthwhile to do this?" He turned to another of Peabody's arguments "that we need a coaling station for our ships. Now it is not generally known that Pearl Harbor, a port in one of the islands, belongs to the United States. All that is needed is a little inexpensive dredging and we shall have a coaling station without annexation."[10]

The positions young Roosevelt took on Hawaiian annexation and Philippine independence are less important than America's self-discovery as a world power that was reflected in these preoccupations. "Whether we wish it or not," Franklin's cousin Theodore Roosevelt proclaimed as president, "we are a great people and must play a great part in the world . . . we have to play it. All we can decide is whether we shall play it well or ill."[11]

In 1905, with quiet British encouragement, President Theodore Roosevelt offered his good offices to Japan and Russia to help end the war between them and, with the assistance of Sir Cecil Spring-Rice, the secretary of the British embassy in Russia who had been best man at Theodore's wedding, brought the parties together at a peace conference in Portsmouth, New Hampshire. Eleanor and Franklin were in England on the last leg of their honeymoon when news of Theodore Roosevelt's diplomatic success was filling the papers. "Everyone is talking about Cousin Theodore," Franklin wrote his mother on September 7, in phrases that reflected potent American nationalism as well as family pride, "saying that he is the most prominent figure of present day history, and adopting towards our country in general a most respectful and loving tone. What a change has come over English opinion in the last few years! Even the French were quite enthusiastic, but the German tone seemed to hide a certain animosity and jealousy as usual."[12]

The concept of Anglo-American friendship did not come easily to young Roosevelt—or so he insisted in October, 1939, after Ernest Lindley, a friendly biographer, had written a column suggesting that a "bias" in favor of the English acquired in youth might make Roosevelt a pawn of British policy. An irked Roosevelt directed his press secretary Steve Early to tell "Ernest" that, if anything, his boyhood bias by family tradition was anti-English. The Roosevelts in 1776 were "revolutionists rather than tories," he said, because their sharpest competitors in the West Indies sugar business were British and French interests. And on the Delano side of the family, "I was brought up on the story of how the Delano family's principal competitors [in the China trade] were the British" and how his grandfather Warren Delano "was the United States agent in China during the whole of the Civil War and spent most of his time fighting against British interests which, at that time, were wholly on the side of the Confederacy." He did not know Britain and France as a boy, his memo to Early went on, "but I did know Germany. If anything, I looked upon the Germany I knew with far more friendliness than I did on Great Britain or France."[13]

Roosevelt's memo, written at the height of the arms-repeal debate in Congress, was a political document. Yet the historian need not question Roosevelt's description of his boyhood sentiments in order to suggest they were no guide to his subsequent feelings and policies. The description, rather, is a reminder that at heart Roosevelt, like Theodore Roosevelt and Henry Cabot Lodge, was an American nationalist who embraced friendship with England as a ruling principle in foreign affairs because it advanced American interests and safety, and who, in his dealings with the British, could drive as hard a bargain as his Yankee trading forebears.

Theodore Roosevelt's mediation in the Russo-Japanese War was not wholly disinterested. Both England and the United States wanted to see the war ended on terms that would assure a balance of power in the Far East rather than Japanese supremacy. An arrangement where Russia would be "left face to face with Japan so that each may have a moderative influence on the other" would best serve Anglo-American interests. When Lodge visited King Edward that year, he was instructed by Roosevelt to inform the king "that we intend to have the United States and England work together [in Europe] just as we are now working together in the Far East." And if England failed to keep the scales level, Theodore Roosevelt privately noted three years before the outbreak of World War I, "the United States would be obliged to step in at least temporarily, in order to reestablish the balance of power in Europe, never mind against which country or group of countries our efforts may have to be directed. In fact we ourselves are becoming, owing to our strength and geographical situation, more and more the balance of power of the whole globe."[14]

Turn-of-the-century dreams of an American *imperium* went hand in hand not only with a large navy and the acquisition of strategically placed islands in the Caribbean and the Pacific, but with the construction of an isthmian canal. "America must have a powerful Navy," Senator Lodge told a Senate which listened to him with respect despite his Harvard accent and imperious demeanor, "and must build a canal across Central America as well. It is sea power which is essential to the greatness of every splendid people."[15]

The canal gripped the imagination of Americans, and of none more so than young Franklin. Not only was its construction finally launched under the resolute and aggressive leadership of "Cousin Theodore," but Colón, the city at the Atlantic terminus of the canal, was originally called Aspinwall, after its founder, William H. Aspinwall, who was Franklin's great-uncle. When Franklin's mother in 1904 took him off on a Caribbean tour in hopes of getting his mind off Eleanor, the latter was writing him from Washington about dining with "Uncle Theodore . . . a very pleasant dinner during which I just sat still and listened while the men discussed the appointments for the Panama Commission." Eight years later Franklin went on another Caribbean cruise, this time with his brother-in-law Hall Roosevelt, a tour that culminated in a week-long inspection of the nearly complete Panama Canal with its great locks and impressive Culebra Cut. "Goethals said in his quiet way last night," Franklin wrote his mother, " 'We like to have Americans come down, because they all say it makes them better Americans.' " The canal was one of the world's wonders, Roosevelt exulted, "greater than the Tower of Babel or the Pyramids."[16]

"How would you like to come to Washington as Assistant Secretary of the Navy?" Josephus Daniels asked Roosevelt the morning of Woodrow Wilson's inauguration.

"How would I like it? I'd like it bully well," Franklin replied. "All my life I have loved ships and have been a student of the Navy, and the assistant secretaryship is the one place above all others I would love to hold."

"He is our kind of liberal," Daniels told the president two days later when he brought up Roosevelt's name. Liberal he was, but neither man was unmindful that Roosevelt had other qualifications. He was related by marriage as well as by name to Theodore Roosevelt, who himself had been assistant secretary of the navy and had established the United States as a major naval power. The young pince-nezed northerner, moreover, whose father and half brother had been well-known Cleveland Democrats, would nicely balance Josephus, a homespun North Carolina editor, pacifist, and prohibitionist who, along with William Jennings Bryan, was the chief representative of the populist tradition in the Wilson administration.

Eleanor and Franklin were loyal Democrats, but the social circles they moved in during their first years in Washington were mostly Republican—the Longworths, the Lodges, Henry Adams, and Henry White, the diplomatist; the Chevy Chase and Metropolitan clubs; and among foreign diplomats the young Roosevelts inherited Uncle Ted's friends, especially the British ambassador Sir Cecil Spring-Rice, "Springy"—poet, widely read and brilliant conversationalist, and favorite of the ladies—who had known Eleanor's parents and who, as a foreign office professional, had been one of the animators of the shift in Anglo-American relations. The Roosevelts and Spring-Rices were neighbors in Washington and their children friends and schoolmates. Their minds met on the subject of Anglo-American friendship.

Roosevelt was thirty-one when he became assistant secretary. He loved the navy and his job, and was bursting with vitality and ambition. "I get my fingers into almost everything and there's no law against it," Daniels once quoted him as saying. He pored over old navy records from sailing-ship days, and his walls began to be covered with naval prints, his shelves filled with naval books. He was so steeped in naval history that the official navy historian, Robert W. Neeser, frequently consulted him. "I talked about every Naval engagement from Salamis to Falkland Islands with him up to 1 a.m.," Roosevelt reported to his wife after one session with Neeser.[17] He delighted in naval ceremonials: the seventeen-gun salute and four ruffles to which he was entitled, the honor guard on the quarterdeck, the specially designed pennant. He did not hesitate to use the *Dolphin,* the dispatch boat assigned to the secretary, for trips down the Potomac. And, during the summer of 1913, naval vessels were turning up at Campobello. He even piloted a destroyer through the Campobello narrows. "As Mr. Roosevelt made his first turn," recalled William F. Halsey, at that time a lieutenant, "I saw him look aft and check the swing of our stern. My worries were over; he knew his business."[18]

When Daniels took over the secretaryship from George von L. Meyer, Adm. Bradley A. Fiske was "the official strategist of the navy." In his view and that of the other senior officers, "there were only two navies that we had cause to fear, the German and the Japanese. We knew, of course, that the British Navy was much stronger than ours; but we saw no reason for coming into collision with it." As the navy's strategist, Fiske's chief concern, especially in 1914, was the unreadiness of the U.S. fleet for war; but on this matter he could get a hearing from Roosevelt only, not Daniels. "Took to Secretary Daniels the paper of the General Board showing that the Department had no plan or system for getting prepared for war," he noted in his diary on March 19, 1914. "I argued for half an hour. I might as well have tried to scratch a diamond with an iron file! . . . Later, I talked to Assistant Secretary Roosevelt. Of course, he understood the principles at stake."[19]

It was "the German Navy that occupied our attention the most," Fiske said of the years that preceded the outbreak of war. Roosevelt was more worried about the Japanese navy. The Panama Canal was not scheduled for completion until 1915. "One closing legacy," Theodore Roosevelt had written his successor, William H. Taft, on his last day in office in 1909, "under no circumstances divide the battleship fleet between the Atlantic and Pacific Oceans prior to the finishing of the Panama Canal." He wrote in a similar vein to Franklin, three months after the latter had become assistant secretary:

It is not my place to advise, but there is one matter so vital that I want to call your attention to it. I do not anticipate trouble with Japan, but it may come and if it does it will come suddenly. In that case we shall be in an unpardonable position if we permit ourselves to to be caught with our fleet separated. There ought not to be a battleship or any formidable fighting craft in the Pacific unless our entire fleet is in the Pacific. Russia's fate ought to be a warning for all time as to the criminal folly of dividing the fleet if there is even the remotest chance of war.[20]

A crisis with Japan did arise in the spring of 1913, occasioned by Japanese indignation over California land-exclusion laws. The navy wanted to take some precautionary steps, but Daniels thought any movement of the Asiatic squadron would be both provocative and impotent. Wilson and Bryan agreed with him. Four U.S. warships were in the Yangtze on a summer cruise north of the Philippines when the crisis erupted, Roosevelt later informed Admiral Mahan. Roosevelt, supporting the admirals, wanted to move the ships nearer to their Philippine base, but Wilson and Bryan feared such a move might endanger negotiations with Japan. Orders were sent, over Roosevelt's protests, to Admiral Nicholson, telling him not to move out of the Yangtze. Had hostilities broken out, they might have been interned or overwhelmed by superior force, Roosevelt contended.[21]

Daniels, who distrusted admirals as much as Roosevelt admired them, suspected Admiral Fiske of wanting to precipitate a war with Japan. Fiske had sent him a confidential memorandum, with a copy to Roosevelt, warning that Japan might launch a sudden attack upon the United States, seizing the Hawaiian Islands and the Philippines and then standing pat until a war-weary America was ready to sue for peace. "Daniels scoffed but Roosevelt listened and remembered," according to Roosevelt biographer Frank Freidel.*[22]

Rear Admiral Fullam also remembered that crisis. "I got very much wrought up about it," he told Senate investigators in 1920.

I was aide for inspection and personnel then, and I drew up a memorandum of things that I thought ought immediately to be done; oh, anybody would say that they should be done. But I did not take that to Mr. Daniels at all. I did not want him to know I drew it up. . . . I took it to Franklin D. Roosevelt, the Assistant Secretary of the Navy, who usually—always—took a lively interest in the Navy. . . . I said, "Mr. Roosevelt, do you approve of this?" He read it over and he said, "Yes every bit of it." I said, "Will you take that as yours, and do not mention my name as ever having written it, and do not let anybody know that I wrote it, and will you present it to the Secretary of the Navy this afternoon?" He said he would and he took it in there.[23]

Japan and Germany were both potential enemies, but the chief danger was in dispersing and dividing the fleet. Roosevelt, fearing there would be pressure to do so when the Panama Canal was opened in 1915, suggested to Admiral Mahan that he write an article on the subject, which Mahan did for the *North American Review*. Entitled "The Panama Canal and the Distribu-

---

* Yet, as we shall see in Chapters 27 and 28, Roosevelt in December, 1941, although prepared for a surprise attack, did not seriously consider Pearl Harbor as one of Japan's targets.

tion of the Fleet," it appeared in September, 1914; its principal theme was "Halve the fleet and it is inferior in both oceans."[24]

As late as the summer of 1914, Mahan still felt that Japan rather than Germany was the main threat to the United States, and Roosevelt agreed with him. "Personally, I feel that our danger in the Pacific much exceeds that in the Atlantic," Mahan wrote Roosevelt. "I wish it were possible to speak quite frankly and in public about the excess of our danger in the Pacific area over that in the Atlantic." "I agree with you most heartily," Roosevelt replied, "that the European Powers are not disposed to interfere with us, though some members of the General Board do not agree."[25]

Even after war broke out, and though all his sympathies were against Germany and "all our interests favor British success," Mahan was concerned, when Japan declared war on Germany, that Japan would seize the German-held islands in the Pacific. "It is one thing to have them in the hands of a Power whose main strength is in Europe, and quite another that they should pass into the hands of one so near as Japan." He addressed himself to Roosevelt on these matters, Mahan explained in a postscript to one of his letters, "because I know no one else in the Administration to whom I should care to write."[26]

In November, 1914, Mahan came to Washington to do some research. He took time out to call on his young disciple. Roosevelt was out, and no one told him of Mahan's call. A few days later Mahan suddenly took ill and died. The two men never met, but Roosevelt had absorbed the admiral's teachings well.

Among the congratulatory notes that young Roosevelt received on his appointment as assistant secretary was one from C. C. Burlingham, the distinguished New York attorney, who ended his note with the caution that Roosevelt not emulate his counterpart in London, the first lord of the admiralty, Winston Churchill, and become too enthusiastic over a big navy. Events proved this an inapt admonition. Historians would say of Churchill's first tenure at the admiralty that one thing could not be taken away from him: when war came, the fleet was ready. The same might be said of young Roosevelt. Although his chief, Daniels, cherished the hope of an international agreement to limit naval armaments, Roosevelt was a big-navy, big-battleship man. "Dreadnoughts are what we need," he told the *Milwaukee Sentinel,* and coupling Germany with England, since Milwaukee had a large population of German descent, he added, "You can't fight Germany's and England's dreadnoughts with U.S. gunboats, strange as it may seem, and the policy of our Congress should be to build dreadnoughts until our Navy is comparable to any in the world."[27]

Roosevelt promptly allied himself with the navy's general board, the advisory body of senior officers headed by Adm. George Dewey, the victor at Manila Bay, that was demanding a naval build-up, and with the Navy League, the society of shipbuilders, arms suppliers, and retired officers, which out of self-interest as much as out of patriotism, beat the drums for a stronger navy and for whose members Daniels with his bow string tie, porkpie hat, and concern for raising the educational level of the enlisted man, was an object of derision. Through Henry Cabot Lodge, the navy's most influential advocate in the Senate, an audacious Roosevelt even encouraged the Republicans to urge a larger naval construction program than was administration policy. And when war broke out and Lodge launched a savage attack on Daniels for fleet unreadiness, Roosevelt supplied him and his Republican son-in-law, Rep. Augustus Peabody Gardner, with information—an act close to insubordination. "He [Roosevelt] had to learn that loyalty essential not only to democracy, but within it also," wrote Jonathan Daniels, the son of Josephus. The father put it a little differently: "He was young then and made some mistakes. Upon reflection, although I was older, I made mistakes too."[28]

Except for Roosevelt and the general board, Admiral Fullam testified after the war,

nobody gave a willing ear to the seriousness of the situation, and the Navy Department proper was exclusively busied with a routine of peace, totally indifferent to a state of war being forced upon us. . . . Mahan's principle, "The Navy Department should be so organized that it can pass from a state of peace to a state of war without a jar in the machinery," was ignored. . . . Mr. Roosevelt was always anxious to forward measures for the fighting efficiency of the Navy. Like his namesake of glorious memory, he seemed to regard the Navy as the first line of the Nation's defense, and he wanted to see it ready.[29]

In mid-1915, after the sinking of the *Lusitania,* Wilson became a convert to preparedness. He was soon calling for "incomparably the greatest Navy in the world" and ordered Daniels to draw up an adequate naval program. Nevertheless, differences between the secretary and his aggressive young aide persisted. For Daniels, navalist meant imperialist; even though he had a romantic attachment to the navy, he had strong convictions about militarism and "an American tradition . . . more important than any naval heritage— 'the supremacy of the civil over the military authority.' " Roosevelt, on the other hand, at a Navy League dinner in May, 1915, at which Daniels had just praised "the forward-looking" Sixty-third Congress, urged faith in the admirals, "Let us learn to trust the judgment of the real experts, the naval officers. Let us insist that Congress shall carry out their recommendations."[30]

Roosevelt's outlook embraced other tenets of the navalist point of view —economic nationalism, the dependence of U.S. prosperity on foreign trade and overseas possessions, and no unilateral disarmament. He was a vigorous advocate of intervention in Mexico. When, in April, 1914, the United States Navy occupied Vera Cruz and a Minneapolis newspaperman asked Roosevelt the meaning of the crisis, he replied readily, "War, and we're ready." "I do not want war," he said the next morning in Milwaukee, "but I do not see how we can avoid it. Sooner or later, it seems, the United States must go down there and clean up the Mexican political mess. I believe that the best time is right now." But Wilson pulled back. "In foreign relations," Lodge wrote Theodore Roosevelt, "he flinches."[31]

Roosevelt cheered the United States purchase of Saint Thomas from Denmark. He wanted to be there on the day of the transfer. "Incidentally, we have simply got to control these islands as a whole—the sooner the better—the next step is to purchase the Dutch interests!" He exulted in the occupation of Haiti by the U.S. Marines in 1915, and on a combination inspection-holiday trip to Haiti at the beginning of 1917 endorsed the work of the marines there and favored substituting open marine rule for the façade of self-government that remained.[32]

Even war, when it finally came, was an adventure, a test of mettle rather than a final failure and tragedy. In this, too, Roosevelt differed markedly from his chief. He was on the train to Washington from Reading, Pennsylvania, where he had dedicated an anchor from the battleship *Maine,* when he heard the news that Germany had declared war on Russia. "These are history-making days," he wrote his "Dearest Babs" (Eleanor), who was in Campobello. "It will be the greatest war in the world's history." It filled him with excitement. There was work for him to do. "A complete smash-up is inevitable, and there are a great many problems for us to consider. Mr. D[aniels] totally fails to grasp the situation and I am to see the President Monday a.m. to go over our situation."

The next day he expatiated over what he found at the department on his return to Washington:

Nobody seemed the least bit excited about the European crisis—Mr. Daniels feeling chiefly very sad that his faith in human nature and civilization and similar idealistic nonsense was receiving such a rude shock. So I started in alone to get things ready and prepare plans for what *ought* to be done by the Navy end of things. Friday I worked all day on these lines, and actually succeeded in getting one ship north from Mexico.

These dear good people like W.J.B. and J.D. have as much conception of what a general European war means as Elliott [Roosevelt's son] has of higher mathematics. They really believe that because we are neutral we can go about our business as usual. To my horror, *just for example,* J.D. told the newspapermen he thought favorably of sending our fleet to Europe to bring back marooned Americans!

Roosevelt then gave his wife a little lecture on naval doctrine straight out of Mahan:

We should unquestionably gather our fleet together and get it into the highest state of efficiency. We still have twelve battleships at Vera Cruz. . . . The rest of the fleet is scattered to the four winds—they should be assembled and prepared. Some fine day the State Department will want the *moral* backing of a "fleet in being" and it *won't be there.*

To his friend Livingston Davis, Roosevelt wrote shortly after the war broke out, "I have had the most interesting ten days of my life."[33]

The dispersion of the fleet worried Roosevelt. He confided his anxieties to Admiral Fiske. The general board had recommended concentration, Fiske replied, but Daniels had refused. Mahan wrote Roosevelt urging that "the fleet . . . be brought into immediate readiness, and so disposed as to permit of very rapid concentration, ready to proceed where desired." The admiral predicted with astonishing prescience that the war would be decided eventually by sea power; Britain's capacity to concentrate strength in the North Sea and impose a blockade would finally beat Germany to her knees. . . . Germany's procedure is to overwhelm at once by concentrated preparation, and impetuous momentum . . . should the Germans defeat both France and Russia on land, they would gain a "respite" which might enable them to build sea power measurable with England's. In that case the world would be confronted by the naval power of a state, not like Great Britain, sated with territory, but one eager and ambitious for expansion. . . . The consideration may well affect American sympathies.

The United States had a stake in a British victory. U.S. neutrality, Mahan urged Roosevelt, should "omit traditional formula which permitted belligerent ships to coal up enough to reach the nearest national port, for that would be to German advantage."[34]

"So-called private property" on the seas should not be exempt from maritime capture, Mahan had written Theodore Roosevelt in 1904.

Great Britain and the British Navy lie across Germany's carrying trade with the whole world. Exempt it, and you remove the strongest hook in the jaw of Germany that the English-speaking people have—a principal gage for peace.

British interests are not American interests; no. But taking the constitution of the British Empire, and the trade interests of the British Islands, the United States has a certainty of a very high order that the British Empire will stand substantially on the same lines of world privilege as ourselves; that its strength will be our strength, and the weakening [of] it injury to us.[35]

Mahan did not wholly persuade Theodore Roosevelt, but the navy's general board went along with Mahan's qualified approach to freedom of the seas.

Woodrow Wilson became increasingly anti-German. "If Germany won," he told Colonel House, his chief foreign-affairs adviser and emissary "it would change the course of our civilization and make the United States a military nation." But Wilson rejected the navy's conception of a neutrality that favored the Allies. "We must be impartial in thought as well as in action," he said, "[we] must put a curb on our sentiments as well as upon every transaction that might be construed as a preference of one party to the struggle before another."[36]

In line with Wilson's proclamation of neutrality, the navy was given the job of "watching things along the coast," as FDR put it. But the application of Wilsonian principles of neutrality to the practical realities of the British blockade proved to be no simple matter, especially since American sympathies were so overwhelmingly on the side of the Allies. "I've been disappointed that England has been unable to force a naval action," Roosevelt wrote his wife a week after the war began. "Of course it is the obvious course for Germany to hold her main fleet back and try to wear out the blockading enemy with torpedo and submarine attacks in foggy and night conditions."[37]

Blockade, as Mahan predicted, was one of the principal weapons of the Allied powers, perhaps the principal one after the battles of Mons and the Marne produced a grinding war of attrition on the western front. But the tightening of the blockade brought Britain into collision with American rights under international law to trade with belligerents and neutrals on land and sea. The object of British diplomacy, wrote Edward Grey, "was to secure the maximum of blockade that could be enforced without a rupture with the United States." Even before the war settled into a stalemate, America's importance to the Allies was obvious. Churchill, for example, in September, 1914, suggested recruiting volunteers from America. "Nothing," he observed, "will bring American sympathy along with us so much as American blood shed in the field." British naval vessels should not approach American ports too closely in their patrols. "They should . . . discharge their duties with tact," he minuted,* "remembering how greatly British interests are concerned in the maintenance of good relations with the United States."[38]

But generally friendship with America was subordinated by Churchill to military considerations. One of the U.S. Navy's jobs after the outbreak of the war was to see to it that no armed ships of belligerents left American ports. This was fine from the admiralty's point of view as it applied to German auxiliary cruisers masquerading as merchant vessels, but Churchill did not want the prohibition applied to British merchant vessels armed for defense. "I should be so glad if you could see your way to making a strong stand against this," he wrote Grey. "It is only when merchant ships are armed and commissioned as auxiliary cruisers, not for purposes of self-defence, but for those of commerce destruction, that we claim they should be treated as ships of war. . . . I would earnestly ask . . . that very great pressure should be exerted."[39]

Germany's reply to the British blockade was a counterblockade of England, announced in February, 1915, in which the submarine was the principal weapon. This blockade was to be enforced with a maximum of ruthlessness short of provoking U.S. intervention.

This counterstrategy of declaring the waters around Britain a war zone might have been effective had it not been undermined by the differences in the U.S. response to the British and the German blockades. The sinking of unarmed British and American passenger liners, particularly those with Americans aboard, quickly raised a storm of indignation in the United States that quite obliterated American irritation with the British for the destruction of some of its best markets. The United States did not resist British violations of international law, including the seizure as contraband of food and cotton, as determinedly as it condemned, and demanded that Germany desist from, unrestricted submarine warfare. Although Wilson in 1914 had called upon the country to be "impartial in thought as well as in action," by 1916 he was in effect "insisting that the Germans obey international law regardless of what their enemies did."[40]

In this policy of discriminating in favor of Britain, Wilson not only was upheld but was prodded and urged on by young Roosevelt, who, although a member of Wilson's administration, privately conferred with and counseled

---

* *To minute* means "to make a note (as of instructions, comment, or record)" on, for example, an ambassador's dispatch. It often serves as a rough draft of a reply (*Webster's Third New International Dictionary*).

the most militant critics of Wilsonian neutrality, especially Theodore Roosevelt and his associates. The latter, whenever Wilson placed the defense of U.S.
commercial rights or mediation in the interests of a compromise peace ahead
of Anglo-American friendship and Allied victory—which, of course, Wilson,
like 90 per cent of the American people, favored—charged him with indecision, timidity, and misjudgment of the American national interest.

"I dined last night with General Wood, Captain McCoy, Gerald Morgan,
and Basil Miles," Franklin Roosevelt wrote his wife in October, 1914, "most
interesting. They seem to feel the Allies will hold out." Roosevelt's dinner
companions were all TR's allies, observed Jonathan Daniels, writing in defense of his father, who, together with his good friend William Jennings
Bryan, were the leading noninterventionists in the Wilson administration.
Jonathan added, "The group almost constituted belligerency unlimited."[41]

On May 7, 1915, the English Cunard liner *Lusitania,* homeward bound
from New York to Liverpool, was torpedoed without warning by a German
submarine off the south coast of Ireland with a loss of 1,198 lives including
those of 124 Americans. The sinking occasioned a crisis in U.S.-German relations and the resignation of Bryan as secretary of state. Bryan opposed the
dispatch of a second note to Germany in which Wilson demanded that
Germany end its "ruthless" submarine campaign and warned that if this were
not done, the United States would henceforth hold Germany strictly responsible. Bryan considered the note tantamount to a declaration of war.

"These are hectic days all right!" an exhilarated Franklin wrote his wife.
"What d'y' think of W. Jay B.? It's all too long to write about, but I can
only say I'm disgusted clear through. J.D. will not resign!" To Wilson he sent
a note of approval and encouragement: "I believe most strongly that the
Nation is overwhelmingly behind you and that you can count on its continued support." Daniels, although he was the member of the cabinet closest
to Bryan, did not resign because, as he wrote later, he "did not believe the
note would lead to war." But he and Roosevelt argued strenuously over the
policy to be adopted toward Germany's U-boat campaign. "This line of talk
and thought is typical," Roosevelt noted after a clash with Daniels on the
subject. "Things can be done which would possibl[y] make Germany realize
our determination. They are military and economic steps. We shall be forced
to think of them, to choose which will best serve our purpose, unless we go
on negotiating—by notes and more notes— But of this there is a limit—witness the war of 1812."[42]

Pressured by U.S. demands, Germany assured the United States that its
submarine commanders would not sink unarmed passenger liners without
warning. Arguments with the British now came to the forefront of State Department anxieties. The British navy was stopping vessels on the high seas
instead of near enemy ports as the traditional rules of blockade required. It
seized U.S. merchantmen bound for neutral countries on grounds that their
cargoes were ultimately destined for Germany. The British government was
continuously adding to the list of contraband goods and in mid-1915 was
about to prohibit the shipment of cotton, a crop important to the U.S. econ-

omy and vital to the South, whose solid support was a foundation and bed-rock of Wilson's political majority.

Throughout this time of tension between the British foreign office and the U.S. State Department, Roosevelt was on cordial terms with the members of the British embassy. He wrote to his wife of a luncheon he had had with Sir Cecil Spring-Rice. The German ambassador, Count von Bernstorff, "was at the next table, trying to hear what we were talking about! . . . I just *know* I shall do some awful unneutral thing before I get through!" Almost every letter to Eleanor contained some reference to "Springy" or some other mem-ber of the British embassy. "Springy spent an hour with me this afternoon," Roosevelt wrote in August, 1915, "and seems very worried over the financial situation, though the cotton troubles seem to be clearing." A few days later, however, the British placed cotton on the contraband list, and, grumpily, the United States accepted this, too. But when, on August 18, the White Star liner *Arabic* was sunk, with the loss of forty-four lives, including two Amer-icans, Roosevelt was up in arms against Germany. "I have seen Lansing today and am worried about the *Arabic*," Roosevelt wrote his wife a few days later, "and I think the President will really act as soon as we can get the facts. But it seems very hard to wait until Germany tells us her version and I personally doubt if I should be so polite."[43]

It is uncertain when Roosevelt decided in his own mind that the United States must go to war. More than once toward the end of 1916, after the re-election of Wilson, Roosevelt would come into Daniels's office and exclaim, "We've got to get into this war." And each time Daniels would reply with equal warmth, "I hope not."[44]

Roosevelt was in Haiti at the beginning of 1917 when German submarine commanders began to carry out the fateful decision of the German Crown Council of January 9 to resume unrestricted submarine warfare. Daniels or-dered him back to Washington. "Late that afternoon we were back in Wash-ington," FDR concluded the log of his 1917 trip. "I dashed to the Navy Department and found the same thing . . . no excitement, no preparation, no orders to the Fleet at Guantánamo to return to their yards on the East Coast."[45]

The German ambassador had been sent home five days earlier. But through February and March, Wilson continued to debate whether or not to declare war. He was resigned to entering, but he knew the price it would exact and wanted it clear for the record that Germany left him no other course.

Daniels shared the president's feelings. "If any man in official life ever faced the agony of Gethsemane, I was the man in the first four months of 1917," he later wrote. "From the very beginning of the war in Europe I had resisted every influence that was at work to carry the United States into the war."

The central issue in Washington at the end of February was whether to arm U.S. merchantmen and prepare for war. Roosevelt believed that Wilson had the power to arm merchant vessels without congressional authorization, as did Secretary of the Interior Franklin K. Lane, the member of the cabinet to whom Roosevelt was closest. "We wait and wait," Lane wrote his brother on February 16. "Daniels said we must not convoy—that would be dangerous. (Think of a Secretary of the Navy talking of danger!)" Roosevelt's own impatience is reflected in a briefly kept diary. "Saw Colonel House at the White House at six," he wrote on March 5, the day of Wilson's inauguration. "I gave him some guarded views about condition of Navy and opposed strongly sending fleet through Canal in event war. Looks like running away. Bad for morale of fleet and country and too far to bring home if Canal blocked or German submarines in Caribbean."[46]

In the Senate, the small band of noninterventionists had conducted a successful filibuster against the bill that would authorize the president to arm merchant ships. Then the Senate adjourned on March 4. "White House statement that Wilson has power to arm and inference that he will use it," Roosevelt noted on Friday, March 9. "J.D. says he will by Monday. Why doesn't President say so without equivocation?" Saturday, Roosevelt was in Boston. "Inspected Charlestown Navy Yard. . . . They had had no replies from Washington to authority asked for [to enrol men and boats in the naval reserve]—6 days—I got it by radio. . . . Lunched with Class of '04 at Harvard Club and spoke quite freely about Navy."

On Sunday in New York, Roosevelt again saw Colonel House. "Outlined principal weaknesses of Navy—J.D.'s procrastination—Benson's [chief of naval operations] dislike of England—failure to make plans with France and England and study their methods—necessity if war comes of going into it with all force—money, troops, etc. He was sympathetic and agreed to main points."

That evening Roosevelt dined at the Metropolitan Club in New York City. Those present were ardent interventionists—and Republicans: Theodore Roosevelt, Gen. Cornelius Bliss, General Wood, J. P. Morgan, Elihu Root, New York City's reform mayor John Purroy Mitchel, and New Jersey Gov. Walter Edge. "Condition of army and navy outlined. Discussion of (1) how to make administration steer clear course to uphold rights, (2) how to get active increase army and navy. Decided to use Governors' Conference to demand this. Root inclined to praise Administration's present course. T.R. wanted more vigorous demand about future course—less indorsement of the past. I backed T.R.'s theory. Left for Wash."

Roosevelt had inspected navy installations in New York as well as in Boston. "Told J.D. things not satisfactory Boston and worse N.Y. He said nothing." Wilson that day ordered armed neutrality on his own executive authority. "Final instructions sent to commanders of armed merchant ships," Roosevelt noted in his Diary, adding with a slight touch of exasperation, "Lansing's suggestion that they be allowed [in the war zone] to fire on ships [submarines] showing no colors was eliminated at Benson's objections. Asked Secretary in presence of Benson that matters pertaining to naval district defense be put under me. To be discussed tomorrow. Something must be done soon to organize and expedite work." Here the diary ends.

On March 18 German submarines torpedoed three American vessels, and the cabinet, including Daniels, advised Wilson to ask Congress to declare war. "The Cabinet is at last a unit," wrote Secretary Lane. But the president, he added, "goes unwillingly." So did Daniels. "Having tried patience," he wrote in his diary, "there was no other course to us except to protest our rights on the seas. If Germans win, we must be a military nation."[47]

Congress was summoned to meet on April 2 in special session "to receive a communication concerning grave matters." There was no alternative to war, a solemn president explained to the reassembled Congress. Autocracy was the foe of liberty.

The world must be made safe for democracy. . . . It is a fearful thing to lead this great peaceful people into this most terrible and disastrous of all wars, civilization itself seeming to be in the balance. But the right is more precious than peace, and we shall fight for the things which we have always carried nearest our hearts.

"I went," wrote Eleanor Roosevelt, "and listened breathlessly and re-turned home still half-dazed by the sense of impending change."[48]

For Franklin it was a time of rousing self-fulfillment and mission. Eleanor accompanied her husband to a Navy League reception for the head of the British naval group, one of the high-ranking Allied officials who came hurry-ing to Washington immediately after the United States entered the war. In Franklin's remarks he sought to awaken the public to Allied needs. The British and French missions had been given "fair words, and again fair words," he said, but they had a right to ask about "the number of men that have left America for the other side. . . . It is time that they [Congress and the people] insist on action *at once*. Action that will give something definite— definite ships, definite men—on a definite day."

Franklin, Eleanor reported to his mother, "said all he has pent up for weeks. It was solemn and splendid and I was glad he did it and I think a good many people were but I shouldn't wonder if the Secretary was annoyed."[49]

The Allied missions pressed urgently for the dispatch of U.S. destroyers. Even before America entered the war, the younger officers and Roosevelt had understood that curbing the submarine was the greatest challenge to the Allied naval forces, and they now supported the Allied missions in their requests. But the senior officers in the Navy Department demurred. They did not want to diminish the U.S. Atlantic fleet as a fighting unit, even though the British navy had the German Grand Fleet safely bottled up in the North Sea. This became another argument with Daniels, who noted in his diary: "Roose-velt . . . proposed that we should send destroyers to England and tell her we would expect her to furnish in return some of her best dreadnoughts. . . . Lansing had made the same suggestion to Cabinet and President has not approved."[50]

As part of an aggressive antisubmarine strategy, Roosevelt pushed a plan to lay a mine barrage across the North Sea to bottle up the submarines in their nests. He was the chief advocate of the plan at a time when Daniels questioned its practicality and the British admiralty dragged its heels.

"I have loved every minute of it," Roosevelt said as the Great War drew to a close.[51]

Twenty-one years later, when, as president, he was seeking to arouse the country to the danger that a Nazi-dominated continent constituted for the United States, he explained to the American Society of Newspaper Editors that the danger was clear to anyone with a knowledge of geography, which in its broadest sense, was the basis of an understanding of foreign affairs.

I was given the privilege, in 1913, by my old chief, of coming down here and learning more geography, not only the country but the world, because the Navy was concerned with the world. It had to do with other things that went with geography, the relative military strength of other nations, the relative economic strength of other nations to conduct a war. There were the strategical and even, in the narrower places, the tactical positions that one country bore to the other countries.[52]

The geopolitical problem in 1939 remained in its essentials what it had been twenty-five years earlier. That was the import of his letter to Churchill.

Chapter Three

Churchill at the Admiralty
1914 and 1939

CHURCHILL was born in 1874, Roosevelt in 1882. Both achieved their first appointment to a high government post when they were thirty-one. In December, 1905, Churchill, who had recently crossed over from the Conservative to the Liberal party benches in the House of Commons, was named undersecretary of state for the colonies in the Liberal party cabinet headed by Sir Henry Campbell-Bannerman. The man under whom he served, Lord Elgin, was twenty-five years his senior. He had been viceroy of India while Churchill was a subaltern there. The uneasy, vigilant, but fruitful relationship between the two at the colonial office from December, 1905, to April, 1908, was not unlike the difficult relationship between Roosevelt and Daniels. Elgin, a modest, tolerant, amiable, and cautious man, full of a "high sense of seriousness and duty," appeared to Churchill's lifelong friend and private secretary Edward March as "a rugged old thane of antique virtue," while Churchill was the "young man in a hurry," as Campbell-Bannerman characterized him, and as "restless, egotistical, bumptious, shallow-minded and reactionary, but with a certain personal magnetism, great pluck and some orginality not of intellect but of character," as Beatrice Webb saw him.[1]

"Undoubtedly Churchill sorely tried Elgin's patience," commented Ronald Hyams, the chronicler of their relationship. "Like Gulliver [Elgin] found 'by experience that young men are too opinionative and volatile to be guided by the sober dictates of their seniors.' " Churchill's gift for arresting statement was already widely known. Brilliantly written minutes within the department were an asset; they became less appealing to Elgin when Churchill's exposed the differences between them, sometimes with wounding levity. A long Churchill memorandum ended grandly, "These are my views." "But not mine," Elgin appended firmly. And, like Roosevelt at the Navy Department, Churchill, for all of his egotism and love of the limelight and fun-loving high spirits, made a contribution to policy, especially to the central issue that confronted the colonial office at the time—namely, how much self-government should be permitted to Transvaal in the new constitution, where the argument for limitation was that the Boer should not be allowed "to regain by the ballot box what he had lost by the sword" and where Churchill's memorandum, dated January 2, 1906, "was a classic statement of the primary principle of the political conduct of the Victorian and Edwardian ruling *elite,* the principle of timely concession to retain an ultimate control."

Churchill was given the honor of announcing the terms of the new constitution in the House of Commons. "He was persuasive, temperate, and restrained through-out, showing a perfect sense of the occasion," recalled Violet Bonham Carter.[2]

Although Randolph Churchill, in his life of his father, said it was "strange" in retrospect that "no one on either side, Boer or British, Liberal or Tory, foresaw any racial issue between black and white" in South Africa, a few paragraphs later, he quoted from a speech his father gave in the House that showed a lively awareness of the racial issue. In the presence of the "black peril," young Churchill said, "all the harsh discordances which divide the European population in South Africa vanish. Farmer and Capitalist, Landlord and miner, and Boer, Briton and Afrikaner forget their bitter feuds and are all united in the presence of what they regard as the greatest peril which they will ever have to face. Even during the worst stresses of the war it was regarded as a nameless crime on either side to set the black man on his fellow foe." In the United States, Churchill noted, the ratio of white to black was eight to one, "and even there I believe there is something sometimes approaching to racial difficulties but in South Africa the proportion is one white man to five natives." The "black peril" had the redeeming feature of causing the European to forget his feuds and "to look with a real feeling of self-restraint and comfort to the armed forces of the British Crown." It was, nevertheless, the intention of the government, added Churchill, "as far as we can, to advance the principle of equal rights of civilised men irrespective of colour" and to speak out "when necessary if any plain case of cruelty or exploitation of the native for the sordid profit of the white man can be proved."

No liberal statesman could have gone further on the racial issue without "completely alienating" the Boers, Randolph Churchill observed. By comparison, in the United States the treatment of blacks during the administration of Woodrow Wilson, a Virginian by birth, retrogressed, without protest from Franklin D. Roosevelt.[3]

In 1908, on the resignation (because of illness) of Campbell-Bannerman as prime minister, the king sent for Henry Asquith, who had been chancellor of the exchequer, and requested him to form a new government. Churchill, impatient for full cabinet rank, wrote to Asquith, arguing his case to head the colonial office. "Practically all the constructive action and all the Parliamentary exposition has been mine. I have many threads in hands and many plans in movement." Asquith overlooked his brashness and self-advertisement, not to mention his disloyalty. He appointed Churchill president of the Board of Trade and, not long afterward, home secretary. Lord Elgin, reviewing his recent relationship with his young aide, wrote in terms that were reminiscent of Daniels's writing about Roosevelt at the end of the navy experience:

I think I may say I succeeded, certainly we have had no quarrel during the two and one half years, on the contrary, he has again and again thanked me for what he learned and for our pleasant personal relations, and I have taken a keen interest in his ability and in many ways attractive personality. But all the same I know quite well that it has affected my position *outside the office,* and the strain has been severe.[4]

As president of the Board of Trade, Churchill succeeded another up-and-coming politician, the radical Welshman David Lloyd George, eleven years Churchill's senior, who had moved on to become chancellor of the exchequer. The political world paired them. Beatrice Webb modified her earlier harsh verdict.

We lunched with Winston Churchill and his bride—a charming lady, well bred and pretty, and earnest withal—but not rich, by no means a good match, which is to Winston's credit. Winston had made a really eloquent speech on the unemployed the night before. He is brilliantly able—more than a phrase-monger, I think.

Lloyd George is a clever fellow, but has less intellect than Winston and not such an attractive personality.[5]

Churchill, as home secretary, allied himself with Lloyd George in a group called the "economists" in opposition to the admiralty's proposals to increase the battleship program. In a printed paper that he circulated to the cabinet, Churchill expressed "his scepticism about the danger of the German challenge," which the admiralty was citing in order to justify the increase. Holding down the military budget was popular with the Liberal rank and file. Asquith complained to his wife that Lloyd George and Churchill "by their machinations have got the bulk of the Liberal press into [their] camp," adding that there were moments "when I am disposed summarily to cashier them both."[6]

But the Moroccan crisis, when Germany, in dispute with France, flexed her muscles by sending the gunboat *Panther* to Agadir, persuaded both Lloyd George and Churchill that Germany's growing navy could be a menace to Britain. And with his appointment to the admiralty in 1911 as first lord, Churchill's absorptions shifted. Men who move happily and naturally in the center of the stage also have the capacity for making the position they occupy or role they are playing or department they are heading the center of the world. "He never gets fairly alongside the person he is talking to," complained Asquith, "because he is always so much more interested in himself and his own preoccupations and his own topics."[7]

Churchill came into his own with his appointment as first lord. "His whole life was invested with a new significance," Asquith's daughter wrote. "He was tasting fulfillment. Never, before or since, did I see him more completely and profoundly happy." Now he became "the extravagant, demanding First Lord," and within a year he was in furious argument with Lloyd George over the size of the budget allocation to the navy, writing on one occasion, although the letter was not sent, "These large issues ought not to affect personal friendships." "He is too concentrated on his particular office," a colleague wrote in his Diary. "He has not got the art of playing in conjunction with others. . . . When we refuse him anything, he talks of resigning."[8]

Churchill's tutor on navy matters was Lord Fisher who had been first sea lord of the admiralty until 1907 and under whose leadership Britain had built a great battle fleet of dreadnoughts. Churchill and Fisher first met when the former was at the colonial office. "He was the First Sea Lord and in the height of his reign," Churchill wrote in *The World Crisis*. "We talked all day long and far into the night. He told me wonderful stories of the Navy and of his plans—all about Dreadnoughts, all about submarines, all about new educational schemes for every branch of the Navy, all about big guns, and splendid Admirals and foolish miserable ones." Fisher was an indefatigable letter writer and bombarded his new protégé with a chain of missives on every variety of naval topic. "My dear Lord Fisher," Churchill promptly wrote him on becoming first lord, "I want to see you very much."[9]

German intentions was the dominant question in 1912 for Britain as a whole and for the admiralty especially. Churchill put the problem succinctly in a speech in Glasgow a few months after he became first lord:

The British Navy is to us a necessity and, from some points of view, the German Navy is to them more in the nature of a luxury. Our naval power involves British existence. It is existence to us. It is expansion to them.[10]

Churchill was upset to find, when he arrived at the admiralty, that "The Royal Navy had made no contribution to naval history" and that "the standard work on Sea Power was written by an American Admiral." But he shared and was deeply imbued with Mahan's central doctrine:

It should not be supposed that mastery on the seas depends on the simultaneous occupation of every sea. On the contrary it depends upon ability to defeat the strongest battlefleet or combination which can be brought to bear. This ability cannot be maintained by a policy of dispersion. The sea is all one, and war is all one. The supreme strategic principle of concentration of superior force in the decisive theatre, and the supreme tactical principle described by Napoleon as "frapper la masse" must govern all naval dispositions.[11]

In his pursuit of the "strongest fleet" Churchill was moving against Liberal tradition and that sizable segment of Liberal opinion which believed that "if Britain would relax the pace of naval building the Germans would do likewise." Lloyd George assailed his colleague's naval estimates on the basis of fiscal soundness and extravagance. "Winston is being bitterly attacked in the Liberal papers," Lord Riddell noted in his diary. "Samuel, Simon and Runciman [all Liberal MPs at this time] are doing their utmost to force him out of the Cabinet." Churchill's aunt, Lady Wimborne, expostulated with him: "You are breaking with the tradition of Liberalism in your naval expenditures;

you are in danger of becoming purely a 'Navy man' and losing sight of the far greater job of a great leader of the Liberal Party." She warned that he was in danger of wrecking his political career. Though a democrat "to the bone," observed Violet Bonham Carter astutely, and "imbued with a deep reverence for Parliament and a strong sense of human rights, he was never quite a liberal. He never shared the reluctance which inhibits liberals from invoking force to solve a problem. And though he revelled in discussion he was by temperament an intellectual autocrat. He never liked having other people's way. He infinitely preferred his own."[12]

Asquith urged Churchill to compromise on the issue of his naval estimates. "Very largely in deference to my appeal, the critical pack (who know very well that they have behind them a large body of party opinion) have slackened their pursuit." Churchill should show "a corresponding disposition and throw a baby or two out of the sledge." Churchill refused to bend. He was not enamored of "this naval expenditure," but "the sledge is bare of babies, and though the pack may crunch the driver's bones, the winter will not be ended."[13]

It was Lloyd George who capitulated, urged to do so by his wife. "Oddly enough, my wife spoke to me last night about this dreadnought business," he greeted Churchill at a reconciliation breakfast:

She said, "you know, my dear, I never interfere in politics; but they say you are having an argument with that nice Mr. Churchill about building Dreadnoughts. Of course I don't understand these things, but I should have thought it better to have too many rather than too few." So I have decided to let you build them. Let's go in to breakfast.

Speaking a few weeks later in Parliament on the naval estimates, Churchill defended them, saying that "our diplomacy depends in great part for its effectiveness upon our naval position, and that our naval strength is the one great balancing force which we can contribute to our safety and to the peace of the world."[14]

Three months later the Austrian archduke Francis Ferdinand was assassinated, and with the Austrian ultimatum to Serbia the war crisis came to a boil. "Everything tends towards castastrophe and collapse," Churchill wrote his "darling one and beautiful," as he addressed his wife Clementine.

I am interested, geared up and happy. Is it not horrible to be built like that? The preparations have a hideous fascination for me. . . . No one can measure the consequences. I wondered whether those stupid Kings and Emperors could not assemble together and revivify kingship by saving the nations from hell but we all drift on in a kind of dull catalyptic trance. As if it were somebody else's operation![15]

"Winston very bellicose and demanding immediate mobilization," Asquith noted. And Asquith's daughter, Lady Violet, recalled that in the rare moments that she saw Churchill during the build-up of the crisis, "I felt in him a sense of tense expectancy and exhilaration—as if an arrow in a bow waiting impatiently to be released."[16]

Not everyone in the British cabinet was for intervention on the Continent even if Germany should attack France and Belgium. His colleagues, according to Churchill, were overwhelmingly pacific; he, however, was strenuously in favor of going in. He had, even while the issue was being debated, ordered the fleet moved to its war station at Scapa Flow. The Grand Fleet had been assembled for review at Portland and, in agreement with its operational chief Prince Louis of Battenberg, Churchill had kept it from dispersing. Now it sailed for its war station on the North Sea, an order that Churchill cleared with Asquith but kept concealed from the cabinet, "which might have objected to it as provocative." This was a fateful move, wrote military historian Liddell Hart, for it positioned the fleet for the blockade and the blockade proved to be "the decisive agency in the struggle."[17]

Lady Violet contrasted the attitudes of her father and Churchill at the approach of war:

Next morning [August 4] the news came that the Germans had invaded Belgium. An ultimatum to Germany, to expire at midnight, was drafted by my father and Sir Edward Grey and dispatched. In his daily notes my father wrote: "The whole thing fills me with sadness."

No one could have described Winston as "filled with sadness." He rose to this greatest of all adventures with glowing zest. (And who can blame him?—though some did.) For three years he had devoted all his powers to preparing the Navy to meet the challenge of this hour, and he knew that he had done it well. The hour had come. He hailed it with cheer. . . . It is true that the dark and tragic certainties to which Grey and my father were alive were hidden from Winston's eyes. Against this he was alive to things which others did not see. His power of concentrating on one aim to the exclusion of all else was at once his weakness and his strength.[18]

The ultimatum expired and Churchill was authorized to signal all ships: "Commence hostilities at once with Germany. . . ." Lloyd George caught the moment as recorded by Asquith's wife Margot:

Winston dashed into the room radiant, his face bright, his manner keen, one word pouring out on another how he was going to send telegrams to the Mediterranean, the North Sea, and God knows where. You could see he was a really happy man.[19]

Churchill's energy and ebullience, combined with a habit of command and disdain for leaders who shrank from the hard decisions that war involved ("the capacity to run risks is at famine prices. All play for safety," he wrote his brother Jack), soon brought him into conflict with many of his colleagues. He made repeated visits across the Channel to France to the British expeditionary force. They gave him a first-hand feeling for what trench warfare was like. But the visits were resented, especially by Lord Kitchener, the secretary of state for war. His colleagues privately were derisive.

Churchill could not overcome Kitchener's opposition to his visits to France,* an opposition that at one point exploded into a threat to resign. "The Army thinks that he mingles too much in military matters," Asquith

* Kitchener had also tried to keep young Churchill out of the Sudan.

wrote to Venetia Stanley,* "& the Navy that he is too much away in what may be critical moments for them. I am so far disposed to agree that I think, after this, I shan't allow him to go again for a long time." When Sir John French, commander in chief of the British expeditionary force, came to London, Asquith cautioned him against Churchill's visits. "I found that [French] was substantially of the same opinion, & with all his affection & admiration for W, estimates his judgement as 'highly erratic.' "[20]

One visit to the Continent in the early weeks of the war—to Antwerp in order to stiffen Belgian resolve to defend that city—had the approval of his colleagues. As Asquith reported to Venetia Stanley:

The intrepid Winston set off at midnight. . . . He will go straightway & beard the King & his Ministers, & try to infuse into their backbones the necessary quantity of starch. . . . I don't know how fluent he is in French, but if he was able to do himself justice in a foreign tongue, the Belges will have listened to a discourse the like of which they have never heard before.[21]

Churchill toured Antwerp's defenses, arranged for the British naval brigade, which was at the disposal of the admiralty, to join the defensive forces, and, caught up in the excitement of prospective combat, telegraphed an astonished Asquith and offered to resign from the cabinet and to take over command of Antwerp's defenses. Earlier that day Asquith had recorded that "Winston succeeded in bucking up the Belges, who gave up their panicky idea of retreating to Ostend. . . . Then comes in a real bit of tragi-comedy," he added, speaking of Churchill's request to resign, and he told how he had reluctantly reported Churchill's request to the cabinet. "I regret to say that it was received with a Homeric laugh."[22]

The request "staggered" Asquith's daughter.

What amazed and shook me was the sense of proportion (or lack of it) revealed by Winston's choice. His desire to exchange the Admiralty, in which for years he had invested all his treasure and which was now faced with its first test and greatest opportunity, for the command of a mere major-general, one of many, in the field seemed to me to be hardly adult. It was the choice of a romantic child. In terms of scope and power the jobs were not comparable. He would be abdicating his part in the grand strategy of the war, which he had always seen in world-wide terms, in order to play a personal part in a small patch of it. . . . Had he imagined life without his telegrams and boxes?—his access to the heart of things? . . . I could not reconcile his wish with his dramatic sense or his imaginative range.[23]

He bewildered his friends; he exasperated his colleagues; the king considered him "irresponsible and unreliable." Yet there was always a recognition that he had some special, unique quality. Men feared the demonic fire that burned in his spirit, but they also warmed themselves by it.

---

* Venetia Stanley (1887–1948) was the youngest daughter of Lord Sheffield, close friend and contemporary of Violet Asquith, and recipient of the prime minister's most intimate confidences. In July, 1915, she married Edwin Montagu, one of Asquith's closest political associates.

"What is it that gives Winston his pre-eminence?" Margot Asquith asked in her diary on his fortieth birthday.

I said long ago & with truth Winston has a noisy mind. Certainly not his judgement. . . . It is of course his courage & colour—his amazing mixture of industry & enterprise. . . . He never shirks, hedges, or *protects* himself—though he thinks of himself perpetually. *He takes huge risks.* He is at his very best just now; when others are shrivelled with grief—apprehensive, silent, irascible & self-conscious morally; Winston is intrepid, valorous, passionately keen & sympathetic, longing to be in the trenches—dreaming of war, big, buoyant, happy, even. It is very extraordinary, he is a born soldier.[24]

He could not bear to be passive personally or on the defensive militarily. An operations officer who dined with Churchill at the admiralty found the first lord "rather oppressed with the impossibility of *doing* anything." By the end of October, 1914, the western front was firmly frozen, and advocates of an aggressive strategy were desperately searching for moves that might give the Allies the military initiative. "His volatile mind," Asquith wrote Venetia Stanley, "is at present set on Turkey & Bulgaria, & he wants to organise a heroic adventure against Gallipoli & the Dardanelles: to which I am altogether opposed."[25]

A static western front made sea power more than ever appear to be the key to victory. There was the blockade whose effects Churchill described graphically: "Germany is like a man throttled with a heavy gag. You know the effect of such a gag. . . . The effort wears out the heart, and Germany knows it. The pressure should not be relaxed until she gives in unconditionally." Churchill and Lord Fisher, the first sea lord, pressed in the cabinet for permission to wage ruthless economic warfare against Germany, even at the risk of antagonizing neutral opinion, especially America's. At the beginning of the war Churchill himself had been quite alive to the dangers of alienating the United States, but as the blockade increased in strategic importance he became less concerned with United States reaction.[26]

Blockade was one arm of a strategy based on sea power; the other arm was an end run around the western front. For a time Churchill pushed a plan to capture the German island of Borkum in the North Sea as a stepping stone for an invasion of North Germany. But the Dardanelles expedition, also fathered by Churchill, proved more attractive to the war council. It would yield richer political dividends and ease the situation of Russia. Moreover Vice-Admiral Carden, in command of the eastern Mediterranean, advised the cabinet that the Dardanelles could be forced by ships alone without troops. Although Churchill doubted that a purely naval operation could succeed, he was so intent on the operation as a whole that he went along with the plans and made himself in the eyes of Parliament and the public their principal sponsor.

This is not the place to recount the story of the Gallipoli disaster. When the naval operation failed and plans for a military landing were approved, control of the operation passed from Churchill to Kitchener, much to the former's unhappiness. The difficulties mounted. Lord Fisher turned against the enterprise and resigned, precipitating a political crisis that was resolved by Asquith's decision, made in order to head off a Conservative onslaught, to reconstitute his government on a coalition basis. He also decided that Churchill had to go. He is "far the most disliked man in my Cabinet by his colleagues," Asquith had told his wife a few weeks earlier.

When the prime minister informed Churchill of his decision to form a national government, he asked him, "What are we to do for you?" indicating thereby that Churchill was no longer to remain at the admiralty. On May 27 Churchill was named chancellor of the duchy of Lancaster, a cabinet post whose only duty was to appoint county magistrates. Not long after that he resigned that post to go to France as a soldier. "The Dardanelles haunted him for the rest of his life," Clementine Churchill said. "He always believed in it. When he left the Admiralty he thought he was finished. . . . I thought he would never get over the Dardanelles; I thought he would die of grief."[27]

Early in 1916 the divisions that had been landed on the Gallipoli peninsula were withdrawn and the enterprise abandoned as a disastrous failure; Churchill was made the scapegoat. Yet the conception was sound. "If the British had used at the outset," wrote Liddell Hart, "even a fair proportion of the force they ultimately expended in driblets, it is clear from Turkish accounts that victory would have crowned their undertaking."[28]

By the end of 1915, the British army had passed from the "easterners" to the "westerners," as the strategists were called who believed that the path to victory was to go "through" rather than "around" the western front's trench barrier. But on the western front it would not make much difference which side attacked. It remained a war of attrition, of immense butchery for negligible gains. In the end it was the blockading navy that was the decisive instrument in bringing about the German surrender—the "gag" had finally done its work.

"Patience is the only grace you need," Sir Winston's wife wrote to Churchill at the beginning of 1916. The events that followed Churchill's loss of the admiralty—his ouster from the cabinet altogether, his departure for France to take his place in the battle line, his restless return to the back benches of Parliament and twenty months "in the wilderness," and his discovery that "they don't want to listen to me, or use me. They only want to keep me out"—began to teach him the lesson of biding his time, of curbing his ego, lessons that Roosevelt learned when polio brought him low.[29]

Churchill held many government posts between the time of the Gallipoli disaster and his return to the admiralty in 1939: minister of munitions, war secretary, and colonial secretary under Lloyd George; and in the twenties, once again a Conservative, he was chancellor of the exchequer. But none had the spice and savor of the admiralty in wartime. For eleven years— from the time of the fall of the Baldwin ministry in 1929—he had been "in the political wilderness," which was a slow kind of death. He had not been too anxious for office in the first years of his opposition to the government.

The revival of German power and threat in the thirties, however, made him eager to lay his hands once more "upon our military machine."

But after Baldwin's landslide victory in 1935, the Conservative party managers said "No." "To me," Churchill wrote, "this definite, and as it seemed final, exclusion from all share in the preparations for defence was a heavy blow." He had to struggle to keep himself under control "and appear serene, indifferent, detached."[30]

Baldwin retired after the abdication crisis and the crowning of King George VI, but Neville Chamberlain, who succeeded him, did not even consider Churchill for his cabinet. Churchill had championed the abdicated king, at times standing almost alone in a hostile House of Commons, and at the end of the crisis had so fallen in public estimation that again "it was the almost universal view that my political life was at last ended." The new prime minister, moreover, came into office with hopes of bringing about a general settlement with Hitler and Mussolini. He was a forceful executive who knew that his ideas were different from Churchill's, and he had always kept Churchill at arm's length. "I had no expectation that [Chamberlain] would wish to work with me; nor would he have been wise to do so at such a time," Churchill later wrote.[31]

By September, 1939, events had proven Churchill right and Chamberlain fatally wrong about Hitler. Chamberlain was distrusted not only by Liberal and Labour, but by a large number of Tory M.P.s. Churchill had known that Chamberlain would not turn to him except as a "last resort." "Churchill's chances [of entering the government] improve as war becomes more probable and *vice versa*," Chamberlain had noted in his diary at the beginning of the summer. On September 1 Hitler's armies invaded Poland. That same day Chamberlain invited Churchill to join the war cabinet. The hostility of Commons toward Chamberlain was made evident on September 2, when Britain and France had not yet declared war on Germany even though Hitler's armies were deep in Poland. "Speak for England, Arthur," was the cry from Conservative benches when Arthur Greenwood arose to give Labour's answer to Chamberlain's marking-time speech.

The next day, Chamberlain, at 11:15 A.M., broadcast that England was at war. Soon afterward the air-raid sirens sounded in London. Churchill and his wife repaired to the shelter, "armed with a bottle of brandy and other appropriate medical comforts." That afternoon Chamberlain offered him the admiralty as well as a seat in the war cabinet. Churchill promptly betook himself to the admiralty and the signal went out to the fleet: "Winston is back."

"So it was that I came again to the room I had quitted in pain and sorrow almost exactly a quarter of a century before, when Lord Fisher's resignation had led to my removal from my post as First Lord." As a government minister, Churchill had always been noted for the volubility of a pen which poured forth advice, dissents, briefs, and minutes to all of his colleagues on their business as well as his own. But now that he was back at the center of power, chastened by his years in the wilderness, he was determined to be the most loyal and supportive of colleagues. "I was anxious to establish a broad basis of common ground with the Prime Minister," and would not jeopardize this effort by a stream of letters to President Roosevelt. He was careful to obtain not only the prime minister's permission before replying to Roosevelt's invitation to correspond, but the consent of the foreign secretary, Lord Halifax, saying to him, as reported by Halifax, "that it was a good thing to feed him [Roosevelt] at intervals. He said he would always show me anything he was sending."[32]

As a further gesture of administrative loyalty, Churchill confined his communications, until he became prime minister, to admiralty business, furnishing Roosevelt, he said, "with a stream of information about our naval affairs." "Stream of information" was a considerable exaggeration. In a correspondence that would total 1,200 communications from Churchill and 800 from Roosevelt, less than twenty-five were exchanged before Churchill became prime minister.

Chapter Four

The Unspoken Naval Alliance

I N MAY, 1939, under conditions of the utmost secrecy, the British admiralty sent a planning officer to Washington to discuss Anglo-American naval dispositions in the event that Britain found herself at war with Germany. In these discussions, according to the U.S. Navy's official account, it was agreed that "command of the western and southern Atlantic, as well as the Pacific, would have to be assured by the United States Fleet."[1]

Several times before the outbreak of the war, Roosevelt, hobbled by congressional resistance to amending the Neutrality Act in favor of the democracies, had used Anglo-American naval cooperation to signal the war offices of the Axis powers that they should not count upon U.S. noninvolvement in or detachment from a war arising out of their aggressions. In 1938, Captain Royal E. Ingersoll, assigned to naval liaison in London, had prodded the State and Navy Departments to agree—and with Roosevelt's support they did—to London's request that four American cruisers attend the ceremonies at the opening of the new British naval base at Singapore.[2] In the spring of 1939 Roosevelt joined the United States fleet, which had been brought from the Pacific for naval maneuvers off the Windward Islands, " 'a fleet problem' to be held in those waters for the first time," he wrote George VI of England. "I imagine that some international significance may be attached to them." He wished the king could join him. Clearly the potential enemy in the exercises was not the British fleet. And after the maneuvers were concluded, the fleet, instead of proceeding to New York harbor for the World's Fair, as it had been scheduled to do, was ordered back to the Pacific. The change in plans was widely interpreted to mean, as Roosevelt intended, that the United States would stand guard in the Pacific and thereby free the English fleet for action in Europe, if necessary.

In June, 1939, King George VI visited Roosevelt, and the president, in a very frank talk about the help he planned to give Britain in the event of war, sketched his ideas of a western Atlantic patrol that, basing itself in Trinidad and Bermuda, would fan out along a radius of 1,000 miles by sea and air. "The idea is that U.S.A. should relieve us of these responsibilities," the king recorded, "but can it be done without a declaration of war?"

A few weeks later Roosevelt secretly proposed to the British that the United States should establish "a patrol over the waters of the Western Atlantic with a view to denying them to the German Navy in the event of war. Although," said the foreign office record of this offer, "the proposal was vague and woolly and open to certain objections, we assented informally as the patrol was to be operated in our interests."[3]

The division of labor between the Atlantic and Pacific was becoming clear. But how could a nonbelligerent, "neutral" United States take on the additional chore of standing guard in the western and southern Atlantic? Roosevelt came up with the idea of establishing a "neutrality zone" around the Western Hemisphere, ranging in depth from 300 to 600 miles, from which the warships of all the belligerents would be excluded. Sumner Welles carried this proposal for a hemispheric "chastity belt" (as some British foreign office people derisively called it) to the Inter-American Conference that gathered in Panama City on September 23 to adopt a hemispheric approach to the war in Europe. The "Declaration of Panama" asserted the right of the twenty-one American republics to have the waters adjacent to them free from hostile acts by any non-American belligerent, and they circumscribed these waters by a line that ran 300 to 1,000 miles out from the coast from the Canadian border south.

It was the president's idea, said Hull. He himself was skeptical. Such a zone had no precedent in international law, and the belligerents could be expected to object. Moreover, it would be difficult to enforce. But since Roosevelt had so "wholeheartedly embraced" the proposal, Hull went along.[4]

The Germans immediately saw that the zone contracted the area in which their commerce raiders—whether U-boat or pocket battleship—could hunt. The "American Closed Zone" plan, a German foreign office analysis concluded, was disadvantageous to Germany, but German officials preferred to let the odium for rejecting it fall upon Great Britain and France. They drew comfort from press accounts that described the English government as unwilling to recognize the closed zone. "English naval opinion is especially critical of the fact that it would cut off England from her American colonies."[5]

The Germans did not know that the zone, in fact, screened a pooling of Anglo-American naval resources. Churchill, signing himself as "naval person," had on October 5, 1939, informed Roosevelt that the neutrality-zone decision, which had been transmitted to him by Ambassador Kennedy, was acceptable to the British government:

We do not mind how far south the prohibited zone goes, provided that it is effectively maintained. We should have great difficulty in accepting a zone which was policed by some weak neutral. But of course if the American navy takes care of it, that is all right.

The British were on the lookout for a German raider off Brazil—either the pocket battleship *Admiral Scheer* or the 10,000-ton cruiser *Hipper,* Churchill went on.

The more American ships cruising along the South American coast the better, as you, sir [meaning Roosevelt] would no doubt hear what they saw or did not see. Raider might then find American waters rather crowded, or may anyhow prefer to go on to sort of trade routes, where we are preparing.

Churchill had brought Adm. Tom Phillips* into the discussion with Kennedy about the neutrality zone, and Phillips sent along a message with Churchill's that enumerated the conditions of British acquiescence: British consent was not to be considered a precedent in international law; British warships would continue to have "free access" to British or Allied territories within the zone; the use of the area as a "sanctuary" would be prevented; the extent of the zone would depend on the possibilities of "effective enforcement"; the British would retain the right of "pursuit" should a raider take sanctuary in the zone; and "we should of course hope to obtain any information concerning the movements of enemy forces within the area since otherwise the operation of the scheme would greatly reduce the possibilities of obtaining real information for ourselves."[6]

Roosevelt's keenness on the neutrality patrol was made evident a few days after he received these messages. He was "disturbed," he wrote Acting Secretary of the Navy Charles Edison, by the

slowness of getting the East Coast, Caribbean and Gulf patrols under way. . . . It is, therefore, necessary to make the following orders clear:

(1) The patrol operations will be rushed to completion by the use of the 18 East Coast and 22 West Coast Priority Number 1 destroyers and by completing the aircraft patrol planes.

(2) When any aircraft or surface ship sights a submarine a report thereof will be rushed to the Navy Department for immediate action. The plane or surface ship sighting a submarine will remain in contact as long as possible. . . .

(3) Planes or Navy or Coast Guard ships may report the sighting of any submarine or suspicious surface ship in plain English to Force Commander or Department.[7]

"We wish to help you in every way in keeping the war out of Americas," Churchill's message had concluded benignly. He was perfectly willing to follow Roosevelt's lead and use the language of neutrality to cover what the official U.S. naval account of Anglo-American cooperation would call an informal arrangement between the British admiralty and the Navy Department for the "exchange of information concerning movements and operations of Axis vessels in the Western Alantic."[8]

The American department of the foreign office erupted angrily when it learned of these messages. Admiral Phillips was reproved for communicating directly with the United States ambassador, and there were suggestions

* Tom Phillips was vice chief of staff under the first sea lord. He went down with the *Prince of Wales* off Singapore after Pearl Harbor.

that Churchill's "private messages" to Roosevelt either be stopped or at least "vetted." The department's anxieties were not wholly eased when Lord Halifax noted, "The First Lord had brought both these messages to Cabinet and he showed them to me for approval which I gave." An American department officer commented:

It is unfortunate that the U.S. Govt sh^d have been led to found their views of H.M.G. to the neutral zone proposals on two entirely unofficial documents, a private & personal message to the Pres from the 1st Lord of the Ad^{ty} and an informal memo. improperly communicated to the U.S. Amb^{dr} by the D.N.I. Although no actual *harm* may have [been] done, (despite Mr. Churchill's remark "If America requests all belligerents to comply we sh^d immediately declare that we w^d respect your wishes") which is more categorical than cases perhaps warrant, this duplication (or triplication) of the channels of communication is undesirable in itself (consequences may not in all cases be as harmless as in the present case) and is likely to be the source of considerable embarrassment to His Majesty's Amb^{dr} and ultimately to H.M.G. (particularly if Foreign Office does not know what is happening! . . . . . It might also be well if Lord Lothian [British ambassador to the United States] were to take some early and suitable opportunity to make it clear that the First Lord's messages to the President are *personal* ones, and sh^d not be regarded as expressing more than personal opinions, or as committing H.M.G. officially to the views set forth.

The head of the American department, David Scott, said that he would be content with the chance to "vet" the first lord's messages. "I do not much like the idea of hinting to the President that H.M.G. may sometimes have to disown Mr. Churchill." Halifax ended this particular discussion with his red-ink comment: "I do not suppose the 1st Lord would have any objection to vetting any personal communications he may wish to make to the President: and I think there is positive advantage in his making such personal contact, subject to Foreign Office knowledge and concurrence. I should like a tactful letter for my signature, putting a good deal on Lord Lothian's difficulties and possible crossing of wires—I think I am partly to blame for the difficulty that has arisen, which Mr. Scott's suggestion would avoid."[9]

Publicly Roosevelt justified the neutrality patrol as a way of keeping war away from the Americas. Privately his concern was with the British fleet and its importance to American security. He hoped that events would enable him in time to educate the American people to the relationship between sea power and American safety. Churchill was emphasizing America's dependence on the British fleet in his talks with Ambassador Kennedy. The British were worried about Kennedy's statements that Britain was certain to be "thrashed" in the war. Halifax advised Lothian:

It has come to our notice from various unofficial sources that Kennedy has been adopting a most defeatist attitude in his talks with a number of private individuals. The general line which he takes in these conversations as reported to us is that Great Britain is certain to be defeated in the war, particularly on account of her financial weakness.[10]

Churchill feared that a German bombing offensive was imminent, reported Kennedy. "I judge," commented the ambassador,

there is a feeling that if women and children are killed as a result of these bombings in England that the United States will tend more toward their side. Churchill said, "After all, if they bombed us into a state of subjection, one of their terms of course would be to hand over the fleet and if we attempted to scuttle the fleet their terms would be that much worse. And if they got the British fleet, they would have immediate superiority over the United States and then her troubles would begin."[11]

Churchill's next message to Roosevelt reported a heavy blow to Anglo-American sea power. A daring German submarine commander worked his way into the British fleet's northern anchorage at Scapa Flow and sank the battleship *Royal Oak,* "a remarkable episode of which I will write you more fully," Churchill said, adding, "it in no way affects the naval balance." It did upset the House of Commons and the British public. Churchill candidly noted in his memoirs that it might have been "politically fatal" to him, except that, newly returned to the admiralty, the Commons did not hold him responsible. And Sir Samuel Hoare, who disliked Churchill intensely, acknowledged to Lothian at the time:

Being for the moment the war hero, he has come through it fairly well. I shudder to think what would have happened if there had been another First Lord and he had been in the Opposition. As it is, the Navy have had a shake-up, and I am sure that there is no risk of such mistakes being made again.[12]*

Churchill's other news to Roosevelt was cheerier. "We have been hitting the U-boats hard with our new apparatus." This is a reference to asdic, later known as sonar, an inexpensive device for locating the position of submarines under water by means of the sound waves that bounce back from any steel structure that they encounter.

We should be quite ready to tell you about our asdic methods whenever you feel they would be of use to the United States Navy and are sure the secret will go no farther. They certainly are very remarkable in results and enable two destroyers to do the work that could not have been done by ten last time.

Churchill also reported that they were still looking for the pocket battleship *Admiral Scheer* which had been at sea before the war began. "It is very odd that *Scheer* should have made no other prizes since September 30. As I told you we are taking some pains in looking for him. He may be anywhere by now." But it was a sister ship, the *Graf Spee,* that was finally sighted on December 1 off Montevideo by a British hunting group that, although outgunned, forced the German ship to scuttle itself in neutral waters.

This was the first, and only, victory the Allies could report during the

---

* Although Churchill had been anxious about Scapa Flow's defenses almost from the moment that he had returned to the Admiralty, he declined to enter into recriminations as to why the base was not better defended. All he said was, "What a wonderful feat of arms."

first winter of the war, and Churchill, a combative soul, did not appreciate the protest against violation of the neutrality zone that the president of Panama, on behalf of all the American republics, addressed to Great Britain and Germany. There were, in addition, direct complaints from the United States because British cruisers in pursuit of German merchantmen near the United States coast had violated the neutrality zone. Churchill cabled Roosevelt on Christmas Day:

Trust matter can be allowed to die down, and see no reason why any trouble should occur unless another raider is sent which is unlikely after the fate of the first. South American states should see in Plate action their deliverance perhaps indefinitely from all animosity. Much of world duty is being thrown on admiralty. Hope burden will not be made too heavy for us to bear. Even a single raider loose in North Atlantic requires employment half our battle fleet to give sure protection. Now unlimited magnetic mining campaign adds to strain upon flotillas and small craft. We are at very full extension till the new war-time construction of anti-submarine craft begins to flow from May onwards. If we should break under load South American Republics would soon have worse worries than the sound of one day's distant seaward cannonade. And you also, Sir, in quite a short time would have more direct cares. I ask that full consideration should be given to strain upon us at this crucial period and best construction put upon action to end war shortly in right way.[13]

The dispatch of this message, a copy of which Churchill had sent to the foreign office, produced a renewed flurry there. Halifax asked to see any such messages in advance so that he could keep Lothian posted and added that it would be best if the messages were sent "through us and Lothian rather than through the U.S. Embassy here and the State Department." "My dear Edward," Churchill replied:

Yours of the 6th instant. Of course I will do what ever you like, but I think it would be a great pity to close down this private line of communication through the American Embassy and the State Department. I have availed myself of your permission to send such messages with the most scrupulous care to keep strictly within the lines of your policy. I told my people to send you at the Foreign Office a copy immediately of what I sent and I imagined the Foreign Office would send a copy accordingly to Lothian. I do not know why they did not do so. Would it not be much better for the communications to go simultaneously by both routes, thus keeping Lothian informed while giving the President the feeling that he has a special line of information?

Halifax agreed to the procedure suggested by Churchill except that he again asked that copies be sent to the foreign office "before, or if this cannot be managed, at the latest at the same time as, the message is sent to the U.S. Embassy."[14]

Roosevelt protested British violations of the neutrality zone reluctantly and primarily for the record. He understood the basic issue. As Lothian wrote to Lady Astor,* "I had lunch with the President the other day. He says he

---

* Virginia-born Nancy Astor was the first woman to sit in the House of Commons. Cliveden, her country house, had been a gathering place for supporters of appeasement, including Lothian, as well as for opponents of the policy.

doesn't think American public opinion yet realizes in the least the risks it is running or what would happen if, by any chance, we and France lost the war." There were some in the State Department who felt that the usefulness of the neutrality zone in keeping the western Atlantic free of U-boats and other commerce raiders was outweighed by the frictions it was engendering between Washington and London as the latter began to tighten the blockade, but Roosevelt was not among them. "Will you let me know," he queried the Navy Department at the beginning of December, "how many of the original forty destroyers—Priority Number 1—are now on patrol or on way to patrol." All forty, he was assured the next day. And when the U.S. minister to Norway, Mrs. J. Borden Harriman, asked Roosevelt to sell some old destroyers to Norway, which was doing exceptional work at sea, Roosevelt turned her down.

First, because the United States has none to spare, all of the destroyers you have in mind are being recommissioned as rapidly as possible for duty in connection with our Neutrality Patrol. Second, because the sale of vessels to a foreign government is prohibited by law.[15]

At the beginning of January, Churchill sent Roosevelt a précis of the reports that he had received on the naval action off Montevideo. It was a moment of mounting acrimony between the State Department and foreign office over what the United States considered British disregard of American rights in the application of its blockade. "In the last war," Lothian confided to Hoare, "however irritated the United States got through the arbitrary exercise of our command of the sea, we could be certain that the Germans would do something far more exasperating. Today this factor no longer exists." It did not exist partly because of the prohibitions of the Neutrality Act, but chiefly because the German navy was under strict orders from Hitler not to interfere with American trade and shipping.[16]

A major point of friction was British search and detention of American ships. The revised Neutrality Act prohibited American ships from going into combat zones, including the waters around the British Isles. But British ships of war were taking American vessels to Kirkwall, Scotland, to be examined for contraband. Public feeling began to mount on both sides of the Atlantic over the issue. "You will have seen from the papers that poor old Britain has had 'the heat turned on' against it recently by the State Department," Lothian wrote Lady Astor. "It is a nuisance because, as you know well, once the American public begins to feel that Great Britain is treading on its corns, it gets easily inflamed because of old memories. . . . We ought to go out of our way to avoid hurting American susceptibilities, while sticking like grim death to everything that is important for winning the war."[17]

Lothian also wrote to Halifax about the "recent minor crisis" in Anglo-American relations:

It is due partly to the feeling that we have been needlessly inconsiderate of American interests, both private and public; that we have been trading upon her good will and, more important perhaps in the long run, the U.S.A. is beginning to feel the old irritation against the way we use our "command of the seas," which has been the constant source of often unreasonable protest to us for the last hundred years. The U.S. feels acutely that she is now a sea power equal to ourselves, and must be treated with the consideration due to this power. She knows, too, that, if she chooses to put down her foot by threatening retaliation, she can probably compel us. I think, therefore, that you must face the fact that the period of easy going that we have enjoyed over here in the past has come to an end, and that the United States, while anxious to do nothing to impede our war effort, will assert itself a good deal more vigorously and will expect to be consulted a good deal more about our policy on all matters which affect her trade and interests. The essence of the case is this. We have got to prove to the U.S.A., which includes public opinion as well as the Administration, that any action we take affecting them is really necessary for the winning of the war.[18]

Churchill understood the need to avoid irritating the United States. On January 29 he cabled Roosevelt in regard to the search and detention of American shipping:

I gave orders last night that no American ship should, in any circumstances, be directed into the combat zone round the British Islands declared by you. I trust this will be satisfactory.

Churchill followed this up the next day with a request that the new directive be kept confidential lest it appear that Great Britain was discriminating among neutrals in favor of the United States. Also, some measures would have to be worked out, he added, "to ensure in advance of their departure that United States ships carry no objectionable cargo."[19]

A few days later Roosevelt weighed into the controversy over American rights directly. He thanked Churchill for sending him the accounts of the River Plate battle and then went on to say that he thought the talks between the United States and Great Britain on search and seizure were

working out satisfactorily—but I would not be frank unless I told you that there has been much public criticism here. The general feeling is that the net benefit to your people and to France is hardly worth the definite annoyance caused to us. That is always found to be so in a nation which is 3,000 miles away from the fact of war.

Roosevelt sandwiched this gentle admonition in between more agreeable sentiments. He thanked Churchill for the "tremendously interesting account of the extraordinarily well fought action of your three cruisers" and ended his letter with the wish "that I could talk things over with you in person—but I am grateful to you for keeping me in touch, as you do."[20]

Churchill was intent on getting along with Roosevelt and the United States. From the time that he had ordered the British fleet not to bring American ships into the combat zone, he informed Roosevelt,

many of the other departments have become concerned about the efficiency of the blockade and the difficulties of discriminating between various countries. The neutrals are all on them and they are all on me. Nevertheless the order still stands and no American ship has been brought by the navy into the danger zone. But you can imagine my embarrassment when Moore-McCormack Line actually advertises in Norway that they do not have to worry about navicerts [certificates of clearance] or Kirkwall, and when all the Scandinavian countries complain of discrimination in American favor. . . . All our experience shows that the examination of mails is essential to efficient control as only in this way can we get the evidence of evasion. I do hope that I may be helped to hold the position I have adopted by the American shipping lines availing themselves of the great convenience of navicerts which was an American invention and thus enable American trade to proceed without hindrance.

Churchill ended his message, as Roosevelt had, on an amiable personal note. "It is a great pleasure to me to keep you informed about naval matters, although alas I cannot have the honor of a talk with you in person."[21]

He was having the complaint against the Moore-McCormack Lines studied, Roosevelt replied, and Adolf Berle, who was handling the matter in the State Department, had informed him that "arrangements could be worked out covering the situation, but they will take a few days."[22]

Argument raged both within and between the British and American governments. There were differences over how much one set of national interests —the British in the blockade and the American in trade—should yield to the national interests that were served by Anglo-American cooperation and friendship. Jay Pierrepont Moffat, the chief of the European division in the State Department, noted in his diary that the slogan of some members of the department, including himself, had become "No help to Germany but no Dominion status for ourselves."[23]

"Nearly everyone was in agreement along these lines," Moffat wrote of a department decision to protest another British action, "except Herbert Feis, who as usual spoke up in bitter opposition to any action on our part which would embarrass England."

Foreign office officials echoed such nationalist sentiments and suspicions. "The American insistence on the Zone proposal," an officer minuted, "is doubtless to be explained partly by the desire to keep the war away from American shores but also to reinforce Pan-American solidarity which implies an increasing economic and political strangle-hold by the U.S. over other American States, which can only, in spite of Lord Lothian's Panglossian optimism, redound to our disadvantage in the long run."[24]

Henry L. Stimson, who had been Hoover's secretary of state but was often consulted by Hull and Roosevelt, regularly talked with Herbert Feis when he (Stimson) was in Washington. In March, 1940, Feis complained to Stimson that the department was allowing "too acrimonious a tone" to get into its diplomatic notes to Britain on the subject of interference with U.S. trade rights. Feis thought the neutrality zone idea "half-baked and dangerous" because it inevitably generated friction with the world's leading sea power.[25] This was the diplomats' view, not that of the British and American navies. In March, 1940, Sumner Welles went to London on his information-gathering mission for Roosevelt. The British government appeared to be backing away from the neutrality zone. Welles, at dinner, was seated next to Churchill and discussed the problem with him. He could not understand why the British did not accept the zone, he told Churchill, "provided Germany likewise agreed to respect the Zone. Mr. Churchill said he agreed; that he had not known of his government's reply and that there were 'too damned many lawyers in the Foreign Office.' I said to Mr. Chamberlain [who was on Welles's other side] and to Mr. Churchill that I believed they would find that the American Republics were becoming more and more determined that the Zone was here to stay, and I hoped a way could be found to prevent any misunderstandings with regard thereto."[26]

Although in the minds of some, the neutrality zone had become an abrasive rather than an emollient in Anglo-American relations, that was not the view of the men at the top who understood what was going on. One of these was the British ambassador in Washington, Lord Lothian, who after a few months of war spoke of America's "present unwritten and unnamed naval alliance with Great Britain" and who saw that Roosevelt, in defense of the Western Hemisphere, was able to make moves beneficial to the Allies that otherwise would have been denied to him. But Lothian's efforts to give a conceptual underpinning to a closer working relationship with the United States occasionally ran afoul of the "foreign office lawyers." They were unhappy that in his speeches Lothian spoke of "democratic" control of the seas. "Even at this moment, if we honestly face the facts," Lothian told American audiences, "our present safety today rests upon the fact that we control the Atlantic and you control the Pacific."

"So far as I know," minuted a foreign office official, "Lord Lothian has received no instructions from this end to preach to his U.S. audiences the virtues of federal union for Europe or the democratic control of the seas." Halifax gently admonished his Washington ambassador: "I doubt if even a Cabinet Minister has to be more careful than you, even though as Winston said a day or two ago, to ask a Cabinet Minister to make a speech without causing offence in some quarter is like telling a centipede to go for a walk and not to put his foot into it! . . . Incidentally your references at Chicago to the democratic control of the seas . . . excited the wrath of some Members of Parliament who threatened to put down what would have been rather awkward questions to answer." Undaunted, Lothian replied, "I can imagine what my speeches would have been like if they had first been minuted by all the veterans of the Foreign Office at home!" He refused to yield on sea power. "I confess that it seems to be obvious that we cannot by ourselves do what we did in the 19th Century. . . . But one reason why the United States of America won't face the fact that the first and best line of defence is the British Navy is the conviction among most Americans that we will *never* share sea power with them—the very case that your die-hard friends put forward."

If the United States ever entered the war, predicted Lothian on the eve of Hitler's assault against the Low Countries, it would be with slogans quite different from 1917. "Her ultimate position is far more likely to be an extension of the Monroe Doctrine to cover the Western democracies and the seas in her own interests than to make the world safe for democracy or anything else."[27]

Chapter Five

The Phony War

POLAND HAD DISAPPEARED. Its blitzkreig destruction bolstered a popular image of Hitler's *Wehrmacht* as an unstoppable, fire-breathing juggernaut.

Western statesmen and military staffs reacted more calmly. Some emphasized the need for rapid and increased rearmament. Others hoped some sort of nonhumiliating peace with the Nazis might still be possible. Both groups comforted themselves with the view that Hitler was now at an impasse—his was the problem of where to move next. "One is left to wonder," Capt. Alan G. Kirk, the United States naval attaché in London, cabled home, "whether the direction of the war on the part of both England and France is in the hands of vigorous, well-trained and resolute men. Inside England there is also an undercurrent of apathy and distaste for the whole war. There is a certain amount of wishful thinking as regards a political collapse inside Germany."[1]

The Allies waited. The six months between Poland's destruction and the Nazi swoop upon Scandinavia in April, 1940, soon became known as the "phony" war—isolationist senator William E. Borah's phrase—the "twilight" war, and in Germany some called it *der kalte Krieg,* the cold war.[2]

Hitler was prepared to use the initiative the Allies relinquished to him. By the beginning of October he had transferred to the West his crack divisions, as many as forty-seven of them, intelligence reported. London and Paris braced for a new Nazi thrust. Churchill thought it would be either a sky-darkening bomber assault or a peace offer. "It would seem our duty and policy to agree to nothing that will help him out of his troubles," a Churchill cabinet memorandum stated on September 25, "and to leave him to stew in his own juice during the winter, while speeding forward our armaments and weaving our alliances."[3]

Roosevelt, trying to figure out what really was going on in Europe's chancelleries, depended in part on his ambassadors in London and Paris—in neither of whom, however, did he have complete confidence.

Kennedy lunched with Churchill and cabled home: "I received the impression that any terms that might be offered by Hitler on a peace basis would be rejected [by Churchill]." The ambassador, who feared the expansion of Soviet power if the war went on, inquired about the Russian threat. "Churchill does not feel that the power of Russia to move out over the world is nearly as dangerous as the Germans and for that reason the Germans under the Nazi regime must be finished off first." But Lord Halifax, the foreign secretary, shared Kennedy's anxieties. "I have just seen Halifax," continued Kennedy. "They have heard nothing from Italy or from Germany on any peace proposals. When they are made . . . unless it is an overt humbug, they propose to give it careful consideration. . . . Halifax also expressed the opinion that if this war continues it will mean Bolshevism all over Europe."[4]

Joe Kennedy gave him "an awful pain in the neck," Roosevelt confided to Morgenthau at their weekly luncheon. "Joe always has been an appeaser and always will be an appeaser. If Germany and Italy made a good peace offer tomorrow," continued Roosevelt, "Joe would start working on the King and his friend, the Queen, and from there on down, to get everybody to accept and," he added, "he's just a pain in the neck to me."

William C. Bullitt, the U.S. ambassador to France, was not appeasement-minded, Roosevelt went on, but mercurial. "The trouble with Bullitt is in the morning he will send me a telegram 'Everything is lovely' and then he will go out to have lunch with some French official and I get a telegram that everything is going to hell." Roosevelt kept Bullitt in Paris and Kennedy in London because he knew when and where to discount the information they cabled home. "The only thing that saves the information is I know my men."[5]

"My own view of the future is the following," Bullitt wrote Roosevelt from Paris at the beginning of October. "France and England will not accept the 'peace ultimatum' that Germany is contemplating. . . . Germany then will attack. . . ." The key to the outcome of such a collision lay in air power. "If American production of airplane motors and bombers can be trebled in eight months, dominance in the air should be in the hands of the French and British by August or September of next year." England and France, Bullitt realized, "might be defeated and destroyed before our American production can be raised to a sufficient point to save them, but I hope that will not be."[6]

Chamberlain's views on the course the war might take were outlined in a letter he sent to Roosevelt on October 4.

My own view is that we shall win, not by a complete and spectacular military victory, which is unlikely under modern conditions, but by convincing the Germans that they cannot win. Once they have arrived at that conclusion, I do not believe they can stand our relentless pressure, for they have not started this war with the enthusiasm or confidence of 1914.

I believe they are already halfway to this conviction and I cannot doubt that the attitude of the United States of America, due to your personal efforts, has had a notable influence in this direction. If the embargo is repealed this month, I am convinced that the effect on German morale will be devastating.[7]

"They all contend," a cynical Kennedy cabled home, "that all they want is revision of the Neutrality Act to give them an opportunity to buy in America, but I do not believe it for a minute. If Germany does not break and throw Hitler out after the passage of the Neutrality Act they will spend every hour figuring how to get us in."[8]

On October 6, Hitler made his peace speech to the *Reichstag*. "Germany has no further aims against France," he declared. He had soft words for Britain. "At no time and in no place have I ever acted contrary to British interests. . . . Why should this war in the West be fought? For restoration of Poland? Poland of the Versailles Treaty will never rise again. . . ." He proposed a conference of Europe's leading nations, adding, "Mr. Churchill and his companions may interpret these opinions of mine as weakness or cowardice, if they like. . . . If [their] opinions . . . should prevail, this statement will have been my last. Then we shall fight. . . . There will never be another November, 1918, in German history."[9]

But few in the West any longer believed Hitler. "I am coming more and more to the view," said Halifax the next day during a cabinet discussion of Hitler's speech, "that my chief war aim is the elimination of Herr Hitler. It is not, however, politic to say so." The French were the first to reply formally. France would not lay down her arms, Premier Édouard Daladier said, without guarantees of "a real peace and general security." A few days later Chamberlain, in a speech to the House of Commons, rejected Hitler's proposals as "vague and uncertain. . . . They contain no suggestions for righting the wrongs done to Czechoslovakia and Poland." No reliance could be placed on the promises "of the present German Government." He called for convincing proof from Hitler that the latter really wanted peace. In other words, the Allies required as a condition of making peace, a change of government in Berlin and a withdrawal of German forces from Poland, Bohemia, and Moravia.

Hitler was prepared either for peace on his terms or war. Three days after his *Reichstag* speech, he met his military chiefs and directed them to prepare an attack on France and Britain through the Low Countries in the event his proposals were rejected. Germany's war aim, he told his generals, "is and remains the destruction of our Western enemies."[10]

Hitler's generals were dubious about the success of an offensive in the West. They held out against him until October 17, when, according to the diary of Army Chief of Staff Gen. Franz Halder, Hitler informed him and his chief, General Walther von Brauchitsch, that "the British will be ready to talk only after a beating. We must get at them as quickly as possible. Date between November 15 and 20 at the latest."[11]

British intelligence was aware of the argument between Hitler and his generals. Churchill cabled Roosevelt:

Our account of Hitler's oil position makes us feel he is up against time limits. This means that either he will make vehement attack on us for which we are prepared or he is being held back by counsellors who see the red light.(?) We propose to see what happens feeling fairly confident that all will be well.[12]

Roosevelt doubted that Hitler was up against a dwindling supply of oil. He had examined Germany's oil potential with Morgenthau and had come to the conclusion it could become self-sufficient. But Roosevelt did believe— as, indeed, did Hitler—that time was on the side of the West and that the Allies were right to stand on the defensive. "It is the opinion of the French General Staff," Bullitt informed him, "that whichever army attacks first the line of fortifications that now divide France and Germany will be defeated." It would be "criminal folly," Henry L. Stimson wrote in his diary, if the Allies "dashed their heads against the Western Wall and slaughtered perhaps two million men on both sides in an effort to invade and capture Germany."[13]

The greatest contribution the United States could make to the siege tactics of the Allies, as Chamberlain and Daladier had indicated, was to repeal the arms embargo provisions of the Neutrality Act and make American armaments, especially planes, available to Britain and France. From the war's outbreak, Roosevelt's chief aim had been revision of the Neutrality Act. He had only delayed calling Congress into special session until his congressional leaders had given him a head count. The Senate secretary, Colonel Halsey, "who has been carefully checking against all records, public utterances, etc.," Steve Early informed Roosevelt, "tells me that sixty senators will support a 'cash and carry' neutrality act; that twenty-five will stand in opposition; that the others are on the doubtful or uncertain list." Behind the scenes, Roosevelt took personal command of the repeal battle, keeping close tabs on the voting inclinations of doubtful senators and representatives, enlisting Archbishop Spellman's help to ease Catholic pastoral opposition to repeal in Brooklyn and Boston, telephoning Thomas W. Lamont, a prominent Wall Street figure, to use his influence on wavering Republicans like Rep. Bruce Barton, meeting with Gov. Alfred M. Landon and Col. Frank Knox, who had headed the Republican ticket in 1936, analysing amendments, rebuking his own vice-president Henry A. Wallace for violating his order for a moratorium on politics.[14]

Roosevelt had as little sympathy as Churchill for a compromise peace that would leave Germany in control of Poland and Czechoslovakia and the Nazis in control of Germany, and he was certainly not going to permit Hitler's peace maneuvers to undercut the drive for revision of the Neutrality Act.

On September 18, the day Soviet troops crossed the Polish border and occupied the eastern half of that unhappy country, William Rhodes Davis, an oilman with holdings in Germany, visited Roosevelt in an effort to enlist the president's help in promoting peace on Hitler's terms. He had obtained his appointment at the request of John L. Lewis, leader of the CIO and the United Mine Workers' Union and Roosevelt's most potent labor backer in the 1936 campaign. The president asked Adolf Berle to sit in on the meeting because he thought it prudent to have a witness present at a meeting with Davis. The "priceless adventurer," as Berle called Davis, told the president that he was in touch with Field Marshal Hermann Göring, who had asked him to ascertain whether Roosevelt would not act as mediator in bringing the war to an end. Roosevelt led Davis on, reported Berle, and though he said he could not move unless officially requested to do so by a government he would be interested to hear any information Davis might bring back. The next day, Berle recorded, Roosevelt telephoned Berle about noon.

[The president] had received an interesting cablegram which had been sent to W. R. Davis. It implemented the intrigue which Davis had sketched out; since it was a request from Goering's secretary, obviously in answer to something Davis had sent him, that Davis influence the President not to revise the Neutrality Act, but support a German peace offer, in return for which the German government would accord to the United States an absolutely free hand in the Far East.

Later, Berle wrote: "The Germans have made an extremely clumsy use of this man in endeavoring to get the President committed to something which would serve their own desire. At present this is a desire to end the West Front war, on their own terms."[15]

There were other pressures on Roosevelt, particularly after Hitler's *Reichstag* speech, to use his good offices to bring about an armistice. King Leopold III of Belgium appealed to him as "the only person in the world who can possibly avert the holocaust." He would only do so, Roosevelt replied, "after it has become abundantly clear that the path towards which we may point does in fact lie in the direction of peace." On October 27, the Senate approved repeal of the arms embargo by a vote of 63 to 31, and a week later the House of Representatives followed suit by a majority of 61.[16]

"I am convinced," Chamberlain wrote Roosevelt, "that it will have a devastating effect upon German morale."[17] This was wishful thinking. Even as Chamberlain was writing this letter, German forces were moving to their jump-off points opposite Holland, Belgium, and Luxembourg for the attack that was scheduled to begin November 12. The attack was postponed because of weather conditions, but the Allies interpreted the postponement as a sign of irresolution, perhaps even of division.

"I do not doubt myself that time is on our side," Churchill said in a broadcast address that bespoke perseverance in making war until the other side had had enough. Although Churchill's colleagues were quick to resent any encroachment by the first lord on their jurisdictions, they recognized he was the government's most effective spokesman—indeed, the only minister whom the general public still considered worth listening to and believing in. "I go so far as to say that if we come through this winter without any large or important event occurring we shall in fact have gained the first campaign of the war . . . because we are all the time moving forward towards greater war strength, and because Germany is, all the time, under the grip of our economic warfare, falling back in oil and other essential war supplies." Russia barred an advance in the East. "They have not chosen to molest the British Fleet . . . they recoil from the steel front of the French Army along the Maginot Line." Instead they were massing along the frontiers of Holland and Belgium. "To both these States the Nazis have given the most recent and solemn guarantees; no wonder anxiety is great." The fate of Holland and Belgium, Churchill went on, "will be decided by the victory of the British Empire and the French Republic. If we are all conquered, all will be enslaved and the United States will be left single-handed to guard the rights of man." Churchill paid his respects to Hitler, of whom he spoke as "a cornered maniac. . . . I have the sensation and also the conviction that that evil man over there and his cluster of confederates are not sure of themselves, as we are sure of ourselves; that they are harassed in their guilty souls by the thought and by the fear of an ever-approaching retribution for their crimes, and for the orgy of destruction in which they have plunged us all." He rejoiced in the treaty of alliance between France and Britain with Turkey and in the repeal of the arms embargo in the United States. "The whole world is against Hitler and Hitlerism," he concluded in an optimistic burst.[18]

But in fact Churchill's speech upset many neutral capitals. From Turkey, Ambassador Franz von Papen reported to Berlin that Şükrü Saracoğlu, the Turkish foreign minister, was in agreement that Churchill's speech revealed who were the warmongers and that his thesis, " 'The war could end only with victors and vanquished,' had destroyed all hopes of peace." In Washington, Lord Lothian informed Roosevelt and Hull that an earlier message that the Belgian government had at last agreed to immediate military conversations with the British and French was inaccurate and exaggerated. And in London, R. A. Butler, a junior minister in the foreign office, assured the Italian ambassador that Churchill's speech "was in conflict with the Government's views. . . . As a matter of fact, he always spoke only as Mr. Churchill."[19]

On November 23, Hitler again convened his military chiefs to hear his thinking on impending events. It was an unbridled display of egomania. Churchill and Roosevelt did not exaggerate when they suspected his goal to be world domination. Hitler reviewed his early struggles. "I had a clear recognition of the probable course of historical events and the firm will to make brutal decisions," he told the assembled generals and admirals, who, knowing of the atrocities and massacres then taking place in occupied Poland, needed no reminder of his capacity for cruelty. He might be charged with simply wanting to "fight and fight again," he went on. He did not reject the impeachment. "In fighting I see the fate of all creatures. Nobody can avoid fighting if he does not want to go under." Germany's goal was "a larger *Lebensraum*" established on a secure basis. "No calculated cleverness is of any help here, solution only with the sword. . . . Since 1870, England has been against us. . . . Basically I did not organize the armed forces not to strike. The decision to strike was always in me."

Hitler's thinking coincided with Churchill's on one point. "Time is working for our adversaries." Russia was not dangerous at the moment. Its army was "of little worth," and would remain ineffective for the next one or two years. Russia would adhere to the Nazi-Soviet pact only as long as it benefitted her. She had "far-reaching goals. . . . We can oppose Russia only when we are free in the West. Further, Russia is seeking to increase her influence in the Balkans and in striving toward the Persian Gulf. That is also the goal of our foreign policy."

He dismissed U.S. aid to the Allies. "America is still not dangerous to us because of her neutrality laws. The strengthening of our opponents by America is still not important."

Another consideration was his own indispensability. "In all modesty I must say I am irreplaceable." The egomania rose to a crescendo. "Neither a military man nor a civilian could replace me," Hitler went on. "Attempts at assassination may be repeated. I am convinced of my powers of intellect and of decision. Wars are ended only by the annihilation of the opponent. Whoever believes differently is irresponsible. . . . The fate of the Reich depends only on me."

He ruled out compromise. "Victory or defeat! The question is not the fate of a National Socialist Germany but who is to dominate Europe in the future. . . . My decision is unchangeable. I shall attack France and England at the most favorable and earliest moment. Breach of the neutrality of Belgium and Holland is of no importance. No one will question that when we have won."[20]

British military planning was for a three-year war. "If Hitler wants a short war," Hoare, who was charged with this planning, advised Lothian,

we ought to go for a long war. If we go for a long war it is obviously unwise to risk our resources, particularly in the air and on the sea, until we reach a decisive moment. Remember that our bombers are now very like our Battle Fleet. It is essential that the two fleets should be kept in being until the decisive moment. That, you will remember, is the basic principle of fighting upon which Mahan insisted, and it may be worth your while to press this point upon your important friends.[21]

It was not, however, just a matter of holding back the Allied bomber fleets until the "decisive moment"; the bomber fleets still had to be manufactured. Allied air inferiority had been the cause of the Munich surrender, Roosevelt believed, and in the Luftwaffe's continued ascendancy he sensed the seeds of an Allied military disaster. "I don't like to say so in a telegram," Bullitt warned him,

but I really believe that there is an enormous danger that the German Air Force will be able to win the war for Germany before the planes can begin to come out of our plants in quantity. I think we should encourage the French and British in every way possible to place the largest conceivable orders. If, before these orders are completed, the French and British shall have been defeated, we shall need the planes for our own defenses.[22]

In the cold aftermath of Munich, Roosevelt had turned to Henry Morgenthau, Jr., to expedite the expansion of America's productive capacity and to see to it that French fighter and bomber orders were filled even before those of the United States Air Force. By the spring of 1939, Jean Monnet, the Frenchman in charge of purchasing, had contracted for 555 planes and had also agreed to subsidize the expansion of the American aircraft industry to a productive capacity of 1,500 planes a year.

Even so, at the end of 1939, the Allies were not in sight of equality and even further from dominance in the air. Despite Roosevelt's invitations, the British had placed no orders at all. With the enactment in November, 1939, of "cash and carry," Roosevelt and Morgenthau expected the situation to change drastically and that there would be a deluge of Allied orders. What would happen, Postmaster General James Farley asked the president at a cabinet meeting at the beginning of December, "if England or France wanted airplanes and we wanted them at the same time?" Would we "insist upon deliveries to us?" The president replied confidentially, "Up to a certain number at any rate, we would let England and France have the first call."[23]

Arthur Purvis, a Canadian, was dispatched to Washington to handle British purchasing. He wrote Monnet about the situation there. He had talked with Roosevelt and Morgenthau and found the president most intent on being helpful. But both men had impressed upon him the need to keep Allied purchase discussions secret:

to avoid stirring the isolationist groups. . . . The President finding in the State Department a reluctance to take as open action in favor of the Allies, as he would like, has turned to Morgenthau as his best channel. . . . Morgenthau is only too happy to play the role.[24]

The British, wishing to conserve dollar balances and worried over the impact of an expanded U.S. capacity on British industry, still hesitated to place large orders for planes in the United States. It took French prodding, especially Jean Monnet's analysis of German air strength, to get them to do so. Finally, "in March 1940, Britain joined France in placing the largest order for American military planes since 1918." However, the U.S. Air Force still resisted giving priority to Allied orders. At one point, in early 1940, Roosevelt had to caution its chief, General Henry H. ("Hap") Arnold, that "there were places to which officers who did not 'play ball' might be sent, such as Guam." And when isolationist Secretary of War Harry Woodring refused to release the latest models, Roosevelt instructed him "either to go along with the program or resign."[25]

After the war, the Allies learned that Hitler was almost as apprehensive as they were about unleashing an air offensive prematurely—both sides felt unprotected against an all-out air bombardment. "I am still inclined to think that we should not take the initiative on bombing," Churchill advised Chamberlain in September, "except in the immediate zone in which French armies are operating, where we must of course help. It is to our interest that the war should be conducted in accordance with the more humane conceptions of war. . . . Every day that passes gives more shelter to the population of London and the big cities." Hitler was less concerned with an attack on Germany's cities than on its war industries. In his October 9 directive to the armed forces to prepare for an attack on the West, he said that "the greatest danger was the vulnerability of the Ruhr. If this heart of German industrial production were hit, it would lead to the collapse of the German war economy and thus of the capacity to resist." The occupation of Belgium and Holland, he told his military chiefs, would give German U-boats and the Luftwaffe "a better starting point" and would also serve as a protective barrier for the Ruhr. "We have an Achilles heel—the Ruhr. The conduct of the war depends on possession of the Ruhr. If England and France push through Belgium and Holland into the Ruhr, we shall be in the greatest danger."[26]

Such a "push" was not under Allied consideration. Although they pressed King Leopold of Belgium to permit their armies to advance into Belgium in order to meet the expected German invasion, they had no plans for an offensive themselves. "Everyone will be expecting dramatic events," Hoare acknowledged when he announced an armaments program based on a three-year war, "and instead there will be a war of nerves constantly playing upon the weaker side of human nature. I am sure, however, that short of an attack upon us, this is the line we must hold."[27] Churchill alone found a siege strategy difficult to accept. Although he did not favor a frontal clash, either of armies or air forces, he probed and pressed for flanking movements that might take advantage of Britain's superiority at sea. As autumn turned to winter, recalled Hoare, "the demand for action of some kind became stronger than ever. Churchill in particular was straining at the leash. Not a week passed without some imaginative proposal from his fertile and brilliant mind."

Almost from the moment the war had begun Churchill had pushed Operation Catharine, a plan to force a passage into the Baltic with naval forces in order to isolate Scandinavia from Germany. The offensive spirit that animated the project was commendable, but it ignored Germany's ability to decimate the expedition by the use of land-based air power. The operation "appealed to the cavalryman in him," wrote Sir Eric Seal, who at the time was Churchill's principal private secretary. "He wanted to disregard the danger of air attack as the famous 'Light Brigade' had disregarded the Russian artillery at Balaklava."

Another project that Churchill stubbornly pursued during the dreary months of the "phony war" was the mining of Norwegian waters. Swedish iron ore, indispensable to Germany's war economy, moved to Germany by means of this corridor in the winter, when ice blocked the Swedish route.

Churchill argued for the proposal at a war cabinet meeting on November 30. He recalled that in the last war, mines had driven the iron-ore vessels out into the open seas where British warships were able to get at them. "The time is coming when we shall have to consider taking similar measures. A few small minefields, each of perhaps three or four square miles, would be enough for the purpose." Halifax thought the Norwegians would refuse to agree to such an operation; nevertheless, preparatory studies were authorized.[28]

"The President's reactions are more favorable than I had hoped," Churchill informed his fellow ministers on December 11. Roosevelt had been thinking about Sweden's iron ore—another example of the similar way he and Churchill viewed the problems of World War II because of their experiences in World War I—when Norwegian territorial waters had been mined. He was glad to know "the Swedish position in regard to neutrality," Roosevelt had written the U.S. minister to Stockholm the previous April.

> At the same time what the democratic countries want to know is whether in the event of a general war Sweden would be really neutral—i.e.—*not* give help to the dictator nations.
>
> This would involve, in all probability, the problem of continued shipments of iron ore or pig iron to Germany.
>
> As I said in my message to Congress in January, there are circumstances where neutrality so-called actually helps an aggressor nation and is, therefore, not neutrality in fact.[29]

Not surprisingly, the Swedes rejected this conception of neutrality. If the iron ore from the Gällivare ore fields in northern Sweden was to be stopped from reaching Germany, it would have to be through Allied occupation of Narvik, the Norwegian port to which the ore was transported for shipment by sea, or through Allied mining of Norwegian territorial waters.

The Gällivare proposal became entangled with that of aid to Finland. Soviet pressure on Finland for territorial and political concessions that would turn that small country into a Soviet satellite had mounted all through November. Churchill had not been unsympathetic to Soviet moves in the Baltic. "No doubt it appears reasonable to the Soviet Union to take advantage of the present situation to regain some of the territory which Russia lost as a result of the last war, at the beginning of which she was the ally of France and Britain. . . . This applies not only to Baltic territories, but also to Finland. It is in our interests that the U.S.S.R. should increase their strength in the Baltic, thereby limiting the risk of German domination in that area. For this reason it would be a mistake for us to stiffen the Finns against making concessions to the U.S.S.R." So Churchill had spoken at a cabinet meeting on November 16.[30]

Two weeks later the Russians launched their attack against Finland. Unlike the geopoliticians, the man in the street, still unforgiving of Russia's switch in alliances, was even more aroused by the spectacle of the clumsy giant clawing its small neighbor. The issue in the British cabinet became one of coming to the aid of Finland. But behind the thinking of Allied strategists was the hope that an expeditionary force to aid the Finns, moving across northern Norway and Sweden, might occupy the Gällivare ore fields and, indeed, outflank the Germans. Churchill, reporting on Roosevelt's favorable reaction to the mining of Norway's waters, told the cabinet:

> I think it would be to our advantage if the trend of events in Scandinavia brought it about that Norway and Sweden were forced into war with Russia. . . . We would then be able to gain a foothold in Scandinavia with the object of helping them, but without having to go to the extent of ourselves declaring war on Russia. Such a situation would open prospects in the naval war which might prove most useful.[31]

Discussion of the mining of Norwegian waters and the dispatch of an expeditionary force to aid the Finns (and, coincidentally, to seize the iron mines) went on in the British cabinet throughout December and January. With his capacity for investing the project he was embarked on with pivotal importance, Churchill was soon depicting the stoppage of ore supplies as a major offensive which justified overriding the expected opposition of small countries. "No other measure is open to us for many months to come," he argued in a cabinet memorandum, "which gives so good a chance of abridging the waste and destruction of conflict, or of preventing the vast slaughter which will attend the grappling of the main armies. . . . Humanity, rather than legality, must be our guide." Finland's initial military successes encouraged the Allied Supreme War Council, headed by Chamberlain and Daladier, to consider an expedition to aid them. "We have a right and, indeed, are bound in duty to abrogate for a space some of the conventions of the very laws we seek to consolidate and reaffirm," Churchill argued in another paper. "Small nations must not tie our hands when we are fighting for their rights and freedoms."[32]

Again Churchill stepped forward to sell the government's policy. In a radio broadcast on January 20, 1940, he addressed himself to the neutrals. He painted the situation of the Allied powers in glowing terms, compared especially to the lot of "the unfortunate neutrals" who, whether in Scandinavia or the Balkans, are "considering which will be the next victim," each one hoping "that if he feeds the crocodile enough, the crocodile will eat him last." But "what would happen if all these neutral nations I have mentioned —and some others I have not mentioned— . . . were to stand together with the British and French Empires against aggression and wrong?" It was an eloquent address but it had a sour reception, especially in Norway. Norway's foreign minister Halvdan Koht told the German minister in Oslo:

It was incomprehensible that one of the ranking members of the Cabinet should have delivered such an address which would drive the neutral countries into opposition to British policy even if they were in sympathy with England.

Koht said he had known Churchill for thirty years "and considered him a demagogue and a windbag."[33]

How fully Roosevelt was kept informed of Anglo-French plans for an expeditionary force in aid of the Finns is unclear. At the end of 1939 he was preoccupied with American apathy and indifference to events in Europe. He unburdened himself to William Allen White of Kansas, the Republican editor who had headed up an effective citizens' committee to repeal the arms embargo. "No human being, with the best of information, has the slightest idea how this war is going to come out," he wrote White. Yet Americans had a great stake in what did ultimately happen, particularly in seeing to it that the war did not end "in a patched-up temporizing peace which would blow up in our faces in a year or two."

Much depended on what had motivated the Nazi-Soviet pact:

One thinks that Germany took hold of the Bear's tail in order to keep England and France out of the war and that Germany today is much concerned over Russia's unexpected policy of action—Eastern Poland, Finland and the possibility of Norway, Sweden, Rumania, Bulgaria, etc.

The other school of thought, with equal reason, believes that there is a fairly definitive agreement between Russia and Germany for the division of European control and with it the extension of that control to Asia Minor, Persia, Africa and the various British, French, Dutch, Belgian, etc., colonies.

If the latter is true, and Germany and Russia win the war or force a peace favorable to them, the situation of your civilization and mine is indeed in peril. Our world trade would be at the mercy of the combine and our increasingly better relations with our twenty neighbors to the south would end—unless we were willing to go to war on their behalf against a German-Russian dominated Europe.

But public opinion in the United States, Roosevelt fretted, instead of thinking about "possible results in Europe and the Far East" is "patting itself on the back every morning and thanking God for the Atlantic Ocean (and the Pacific Ocean)" and thanking God for Roosevelt and Hull who, "no matter what happens, . . . will keep us out of war."

Therefore, my sage old friend, my problem is to get the American people to think of conceivable consequences without scaring the American people into thinking they are going to be dragged into the war.[34]

Roosevelt's own apprehensions that the war on the western front would at any moment erupt into full fury were reflected in letters that he wrote at the turn of the year to Queen Wilhelmina of the Netherlands and to King Leopold of Belgium, renewing an offer of refuge to their families should their countries be invaded, an offer that he had first extended on November 11, when an invasion of the Low Countries appeared imminent. This time, in addition to Wilhelmina and Leopold, he wrote to Crown Prince Olaf of Norway.

But Roosevelt had larger schemes in mind, and the last paragraph of his letter to White was a clue to his thinking. Like Churchill, he was an activist. Like Churchill, politics and leadership were vocations into which he had moved as inevitably and naturally as a fledgling bird takes to the air. From the moment he had come into office in March, 1933, he had taken direct, personal command of U.S. foreign policy. The rise of the totalitarians, whose successes in Europe and Asia he felt endangered American safety, had deepened his determination to exert American leadership in world affairs. And since a deeply isolationist public and Congress circumscribed his ability to associate America's warmaking powers with the forces resisting aggression, he had had recourse to the role of mediator and peacemaker, exercising his few opportunities to assert an American presence on the world stage in ways that he hoped might strengthen the hands of the democracies.

Now, in the winter of 1939–1940, seeking, as he wrote White, to awaken the American people to America's stake in preventing a peace dictated by Germany and Russia and, as the world's leading neutral, using that word in the sense of noninvolvement in the hostilities, he was groping his way toward a formula by which the United States, leading the neutrals, could intervene on the side of the democracies to ensure a peace settlement acceptable to the democracies. "We do not have to go to war with other nations," he said in his annual message to Congress, "but at least we can strive with other nations to encourage the kind of peace that will lighten the troubles of the world, and by so doing help our own nation as well."[35]

Germinating in his mind was the possibility of organizing a fact-finding mission, headed by Sumner Welles, to find out whether there was a peace formula acceptable to the Allies and the Axis that a neutral bloc led by the United States might put forward. It was a project that upset Chamberlain, seemed unrealistic to Churchill, but appears not to have disturbed Lord Lothian, the British ambassador in Washington. That extraordinarily intelligent man, tutored perhaps by such friends of Versailles Peace Conference days (when he was secretary to Lloyd George) as Walter Lippmann and Felix Frankfurter, had achieved a sensitive understanding of the complex, oblique ways by which Roosevelt moved toward his goals and the large part that the movement of public opinion played in what Roosevelt could and could not do. "In previous dispatches," Lothian cabled London,

I have endeavored to record the movement of American public opinion about international affairs since the war began. I say "public opinion" deliberately, because in this country, owing to the constitutional equality of status of the Executive and the Legislature, it is public opinion itself which is continually decisive. Under the parliamentary system the Government of the day, provided it can keep the support of its own majority and does not provoke by its policy a violent agitation in the country, can make its own policy prevail. Under the American system, whatever the policy of the Administration, Congress and, in the case of foreign affairs, the Senate, both of which are always extremely jealous of their independent responsibility, can always in fundamentals block the Executive until public opinion, expressing itself through the newspapers, through deluges of telegrams to Washington, and through ordinary party and political channels, expresses a clear opinion.[36]

This dispatch was minuted by a newcomer to the American department of the foreign office, Harvard professor T. North Whitehead, the son of the philosopher Alfred North Whitehead:

The close dependence of the Administration upon public opinion accounts for the baffling phenomenon of an Administration clearly sympathetic and yet liable to object to our particular actions whenever we have failed to retain the sympathy of the nation at large.

Lord Lothian ends a brilliant survey with an appeal for us to avoid our usual tendency to tell the Americans what they should think or do. "Anything that looks like British propaganda designed to influence American policy creates a cold fury in the American mind. It resents not being left alone to make up its mind on the most important issues before it, for itself and by itself."

Lothian understood that Roosevelt's effort to rally the neutrals was another way of trying to exert United States influence on European events within the limits imposed upon him by the Neutrality Act and isolationist public opinion. Lothian himself had been preaching to Americans high and low—and he must have felt that the doctrine was acceptable to Roosevelt—that an early peace "really depends upon the neutrals." If they stood aloof, a fight to the finish could not be avoided, but if they associated themselves in some form with the war aims of the Allies, whose basic objective was "a guarantee of security, . . . and against an early return of world war," that might affect politics inside Germany, producing perhaps a conservative, non-Nazi regime with which a negotiated peace might be possible.

Lord Lothian notwithstanding the foreign office was opposed to the Welles mission. A foreign office minute on a conversation at Ditchley, the country house of Ronald Tree,* on what the United States minister Walton Butterworth, just back from Washington, had to say about Welles's purposes confirmed the office's anxieties:

This interesting conversation confirms our views generally. The argument seems to be as follows—

The President and those surrounding him think that we can't win.

The United States can not afford to let us lose and would not like to see us defeated.

The only way to prevent our defeat is either to come to our help and declare war on Germany—and this is the last thing they want to do—or to make us accept peace.

If the President can somehow stop the war his own domestic position will be enormously strengthened. (And though, to do him justice, I don't believe he would set his own personal position before what he thought were our interests, we should remember how passionately he must wish for another Democratic term to carry on the work of the New Deal.)

This is the last moment before the much heralded spring offensive and the latest moment suitable from an internal domestic standpoint for conducting a peace offensive.

He therefore has decided to send Mr. Summer Welles and even if we assure him that the mere mention of the visit will affect our interests injuriously he will no doubt, secure in his conviction that we can't win, disregard our remonstrances and feel that he is saving us from ourselves.[37]

It is doubtful that at this time Roosevelt thought the Nazis could breach the Maginot Line. But there was widespread feeling among America's leaders that Britain and France could not win. An "estimate of the foreign situation as it exists today" that Adm. Harold Stark, the chief of naval operations, handed to Roosevelt on March 9, 1940, as the president's "light reading" for the week end, asserted as its first conclusion "that a successful attack by either belligerent on the fortified Western Front is considered highly improbable." Stark's general conclusion was "that either oil or finance, or both, may be deciding factors, and perhaps to this should be added morale. Any one or any combination of these could bring peace without a definite military decision having been reached."[38]

---

* Conservative M.P. Ronald Tree was the grandson of Marshall Field and a member of the "Eden" group in the House of Commons that was pressing for more vigorous governmental leadership.

Chamberlain sent off two telegrams to Roosevelt, showing them to Churchill, who endorsed them with gusto. In them, the prime minister set forth the dangers to the Allied cause of the Welles mission. He suggested that "the inevitability of a tremendous offensive in the spring . . . has for some time past been put about by German propaganda as part of the war of nerves on which they are engaged," designed in part to keep the neutrals "on tenter-hooks" and to dispose them to go along with a peace dictated by Germany. Chamberlain minimized the likelihood of an attack even though, on January 10, German plans for an offensive scheduled to be launched on January 17 had fallen into Western hands when a German aircraft became lost in the clouds over Belgium and was forced to land. Because of the capture of the plans and a deterioration in the weather, the offensive was again postponed, and the Allies assumed the incident had been staged as part of the war of nerves. Chamberlain agreed with Roosevelt that the "kernel of the difficulty" was "to find some means of assuring Europe" that a settlement "could not be followed sooner or later by a renewed attack on the rights and liberties of the weaker European states," but he was unable to imagine "how such an assurance could be attained so long as Germany remains organized on the present lines and is under the direction of her present rulers." To demand that the German people throw off Hitler's regime as a condition of peace talks was unrealistic, "and to be quite frank there would be the utmost difficulty in persuading people of this country and I believe France that *any* settlement is worth signing with Hitler or the present regime." German public opinion was "dragooned and controlled," and the Welles mission, he feared, was more likely to arouse false hopes and emphasize divisions in the democracies than in the dictatorships.

Chamberlain's second telegram to Lothian for Roosevelt "entrusted [Roosevelt] with a secret that has been divulged to no one." The Allied Supreme War Council, at a meeting on February 5, had agreed to dispatch a Franco-British expeditionary force across northern Scandinavia to assist the Finns. This required the cooperation, "or at least consent," of Norway and Sweden. "What we fear is that if the Governments of Sweden and Norway get the idea that some peace suggestions are likely to be set on foot, they will refuse the facilities we want in order to save Finland."[39]

Welles's first stop was in Rome where, on February 26, Mussolini received him and the United States ambassador William Phillips at the Palazzo Venezia. Phillips was shocked by Mussolini's "ponderous" appearance. He seemed fifteen years older than his fifty-eight and "moved with elephantine motion," his close-clipped white hair heightening the fleshiness of his face. But Welles came away from the meeting believing that Mussolini was "a man of genius" who might just conceivably be an ally in an effort to restore peace. Welles then went on to Berlin for a meeting with Hitler before proceeding to London and Paris.

Insofar as Welles's trip represented a belief held by Roosevelt that Hitler could be deflected from launching a tremendous offensive in the spring by means of an Allied-Axis agreement on a "security plus disarmament" formula that would be sponsored by a neutral bloc headed by the United States, the mission was, as Welles's published account acknowledged, "a forlorn hope." Roosevelt evidently recognized this after Welles's interview with Hitler, for he commented to Morgenthau that "Welles did all right in Italy, but in Germany they just wanted everything. He shook his head two or three times and said 'Not so good.' "[40]

Churchill, when Welles reached London, gave him little comfort, and Welles's reports to Roosevelt included an unflattering account of his talk with the first lord of the admiralty:

When I was shown into his office Mr. Churchill was sitting in front of the fire, smoking a 24-inch cigar and drinking a whiskey and soda. It was quite evident that he had consumed a good many whiskeys before I arrived. As soon as the preliminary courtesies had been concluded, Mr. Churchill commenced an address which lasted exactly one hour and fifty minutes, during which I was never given the opportunity to say a word. It constituted a cascade of oratory, brilliant and always effective, interlarded with considerable wit. It would have impressed me more had I not already read his book "Step by Step" (of which incidentally, he gave me an autographed copy before I left) and of which his address to me constituted a rehash.

The gist of Mr. Churchill's remarks was that he was sitting in the same office in which he had sat twenty-five years before, confronted by exactly the same situation. The reason for it was that British Governments during the past twenty years had refused to follow a realistic policy towards Germany. The objectives of the German people had not changed, and would not change. These were world supremacy and military conquest; objectives which endangered the security of the United States as much as they imperilled the safety of the British Empire. He had foreseen the present crisis; time and again he had pointed out to previous British Governments the dangers they were incurring, but he had not been listened to and now the crisis was once more upon them. There could be no solution other than outright and complete defeat of Germany; the destruction of National Socialism, and the determination in the new Peace Treaty of dispositions which would control Germany's course in the future in such a way as to give Europe, and the World, peace and security for one hundred years. Austria must be reconstituted, Poland and Czechoslovakia re-created, and Central Europe made free of German hegemony. Russia, to him, offered no real menace and no real problem.

At the conclusion of this address, Welles went on, Churchill turned to the war at sea, saying that 770,000 tons of shipping had been destroyed, but that this was offset by 550,000 tons of new construction. German magnetic mines had been completely defeated, forty-three submarines had been sunk, and the Germans were producing one submarine a week. "Aviation he recognized as the chief danger." Churchill then took his visitor to the other end of the building to see the War Maps Room. "Mr. Churchill expressed his deep regret that the President himself could not see this room, since he knew how interested he would be in the systems of protection for shipping which had been devised."

There was another reference to Churchill in Welles's reports. He talked with Paul Reynaud in Paris, a man who impressed him as having "a greater grasp of foreign relations, and . . . a keener mind than any other member of the present French Government." Reynaud described himself as "rightly regarded as the 'hardest' man in the French Government with regard to French relations with Germany." Nevertheless, he too was critical of Churchill, who had

paid him a midnight visit two nights before. Mr. Churchill's point of view was utterly intransigent. M. Reynaud felt that while Mr. Churchill was a brilliant and most entertaining man, with a great capacity for organization, his mind has lost elasticity. He felt that Mr. Churchill could conceive of no possibility other than war to the finish—whether that resulted in utter chaos and destruction or not. That he felt sure was not true statesmanship.

Welles's critical references to Churchill in his reports suggest that he had, especially after his initial talk with Mussolini, begun to believe there was a real possibility of heading off the great military showdown by some patched-up peace. He saw Mussolini again on March 16 at the end of his mission. The Italian dictator told him that he was meeting Hitler in two days at Brenner Pass. Could he communicate to Hitler the impressions Welles had formed in London and Paris of the possibility of a negotiated solution of political and, especially, territorial questions? That would require specific instruction from the president, whom he would telephone, replied Welles.

Welles did call the president. "I expressed to the President my belief that he should authorize me to say to the Duce that the President did not feel that he possessed sufficient information with regard to the views which had been expressed to me in my visits to Berlin, Paris and London, to make it possible for him to agree to permit Mussolini to convey to Hitler any impressions which I myself had formed with regard to any possible territorial adjustments." Roosevelt agreed to this statement but said Welles should further say that the problem of security and disarmament was the fundamental issue. Roosevelt's reply was conveyed to Ciano, minister of foreign affairs, and Welles offered to delay his return in order to get from Ciano an account of the Brenner meeting.

In the interim, Welles saw the pope, who told him that the president's greatest service would be to influence Mussolini to remain a nonbelligerent. The pope did not think a peace move practicable at this time, but when the moment became propitious the United States, Italy, and the Vatican might act together. Ciano returned from Brenner to inform Welles that Hitler was unreceptive to the idea of a negotiated peace, but that, because of "weather" and other "momentary" obstacles, neither was an offensive imminent. Welles should tell the president, Ciano said in parting, "that so long as I remain Foreign Minister, Italy will not enter the war on the side of Germany, and that I will do everything in my power to influence Mussolini in that same sense."[41]

The Welles mission had indeed set the rumors flying that the president was preparing a move for peace that would in effect ratify Hitler's gains. Churchill, for example, wrote to Gen. Maurice Gamelin, the French commander in chief, on March 16, to plead again that the French expedite his proposal to mine Germany's inland waterways. He argued that "after the fiasco in Scandinavia and . . . the sinister lull now prevailing, the effect of our appearing bankrupt in all forms of positive or offensive action may be bad upon the neutrals, and give encouragement to the movements for a patched-up peace, which gather around the mission of Mr. Sumner Welles." The rumors had reached such a stage that Roosevelt and Hull agreed the president had better make a speech correcting them. On March 16, the day that Welles had telephoned Roosevelt, the president, in a broadcast from the White House, stated in regard to a negotiated settlement, "it cannot be a lasting peace if the fruit of it is oppression, or starvation, or cruelty, or human life dominated by armed camps. It cannot be a sound peace if small nations must live in fear of power neighbors."[42]

Hull had little use for Welles, whose access to Roosevelt he resented. He felt satisfied, he later wrote, that Welles had asked the president to send him on this mission. So did Ambassador Bullitt in Paris, who felt that it violated an understanding that Bullitt had with Roosevelt which made him the principal White House adviser on European affairs. Bullitt painted a malicious picture of French reaction to Welles's mission, one that suggested the French, including Reynaud, were as intransigent as Churchill. He wrote Roosevelt on April 18:

I had hoped that the repercussions caused here by Welles' trip would have died down completely before my return; but Reynaud, Daladier, Chautemps [minister of state], Blum and all the rest of the French politicians, to say nothing of all the diplomats here have insisted in talking about the trip. They have all said the same thing; to wit: that Welles "eulogized" Mussolini to everyone and in discussing Germany, produced the impression that Germany could not be beaten. Daladier used the word "eulogy"; Reynaud used the word "commendation"; Chautemps used the word "praises," etc. The meaning was the same.

Daladier said that the impression Welles produced was that you thought Germany was invincible and that France and England ought to try to get a peace of compromise which would leave Germany in control of Central and Eastern Europe by using the good offices of a great man—Mussolini. Daladier was a bit shocked and sore; Chautemps went so far as to say that he was much too intimate a friend of mine not to let me know that the visit had been exceedingly damaging to your influence in France and to my influence, since the impression had been produced either that you were unaware of Mussolini's real character and intentions or that I was unaware of what was in your mind.

I replied in the same tone to everyone; that I was entirely certain that neither you nor Welles had the slightest intention of using Welles' visit to persuade the French and British to stop fighting and leave the fate of Europe to Mussolini as arbiter. I added that I could not believe that Welles had praised Mussolini in any terms which would suggest that you thought Mussolini should be entrusted with the peace-making.[43]

Bullitt never eased his attacks on Welles for the latter's praise of Mussolini and his efforts to find a formula for a negotiated peace. It is doubtful, however, that Welles would have ventured any opinion in Europe that he did not believe reflected Roosevelt's own views and hopes. In attacking Welles as bitterly as he did, Bullitt was laying the basis for Roosevelt's subsequent re-luctance to give him a new post of consequence. Moreover, within a few weeks Reynaud, Churchill, and Roosevelt would all be offering all kinds of blandishments to Mussolini in a vain effort to keep him out of the war.

Welles published his account of the mission in 1944 while Roosevelt was still alive. His final verdict, one suspects, was not too far from Roosevelt's.

Looking back now with a fuller knowledge of the overwhelming confidence of the Nazi leaders, it is obvious that no verbal interposition by the United States in the winter of 1940 would have been effective. Only one thing could have deflected Hitler from his purpose; the sure knowledge that the power of the United States would be directed against him if he attempted to carry out his intention of con-quering the world by force. And only that same knowledge could have dissuaded Mussolini—as distinguished from the Italian people—from his fatal adventure at the side of Hitler.

At that time no representative of this government could have been authorized to intimate any such thing. . . . My mission, therefore, was a forlorn hope.[44]

Chapter Six

"Former Naval Person"

I T IS IRONIC that the shattering events that brought Churchill to the prime ministership and converted his correspondence with Roosevelt into that between president and "former naval person" began with a military adventure sponsored by Churchill himself.

The Norwegian fiasco that finally toppled Chamberlain was Churchill's invention, insisted on by him in the face of the waverings of other cabinet ministers and guided by him as head of the admiralty in its day-to-day operations. He was as deeply involved in Norway as he had been in Gallipoli, but while the latter led to political exile, Norway brought him to the pinnacle of power.

The Finnish-Russian War of 1939–1940 ended on March 12 with Finland's capitulation to Soviet terms. The surrender of the gallant Finns cast a pall over the West, where it was regarded as new evidence of the inability of the democracies to stand up to the dictators. "Cabinet 10:30. Everyone very gloomy, particularly, of course Winston," Cadogan, the permanent undersecretary of the foreign office, recorded in his diary. "I suppose we *have* suffered a reverse over Finland." Churchill, whose mettlesome temperament and powerful, thrusting imagination had engendered one scheme after another by which the West might seize the military initiative, lamented in the cabinet, "I fear we shall never get another opportunity of gaining a foothold in Scandinavia."[1]

In retrospect, it was fortunate that the Allies were unable to consummate their plans to send an expeditionary force across Norway and Sweden. Not only might such an operation have provoked a counterinvasion by Germany, a sequence that would not have alarmed Churchill for he had argued that "we have more to gain than to lose by a German attack on Norway and Sweden," but it might have risked military collision with Russia. "Switching" the war was what some Allied leaders wanted, but not Churchill. "I am not recorded as having said a word," Churchill wrote of the Supreme War Council meeting in Paris, February 5, at which the decision was made to send aid to Finland, including troops. This unwonted silence may have reflected Churchill's awareness that his famous volubility was not always appreciated by Chamberlain rather than misgivings about the Finnish operation. In any event, he wanted a way to stop ore shipments from the Gällivare mines, and the expeditionary force gave it to him. The foolhardy operation to aid the Finns was balked by the refusal of the Swedes and Norwegians to consent to the passage of the Allied expeditionary forces across their territories. When the Finns made peace, Churchill's chief anxiety was about his plan to seize the Gällivare fields, which was now up in the air. "Up till now we have had assistance to Finland as 'cover.' . . . We have now lost this justification." He proposed that Britain take the line that "our national interests are directly threatened."[2]

Germany, whose own admirals had been pressing for an operation against Norway not only to forestall the British but, as Hitler put it, to "give our Navy and Air Force a wider starting line against Britain," also was somewhat disconcerted by events. "Conclusion of peace between Finland and Russia deprives England, but us too, of any political basis to occupy Norway," Gen. Alfred Jodl noted in his diary. Even if the danger of British landings no longer was acute, Grand Adm. Erich Raeder warned Hitler at a military conference in Berlin, one British objective "has been and still is to cut off Germany's imports from Narvik."[3]

The disappearance of a "pretext" deterred neither side. "It cannot be too strongly emphasized that British control of the Norwegian coastline is a strategic objective of first-class importance," Churchill had minuted to the cabinet in December, 1939. As late as the end of February Cadogan noted that the cabinet was "still undecided about minefields in Norwegian waters. Of course it is really only a Winston stunt," he added, "tho' I shouldn't mind doing it," which was having the best of both worlds. Churchill first proposed mining Norwegian waters in September and could comment justly, "They [the cabinet members] certainly were very long in reaching a decision." The plan was finally approved at a meeting of the Supreme War Council on March 28. France was represented for the first time by Paul Reynaud, Daladier having fallen as premier because of French unhappiness over Allied passivity in the face of Finland's agony. Confronted with a rising public clamor for action, the council approved two of Churchill's "stunts," as Cadogan called them. It set April 5 as the day for the mining project and also approved the "Royal Marine Operation," a Churchill inspiration to sow mines in Germany's inland waterways, especially the Rhine. But French hesitancy over the Royal Marine Operation, which its leaders feared would provoke the Luftwaffe to retaliate by bombing France, caused the Norwegian operation date to be postponed until April 8. Hitler, in the meantime, had approved April 9 as the date for the German invasion of Norway. "A race is beginning for Scandinavia between ourselves and Britain," the German Naval Staff diary noted on April 3. After the war, the Allies learned that German intelligence had broken British signals and had a rather accurate reading of British plans and intentions in Norway. The British, too, were receiving signals of German concentrations in the Baltic, but failed to give them their due weight. Churchill anticipated—indeed, hoped (and his expectations were approved by the cabinet)—that mining Norway's waters would provoke the Germans to react, thereby giving the Allies a reason to land troops at Narvik, Trondheim, Stavanger, and Bergen; and the preparations for the mining of Norway's waters included preparations for follow-up landings. So optimistic was the British cabinet that on April 3, Chamberlain imprudently exulted to the conservative central council:

After seven months of war, I feel ten times as confident of victory. I feel that during the seven months our relative position towards the enemy has become a great deal stronger than ever.

This statement was made in utter disregard of Reynaud's declaration at the Supreme War Council meeting of March 28 that the number of divisions on the German side was increasing faster than on the Allied side and that the signs from the frontiers of the Low Countries and France indicated that the time of the testing of nations was just at a beginning. Chamberlain thought it "extraordinary" that Hitler had not taken advantage of Germany's lead in preparations at the beginning of the war. "One thing is certain: he missed the bus." "This proved an ill-judged utterance," Churchill later wrote. The prime minister seemed impervious to the signs of impending events, "whereas it seemed almost certain to me that the land war was about to begin." "All's quiet on the Western Front," Churchill said in a broadcast address on March 30. "But more than a million German soldiers, including all their active divisions and armored divisions, are drawn up ready to attack, at a few hours' notice, all along the frontiers of Luxembourg, of Belgium and of Holland."[4]

Four days later, on April 7, powerful German naval forces were spotted at sea, headed, it was thought, for Narvik, but also, it was soon learned, pressing on for Trondheim, Bergen, and Oslo. Waiting at these ports disguised as ore vessels at Narvik, and merchant ships elsewhere, were German transports loaded with troops. As reports came into the admiralty of German battle-cruiser and destroyer sightings, the British home fleet steamed out of Scapa Flow to intercept them. "Winston is back from France full of blood," Maj. Gen. H. L. Ismay noted. "He was like a boy this morning describing what he had done to meet the Germans." "It is an honourable tradition of the Royal Navy," commented the official British historian, "that a British fleet should seek to bring the enemy's strongest force to battle at the first opportunity. It is possible, however, that by doing so it may be playing the enemy's game, and such turned out to be the case in the present instance." The plans for British troop landings in Norway's ports, which were to be set in motion in the event the Germans retaliated for the mining of Norwegian waters, were jettisoned—so hastily that the First Cruiser Squadron, which had been embarking troops for Norway, marched the four battalions ashore and steamed out to sea with their equipment, immobilizing them for five days. This fateful decision to subordinate the landings to clear the seas of the enemy was a unilateral admiralty decision, concurred in—and perhaps, judging by Ismay's recollection, spurred by—Churchill.[5]

By five in the morning on April 8, the British mine fields had been successfully laid and the news was announced to the world. But as the admiralty was congratulating itself on this successful action and the Norwegian foreign office was drafting a protest against Britain's violation of Norway's neutrality, more ominous sounds began to dominate the scene. There were increasing reports of sightings of German warships speeding northward. A German transport was sunk off the Norwegian coast. The British destroyer *Glowworm,* 150 miles southwest of the Narvik fiord, reported sighting one, then two, German destroyers and engaging them in action. Early on the morning of April 9 the chiefs were routed out of their beds to learn of German landings at Oslo, Stavanger, Bergen, and Trondheim, and by 6:30 the hurriedly assembled military leaders began to grapple with a German invasion that was not too different from the German "reaction" to the British mining operation that they—Churchill and the war cabinet—had expected, even desired.

The German stroke was swifter, more audacious, more ruthless, and larger in scope than had been anticipated; but that was a flaw in Allied planning, which had been guided by Churchill more than by any other strategist. A week earlier, an uneasy Gen. Maurice Gustave Gamelin, the French commander in chief, had urged Gen.. Sir Edmund Ironside, the chief of the Imperial General Staff, to speed up the dispatch of troops to Norway, only to be told "With us the Admiralty is all-powerful. It likes to organize everything methodically. It is convinced that it can prevent any German landing on the west coast of Norway."[6]

Of the emergency meeting of the chiefs of staff, no one, Ismay wrote on April 9, had a "plan of action," and up to the time that they rose two hours later to move to Number 10 Downing Street for a meeting of the war cabinet, there had not been "a single constructive suggestion." Ismay's recollection reflects the disarray and muddle caused by Hitler's surprise thrust. It must be qualified as a description of the navy's response to the invasion. Indeed, as a German task force headed into Bergen, the British main fleet, under the command of Adm. Sir Charles Forbes, had arrived off Bergen. Forbes notified the admiralty that he was ready to send in a force to attack the German warships and transports, and the admiralty authorized him to prepare to do so and also to prepare plans for an assault on the German forces at Trondheim. Churchill reported these preparations at the war cabinet meeting to which the chiefs had repaired and was authorized to tell Forbes to go ahead. By the time Churchill returned to the admiralty, however, the first sea lord, Adm. Sir Dudley Pound, had decided the risks were too great. There were two cruisers in the harbor instead of one, and Norwegian shore batteries were thought to be in German hands. Churchill studied the information and agreed with Pound to cancel the attack although Forbes was prepared to take the risk. "Looking back on this affair," Churchill later wrote, "I consider that the Admiralty kept too close control upon the Commander-in-Chief."[7]

The initial German invading force was small, and a frontal assault on Bergen, we now know, would have been successful. Instead, the British fleet steamed northward to be out of range of German aircraft and to concentrate on the northern ports. The enemy was left to consolidate its positions in the south.

For all the failure of command wisdom the British fleet performed heroically. Despite foul weather and blinding fog, despite the vast areas in which the German ships maneuvered and the deep fiords in which they took refuge, before the action was over the Germans had lost three cruisers and ten destroyers; three battleships were severely damaged. Although the German fleet was crippled, German forces had successfully landed in the meantime.

As the world reeled from the news of the German invasion of Denmark and Norway and the occupation of Norwegian ports as far north as Narvik, the immediate question asked by everyone was how the Germans could have done it in the face of British naval supremacy in the North Sea. "The immediate reaction, among Americans and foreign naval attachés," wrote the U.S. naval attaché in Berlin, "was—where in hell was the British Navy? They got caught flat-footed!" And in a cable that ended up at the White House, Capt. Alan G. Kirk, the naval attaché in London, reported: "The operations of the Germans in Scandinavian attack is a fine example of the importance attached to speed of operations which is the present Nazi technique." Washington was as baffled as European capitals by the failure of the British fleet. "The thing that has made me hopping mad," Roosevelt said to Henry Morgenthau, "is where was the British Fleet when the Germans went up to Bergen and Oslo. It is the most outrageous thing I have ever heard of."

On April 9 Chamberlain had made a brief statement in the House of Common. "It is rather well done," Nicolson, no admirer of the prime minister, reported, "and he admits quite frankly that the Fleet is out and that we do not know exactly what is happening. . . . The House is extremely calm and the general line is that Hitler has made a terrible mistake." There was general relief that the twilight war had been brought to an end and that Allied forces were in action. Above all, the country was confident that the British navy would prevail in a battle that was being fought, it was presumed, chiefly at sea. But as the report of German successes sank in, including, most incredible of all, German occupation of Narvik, the public became uneasy. "The news is bad," Nicolson noted on April 10.

The war cabinet decided that a full statement had to be made in the House and that the government's spokesman should be the minister the House was most eager to hear and who, in fact, carried the largest responsibility for the military operations then taking place.[8] "Winston comes in [to address the House]," as Sir Harold Nicolson described the scene.

He is not looking well and sits there hunched as usual with his papers in his hand. When he rises to speak it is obvious that he is very tired. . . . I have seldom seen him to less advantage. The majority of the House were expecting tales of victory and triumph, and when he tells them that the news of our reoccupation of Bergen, Trondheim and Oslo is untrue, a cold wave of disappointment passes through the

House. . . . One has the impression that he is playing for time and expects at any moment some dramatic news will be brought to him. It is a feeble, tired speech and it leaves the House in a mood of grave anxiety.[9]

Churchill had a different impression of the House's reception. It listened, he wrote, "with growing acceptance," to his account of the naval battles, the difficulties the fleet had encountered, the obstacles to vigorous Allied planning engendered by Norwegian neutrality.

It is not the slightest use blaming the Allies for not being able to give substantial help and protection to neutral countries if we are held at arm's length until those neutrals are actually attacked on a scientifically prepared plan by Germany.

Then, in a warning to Belgium, which, despite German troop concentrations on the frontiers of the Low Countries, still refused to allow British and French troops to enter the country and prepare an advance defense line, Churchill said that he trusted that the Norwegian experience

will be meditated upon by other countries who may tomorrow, or a week hence, or a month hence, find themselves the victims of an equally elaborately worked-out staff plan for their destruction and enslavement.

But what most interested and buoyed up the House—and the country—was the optimistic note at the end of Churchill's ninety-minute statement:

In my view, which is shared by my skilled advisers, Herr Hitler has committed a grave strategic error in spreading the war so far to the north and in forcing the Scandinavian people, or peoples, out of their attitude of neutrality . . . we shall take all we want of this Norwegian coast now, with an enormous increase in the facility and in the efficiency of our blockade.

In the upshot, it is the considered view of the Admiralty that we have greatly gained by what has occurred in Scandinavia and in the northern waters in a strategic and military sense. For myself, I consider that Hitler's action in invading Scandinavia is as great a strategic and political error as that which was committed by Napoleon in 1807, when he invaded Spain.

As Churchill sat down, it seemed to him that the House was "very much less estranged."[10]

The speeches of the opposition spokesman justified Churchill's satisfaction. "What we are most afraid of," said A. V. Alexander, a member of Labour's shadow cabinet and its chief spokesman on naval matters, "is lest the vigour and the intentions expressed by the First Lord should not be continuous day by day, in season and out of season, because of any lack of heart or spirit in other elements in the Government." Liberal leader Sir Archibald Sinclair immediately associated himself with these comments, adding, "In a debate on Finland the other day I referred to the impression made by many recent events on the minds of the neutrals that while the Germans are evil, they are swift, terrible and efficient, and that while we are good, we are slow, vacillating, and ineffective." The majority of the House clearly thought Churchill was the man to change that, "and by prompt and vigorous action to efface that impression once and for all."[11]

With southern Norway in German hands, Allied hopes now rested on the ejection of the German forces from Trondheim and Narvik, the latter a project that seemed not too difficult after the British navy's successful attack on those German warships that had accompanied the troops to that distant port. Narvik was Churchill's "pet." But the Norwegians, though taken by surprise and unable to mobilize, and who gallantly were trying to establish a line of resistance, felt that Trondheim was of greater strategic importance. It was the "key" to central Norway from which the German advance northward could be blocked and would give access to Sweden by rail. At the war cabinet meeting on April 13, Halifax, supported by Chamberlain, argued that Trondheim be given priority—"the action at Narvik can wait." Churchill defended his "first love." "I am very apprehensive of any proposals which might weaken our intentions to seize Narvik. . . . Trondheim is, on the other hand, a much more speculative affair. . . . There is a grave danger that we shall find ourselves committed to a number of ineffectual operations along the Norwegian coast, none of which will succeed." He was outvoted; but instead of subordinating the Narvik operation to the Trondheim assault, Narvik still held for him the highest priority. "Winston reluctantly sent a telegram to Paris asking for power to divert Chasseurs Alpins from Narvik to elsewhere," Cadogan noted. The French ardently backed an all-out effort in Scandinavia. "Want to make it a scene of major operations," commented Cadogan, sardonically adding, "so as to remove the war from France!" Churchill, despite what Cadogan called his "interminable speeches" in favor of Narvik, was not sure of himself. General Ironside, who had been delighted that in the cabinet debate "Winston backed me up in saying that we must deal with Narvik first," reported that at two the next morning Churchill, accompanied only by the deputy chief of the naval staff Adm. Tom Phillips, came to his room at the war office. "Tiny, we are going for the wrong place," Churchill exclaimed. "We should go for Trondheim. The Navy will make a direct attack on it and I want a small force of good troops, well led, to follow up a naval attack."[12]

While the attack on Narvik marked time, planning went forward for an amphibious assault on Trondheim, provisionally set for April 22. Diversionary landings were made north and south of Trondheim at Namsos and later at Åndalsnes. Churchill threw himself into these operations with his wonted vigor and enthusiasm. But as he became a convert, his military advisers cooled on the venture. On April 19 they recommended unanimously against a direct assault, preferring instead to turn the diversionary landings at Namsos and Åndalsnes into an enveloping pincers movement. Churchill was "indignant" but did not feel he could override the unanimous view of his professional advisers.

"He is so like a child in many ways," Ironside commented. "He tires of a thing and then wants to hear no more of it. He was mad to divert the Brigade from Narvik to Namsos and would hear of no reason. Now he is bored with the Namsos operation and is all for Narvik again. It is most extraordinary how mercurial he is."[13] Mercurial or flexible? The chief characteristic of Allied military leaders at this time was an inability, perhaps fear, of improvisation. Years of peacetime drilling punctuated by starchy war games and memories of frozen fronts in World War I had unfitted them for a war of surprise and lightninglike movement.

Within a week the situation at Namsos and Åndalsnes had so deteriorated that Chamberlain was reporting to his cabinet that plans had to be prepared for the total evacuation of Norway, except at Narvik. Cadogan's diary records the somber onset of awareness that Britain had been defeated.

27 April: Cabinet at 10:30. Lasted all morning. Very gloomy. We must get out, but it's an awful debacle. But there it is, and must be faced. . . .

28 April: Everything as black as black. . . .

And Chamberlain, who at the beginning of the week had still been hopeful that Trondheim would be "practically captured" before the week was over, sadly wrote: "This has been one of the worst, if not *the* worst, weeks of the war."[14]

Now the public and Parliament, whose expectations had been buoyed by Churchill's optimistic assessment on April 11, began to stir uneasily. Members of the House, including the steady and sobersided leader of the Labour party Clement Attlee, inquired of Chamberlain when the House might expect a statement on the British position in Norway. Admiral of the Fleet Sir Roger Keyes, veteran of the effort to force the Dardanelles and hero of Zeebrugge, told confidants in Parliament how he had gone to the admiralty to implore it to attack Trondheim, volunteering to lead the assault himself. A close friend of Churchill, he had come away, he reported, "in despair." "He [Keyes] says," recorded Harold Nicolson, "the Admiralty Board refused to take naval risks since they were frightened by the possible attitude of Italy. . . . He says that Winston's drive and initiative have been undermined by the legend of his recklessness. Today, he cannot dare to do the things he could have dared in 1915."[15]

Keyes, who was passionately devoted to Churchill and wanted to see him prime minister, returned to the Gallipoli theme in his speech in the House of Commons in the fateful debate of May 7–8 that resulted in Chamberlain's downfall.

The Gallipoli tragedy has been followed step by step. . . . It was a brilliant conception of the First Lord of the Admiralty to circumvent the deadlock in France and Belgium. It was defeated first by his Principal Naval Adviser. . . .

I have great admiration and affection for my right honourable Friend the First Lord of the Admiralty. I am longing to see proper use made of his great abilities. . . . A great friend of the First Lord remarked to me that the iron of Gallipoli had entered into the soul of my right honourable Friend, after he was submerged in the political upheaval which followed his difference of opinion with his Principal Naval Adviser. . . .

For Churchill to have agreed to Keyes's offer to lead an assault on Trondheim would have meant the resignation of Sir Dudley Pound, the first sea lord, and probably of Admiral Forbes, the fleet commander. It was not true that he had lost the capacity to dare, Churchill wrote of Keyes's Gallipoli thrust, but that "the difficulties of acting from a subordinate position in the violent manner required are of the first magnitude."[16]

"The situation in Norway," Ambassador Kennedy cabled Roosevelt and Hull, "which some people are already characterizing as the second Gallipoli, has caused Mister Churchill's sun to set very rapidly. . . . Churchill, confidentially, on being catechized last night about the terrible mess in Norway, complained that he did not have executive authority. I do not know what he meant, but I am sure he is wrong, because with the terrific popular pull he had behind him, he was running high, wide and handsome in the Cabinet." Everybody wanted to get rid of the Chamberlain cabinet, Kennedy went on, "but when you ask whom they would put in, they have not the slightest idea."

Roosevelt was disturbed. For the first time Americans were worrying over the outcome of the war, he wrote his old friend, Arthur Murray, whom he used occasionally to convey messages to Chamberlain and Halifax. "Frankly, I wish things could be speeded up a bit on your side—because the only way to meet the product of an almost perfect machine is to build an equally perfect machine."[17]

The political no less than the military battle field is ever primed with surprises. Even as the Conservative whips were "putting it about that it is all the fault of Winston,"[18] opinion in the House of Commons, led by the members closest to the services, was crystallizing in favor of Churchill's succeeding Chamberlain. The finger of fate wrote paradoxically, but the paradox reflected a keen discernment of the gifts and capabilities that England's supreme moment of peril required of her leader.

Parliament turned to Churchill because it believed that the direction of the machinery of war had never been placed firmly and clearly in his hands. He had first advocated the mining of Norwegian waters in September, 1939; the government havered and hovered for over six months; the service chiefs were ingenious at finding reasons not to move, Churchill at one point impatiently characterizing them as a "machinery of negation." When the Norwegian operation finally was authorized, the task of coordinating the services and approving operational plans belonged in the first instance to the Military Co-ordination Committee and, above them, to the war cabinet.

In early April, Chamberlain, yielding to demands for a more vigorous military policy, had appointed Churchill chairman of the MCC. But Churchill had been without power to implement his views, and because he headed the navy, his views as chairman were somewhat suspect with the army and air force. Once, after spending a night with Churchill at Chartwell before the war, General Ironside had remarked in his diary: ". . . very surprised at how Winston was so navally-minded. All his schemes came back to the use of the Navy." Ironside went on to refer to Churchill as "a grand strategist," and that was how most service chiefs felt about him. But his repute as a strategist did not enable him to impose a unified direction and plan on the competing services, whose representatives arrived at meetings of the MCC with their minds made up on the basis of preliminary discussions within their departments. In a fluid battle situation, where the unforeseen is the customary, the ability to respond swiftly and flexibly can be critical. But the cumbersome machinery of the MCC reporting to a war cabinet entailed endless meetings, and events constantly outran the decision-making process. The army, represented by both Secretary of State for War Oliver Stanley and Chief of the Imperial General Staff Ironside, fought Churchill at the meetings of the MCC:

One of the fallacies that Winston seems to have got into his head is that we can make improvised decisions to carry on the war by meeting at 5 p.m. each day. . . . [Oliver Stanley] is going to see the Prime Minister today and tell him that war cannot be run by the staffs sitting around a table arguing. . . . We cannot have a man trying to supervise all military arrangements as if he were a company commander running a small operation to cross a bridge.[19]

Chamberlain could have cut through this interservice squabbling by making Churchill minister of defense, but he and his political allies feared this would quickly turn Churchill into the most powerful man in the government. In mid-April, Churchill told Chamberlain that he was unable to make the MCC function and he wanted the prime minister to chair its meetings. Chamberlain did so for a few weeks, partly to bolster Churchill's authority, but the tactic was not fruitful.

Knowledgeable men in London, especially those in touch with the services, knew much of this. A significant group of peers and M.P.s, chiefly Conservative, had established a "watching committee" which met regularly at the home of Lord Salisbury, a much-respected elder statesman, "a man of splendid courtliness," who carried much weight among Conservatives in the House of Lords. Although not fully in the confidence of the government, for the group was persuaded that the war would never be conducted vigorously under Chamberlain, it had a pretty clear picture of what was going on. Nicolson, a member of the group, wrote on April 23 in his diary:

Lord Salisbury tells us that he had been to see Winston Churchill and had asked him quite formally whether he believed he could carry on concurrently the job of First Lord and Co-ordinator of Defence. Winston told him that he is feeling in perfect health, and that he would die if the Admiralty were taken away from him, and that the press had much exaggerated his role as Co-ordinator of Defence, which was little more than Chairman of a Committee of the fighting services. . . . Salisbury gave him the names of our Committee and he purred like a pleased cat.[20]

"The group to which I belonged in the House of Commons," wrote Maj. Gen. Sir Edward Spears, witty and urbane confidant of Churchill, whom he advised on French matters, "believed in Winston Churchill. We felt he was the only leader we had, and we were anxious lest he should become hopelessly compromised by the company he was in. Not the least distressing aspect of the situation was his sense of loyalty." No doubt Churchill had loyalty, but as an astute parliamentarian and practiced politician he knew, too, after his return to office in September, 1939, how greatly the Conservative machine distrusted and disliked him. Nor had Labour forgiven him for "Tonypandy" when, as home secretary, he was supposed to have sent in the troops in a labor dispute* or for the gusto with which he had pitched into breaking Labour's general strike in 1926. Churchill knew how reluctant Chamberlain had been to bring him into the cabinet. He had set about using his great force and charm to make an ally of the prime minister. His first reward for this exercise in loyal self-subordination had been Chamberlain's invitation to him to participate in the meeting of the Supreme War Council in Paris in February. Churchill was in high spirits when the ministerial party gathered to cross the Channel on that occasion. Chamberlain and Halifax were preoccupied at the time with how to head off Roosevelt's proposal to send Welles on his mission to Europe, an idea that Cadogan labeled "awful, half-baked." Chamberlain showed Churchill Roosevelt's telegrams and the reply that Cadogan had drafted. "Winston—after a second sherry—read them through and, with tears in his eyes, said 'I'm *proud* to follow you!' "[21]

Churchill's jubilant behavior was further described by the secretary of the MCC, General Ismay:

We were a large party—the Prime Minister, Lord Halifax, Mr. Churchill, the three Chiefs-of-Staff and myself. Mr. Churchill, attired as an elder brother of Trinity House† (Cadogan called it "a strange spurious naval costume"), made it clear from the outset that the journey was a naval occasion, that he, as First Lord, was our host, and that "a good time was going to be had by all." He must have travelled in scores of destroyers and crossed the Channel on almost innumerable occasions, but his enthusiasm that morning was spontaneous and infectious. The Prime Minister and Lord Halifax were led directly to a post of honour on the bridge, and the rest of us were given to understand that we would be missing a great treat if we retired to the ward room instead of staying on deck. As luck would have it, a stray mine was spotted, and the orders went forth that it was to be destroyed by rifle fire. Winston insisted on planting a helmet on Mr. Chamberlain's head to protect him against the splinters. The combination of this ill-fitting head gear and the well-known, badly-rolled umbrella was somewhat incongruous. At the Council meeting that morning, Churchill was scrupulously careful to leave the lead in Chamberlain's hands. Indeed I cannot remember that he intervened in the discussions at all. That night the whole embassy party took themselves to bed at an early hour but Lord Halifax told me the next morning that just as he was about to turn out his lights Churchill had arrived in a dressing gown and observed that it was very seldom that two intelligent people got the chance of a nice uninterrupted talk. He did not say how long the talk lasted, but he looked extremely sleepy.[22]

In response to Churchill's loyalty, as well as to his inexhaustible flow of military suggestions and the brilliance of his speeches expounding government policy, Chamberlain thawed to such an extent that Churchill wrote of

* Tonypandy was the scene of a pitched battle in 1911 in the coal fields of south Wales. Although it became part of Labour mythology that this episode showed Churchill's "whiff of grapeshot" attitude, his influence appears to have been a moderating one.

† Trinity House is a venerable society that looks after lighthouses and lightships. To be made an "elder brother" is an honor conferred by the society on persons connected with the sea. The attire consists of a reefer with brass buttons and a visored flat blue cap with an appropriate badge.

the March 28 meeting of the Supreme War Council, when Chamberlain took the lead in pressing for Churchill's proposals on Norway and the mining of the Rhine: "I listened to this powerful argument with increasing pleasure. I had not realised how fully Mr. Chamberlain and I were agreed." And speaking of the next few weeks, which covered the operations in Norway, Churchill wrote: "The Prime Minister was so favourable to my views at this juncture that we seemed almost to think as one."[23]

Churchill's stanchness and loyalty as a player on Chamberlain's team now was to be rewarded. When the realization came to Chamberlain that he had to step down, Churchill, although still not the preferred successor, was an acceptable one at a time when, as Nicolson observed, "Churchill is undermined by the Conservative caucus."

The basic reason, however, why Parliament and country turned to Churchill despite his responsibility for the Norwegian disaster was their recognition that he was a war leader. "His personal minutes and 'prayers,'" wrote his principal private secretary at the admiralty of his messages beginning "Pray inform me . . .," "made everyone feel that he was watching them, but these would have been of little use if we had not felt that he was imbued with the spirit of pugnacity, and with the offensive spirit to be 'up and at 'em.'" General Spears reported his bewilderment in Paris in February at hearing Paul Reynaud, the aggressive French minister of finance, attacked as "'belliciste' . . . a strange accusation for a political leader to level at a Minister in office in war-time."[24] Churchill was *belliciste,* and that was why Parliament, which had formerly been pacifist, turned to him.

"The House is crowded," Nicolson wrote of the tense, momentous debate on "The Conduct of the War" that began on May 7, "and when Chamberlain comes in he is greeted with shouts of 'Missed the bus!' He makes a very feeble speech and is only applauded by the Yes-men."[25] Chamberlain sought to mollify the House with the announcement that changes were being made in the direction of military operations, that Churchill, as chairman of the MCC, had been authorized to give guidance and direction to the chiefs of staff. But the House was not to be appeased. "This is a reverse," Major Attlee began his speech to the House. Mining Norway's waters had been long under consideration and had always held the possibility of "a hit back by Germany. I want to know what care was exercised in planning the means for defeating that stroke if it should come." That was, if the truth had been known, a thrust at Churchill. But Churchill was exempted from Attlee's attack. Attlee questioned the new setup of the MCC. "It is like having a man commanding an army in the field and also commanding a division. He has a divided interest between the wide questions of strategy and the problems affecting his own immediate command. The First Lord of the Admiralty has great abilities, but it is not fair to him that he should be put into an impossible position like that." Attlee finished on a note that united Labour, Liberals, and Conservative backbenchers. The country was "not satisfied that the war is being waged with sufficient energy, intensity, drive and resolution."

Liberal party leader Sir Archibald Sinclair concentrated on Trondheim:

"If it was a feasible operation, it ought to have been undertaken with ruthless determination. The Germans may have sacrificed a third of their fleet, but that fleet has helped to win a campaign, which is more than the Kaiser's greater fleet ever succeeded in doing." Sinclair quoted his favorite historian, Macaulay: "To carry the spirit of peace into war is a weak and cruel policy; a languid war does not save blood and money, but squanders them."[26]

The debate had begun at three. "There is no reason to believe Chamberlain will not weather the present storm," Kennedy cabled Washington at the end of the afternoon. But as evening shadows began to filter through Westminster, Admiral of the Fleet Sir Roger Keyes, "dressed in full uniform with six rows of medals," came into the House and rose to speak. He was there in uniform, he explained, "because I want to speak for some officers and men of the fighting, sea-going Navy who are very unhappy." Keyes made, records Nicolson, "an absolutely devastating attack upon the naval conduct of the Narvik episode and the Naval General Staff. The House listens in breathless silence when he tells us how the Naval General Staff had assured him that a naval action at Trondheim was easy but unnecessary owing to the success of the military; there is a great gasp of astonishment. It is by far the most dramatic speech I have ever heard and when Keyes sits down there is thunderous applause." Keyes, too, in his concluding remarks, exempted Churchill. Churchill's opportunity was coming, Keyes predicted. The whole country was looking to him to help win the war. "I am certain that tomorrow night he will deliver a very fierce counter-attack on me, because he is always loyal to his friends and colleagues, but having done that I do hope he will accept my view."[27]

The House was still reverberating to Keyes's hammer blows when Leopold Amery, Conservative, former government minister, and member of the Privy Council—"the most respected, the most experienced and probably the wisest amongst us," wrote General Spears—rose to administer the *coup de grâce*. He did not exempt Churchill, and, as Churchill later wrote, it was a "miracle" that he survived the military disaster and the debate that followed it. The whole world knew the Allies were planning some operation in the waters close to Germany, Amery began. "What did we expect to follow? Did we know Hitler and his merry men so little as to think their rejoinder would be slow or half-hearted? . . ." British intelligence knew as early as January that Admiral Raeder wanted the indented, deep-water coast of Norway "for the purposes of his air and submarine warfare." To mask the German convoy of troops to Norway, Admiral Raeder two days earlier had sent a large part of his fleet up the west coast of Norway, and "the Navy went off in hot pursuit after that German decoy. Rarely in history can a feint have been more successful." It was "a bad story, a story of lack of provision and of preparation, a story of indecision, slowness and fear of taking risks. If it only stood alone." The problem was the men who constituted the war cabinet. "Just as our peace-time system is unsuitable for war conditions, so does it tend to breed peace-time statesmen who are not too well fitted for the conduct of war. Facility in debate, ability to state a case, caution in advancing an unpopular view, compromise and procrastination are the natural qualities—I might almost say, virtues—of a political leader in time of peace. They are fatal qualities in war. Vision, daring, swiftness and consistency of decision are the very essence of victory." Amery ended on a note of anathema, quoting Cromwell's accusatory dismissal of the Long Parliament: "You have sat too long here for any good you have been doing. Depart, I say—let us have done with you. In the name of God, go."

He had never seen Commons in graver mood, commented the deputy leader of Labour Arthur Greenwood. The Speaker adjourned the House at 11:30. "There is no doubt that the Government is very rocky and anything may happen tomorrow," Nicolson recorded.[28]

When debate resumed the next afternoon, Churchill's most devoted supporters were on tenterhooks lest Churchill, who was scheduled to wind up the debate for the government, repudiate the efforts of its critics to draw a line between him and his colleagues and affirm his loyalty to Chamberlain in such thumping phrases as to make it impossible to salvage him from the Chamberlain wreckage. The continuation of Chamberlain in office became the issue as soon as Herbert Morrison, the lead-off speaker for Labour, requested a division at the end of the debate, in effect turning the issue into one of a vote of confidence. Chamberlain, who that morning had seemed to Cadogan well and quite cheerful, his sallow face slightly flushed, immediately accepted the challenge. "I welcome it indeed. At least we shall see who is with us and who is against us, and I call on my friends to support us in the lobby tonight." The House gasped. It was a moment of national peril. The critics of the government were speaking in terms of the national interest and Chamberlain, by his appeal "to my friends in the House—and I have friends in the House," was seeking to turn the debate into partisan channels, making it an issue of party rather than of nation. "This really horrifies the House," wrote Nicolson, "since it shows that he always takes the personal point of view." Chamberlain knew he was in trouble. His parliamentary private secretary approached representatives of the Tory rebels to say that the prime minister was prepared to meet with them next morning in order to satisfy their demands on the conduct of the war. But the conviction was now deep-rooted that Chamberlain himself was the obstacle to winning the war. That was stated most effectively by Churchill's colleague of World War I days, Lloyd George. He, too, exempted Churchill. The first lord, he remarked, could not be held "entirely responsible" for all the things that had happened in Norway. Immediately, as Churchill's friends feared, he was on his feet. "I take complete responsibility for everything that has been done by the Admiralty, and I take my full share of the burden."

"The right honourable gentleman," Lloyd George countered chivalrously, "must not allow himself to be converted into an air-raid shelter to keep the splinters from hitting his colleagues." Then he directed a deadly shaft at Chamberlain. The prime minister had "appealed for sacrifice. The nation is prepared for every sacrifice so long as it has leadership. . . . I say solemnly that the Prime Minister should give an example of sacrifice, because there is nothing which can contribute more to victory in this war than that he should sacrifice the seals of office."[29]

Now it was up to Churchill. He was preceded by Alfred Duff Cooper, who had resigned as first lord of the admiralty at the time of Munich because of his disagreement with Chamberlain's policy. He cautioned his colleagues against being beguiled by Churchill. "He will be defending with his eloquence those who have so long refused to listen to his counsel, who treated his warnings with contempt and who refused to take him into their own confidence. He will no doubt be as successful as he always has been, and those who so often trembled before his sword will be only too glad to shrink behind his buckler."

Churchill's summation was the government's familiar case. If neutrals like Norway had been more cooperative, advance preparations could have been more consistent and sure-footed. He hoped that Belgium would not be the next victim of neutrals' wishful thinking. In the military sphere, the enemy's air superiority had been decisive, and those who had resisted larger defense budgets in peacetime carried a share of the responsibility. Trondheim was the place to go, but the diversionary landings had made such splendid progress and direct attack involved such heavy risks that it seemed easier to capture Trondheim by envelopment. The decision to abandon the attack on Trondheim "saved us in the upshot from a most disastrous entanglement. . . . We must be careful not to exhaust our air force in view of the much greater dangers which might come upon us at any time." He took the "fullest responsibility . . . for having accepted the unanimous view of our expert advisers."*

Churchill's mention of air power was the key. This was the new element in warfare—the proper use of air power—and here Churchill had been considerably less than candid with the House of Commons. He had spoken of German "numerical" superiority in the air, but the admiralty's analysis behind closed doors, as conveyed to Captain Kirk, U.S. naval attaché in London, by "an officer of high rank, wide experience and considerable responsibility," placed its main emphasis on Britain's failure to use its sea and air power correctly. "The ability of the Germans to coordinate their air power with their military operations was something the British Army and the Royal Air Force had still to learn." There was another factor: Churchill and the admiralty had not realized the vulnerability of warships to land-based air attack. Churchill assumed that a warship's air-attack defenses provided sufficient protection.

Churchill ended his speech with a statement intended to defuse the sharp hostility engendered by Chamberlain's appeal to his friends. "Exception has been taken because the Prime Minister said he appealed to his friends. He thought he had some friends, and I hope he has some friends. He certainly had a good many when things were going well."[30]

* Churchill's views about the dangers of clinging to the positions in central Norway were later sustained by Hitler, who on May 3 wrote to Mussolini that "I had a slight hope that the English would allow themselves to be lured into holding on to their positions in Central Norway somewhat longer so as to allow the affair to develop gradually into one where British prestige was at stake. There could not have been a better opportunity of gradually decimating the British fleet by daily attacks."

Churchill's own friends breathed more easily. "He has an almost impossible task," Nicolson wrote of Churchill's performance. Nicolson had considered it impossible for the first lord to sum up for the government "without losing some of his own prestige." Yet Churchill had managed to do so "with absolute loyalty and apparent sincerity, while demonstrating by his brilliance that he has really nothing to do with this timid and confused gang."[31]

House members pressed into the division lobbies. Tension became almost palpable. Feelings rose. When the figures were disclosed, the government's majority of 213 had dwindled to 81. Pandemonium broke loose. Major Wedgwood, a Labourite, began to sing "Rule Britannia," and the singing gradually gave way to the chant, "go, go, go, go!"

The nation had spoken. The moment of cabinet reconstruction had arrived. Chamberlain, who had stalked out of the chamber of the House chalky-faced, outwardly sardonic but inwardly a shaken figure, asked Churchill to come to his room; they talked until midnight. The prime minister stated that a national government had to be established but that Labour would be unwilling to serve under him. Churchill urged him not to step down, on which note they parted.

"Everybody is mad and all wanting to do something and go places," Kennedy cabled after the vote, "but nobody has the slightest idea of what should be done." If Chamberlain did resign, "the politicians and conservative party would much prefer Halifax. The public would definitely prefer Churchill."[32]

Churchill is quite vague about what happened the next day, May 9, before his 4:30 meeting with Chamberlain and Halifax to discuss the creation of a coalition government. The fullest picture is given by Sir Anthony Eden, who was serving as secretary for the Dominions and who had been unsuccessfully pushed by Churchill for one of the service ministries during a minor reorganization of the cabinet in late March:

May 9th: Winston rang me up about 9:30 and said that he wanted to see me as soon as possible and while shaving he rehearsed to me the events of the previous evening. He thought that Neville would not be able to bring in Labour and that a National Government must be formed. Later I lunched with him and Kingsley [Wood, Lord Privy Seal and a confidant of Chamberlain's], when they told me that Neville had decided to go. The future was discussed. Kingsley thought that W. should succeed, and urged that if asked he should make plain his willingness.[33]

Eden was surprised that Wood, one of the men of Munich, should now be with Churchill to the point of alerting him that Chamberlain would want Churchill to concur in his preference for Halifax. "Don't agree and don't say anything," Wood advised Churchill. Eden was shocked that Wood should talk in this way, "for he had been so much Chamberlain's man, but it was good counsel and I seconded it."

Chamberlain had spent the morning trying to shore up his own position. The prime minister was on the telephone, wrote Labour leader Hugh Dalton, "from 8 a.m., trying to conciliate opponents, offering to sacrifice Simon,

Hoare, even Kingsley Wood, offering Leo Amery his choice of any position in the Cabinet except the Prime Ministership if he would bring his rebels in."[34]

Chamberlain's meeting with Churchill and Halifax at 4:30 was to agree on what would be said to Labour party leaders Attlee and Greenwood when they came in at 6:15. Captain Margesson, the Conservative chief whip, was also present. Chamberlain recapitulated the position as he saw it. There had to be an all-party government. He doubted that Labour would serve under him. He expressed his readiness to serve under either Halifax or Churchill. Chamberlain preferred Halifax, and he mentioned Labour's hostility to Churchill, noting their sharp interruptions of the first lord's speech the previous evening. That seemed ungenerous to Churchill, since the fierce thrusts that had provoked the Labour benches were made in defense of Chamberlain's government; but heeding the advice of Wood and Eden he kept his silence. It had been generally bruited about that Labour preferred Halifax to Churchill and Halifax had a note from Cadogan, saying,

Dalton called to see me at dinner time yesterday evening and told me that his party would come into the Government under you but not under the Prime Minister. . . . Dalton said there was no other choice but you. Churchill must "stick to the war."

But Churchill knew, from a talk that his devoted friend Brendan Bracken had had with Attlee, that while Labour would prefer Halifax it would not, despite "Tonypandy" and the like, refuse to serve under him.[35]

Though Labour at that point seemed to prefer Halifax, the foreign secretary saw difficulties in becoming prime minister. He would have no access to the House of Commons, he told the group in Chamberlain's room. Winston would be running Defence. He, Halifax, would speedily become a "more or less honorary Prime Minister." "If I was not in charge of the war and if I did not lead in the House, I should be a cypher," he later told Cadogan. "I thought Winston was a better choice. Winston did not demur. Was very kind and polite but showed that he thought this was the right solution. Chief Whip and others think feeling in the House has been veering towards him."[36]

Halifax and Churchill had a cup of tea in the garden while the prime minister attended to some other business. At 6:15 Attlee and Greenwood arrived. Chamberlain presented the situation to them and, to their surprise, invited them to join an all-party government under himself. Greenwood swiftly and somewhat tartly reaffirmed Labour's objections to serving under Chamberlain. "It is not pleasant to have to tell a Prime Minister to his face that he must go," Attlee later said, "but I thought it the only thing to do. I said, 'Mr. Prime Minister, the fact is our party won't come in under you. Our party won't have you and I think I am right in saying that the country won't have you either.' " Attlee told Chamberlain the decision to serve in a national government would have to be taken by the party executive, which was then at the Labour party conference in Bournemouth. Chamberlain asked him to canvas the executive on two questions: (1) Would they enter a government under the present prime minister? (2) Would they come in under someone else? Attlee promised to communicate the replies by telephone the next day, but he also made it quite plain that he already knew the answer to the first.[37]

At the end of the day Churchill dined with Eden. He sensed that fate was moving toward him and that Chamberlain the next day would advise the king to send for him. He hoped Chamberlain would stay, he told Eden, to lead the House of Commons and the party. "Winston would be Minister of Defence as well as Prime Minister," Eden recorded. "Winston quiet and calm. He wishes me to take war."[38]

The next morning England awoke to the news that Germany's vast armies had finally been unloosed on the Low Countries. Immediately the Chamberlain group seized on this as a reason to delay reconstruction of the government. "I had fully made up my mind as to the course I should pursue and fully agreed it with Winston and Halifax," Chamberlain wrote Lord Beaverbrook. "But as I expected Hitler has seized the occasion of our diversions to strike the great blow and we cannot consider changes in the Government while we are in the throes of battle." Sinclair, the Liberal leader, agreed, but Attlee thought "a change more urgent than ever if the nation was to be united." Joseph Kennedy, to whom Beaverbrook had shown Chamberlain's letter, was struck by "the drama of the situation. Here was Churchill realizing his life's ambition to become Prime Minister, spending the night arranging his Cabinet, arranging to announce it at six o'clock tonight, and Hitler invades Holland. . . . I do not know what Churchill's opinion will be but I am definitely sure he is not going to be very happy and this may result in another bitter fight while the world is burning."

"Just before 11:30 Cabinet," recorded Eden, "I was talking to Maurice Hankey [Lord Hankey, minister without portfolio] when Simon [i.e., Sir John Simon, chancellor of the exchequer] came up and said he understood that, despite the attack in Flanders, Churchill was pressing for early changes in the Government. He was indignant." Chamberlain felt, as he confided to Halifax, "that Winston did not approve of the delays, and left me guessing as to what he meant to do." Some Chamberlain supporters, however, notably Kingsley Wood, urged him to advise the king to send for another prime minister. Then the telephone call came from Bournemouth, saying that Labour would serve in a government of national unity but not under Chamberlain. "All of us felt," wrote Dalton, in view of Hitler's massive offensive, "it *must* be Churchill not Halifax. Regardless of all else, the strongest and most vigorous man must lead."

The prime minister had changed his mind, Kennedy reported "and within a few hours he will resign and Churchill become Prime Minister. Churchill is going to insist that Chamberlain be included in the Government and we will have to see whether Labour will come in on that basis. The general impression is that they will if Churchill is firm enough."[39]

Chamberlain had his final audience with the king. "I accepted his resignation," King George noted, "and told him how grossly unfairly I thought he had been treated. . . . We then had an informal talk over his successor. I, of course, suggested Halifax, but he told me that Halifax was not enthusiastic, as being in the Lords he could only act as a shadow or a ghost in the Commons, where all the real work took place. . . . Then I knew there was only one person whom I could send for to form a Government who had the confidence of the country, and that was Winston." The king then described his summons to Churchill, Churchill's acceptance, and ended his entry, "He was full of fire and determination to carry out the duties of Prime Minister."[40]

The responsibility was awesome, but Churchill was "full of fire" to shoulder it. As for Chamberlain and Halifax, they were relieved not to have to do so. Chamberlain was "a good deal shaken by political events, but very good," Halifax noted in his diary after the change-over had been effected.

He told me that he had always thought that he could not face the job of being Prime Minister in war, but when it came he did; and yet now that the war was becoming intense he could not but feel relieved that the final responsibility was off him. He said, what is quite true, that in the last resort the Prime Minister could nearly always impose his will on the Cabinet, hence the responsibility.[41]

Halifax shrank from the responsibility even more than Chamberlain. In the fateful discussions on May 9 he had been so disturbed at the prospect of becoming prime minister that he had felt sick to his stomach. When Chamberlain, on the morning of May 9, had dismissed his argument that it would be difficult to lead the government from the House of Lords, Halifax recorded that "the evident drift of his mind left me with a bad stomach ache."[42]

As for Churchill, when he went to bed about three in the morning, "I was conscious of a profound sense of relief. At last I had the authority to give directions over the whole scene. I felt as if I were walking with Destiny, and that all my past life had been but a preparation for this hour and for this trial."[43]

Chapter Seven

The Third Term

THE NEWS OF Chamberlain's resignation was handed to Roosevelt while the president was meeting with his cabinet to discuss the German blitz against the Low Countries. Henry Morgenthau, who found the president "very quiet and self-contained" on that turbulent day, makes no mention of the British political crisis, but Harold Ickes recorded that there was discussion of who might take Chamberlain's place. "We assumed that Churchill would be charged with organizing a new Cabinet, and the President said that he supposed Churchill was the best man that England had."[1]

It was not an ardent, all-out endorsement, although endorsement it was, more perhaps because of distrust of Chamberlain (whom Ickes called the "evil genius" of Western civilization) than admiration of his successor. The British navy's mistakes in the Norwegian campaign had shaken Roosevelt. Sumner Welles and Lord Lothian in Washington, the president's ambassadors in London and Paris, all were unflattering about the first lord. Lothian had dropped in to see Welles on May 5 and had "hazarded a guess that the Chamberlain government might well go under on Tuesday, but there was no one else who could act as Premier." Welles agreed on the British lack of alternatives. He was quite caustic about Churchill. On the first of the two evenings that he had seen the first lord, Welles told Adolf Berle, "[Churchill] was quite drunk." Berle inquired whether "in his peregrinations [Welles had seen] any indication of clear-cut leadership. Welles answered that he saw none."[2]

Joseph Kennedy's most intimate cronies in London were people who deprecated Churchill. The night that the House of Commons spurned Chamberlain, Kennedy telephoned Roosevelt from Lord Beaverbrook's rooms. Although the great Tory press lord was an old friend of Churchill, it was not at all clear, according to his official biographer, that on the eve of the shift of power "he preferred Churchill to Chamberlain. He doubted whether the bulk of the Conservative party would support Churchill. Maybe too he was disturbed by Churchill's 'harebrained' strategy in Norway."[3]

William C. Bullitt had confided his disapproval of Churchill to friends during the leave of absence that brought him to Washington early in 1940. "Bill has no use for Chamberlain," reported Ickes, who had suggested to Roosevelt that the president make Bullitt secretary of war, "and almost none for Churchill." Ickes went on: "There are no real leaders, as he sees it, in all of England in this time of grave crisis."

Bullitt's distrust of British leadership, including Churchill, was shared by the French government. "Both Reynaud and Daladier are bitter about the manner in which the Norwegian affair has been handled," he wrote Roosevelt. "They both favored the idea, but insist that the British made no proper preparations and have handled and are handling the expedition with complete lack of intelligence, although with courage. Reynaud is violent on the subject of lack of brains in the British Government and the British High Command. Daladier . . . blames Reynaud as well as the British for not foreseeing the German riposte, and preparing adequately to meet it."[4]

But Roosevelt had little disposition and less time to sit in judgment on British leadership. The crisis in Europe called for decisions in Washington, decisions that Roosevelt had long postponed either because he could not see his way clearly or because Congress and the public were not prepared to follow him or because his sense of political timing told him not to jeopardize short-range objectives by proclaiming ultimate possibilities and preferences. There was the basic and urgent question of how far to go in aiding Britain and France and—"shuddering possibility" as Berle called it—how to defend America if England and France both went down. There were questions relating to America's rearmament. Until the end of the Norwegian campaign, the president's formula for the restraint of Nazism in Europe had been a "trinity of French land power, British sea power, and American industrial power, expressed chiefly in terms of aircraft re-enforcement of the European allies." In his annual message Roosevelt had said: "I can understand the feelings of those who warn the nation that they will never again consent to sending American youth to fight on the soil of Europe. But, as I remember, nobody has asked them to consent—for nobody expects such an undertaking." He meant the latter.

Navalist in background, alive to the importance of air power, he had scanted the army. At the White House, as Nazi armies blitzed through the Low Countries, Morgenthau said to Army Chief of Staff Gen. George C. Marshall, "I understand you could only put into the field today, fully equipped, 75,000 troops." "That's absolutely wrong," Marshall said. "Well, how many could you put into the field today?" Morgenthau pressed the dour chief of staff. "80,000," he said. Noting that the president was spending more time on the army's needs than ever before, Morgenthau commented, "The President has to take a great deal of responsibility that the Army is in bad shape as it is."

There were other decisions relating to American preparedness that Roosevelt had to take: how and when to reorganize his own cabinet so that it would function more effectively as an instrument of American mobilization; whether to recommend compulsory military service, as friends of the army were urging; and which businessmen to invite down to Washington to head up the vast and imperative expansion of military production.[5]

Enveloping every other issue was that of the presidential succession itself—how to ensure a continuation of his foreign and domestic policies without himself running for a third term. All winter and spring he had been plagued by colds, flu, and inflamed sinuses—afflictions to which his system was particularly vulnerable when there were actions that had to be taken and which he could not take because the country and Congress were not ready for them.

Back in mid-1939 Henry Morgenthau, one of the most sedulous president-watchers in a city full of them, had noted that the president was bored. But a few months later, with the outbreak of the war, Morgenthau sensed a quickening of spirit in his friend, who remarked to him, "I like it when something is happening every minute." But that did not mean he liked the stimulation and excitement of wielding presidential power enough to stay on in the presidency. He was at heart a traditionalist who would not, for such strictly personal reasons as the enjoyment of the power and the perquisites of the presidential office, violate the two-term tradition.[6]

That had been his attitude all through his second term. Early in 1938, shortly after Congress defeated his plan to enlarge the Supreme Court and a coalition of Republicans and conservative southern Democrats solidified in order to block all reform legislation, Roosevelt concluded that a conservative trend had set in which would continue until 1940 and would bring a conservative into the presidency. The conservatives would have no program, he was sure, and the New Dealers should be ready with one—especially to end unemployment.

Roosevelt intended to comment and write from the sidelines at Hyde Park and set about building a library there that would house his books and papers, himself, and his secretaries. When Harry Hopkins fell ill and had to have part of his stomach removed at the Mayo Clinic, Roosevelt spoke of Hopkins helping him at the library at Hyde Park. "I'm going to give him one of the cottages on my place and I'm going to ask [President] MacCracken to make him a professor at Vassar," he told Morgenthau, meaning he hoped to have Harry nearby for Hopkins was a congenial companion. Originally a social worker, Hopkins had been brought into the inner family circle as much as a result of Eleanor Roosevelt's fondness for him as the president's. Hopkins was a down-to-earth, unsentimental reformer who understood the political game—indeed, saw things so much the way the president did that Roosevelt, as part of an effort to build him up for the presidency, appointed him secretary of commerce to take the "social worker" stamp off of him. But the campaign collapsed with Harry's health, and for six months Hopkins had been unable to attend a cabinet meeting. Roosevelt was a lonely man who did not disclose his innermost thoughts and feelings to anyone. Yet he was also the most gregarious of men, needing the company of people, like Hopkins, who shared his outlook and respected his reticence. And as it became clear that Hopkins could no longer think of a career for himself, he abandoned all ambition except to serve Roosevelt and Roosevelt's purposes, which were also his own. He provided Roosevelt with the disinterested companionship that the president so desperately needed.

Roosevelt's talk of Hopkins getting a professorship at Vassar was another indication that FDR did not intend to run in 1940.[7] So was his decision in 1938 to build himself a retreat at Hyde Park four miles east of the Big House, behind Mrs. Roosevelt's Val-Kill cottage, on wooded hills from which the distant Catskills could be glimpsed. He sketched out the low Dutch-style cottage that he wanted, and Henry Toombs, the architect who had built Val-Kill, drew up the plans. Roosevelt kept close tabs on its progress, as he did on the progress of the library. Like Churchill at Chartwell, the builder's impulse was strong in him; and no doubt if polio had not prevented it, he too, like his British contemporary, would have even wielded a bricklayer's tools. "We think much of you both and we are counting on you and Arthur at Hyde Park just as soon as peace comes," he wrote the Murrays in mid-April, 1940. "You will probably find me sitting there doing little and praying that my successor will carry on the general policies of this Administration. . . . I will send you a snapshot of the new Library and of the cottage with its new shrubs, when I go up in May."

Roosevelt could become quite angry with New Dealers who talked of his indispensability. In May, 1939, Tom Corcoran, a leading New Dealer, tried to enlist Sumner Welles in a "draft Roosevelt for a third term" movement. Welles took it up with the president. "The President got emotional about it," Berle recorded in his diary. "He said he had nothing to do with third term talk; he did not consider it; did not want it; and was violently and vividly opposed to it."[8]

This accorded with Eleanor Roosevelt's impressions of her husband's attitude toward a third term. Hopkins and his small daughter Diana lunched with her on May 28, 1939, and for three hours she and Harry discussed the state of the nation.

Mrs. Roosevelt was greatly disturbed about 1940. She is personally anxious not to have the President run again, but I gathered the distinct impression that she has no more information on that point than the rest of us. She feels the President has done his part entirely. That he has not the same zest for administrative detail that he had and is probably quite frankly bored. She thinks that the causes for which he fought are far greater than any individual person, but that if the New Deal is entirely dependent upon him, it indicates that it hasn't as strong a foundation as she believes it has with the great masses of people. Mrs. Roosevelt is convinced that a great majority of voters are not only with the President, but with the things he stands for, and that every effort should be made to control the Democratic convention in 1940, nominate a liberal candidate and elect him. She has great confidence in his ability to do this, if, and it seems to be a pretty big "if" in her mind, he is willing to take off his coat and go to work at it.[9]

Roosevelt agreed with his wife. As 1939 ended he was determined not to run himself but to impose his choice of a successor on the convention. He diverged from his more ardent liberal backers, however, in thinking that his successor, in view of the war and the importance of foreign affairs in the next executive's agenda, should be his secretary of state Cordell Hull, a conservative on most domestic issues. Roosevelt's daughter Anna and her husband John Boettiger, who ran the *Seattle Post Intelligencer,* came to the White House for the Christmas holidays and talked with the president about 1940. Their closest friends in Washington at the time were Jane and Harold Ickes. The latter was one of the most ardent advocates of a third term as the only way to ensure a continuation of liberalism in the United States. John Boettiger, after his talks with the president, cautioned Ickes that he was convinced FDR would not run in 1940. "John said the thing to bear in mind was the possibility of Hull as a candidate for President, with a young liberal, [Attorney General Robert] Jackson or [Justice William O.] Douglas, on the ticket for Vice President. He thinks that this is what is running in the President's mind and he warned me several times to be on guard in this respect."[10]

"I should not feel much cheered by the prospect of Mr. Hull," Halifax commented when advised by Lothian that the president preferred Hull to Vice-President Garner. "The general impression now is that the President himself does not want a third term," Lothian wrote at the end of 1939, adding, however, that "in the long run the issue will be determined by the foreign situation." Lothian was asked by Halifax whether the foreign office was correct in thinking that "if, contrary to the expectations of his friends, Mr. Hull were to run as a candidate, it would suit our books better that he should be chosen as the Democratic nominee rather than Mr. Garner?" That would be understating it, the Washington embassy replied, but "the only man who could rally the Democratic party on both the foreign and domestic front is the President himself—though there is a widespread prejudice against the Third Term." Cadogan dissented about Hull being preferable to Garner. "Mr. Hull, no less than Mr. Garner would be a disastrous President for the U.S. & for us. He is incapable of making up his mind."[11]

Another reason for Roosevelt's reluctance to run was his conviction that he would have much more trouble with Congress in a third term than he had had in his second term. He so advised Sen. George Norris, the Nebraska progressive known as the father of TVA and an enthusiastic advocate of a third term. FDR told Tom Corcoran while working on his annual message to Congress that he felt he had "probably gone as far as he can on domestic questions." Bullitt had several talks with Roosevelt during the late winter and at the end of his home leave told a close friend "that F.D.R. is tired out and has no more enjoyment out of the Presidency, and doesn't want to run; that he is going to back Hull; that he still hangs on so as not to throw away all chances for himself, but W.C.B. [William C. Bullitt] thinks he will not run."[12]

But none of this meant that Roosevelt was prepared to show his hand publicly and yield to Republican and conservative Democratic demands that he rule out a third term. To do so would mean to lose all control over Congress and, equally important, much of his influence over the selection of a candidate and the writing of a platform at the Democratic convention. He not only went along cheerfully with the moves to get delegation slates pledged to him so long as they did not require any declaration of intentions from him, but in several instances quietly managed this movement. Moreover, he had liberals like Ickes, Jackson, Corcoran, and Cohen in for dinner meetings at which they worked on a draft platform and planned the organization of the convention. His strategy, Roosevelt told Morgenthau, reflected advice from the wife of one of his officials to keep his mouth shut. This was not only sound from the point of view of keeping political control in his hands, but would keep open the option of running again should things get much worse in Europe. He agreed with Morgenthau that he did not have to make up his mind until the last moment.[13]

Roosevelt's deft moves to keep the situation fluid were necessarily veiled in secrecy. If they were disclosed, a hostile press would seize upon them as confirmation of an intention to seek a third term, and every initiative in the fields of foreign and defense policy would be read in the framework of United States domestic politics. That had disadvantages as well as advantages. Everyone in London had been gracious and kind to Sumner Welles, and Chamberlain had sent Roosevelt a hand-written note expressing his gratitude for Welles's visit. But the prime minister's real feelings and those of the foreign office were disclosed thirty years later when the wartime archives of the foreign office were opened. In a memorandum of Sir Robert Vansittart, the chief diplomatic adviser of the government wrote:

It is now pretty clear as the Prime Minister says in these minutes, that President Roosevelt is ready to play a dirty trick on the world and risk the ultimate destruction of the Western Democracies in order to secure the re-election of a democratic candidate in the United States. It is not only the Prime Minister who has drawn this deduction; it is the general expectation of everybody that I know who knows anything of the American situation. . . . I feel strongly that we should exert the greatest and most immediate pressure on President Roosevelt to prevent him from selling the world for his own particular mess of pottage.[14]

The Nazis even more than the British read domestic politics into every move Roosevelt made. FDR dispatched Myron Taylor, eminent Episcopalian and former chairman of U.S. Steel, as his special envoy to the pope because of the uniqueness of the Vatican as a diplomatic listening post, because the pope shared an interest with the United States in keeping Mussolini out of the war, and because the president hoped that the gesture might induce a more favorable attitude among American Catholics toward his foreign policy. But Hans Dieckhoff, the former German ambassador to the United States, saw it differently. He cautioned his superiors that it was

a tactical move with the *elections* in mind. The President has always shown universally great consideration for the Catholic element in the United States (although, or perhaps because, he has many adversaries particularly among the

Catholics, e.g., Father Coughlin,* etc.) and he now emphasizes this tendency in view of the coming election.[15]

The German chargé in Washington, Hans Thomsen, concluded by early February that Roosevelt would bid for a third term. "The war in Europe was probably decisive in making up Roosevelt's mind. In addition to his strongly developed pretensions to leadership and his vanity vis-à-vis world opinion, he believes that in these critical times he must make the 'sacrifice' of another four-year term to the American people." And the next day when Welles informed Thomsen of Roosevelt's decision to send him to Europe, Thomsen advised Joachim von Ribbentrop, German minister of foreign affairs, that "the President's decision appears noteworthy, among other reasons, because it permits the inference that Roosevelt's policies are planned well in advance, and thus it is necessary to reckon with his re-election next fall."

Hitler classified Roosevelt, along with Churchill, as a warmonger, meaning only that Roosevelt was an unyielding opponent of Hitler's policies. Just before Hitler had received Welles, he had had a long talk with Colin Ross, a German "expert" on the United States who had recently returned from a propaganda trip there. According to the shorthand notes of Dr. Paul Schmidt, Hitler's interpreter,

Colin Ross then talked about Roosevelt, whom he believes to be an enemy of the Fuehrer for reasons of pure personal jealousy and also on account of his personal lust for power. . . . He had come to power the same year as the Fuehrer and he had had to watch the latter carrying out his great plans, while he, Roosevelt . . . had not reached his goal. He too had ideas of dictatorship which in some respects were very similar to National Socialist ideas. Yet precisely this realization that the Fuehrer had attained his goal, while he had not, gave to his pathological ambition the desire to act upon the stage of world history as the Fuehrer's rival. . . .

After Herr Colin Ross had taken his leave, the Fuehrer remarked that Ross was a very intelligent man who certainly had many good ideas.[16]

The Nazis made open and secret efforts to oppose Roosevelt's policies and renomination. The most ambitious public move was the publication of a German white paper containing documents allegedly found in the archives of the Warsaw foreign office. Polish ambassadors in Washington, Paris, and London reported supposed conversations with American ambassadors, particularly with Bullitt and Kennedy, in which the Poles were encouraged to take an intransigent attitude toward German demands, implying that the United States would join the war on the side of Britain and France. "Should war break out," Bullitt was quoted as saying, "we shall certainly not take part in it at the beginning but we shall end it."

Nazi newspapers were advised in Berlin: "We inform you in confidence that the purpose of publishing these documents is to strengthen the American

---

* At the height of his power, Father Charles E. Coughlin, the "radio priest," commanded a listening audience of millions, published a weekly newspaper entitled *Social Justice,* and led the National Union for Social Justice—all in support of a program that was rabidly isolationist and anti-Semitic.

isolationists and to place Roosevelt in an untenable position, especially in view of the fact that he is standing for re-election."[17]

Ribbentrop was very much taken with the documents. "These reports brought out two things in particular," he told Mussolini. "First, the monstrous war guilt of the United States, and second, the tremendous hatred of National Socialism together with a boundless will to destroy that regime. This outlook governed all actions of the British, the French, and unfortunately also the American plutocracies."

Mussolini was less impressed. The documents, "while certainly very interesting, offered nothing essentially new, since it had been known all along that France, England, and the United States were opposed to the authoritarian regimes."[18]

"The German publication hit political circles like a bombshell," Thomsen reported home, adding the next day that "it can be seen from the unusual haste of the disavowals, especially by Roosevelt and Hull, how extremely embarrassing to the American Government the German propaganda attack is; it feels that it is being driven into a corner and that Roosevelt's foreign policy is being exposed." Thomsen, acting through intermediaries, arranged to underwrite with a hundred-thousand-dollar guarantee the publication of the white paper by a respectable American publisher with a foreword by one of the "most distinguished American scholars and research workers on war guilt questions." At the same time, isolationist congressmen tried to use the documents to bring about a congressional investigation. Rep. Hamilton Fish said that "if upon investigation the facts warrant impeachment of any American Ambassador or Minister, or even of the President, for making secret commitments that might jeopardize our neutrality and involve us in war, then it is the duty of the House of Representatives to initiate impeachment proceedings." In the Senate, Robert F. Reynolds of North Carolina echoed the call for investigation. The executive branch of the government, he argued, does not have "unlimited powers to conduct the foreign relations of the United States as it sees fit." The Constitution gave Congress, especially the Senate, a voice in setting foreign policy. But they were alone, even though top State Department officials admitted to "a sneaking suspicion . . . that there is more truth than fiction in some of the reported conversations."

Whatever interest there was in the German allegations was soon snuffed out by the Norwegian events. Thomsen sadly reported that "it is not yet possible to judge whether the prejudicial effect on Roosevelt's chances of re-election achieved through our propaganda attack by means of the Polish documents has been weakened by the military operations in Scandinavia. Roosevelt's position of leader and his chances of re-election have certainly been considerably improved for the moment."[19]

A more sinister effort to prevent the renomination of Roosevelt was that in which oilman William Rhodes Davis was involved. It was Davis who had come to Roosevelt in September, via John L. Lewis, in order to enlist the president's help on behalf of a Nazi-inspired peace initiative after the destruction of Poland. Now he was boasting to his German sponsors how he could assure Roosevelt's defeat through Lewis. The mine leader on January 24, 1940, had broken with Roosevelt. He had recommended that the United Mine Workers refrain from endorsing a third term and had predicted "ignominious defeat" for Roosevelt if the Democratic national convention "could be coerced or dragooned into nominating him." Thus, Lewis's private dissatisfaction with Roosevelt, who he felt slighted and patronized him, took public form.

Although most political observers interpreted Lewis's broadside as a warning to the Democrats to give him a voice in selecting the 1940 nominee, darker forces moved in to deepen and exploit the breach. The Communists, who were in their "Yanks are not coming" phase, swung in gleefully behind Lewis. At the Washington "pilgrimage" of the American Youth Congress (in which there was considerable Communist influence), after Roosevelt's speech to a drenched gathering of young people standing on the White House lawn in which the president denounced as "unadulterated twaddle" a Youth Congress resolution condemning loans to Finland as an attempt to force the United States into an imperialistic war, Lewis taunted Roosevelt, saying the Mine Workers had passed a resolution essentially like the one the president had criticized, and invited the Youth Congress to take shelter under his organization's Labor's Nonpartisan League.

Roosevelt interpreted Lewis's public opposition as a bid to obtain the nomination for Sen. Burton K. Wheeler, a leader of the western progressives until he had parted company with Roosevelt over the Supreme Court and now the ablest of the isolationists in Congress. FDR considered the Wheeler candidacy sufficiently likely to request his secretaries to digest the senator's voting record for him. "Lewis is backing Senator Wheeler for the Democratic nomination," Ickes noted, "and, according to [columnist Robert] Kintner, he has in the bank more than a million dollars, representing an assessment of the miners' union, to be put on Wheeler."

According to Dr. Joachim Hertslet, an agent of Field Marshal Göring and an associate of oilman Davis, he met with Lewis in the spring of 1940 to discuss how Germany might be helpful in the labor leader's campaign against Roosevelt. Hertslet, after the war, talked of millions secretly sent over to defeat Roosevelt. How much was spent and through what channels—indeed, how much was available—has never been clearly established. What is clear is that the Nazis wanted Roosevelt beaten and were in touch with Lewis. As Dieckhoff said: "We thought that anybody would be better than Roosevelt."[20]

Roosevelt, in the winter and early spring of 1940, was walking not one but two tightropes. In one ring he sought to keep the politicians guessing about his ultimate presidential intentions while maneuvering, usually behind the scenes, to ensure that the convention and platform would be controlled by the liberal forces in the Democratic party. And, as if that were not a sufficiently intimidating balancing act, in another ring he had to educate a resistant and wishful-thinking American public to the country's stake in the Allied cause. It took events—catastrophes, unhappily—to place him on firmer ground.

The invasion of Scandinavia was one such event. The morning that the newspapers were black with headlines announcing the Nazi pounce on Denmark and Norway, the press trooped into Roosevelt's office. Did these developments bring the war closer to the United States? the reporters wanted to know. "You can put it this way," the president replied guardedly, "that the events of the past 48 hours will undoubtedly cause a great many more Americans to think about the potentialities of war." That was all that he dared to say. There was the customary question about presidential politics. Had he heard anything from the Nebraska and Illinois primaries? That gave Roosevelt a chance to reaffirm his own priorities: "There are certain things like primaries and politics, which sort of get eclipsed by the news of the last 48 hours. They don't seem to have quite the same relative importance that they had before—except as space fillers."[21]

"The situation is dominated by the silence of President Roosevelt," Professor Whitehead minuted in the foreign office. "No one knows whether he will stand and guesses are useless, but if he does stand the general expectation is that he will get in, only very ardent Republicans believe otherwise." Another member of the American department minuted more cynically: "The decision of the President about a third term will, it seems clear, be determined by the way the war develops between now and July—the tired Caesar is biding his time and leaving it to events and the wishes of his party to resolve whether he is to accept the crown."[22]

During the next few weeks, as an appalled American public watched the Nazis triumph in Norway with the same remorseless efficiency that their armies had displayed in Poland, Roosevelt repeatedly used his press conferences as a classroom in geopolitics. Suppose the Germans occupied Greenland? a correspondent asked. Roosevelt and his advisers were themselves concerned with that very question and were studying how an American presence could be established in that Danish dependency. But Roosevelt did not know how far the public and Congress were prepared to go. So he evaded an answer. The question was "awfully hypothetical," he countered. Yes, but it was being discussed everywhere, the reporter persisted. "I think it is grand that the American people are learning something about a subject that very, very few people have thought of before," Roosevelt came back in a reply that in effect said yes, we were worried about Greenland, but said it in terms so mild and lulling as not to fire up an isolationist storm or alarm the Germans. "The number of people in the last three days or two days that have come to me and said, 'My gosh, have you looked at the map?' Sure, I have been looking at the map." But the reporters wanted something more concrete. Was Greenland covered by the Monroe Doctrine? Again, Roosevelt parried. That question was "very, very premature." The geographers to whom he had talked told him that "from the point of view of very, very ancient history, the Island of Greenland, in its fauna and its flora and its geology, belongs to the European continent." He evidently had meant to say "American continent," and the fumble was evidence of his anxiety over how the country might take his next announcement, which was that the United States did have a humanitarian interest in the 17,000 Eskimos who were now cut off from Danish supplies and that he had asked the Red Cross to take over the "relief" job that the Danes had previously performed.

He had misjudged American psychology, he confessed a week later. "The press came in the other day and asked me whether Greenland belongs in the Monroe Doctrine. I stalled. . . . I took a very righteous tone, saying that I am more interested in the humanities of it, in the 17,000 splendid Eskimos who are living in Greenland, than I am in the Monroe Doctrine, and I am still stalling." The newspaper editors to whom he made this confession laughed sympathetically. Encouraged, Roosevelt opened a shutter on his mind: "Where I went wrong is this: I did not think the American people would support me if I said that Greenland belongs to the Monroe Doctrine. But the American people are way out ahead of me and I think I am right in saying that most of the American people today, as most of you sense, would O.K. it if this Government said tomorrow that Greenland is inside the Monroe Doctrine. They are ahead of their Government. Now, that is the actual fact."[23]

Roosevelt used his annual meeting with the American Society of Newspaper Editors to prod them—and through them their readers—into recalling that the previous year they had thought him an "alarmist" and "all wet" when he had expressed fears that war would break out. "But the fact remains that I was right and most of you, the majority of you, were wrong." In the past couple of weeks he had sensed "an increased desire, a willingness on the part of the American public, to think things through." His wife had just returned from a three-week lecture tour "and she noticed, even in the past week, that people were beginning to take their heads out of the sand and beginning to say to themselves and in questions to her, in the last week of this trip: 'What is going to happen if? What is going to happen if?' . . . That is the first time I have seen a more general willingness on the part of the American public to say, 'What is going to happen if?' "

He had been trying to get the American public and Congress to face up to that question ever since he had delivered his "quarantine the aggressor" speech in October, 1937. His annual message, whose delivery opened the 1940 session of Congress, had challenged the widely shared notion that "the United States of America as a self-contained unit can live happily and prosperously, the future secure, inside a high wall of isolation while, outside, the rest of civilization and the commerce and culture of mankind are shattered." What would life be like for America's children "if the rest of the world comes to be dominated by concentrated force alone?"

Defense in depth. Roosevelt had been trying to tutor the public, his New Deal associates, and his generals and admirals in the meaning of that concept, especially in the implications of air power for American safety. In late February, attended by a small pool of reporters, he had boarded the U.S.S. *Tuscaloosa* for a combined-operations exercise designed to test the Panama Canal's defenses against an invading fleet and expeditionary force. The new element, he explained to the reporters, was the airplane, whose interception required long-distance air patrolling and the establishment of bases several hundreds of miles from the canal zone. Defense, the president-as-professor continued, was not a static matter of coastal fortifications, of lining up the fleet and cannonading away at an approaching enemy fleet. It meant command of wide areas of the ocean where there would be room for maneuver and concentration. And as for planes, "it is better policy to get them on the way in than to wait until they get to their objectives."[24]

FDR was himself going to school in the proper use of air power, the new element in warfare. He had been struck by Capt. Alan G. Kirk's analysis of the reasons for the Norwegian fiasco, so much so that he had instructed Missy LeHand to keep it in his confidential file at the White House and not to let the navy have it back. The admiralty was still fighting the last war, Kirk was told by an admiralty officer "of high rank." The admiralty was prepared for fleet actions and for contests for "command of the seas," which, Kirk's informant pointed out, "lay in Allied hands from the very beginning. The shadow of a [German] 'Grand Fleet' still persisted and prevented seizing opportunities to inflict severe damage on the enemy by local operations." The officer then told Kirk about German air tactics. "The ability of the Germans to coordinate their air power with their military operations was something the British Army and the Royal Air Force had still to learn." The RAF, husbanding its resources for "long-range bombing excursions deep into Germany" and "short-range fighter operations in England," had failed to appreciate "the vital part the British air forces must play if the Norwegian operations were to succeed." The fleet air arm had done a splendid job, but with "indifferent equipment. The lack of suitable types, especially carrier fighters, was felt a serious handicap. . . . The point here stressed was the fact that in order to make hits the German planes had been obliged to come down so close to the ship that it amounted almost to 'throwing a brick down the funnel.'" An attacking aircraft could employ such tactics only against a vessel that was unarmed and unescorted, the officer said. A subsequent dispatch of Kirk put the lesson to be learned succinctly: "naval units cannot be maintained in sea areas close to shore-based enemy aircraft unless, and until, control of the air has been wrested from the enemy."[25]

On the surface Roosevelt was buoyant, optimistic, always the educator, ever able to extract some element of hope out of the most intractable of situations. Yet he, too, had his dark moments as the enormity of the Allied reverse in Norway and the revelation of Allied impotence and incompetence unfolded. He cut short a stay in Warm Springs at the end of April because he had the "jitters about the European situation" and feared that "if things kept up the way they were going, the English were going to get licked." He was deeply worried that Mussolini was about to enter the war. Lord Lothian had passed on information from secret sources in the Vatican that the Fascist grand council had met and that Mussolini "had carried the day" for entering the war. "Lothian was very blue," noted Adolf Berle.[26]

"I can't get out any orders telling everybody to take a very, very gloomy and serious attitude towards the matter," Roosevelt told Morgenthau, who saw him that day, "but I feel that's what we should do." Morgenthau remonstrated: "Well, frankly, Mr. President, I don't see why you want us to take that attitude." By taking the attitude, Roosevelt replied, "that England is going to get licked we prepare sentiment in this country." Morgenthau was so upset by his old friend's "defeatism," as he described it, that he resolved to ask Eleanor Roosevelt to work on her husband.

Given the possibility of an Allied disaster, Roosevelt's problem was how to take the military steps he considered necessary, when public opinion refused to see how an Allied overthrow would imperil the United States. The same day that Roosevelt spoke so gloomily, Lothian sent the British foreign office one of his periodic surveys of American attitudes. "The United States is 95 percent anti-Hitler, is 95 percent determined to keep out of the war if it can, and will only enter the war when its own vital interests are challenged, though those vital interests include its ideals." The Americans had been shaken by the swift Nazi victory in Scandinavia. On the other hand, "the hysteria about keeping out becomes more intense as the precipice seems to be nearer." In summary, wrote Lord Lothian,

The United States is still dominated by fear of involvement and incapable of positive action. On the other hand, the war is steadily drifting nearer to them and they know it. They are not pacifists; on the contrary, they are highly belligerent by temperament. The point at which they will be driven to say, as we did after Prague, "Thus far and no farther" depends mainly on the dictators and the events they precipitate. The President would like to take action vigorously on the basis of his own principle "Everything short of war." This is also true of Mr. Hull. All the other candidates, and especially the Republicans, none of whom are familiar with international affairs, are paralyzed with a fear of being charged with a desire to get the United States into war. That does not mean that if they were elected they would not deal with the situation in a practical and realistic manner.[27]

For a man of Roosevelt's temperament, an inability to work his will in matters that he considered paramount for the national safety was oppressive and dispiriting. When an American Youth Congress questioner taxed him for failure to move ahead with legislation of importance to his progressive supporters, Roosevelt interrupted to ask the young man whether he had read Carl Sandburg's biography of Lincoln. "I think the impression was that Lincoln was a pretty sad man," Roosevelt followed up, "because he could not do all he wanted to do at one time, and I think you will find examples where Lincoln had to compromise to gain a little something. . . . If you ever sit here, you will learn that you cannot, just by shouting from the housetops, get what you want all the time."[28]

Another source of malaise was Roosevelt's aversion to firing people, especially at a time when he knew he should get rid of associates like arch-isolationist Secretary of War Harry Woodring and re-form his cabinet on a coalition basis, as he had wanted to do since the outbreak of the war. His most loyal supporters—Hopkins, Morgenthau, and Ickes—were pressing him to do so, but his natural inclination was to please and captivate. More important, in this instance, was a desire not to stir up the press, with whom Woodring was in close touch, and the isolationists in Congress. To do so risked giving the isolationist forces in the Democratic party a rallying point and issue before the Democratic convention and might even slow down aid to the Allies at a critical moment. Roosevelt knew that to bring Republicans into the cabinet would be pounced upon as certain evidence that he intended to run for a third term. Yet at the end of April, on the eve of the German assault upon the West, he was as resolved as he had been all winter and spring not to run again. Welles confided to Berle at the Metropolitan Club at one in the morning that he, Welles, understood that Roosevelt, "unless the situation changes, will wait until the last minute and then issue a statement in favor of Mr. Hull."[29]

That was the night of May 8, and what had routed Welles out of bed after taking two sleeping draughts was one cable from Berlin alerting Washington to the fact that the German army had its orders to invade the Low Countries and one cable from Queen Wilhelmina to Roosevelt, inquiring about whether his November offer of a cruiser to take her to safety if the need should arise also held for her daughter, Princess Juliana.

Roosevelt intended to declare for Hull, Welles said, unless the situation changed. It was changing—how cataclysmically few dreamed that night. At the end of the previous week's cabinet meeting Hopkins had stopped Morgenthau and had said, "The only thing that matters is to take care of the war situation. Nothing else." Hopkins then added, "I am not saying that Hull could not be elected President, but the only man who understands the situation is Roosevelt and he has got to run."[30]

The New Dealers could not draft him, but international developments imperiling the nation's safety could, and they were beginning to unfold.

"The third term," Cordell Hull wrote in 1948, "was an immediate consequence of Hitler's conquest of France and the specter of Britain alone standing between the conquerors and ourselves. Our dangerous position induced President Roosevelt to run for a third term." Hull was in a position to know. On the morning of May 10, with the reports flooding in from Allied capitals of the Nazi blitz against the Low Countries and France, Hull took time off to talk a little presidential politics with Breckinridge Long, an old hand in the Democratic party and Hull's political confidant in the State Department. "He [Hull] now recognizes that there is practical unanimity of unofficial agreement upon him as the person to be nominated in case Roosevelt is not," Long recorded afterward. Hull wanted to be president. Two months earlier he had complained to Long about the "cabal" against him in his home state of Tennessee, where the party leaders were putting together "a delegation instructed for Roosevelt simply as a slap at him and to indicate that he has no support in his own state." Hull wanted it, even though he protested to the contrary.[31]

Politics does not adjourn for the collapse of civilizations; on the contrary, changes of leadership register the cataclysms. So it had happened in Britain. So it would now happen in the United States in Roosevelt's coming to a decision to run for a third term. On May 13, by which date Holland had been subjugated, Belgium was reeling, and the Nazis were beginning their decisive assault at Sedan, Long reported that "Hull thinks now the President has decided to accept the nomination himself. He has been talking with [Attorney

General Robert H.] Jackson and Jackson told him that the President had so decided." In explanation of Jackson's knowledgeability, Long noted that the attorney general had spent the previous day on the presidential yacht *Potomac* with the president. There is no other record of this talk, and men much closer to Roosevelt than Jackson—indeed, Hull himself in his *Memoirs*—portray the president as making up his mind in late May or early June.

During the first week of the Nazi invasion there were more pressing matters than presidential politics to claim Roosevelt's attention—in particular, the need to strengthen America's defenses. It will run "to a large sum of money," Roosevelt told his press conference after almost a week of conferring with his military chiefs. He decided to deliver his defense message to Congress in person and talked over its contents with Harry Hopkins. The latter had come to dinner on May 10, still an ill man, and at Roosevelt's request stayed on as a permanent guest. Hopkins knew politics and social welfare; he knew some economics and was an energetic administrator. Roosevelt now proceeded to instruct him in military tactics and strategy and the significance of the plane and motorized infantry for American foreign policy. Roosevelt talked and Hopkins took notes:

a defense which depends solely on repelling the offensive of an enemy against so-called impregnable forts—and never makes a countercharge is doomed to failure. A defense which allows an enemy to consolidate the approach lines without hindrance always loses. A defense which makes no effort to hamper the line of supply of enemy in the rear is inadequate. . . .

The Atlantic and Pacific were adequate defensive barriers while fleets under sail would move at an average speed of 5 miles an hour—tho sudden forays like the burning of our national capital were possible. The oceans gave strength to defense as long as steam fleets and convoys at 15 or 20 miles an hour—

But the new element—air navigation—steps up the speed of possible attack enormously—to 200 or 300 miles an hour. Furthermore it brings new possibilities of the use of much nearer bases from which to attack the continent itself.

The fjords of Greenland are only X miles from Newfoundland, X from Nova Scotia, New Brunswick and Quebec, only X miles from New England.

The Azores are but . . .

The islands of S. Pacific are not too far removed from the West Coast of South America to prevent them from becoming bases of enormous strategic advantage to attacking forces.

People assumed last year—there would be no war—and when it came they thought [it] would be conducted like World War I—there would be impregnable lines and settle down to long contest of endurance.

Our whole concept revamped.

Today we see motorized armies moving 200 miles a day—We see air armadas successfully landing thousands of troops—miles in rear of defending front. We see attacks capable of destroying airplane factories—munitions—hundreds of miles [behind the lines].

Complete re-orientation.[32]

Geopolitics was a discipline that Roosevelt understood better than anyone else in Washington. His "grasp of the principles of geopolitics" impressed

Welles as being "almost instinctive." When it came to Keynesianism or medical economics or the ever-normal granary, the New Dealers tutored him; in the field of military strategy and world politics, he taught his advisers. And when he went up to Congress to deliver his defense message, he overrode the reservations of some of his advisers* and capped his lecture on how to keep war at a distance in the day of the airplane and the blitz by asking Congress to authorize the building of 50,000 planes in the next twelve months and a productive capacity of 50,000 planes a year.

Congress cheered—Republicans as well as Democrats. When Roosevelt returned to his office, a scrawled note from the chief of naval operations was on his desk:

Dear Mr. President

—————————————————

—G R E A T—

—————————————————

Betty [Stark]
(for all of us)

"Magnificent," wrote Ickes on the speech. "He had the finest reception that he has been accorded by a joint session of Congress for five or six years." And though isolationists in Congress charged Roosevelt with fomenting hysteria, Long confidently predicted that Congress "will vote everything he asked."[34]

Leadership was again possible. Events had vindicated him. "A year and a half, two years ago," Mrs. Roosevelt said to a group of young people whose isolationism worried her and the president,

—I think you could pick out members of Congress—to whom he said, "We should do thus and so now." And they said, "Oh, no; oh, no, you are dreaming Mr. President. No, these things are not ever going to happen. No, Mr. President. Such a thing is ridiculous to contemplate."

Today they are all running to him because the circumstances, the life of the world, have hit them in the face, and they are all saying, "Oh, Mr. President, yes, we are ready to do it."[35]

People were turning to Roosevelt, Republicans as well as Democrats. Stimson and Knox were among those who wrote to him approvingly of his speech to Congress, confirming an idea that he had nurtured since the out-

---

* "The part that worries me most is the President's statement that he wants to have 50,000 planes and wants the Government to build a lot of factories. I just can't see it and I told him so. No one has thought the plan through," wrote Morgenthau. Hull asserted that it was he who suggested the 50,000 figure and struck the president "literally speechless." "The President then told me," recorded budget director Harold D. Smith, "that the old man from Tennessee, referring to the Secretary of State to whom the President had referred his preliminary draft of the message in which he referred to the fact that this country should develop the production of airplanes at 50,000 a year, had come over to see him with the suggestion that the President say not only that, but say that this country should have 50,000 airplanes. He said that the Secretary of State thought that that statement would be heard in Tokio [*sic*] and Rome." In 1943, the United States produced 90,000 planes.[33]

break of the war—that he should bring Republicans who shared his attitude toward world politics into his cabinet. The most gratifying sensation was that he could again influence events and exercise leadership in a great national crisis. As Churchill felt when the king sent for him that he was walking with destiny, so Roosevelt now felt as events bore out his warnings and the nation again responded to him that fate had saved him for this moment of supreme crisis. In telling intimates that he did not want to run, he had always added, "unless . . . things get very, very much worse in Europe." The question of whether Roosevelt would run, wrote Berle on May 15, "is being settled somewhere on the banks of the Meuse River."[36]

Chapter Eight

Acts of "Faith and Leadership"

O N MAY 10, according to Ciano, Mussolini was so certain of the rapid success of the Nazi invasion that he heard the news of Churchill's accession to power "with absolute indifference." And, indeed, Churchill had not even completed the formation of his cabinet when the astonishing Nazi breakthrough at Sedan raised the specter of an Allied collapse as swift as Poland's. A frantic Churchill turned to the United States and to its president, whose democratic sympathies and realistic geopolitical understanding of America's stake in the outcome of the battle about to be fought in Flanders would dispose him to do his utmost to aid the reeling and beleaguered Allies. The correspondence during Chamberlain's time between Roosevelt, the head of the United States government, and Churchill, a subordinate minister, had been unconventional. The intimate relationship that now developed via the cables between an embattled Allied prime minister and the president of the officially "neutral" United States was even more unorthodox and carried formidable political risks for Roosevelt, risks that he was the more willing to shoulder as Churchill's indomitable spirit and incomparable oratory inspired free men everywhere and gave hope that Great Britain would not capitulate.

On May 13 Parliament assembled to hear a statement from the new prime minister and to approve formally the war cabinet that he announced. "When Chamberlain enters the House, he gets a terrific reception," recorded Nicolson, "and when Churchill comes in the applause is less." Churchill's applause came mostly from the Labour benches. It was not until July that the Tory "regulars" relented and the whole House cheered a Churchill report. Because of the battlefront developments, Churchill's mood on May 13 was one of the profoundest anxiety. "I would say to the House as I said to those who have joined this Government: 'I have nothing to offer but blood, toil, tears and sweat.'" Lloyd George, his old colleague of Asquith days, welcomed the new prime minister affectionately, and Churchill, sitting between Chamberlain and Attlee, "cries slightly and mops his eyes."

That same day, a few hours earlier, Queen Wilhelmina had awakened King George VI with a telephone call pleading for aircraft. "It is not often one is rung up at that hour, and especially by a Queen," the king noted. "But these days anything may happen."[1] By the end of the day the Germans had devastated Rotterdam with ruthless bombing assaults that killed thousands, thus effectively ending Dutch military resistance.

Worse battlefront news arrived from Reynaud the next day. He implored Churchill to send "ten more squadrons" of British fighters to help the French army contain the German breakout at Sedan. A few hours later Churchill was awakened to be told by Reynaud over the telephone, "We have been defeated. We are beaten. We have lost the battle."

Churchill "is sending you a message tomorrow," Joseph Kennedy advised Roosevelt by a cable that was sent even before Reynaud's "alarmist" message, as Churchill characterized it, was received. Kennedy had left Churchill at 1:00 A.M. on May 15. The encounter only confirmed Churchill's distrust of the ambassador, and the reason could be seen in Kennedy's dispatch describing his talk with the prime minister. "[Churchill] said the German push is showing great power and although the French are holding tonight they are definitely worried. They are asking for more British troops at once, but Churchill is unwilling to send more from England at this time because he is convinced within a month England will be vigorously attacked." Churchill was cabling Roosevelt directly, Kennedy went on, because the prime minister needs help. "I asked what the United States could do to help that would not leave the United States holding the bag for a war in which the Allies expected to be beaten. It seems to me that if we had to fight to protect our lives we would do better fighting in our own backyard." Even if the United States could find the planes and the overage destroyers to send, they would serve little purpose "if this is going to be a quick war all over in a few months." Kennedy's defeatism provoked Churchill to a declaration of resolution and defiance. "He said regardless of what Germany does to England and France, England will never give up so long as he remains a power in public life even if England is burnt to the ground. Why, he said, the government will move to Canada and take the fleet and fight on. I think this is something I should follow up."[2]

Churchill's "most secret and personal" telegram for the president from the "former naval person" was sent at 6:00 P.M., May 15, London time. It was a plea for all-out American help short of the dispatch of armed forces before it was too late.

Although I have changed my office, I am sure you would not wish me to discontinue our intimate, private correspondence. As you are no doubt aware, the scene has darkened swiftly. The enemy have a marked preponderance in the air, and their new technique is making a deep impression upon the French. I think myself the battle on land has only just begun, and I should like to see tanks engaged. Up to the present, Hitler is working with specialized units in tanks and air. The small countries are simply smashed up, one by one, like matchwood. We must expect, though it is not yet certain, that Mussolini will hurry in to share the loot of civilization. We expect to be attacked here ourselves, both from the air and by parachute and air-borne troops in the near future, and are getting ready for them. If necessary, we shall continue the war alone and we are not afraid of that. But I trust you realize, Mr. President, that the voice and force of the United States may count for nothing if they are withheld too long. You may have a completely subjugated, Nazified Europe established with astonishing swiftness, and the weight may be more than we can bear. All I ask now is that you should proclaim non-belligerency, which would mean that you would help us with everything short of actually engaging armed forces. Immediate needs are: first of all, the loan of forty or fifty of your older destroyers to bridge the gap between what we have now and the large new construction we put in hand at the beginning of the war. This time next year we shall have plenty. But if in the interval Italy comes in against us with another hundred submarines, we may be strained to the breaking point.* Secondly, we want several hundred of the latest types of aircraft, of which you are now getting delivery. These can be repaid by those now being constructed in the United States for us. Thirdly, anti-aircraft equipment and ammunition, of which there will be plenty next year if we are alive to see it. Fourthly, the fact that our ore supply is being compromised from Sweden, from North Africa, and perhaps from northern Spain, makes it necessary to purchase steel in the United States. This also applies to other materials. We shall go on paying dollars for as long as we can, but I should like to feel reasonably sure that when we can pay no more, you will give us the stuff all the same. Fifthly, we have many reports of possible German parachute or air-borne descents upon Ireland. The visit of a United States squadron to Irish ports, which might well [be] prolonged, would be invaluable. Sixthly, I am looking to you to keep that Japanese dog quiet in the Pacific, using Singapore in any way convenient. The details of the material which we have in mind will be communicated to you separately.

With all good wishes and respect.[4]

Churchill's telegram, although the foreign office had been consulted about it, was Churchillian in style and vigorous marshaling of argument. Roosevelt's answer the next day, drafted by Sumner Welles, was more impersonal, the bureaucratic product of consultations with Hull, Admiral Stark, and Secretary of the Navy Edison, although it sought, within the limits of the president's powers, to give an affirmative answer to Churchill's requests.

URGENT. STRICTLY CONFIDENTIAL FOR THE AMBASSADOR.
Your 1216, May 15, 6 p.m.
Please transmit the following message from the President to the former naval person:

QUOTE. I have just received your message and I am sure it is unnecessary for me to say that I am most happy to continue our private correspondence as we have in the past.

* Sir Ronald Campbell, the British ambassador in Paris, had advised Churchill that day: "Mr. Bullitt told me that at his suggestion President Roosevelt was seeing whether he could legalise sale to France of twelve old destroyers by having them classed as obsolete. There were plenty more such vessels and [if?] sale to France went through he wondered whether H.M.G. would like some. He mentioned fifty or even one hundred."[3]

I am, of course, giving every possible consideration to the suggestions made in your message. I shall take up your specific proposals one by one.

First, with regard to the possible loan of forty or fifty of our older destroyers. As you know a step of that kind could not be taken except with the specific authorization of the Congress and I am not certain that it would be wise for that suggestion to be made to the Congress at this moment. Furthermore, it seems to me doubtful, from the standpoint of our own defense requirements, which must inevitably be linked with the defense requirements of this hemisphere and with our obligations in the Pacific, whether we could dispose even temporarily of these destroyers. Furthermore, even if we were able to take the step you suggest, it would be at least six or seven weeks at a minimum, as I see it, before these vessels could undertake active service under the British flag.

Second. We are now doing everything within our power to make it possible for Allied governments to obtain the latest types of aircraft in the United States.

Third. If Mr. Purvis may receive immediate instructions to discuss the question of anti-aircraft equipment and ammunition with the appropriate authorities here in Washington, the most favorable consideration will be given to the request made in the light of our own defense needs and requirements.

Fourth. Mr. Purvis has already taken up with the appropriate authorities here the purchase of steel in the United States and I understand that satisfactory arrangements have been made.

Fifth. I shall give further consideration to your suggestion with regard to the visit of the United States Squadron to Irish ports.

Sixth. As you know, the American fleet is now concentrated at Hawaii where it will remain at least for the time being.

I shall communicate with you again as soon as I feel able to make a final decision with regard to some of the other matters dealt with in your message and I hope you will feel free to communicate with me in this way at any time.

The best of luck to you. UNQUOTE.[5]

The answer was totally unresponsive to Churchill's chief request that the United States proclaim its nonbelligerence. Roosevelt knew, Churchill must have, too, and certainly Lothian knew, that the American people, although prepared to support Roosevelt's defense requests and increasing aid to the Allies, recoiled abruptly from any step that meant U.S. involvement in the war. "The U.S. is at last profoundly moved and frightened," Lothian wrote Lady Astor. "The old isolationism is dead. Nobody is against a vast armament programme. . . . We shall doubtless get what help we want, short of war. But USA won't enter the war, unless and until its own vital interests are affected and that, I think, Hitler and Goebbels are too clever to do for the present."[6]

Roosevelt's reply arrived in London while Churchill and his military advisers were in Paris. Sir Winston's decision to go is graphically described in Cadogan's diary:

The blackest day I have ever lived through. But there are doubtless worse to come. . . . Cabinet in morning at which we received black and blacker news from France. Finally Dill explained plans for withdrawal in Belgium. This infuriated Winston who said we couldn't agree to that, which could jeopardize our whole army. Sprang up and said he would go to France—it was ridiculous to think that

France could be conquered by 120 tanks (but it may be!). He said he would leave after lunch, and asked Neville Chamberlain to mind the shop.[7]

Just as the Norwegian campaign had begun with Germany sending its fleet far north in order to draw off the main British fleet while its troops landed in Norway, so the invasion of the Low Countries masked its main thrust, an attack through the Ardennes, where it was least expected by the Allies because of the terrain's woods and hills, with the objective of encircling the Allied armies that had rushed forward into Belgium. Churchill's opposition to the withdrawal of the Allied forces from Belgium reflected his fighting spirit, but not wise tactics. Nor did Churchill fully appreciate the technique of the blitzkreig: "I did not comprehend the violence of the revolution effected since the last war by the incursion of a mass of fast-moving heavy armour. I knew about it, but it had not altered my conviction as it should have done." Brendan Bracken's explanation of Churchill's failure to grasp the significance of the tank was "Bear in mind that Winston always remains the 4th Hussar."[8]

Until Churchill arrived in Paris, where he saw Quai d'Orsay officials already burning archives, he underestimated the gravity of the situation in Flanders. So did State Department officials in Washington. Bullitt's agitated cables about nothing standing between the Nazi panzers and Paris provoked disbelief. "Somehow or other," wrote Berle, "I cannot make out whether there is a mass of hysteria in Paris, or whether things are really extremely bad. Sumner is inclined to think they are really bad." Berle also described Churchill as having spoken to Kennedy "rather wildly of fighting to the last ditch and moving the fleet to Canada, and keeping it up, even there."[9]

Cadogan's diary entry for May 16 about Churchill's dash to Paris went on: "Cabinet under Neville Chamberlain assembled at 11. Winston's message showed situation desperate and endorsed appeal by French for all the Fighters we can give them. Agreed by midnight to send six squadrons" (in addition to the four the cabinet had agreed to earlier in the day).[10]

Although Churchill was dismayed by the situation he found in Paris, he gave no sign of despair or defeatism. "Mr. Churchill," wrote Paul Baudouin, secretary to the French cabinet, "was remarkable for his energy and vehemence as, crowned like a volcano by the smoke of his cigars, he told his French colleagues that even if France was invaded and vanquished, England would go on fighting until the United States came to her aid."[11]

Back in London, Churchill gave the cabinet an account of his trip. Then he saw Kennedy, who handed him Roosevelt's reply to his appeal. "I'm quite convinced that the President will do all he can," Cadogan wrote, "but he can't go ahead of his public. And even then, what can they do to affect *this* battle? . . . Never did I think one could endure such a nightmare."[12]

"Many thanks for your message for which I am grateful," Churchill replied to Roosevelt on May 18. "I do not need to tell you about the gravity of what has happened. We are determined to persevere to the very end whatever the result of the great battle raging in France may be. We must expect in any case to be attacked here on the Dutch model before very long and we hope to give a good account of ourselves. But if American assistance is to play any part it must be available."[13]

Roosevelt did not reply to this directly, but instructed Morgenthau to arrange with General Marshall to turn over to the French Curtiss P-36s that the army had on hand in exchange for foreign-ordered planes scheduled for delivery beginning in July. That would slow up U.S. air rearmament, but the P-36s could be shipped immediately. "Work it out on swap," Roosevelt told Morgenthau, "after all we will not be in for *60 or 90 days.*" (The emphasis is Morgenthau's.)[14]

Another reason Roosevelt may not have thought it necessary to respond directly to Churchill's May 18 cable was that he had talked quite frankly with Lothian, even raising the subject of British fighter aid to the French. He did so gently. It was hardly fitting for the United States, which was not in the battle, to upbraid those who were. He informed Lothian that the French had been "very critical" of British failure to commit more of its air force to the Battle of France. That was stating it mildly. Bullitt, on May 16, had come close to charging the British with a sellout. "The British, who have not yet sent to France the quantities of pursuit planes that they have in England to protect their factories (they have exactly two squadrons in France), are already beginning to be critical and contemptuous of the French . . . you should have in mind the hypothesis that, in order to escape from the ultimate consequences of absolute defeat, the British may install a government of Oswald Mosley and the Union of British Fascists which would cooperate fully with Hitler. That would mean that the British navy would be against us." The president "ought to try to make certain that in case the war goes badly, as it may, the British fleet would base itself on Canada for the defense of the dominion which might become the refuge of the British Crown."[15]

Sir Hugh Dowding, head of the RAF fighter command, was, like Lord Beaverbrook, whom Churchill was shortly to put in charge of aircraft production, "an isolationist by virtue of his position, caring only for the defence of Great Britain and regarding allies as an embarrassment. On the fall of France, he said to Halifax 'Thank God we are now alone.' " But that was not Churchill's position and he carried the war cabinet with him. The French were now "far better satisfied," Roosevelt said to Lothian. He then went on to discuss what he had been unwilling to put into a cable about Churchill's plea that the United States declare itself a nonbelligerent ally of Britain and France. The United States was doing everything possible to keep Mussolini out of the war. The American program of 50,000 planes was designed to deter both Italy and Japan. The size and efficiency of America's neutrality patrol were increasing, and, Roosevelt added, although guardedly, Britain could leave the protection of its Caribbean interests to the United States Navy. If a German ship appeared in West Indian waters, the United States Navy would not hesitate to deal with it.[16]

But Lothian pressed for more, as he cabled London. Suppose Britain were left to stand alone, subjected to continuous bombardment. British command of the Atlantic was as much in the interests of American as of British security. For without it, if the U.S. Navy were held in the Pacific, Germany and Italy could establish themselves in Brazil with the help of German and Italian "fifth columns" already in the country. They would then be within bombing distance of the Panama Canal. And if the American navy were shifted to the Atlantic, the Japanese could dismember Hawaii and Alaska. If the navy were divided, the United States might be in a position of inferiority in both oceans. The United States had a vital stake in helping the British navy maintain command of the Atlantic, argued Lothian, and the way it could help was to supply food, destroyers, and planes, and to press Spain not to enter the war.

Roosevelt did not demur from this analysis but, referring especially to the transfer of overage destroyers, said he could not move without congressional concurrence. Nor had public opinion as yet grasped the strategic situation. He doubted that Hitler would lightheartedly take on the United States. And then the president broached the most delicate subject of all. If worst came to worst—meaning if Britain were subjugated by Hitler—the British fleet might cross the Atlantic to Canada or the United States. Such a transfer, Lothian quickly interjected, would depend on whether the United States had entered the war. He doubted that British public opinion would entrust the fleet to a neutral United States. Mr. Roosevelt, commented Lothian, "seemed impressed by this possibility."

The line taken by Lothian on transfer of the fleet was worth pursuing, commented the American department. "It is true that, in the event of our defeat, the future existence of the rest of the Empire as independent nations would probably depend largely on the combination of the United States and our fleet and Mr. Roosevelt must know that we believe this to be so. But none the less we must continue to play on the idea that unless the United States was a belligerent—and that too very soon—we should probably elect to send our fleet to Australia and New Zealand as being that part of the Empire where British ideals and ways of life would have the best chance of survival. This is rather like blackmail, and not very good blackmail at that, but I think we are justified in planting the idea rather more firmly in Mr. Roosevelt's mind."[17]

By the time Lothian's cable arrived in London, the British chiefs of staff were planning "British strategy in a certain eventuality," meaning France's defeat and Italy's joining the war. Could Britain hold out until help came from the United States? the report asked. "Our only hope, it seems to me," Chamberlain wrote that same day, May 19, "lies in Roosevelt and the U.S.A. But unfortunately they are so unready themselves that they can do little to help us now." That night Churchill broadcast to the Empire for the first time as prime minister. He spoke of "the tremendous battle" in Flanders, the remarkable German breakthrough, "the gravity of the hour." He did not want to speak too discouragingly about the situation in France. He expected the front there to be stabilized. But he also placed on public record that he had received from "the Chiefs of the French Republic, and in particular from its indomitable Prime Minister, M. Reynaud, the most sacred pledges that whatever happens they will fight to the end, be it bitter or be it glorious." Churchill also prepared his countrymen for a Nazi invasion: "We must expect that as soon as stability is reached on the Western Front, the bulk of that hideous apparatus of aggression which gashed Holland into ruin and slavery in a few days will be turned upon us."[18]

"Listened to Winston's broadcast," noted Cadogan. "We must fight on, whatever happens. I shall count it a privilege to be dead if Hitler rules England." In the United States, Churchill's broadcast was heard just after lunch on Sunday. Archibald MacLeish, poet and librarian of Congress, and Justice Frankfurter were lunching with Ickes. "At three o'clock we all went upstairs, where the good radio is, and listened," Ickes wrote. "Churchill's speech affected all of us. . . . We were glad that a man who could say what he said, in a manner that he said it, was at the head of the British government instead of Chamberlain. But all of us realized more than ever what a tremendous task he has undertaken."[19]

Churchill's stoutness of spirit, his determination to fight to the end, was becoming a pivotal factor in Roosevelt's strategic thinking. Just as the British leader's readiness to throw into the Battle of France Britain's dwindling fighter force was necessarily influenced by his assessment of the French leadership's resolution, so Roosevelt's willingness, as it became clear that France was defeated, to take risks in supplying war matériel to the British at the expense of America's own rearmament was affected by his and his associates' appraisal of Churchill's resolve.

"Lothian has reported his conversation with you," Churchill cabled the president on May 20.

I understand your difficulties but I am very sorry about the destroyers. If they were here in six weeks they would play an invaluable part. The battle in France is full of danger to both sides. Though we have taken heavy toll of the enemy in the air and are clawing down two or three to one of their planes, they have still a formidable numerical superiority. Our most vital need is therefore the delivery at the earliest possible date of the largest possible number of Curtiss P-40 fighters now in the course of delivery to your Army. With regard to the closing part of your talk with Lothian, our intention is whatever happens to fight on to the end in this Island and, provided we can get the help for which we ask, we hope to run them very close in the air battles in view of individual superiority. Members of the present administration would likely go down during this process should it result adversely, but in no conceivable circumstances will we consent to surrender. If members of this administration were finished and others came in to parley amid the ruins, you must not be blind to the fact that the sole remaining bargaining counter with Germany would be the fleet, and if this country was left by the United States to its fate no one would have the right to blame those then responsible if they made the best terms they could for the surviving inhabitants. Excuse me, Mr. President, putting this nightmare bluntly. Evidently I could not answer for my successors who in utter despair and helplessness might well have to accommodate themselves to the German will. However there is happily no need at present to dwell upon such ideas. Once more thanking you for your good will.[20]

Roosevelt made no reply to this plea, and, except for Lothian's talks with Welles and Roosevelt, there was a hiatus in the Roosevelt-Churchill correspondence until June 12. Churchill had instructed Lothian to forward to the president the highly secret appreciations of the military situation that were dispatched to the British ambassador almost daily. This gave Lothian a chance to append several notes to these estimates. On May 22, for instance, he wrote: "My Government understands that there are now two or three U.S. warships at Lisbon. They think it would be very useful if they could be kept there for the present." "You will note the steady loss of destroyers," he post-scripted on June 3. "The damaged ones are also piling up in our repair yards."

Both the principals were preoccupied, Churchill with extricating the British expeditionary force from France—the "miracle of Dunkirk"—and Roosevelt with efforts to keep Mussolini out of the war and with America's own strategy and rearmament. They were further constrained, Roosevelt especially, by the discovery that Tyler Kent, a code clerk in the U.S. embassy at London, was turning over to Fascist sympathizers in London the most secret United States–British diplomatic cables, including Churchill's correspondence with Roosevelt. In turn, Kent's confederates handed the material on to the Italians, who conveyed some of their contents to the German ambassador in Rome. "He comes from an old Virginia family," a horrified Breckin-ridge Long noted in his diary, "was recommended by [Sen.] Harry Byrd, had been in the Service for some time . . . was once denied admission to the Diplomatic career service." Two days after the British raid on his apartment, Kent was formally arrested, dismissed from the foreign service, and stripped of diplomatic immunity. "A dispatch from London catalogues the papers found in Kent's rooms. They are a complete history of our diplomatic correspondence since 1938. It is appalling. . . . It means not only that our codes are cracked a dozen ways but that our every diplomatic maneuver was exposed to Germany and Russia. It is a terrible blow—almost a major catastrophe. No doubt the Germans will publish another White Book during our political campaign which will have as its purpose the defeat of Roosevelt."[21]

The United States did not ask for Kent's extradition. The administration preferred to have the case handled by the British, who would keep it out of the press. He was tried *in camera* in October and sentenced to seven years. Kent's defense was the right of Congress and the American people to know how far Roosevelt had gone in his commitments to the British and French. If that was his purpose, his method of communication with Congress, via the Italians, was indeed roundabout. He was, in fact, a Fascist sympathizer. Service with the embassy in the Soviet Union had turned him bitterly anti-Communist. When right-wing isolationists in the United States learned of his case, they made a hero out of him, describing him as a victim of a Roosevelt-Churchill-Jewish conspiracy.

As an immediate consequence of the Kent case, Welles suggested to Lothian that for security reasons the safest channel of transmission of Churchill-Roosevelt messages would be through the British embassy in Washington rather than through the United States embassy in London. The British foreign office heartily concurred not only because of the Kent leak, but because Joseph Kennedy's openly expressed defeatism made it uncomfortable (although he, too, was appalled by the Kent affair). The foreign office dossier on Kennedy, composed by Vansittart, ended: "Mr. Kennedy is a very foul specimen of double-crosser and defeatist. He thinks of nothing but his own pocket. I hope that this war will at least see the elimination of this type."[22]

Despite the Kent breach of security, Churchill soon returned to transmitting his messages to Roosevelt via Kennedy. He did not want to hurt Kennedy's feelings, he explained. "I should have thought in order to keep him sweet, he could inform Kennedy," Halifax commented. New reports came in that Kennedy had talked "abject defeatism" to American journalists and of new proposals that he should be cut out of the line of communication between Roosevelt and Churchill. But Halifax had changed his mind. "He can do us a good deal of harm if we put him wrong and I think the President has the right hang of things here which is what matters." Lothian objected. "The President is so overworked at the present moment that it is not easy for me to see him unless I have some specific message to deliver or discuss." Tell Lothian, directed Halifax, that "when messages were sent otherwise than through the American Ambassador, Mr. Kennedy became distressed. Therefore it is thought better to send personal messages through him for the present, duplicating to Lothian."[23]

One consequence of the Kent security leak was a State Department decision to check out its foreign-service personnel. Hull and Welles discussed with Long and Gen. Sherman Miles, the new head of military intelligence, how to carry through such an inspection. J. Edgar Hoover was brought in, and he and Miles said they could supply the inspectors, who did their job disguised as "couriers."

The Kent case contributed to Roosevelt's growing concern with spies and fifth columnists. Secretary of Labor Frances Perkins, the president told businessmen who were coming in to help with defense production, had been ready to employ a top official in the Labor Department, a man who had turned out to be "absolutely 100 percent affiliated and associated with the Communist movement in this country. You have to be careful on that. Also to be careful not to get pro-Germans. . . . We even have them in the ranks of the officers of the Army and Navy." Any prospective employee could be investigated very quickly by the FBI, broke in Attorney General Robert Jackson.[24]

Few questioned that the government should monitor the communications of hostile or potentially hostile powers. The problem was rivalry among the various investigative agencies. The FBI, Henry Morgenthau found, wire-tapped the Japanese and German consulates, but not the embassies. "That is with the Army. The Army never tells FBI what they hear. I'm interested in where this money goes and I only get half the story because I get what FBI has and not what the Army has." In the area of domestic wire tapping, the issue was not who should do it but whether it should be done. Morgenthau recorded:

I spoke to J. Edgar Hoover, and asked him whether he was able to listen in on Nazi spies by tapping the wires and he said no; that the order given by Bob Jackson stopping him had not been revoked. I said I would go to work at once. He said he needed it desperately.

He said there were four Nazi spies working in Buffalo across the Canadian border and the Royal Mounted Police had asked for his assistance and he had been unable to give it.

I called up General Watson and said this should be done and he said, "I don't think it is legal." I said "What if it is illegal?" He called me back in five minutes and said he told the President and the President said, "Tell Bob Jackson to send for J. Edgar Hoover and order him to do it and a written memorandum will follow."

(I spoke to Bob Jackson about this at Cabinet last Friday, the 17th, and he said that he was not going to do anything about it until after Congress goes home.)[25]

Roosevelt's memorandum to Jackson broadened considerably the government's surveillance activities.

I have agreed with the broad purpose of the Supreme Court decision relating to wire-tapping in investigations. The Court is undoubtedly sound both in regard to the use of evidence secured over tapped wires in the prosecution of citizens in criminal cases; and is also right in its opinion that under ordinary and normal circumstances wire-tapping by Government agents should not be carried on for the excellent reason that it is almost bound to lead to abuse of civil rights.

However, I am convinced that the Supreme Court never intended any dictum in the particular case which it decided to apply to grave matters involving the defense of the nation.

It is, of course, well known that certain other nations have been engaged in the organization of propaganda of so-called "fifth columns" in other countries and in preparation for sabotage, as well as in actual sabotage.

It is too late to do anything about it after sabotage, assassinations and "fifth column" activities are completed.

You are, therefore, authorized and directed in such cases as you may approve, after investigation of the need in each case, to authorize the necessary investigating agents that they are at liberty to secure information by listening devices direct to the conversation or other communications of persons suspected of subversive activities against the Government of the United States, including suspected spies. You are requested furthermore to limit these investigations so conducted to a minimum and to limit them insofar as possible to aliens.[26]

In October, 1938, when a federal court had convicted members of a Nazi spy ring in the United States and Roosevelt was asked what he intended to do to combat the activities of foreign agents, his answer had emphasized the protection of individual rights: "We do not need any secret police in the United States to watch American people, to watch our own people, but we do need our own people to watch the secret police of certain other nations, which is a very excellent distinction to make, and therefore we are going to ask for more money so that our people can check up on the activities of the secret police of other nations." By the end of May, 1940, however, the experience of other democratic nations with fifth columnists and spies had mandated harsher precautions.[27]

Roosevelt also ordered the FBI, army intelligence (i.e., G-2), and naval intelligence (ONI) to coordinate their activities. Berle took part in these meetings as the representative of the State Department and to give political guidance in the light of the president's overall objectives. Another Roosevelt directive was reported to Churchill by William Stephenson, the newly arrived chief of British intelligence operations in the United States:

The President has laid down the secret ruling for the closest possible marriage between the FBI and British Intelligence. The fact that this cooperation was agreed upon is striking evidence of President Roosevelt's clarity of vision. The fact that it has to be kept secret even from the State Department is a measure of the strength of American neutrality. It is an essential first step toward combatting enemy operations but it is insufficient to meet the demands of the situation. The Nazis in America are already well organized and well entrenched. They realise the extent of British dependence on American material aid, and so direct their subversive propaganda toward buttressing the wall of traditional isolationism by which the President is encompassed.

The FBI was new to the business of counterintelligence and espionage. The line between enemy propaganda and legitimate isolationist activity was not easy to draw. J. Edgar Hoover prided himself on his good relations with Congress in which isolationism was heavily entrenched. The alliance with Stephenson, who operated with greater experience and freedom, was a godsend.*

Norway had its Quisling, as had every country overrun by the Nazis. The current flabbiness of France was due as much to the defeatism of the Communists and of the anti-Communists who preferred Hitler to Léon Blum as to the rigidities and blunders of the French general staff. Churchill, preparing the country against invasion, not only initiated measures for the control of aliens, but directed that "action should also be taken against Communists and Fascists, and very considerable numbers should be put in protective or preventive internment, including the leaders. These measures must, of course,

---

* It is almost impossible on the basis of material available to American scholars to establish what is true, inflated, or deliberately distorted in William Stevenson's *A Man Called Intrepid*. A more sober account of Stephenson's operations was published in 1962 in *Room 3603* by H. Montgomery Hyde. In Hyde's book, Stephenson's first, and perhaps only, meeting with Roosevelt took place in early June, 1940, and appears to have focused on British anxiety about safeguarding their defense orders against sabotage. Stevenson's book states that Stephenson had his first meeting with Roosevelt when he came to the United States in early spring, 1940, and that Stephenson informed the president at that time of British guerilla-warfare techniques "which will get us back into Europe." But the account is seriously flawed. The German invasion of the Low Countries only began May 10, 1940, and British armies were only forced off the Continent early in June, which was long after Stephenson's first visit to the United States. Hyde's account—that on his first visit Stephenson saw Hoover and only heard through intermediaries about Roosevelt's reaction to the proposal that he and Hoover cooperate—seems more plausible. The Stevenson book must be treated with great circumspection.

be brought before the Cabinet before action." In the interests of national security, the innocent were swept up along with the guilty. He knew, he said two weeks later, at the time of Dunkirk, that there were "a great many people affected by the order which we have made who are the passionate enemies of Nazi Germany. I am very sorry for them, but we cannot at the present time and under the present stress, draw all the distinctions which we should like to do."[28]

For Roosevelt there was also the problem of Col. Charles A. Lindbergh, youthful, engagingly shy, a folk hero, and emerging as a virulent spokesman of isolationism. Lindbergh, while advocating adequate hemispheric defense, was seeking to counter the powerful impact of Roosevelt's May 15 call for rearmament by denouncing the hysterical chatter of calamity and invasion. "We are in danger of war today, not because Europeans attempted to interfere in our internal affairs, but because Americans attempted to interfere in the internal affairs of Europe." "The President said to me at lunch to-day," noted Morgenthau, " 'If I should die tomorrow, I want you to know this. I am absolutely convinced that Lindbergh is a Nazi.' "[29]

The grimmest bulletins were pouring in from Paris. On May 20 it became clear that German panzers were not heading for Paris but for the Channel ports, their purpose being to cut off the British expeditionary force and the French First Army. Churchill again rushed to France to find out exactly what was taking place. Back in London by nightfall, he reported to the cabinet that he had worked out a plan with the new French supreme commander, Gen. Maxime Weygand, under which the British expeditionary force and the French First Army would attempt to escape encirclement by attacking in a southerly direction at the same time that a new French army group would strike north from the Somme, placing the German panzers between a hammer and anvil. But nothing happened, no attack developed. A stern telegram flew from Churchill to Reynaud: "Strong enemy armoured forces have cut communications of northern armies. Salvation of these armies can only be obtained by immediate execution of Weygand's plan. I demand that French commanders on North and South and Belgian HQ be given the most stringent orders to carry this out and turn defeat into victory. Time vital as supplies are short."

Clement Attlee saw a larger peril. "Are we not in danger of falling between two stools," he asked in the war cabinet, "neither the plan agreed with General Weygand will be carried out, nor will we use our forces to best advantage in retaining our hold on the Channel Ports?" He suggested that the British expeditionary force retreat to these ports. Churchill demurred. "I feel . . . that we have no choice in the matter but to do our best to conform to General Weygand's plan. Any other course would wreck the chance of General Weygand's plan succeeding." That same day Gen. Sir Alan Brooke, corps commander with the British northern armies, wrote in his diary: "Nothing but a miracle can save the BEF now, and the end cannot be far off." The U.S. naval attaché in Paris conveyed the same impression to Roosevelt: "German advance going north. . . . Allied counterattack to south between

Cambrai and Arras moving slowly. Outlook most grave unless Allied attack succeeds."[30]

In Washington, Arthur Purvis, the Canadian head of the British purchasing mission, who in a brief time had established a fine rapport with Morgenthau and the army and navy officers concerned with supply, urgently sought the transfer to Britain of two hundred P-40 fighters, as many bombers as the army could spare, and various types of arms and munitions. By instruction of the president, Welles informed Lothian, General Marshall had visited Purvis that morning and shown him a tentative list of rifles, field pieces, mortars, and ammunition that the War Department could sell to Britain by declaring them surplus stocks, not needed for the defense of the United States. The matériel would be transferred to private manufacturers for resale to the British. This roundabout procedure was conceived because the Neutrality Act, even as revised, allowed the Allies to purchase war materials from private manufacturers in the United States, but not from the government.

Roosevelt faced other difficulties in meeting the pleas of the Allies for quick dispatch of matériel. His army and navy chiefs resisted pressures to transfer war stocks, especially planes and destroyers, arguing that to do so would delay America's rearmament as approved by Congress. "It is a drop in the bucket on the other side and it is a very vital necessity on this side and that is that," Marshall had told Morgenthau on May 17, adding, "Tragic as it is, that is it."[31]

Britain's request for planes and destroyers, Welles told Lothian, could not be handled by the "surplus" procedure and would depend on the willingness of Congress to make a "radical departure" from the policies embodied in the Neutrality Act as well as on the president's interpretation of international law. After Welles had stated what the United States was prepared to do, Lothian brought up what the attitude of the British government would be in the event France were defeated and Britain invaded:

The Ambassador in very vigorous terms stated that it was his positive conviction that so long as the British and French fleets remained intact and out of German hands and so long as the United States fleet remained in the Pacific . . . as a counterpoise to Japan in the Pacific, Germany could not eventually win the war. He said that he was further confident that no British Government would surrender the fleet and that high ranking officers in command of the fleet would never agree to surrender the fleet even if ordered to do so. He said that he was positive that even if a majority of the House of Commons voted in a new government which would agree to surrender the fleet, the present British Government would refuse to acquiesce in any such decision and would remove to Canada, where the British fleet could at least in part be based, other portions of the fleet being based on the British West Indies or perhaps off South Africa.

Welles commented in his memorandum that he had the definite impression "from the positive terms" in which the ambassador spoke that Churchill had instructed him to do so in reply to the president. The British attitude on the fleet soon changed and the United States would again be informed that it could not assume that if it stayed aloof from the struggle, sending the British a handful of World War I equipment, it would inherit the great British fleet. Some hard bargaining was ahead, especially after Lord Beaverbrook, isolationist and imperialist, came into Churchill's government as minister of aircraft production and one of his most intimate advisers. His attitude, not unlike Joseph Kennedy's, was give nothing "except for money received."

Lothian cabled home on May 30:

During the last week, we have noted that the President's anxiety about eventual disposition of the British Fleet seemed to have lessened and I am now sure that the reason has been that he has persuaded himself that the Empire can be relied upon to get the British Fleet across the Atlantic before it is too late. . . . The expert politician in the President is always trying to find a way of winning war for the Allies and if he fails to do that of ensuring the security of the United States without the United States itself having to take the plunge into the war. In so far as I discreetly can I try to make everybody here see that the only way in which the United States can build up resistance to Germany and keep in being two-navy protection of its own interests is by doing everything possible, including entering the war on the side of the Allies, to preserve an effective Franco-British front in Europe, which alone gives them time in which to arm to the limit. I think that Casey's interview coming from one who can speak authoritatively for the Empire, will do much to shatter the paralysing illusion in the President's mind.

Speaking with Welles about the real possibility of an invasion of Britain, Australian minister Casey, in reply to Welles's query about what would happen to the British fleet, had said it would not surrender "but they would probably immolate themselves by an attack on German ports." That would be "illogical," Welles had protested. "People aren't logical in such circumstances," commented Casey, and the only thing that might change their view was if they saw some eventual chance of the United States entering the war.

"We must be careful not to let Americans view too complacently prospect of a British collapse," Churchill advised Canadian Prime Minister Mackenzie King, "out of which they would get the British Fleet and the guardianship of the British Empire, minus Great Britain. . . . Although President is our best friend, no practical help has [reached us] from the United States as yet."[32]

On the eve of Dunkirk, appeasement pressures again came to the surface in Britain. The issue was an approach to Italy to intercede with Germany for an all-European conference. This move grew out of, but was distinct from, Allied efforts, backed by Roosevelt, to "buy off" Mussolini from entering the war. Allied fears on this score first came to a head during the Norwegian debacle, and Roosevelt, on April 29, at the Allies' request as well as that of the Vatican, had agreed to urge Mussolini not to enter the war. In the State Department, Welles and Moffat alone had been opposed to this tactic. "After all, any message would imply that we disbelieved the assurances that Mussolini had given Sumner Welles six weeks ago," wrote Moffat. But Roosevelt overruled them. "Mussolini received Phillips and gave him the completest assurances that he does not intend to enter the war," recorded Adolf Berle. "He treated the gesture as a very friendly one. Welles thinks this ends the Mediterranean crisis."

Ciano gave the German ambassador in Rome a very different picture. "The Duce had been very annoyed at Roosevelt's message and had felt the whole of the Ambassador's visit to be so importunate that he had told him, Ciano, afterwards, that he would not in the future receive any Ambassador— except the German one—in order to receive such a message or any other letter." So the German ambassador informed Ribbentrop. The Italian ambassador in Washington was instructed to convey to Roosevelt Mussolini's reply, which Ciano described as "cutting and hostile."[33]

Two weeks later, when the Germans shattered the French front, almost all official Paris appealed to Roosevelt via William Bullitt to make a final effort to keep Mussolini out. Berle, on his way home from a Toscanini concert, saw the lights on in Hull's office and went in to find the secretary working on the draft of a message to Mussolini. While Berle was with Hull the president telephoned and gave Hull his draft of what should be said. It was, commented Berle, "as usual, better than anyone else[s]. . . . One sentence deserves to be famous. He said, as nearly as I can remember, 'I am a realist. As a realist, I know that if this war becomes general, it will be impossible for chiefs of state to keep it in control, and no one is wise enough to foresee the ultimate results.' " "Sumner tells me," Berle added the next day, "that our communication to Mussolini was received in entire friendliness." This was wishful thinking, as Roosevelt suspected. Mussolini, as he had told the Germans, refused to receive Ambassador Phillips. The Duce did not reply until May 18 and then said pointedly that as a realist the president should understand "that Italy is and intends to remain allied with Germany and that Italy cannot remain absent at a moment in which the fate of Europe is at stake."[34]

On May 16, Churchill also tried his hand at dissuading Mussolini, assuring the Duce that he had never been an enemy of Italian greatness or at heart a foe of his, adding, however, that whatever the outcome of the battle in France, Britain would in the end prevail with the help of the United States and of all the Americas. "It is a message of good will," commented Ciano, "couched in vague terms, but nonetheless dignified and noble. Even Mussolini appreciates the tone of it, and he means to answer that, like England, he, too, intends to remain true to his word." But, according to Ciano, Mussolini's reply two days later, May 18, influenced perhaps by the speed of the German advance, was "brief and needlessly harsh in tone." It was, cabled Kennedy from London, "not even a polite 'Go to Hell.' "[35]

But these interventions with Mussolini took a different turn a week later. Lord Halifax, on May 25, talked with the Italian ambassador in London, Signor Bastianini. In line with British policy, Halifax assured the envoy of British willingness to satisfy reasonable Italian demands. Then, with Bastianini in the lead and Halifax quite acquiescent, the discussion turned to an all-European conference to provide a settlement that would provide a "secure peace in Europe," a settlement that would protect European peace for a century. When Halifax reported Bastianini's soundings to the war cabinet the next day, Churchill angrily commented that "peace and security might be achieved under a German domination of Europe. That we could never accept." The same day Reynaud came to London to advocate an approach to Italy. "The only one who understands is Halifax," Reynaud said on his return to Paris. He "is clearly worried about the future and realizes that some European solution must be decided. Churchill is always hectoring and Chamberlain undecided."

After Reynaud left, a violent altercation broke out between Churchill and Halifax. Britain should take care, Churchill advised, not to be forced into a weak position in which she invited Mussolini to go to Hitler and ask him to "treat us nicely." Halifax coldly replied that he attached rather more importance to the desirability of allowing France to try out the possibilities of European equilibrium. He was not quite convinced that it was in Hitler's interest to insist on "outrageous terms." Mussolini would regard such an approach with contempt, Churchill argued. Halifax, joined by Chamberlain, demurred. The French should at least be free to pursue the idea, and the war cabinet agreed to send a noncommittal message of vague support to Reynaud.[36]

On May 27 the war news turned even darker. The Belgians, on whom the British relied to protect their flank, indicated abruptly that they intended to surrender. They ceased firing at four the next morning, giving one hour's notice to the British commander. Again the French appealed to Britain to support more vigorously an approach to Mussolini, and again Churchill objected: "The French are trying to get us on the slippery slope. The position will be entirely different when Germany has made an unsuccessful attempt to invade this country. . . . Nations which go down fighting rise again, but those which surrender tamely are finished." Chamberlain thought Churchill too hard on the French, and the war cabinet delegated him and Halifax to draft the message to the French. "We are convinced that at this moment, when Hitler is flushed with victory and certainly counts on early and complete collapse of Allied resistance, it would be impossible for Sr. Mussolini to put forward proposals for a conference with any success . . . without excluding the possibility of an approach to Sr. Mussolini at some time, we cannot feel that this would be the right moment."[37]

Halifax was furious with Churchill. He wrote in his diary:

At Cabinet we had a long and rather confused discussion about, nominally, the approach to Italy, but also largely about general policy in the event of things going really badly in France. I thought Winston talked the most frightful rot, also Greenwood, and after hearing it for some time I said exactly what I thought of them, adding that, if that was really their view, and if it comes to the point, our ways must separate. . . . I despair when [Churchill] works himself up into a passion of emotion when he ought to make his brain think and reason.

Halifax unburdened himself to Cadogan. "I can't work with Winston any longer." "Nonsense," retorted Cadogan, "his rhodomontades probably bore

you as much as they do me, but don't do anything silly under stress of that."
Later Halifax came to have tea with Cadogan. "Said he had spoken to W.,
who of course had been v. affectionate!" Although Halifax complained of
Churchill's yielding to sentiment instead of using his brain, Cadogan, whose
brain was among the coolest, agreed with Churchill about the futility of an
appeal to Mussolini. When Lord Lothian reported that Mussolini's reply to
Roosevelt's May 27 offer to mediate and guarantee Allied offers to Italy was
"entirely negative," Cadogan commented: "Of course Mussolini is not going
to, and in fact, dare not make any separate agreement with the Allies, even if
he wanted to. He is simply wondering how much of the general 'share-out' he
will be allowed by his 'Ally' to take, and whether he will ultimately get more,
or less, by spilling Italian blood for it. We can't tell which way he'll jump, but
I hope we shan't delude ourselves into thinking that we shall do ourselves any
good by making any more 'offers' or 'approaches.' "[38]

Mussolini's attitude was worse than even the hardheaded Cadogan surmised. "I answer Phillips that Roosevelt is off the track" with his offer of
mediation, Ciano noted. "In fact, it is not that [Mussolini] wants this or that;
what he wants is war, and even if he were to obtain by peaceful means double
what he claims, he would refuse."[39]

The new appeasement pressures within the British government had not
escaped Roosevelt. A cable from Kennedy sympathetic with the appeasement
line put him on his guard:

Only a miracle can save the BEF from being wiped out or, as I said yesterday, surrender. I suspect that the Germans would be willing to make peace with
both the French and the British now—of course on their own terms but on terms
that would be a great deal better than they would be if the war continues. . . .

I realize that this is a terrific telegram, but there is no question that it's in the
air here. The result of that will be a row amongst certain elements in the Cabinet
here; Churchill, Attlee, and others will want to fight to the death but there will
be other members who realize that physical destruction of men and property in
England will not be a proper offset to a loss of pride. In addition to that the
English people, while they suspect a terrible situation, really do not realize how
bad it is. When they do, I don't know what group they will follow—the do or die,
or the group that wants a settlement.[40]

In Washington Colonel Knox warned Roosevelt that, on the basis of
information received from his London bureau, "a certain group of politicians
in London are talking of a possible negotiated peace."[41]

"It is extremely serious for Britain and France," Roosevelt told the
Advisory Commission to the Council on National Defense, which he had set
up to coordinate the huge defense production effort that was getting under
way. "We are not saying so out loud because we do not want to intimate in
this country that England and France have gone." But he expected Italy to
come into the war soon, which would mean the complete domination of
Europe and Africa by the Fascists and an all-out drive "to destroy the power
of the British Empire and England especially." That did not mean that Fascist
forces necessarily "will be coming over here," but the president did see a drive

to dominate Central and South America economically and politically. Nor did he exclude larger ambitions. Hitler might not at the beginning think he is

going to conquer the whole world but, when the time comes and he has conquered Europe and Africa and got Asia all settled up with Japan and has some kind of practical agreement with Russia, it may be human nature for victors of that kind to say, "I have taken two thirds of the world and I am all armed and ready to go—why shouldn't I go the whole hog and control, in a military way, the last third of the world, the Americas?" And there is no one of us can guess definitely as to what will be the decision on the part of Germany and Italy if they completely control all of Europe, including the British Isles. We don't know. That's the reason for this program. It is because we don't know. That is the primary reason. A good many other victors and conquerors in the world have said, "I only want so much," and when they got that they said, "I want only so much more," and when they got that they said, "I want all the whole known world."*[43]

Would Britain, in the event of a French collapse, continue to fight? Would it be able to withstand a Nazi onslaught against the islands? These were the questions that preoccupied Roosevelt and his advisers at the end of May.

The "deliverance" at Dunkirk, as Churchill called it, now gripped the Atlantic world's mind and heart. The English-speaking peoples hung breathless on an evacuation that seemed as miraculous as the passage of the Israelites through the Red Sea. The word "seemed" is used advisedly. Not to detract from the heroism of the men engaged in the operation, but, as was learned after the war, a contributing factor to the "miracle" was Hitler's decision to halt his armed spearheads sweeping along the Channel coast. German Army Chief of Staff Halder had noted Hitler's jitteriness the week before. "A most unfortunate day. The Fuehrer is terribly nervous. He is frightened by his own success, is unwilling to take any risks and is trying to hold us back." "Dunkirk was one of Hitler's most decisive mistakes," wrote General von Manstein of Hitler's order holding up his panzers in the vicinity of Dunkirk.[44]

Dunkirk, and Churchill's extraordinary speech at the end of that heroic operation, exercised a powerful impact on American opinion. The evacuation

---

* This was the viewpoint of most Americans. As early as the collapse of Poland, 63 per cent of those polled by the American Institute of Public Opinion were convinced that if Germany was victorious in Europe, it would eventually attack the United States; and after France's collapse, 63.1 per cent expected an immediate attempt to seize territory in the Western Hemisphere and 42.5 per cent expected an immediate attack on the United States. Nevertheless, according to a *Fortune* poll published May 29, 1940, only 7.7 per cent favored entry into the war at once; 19 per cent believed that the United States should intervene to prevent defeat of the Allies; and 40 per cent opposed U.S. intervention under any circumstances. On the subject of increased aid to the democracies, 71 per cent of those polled by Hadley Cantril's Princeton group favored it while 23 per cent opposed aid to one side in the conflict.

Although Roosevelt did not expect an immediate military attack on the Western Hemisphere, he directed Admiral Stark on April 30, 1940, to prepare to occupy the island of Fernando de Noronha, a Brazilian penal colony situated off the easternmost bulge of Brazil, in an emergency and to be ready to destroy its airfield "so that it cannot be used by land planes or amphibians." [42]

began the night of May 26 and by the end of the twenty-seventh over 7,000 had been safely embarked. The next day, nearly 18,000 got off the beaches into the diverse small craft that had pushed across the Channel to take part in the rescue operation—the official figure was 222 naval vessels and 665 ships and boats. On May 29 the number of evacuated rose to 50,000, and the next two days to over 60,000.

On May 31, Churchill and Attlee went to France for a meeting of the Allied Supreme War Council, where Churchill described the evacuation. "The meeting was affecting," wrote Baudouin, "for Mr. Churchill twice had tears in his eyes when he was describing the martyrdom of the armies in the north, the terrible suffering of the men and the loss of matériel which were saddening England. His voice broke down when he told us that in order to form a new army, he had given orders to embark the wounded last." "It seems to me," minuted a member of the American department, "that the way the retreat to Dunkirk is being managed should convince the Americans that we are worth saving and that Germans are not invincible supermen."[45]

The operation was officially completed on June 4. "The Prime Minister informed the War Cabinet that the personnel of the BEF had now been withdrawn to this country practically intact." A total of 338,226 troops had been rescued, 225,000 of whom were British. "My darling," Nicolson wrote his wife Vita, "how *infectious* courage is. I am rendered far stronger in heart and confidence by such bravery." At the war office, Eden had sterner thoughts. "My own view is that now we have got off such a large proportion of the BEF we should send some additional troops to France." Both he and Churchill were deeply aware of the disparity between the dozen divisions Britain had in France in 1940 and the more than fifty divisions sent to France in the first year of the First World War.[46]

Dunkirk was the setting for Churchill's great speech of June 4. It was preceded by a French suggestion of a joint appeal to the United States for help.* The British war cabinet feared such an appeal would suggest weakness, even panic, to the Americans. But it did agree to sound out the president on an appeal along lines suggested by General Smuts of South Africa—that the Allies intended to fight on in any circumstance, and that they wanted nothing for themselves but were concerned with the defense of liberty against Nazi domination. Would the United States help, or would it stand aside and take no action in defense of the rights of man? Roosevelt, consulted by Lothian, did not consider such an appeal desirable. It would hinder him in getting matériel to the Allies and would slow down the crystallization of American opinion in favor of aid because it would be interpreted as an attempt by foreigners to influence the United States in the direction of war. However, Roosevelt felt

* William Bullitt had encouraged such an appeal, which elicited a tart comment from Professor Whitehead: "Monsieur Reynaud's suggestion for a combined Anglo-French appeal to the U.S. seems most ill-judged from every point of view. In the first place Mr. Bullitt's belief that U.S. public opinion has outstripped the President is worth very little. For many years the President has shown an uncanny knowledge of American opinion whereas Mr. Bullitt is an emotional enthusiast living 3,000 miles from his own country."[47]

that a broadcast by Churchill (which had also been suggested by the war cabinet) might be useful, with the qualification that it should be addressed to the British Empire. Lothian was informed that Churchill would probably speak in the House of Commons on June 4 and that his speech would subsequently be broadcast.[48]

Churchill had warned Parliament at the time of King Leopold's surrender that it should prepare itself for "hard and heavy tidings," and it was a solemn and somber house that assembled on June 4 to hear his report. The prime minister sat, as usual before a speech, hunched up, shuffling his papers, stooping over nervously to pick up a fallen scrap. He then rose to deliver what Nicolson described as "the finest speech I have ever heard."

A week ago, Churchill began, he had thought that he would have to announce today "the greatest military disaster" in British history, the capitulation of the British expeditionary force. But thanks to the Royal Navy and the Royal Air Force, that calamity had not befallen the Allies. "We must be very careful not to assign to this deliverance the attributes of a victory. Wars are not won by evacuations. But there was a victory inside this deliverance which should be noted. It was gained by the Air Force." Hurricanes, Spitfires, and Defiants had turned back wave after wave of the Luftwaffe, inflicting losses in the ratio of four to one and demonstrating the superiority of the British fighter to anything Germany has at present. "When we consider how much greater would be our advantage in defending the air above this Island against an overseas attack, I must say that I find in these facts a sure basis upon which practical and reassuring thoughts may rest." But what had happened in Belgium and France was "a colossal military disaster," and the rescued British force was denuded of equipment—guns, transport, armored vehicles, all were lost. Churchill went on to speak of the steps being taken to brace the island for invasion, and then soared to a peroration that buoyed and exalted men's spirits throughout the English-speaking world:

Even though large tracts of Europe and many old and famous States have fallen or may fall into the grip of the Gestapo and all the odious apparatus of Nazi rule, we shall not flag or fail. We shall go on to the end, we shall fight in France, we shall fight on the seas and oceans, we shall fight with growing confidence and growing strength in the air, we shall defend our Island, whatever the cost may be, we shall fight on the beaches, we shall fight on the landing grounds, we shall fight in the fields and in the streets, we shall fight in the hills; we shall never surrender, and even if, which I do not for a moment believe, this Island or a large part of it were subjugated and starving, then our Empire beyond the seas, armed and guarded by the British Fleet, would carry on the struggle, until, in God's good time, the New World, with all its power and might, steps forth to the rescue and liberation of the old.[49]

The reaction in the United States to Churchill's roar of defiance was profound. "Winston Churchill made a speech to Parliament yesterday," Ickes noted in his diary, "in which he served notice that England would go on fighting to the very end and that if the Island itself were conquered, England would move to some other part of the Empire and fight from there until the new world should come to the rescue. It was a great speech. He really served notice that the British fleet, whatever might happen, would not be surrendered to Hitler. This phase of his speech was quite reassuring to me."⁵⁰

It was equally so to Roosevelt. He had been disturbed by a message from Churchill to Mackenzie King, the prime minister of Canada, in which Churchill had again refused to be categoric about the fleet, saying that "if America continued neutral, and we were overpowered, I cannot tell what policy might be adopted by a pro-German administration such as would undoubtedly be set up." Churchill had written that message, the president told Moffat, the new U.S. minister to Ottawa, before his speech of June 4 and that speech was firmness itself. The president and he were persuaded after that speech, wrote Hull, that Britain under Churchill "intended to fight on. There would be no negotiations between London and Berlin. The President and I believed Mr. Churchill meant what he said. Had we had any doubt of Britain's determination to keep on fighting, we would not have taken the steps we did to get material aid to her."

Lothian, however, was unhappy over Churchill's references to the fleet. "Unfortunately many Americans including some in the Administration try to persuade themselves that somehow or other the rest of the Empire is going to get the fleet for the United States even if Britain is overrun and that the U.S. need not face war until after this has taken place."⁵¹

U.S. public sentiment was changing. "Moves designed to aid the Allies now command overwhelming support in Middle West," Knox cabled the president from Chicago. "You have the country back of you in measures designed to help now in such critically decisive hours when fate of civilization hangs in balance." But a favorable public opinion did not necessarily mean votes in Congress, nor did it influence some of Roosevelt's recalcitrant advisers. The overage items that Marshall had declared surplus on May 23 sat in army warehouses until June 3 because Secretary of War Woodring and the legal adviser of the State Department had ruled that there had to be prior public advertisement before the matériel could be sold to private firms. Finally, on June 3, the attorney general upheld the legality of the exchange or sale of overage or surplus equipment without prior advertisement. On June 5, the Senate Foreign Relations Committee rejected an administration proposal to authorize the government to sell to Britain ships and planes as well as rifles, guns, and ammunition. Two days later, at a rousing keep-out-of-war rally in Washington, isolationist senator Burton K. Wheeler charged that Roosevelt was doing "by indirection" through the attorney general's ruling what the Senate Foreign Relations Committee had said "we should not do when its members voted 19 to 2 against the Pepper resolution which sought to do this very thing." And, of course, Roosevelt was.⁵²

"Actually, I am adopting the thought," the president wrote Lewis Douglas, a conservative banker who had broken with him in 1933 over gold policy but who was now urging immediate aid to Britain, "that the more effective usable matériel we can get to the other side will mean the destruction of an equivalent amount of German matériel—thereby aiding American defense in the long run. So you see I am doing everything possible—though I am not talking very much about it because a certain element in the press . . . would undoubtedly pervert it, attack it, and confuse the public mind." At a cabinet meeting that same day, Roosevelt impatiently overruled the secretary of the navy, who reported that the dispatch of certain materials to the Allies had been delayed because the navy's judge advocate general had ruled the transaction illegal. Roosevelt brusquely called the judge advocate general a "sea lawyer" and advised Secretary Edison to send him on vacation; and if the man next in line did not know any more law, he should also be sent on vacation; and so on down the line. When Edison tenaciously repeated to Roosevelt that the judge advocate general had ruled the transaction illegal, Roosevelt pre-emptorily ordered "forget it and do what I told you to do."[53]

The next day it was the War Department that balked. Woodring and Louis Johnson, the assistant secretary, were refusing to release 750 bombs to the French to go along with 50 dive bombers that they had purchased, Morgenthau informed Roosevelt, who that week end was cruising down river on the U.S.S. *Potomac*. "It seems obvious that bombs are a necessary part of plane equipment," Roosevelt answered via naval communications, "and should go along with the fifty Navy Bombers. Show this to Woodring as authority to release."[54]

Roosevelt knew he was skating on dangerously thin ice. A few days earlier he had explained the delicacy of his position to Ickes, who had pressed to transfer obsolete destroyers to Britain. "If we should send some destroyers across, they would be of no particular use to the Allies but they might serve further to enrage Hitler. We cannot tell the turn the war will take and there is no use endangering ourselves unless we can achieve some results for the Allies." Ickes acknowledged Roosevelt's dilemma. "If you do send some help with bad consequences to ourselves, the people will blame you just as they will blame you if you don't send help and the Allies are crushed." "The degree to which the U.S.A. will come to our assistance rather than concentrate upon the defence of her own hemisphere," advised John Balfour of the American department, "depends in the highest degree upon our ability to prove that we are vigorously prosecuting the war and are capable of winning it in spite of the reverses we have sustained."[55]

"The President is afraid," Lothian wrote his good friend Lady Astor during Dunkirk, "that if he goes too fast you will get another 'battalion of death' in the Senate like Wilson did over the League of Nations—a group which will exploit the natural human reluctance to war, excite the women (saying they are going to keep their boys out of the war) and get the Senate so balled up as to produce complete paralysis of action in any direction."[56]

When Maj. (later Lt. Gen.) Walter Bedell Smith took to the White House an Allied request for 500 75-mm guns and appropriate ammunition, "Pa" Watson asked him what he thought of the transaction. "I replied that if the War Department could be assured that we would not be called upon for a general mobilization within two years . . . the transaction was perfectly safe, but that if we were required to mobilize, after having released guns necessary for this mobilization and were found to be short in artillery matériel . . . everyone who was a party to the deal might hope to be found hanging from a lamppost. Whereupon General Watson took the paper in to the President, who ok'd the transaction."[57]

Balky war and navy officials, a Congress which at key points was controlled by the isolationists, a cautious State Department, an unpredictable international situation—these were the daunting forces standing in the way of a clear United States commitment of all-out aid to the Allies. The commitment was now supported by public opinion. Roosevelt appreciated better than anyone how volatile that could be, yet he had decided not only to make the commitment, but to make it public. The occasion was a commencement address on June 10, at the University of Virginia in Charlottesville, where his son Franklin, Jr., was completing his law studies. June 10 also turned out to be the day that Italy entered the war. In preparing his speech Roosevelt had struggled with his State Department advisers—Welles in particular—over the reference to Mussolini's grab for spoils as a "stab in the back," a phrase that had been used by Reynaud and Bullitt. On his way down to Charlottesville, however, after having removed the phrase, Roosevelt reinserted it, and, said his wife, felt a sense of relief and satisfaction. It was the phrase by which the speech would be remembered; it elicited "a deep growl of satisfaction" from Churchill, who went to the admiralty's war room at midnight to listen to a broadcast of the speech. But the speech's real significance lay in its declaration of intent:

On this tenth day of June, 1940, the hand that held the dagger has struck it into the back of its neighbor.

On this tenth day of June, 1940, in this University founded by the first great American teacher of democracy, we send forth our prayers and our hopes to those beyond the seas who are maintaining with magnificent valor their battle for freedom.

In our American unity, we will pursue two obvious and simultaneous courses: we will extend to the opponents of force the material resources of this nation; and, at the same time, we will harness and speed up the use of these resources in order that we ourselves in the Americas may have equipment and training equal to the task of any emergency and every defense.[58]

Before he went to bed, Churchill cabled Roosevelt. An impulsive man himself, especially attracted by bravery, he appreciated the intrepidity of words that risked affronting the Italian-American vote on the eve of a presidential election:

We all listened to you last night and were fortified by the grand scope of your declaration. Your statement that the material aid of the United States will be given to the Allies in their struggle is a strong encouragement in a dark but not unhopeful hour. Everything must be done to keep France in the fight and to prevent any idea of the fall of Paris, should it occur, becoming the occasion of any kind of parley.

Churchill renewed his plea for matériel. As soon as divisions of the British expeditionary force could be re-equipped they would be sent to

France. The need was for destroyers, a need made more pressing by Italy's entry into the war.

The next six months are vital. If while we have to guard the East Coast against invasion a new heavy German-Italian submarine attack is launched against our commerce, the strain may be beyond our resources, and the ocean traffic by which we live may be strangled. Not a day should be lost. I send you my heartfelt thanks and those of my colleagues for all you are doing and seeking to do for what we may now, indeed, call the Common Cause.[59]

Without Churchill, Britain might have gone the way of France and, despairing of the United States, solicited a compromise peace with Hitler. Without Roosevelt the United States might have pursued a "fortress America" policy, leaving the totalitarians free to destroy England and to consolidate their positions on the continents of Europe, Asia, and Africa. What emerges from these initial exchanges between the "former naval person" and the president of the United States is that among their respective associates Churchill and Roosevelt had the broadest vision and the bravest hearts. Therein lay their greatness.

Chapter Nine

France Leaves the War

THE BATTLE OF Flanders was lost. The effort to stabilize an Allied front faltered. Italy, as feared, had jumped in to grab its share of the booty. Roosevelt's offer of material aid to the Allies was not enough; Allied pressures soon mounted on him to enter the war.

On June 4 William Bullitt had reported on a dismaying luncheon he had had with Marshal Pétain, now vice-president of the council. That surrender-minded member of Reynaud's cabinet, bitter about the British, accused them of intending "to permit the French to fight without help until the last drop of French blood should have been shed" and then, under a Fascist leader, to make a compromise peace with Hitler, using as bargaining counters their planes, troops, and fleet.[1] By the next day Bullitt, reporting a talk with Reynaud, seemed to have adopted Pétain's viewpoint on Britain. British willingness to send fighter planes to France was the "touchstone" by which to gauge future British policy, Bullitt advised Roosevelt. If the British refused to commit their fighters, it meant that they were conserving their forces so that before or after a German attack on England they could install a Fascist government "and accept vassalage to Hitler."[2]

Churchill had been the strongest advocate within the war cabinet of aid to France. But now, in view of the disintegration of French resistance, he, too, was unwilling to commit Britain's remaining fighters to a last-ditch effort to save the situation. Even General Smuts, the South African leader whose wisdom Churchill valued to the point of reverence, was unable to budge him. "I see only one way through now," Churchill explained, "to wit, that Hitler should attack this country, and in so doing break his air weapon. If this happens, he will be left to face the winter with Europe writhing under his heel, and probably, with the United States against him after the Presidential election is over."[3]

On June 10 a desperate Reynaud sent a ringing appeal, reminiscent of Churchill's, to Roosevelt. The enemy was almost at the gates of Paris. "We

shall fight in front of Paris; we shall fight behind Paris; we shall close ourselves in one of our provinces to fight and if we should be driven out of it, we
shall establish ourselves in North Africa to continue the fight and if necessary
in our American possessions." He begged the president to explain French
determination to the American people, and, "at the same time that you explain this situation to the men and women of America, I beseech you to declare publicly that the United States will give the Allies aid and material support by all means short of an expeditionary force. I beseech you to do this
before it is too late." Roosevelt turned over Reynaud's cry for help to the
State Department to draft a reply. Two days were to elapse before there was
agreement on what could be said to him.[4]

Sensing that surrender sentiment was rising around Reynaud, Churchill,
accompanied by Eden and Generals Dill and Ismay, flew to General Weygand's headquarters near Orléans. Landing on a crude air strip, they were
met by an uncommunicative colonel who conducted them to a nearby château
where they found Reynaud, Pétain, and Weygand. The British felt that their
"presence was not really desired." Churchill sought to fire up the offensive
spirit of the French. They should defend Paris as Madrid had been defended.
He reminded them of Clemenceau's World War I slogan: "I will fight in
front of Paris, *in Paris* and behind Paris." (He did not have to add that
Reynaud's message to Roosevelt had omitted the middle phrase.) Weygand
answered Churchill that in 1941 there had been sixty British divisions in the
line compared with the handful that remained in France now. The destruction of Paris would not affect the final outcome. The battle was being waged
outside of Paris and the whole British fighter force should be thrown into it.
"Here," Weygand said, "is the decisive point. Now is the decisive moment. It
is therefore wrong to keep any squadrons back in England."[5]

Churchill demurred. "This is not the decisive point and this is not the
decisive moment. That moment will come when Hitler hurls his Luftwaffe
against Great Britain. If we can keep command of the air, and if we keep the
seas open, as we certainly shall keep them open, we will win it all back for
you." Air Marshal Sir Hugh Dowding had said—and the war cabinet, including Churchill, had agreed—that twenty-five fighter squadrons were the
minimum essential to fight the Battle of Britain. Churchill's British colleagues
indicated relief as he told the French that Britain would not yield on this. The
British had been fearful, wrote General Spears, who idolized Churchill, "that
French eloquence and the magnitude of the French disaster, which had so
obviously awakened his deepest sympathy, might cause him to give way."
The German attack on the United Kingdom would in all probability bring the
United States into the war, Churchill continued. It was essential to keep intact the weapon and instrument on which United States intervention depended. His preoccupation, concluded Spears, is with keeping the war going
until the United States joined in the conflict. Churchill's rousing words did
not dispel the gloom of the French military, and before the British left, Reynaud informed Churchill that Pétain had already written a memorandum on
why it was necessary to seek an armistice.

To a stunned war cabinet back home Churchill reported that "France was near the end of organized resistance." Before he went into that meeting, Eden had sent him a note saying, "I am more than ever convinced that the chances of Reynaud's survival and of France staying in the war are to a large extent dependent upon the attitude of the United States. If Roosevelt could go a stage further and break off relations with Germany, even without declaring war, if such an action be possible, he would perhaps give our hard-pressed French friends just that spice of encouragement they need." Churchill's relations with Roosevelt, Eden then added, were "so good, and he is so heart and soul with us," that Churchill might be willing to risk telegraphing him along these lines.[6]

Churchill drew back from urging Roosevelt to break relations with Germany. Instead, his message to Roosevelt stressed the gravity of the French situation.

The aged Marshal Pétain who was none too good in April and July 1918 is I fear ready to lend his name and prestige to a treaty of peace for France. Reynaud on the other hand is for fighting on and he has a young general de Gaulle who believes much can be done. Admiral Darlan declares he will send the French fleet to Canada. . . . This, therefore, is the moment for you to strengthen Reynaud the utmost you can and try to tip the balance in favour of the best and longest possible French resistance. . . . If there is anything you can say publicly or privately to the French now is the time.[7]

The message was transmitted through Joseph Kennedy, who added a footnote stating that the prime minister "urged me strongly to present again his crying need for destroyers." A few hours later, Kennedy forwarded his own views, stressing the bleakness of Allied prospects. The British had little left except courage with which to oppose Hitler. "Unless France and England are dealing or will deal Germany really crippling blows at her industrial production and seriously affect her strength in the air and in tanks as a result of these battles, the United States will have plenty to worry about in their own country. The cry should be to prepare for anything right there, right now."[8]

The next morning Churchill again cabled Roosevelt. "French have sent for me again, which means that crisis has arrived. Am just off. Anything you can say or do to help them now may make a difference. We are also worried about Ireland. An American squadron at Berehaven would do no end of good I am sure." The news that sent Churchill back to France, accompanied by Halifax, Beaverbrook, and Ismay, were reports of pressure on Reynaud by Weygand and Pétain to start armistice negotiations. This time, when the British landed at Tours, there was no one to meet them. They made their own way from the airport, found lodgings and a meal, and at last were able to make contact with the French government. Reynaud and Churchill fought a delaying action against those who wanted to surrender. Reynaud said he was again appealing to Roosevelt—"the last hour had come" and the fate of the Allied cause lay in American hands. Unless the United States intervened, he would be unable to persuade his associates to continue the war. Churchill agreed that the first step was to send the message to Roosevelt and to wait the answer before considering alternatives. Reynaud should put the case in the strongest terms and he, Churchill, would support him. Until Roosevelt's reply was received, Churchill refused to discuss Britain's willingness to release France from its solemn undertaking not to make a separate peace.[9]

Churchill and his group then returned to London where he was handed Roosevelt's reply to Reynaud's earlier June 10 cable. Hull, cautious as always, had favored a guarded reply, heavy on the rhetoric of common goals and the like but chary of specific promises. This had not satisfied Roosevelt, whose concern over the disposition of the French navy mounted hourly. If it went to the Germans, control of the Atlantic would be endangered and Hitler could starve England into submission. FDR pressed Hull and Welles to go much further in pledges to the French. Welles supported the president, and Hull was silenced although by no means convinced. And he was furious that Welles had overruled him at the White House. "There is a difference of principle," commented Adolf Berle. "Welles and the President are emotionally much more engaged than the Secretary."

In the end, the message was drafted by Roosevelt in his handwriting:

Send to
Kennedy

Get following to P.M. as quickly as possible but with full secrecy: Quote I have sent following to Reynaud subquote

> I am personally particularly impressed by your declaration that France will continue the fight on behalf of democracy even if it means slow withdrawal even to N. Africa and the Atlantic. It is most important to remember that the French and British fleets continue the mastery of the Atlantic and other oceans. Also to remember that vital materials from the outside world are necessary to maintain all armies.

> I am also greatly heartened by what Prime Minister Churchill said a few days ago about the continued resistance of the British Empire and this determination would seem to apply equally to the great French Empire all over the world. Naval power in world affairs still carries the lessons of history, as Admiral Darlan well knows.

To the message to Reynaud was appended a reply to Churchill about Ireland:

I cannot send squadron to Berehaven as we have squadron off Portugal and another visiting East Coast South America—
Atlantic Patrol from Nova Scotia to Trinidad is in my judgment important as it continues to provide wide safety zone. I think you will agree that maintenance main fleet in Hawaii is vital.

All that was left of the State Department draft reply to Reynaud was the pledge that the United States would redouble its efforts to make war materials available to the Allies.[10]

Churchill caught at Roosevelt's reply, terming it "remarkable." He undertook to interpret it in a way that was even more remarkable. It "came as near as possible to a declaration of war," he said in a discussion with the war cabinet, "and was probably as much as the President could do without Congress. The President could hardly urge the French to continue the struggle, and to undergo further torture, if he did not intend to support them." His cabinet associates agreed, but thought the French would want something more definite and proposed that Churchill interpret the message to them. He would tell Reynaud, said Churchill, that the message fulfilled every hope and could only mean the United States would enter the war.

Churchill then left the cabinet meeting to ask Kennedy to obtain Roosevelt's consent to the publication of his message to Reynaud. The prime minister also sent a cable to the president, telling FDR of his meeting at Tours. The French were "very nearly gone." They had asked to be released from their obligation not to make a separate peace, but he had not hesitated "to refuse consent to an armistice or separate peace." Reynaud felt he was unable to urge his people to fight on "without hope of American intervention up to the extreme limit open to you." Churchill then referred to Roosevelt's "magnificent" message, "but Mr. President, I must tell you that it seems absolutely vital that this message should be published tomorrow, June 14, in order that it may play the decisive part in turning the course of world history."[11]

On June 14, however, an unhappy Churchill was obliged to inform the war cabinet that Kennedy had telephoned the president, who was willing to allow publication of his message, but that Hull was opposed, and the president had gone along with Hull. "Churchill was obviously terribly disappointed," Kennedy reported. "I told him of your desire that any misapprehension which might exist in the minds of French officials regarding the meaning of the message be cleared up. . . . [He] said he was afraid conveying such a message now to the French would merely dampen what fires remained." Churchill, hoping that the message he had sent after Kennedy's telephone call might have changed Roosevelt's mind, asked whether there was any reply yet to it. Not so far, Kennedy answered.

The ambassador, in the meantime, had cabled Roosevelt and Hull:

The danger of publication of your note to Reynaud as I see it is that Churchill sees in your note an absolute commitment of the United States to the Allies that if France fights on the United States will be in the war to help them. . . . I realize the tragedy of the present moment and how important it is for the success of these poor people that their morale should be built up; nevertheless I see a great danger in the message as a commitment at a later date.[12]

Roosevelt, concerned not only with Allied morale but with the French fleet and the continued resistance of the French Empire, was prepared to take risks. But he knew he could not give, or appear to give, a commitment to go to war. Hull had cautioned him that his message might be so construed. And as Hull's warnings were borne out, the president retreated. To reinforce the telephoned ban on publication, a cable went to Kennedy for Churchill:

"As I asked Ambassador Kennedy last night to inform you, my message of yesterday's date to the French Prime Minister was in no sense intended to commit and did not commit this Government to military participation in support of Allied governments. You will know that there is, of course, no authority under our Constitution except in Congress to make any commitment of this nature." The president was more than ever concerned about the French fleet and suggested to Churchill a maneuver by which it might be kept out of Nazi hands. "As naval people you and I fully appreciate [that] the vital strength of the fleet in being and command of the seas means in the long run the saving of democracy and the recovery of those suffering temporary reverses." If the French government sought an armistice, it would be unable to avoid inclusion of the fleet in the terms discussed. "On the other hand if a general seeks an armistice for his land forces, he does not control or include the disposition of naval forces."[13]

Churchill read Roosevelt's chilling words to the war cabinet on June 15. His own reply was candid, almost stern. And when he published it after the war in his memoirs he preceded it with some mitigating words:

Around our table we all fully understood the risks the President ran of being charged with exceeding his constitutional authority, and consequently of being defeated on this issue at the approaching election, on which our fate, and much more, depended. I was convinced that he would give up life itself, to say nothing of public office, for the cause of world freedom now in such awful peril. But what would have been the good of that? Across the Atlantic I could feel his suffering. In the White House the torment was of a different character from that of Bordeaux or London. But the degree of personal stress was not unequal.

These compassionate and understanding words were written in 1948. On June 15, 1940, impending calamity drove Churchill's pen:

I understand all your difficulties with American public opinion and Congress, but events are moving downward at a pace where they will pass beyond the control of American public opinion when at last it is ripened. Have you considered what offers Hitler may choose to make to France? He may say, "surrender the fleet intact and I will leave you Alsace Lorraine," or alternatively, "if you do not give me your ships I will destroy your towns." I am personally convinced that America will in the end go to all lengths but this moment is supremely critical for France. A declaration that the United States will, if necessary, enter the war might save France. Failing that in a few days French resistance may have crumbled and we shall be left alone.

Although the present government and I personally would never fail to send the fleet across the Atlantic if resistance were beaten down here, a point may be reached in the struggle where the present ministers no longer have control of affairs and when very easy terms could be obtained for the British islands by their becoming a vassal state of the Hitler empire. A pro-German government would certainly be called into being to make peace and might present to a shattered or a starving nation an almost irresistible case for entire submission to the Nazi will. The fate of the British fleet as I have already mentioned to you would be decisive on the future of the United States because if it were joined to the fleets of Japan, France, and Italy and the great resources of German industry, overwhelming sea power would be in Hitler's hands. He might, of course, use it with a merciful moderation. On the other hand he might not. This revolution in sea power might happen very quickly and certainly long before the United States would be able to prepare against it. If we go [down?] you may have a United States of Europe under the Nazi command far more numerous, far stronger, far better armed than the new [world?].

I know well, Mr. President, that your eye will already have searched these depths but I feel I have the right to place on record the vital manner in which American interests are at stake in our battle and that of France.

The argument for U.S. intervention, however compelling intellectually and emotionally, was up against the hard facts of the resistance of the American public and Congress. Having put the argument on record, Churchill proceeded to plead once again for the dispatch of thirty-five destroyers:

The changed strategical situation brought about by the possession by the enemy of the whole coast of Europe from Norway to the channel has faced us with a prospect of invasion which has more hopes of success than we had ever conceived possible. While we must concentrate our destroyers on protecting the vital trade, we must also dispose our naval forces to meet this threat.

If this invasion does take place, it will almost certainly be in the form of dispersed landings from a large number of small craft and the only effective counter to such a move is to maintain numerous and effective destroyer patrols. . . .

We must ask therefore as a matter of life or death to be reinforced with these destroyers.[14]

A few hours after dispatching this impassioned plea, Sir Ronald Campbell, the British ambassador in Bordeaux, warned Churchill that Pétain was determined to resign unless the French government asked for an armistice or the United States declared war. Off went another appeal to the president from the "former naval person":

Since sending you my message this afternoon I have heard that Monsieur Reynaud, in a telegram which he has just sent to you, has practically said that the decision of France to continue the war from overseas depends on your being able to assure the French Government that the United States of America will come into the war at a very early date.

When I sent you my message just now I did not know that Monsieur Reynaud had stated the dilemma in these terms, but I am afraid there is no getting away from the fact that this is the choice before us now.

Indeed, the British Ambassador in Bordeaux tells me that if your reply does not contain the assurance asked for, the French will very quickly ask for an armistice, and I much doubt whether it will be possible in that event for us to keep the French fleet out of German hands.

When I speak of the United States entering the war I am, of course, not thinking in terms of an expeditionary force, which I know is out of the question. What I have in mind is the tremendous moral effect that such an American decision would produce not merely in France but also in all the democratic countries of the world and in the opposite sense on the German and Italian peoples.[15]

In Washington, Roosevelt and Hull met with the British and French ambassadors. What reply did Roosevelt feel able to make to Reynaud's June 14 appeal? Lothian inquired. Hull read off a list of material and supplies that had been sent off that day. The question of entering the war, Roosevelt picked up, rested with Congress. It would be useless to initiate a campaign by radio and platform in favor of a declaration of war, as Lothian had urged, when he was certain that it would result in the swift political destruction of the authority of his government. Hull agreed.

Roosevelt then turned to the French ambassador. The United States was in no position to offer advice to France, but in his opinion, the French would be no worse off if they did not ask for an armistice, allowed Germany to occupy the whole of the country, while the government, part of the army, and the fleet moved across to Africa to continue the struggle. Roosevelt stressed the importance of not allowing Hitler and Mussolini to get hold of the French fleet. As long as Britain, France, and the United States controlled the oceans, the blockade would eventually be effective. This offered cold comfort to a France in agony, its ambassador commented. Britain might soon be in the same position as France, Lothian picked up from his French colleague, and its decision about making peace and disposing of its fleet, like that of France at the moment, might depend on the possibility of seeing "light at the end of the tunnel," meaning U.S. entry into the war. What were the chances of the United States being at war with Hitler before the final and critical decision had to be made? he asked. No one could answer that question, Roosevelt replied, since the answer depended on the movement of American opinion and, even more, "on whether before that time the Dictators had taken some action which compelled the United States to go to war in self-defense." The president implied that this last would be the case in the event of an imminent British defeat; but again it was only conjecture. "U.S. looks pretty useless," commented Cadogan fatalistically. "Well, we must die without them."[16]

Could Roosevelt have gone further? Public opinion had shifted dramatically. "The change has been staggering in the last fortnight," Lothian wrote Nancy Astor. "It would take very little to carry them in now—any kind of challenge by Hitler or Mussolini to their own vital interests would do it." Ickes was astonished to hear Archibald MacLeish say that he was in favor of declaring war. MacLeish was one of the young intellectuals who in the twenties had preached war's futility, Ickes noted. But he himself, Ickes confessed, would support a resolution declaring war and sending the Allies everything short of an expeditionary force.

Yet there was another current of opinion in the United States that was demonstrating its power to hamstring Roosevelt's efforts to send even material aid to the Allies. Roosevelt had resisted Churchill's pressure for destroyers, but at the end of May he had approved, with Admiral Stark's concurrence, the sale to Britain of twenty fast motor torpedo boats that were being built for the U.S. Navy and were scheduled to be delivered to it in July. The transaction came to the ears of Sen. David I. Walsh of Massachusetts, Irishman, isolationist and chairman of the Senate Naval Affairs Committee. An agitated Charles Edison, secretary of the navy, sent in a note to the president: "Senator Walsh is reported to me 1 P.M. as in a towering rage about sale of Navy stuff to Allies. He is threatening to force legislation prohibiting sale of anything. Elco boats started rumpus—everything else came in later—whole Committee in a lather."

Walsh went to the press, denouncing the transaction as "a grievous wrong, especially to our American youth who may be called upon to fight for the defense of our country." Questions were raised about the legality of the transaction. It was referred to the attorney general, who held that it was "absolutely illegal," and Roosevelt felt obliged to cancel the deal. Walsh was not placated. On June 28, prodded by him, the Senate amended the navy expansion bill to forbid the disposal of any army or navy matériel unless the chief of staff or the chief of naval operations should certify them as "not essential to the defense of the United States."[17]

Reminded thus of the isolationists' strength in Congress, it was little wonder that Roosevelt moved cautiously on Churchill's pleas for destroyers, not to mention the *in extremis* appeals that he bring the United States into the war.

Hitler understood the relationship between continued British resistance and its hopes of U.S. intervention. He was also aware of the asset that U.S. isolationism represented. In mid-May, worried by the shift in U.S. sentiment, especially by the polls showing that Americans were "beginning to believe in the danger of a German attack on the Western Hemisphere, either direct or by infiltration through Latin America after a possible Anglo-French defeat," the German chargé in Washington urged Berlin to issue a hands-off pledge with regard to Allied colonial possessions in the Western Hemisphere and a declaration of readiness to respect Latin American sovereignty. That will take "a lot of wind out of the sails of the President's policy," the chargé advised. The German foreign office agreed. "Such a declaration could be made in an interview with the Foreign Minister and I think that would take the wind out of the President's sails." That was in May. By June the Germans were so eager to shackle Roosevelt that they decided to issue the declaration in the form of a purported interview with Hitler. The interview was given to a friendly American newspaperman, Karl von Wiegand, the chief foreign correspondent of the Hearst newspapers. He was well known in the German foreign office. In 1939, Fritz Wiedmann, German consul general–designate in San Francisco, wrote that "Wiegand, to whom I talked in Berlin shortly before my departure, said to me at the time: 'The Fuehrer must clearly understand that President Roosevelt is his most dangerous opponent. President Roosevelt fights for his democratic aims with the same fanatic idealism as does the Fuehrer for National Socialism. Britain and France are no longer dragging America behind them: today America is driving them before her.' "

Wiegand's alleged interview with Hitler began:

With the German armies nearing Paris, June 14—"The Americas to Americans, Europe to Europeans." This reciprocal, basic Monroe Doctrine, mutually observed, declared Adolf Hitler to me here, not only would insure peace for all times between the Old and New Worlds, but would be a most ideal foundation for peace throughout the whole world. In caustic language, with scorn and indignation, he denounced "the lies" that he has or ever had in "dream or thought" played with the fantastic idea of interfering in the Western Hemisphere by any manner or means.

The *Washington Times-Herald* headline on this story was:

> HITLER DISCLAIMS ANY DESIRE TO INVADE THIS
> HEMISPHERE—TERMS "FIFTH COLUMN" FEARS AS
> STUPID; DENIES AIM TO SMASH BRITISH EMPIRE

This interview, questions and answers, was processed in the American committee of the German foreign office, as United States investigators learned after the war from Dr. Paul K. Schmidt, Hitler's interpreter. The German press bureau prepared the questions; the foreign office drafted the answers and submitted them to Hitler, who made some changes; and the final result was the Wiegand interview. It was a propaganda handout, not an interview, and Schmidt doubted that Wiegand even saw Hitler on this occasion.[18]

Asked to comment on Hitler's denial of any thought of doing anything to the Americas, Roosevelt, referring to the Führer's pledges of nonagression in the past, merely said, "It brings up recollections." Then, as the press corps laughed appreciatively, the president added: "I think that is quite sufficient comment. It can be enlarged on with dates and nations, et cetera and so on, going back for quite a period of years." And later that morning, talking with business paper editors, Roosevelt described how domination of a large part of South America could be achieved without the dispatch of troops, through the manipulation of imports and exports. Yet the president feared that as a result of the Wiegand story "a lot of gullible Americans . . . will say, 'You see, he won't do anything over here. Why shouldn't we go easy?' "[19]

Hitler had two primary objectives after Reynaud resigned on June 16 and France sued for an armistice: to keep the French fleet out of British hands and to persuade the British to make peace so that he could consolidate his mastery of the Continent. "You should tell the President," Churchill cabled Lothian on June 16, that Britain is willing to release France from its obligations not to negotiate separately "provided, but only provided, that French fleet is sailed forthwith for British harbours pending negotiations." He asked Roosevelt to support the British position. Roosevelt did not need to be urged. United States Ambassador Biddle, who was with the French government in Bordeaux (Bullitt romantically having elected to stay behind in Paris), cabled Hull that Paul Baudouin, the foreign affairs minister in the new Pétain government, had formally assured him the fleet "would never be surrendered to Germany; as guarantee Admiral Darlan whose views he said are well known on this subject had been named Minister of Marine."

Roosevelt and Hull were not reassured, and Biddle was instructed to see Darlan immediately and tell him that if in pursuing an armistice the French government failed to keep the fleet out of the hands of Germany, "the French Government will permanently lose the friendship and good-will of the United States."[20]

On June 18, Hitler met Mussolini at Munich and shocked the Duce by the leniency of the armistice terms proposed for France. "I find Mussolini dissatisfied," Ciano recorded the day before the meeting. "This sudden peace disquiets him." According to the German documents about the meeting, "The Fuehrer explained in detail what a great increase in strength the French fleet would represent for England, if it were to put itself at Britain's disposal . . . the French fleet must, above all, be prevented from reaching England." It should either be neutralized in some country such as Spain or scuttled. The French fleet was indispensable to England's plan of survival, particularly to the protection of its convoys. "England was of the opinion that if she could hold out in the British Isles themselves for just one year, the war would be lost to Germany, for within that time she could count on the active cooperation of America." "Hitler makes many reservations on the desirability of destroying the British Empire," Ciano noted. "Hitler is now the gambler who has made a big scoop and would like to get up from the table, risking nothing more."[21]

Also on June 18, Churchill again spoke in the House to prepare the country for the Nazi assault. The speech was later broadcast. It was another extraordinary performance. Churchill's final sentences pealed forth with Elizabethan grandeur. The Battle of France was over, the Battle of Britain about to begin.

The whole fury and might of the enemy must very soon be turned on us. Hitler knows that he will have to break us in this island or lose the war. If we can stand up to him, all Europe may be free and the life of the world may move forward into broad, sunlit uplands. But if we fail, then the whole world, including the United States, including all that we have known and cared for, will sink into the abyss of a new Dark Age, made more sinister, and perhaps more protracted, by the lights of perverted science. Let us therefore brace ourselves to our duties, and so bear ourselves that, if the British Empire and its Commonwealth last for a thousand years, men will say, "This was their finest hour."[22]

"I think it is practically certain that the Americans will enter the war in November, and if we can last till then, all is well," Nicolson wrote to his wife. "Anyhow as a precaution, I have got the bare bodkin (lethal pills). I shall bring down your half on Sunday."

" 'Personally I feel happier now that we have no allies to be polite to and pamper.' " King George wrote Queen Mary and, adds his biographer, "in these sentiments was at one with the vast majority of his subjects." He had shooting ranges laid down in the gardens of Buckingham Palace and at Windsor, "at which he and other members of his family and his equerries practised regularly with rifles, pistols and tommy guns."[23]

On June 20, Churchill spoke at a secret session of the House (no stenographic notes were made, but Churchill's notes for the speech have survived): "If Hitler fails to invade or destroy Britain he has lost the war. . . . If we get through next three months, we get through the next three years." He spoke of the attitude of the United States. "The heroic struggle of England best chance of bringing them in. . . . A tribute to Roosevelt. It depends upon our resolute bearing and holding out until Election issues are settled there."[24]

British and American pressure on the Pétain government to keep the French fleet out of Hitler's control was unavailing. On June 22, the armistice was signed in the forest of Compiègne in the same railway car in which the Germans had surrendered in 1918. Under its terms, the French fleet was to assemble in specified ports where it would be demobilized and disarmed under German or Italian supervision. The German government piously asserted that it had no intention of using the fleet for its own purposes. When the British ambassador saw a copy of the terms, he called those dealing with the fleet "diabolically clever." What the armistice boiled down to was trusting the word of Hitler and accepting the assurances of Darlan.

"In a matter so vital to the safety of the whole British Empire we could not afford to rely on the word of Darlan," Churchill said in an ensuing war cabinet discussion over possible British attack on and destruction of France's modern battleships as insurance against their escape from Oran, Casablanca, and Dakar, ports outside German control. But Churchill, who advocated the attack, was at first opposed by most of the war cabinet as well as by the first sea lord, Sir Dudley Pound, and members of the naval staff, who believed British interests would be better served by trusting in Darlan's assurances. "A most scarifying 48 hours," Cadogan called this discussion. "Everyone all over the place and WSC endorses any wild idea."

One man did not consider it a "wild idea," and he, at the time, was the most important man on Churchill's horizon. When, two weeks later, with cabinet authorization, Churchill ordered an attack on the French fleet at Mers-el-Kebir and Oran if it refused to join the British fleet or to sail to some French port in the West Indies, Lothian, forwarding the daily military report to Roosevelt, wrote in longhand at the bottom: "You will see that Winston Churchill has taken the action in regard to the French fleet which we discussed and you approved." The British attack immobilized, except for the units at Toulon, a considerable part of the French fleet. It proves, Ciano observed to his diary, "that the fighting spirit of His British Majesty's fleet is quite alive."[25]

If Roosevelt had any doubts about Britain's pre-emptive attack, a report from Bullitt, who on July 1 finally reached Vichy, would have dispelled them. After talks with Pétain, Darlan, and other members of the new French regime, a disillusioned Bullitt wrote: "their physical and moral defeat has been so absolute that they have accepted completely for France the fate of becoming a province of Nazi Germany. Moreover in order that they may have as many companions in misery as possible they hope that England will be rapidly and completely defeated by Germany. . . . Their hope is that

France may become Germany's favorite province—a new Gau which will develop into a new Gaul."[26]

The swift disintegration of France, which a few weeks earlier had been considered by U.S. military leaders to have the most powerful land army in the world, heightened the "fortress America" psychology among U.S. military planners. On June 17, Gen. George V. Strong, head of the U.S. War Plans Division, recommended to Gen. George C. Marshall a military posture calling for a purely defensive position in the Pacific, no further aid commitments to the Allies, and concentration on hemispheric defense. "This is a recognition of the early defeat of the Allies," Strong explained, "an admission of our inability to furnish means in quantities sufficient to effect the situation and an acknowledgement that we recognize the probability that we are next on the list of victims of the Axis powers and must devote every means to prepare to meet that threat." Marshall thought the recommendations too gloomy, and he and Admiral Stark toned them down somewhat before presenting them to Roosevelt. Their proposals and Roosevelt's oral comments, jotted down by Marshall, demonstrated that Roosevelt had his own estimate of what was likely to happen and that it was more optimistic and broader-visioned than that of his military chiefs. He was determined to act on the assumption that Britain would and could hold out.

Marshall and Stark proposed that if the French fleet should pass to German control, the main United States Fleet should be transferred from Pearl Harbor, where it was meant to deter Japan, to the Atlantic. (This was before the British attack on the French fleet.)

"Yes," commented Roosevelt, "but decision as to return of the fleet from Hawaii is to be taken later."

The military chiefs recommended that the United States make no further commitments of matériel to Great Britain, and that private manufacturers should be prohibited from accepting munitions orders which would retard American procurement.

"In general, yes," but the services should "continue to search over our matériel" to see if there was something "to release . . . decision would have to depend on the situation." If "a little help" seemed likely to carry Britain through the next year, "we might find it desirable from the point of view of our defense to turn over other matériel."

The chiefs recommended occupation of Allied possessions in the Western Hemisphere if necessary to keep them out of the hands of Germany. Roosevelt agreed, but only "after consultation with, and if possible in agreement with the other American Republics."

To speed up arms production, Marshall and Stark recommended a longer work week and the establishment of two-shift and three-shift operations until more workers were trained. Roosevelt would have none of this. Until more unemployed were put to work, he would not alter the existing five-day week.

Finally, Marshall and Stark recommended military conscription, followed by complete military and naval mobilization.

Roosevelt softened "complete" to "progressive" and opposed a purely military draft outlining "at considerable length" a universal youth service program. Some would be in the army and navy, some in production work in arsenals and factories, some in mechanical training; all should be "in camp" during their service.

Marshall and Stark redrafted the proposals and handed them to Roosevelt on June 27, incorporating his suggestions and, in order to assure concerted action with other nations opposing Germany, Italy, and Japan, calling for the preparation of plans for the "almost inevitable conflict" with the totalitarian powers.[27]

Lothian must have heard of the debates among the military planners. It is difficult otherwise to explain his June 26 dispatch to Churchill reporting a wave of pessimism passing over the United States—infecting even the president—to the effect that the defeat of Britain was inevitable. He suggested a "cheering broadcast" by the prime minister. Churchill replied to Lothian:

No doubt I shall make some broadcast presently, but I don't think words count for much now. Too much attention should not be paid to the eddies of United States opinion. Only force of events can govern them. . . . Never cease to impress on President and others that, if this country were successfully invaded and largely occupied after heavy fighting, some Quisling Government would be formed to make peace on the basis of our becoming a German Protectorate. In this case the British Fleet would be the solid contribution with which this Peace Government would buy terms. Feeling in England against the United States would be similar to French bitterness against us now. We have really not had any help worth speaking of from the United States so far. We know President is our best friend, but it is no use trying to dance attendance upon Republican and Democratic Conventions. What really matters is whether Hitler is master of Britain in three months or not. I think not. But this is a matter which cannot be argued beforehand. Your mood should be bland and phlegmatic. No one is downhearted here.[28]

Was Lothian projecting on to Roosevelt and the American people his own sense of discouragement? A few days after this dispatch, Roosevelt accepted a British proposal for joint military staff talks, stipulating only that there must be no publicity in view of the presidential election. That was not the move of a leader who lacked faith in British prospects.

Donald Nelson, later head of industrial mobilization, wrote of the June, 1940, days:

Who among us except the President of the United States really saw the magnitude of the job ahead? . . . All the people I met and talked to, including members of the General Staff, the Army and Navy's highest ranking officers, distinguished statesmen and legislators, thought of the defensive program only as a means for equipping ourselves to keep the enemy away from the shores of the United States. None of us—not one that I know of except the President—saw that we might be fighting Germany and Japan all over the world. He took his stand against the advice of some of the country's best minds, but his foresight was superior than theirs, and this foresight saved us all.[29]

Chapter Ten

"Today all private plans... have been... repealed"

Henry morgenthau was at the White House on June 28. Missy LeHand stopped him, and what she said seemed to the secretary of such historical import that he picked up White House stationery and made a few notes.

Missy asked me did *I* think the Pres. was going to run. I laughed and said why ask me. She said again what did I think. I said I believed that sometime during the last thirty days he had made up his mind to run. . . . She said she hated to ask the Pres. and she really did not know herself whether he was going to run. But she did not contradict me when I said during the last 30 days he had made up his mind to run.

Some of Roosevelt's associates fixed the date of decision as June 10. That was the day of Roosevelt's "stab in the back" speech after Mussolini's entry into the war. While Churchill marveled at the president's intrepidity, risking a statement that might affront Italian-American voters on the eve of a presidential election, the prime minister "knew that Roosevelt was a most experienced American party politician, although never afraid to run risks for the sake of his resolves."

Adolf Berle was with Harry Hopkins when Roosevelt returned to the White House from Virginia. "The President was full of the élan of his Charlottesville speech," Berle recorded. "He had said for once, what really was on his mind, and what everybody knew; and he could speak frankly, and he had done so. I observed that as the situation now stood, it seemed to me that there were only two men left in the world, himself and Hitler, with a number of lesser Gauleiters in between. That, said the President, is a terrible responsibility."[1]

Edward J. Flynn, the urbane "boss" of the Bronx whose association with

Roosevelt went back to the twenties, was the professional politician most privy to Roosevelt's thinking. He dated Roosevelt's shift in feeling about a third term to the latter part of May. There is some supporting evidence in the energetic moves Roosevelt made at that time to broaden his government. After his speech to Congress calling for 50,000 planes, Roosevelt, much to the distress of New Dealers like Ickes, set about bringing into government business leaders capable of achieving his production targets. Experience in the previous war had shown him that it was one thing to call for steeply increased output and quite another to get it. Since the outbreak of the war, Roosevelt had been in close touch with Frank Knox, the Chicago publisher and 1936 Republican vice-presidential candidate, about his coming into the cabinet. He now summoned Knox to Washington to sound him out on his becoming secretary of the navy. He also asked Knox, as he had asked others, to send him lists of industrialists known for their organizing ability. These men, Roosevelt knew, would have to be appealed to on the basis of patriotic duty. And in asking them to leave distinguished law practices or powerful production jobs or lucrative positions on Wall Street, he would to some extent be limiting his own freedom with regard to staying in harness. Although some who responded to his appeal, like Henry Stimson, would have been happier if the president had read it as his duty to reject a third term, others, like Knox, felt differently, and in enlisting for the duration expected Roosevelt to do the same. In any event Roosevelt's appeal to businessmen and industrialists, Republicans and mugwumps, to lay aside partisanship and join his administration raised the question in his own conscience, if not theirs, of his right to retire in the middle of a grave national emergency.

At the first meeting of the advisory commission to the Council of National Defense, established by Roosevelt to spur the nation's economic mobilization, New Dealers Ickes and Jackson were troubled by the inclusion of great industrialists like William S. Knudsen, the General Motors production wizard, and Edward R. Stettinius, the head of U.S. Steel. "All of us realize," Ickes wrote two weeks later after a lunch attended by several New Dealers, "that the whole New Deal accomplishment to date has been placed in grave jeopardy."

Roosevelt brushed aside such qualms. Not that he was without anxiety himself. But the whole setup of the advisory commission was framed to keep the power in his own hands. He had instructed Harold D. Smith, the imperturbable director of the budget, to prepare an emergency defense organization plan that would appease "those who were yelling for industrialists" without, however, turning the government over to them. Smith returned with a commission blueprint that, as he described it, "avoided any super-government independent of the President" and that had the president "as kingpin in the organization."

"Who is our boss?" Knudsen asked at the end of the first meeting of the advisory commission. "Who is your boss?" Roosevelt echoed back. "Well, I guess I am." If industry was to cooperate in the vast preparedness program that FDR had launched, then its leaders had to be brought into the government. As for their using the commanding heights of the defense effort to undermine the New Deal, Roosevelt was, in the final analysis, in command. He did not sound like a man weary of the strains and stress of office, someone about to relinquish the reins of power.[2]

Another sign that he was persuading himself (and being persuaded) to run for office again was the startling announcement made on June 20, on the eve of the Republican convention in Philadelphia, that he was appointing to his cabinet two distinguished Republicans—Henry L. Stimson, who had been Taft's secretary of war and Hoover's secretary of state, and Col. Frank Knox, the Chicago publisher who had been one of Theodore Roosevelt's Rough Riders.

Roosevelt's most intimate associates had known for weeks that the president was casting about for replacements for Charles Edison, the secretary of the navy, and Harry Woodring, the secretary of war (Edison because he was ineffective, Woodring because he was an arch isolationist).* For the War Department post, Roosevelt had discussed, probed, and analyzed the assets and disadvantages of men as various as the ebullient mayor of New York Fiorello La Guardia, the former liberal Republican governor of New Hampshire Gil Winant, Knudsen, Averell Harriman, Ickes, and even the conservative Texan Jesse Jones.

Early in April, when Morgenthau had been after him to get rid of Woodring, Roosevelt had surprised him by saying that "if things get worse I will form a National Cabinet," and a few weeks later, on the heels of the debacle in Norway, had indicated he was thinking of Stimson as a replacement for Woodring. "And you tell me," Morgenthau's wife commented, "the President isn't interested in re-election if he has Stimson in mind?"[4]

As for the navy, Roosevelt first asked Knox, then half promised it to Bullitt, but in the end decided that Knox would add more strength to his administration. Getting rid of Edison presented no problem. The president arranged with Frank Hague, the mayor of Jersey City and powerful "boss" of New Jersey, to nominate Edison for governor. But Woodring was a different matter. He had potent political allies and clung to his job. When Roosevelt finally did request his resignation, isolationists immediately charged that Woodring had been ousted because he refused to allow the transfer to the Allies of military equipment which he believed was needed by the United States Army. Sen. Bennett Clark, calling Woodring the "biggest man in America," suggested that he might easily emerge as the Democratic candidate

---

* In September, 1937, Woodring sent Roosevelt a long memorandum on "An American National Policy That Is Unqualifiedly Pro-American," and the first point was: "It is evident that the influences which led America into the World War are again at work. The arguments used are somewhat altered. The objective is the same—to commit the U.S. to the employment of armed force to any extent necessary to support British policy in the present world situation. The proponents of this policy assume that the fate of America depends upon that of the British Empire. They do not know and they do not enquire what sacrifices in American life and resources will be involved." The collapse of France and Hitler's domination of Europe did not alter Woodring's view.[3]

for president. A few weeks later Woodring was denouncing a draft bill, introduced at the behest of General Marshall, calling it unwarranted and unjustified by military necessity, a measure that "smacks of totalitarianism," imposed on Marshall by Roosevelt.

In contrast to Woodring, both Stimson and Knox, in speeches two days before their appointments, had called for compulsory military service. Knox, in addition, urged an army of a million men, American control of the Atlantic, construction of the most powerful air force in the world, and the dispatch of as many planes as possible to the British. Stimson, in his speech at New Haven, urged abrogation of the neutrality act: not only should the United States send Britain munitions and supplies, but, if necessary, the U.S. Navy should convoy them. He and Knox would be powerful allies, not only against the isolationists, but against the military chiefs. (Marshall, when his opinion was solicited by Roosevelt, that same day had disapproved of the release of any flying fortress bombers to the British.)

It was indicative of the president's private thinking (although not yet his declared public policy) that the two most isolationist members of the cabinet were replaced by men who were more militantly interventionist than any member of his official family except Morgenthau. It was a characteristic Roosevelt stratagem: the interventionist impetus of his government was invigorated, but not in a way the isolationists could effectively challenge. The British were enthusiastic about the appointments. "Mr. Stimson could hardly be more interventionist and Mr. Knox could hardly be more bellicose," a member of the American department minuted. "With such protagonists we hardly need propagandists," commented another.[5]

Alfred M. Landon, the Republican presidential candidate in 1936, whistling in the dark, said that Roosevelt's appointment of Stimson and of Knox, his own running mate of 1936, meant that the president would not run for a third term. When Felix Belair of the *New York Times* put that comment up to Roosevelt, the press corps exploded in laughter while Roosevelt kept his own counsel, benignly disavowing that he was moved by anything but patriotism. By the end of June, Roosevelt was meeting with Democratic party leaders like Ed Flynn, Frank Walker of Montana, who would become chairman of the Democratic National Committee and postmaster general, and Mayor Edward J. Kelly of Chicago, whose clearance he had obtained before appointing Knox. Almost daily he discussed political strategy with Harry Hopkins, who was living at the White House and who regularly lunched with Mrs. Roosevelt and spent the evening with the president.

Also, by the end of June, the Republican convention had met and, to the astonishment of the political world, had nominated Wendell Willkie, a former Democrat and utility magnate, a man of great personal charm and rugged strength, and an advocate of aid to Britain. That was not emphasized at the time. However, the British embassy was very aware of Willkie's position. "[Walter] Lippmann said that he thought Willkie would suit our book better as President than Roosevelt," Nevile Butler wrote John Balfour. "Reason: the real work is re-organising the industry of the country for war purposes and administering it. The New Deal had shown conclusively in 7 years that they don't understand administration."

"Nothing so extraordinary has ever happened in American politics," noted Ickes about the Willkie phenomenon. "You are the only one who can beat Willkie," Justice Douglas advised Roosevelt, "he will be a tough campaigner." Roosevelt and his cabinet, meeting after the Republican convention, concurred unanimously that the Republicans had nominated their strongest possible ticket. Far from dismaying Roosevelt, it added to the zest of the battle ahead. "The President is the natural leader in such a fight," observed Ickes, "and the best possible leader. It is heartening that apparently he is preparing for such a fight and is looking forward to it with keen anticipation."[6]

The abandonment of the two-term tradition bothered Roosevelt. He would like to have it manifest for the purposes of history and his own conscience that he was accepting a call. But Archibald MacLeish, to whom Justice Frankfurter turned for suggestions for Roosevelt's acceptance speech, thought it a mistake. "The more I turn it over on my tongue the more certain I am that the President should not 'accept a call.' Undoubtedly the actual truth is that he will be doing exactly that. But to put it that way is to lead with the chin. I can see the cartoons from here."[7]

To some, Roosevelt appeared to verge on the disingenuous. On July 9, six days before the opening of the Democratic convention in Chicago, the president had his closest political associates to dinner. He invited those present—Hopkins, Flynn, Walker, Mayor Kelly, and Sen. James Byrnes of South Carolina—to discuss convention strategy. According to Byrnes (whose account cannot be fully credited because when he wrote it he was bitterly hostile to Roosevelt), the president began the discussion with a reference to the pressures on him to run for a third term and his own misgivings, as well as those of some of the leaders of the party, about doing so. He disliked to break tradition, he told the group, but the fact remained that he had failed to develop anyone else in the party who he thought could win. Under the circumstances, he did not know whether to permit his name to be advanced at the convention and requested the opinion of those present.

A privately skeptical Byrnes found it difficult to credit Roosevelt with sincerity. "I thought that he had perhaps become a little frightened about the third term issue and wanted to be 'persuaded' to make the race." Byrnes reminded the president that he had in effect drafted men like Knudsen and that his retirement now to Hyde Park would be contrary to the spirit of his appeal to the patriotism of such men to serve because of the national peril. Roosevelt "professed" to be impressed by that argument, Byrnes added cynically. "In any event after general discussion during which the President expressed some doubt about whether he could be elected because of the widespread feeling against a third term he said he would make the race."[8]

Judge Samuel I. Rosenman, Roosevelt's principal speech writer, arrived at the White House the next day. He was to live there throughout the convention. Hopkins brought the judge up to date and informed him that "the Boss" was determined to send a message to the convention to be read at its opening, releasing the delegates committed to him. "The President has never had, and has not today, any desire or purpose to continue in the office of President, to be a candidate for that office, or to be nominated by the Convention for that office," the message as reshaped by Rosenman read, and the delegates were "free to vote for any candidate." At Chicago, the group that had met at the White House (and whose chief link with the president was over a direct line that ended up in the hotel bathroom of Harry Hopkins, who was the president's personal representative in Chicago) advised urgently against that message being sent. The delegates were in a restless, refractory mood, they warned. "The President insisted on sending the message," Rosenman wrote. "I have never seen the President more stubborn."

When Sen. Alben Barkley, at the end of his address as permanent chairman, transmitted Roosevelt's message, Ickes was as derisory as Byrnes had been at the July 9 dinner. He was disaffected anyway because Roosevelt's personal representative at the convention was Hopkins and not he, and Roosevelt's choice for vice-president was Wallace and not he. "If an antagonist of the President" had been in the chair, he commented caustically, "he might have turned the convention against the President because what Barkley said on behalf of the President was ambiguous although any knowing person could see at once that he was leaving the door wide open."[9]

Why was Roosevelt so insistent on the message? He was not an autocrat or of dictatorial bent. He believed, and he wanted it made evident to all, that the catastrophes to which he was responding by accepting a third-term nomination were those to which his countrymen were responding by offering him that nomination. His decision to run for an unprecedented third term had to have a democratic sanction for his conscience and strong sense of tradition to rest easy. He would bring it all into focus in his acceptance speech.

But there was a moment still ahead in the convention when it was touch and go as to whether he would accept the nomination that the convention tendered him by the overwhelming vote of Roosevelt 946 ½, Farley 72 ½, Garner 61, and Tydings 9 ½. The crisis arose over the maneuvers of the Farley-Garner forces to prevent the nomination of Roosevelt's choice of Henry Wallace as his running mate. "Well, I suppose all the conservatives in America are going to bring pressure on the convention to beat Henry," Roosevelt commented to Judge Rosenman, who informed him at breakfast of a swelling mood of ugliness at Chicago against Wallace. "The fellow they really want is either Jesse [Jones of Texas] or [Speaker William B.] Bankhead [of Alabama]. I'm going to tell them that I won't run with either of those men or with any other reactionary—I've told them that before and I'll tell them again."

That was at breakfast. All day the reports came in from Chicago of the sordid atmosphere at the convention as factions intrigued against Wallace. Phoning from Chicago, Frances Perkins got Eleanor Roosevelt, who was at Hyde Park, to fly out there to help lift the convention out of the gutter. Mrs. Roosevelt's speech did precisely that, reminding the delegates that whoever became president faced a heavier responsibility, perhaps, than any man has ever faced before in this country. . . . You cannot treat it as you would an ordinary nomination in an ordinary time. . . . So each and every one of you who give him this responsibility, in giving it to him assume for yourselves a very grave responsibility because you will make the campaign. You will have to rise above considerations which are narrow and partisan. This is a time when it is the United States we fight for.

"Thanks to her," the *Daily News* reported, "the roll call began in a fairly dignified atmosphere."[10]

The responsibility Mrs. Roosevelt had stressed did not trouble the president as long as he would have the power with which to fulfill it. He did not want to be a third-term president, impotent to carry out his programs. There were "two kinds of Presidents," Roosevelt told Ickes a couple of weeks earlier, "one like himself who kept track of everything and the other like Woodrow Wilson, who did not know what was going on but who let his Cabinet run the show." Either he was going to "run the show" or he did not wish to continue as president. That was the issue, as he saw it, in the efforts of the party conservatives to deny the nomination to Wallace.

Back in the Oval Room at the White House where the president's official family had assembled to listen with him to the proceedings, it did not seem to Roosevelt that Wallace's victory was assured. Byrnes had telephoned to warn that "a real fight" was shaping up. Byrnes should tell the delegates, Roosevelt had snapped, that if there was such a lack of confidence in him that the delegates would deny him the traditional prerogative of naming his running mate, he would not accept the nomination for president. Now he sat at a card table grimly waiting for the vice-presidential roll call, listening to the radio, and playing a game of solitaire. He did not like what he heard and suddenly turned to Missy, asked her for a pad and pencil, and then proceeded to cover five pages with his strong, bold handwriting. As everyone in the room wondered what was going on, he handed the pad to Judge Rosenman with instructions to "smooth it out." This is what Rosenman, joined outside by Missy and "Pa" Watson, read:

July 18, 1940

Members of the Convention:

In the century in which we live the Democratic Party has received the support of the electors only when the Party has been, with absolute clarity, the champion of progressive and liberal policies and principles of government.

The party has failed consistently when by political tricks it has been controlled by those interests, personal and financial, which think in terms of dollars instead of in terms of human values.

The Republican Party has made nominations dictated as we all know by those who put dollars ahead of human values.

The Democratic Party, as appears clear from the events of today, is divided on this fundamental issue. Until the Democratic Party makes clear its overwhelming stand in favor of liberalism, and shakes off *all* the shackles of control by conservatism and reaction, it will not continue to march to victory.

It is without question that certain influences of conservatism and reaction

have been busily engaged in the promotion of discord since this Convention convened.

That being the fact and the case, I in all honor cannot and will not condone or
go along with the fact of that party dissension.

It would be best not to straddle ideals.

It would be best for America to have the fight out.

Therefore, I give the Democratic Party the opportunity to make that historic
decision by declining the honor of the nomination for the presidency. I so do.

This robust message was never sent. By the time it was in final form and
typed, Wallace had been nominated and the copies of the message were
whisked out of sight by an alert secretary. But the document is more than an
historical oddity.[11] On the surface it seemed to demonstrate Roosevelt's attachment to the progressive policies with which his administration was identified. That was partly the case. Yet a few weeks earlier he had tried to persuade
Cordell Hull, decidedly not a New Dealer, to run with him as vice-president.
That would have been a strong ticket and undoubtedly that was the compelling consideration with Roosevelt. But Hull was a conservative. Why, then,
was he making such an issue of Wallace? The forces aligned against Wallace
—Farley, Garner, Bankhead, and Jesse Jones—not only were ideologically
conservative but challenged Roosevelt's control of the party and of Congress.
The president did not want the nomination if the Democratic party was not
prepared to support him and his policies, and that is what defiance of his
wishes to have Wallace as a running mate would have signified. And so he
prepared to unfurl the old, tattered New Deal banners.

How much of a New Dealer was he on the eve of acceptance of the third-
term nomination? Back in September, 1939, Early had put out the word that
the "brain trust is out of the window." And while Roosevelt had denied the
story, saying the press had made it up, there was, as the convention neared,
less evidence of Tom Corcoran and Ben Cohen working as agents of the
White House. They had been deeply involved in the third-term drive and the
preparations for the convention—that is, up to the point when Roosevelt decided to run for a third term. Then they were frozen out (much to the embarrassment of Rosenman, who had worked with them in the preparation of
many Roosevelt speeches). They had become objectionable symbols to the
organization men. Even loyalists like Ed Flynn and Frank Walker made it
clear to Roosevelt that they did not want Corcoran and Cohen mixing in party
affairs—and Roosevelt went along.

Yet there was another side to the portrait of this complex and subtle
man. In the congenial, relaxed surroundings of Hyde Park two weeks before
the opening of the convention, a reporter had asked Roosevelt to discuss his
long-range peace objectives. The president thought out loud, groping his way
toward a formula that would be widely understood. He associated aggression
with systems of government—German, Italian, Russian—that had abolished
freedom in the interests of efficiency. Basic to a peaceful world, he thought,
was the acceptance of "certain freedoms." He identified five that day; later
they would be reduced to four: "freedom of information . . . because you

will never have a completely stable world without freedom of knowledge, freedom of information"; "freedom of religion"; "freedom of expression"; "freedom from fear, so people won't be afraid of being bombed from the air or attacked . . . in other words disarmament"; and "freedom from want."[12] He might sidestep the New Deal label as a symbol that had become a political liability and fight shy of New Dealers because the professional politicians, whose support he needed, insisted upon it, but Roosevelt's definition of peace objectives was that of a democratic leader who understood the forces loose in contemporary society and who sensed sympathetically the rising expectations of the common man.

Roosevelt knew that at that moment the important thing in the scheme of world politics was his renomination and re-election. That now had the highest priority. That governed him, too, much to Hull's unhappiness, in the writing of the foreign-affairs plank. At the Republican convention, the isolationists had succeeded in writing into the platform, as the German chargé cheerfully boasted, the declaration that the United States "will not let itself become entangled in a European war. Nothing has leaked out about the assistance we rendered in this."

Roosevelt was determined not to permit the "war party" label to be pinned on him and the Democrats. How much so became clear to the budget director Harold Smith in the course of helping to draft Roosevelt's request in early July for a new defense authorization, the third in two months, this one for $5 billion. Smith and his associates proposed inclusion of the following statement:

That we are opposed to war is known not only to every American, but to every Government in the World. That we will not use our arms in a war of aggression is known not only to every American but to every Government in the World.

Roosevelt revised the last sentence to read:

That we will not use our arms in a war of aggression, that we will not wage war in Europe, Africa, or Asia is known not only to every American but to every country in the World.

Smith, joined by Harry Hopkins, strenuously objected to Roosevelt's formulation. As worded, they pointed out, it was practically a commitment that Japan could do anything it liked in Asia without interference from the United States. Even in a war of defense it might be necessary to wage war in another hemisphere. Hopkins persuaded Roosevelt to make some change. But the final draft, when Steve Early showed it to Smith the next morning, read:

We will not use our arms in a war of aggression; we will not send our men to take part in European Wars.

This "appeared to be a concession to the isolationists," Smith sadly noted.[13]

A similar issue now arose at Chicago. Isolationists managed to prevail in a subcommittee of Sen. Robert Wagner's platform committee and came out with the plank:

We will not participate in foreign wars.
We will not send our armed forces to fight in lands across the seas.

Hull, deeply upset by this development, asked his representative at the convention, Breckinridge Long, "to try to get it softened to the point where it would not preclude our use of naval or air forces abroad if necessary—not that he wanted to use them but for the effect on Germany and Japan he did not want a commitment which would announce in advance that they could do as they pleased with American rights." There were many discussions back and forth between Roosevelt and Hull in Washington and Hopkins and Byrnes in Chicago. The latter, in turn, were holding discussions with two isolationist leaders at the convention, Sen. Burton K. Wheeler of Montana and Sen. David I. Walsh of Massachusetts. Wheeler and Walsh threatened that isolationists would bolt the convention if the formula were softened or rejected. Roosevelt settled the matter by adding the phrase "except in case of attack," and that was the way the convention adopted it. Whatever foreign-policy plank was adopted, the president reassured Hull, he would be defining U.S. foreign policy in his acceptance and other speeches. "The foreign policy plank," Lothian cabled London, "emasculated to placate the powerful Senator Wheeler of Montana, was little better than the Republican, which it closely resembles and fortunately neither will much matter."[14]

It was half past midnight when Roosevelt, via radio, delivered his acceptance speech from the White House to the delegates in Chicago. The delegates cheered it all, but it was the personal notes to which they were most responsive. No call of party alone, FDR said firmly, would have prevailed upon him to accept re-election to the presidency. But when he, as president, was drafting people into the service of the nation, could he shoulder less than his share?

Lying awake, as I have, on many nights, I have asked myself whether I have the right, as Commander-in-Chief of the Army and Navy, to call on men and women to serve their country or to train themselves to serve, and, at the same time, decline to serve my country in my own personal capacity, if I am called upon to do so by the people of my country.

This was not "an ordinary war." Successful armed aggression dominated the world,

successful armed aggression, aimed at the form of Government, the kind of society that we in the United States have chosen and established for ourselves. . . . Like most men of my age, I had made plans for myself, plans for a private life of my own choice and for my own satisfaction, a life of that kind to begin in January, 1941. These plans, like so many other plans, had been made in a world which now seems as distant as another planet. Today all private plans, all private lives, have been in a sense repealed by an overriding public danger. In the face of that public danger all those who can be of service to the Republic have no choice but to offer themselves for service in those capacities for which they may be fitted.

Those, my friends, are the reasons why I have had to admit to myself, and now to state to you, that my conscience will not let me turn my back upon a call to service.

Roosevelt realized that the convention, and the events preceding the convention, did not constitute a "draft."

The right to make that call rests with the people through the American method of a free election. Only the people themselves can draft a President. If such a draft should be made upon me, I say to you in the utmost simplicity, I will, with God's help, continue to serve with the best of my ability and with the fullness of my strength.[15]

The British press, reflecting the national mood, officials, and private citizens, jubilated in Roosevelt's renomination. "People felt as relieved," wrote *New Yorker* correspondent Mollie Panter-Downes, "as though a public-spirited and kindly neighbor had decided that perhaps he wouldn't move out of the district after all. The President's personal popularity and the trust which millions of English place in him are immense."[16]

The German press was instructed to refrain from comment, but the foreign office was under no illusions about the danger that Roosevelt's renomination represented to Germany's ambitions. "Never before has Roosevelt in a speech or other utterance spoken so plainly and undisguisedly about the aims and intentions of his foreign policy," former Ambassador Hans Dieckhoff wrote of Roosevelt's acceptance speech in a memorandum in the German foreign office.

The President points with pride to the fact that he had at an early date taken a stand against these [totalitarian] countries, that he had encouraged and strengthened resistance against them and had always stood for the view that in dealing with them the proper course was one not of yielding and appeasement but only resistance. He calls this policy striving to preserve the peace, while it was actually encouragement of the encirclement of Germany and incitement to opposition, that is to war.

Persistent continuation of such incitement is one of the chief aims of this speech, at least of the part dealing with foreign policy. England is to be prevented from changing her course, English resistance is to be strengthened and the war is to be continued. . . . Never has Roosevelt's complicity in the outbreak and the prolongation of this war come out so clearly as in the speech of July 19. The speech shows how correctly we have always judged Roosevelt and proves how baseless was Sumner Welles' remark to the Fuehrer in the conversation of March 2, that Roosevelt was no enemy of Germany.[17]

Chapter Eleven

The Two Men Compared

ROOSEVELT'S acceptance speech on July 19, Mollie Panter-Downes wrote in her *New Yorker* Letter from London, "effectually drowned out the second oration of the day, Hitler's address to the Reichstag, which to most listeners sounded like the old, old story cooked up again—the denunciation of democratic warmongers, the last appeal to Britain to stop an unnecessary war, and the familiar attack on Mr. Churchill." With Roosevelt renominated and Churchill firmly installed as prime minister, the English-speaking democracies were now headed by men every bit as charismatic, stubborn, eloquent, and wily as the totalitarian despots; they both possessed what David Lilienthal has called "a kind of historic purposefulness."[1]

Churchill was sixty-five, Roosevelt fifty-eight. There were resemblances and contrasts in their styles of leadership. Both had been shaped by turn-of-the-century societies that were fast disappearing—Churchill by a tightly knit aristocracy that for several hundred years had ruled a vast empire in the name of king and country; Roosevelt by a WASP elite, more dispersed than the British, without a monarch on whom to focus its loyalties, but just as self-confidently the governing class of a puissant nation.

Both enjoyed and were skilled in the uses of power. Roosevelt, coming to office in the great national crisis of the depression, had declared that "I shall ask the Congress for broad executive powers to wage a war against the emergency as great as the power that would be given to me if we were in fact invaded by a foreign foe." The nation and Congress had given him the power, and he had used it. And when war had broken out in September, 1939, even though the United States was not directly involved, he had immediately asked the Department of Justice to list the powers conferred upon the president by the Proclamation of a National Emergency which two days later he issued in limited form. Churchill, summoned to office in the middle of a great catastrophe, bid Parliament give him vast emergency powers, which it did; and by becoming defense minister as well as prime minister, he centralized the conduct of the war in his hands.

The recourse to emergency powers to deal with a crisis bespoke an energizing spirit as well as a policy. Col. E. W. Starling, the head of the White House Secret Service detail, described the startling invigoration of the White House on Inauguration Day, 1933, between the time he escorted the Herbert Hoovers to the railroad station and returned to find it "transformed during my absence into a gay place, full of people who oozed confidence." In the next "hundred days," the spacious hall outside the president's bedroom in the upstairs living quarters of the White House saw huddles of excited and dignified gentlemen waiting to confer with a president still in bed, a navy cape thrown over his shoulders, cigarette holder poised at a jaunty angle. The visitors wanted consents, demurrals, and commands, which he was rarely reluctant to issue. This was in the morning. At midnight the same groups, now in dinner jackets, were in the president's Oval Study, while Eleanor Roosevelt, having said good night to their dinner guests, excitedly awaited the end of her husband's meetings so that she might go in to say good night—and also to find out what new vast plan had been launched. The scene was to be re-enacted time after time in moments of crisis and never more so than in the recent peril-laden weeks attendant upon the collapse of France.[2]

Churchill had a similar ability to infuse administration with his own optimism and energy. John Colville, Neville Chamberlain's assistant private secretary who had continued on at Number 10 Downing Street with Churchill (whose arrival Colville had viewed with a "cold chill"), was turned into an idolator within a fortnight, stirred by Churchill's ceaseless outflow of minutes and questions to which the red tag "Action This Day" was attached. Regular hours and country week ends ended. An administration whose pace had scarcely quickened from peacetime was galvanized, "respectable civil servants were actually to be seen running along the corridors." After six weeks of Churchill's leadership, the *Economist,* voice of the establishment, exulted that "the spirit of Mr. Churchill's administration is as different from Mr. Chamberlain's as petroleum is from bilge water."[3]

For a time Churchill's efforts to get his cabinet colleagues and top civil servants to adjust to his pace and working habits almost produced revolt. "The meeting Winston called for 6:30 was put off until 10:30," complained Halifax, "quite intolerable, but one must acquiesce during these two or three days. After that I shall tell him that if he wants midnight meetings he can have them without me." Later, Halifax added wearily, "I am seeking to organize a rebellion with Neville on the subject." On the way back from lunch in mid-July Cadogan met a "Miss X—employed at No. 10 since Lloyd George's days. Asked about her present turbulent conditions of work, she described Winston's late meetings as the 'Midnight Follies!' " Cadogan's great fear was that "Winston will build up a 'Garden City' at No. 10 of the most awful people—including Brendan Bracken." This was a reference to Lloyd George's bypassing of the regular departments by the use of his own men whom he housed in a temporary building in the garden at Number 10 Downing Street—an administrative technique not unlike Roosevelt's recourse to New Deal loyalists like Hopkins, Berle, Corcoran, and Cohen, or Treasury

Secretary Morgenthau's, to push the War and Navy Departments. Cadogan, wrote David Dilks, the editor of Sir Alexander's tart-spoken diaries, "quickly came to place Churchill in a class apart from any statesman he ever served." But his initial reactions to Churchill's methods of administration were caustic. "Told [Halifax] this can't go on. No. 10 is like behind the scenes at the circus and every crank in the world is getting hold of Prime Minister and getting half-baked decisions. I won't go on unless this is stopped." Similarly, Harold Ickes complained of "the back door" to the White House provided by Eleanor Roosevelt.[4]

The military professionals likewise reacted with dismay to Churchill's methods "because the smooth working of the machine was upset" and the flow of minutes and questions "fitted into no Committee pattern." Gen. "Pug" Ismay, who had become Churchill's chief liaison officer with the military staffs, "had to be there constantly and to make his presence felt, and to make sure that anything with a military flavour was safely channeled into the right machine. He had to jostle the friends and adherents of Churchill who were at first like bees around a honey pot."[5]

Both Churchill and Roosevelt understood that information was not only essential to wise judgment, but conferred authority on its possessor. Churchill, out of government in the thirties, had managed to keep himself almost as well informed on defense and foreign policy as the ministers, and as minister would not permit anyone else access to the red dispatch case to which he had the key. Both men refused to be confined to official channels in obtaining their information, although Roosevelt, perhaps because of his crippled state, was in this regard more a sinner, as officialdom viewed it, than Churchill. He not only read the State Department's cables, but he carried on a personal correspondence with some of his ambassadors, to which Hull and Welles might or might not be privy. Bullitt's letters to the president were fuller and franker than his cables to the department. Nor did Roosevelt's skimpy replies dampen his ardor as a correspondent, any more than it did Felix Frankfurter's. Information and advice poured in on him from all sides, a phenomenon that was the more remarkable because the president gave so little of himself in return as regards his innermost thoughts and purposes, leaving it to his correspondents to assume that these were sympathetic to their own. In this he differed markedly from Churchill, whose inner being demanded exposition whether in letter, column, book, or speech.

The administrative methods of Roosevelt and Churchill were unorthodox, sometimes untidy. Their associates would later agree that neither Churchill nor Roosevelt was a good administrator. Elder-statesman Henry Stimson admired Henry Morgenthau, whose point of view he found most sympathetic to his own. Yet Stimson was aghast at the way the treasury secretary encroached upon the jurisdictions of the Departments of State and War. But Morgenthau did so at the instigation of Roosevelt, who was dissatisfied with the sluggish responsiveness of those departments to his policy of aid to Britain. The argument Roosevelt used with Adolf Berle to persuade the latter to come back to Washington to work for him at the State Department was that the department needed "a Brain Truster. Hull was magnificent on principle but timid; Sumner was fundamentally a 'career man.' "

Roosevelt's mental picture of the State Department as a haven of routineers and paper shufflers was reflected in his exasperated handling of a dispute between his budget-management people and the department over the latter's surrendering some space to the White House. Roosevelt was sure the State Department could find space by simply packing off musty old files to a warehouse. The State Department balked until suddenly one day Hull was informed over the telephone that the president was on his way over. Hull and Welles had scarcely arrived on the sidewalk when the president's limousine drew up. As Roosevelt was transferred to his wheel chair, he indicated that he wanted to make a personal inspection of the State Department precincts. Welles, sartorially splendid and erect and barely able to conceal his distaste for the whole proceedings, accompanied the president down the lofty-ceilinged, gloomy corridors. The president, as if he were inspecting the kettles in a ship's galley, picked at random the offices he wished to enter, had himself wheeled in, and opened the file drawers himself. Welles, in a gesture of passive resistance and disapproval, remained outside. The first file Roosevelt opened dealt with wild horses in China. Was that considered a "current" file? the president wanted to know. Roosevelt did not open up all the rooms, commented budget director Harold Smith, but enough "to give him a view of the space available and the situation with respect to files." Smith was alternately amused, sympathetic, "when I saw the face of Cordell Hull and Summer Welles," and admiring of Roosevelt's stamina. "Few men without his physical handicap would have had the energy after a hard day's work to undertake such an inspection."

"The Treasury," Roosevelt once complained to Marriner Eccles, head of the Federal Reserve Board, "is so large and far-flung, and ingrained in its practices that I find it almost impossible to get the action and results I want— even with Henry there. But the Treasury is not to be compared with the State Department. . . . But the Treasury and the State Department put together are nothing as compared with the Na-a-vy. The admirals are really something to cope with—and I should know. To change anything in the Na-a-vy is like punching a feather bed. You pound it with your right and you pound it with your left until you are finally exhausted and then you find the damn bed just as it was before you started punching."[6]

Churchill's exasperation with government departments could be equally pronounced. "He suspected them of pursuing their own policy, irrespective of what the Government might wish, and he mistrusted their judgment," wrote John Colville. Colville once asked Churchill which department the latter disliked most—the treasury or the foreign office. "After a moment's thought, [Churchill] replied: 'The War Office!' " "He greatly distrusted the inertia and orthodoxy of the Government Departments and the Services," Sir Ian Jacob, the military assistant secretary to the war cabinet, wrote of Churchill's attitude toward administration. Issues of administration are inseparable from those of policy, especially under strong leaders. "We were too inclined to respect order and method and to discount initiative and leadership," Sir Ian acknowledged.

In the end Churchill worked out a *modus vivendi* with the professional staffs: they submitted to him. The consequence was indirectly summed up by Churchill in an expressive statement about his communications with Roosevelt:

My relations with the President gradually became so close that the chief business between our two countries was virtually conducted by these interchanges between him and me. . . . As Head of the State as well as Head of the Government, Roosevelt spoke and acted with authority in every sphere, and carrying the War Cabinet with me, I represented Great Britain with almost equal latitude.[7]

In December 1939, Ickes had predicted that if Europe were to blaze up, Roosevelt would run for a third term because, "with the keen interest that he has in foreign affairs and the grasp that is his, he would regret having to surrender command to another in such a situation." FDR's correspondence with Churchill was his main level for effectuating that command.[8]

An old Chinese proverb holds that "the great man is a public misfortune," and Lord Acton, in his reflections on the corruptions of power, thought that "great men are almost always bad men." Sociologist Robert Michels, in his classic work on "the iron law of oligarchy," in which he contended that power "issuing from the people . . . ends by raising itself above the people," also argued that "the consciousness of power always produces an undue belief in personal greatness" and, to support this view, quoted Bakunin: "the possession of power transformed into a tyrant even the most devoted friend of liberty."

Yet a striking characteristic of both Roosevelt and Churchill was the sheer irrelevance of such gloomy maxims to their employment of power. This was partly due to the workings of the British and American systems of government, in which each sought to balance chastening mechanisms on leaders with grants of authority that would enable them to manage the national estate with energy, coherence, and purpose. This characteristic was also partly due to Churchill's and Roosevelt's temperaments and their ways of relating to the people and to their associates. Mussolini was contemptuous of the Italian people. "It is material that I lack," he complained to Ciano. "Even Michelangelo had need of marble to make statues. . . . A people who for sixteen centuries have been an anvil cannot become a hammer within a few years." Hitler extolled the Germans as a race of supermen, but did not allow them to shape their own destiny. Roosevelt's reference point as to what action was "feasible" in the national interest, even in the precarious months before Pearl Harbor, was always the American people rather than Congress or an elite group of advisers. He was a master at "shaping and expanding" the dimensions of the feasible, Abe Fortas has pointed out, but he rarely moved beyond them. And Churchill, when he was later praised for his indomitability in the months that Britain stood alone, insisted it was the pluck of the British people. "I was only privileged to give the roar."[9]

Both Roosevelt and Churchill had to be in command, but neither equated cooperation with sycophancy. "Always stand up to him," Halifax advised Cadogan. "He hates doormats. If you begin to give way he will simply wipe his feet upon you." It was a formidable matter to stand up to Churchill. "The strength of his powers of persuasion had to be experienced to realise the strength that was required to counter it," wrote Gen. Sir Alan Brooke (later Lord Alanbrooke), commander of the British force that was sent back to France after Dunkirk and, later, Chief of the Imperial General Staff. "The P.M. does not want you to do that," General Dill ordered him over the phone from London. "What the hell does he want?" Brooke fired back. "He wants to speak to you." Churchill took the phone and they argued back and forth for almost half an hour, Brooke almost losing his temper when some of Churchill's arguments against evacuation suggested the general might be suffering from "cold feet." Finally, Churchill subsided and told an exhausted Brooke, "All right, I agree with you." Once, after a row with Brooke, Churchill declared that the field marshal, who by then had been promoted to CIGS, hated him and had to go. Ismay went to Brooke to make peace between them. "I don't hate him, I love him; but when the day comes that I tell him that he is right when I believe him to be wrong, it will be time for him to get rid of me."[10]

In the hectic conferences after May 10, when Roosevelt was preparing his first huge defense request to Congress, General Marshall asked Morgenthau's advice on how to get the president to pay as much attention to the army's requests as he did to the navy's (the president so completely identified with the navy that in talking of it he used the term "we"; but the army was "they"). "When you go to see the President," Morgenthau counseled, "stand right up and tell him what you think and stand right there. There are too few people who do it and he likes it." After the meeting, Morgenthau added in his diary entry that he had been "tremendously impressed with General Marshall. He stood right up to the President." Roosevelt had first opposed Marshall's requests, partly, Morgenthau thought, because the army memorandum had taken him "entirely unawares." When Morgenthau spoke out strongly for the army, the president, "with a sort of smile and a sneer," had said, "I am not asking you. I am telling you." "Well, I still think you are wrong,"' Morgenthau persisted. "Well, you filed your protest," Roosevelt curtly ended the discussion, but, added Morgenthau, before the meeting was over the President had accepted "everything in Marshall's program."

Among Roosevelt's responsibilities under the Constitution was that of commander in chief. In this area, as in others, he used the powers of his office to the full, in several cases overruling the views of his chiefs of staff. Over the protests of the army and navy chiefs, who feared unbalanced rearmament, he had ordered the increase of war-plane production facilities—to 10,000 combat planes a year in November, 1938, and to 50,000 in May, 1940. His insistence in June, 1940, on giving all-out military aid to Britain was again over the objections of the military heads of the army and navy who believed that Britain was doomed. He ordered that the fleet be kept at Pearl Harbor to deter the Japanese, despite protests from the admiral commanding the Pacific Fleet. The policy of steadily pushing the United States frontier eastward in the Atlantic was his. But unlike Churchill, Roosevelt preferred to get his way by in-direction instead of argument or confrontation with his advisers. He let the logic of events do the work of persuasion, but he could be firm with his Joint Chiefs when his mind was made up. "I am a pig-headed Dutchman, Bill," he said to Admiral Leahy, whom he would later appoint as his liaison officer with the chiefs of staff, "and I have made up my mind about this. We are going ahead with this and you can't change my mind."[11]

Roosevelt expected members of his official family to argue strenuously for their viewpoints, but after he had made a decision, he also expected them to go along, not to carp or sulk. Associates like Eleanor Roosevelt, Hopkins, and Morgenthau stood up to him, but in ways that the president found ac-ceptable, the most important of which was to sense when to stop. Ickes was unable to make such an accommodation. Although Roosevelt admired his pugnacity and tenaciousness when employed against Roosevelt's foes, he was less enamored of them when they were turned against him. "While I thought of making him Secretary of War last week," Roosevelt explained to Morgen-thau, "I have changed my mind because there won't be a day or two that he won't be fighting with everybody and he's doing very well at his own job."

If Ickes was too contentious, the more normal pattern among Roosevelt's associates was to hold back or to permit Roosevelt's magnetism to divert them from their purposes, if they differed from his. Roosevelt's ability to charm "the bird off the tree" was legendary among his friends and associates. The Felix Frankfurters, in the summer of 1940, adopted for the duration of the war two English children, refugees from the blitz. Soon the justice was re-galing Washington with stories about them. He would love to see these mar-velous youngsters, the president remarked. At this, shepherded by their nanny, they called at the White House. Later the justice called Roosevelt to thank him and to report that although the president had made a conquest of the girl, her younger brother was holding out. That bothered Roosevelt. "Send him over and give me half an hour with him alone," Roosevelt demanded. The idea that anyone, male or female, could resist him really disturbed him. Few people did. People would complain to Mrs. Roosevelt about a presiden-tial policy and she would arrange an appointment with the president. They would go into his study asserting that they intended to tell him exactly what they thought, and emerge later, purring contentedly, having been so beguiled by him, she would learn, that they had never voiced their disagreements at all. During a ninety-minute lunch with the president, Stimson recorded in his Diary, they had the "best talk" in months. Stimson had gone in "fully pre-pared," because the president himself "always has so many ideas that he wants to talk about that it is very hard for a visitor to get in the important positions of his own errand but this time I had a memorandum made out and I went pretty well through it—perhaps about two-thirds."[12]

The position of the president in the American system of government al-most entailed aloofness and distance. Like the British sovereign, the president personified the nation, providing a focus for its loyalties and patriotism. That alone set him apart from all other officials. A British prime minister shared the burdens of decision with his cabinet; responsibility was collective. The president's cabinet was advisory only. "The eminence of his position is so great, the calls upon him so numerous," wrote Harold Laski, a long-time observer of the American system, "that it is not easy for him to avoid a sense of profound separation from his fellows. He cannot cultivate the kind of intimacy with his critics that is born of the almost instinctive good-fellowship of the House of Commons. He is rarely dealing, either in his cabinet or in his party relations, with men to whose initimate friendship he has become accustomed by long experience."

Felix Frankfurter, a friend, incidentally, of Laski's, sensed the president's loneliness. Seek him out, he urged Henry Stimson. Talk to him alone. The president would welcome it. He had been keeping away, Stimson explained, "because I did not like to bother him. [Frankfurter] said that was wrong—that [the president] was a very lonely man and that he was rather proud and didn't like to ask people to come to him but that he was sure that he would welcome my approaches if I would make them."[13]

Powerful restraints on autocratic tendencies in their leaders were structured into both the British and American systems. The mechanisms of accountability were different in both, and the way they operated varied with the holders of the office. The British constitution was designed to enable governments to govern; the United States Constitution, drafted after the American colonists' brush with despotism, was framed to limit government. A system of checks and balances deliberately encouraged an adversary relationship between president and Congress, and even though Roosevelt's party in 1940 commanded a majority in both the Senate and House of Representatives, the president did not command that majority. He had in 1933; indeed, at that moment of economic paralysis, both parties in both houses besought him to take command and to lead. Roosevelt did; but with the passage of the emergency, Congress reasserted itself. By the end of the thirties it had become the burial ground of presidential domestic initiatives, and even in foreign affairs, its neutrality legislation had severely reined in Roosevelt's impulse to act on the Jeffersonian maxim that "the transaction of business with foreign Powers is executive altogether."

Roosevelt had certain levers of influence over Congress—patronage, party allegiances, the veto, and the appeal to public opinion—but none compared with a British prime minister's power to compel Parliament under threat of dissolution to support him. The stalemate resulting from this built-in conflict between executive and legislature led the normally sober-spoken *Economist* to write in June that "the American Constitution, which is perhaps as responsible as any other single factor for the outbreak of the war nine months ago, will continue to exert its baneful influence through the summer." "The Constitution is a disaster," commented Cadogan on Professor Whitehead's account of how American presidents were nominated and chosen. But the American system of checks and balances, of which congressional independence was a vital constitutent, was the chief check on executive despotism, if a president should be so minded. And beyond the legislature—and the judiciary, which also was independent and equal—there was, as Roosevelt had noted in his third-term acceptance speech, the ultimate safeguard against a president's subversion of the democratic process, the retribution that would fall upon him at the polls if the electorate suspected him of seeking to become a dictator.[14]

In the British system, the restraints on a strong and masterful leader like Churchill worked somewhat differently. They began with the cabinet. A prime minister was expected to submit major policy issues to the cabinet for discussion and decision, and the responsibility for those decisions was shared. During Churchill's dashes to France, he carefully referred back to the cabinet for decision the urgent French appeals for more divisions and planes, and the cabinet in London sat in almost continuous session in order to be able to return a prompt reply. The prime minister needed the consent of his colleagues on such matters, and the cabinet as a whole was answerable to the House of Commons, and, beyond the Commons (and this was the fundamental accountability), to the voters. The British system, however, was meant to facilitate strong government, and every channel of accountability contained built-in safeguards against blockage. The prime minister was usually the head of his political party. In normal circumstances it would have been under his leadership that the party gained a victory at the last general election, on the basis of which the sovereign had sent for him to form a government. He selected his cabinet; and through his control over a parliamentary majority and his power to dissolve Parliament, he had a mastery of the House of Commons that no president had of Congress.

Of course, Churchill had not become prime minister as a result of a general election, and he was the head of a coalition, not of a single-party government. The Labour and Liberal parties had named their representatives in his cabinet. "The Dictator, instead of dictating," wrote Lord Hankey impatiently on May 12, "was engaged in a sordid wrangle with the politicians of the left about the secondary offices. Neville Chamberlain was in a state of despair about it all." Hankey, not one of Churchill's admirers, saw the only hope "in the solid core of Churchill, Chamberlain and Halifax, but whether the wise old elephants will ever be able to hold the Rogue Elephant I doubt." On the Conservative benches, the loyalties still went, in early July, to Chamberlain. No Conservative prime minister, Hoare later wrote of Chamberlain, "ever had so strong a hold on his party in the House of Commons." It was only in July that loyalties shifted. For Churchill the moment was memorable. It was on July 4, when he reported to the House the doleful events surrounding the attack on the French fleet at Oran. "The House was very silent during the recital," Churchill wrote, "but at the end there occurred a scene unique in my own experience. Everybody seemed to stand up all around, cheering for what seemed a long time. Up till this moment the Conservative Party had treated me with some reserve, and it was from the Labour benches that I received the warmest welcome when I entered the House or rose on serious occasions. But now all joined in solemn stentorian accord." In Churchill, explained Ismay, "we had found a leader to match the hour . . . and it is no reflection on others to say that in less than two months he had revolutionised the situation. From the outset he had done the right thing and struck the right note."[15]

He had made himself minister of defence and had arranged to have direct access to the chiefs of staff, whose chairman he, in effect, became. He thus had gained personal command of the war-making powers of the government. "As confidence grew," wrote Churchill, "the war Cabinet intervened less actively in operational matters, though they watched them with close attention and full knowledge. They took almost the whole weight of home and party affairs off my shoulders, thus setting me free to concentrate upon the main theme." Churchill's personal correspondence with the president of the United States further fortified his control over not only war but foreign policy. He had held many great offices of state, Churchill wrote later, but freely acknowledged that he liked best being prime minister. "Power for the sake of lording over fellow creatures or adding the personal pomp, is rightly judged base. But power in a national crisis, when a man believes he knows what orders should be given, is a blessing. In any sphere of action there can be no comparison between the position of number one and number two, three, or four. . . . Ambition, not so much for vulgar ends, but for fame, glints in every mind."[16]

In Churchill's first and only novel *Savrola,* written when he was a twenty-three-year-old subaltern in India, the hero, a political man, asks himself "for what" the struggle, the labor, the constant rush? "A people's good! That, he could not disguise from himself was rather the direction than the cause of his efforts. Ambition was the motive force and he was powerless to resist it." And even at twenty-three he foresaw that ambition would be most powerfully served by the gift of words. The chapter in which Churchill of the Fourth Hussars described Savrola's mastery over his followers was entitled "The Wand of the Magician." Crowds stirred Savrola's blood. "He showed, or perhaps he feigned, some nervousness at first, and here and there in his sentences he paused as if searching for a word." His passion ignited the crowd's, but "he withheld from them the outburst of fury and enthusiasm they desired. . . . Then at last he let them go. For the first time he raised his voice, and in a resonant, powerful penetrating tone which thrilled the listeners, began the peroration of his speech."

For Roosevelt, public speaking was a skill, one he had mastered in order to get men to do his bidding; for Churchill, it was a compulsive manifestation of personality. "His ideas began to take the form of words," Churchill wrote of Savrola preparing a speech. The words began "to group themselves into sentences; he murmured to himself; the rhythm of his own language swayed him; instinctively he alliterated. Ideas succeeded one another, as a stream flows swiftly by and the light changes on its waters. He seized a piece of paper and began hurriedly to pencil notes. That was a point; could not tautology accentuate it? He scribbled down a rough sentence, scratched it out, polished it, and wrote it in again. . . . The sound would please the ears, the sense improve and stimulate their minds. What a game it was!" Critics would later say of Churchill, as Lord Esher did in 1917, that "he handles great subjects in rhythmical language, and becomes quickly enslaved by his own phrases."

For Churchill, literary composition, whether in speech or essay form, was a necessity of the spirit; for Roosevelt, it was a burden. In the early twenties, Roosevelt, recuperating from polio, found time hanging heavy on his hands. He embarked upon several writing projects: a biography of John Paul Jones ("a little volume" that would show that much of the published material about Jones was "romance") and a history of the United States. He wrote five pages of the first and fourteen of the second. The fragments are of interest not because of any distinction of style or thought but because their author became one of America's greatest presidents. Churchill, after the end of World War I, also set to work on an account of *The World Crisis*. Despite a hectic public life, he produced six volumes, a minor classic, of which John Maynard Keynes wrote that it reflected "energies of mind" and springs of "elemental emotion" in the narration of events "which are part of the lives of all of us of the war generation, but which he saw and knew much closer and clearer. . . . Mr. Churchill was, perhaps, the most acute and concentrated intelligence which saw the war at close quarters from beginning to end with knowledge of the inside facts and of the inner thoughts of the prime movers of events." This was no small praise from one of the best minds of the twentieth century. And before the 1920s were finished, Churchill had also written *A Roving Commission,* an autobiographic gem.*[17]

Roosevelt and Churchill were both good impromptu speakers, Churchill as a result of long training in the House of Commons, Roosevelt as a result of the give and take of his twice-a-week press conferences. Roosevelt had a gift for simplifying the most complex ideas of government and politics. Through his fireside chats and his flair for the homely illustration, he made the American people participants in the processes of government. A patrician accent adorned a workaday substance.

Churchill had a love for language. He was, wrote Spears, "a master at clothing with apt words any idea that crossed his mind." And. moved by emotion, which on occasion surged from him "in great torrents," he was able to hold his hearers spellbound, as he had both British and French members of the Supreme War Council in Paris during the Dunkirk days, when he brought the meeting to an end with a surge of vivid imagery. "Even if one of us is struck down, the other must not abandon the struggle. Should one of the comrades fall in the battle, the other must not put down his arms until his wounded friend is on his feet again."[18]

Churchill prepared his own speeches. Departments provided data and checked the drafts for accuracy, but the organizing intelligence and the emotion that fused the cold data into sparkling vehemence were uniquely his; nor would he permit it to be otherwise. Roosevelt knew what he wanted to say, but had neither the time nor the aptitude for the winged utterance. When Frankfurter had asked MacLeish to suggest some paragraphs that might go into Roosevelt's speech accepting a third-term nomination, the poet had done so, ending with a gentle demurral the letter transmitting his suggestions: "But

* The British title is *My Early Life.*

you see, Felix, how impossible it is to go on with this. For if ever there was a personal document it is this document of which we are thinking. It can be, if it deeply derived from the emotions and convictions of the man who speaks it, one of the most moving and convincing utterances of which history had record. It can also be something very different."

MacLeish's draft paragraphs sounded precisely the note Roosevelt had been searching for, and they were incorporated into his speech. It said what had to be said and said it well. But, as MacLeish foresaw, it was not a memorable utterance.[19]

When he was of a mind to, Roosevelt wrote with directness and force. His associates marveled at his ability to reduce bureaucratese to crispness and clarity. He used speech writers, but the policy was his; often the most striking phrases were his. His mastery of the press conference, his delight in the exchanges that took place there, indicated that he would have been able to hold his own in the House of Commons.

But still Churchill excelled as an orator and writer. Churchill had a style in which sentence, paragraph, and chapter moved with his thought and feeling, in which the phrases were apt and arresting and the imagery lush and majestic. Churchillian prose is nicely described by some phrases of Flaubert: "bombasts, lyricism, eagle flights, sonorities of phrase and the high points of ideas." For Flaubert, master of the austerely precise phrase, these were excesses to be avoided; but in a public man they represented an enviable achievement.

Churchill's facility with the pen was reflected in his administrative methods. He was, he wrote, "a strong believer in transacting official business by *The Written Word.*" During the morning session in bed, he would browse in the box of papers his secretary had left at his bedside the night before and then dictate to a secretary a flow of minutes and directives that embodied the results of "his ruminations . . . on the papers in the box or on anything which occurred to him—large or small, grave or gay." At the Admiralty his stream of memoranda had become known as "the first lord's prayers" because they often began with "Pray inform me" or "Pray why has" and usually ended in a demand for an answer by a certain time. "If the required report was a good one (and it would not necessarily be one's fault if it were not) one might get a reply in red ink—'v.g. press on.' It was like the stone thrown into the pond, the ripples go out in all directions, galvanising people at all levels to 'press on'—and they did."[20]

It was standard usage in the British government to write everything down in the form of "minutes"—a great convenience to administrators and a boon to historians. U.S. administrative policy was much looser. No minutes were kept of cabinet meetings and discussions or of important conversations, whether face to face or over the telephone. And in this regard Roosevelt was the worst sinner in his administration. Were it not for the diaries kept by others, notably those of Morgenthau, Ickes, and Stimson, much that took place at the highest levels of the United States government would have gone unrecorded.

As it is, the thoughts and feelings of Roosevelt, an extraordinarily subtle and complex man, must often be reconstructed. Where Churchill, his mind and sensibility awash in his own ideas and images, often missed the beacon lights and signals from the shores of other personalities, Roosevelt's system vibrated to those around him, registering their vulnerabilities and their strengths. Every man who talked with Roosevelt, an early observer of the New Deal commented, came away "with the belief that he has convinced the President. Actually, all that has happened is that Roosevelt has explored the dimensions and character of the interest which that man represents and which the President must reconcile with other national interests. This is not weather-cock politics; it is honest brokerage."[21]

Churchill was not a good judge of people. In his novel *Savrola,* the characters are wooden, almost cartoonlike. Historian J. H. Plumb wrote of Churchill's six-volume *Marlborough:* "If the human or political situation became complex—a mixture of conscious or unconscious motives, of good and evil, of treachery and patriotism, existing side by side—then he tended to stumble or to evade the issues. That is why the overall pictures both of Marlborough and Lord Randolph are too simple, too direct." As Lloyd George remarked to a friend who vainly urged him to accept Churchill's invitation to join the coalition cabinet: "Winston has intellectual and rhetorical power and resource but he has no psychological insight."[22]

Roosevelt's and Churchill's types of greatness are illuminated by Freud's remark in the latter's essay on Moses: "The great man influences his contemporaries in two ways: through his personality and through the ideas for which he stands"; and those ideas "may lay stress on an old group of wishes in the masses, or point to a new aim for their wishes."[23]

Roosevelt and Churchill were both charismatic personalities. But Churchill's greatness in the field of ideas rested in the perfection with which he embodied an "old group of wishes," whereas Roosevelt pointed to the new. Not that he was an originator of policies. "[Roosevelt] does not and cannot invent his policies. Instead he listens to everyone and reduces what he has heard to an action calculated to represent the public will." Of Asquith, Churchill wrote, and it was his highest encomium: "he stood firm and unflinching for King and Country." Churchill was outraged by the Oxford Union's resolution not to fight for king or country and denounced it as an "abject, squalid, shameless avowal." But in 1940, when England stood alone, his traditionalism, his patriotism, even his pugnacious advocacy of empire, turned into strengths. "I was listening to Churchill as I sat in the diplomatic gallery," wrote Soviet ambassador Ivan Maisky of Churchill's "blood, toil, tears and sweat," speech, and thought, "Yes, this is the whole Churchill, a British imperialist to the marrow of his bones—yet at this turn of history he is doing a great service."[24]

Not that Churchill was unresponsive to the social and economic ideas that have come to be associated with the "welfare state." Indeed, in 1908 and 1909, as head of the Board of Trade and allied with Lloyd George, who, as chancellor of the exchequer, represented the left wing of the Asquith cabinet, Churchill was in advance of most of his Liberal colleagues in pressing for social reforms. His speeches, collected under the title *Liberalism and the Social Problem,* were aggressively militant, almost radical: "The cause of the Liberal Party is the cause of the left-out millions. . . . We want to draw a line below which we will not allow persons to live and labour, yet above which they may compete with all the strength of their manhood." His attacks on the Tory-dominated House of Lords for interposing a veto on Liberal measures enacted by the House of Commons were fierce. Many of Churchill's speeches were avowedly aimed at keeping the trade unions from affiliating with the growing Labour party He gave free reign to his reforming impulses up to the point where the working man wanted power in his own right. In *Savrola,* the hero's campaign to overthrow Laurania's military dictatorship in the moment of victory is captured by socialist extremists who reject Savrola's counsels of moderation and his wish, in the interests of civil peace and social comity, to spare the lives of the dictator and the dictator's closest associates. In the politics of Laurania, even under the dictatorship, social amenities were preserved among the leaders; the fearsome force was the secret society of socialists, whose leaders, aims, and methods were beyond the influence of Laurania's traditional politics. *Savrola* was published in 1900. Churchill's foreboding prophecy of underground extremists capturing liberal, democratic movements was fulfilled when the Bolsheviks overthrew Kerensky. This fear of demonic forces threatening established society was always powerful with Churchill. It abetted an elitist approach to politics, a Churchillian characteristic that has been perceptively noted by Robert Rhodes James, who quotes Churchill's 1930 description of a political rally in 1900: "I must explain that in those days we had a real political democracy led by a hierarchy of statesmen, and not a fluid mass distracted by newspapers. There was a structure in which statesmen, electors and the Press all played their part."

This elitist note crept into Churchill's first appraisal of Roosevelt in 1934: "He stooped to conquer. He adapted himself to the special conditions and to the humiliations which had long obstructed the entry of the best of American manhood into the unsavory world of politics. He subscribed to the Democratic ticket and made himself the mouthpiece of party aims without losing hold upon the larger objectives of American public life." The time came when Churchill took a more benign view of the Democratic party, declaring himself in private "a Democrat in American politics" (that was almost a decade later after some gentle tutoring by such emissaries of Roosevelt as Hopkins and Harriman, not to mention Roosevelt himself). But in 1934, while hailing Roosevelt's vigorous leadership and the "renaissance of creative effort with which the name Roosevelt will always be associated," Churchill was dubious about the attempt "within the space of a few months to lift American trade unionism by great heaves and bounds to the position so slowly built up—and even then with much pain and loss—in Great Britain," and he deplored "the disposition to hunt down rich men as if they were noxious beasts." He cautioned the president against sinister forces of the sort that overtook Savrola: "To a foreign eye it seems that forces are gathering under his [Roosevelt's] shield which at a certain stage may thrust him into the background and take the lead themselves." Lloyd George, who had stronger claims than Churchill to fathering Britain's welfare state, also appraised Roosevelt's leadership in 1934. It was in the course of a visit paid to him by Adm. Cary T. Grayson, who had been Woodrow Wilson's personal physician. Lloyd George "begged" Grayson "to send [Roosevelt] a message to tell him *not* to give way to the money bags, and not, on any account to be persuaded to fire on the strikers."[25]

The contrasting attitudes of Roosevelt and Churchill toward the working class and the trade unions showed Roosevelt's openness and Churchill's resistance to social change. The unions were among Roosevelt's chief political supports. He helped them achieve their political goals, not, however, at the price of the public interest. Roosevelt regarded the presidency as expressive of that interest, an embodiment of what united rather than divided the nation. His wealthy patrician friends of childhood and youth had been habituated by family tradition, by Groton and Harvard, by the Episcopal Church and New York society, to identify the national interest with their own. And after the 1933 economic paralysis, once they recovered their nerve, they denounced Roosevelt as a traitor to his class. Yet Roosevelt did not hesitate in the sitdown strikes of the mid-thirties, when labor seemed to him to endanger the public interest, to pronounce a "plague on both your houses."

The conception of a national interest to which labor as well as business had to subordinate itself was an old one with Roosevelt. Back in 1918, as assistant secretary of the navy, he had gone to London on official navy business. His letters to his wife and mother told of an audience with the king, a dinner at Gray's Inn in honor of the war ministers. (Churchill had been there, and it would later rankle Roosevelt, who had been called upon to speak for the Allies, that Churchill did not remember the occasion. But, then, neither did Roosevelt consider Churchill's presence sufficiently special to mention his name.) The letter was full of a talk he had had with the prime minister, Lloyd George, at a luncheon given in his (Roosevelt's) honor the next day by Ambassador Walter Hines Page.

I had a very good time with Lloyd George. Lloyd George is just like his pictures; thick set; not very tall; rather a large head; and rather long hair; but what impressed me more than anything else was his tremendous vitality. There is no question that the great majority of Englishmen are standing solidly behind him on the sole issue of winning the war. The Conservatives who used to despise him as a demagogue; the Liberals who used to fear him as a radical; and most of the Labor people who now look on him as a reactionary, may hate him just as much as ever and be unwilling after the war to trust reconstruction to his hands, but they will stand by him just as long as his administration keeps the winning of the war as its only political aim. Strikes are threatened at the present time at a number of munitions plants and shipyards. Mr. Lloyd George and I talked over the labor situation here and at home. He said of course the weakness of the British Government's position has all come from the failure to adopt conscription at the outbreak of the war and I suggested to him that in the same way we should have had

vastly more trouble if we had not had the selective draft law as the final lever to insure continuation of work. I ventured to suggest that in my opinion the British
Unions would obtain no sympathy from our Federation of Labor in any action
involving a tie-up of war work and that on the contrary a firmer attitude on the
part of the British Government would receive hearty applause from the United
States. He seemed very greatly pleased and intimated that he had decided on a
firmer stand in the future.[26]

Roosevelt's and Churchill's attitudes toward the trade unions were not
too different at the time. Both were for firmness when they considered the
unions to be jeopardizing the national interest. But there was a bite to Churchill's dealings with the trade unions that was a product of cocksureness, class
feeling, and natural pugnacity that turned the unions into bitter antagonists.
Roosevelt, on the other hand, gained them as allies. In the twenties, moreover, Churchill, breaking with the Liberals, not only returned to the Conservative fold but, ever the master of invective, stooped to an almost vulgar
anti-Socialism in his attacks on the Labour party, attacks that culminated in
a kind of strikebreaking personal vigilantism during the 1926 general strike.
Roosevelt, during those years, moved in the opposite direction. His bout with
polio had tempered and disciplined him: "A figure tall and proud even in
suffering . . . a man softened and cleansed and illumined with pain" was the
way Will Durant saw him in 1928, the year Roosevelt returned to active politics and was elected governor of New York.

The struggle against paralysis had taught Roosevelt patience. It had
also activated an innate sense of justice and fairness. His wife's work with
the Women's Trade Union League and the union leaders, especially the
women among them whom she had brought to him in New York and Hyde
Park, had given him a sympathetic view of workers as individuals and of the
problems confronting their unions. To him, unions and unionists were an economic and political force to be managed in the interests of the nation and
his own ambitions; they were not, as Churchill often saw them, a hostile, almost sinister, force that menaced the foundations of civilized society. They
represented, in fact, people needing help. They were allies, and their needs
shaped his aims.

Both Churchill and Roosevelt were endowed with magnetic personalities
that drew people to them, the prime minister's authority being fed by inner
fires of imagination, instinct, and intuition, and the president's by a superb
sensitivity to men and their dreams. Churchill was usually impatient and impetuous. Roosevelt, chastened by polio, had learned to bide his time. He,
better than Churchill, had reconciled himself to await what William James
had called "the receptivities of the moment" upon which effective leadership
was dependent. His nomination for a third term on a platform of aid to Britain
was only the latest testimony to a genius for pacing his purposes to events
that disposed public and Congress to support them. Churchill understood
that leadership was conditioned by opportunity. "In 1915 and 1916 he broke
his teeth upon the Impossible," Churchill wrote of Foch. "But 1918 was
created for him."[27] But driven by inner demons, Churchill could not wait,

and in May, 1940, when war and disaster had amply confirmed his warnings of dangers imminent, it had been touch and go whether he would be summoned to the supreme leadership.

Spontaneity characterized Churchill's approach to men and events, self-control Roosevelt's. In respect to concealing his innermost feelings, Roosevelt was more like the typical Englishman than Churchill, whose passions and affections constantly welled to the surface, sometimes to the point of tears. Even those closest to Roosevelt were always asking, "What does he really think? What does he really feel?" That rarely was said of Churchill, who took pleasure in disclosing himself. The young Franklin, Eleanor Roosevelt once explained to her son James, had had to protect himself against a very possessive mother and so had learned to hide his innermost purposes and feelings. Churchill, in childhood and youth—and in this respect he was like the young Eleanor Roosevelt—could never get enough parental affection and attention. His mother, Churchill wrote, shone for him "like an Evening Star. I loved her deeply but at a distance." His father, too, kept him at arm's length. Yet of his death Churchill, who was twenty when it occurred, wrote: "All my dreams of comradeship with him, of entering Parliament at his side and in his support were ended. There remained for me only to pursue his aims and vindicate his memory."[28]

Franklin Roosevelt's father was seventy-two when he died; his son, a freshman at Harvard, was nineteen. The bonds between father and son were affectionate, but Roosevelt never spoke of his father in the passionate terms that Churchill did of his father. Roosevelt's closest ties were with his mother. Half the age of her husband, she was a woman of daunting command whom her son had learned to manage by charm and stratagem. Roosevelt had his moments of disappointment and despair—when he failed to be chosen for Porcellian, Harvard's most exclusive club and, more important, when he was struggling to recover from polio—but he was never subject to fits of depression as was Churchill. FDR was the "gay cavalier"—some thought him all surface, and his Oyster Bay cousins derided him as "handkerchief-boxy"—but he had his purposes and a will as determined as his mother's to see them realized. He wanted to succeed. And if the inner promptings of feeling, intellect, and memory were not as clamant as Churchill's, that very fact permitted a cool, ruthless realism in pursuit of the targets suggested for his ambitions by family, Groton, Harvard, the example of "Uncle Ted," the gentle proddings of his wife, and the interests of his Democratic constituents.

To the world Churchill in 1940 embodied the old; he did so magnificently. But Roosevelt represented the new. Churchill himself had sensed this in 1934, for his appraisal of Roosevelt at that time had ended:

Will he succeed or will he fail? This is not the question we set ourselves, and to prophesy is cheap. But succeed or fail, his impulse is one which makes towards the fuller life of the masses of the people in every land, and which as it glows the brighter may well eclipse both the lurid flames of German Nordic self-assertion and the baleful lights which are diffused from Soviet Russia.[29]

Chapter Twelve

Getting a Little More Mixed Up Together

ONE ENGLISHMAN who was not persuaded of Roosevelt's indispensability to the British cause was the British ambassador in Washington, Lord Lothian. He breathed more easily when Roosevelt and Willkie emerged as the candidates of the two major parties in the United States. The two men thought alike about the war, Lothian advised friends in England, and it would not make much difference to Britain which one won. This view surprised his official biographer, Britain's distinguished military historian J. R. M. Butler, who found it "difficult to believe that [Roosevelt's] rival could have handled day-to-day questions of tactics with the skill and ability of Franklin Roosevelt, or that the Ambassador believed it. And in fact negotiations of the highest importance were beginning." Butler referred to the destroyers-for-bases deal, which, he observed, "gave striking proof of the President's powers as a tactician."

Lothian's reading of the American political situation would have astonished most of his countrymen. As the carefully spoken London *Economist* noted: "Mr. Roosevelt has trained up a newly-aware public opinion with great skill." And, indeed, Willkie's victory in an isolationist-dominated Republican convention "owed much to the spreading consciousness of danger, underlined by the dramatic course of events abroad, that Mr. Roosevelt's leadership has evoked." Even if Willkie could free himself from the influence of the isolationist wing of his party, Britain's first necessity was to survive the summer. "My general strategy at present is to last out the next three months," Churchill cheerfully informed Soviet Ambassador Maisky as he puffed away at a cigar that filled the room with bluish smoke. Any hesitation or hiatus in United States aid would be fatal to such a strategy.[1]

On June 15, Churchill had dispatched an almost desperate plea for overage destroyers. With the Channel ports and the coast of Norway in German hands, Britain faced the prospect of invasion with only 68 destroyers fit for service after Dunkirk, in bleak contrast to the 433 destroyers that had been in service in 1918. Britain's shipping lanes were more vulnerable to German submarine attacks than before the fall of France, and Italy's entry into the war had turned the Mediterranean into a zone of danger. "We must ask therefore as a matter of life or death, to be reinforced with these destroyers." "After reading this, unless we do something to give the English additional destroyers," Morgenthau exhorted the president, "it seems to me it is absolutely hopeless to expect them to keep going."[2]

But this was the period when Roosevelt's chief military advisers, Marshall and Stark, feared that matériel sent from the United States would not suffice to save Britain and would leave America naked. Even the normally interventionist Sen. Key Pittman, chairman of the Foreign Relations Committee, called upon Churchill to send the British fleet to the New World immediately, outraging the British with his defeatist argument:

It is no secret that Great Britain is totally unprepared for defense and that nothing the United States has to give can do more than delay the result. . . . It is to be hoped that this plan [to transfer the British fleet] will not be too long delayed by futile encouragement to fight on. It is conclusively evident that Congress will not authorize intervention in the European war.

Over at the Navy Department, its general board of admirals blamed what it called America's vulnerability on the nation's failure to rely "wholly . . . upon our Fleet, but instead have relied to a certain extent on the Fleet of another nation." The admirals demanded that the United States Navy be built up "to a point where it will be able to exercise dominant strength in both the Atlantic and Pacific Oceans at the same time." The chief of naval operations, Admiral Stark, confronted with demands for a two-ocean navy, dubious about Britain's capacity to hold out (although he normally saw naval matters pretty much as Roosevelt did), resisted handing over any overage destroyers to the British. Such a transaction was likely to provoke an uproar in Congress, he feared, which had been assured by him that the old destroyers were absolutely essential to the American navy. "On a certain afternoon last week we had before us a naval officer," Chairman Walsh of the Senate Naval Appropriations Committee informed his colleagues. "We talked about destroyers, and he vehemently said that the Navy would never give up its destroyers, that we would not be equipped for war for two years, and that the Navy would not approve of such action." The Senate chamber in early July was still echoing to the angry debate that had been precipitated by Senator Walsh's discovery that the administration was using a 1917 statute to sell mosquito boats to the British. "Now, Senators, see how careful we shall have to be in our legislation," the isolationist senator from Massachusetts had cautioned his colleagues. "Who, in God's name, in Congress or in the country thought, when such a power was given [to modify contracts], that these contracts for our own protection would be modified or changed in order to assist one side or the other, or all sides, of belligerents at war?" It was symptomatic of the jumpy mood of the Senate that it approved by a voice vote the Walsh amendment to the Senate naval appropriations bill, which gave to the president's subordinates, Stark and Marshall, vetoes over his power to transfer military items to foreign governments.[3]

Among the fears that fueled this hobble on the presidency (Basil Rauch appropriately labeled it "a constitutional monstrosity")[4] were doubts that Britain would hold out, the same doubts that had caused Churchill to refuse additional planes to France.

The Walsh amendment demonstrated anew to Roosevelt how gingerly he had to move in pursuit of his policy of aid to Britain. A memorandum from Benjamin Cohen showing "that there really is no legal barrier, by reason of our own statutes or the law of nations, which would stand in the way of the release of our old destroyers from our naval service and their sale to the British" impressed Roosevelt. It is "worth reading," he advised Knox, but "in view of the clause in the big authorization bill I signed last Saturday which is intended to be a complete prohibition of sale, I frankly doubt if Cohen's memorandum would stand up. Also I fear Congress is in no mood at the present time to allow any form of sale."[5]

To most British observers it was evident that if Roosevelt, wise in the ways of Congress and the military bureaucracy, hesitated to proceed with the transfer of the destroyers, it would take Willkie, who had never held elective office and who was dependent on a party that was committed to isolationism, considerably longer to move ahead on aid to Britain should he be elected president. Churchill appreciated Roosevelt's essentiality to British fortunes and to his own policy of resistance—whether to the blandishments of a compromise peace that would leave Hitler in control of the Continent or to the scourge of invasion.

Britain, in the six weeks after the fall of France, had such a choice, and there were men in the highest British councils who were tempted to explore the possibilities of peace. This, too, was part of the July backdrop against which the drama of the destroyers-for-bases negotiations unfolded. Hitler's well-orchestrated peace offensive began even before the French armies had surrendered. On May 24, according to the German chief of operations Gen. Günther Blumentritt, Hitler startled his generals by his admiring references to the British Empire, "of the necessity for its existence, and of the civilization that Britain had brought into the world. . . . He said that all he wanted from Britain was that she should acknowledge Germany's position on the continent." When Hitler and Mussolini conferred in Munich on June 18, Ciano was impressed by Ribbentrop's "mood" regarding England:

If London wants war it will be a total war, complete, pitiless. But Hitler makes many reservations on the desirability of demolishing the British Empire, which he considers, even today, to be an important factor in world equilibrium. I ask von Ribbentrop a clear-cut question, "Do you prefer the continuation of war or peace?" He does not hesistate a moment. "Peace." He also alludes to vague contacts between London and Berlin by means of Sweden.[6]

In Berlin, the Italian ambassador approached the U.S. chargé. The Axis had "neither the desire nor the interest . . . to destroy England," he assured the American. "There yet remained a few days in which the catastrophe might be averted," and the ambassador suggested the United States take a hand in persuading the British to ask for the Axis terms. In Rome, exiled King Alfonso XIII of Spain approached United States Ambassador Phillips and offered his services to the president to help initiate peace talks and forestall "the blow from falling on England." In Madrid, the duke of Windsor told U.S. embassy officials to end the war before thousands more were killed or maimed to save the faces of a few politicians. "These observations have their value if any," Ambassador Weddell commented, "as doubtless reflecting the views of an element in England, possibly a growing one who find in Windsor and his circle a group who are realists in world politics and who hope to come into their own in the event of peace." The pope at the end of June addressed parallel communications to Hitler, Mussolini, and Churchill, offering his good offices in the quest for a "just and honorable peace," stating, however, that before initiating such a step he wished to ascertain confidentially how it would be received. A similar offer was made by the Swedish king.

These initiatives were not all of them necessarily German-inspired, but they fitted in with Hitler's hopes for a compromise settlement that would leave him free to consolidate his victories. They evoked some sympathetic resonance in London. "The Pope is making tentative half-baked suggestions for agreement," Cadogan noted acidly in his diary. "Silly old H[alifax] evidently hankering after them." According to Chamberlain's biographer, rumors that British appeasement groups were stirring again became so widespread, disseminated by isolationists who wished to show that Roosevelt was helping a country not worth saving, that Chamberlain, already ailing from the cancer that was to kill him a few months later, went on the radio to declare that "we are a solid and united nation, which would rather go down to ruin than admit the domination of the Nazis."

Hitler, reluctant to give the order to invade Britain because of the hazards involved, could not fathom "what on earth Churchill could be counting on." He postponed his *Reichstag* speech "again and again in order to give England time and room enough to make the hoped-for decision to ask for terms." It was inconceivable, he told the Italian ambassador, that "anyone in England" still seriously believed in victory. "If the English still entertained any thought of winning, they did so only because they counted on support from third countries, presumably mainly from the United States, but perhaps also with a secret hope as to Russia."[7]

On July 16, Hitler finally directed his military chiefs to prepare to invade England if she continued to refuse to come to terms. And on July 19, he addressed the *Reichstag*. Even though he vilified Churchill as a nation wrecker who would flee to Canada with his money, the tenor of Hitler's speech was peace. "In this hour I feel it to be my duty before my own conscience to appeal once more to reason and common sense in Great Britain as much as elsewhere. . . . I can see no reason why this war need go on. I am grieved to think of the sacrifices it must claim." When the BBC quickly broadcast a terse rejection, the disappointment in Berlin was palpable. "Late in the evening, when the first cold English reaction to the speech arrives," Ciano recorded, " a sense of ill-concealed disappointment spreads among the Germans." British obduracy was blamed equally on Churchill and Roosevelt. "According to opinion here," the German minister in Eire reported to Berlin, "the English attitude would be influenced considerably by a reasonable attitude on the part of Roosevelt, whose speech of July 19 was therefore much regretted here." The July 19 speech was Roosevelt's acceptance of the Democratic nomination for a third term. Its "most important passage," the German embassy in Washington cabled home, "was that which declines a peaceable understanding or even a compromise with the new Germany. . . . Roosevelt wants England to continue fighting and the war to be prolonged."[8]

A few days later, Britain's rejection of Hitler's olive branch was made official. It stung Hitler that Churchill himself did not even deign to reply but left it to Halifax. Lothian sought to soften the rejection. He "telephones wildly from Washington in the evening begging Halifax not to say anything in his broadcast tonight which might close the door to peace," a disgusted Nicolson noted. "Lothian claims that he knows the German peace terms and that they are most satisfactory. I am glad to say that Halifax pays no attention to this and makes an extremely bad broadcast but one which is perfectly firm as far as it goes." "One important peace feeler came to our knowledge," Ernst von Weizsäcker, the German state secretary for foreign affairs, recalled.

The British Ambassador in Washington, Lord Lothian, proposed that contact should be made through a certain Quaker. This step, in the manner of British diplomacy, had to be specially authorized. We responded to this to the extent of agreeing to the Quaker arranging a meeting between Lord Lothian and our *chargé d'affaires* in Washington. After this it was a disappointment when Churchill did not reply to Hitler's Reichstag speech of July 19, 1940, and Lord Halifax returned a negative answer which seemed to amount to a disavowal of Lothian's feeler. Our *chargé d'affaires* was now forbidden to have any conversation with Lothian.

The ban on talks was mutual. "I do not know whether Lord Halifax is in town today," Churchill notified the foreign office, "but Lord Lothian should be told on no account to make any reply to the German Chargé d'Affaires' message."[9]

Churchill's chief concern in July was to invigorate British preparations to meet the assault that everyone assumed would soon be launched. The problem was neither morale nor manpower but rather proper deployment and, above all, re-equipment. An "Action This Day" memorandum to the secretary of state for war read: "I was disturbed to find the 3rd Division spread along thirty miles of coast, instead of being as I had imagined held back concentrated in reserve, ready to move against any serious head of invasion." London was to be defended the way Madrid had been. "I have a very clear view that we should fight every inch of it, and that it would *devour* quite a large invading army." Pugnacity was his keynote. "I cannot understand how we can tolerate the movement at sea along the French coast of any vessels without attacking them. . . . We really must not be put off from asserting our sea power by the fact that the Germans are holding the French coast."

Eden recommended that Brooke should replace Ironside as commander of the home forces. Churchill decided to spend an afternoon with Brooke, with whom he had clashed when the general commanded the British forces in France after Dunkirk. The prime minister visited Brooke's southern command, watched a tank exercise for which Brooke was able to muster twelve tanks, and drove about with Brooke. "He was in wonderful spirits," Brooke wrote, "and full of offensive plans for next summer."

Re-equipment had the highest priority. "I want my 'S' Branch to make a chart of all the thirty divisions showing their progress towards complete equipment. . . . I should like to see this chart every week," Churchill directed. American weapons began to arrive. "I have asked the Admiralty to make very special arrangements for bringing in your rifle convoys. They are sending four destroyers far out to meet them, and all should arrive during the 9th. . . . At least one hundred thousand ought to reach the troops that very night, or in the small hours of the following morning. Special trains should be used to distribute them and the ammunition." Another convoy approached at the end of July. It should be guarded with special care, he alerted the admiralty. "Do not forget that two hundred thousand rifles mean two hundred thousand men, as the men are waiting for the rifles." By the end of July Britain was again "an armed nation, so far as parachute or air-borne landings were concerned."[10]

The long war that Hitler was seeking to avoid, the war involving more and more of the world, the war of continents that gave a marked advantage to the nations with superior sea power, seemed to be coming closer to realization. The blockade of World War I had bred a respect for British sea power into German bones. Back in early June, Dr. Hjalmar Schacht, who was in touch with the American chargé in Berlin, had stressed sea power in contemplating the future: "If, with or without American collaboration, Britain continued sea warfare and a blockade of Europe, then eventually Germany would have to come to a negotiated peace because neither Germany nor Europe could indefinitely exist without tropical products." In the armistice negotiations with France, Hitler's major solicitude had been to keep the French fleet out of British hands. The British fleet was a formidable obstacle to a cross-Channel attack. Hitler had given the order to prepare to invade, but his generals were full of doubts, his admirals even more so. They stipulated, and he agreed, that German command of the air was a precondition for invasion. German hesitations even surfaced publicly. A minor sensation was created in Rome when Virginio Gayda, a leading Fascist publicist, wrote: "The war in England could not be lightning, spectacular and massive like the conquest of France. It must be a process of hammering and wearing down." And in Berlin, the head of the German Labor Front, Dr. Robert Ley, emphasized Britain's powers of resistance and warned Germans to be prepared for a "hard fight."[11]

German uncertainties produced a fateful strategic decision at the end of July during a conference in Hitler's Berghof. Hitler agreed that everything hinged on gaining mastery of the air. But if that was not achieved he planned to subdue England by a more circuitous route. As recorded in General Halder's diary, Hitler reasoned that "England's hope is Russia and America. If hope in Russia is eliminated, America is also eliminated, because enormous increase in the importance of Japan in the Far East will result from the elimination of Russia." A powerful Russia, Hitler argued further, was England and America's "Far Eastern sword against Japan." Eliminate Russia, and Japan becomes Germany's far eastern sword against America. "Decision: in the course of this contest Russia must be disposed of. Spring '41." The German ambassador in Tokyo was instructed to press Japan more urgently for a military alliance.[12]

Back in June, when France was disintegrating, Roosevelt had dictated a memorandum that reflected his own strategic outlook in the assumptions he made about the situation that might exist in the fall and winter of 1940:

The surviving forces of the British and French navies, in conjunction with United States Navy, are holding the Persian Gulf, Red Sea and the Atlantic from Morocco to Greenland. Allied fleets have probably been driven out of the Eastern Mediterranean and are maintaining a precarious hold in the Western Mediterranean. Russia and Japan are inactive, taking no part in the war.

The United States active in the war, but with naval and air forces only. Plane production is progressing to its maximum. America is providing part of Allied pilots. Morocco and Great Britain are being used as bases of supplies shipped from the Western Hemisphere. American shipping is transporting supplies to the Allies. U.S. Navy is providing most of the forces for the Atlantic blockade (Morocco to Greenland).[13]

Roosevelt had asked army and navy intelligence whether his hypotheses were a reasonable projection of the present situation. They were more than hypotheses, however. It was reasonable to speculate about what the situation of other powers might be by the fall and winter, but the United States response to the developing events depended in part on America's—notably on Roosevelt's—decisions. Implicit in his memo was a guide to his own maturing program: (1) the arsenal-of-democracy concept; (2) convoying; and (3) U.S. naval and air-force participation on the side of the Allies in order to prevent an Axis victory in the Atlantic. Precisely what Hitler feared the most—a war of continents in which American sea power and production would be ranged on the side of the British—was in the back of Roosevelt's mind.

Whether and how soon such a program would be consummated depended on world developments, on political realities at home—that is, the readiness of the American people to support it—on British survival, and, not the least, on the concurrence of the president's chief military advisers. Central to Roosevelt's strategic thinking was an absolute conviction that the United States had a vital stake in keeping the command of the Atlantic in friendly hands. In June, 1939, during King George's visit to Hyde Park, Roosevelt had broached the idea of a neutrality patrol that would protect the Atlantic approaches to the Western Hemisphere and would be in the best interest of Britain as well as America. In that connection, he had confided to the king, he hoped the British, in the event of war, would give the United States base rights in the Caribbean Islands, Bermuda, and Newfoundland. The navy had long pressed him to acquire such rights; and the isolationists, in the hopes of driving a wedge between the United States and its allies, had advocated acquisition of British and French possessions in the Western Hemisphere in return for cancellation of the war debts.

Lothian, sensing the pressures in the United States for acquisition of base rights, had already in May suggested to his government that it make a spontaneous, voluntary offer of leases to the bases as a contribution to American security.

American anxiety about its own security has brought to the fore in public discussion the question of the future of British and French islands off eastern coast of America. Many suggestions are being made for their disposal to U.S. in part payment of war debts. President has always discouraged such discussion. . . . H.M.G. should seriously consider officially a formal offer to US. to allow it to construct aerodromes and naval stations in British islands which are important to its security.

Halifax, in a war cabinet discussion of the proposal, favored examining it, but Churchill was opposed to a proposal "that we should offer such facilities except as part of a deal." The United States, he said, "had given us practically no help in the war, and now that they saw how great was the danger their attitude was that they wanted to keep everything which would help us for their own defence." Two days later it was again discussed in the war cabinet, and the first lord of the admiralty said that he continued to be opposed "more particularly as the proposal for the sale of American destroyers had been rejected by the Americans." The war cabinet informed Lothian that it felt that "a definite assurance of American assistance should be a prerequisite of any concessions on our part," and asked for the reasons he had for thinking that if the political objections to the proposal could be overcome, "really substantial advantages would accrue to us from the proposed offer to the United States."[14]

Lothian told London that for the time being he would not press his proposal on bases. But he did continue to discuss with Roosevelt Britain's need for destroyers. The president pointed out to Lothian the difficulty he was having with the Senate to get it to agree to the release of the motor torpedo boats, and "in the present anxiety about defense it would be impossible to get Congress to release destroyers."

Had not the time come, inquired Lothian, for secret staff talks as to how the British and American navies might deal with certain eventualities? "The President said he thought that this would be a good thing and that it ought to take place at once." But when Halifax presented this proposal to Churchill, the prime minister demurred: "I think they would turn almost entirely on the

American side upon the transfer of the British Fleet to trans-atlantic bases. Any discussion of this is bound to weaken confidence here at the moment when all must brace themselves for the supreme struggle. I will send the President another personal telegram about destroyers and flying boats a little later on." Hull also demurred, but for different reasons. He feared leakage to the newspapers, which would be very damaging during a presidential election. Hull's backing off was what Halifax feared: "Generally speaking it is sound policy to go as far as we feel we safely can," he advised Churchill, "to fall in with any reasonably practical suggestion put forward or known to be favoured by the President. If we fail to take up one of his suggestions while it is still warm in his imagination, it may cool—or be cooled for him by outside influences—and we may never get a chance to revive the discussion when we judge the moment ripe." Churchill accepted this argument. "Please inform the President," Halifax cabled Lothian, "that the Prime Minister warmly welcomes his suggestion." The talks might be held in London, where there was a lesser risk of their attracting public notice. "I saw the President this afternoon," Lothian cabled back. "He agreed that it was very important to have technical discussions as soon as possible as to what the situation would be if the British Navy were forced to relinquish Gibraltar, if French Fleet passed into German hands, if Germans and Italians were able to base their blockade operations upon French Channel and Atlantic ports, etc., so that if and when a crisis arose British and American Governments could come to decisions based upon a similar estimate of facts. He thought it imperative, however, that there should be no publicity especially owing to election. He is consulting the Secretary of State and Chief of Staff tonight as to the best method of holding discussions in London." A subsequent cable notified London that "in order to avoid publicity a United States Admiral will proceed to London as part of routine exchange."[15]

In the end, the observer's mission to England included representatives of the army and air force. But it was symptomatic of the centrality that sea power held in Roosevelt's strategic preoccupations at that time that the military observer with whom he spent the most time before the group left for London was Admiral Ghormley. The U.S. defense program was based on three alternative possibilities, Roosevelt advised Ghormley:

(1) Great Britain would be defeated by an air attack followed by invasion—which would be followed within six to twelve months by Axis intervention in Latin America and further Japanese expansion in the Pacific.

(2) A Great Britain weakened by attack or invasion would still continue a defensive war—with the Government and perhaps the Royal Navy perhaps transferred to Canada.

(3) Great Britain defends itself successfully in the British Isles and from this base would continue the war, with naval command of European waters and Atlantic, growing air power, etc.

"[Roosevelt] was not convinced," recorded naval historian Kittredge, "that the United States would be forced to intervene as a belligerent in the war against the European Axis, or would be forced to fight Japan in the Pacific to prevent continued Japanese expansion. . . . The conversations which Admiral Ghormley was to undertake in London were therefore to be purely personal and unofficial. While military services must necessarily work out detailed plans in advance to meet any contingencies which national policy and world developments might produce, the most complete secrecy had to be observed." "Today I informed the First Sea Lord, on my own responsibility that I would like information as to the Admiralty ideas of the part our Navy should take, in cooperation with the British, should we become involved in the present war," Ghormley reported to Washington. "I was informed that since June a special Admiralty Board has been making a study of such action. Have just been handed a copy of this paper."[16]

Roosevelt's readiness for joint staff talks disposed the foreign office to take a more favorable attitude toward the United States desire for base rights. There were few exchanges between Roosevelt and Churchill in July. The former was busy with politics, the latter with preparing the island's defenses. Churchill also may have been impressed with Kennedy's advice not to push Roosevelt too hard on destroyers. Halifax had shown the ambassador a message stating that Churchill planned to ask Lothian to take up the destroyer question again. "I pointed out that the President had all the information in regard to destroyers and that he would settle it in his own way in his own time and that to try to give him the 'hurry up' or to put out again the dangers to America was not likely to influence him much. . . . I said I had known the President for quite a while and had never found him subject to a 'rush aggression.' "[17]

At the beginning of July, Lothian had again alerted the foreign office on the subject of base rights. Public clamor was on the increase for acquisition of the Caribbean Islands. Frank Knox, the newly appointed secretary of the navy, had publicly referred to the possibility that Britain might be forced to sell the islands to pay for war materials. At the forthcoming inter-American meeting at Havana there doubtless would be moves to place the islands under American control. Departments that had opposed the grant of base rights began to weaken. The dominions and colonial offices suggested that "facilities" might be offered to the United States in return for second-hand naval craft, a relaxation in the cash-and-carry requirements of the Neutrality Law, and landing rights in Honolulu. That, the foreign office thought, was impractical.

Lothian talked with Knox. The secretary asked about bases in return for cancellation of war debts. The ambassador shrugged and suggested instead that base rights should be discussed in the context of "the kind of naval problems which might confront both our countries in the near future." But Lothian cautioned London that the sooner Britain made an offer to meet American wishes on bases "without surrendering our sovereignty the less likely will there be an imperious demand upon us, backed by a panic stricken public opinion." Vansittart was outraged. The ambassador has "lost his balance. . . . Surely 'an imperious demand upon us' would be the very method of Hitler himself, and is hardly to be foreseen or countenanced on the part of a peace-loving and peace-professing democratic State." But Professor Whitehead, whose reading of American reactions was being more and more listened to, disagreed. "The Americans drive a hard bargain, on the other hand they are generous friends, and if we could have seized the opportunity to offer freely and without bargain or quibble the facilities suggested in Lord Lothian's earlier telegram of the 24th May, I venture to predict that this might well have constituted a significant step towards the building up of genuinely cordial and collaborative relations between the two countries." "I entirely agree," wrote David Scott, the head of the American desk. "As I wrote some time ago, 'there is a traditional Yankee pride in driving a hard bargain. . . . On the other hand the Americans are both sentimental and genuinely large hearted, and the same men who will be unable to resist driving a hard bargain are also capable of acts of great and sustained generosity if approached in a spirit of friendly collaboration."

Vansittart meanwhile had revised his view: "We should certainly get the destroyers and the MTB's as a very minimum."[18]

In the United States, public pressure on Roosevelt was building up—with the encouragement of Roosevelt—by such groups as William Allen White's Committee to Defend America by Aiding the Allies and the Century Group* for the transfer of overage destroyers to the British. The political conventions were over, Lothian advised London, and he was being asked by "various influential people including members of the administration what the United States ought to do. I have replied, privately of course, 'Send 100 destroyers at once to Britain and some flying boats manned by Americans, if necessary volunteers.'" Nine days later, Lothian signaled Churchill: "Now is the moment to send [Roosevelt] most moving statement of our needs and dangers in respect of destroyers and flying boats you can, if you have not already." Churchill drafted a cable to Roosevelt, sent it over to Halifax, and, remembering Kennedy's warning against too much pressure, commented: "I am sure that this is the moment to plug it in, and it may well be that we were wise to hold back the previous draft. But pray let this go now."

"It is some time since I ventured to cable personally to you, and many things both good and bad have happened in between. It has now become most urgent for you to let us have the destroyers, motor boats and flying-boats for which we have asked." Churchill again reviewed the considerations that made acquisition of the destroyers urgent. "In the last ten days we have had the following destroyers sunk: *Brazen, Codrington, Delight, Wren,* and the following damaged: *Beagle, Boreas, Brilliant, Griffin, Montrose, Walpole, Whitshed,* TOTAL 11. All this in the advent of any attempt which may be made at invasion." He hoped the "frank account" would persuade Roosevelt "to ensure that 50 or 60 of your oldest destroyers are sent to me at once. . . .

* It was known as the Century Group because it often met at the Century Club in New York. It originated when thirty prominent Americans on June 10, 1940, in "A Summons to Speak Out," had called on the United States to enter the war against Germany. Later, the group formed the Fight for Freedom Committee, whose program, wrote Herbert Agar, one of its leaders, was "to say much more than [Roosevelt] could dare endorse and to ask for much more than he could hope to accomplish." [19]

Mr. President, with great respect I must tell you that in the long history of the world, this is the thing to do now. Large construction is coming to me in 1941, but the crisis will be reached long before 1941. I know you will do all in your power but I feel entitled and bound to put the gravity and urgency of the position before you."[20]

The night after the receipt of Churchill's message, Lothian, unaware as yet of the cabinet's decision giving him the green light on bases, met with Knox. "Lothian had been almost tearful in his pleas for help and help quickly," Knox told Ickes over the telephone the next morning. Knox had been sympathetic: "We realize your situation and we want to help. However, we can't do anything without legislation and we can't hope to get a bill through Congress without showing that we have received adequate consideration from England." Knox had then advanced the destroyers-for-bases formula. He personally favored such a deal, Lothian replied, but he could not commit his government. Knox informed Ickes that he intended to bring the matter up at the cabinet meeting that day. Stimson was ready to support him, and he hoped he would have Ickes's help, too. Ickes readily agreed, and later described the cabinet discussion as "one of the most important Cabinet meetings that I have attended since the President came into power." Stimson, a veteran of cabinet meetings under Taft and Hoover, shared this opinion as did Roosevelt, who considered the meeting sufficiently momentous to make his own record of it:

At Cabinet meeting, in afternoon, long discussion in regard to devising ways and means to sell directly or indirectly fifty or sixty World War old destroyers to Great Britain. It was the general opinion, without any dissenting voice, that the survival of the British Isles under German attack might very possibly depend on their getting these destroyers.

It was agreed that legislation to accomplish this was necessary.

It was agreed that such legislation if asked for by me without any preliminaries would meet with defeat or interminable delay in reaching a vote.

It was agreed that the British be approached through Lord Lothian to find out if they would agree to give positive assurances that the British Navy, in the event of German success in Great Britain, would not under any conceivable circumstances fall into the hands of the Germans and that if such assurances could be received and made public, the opposition in the Congress would be greatly lessened. I suggested that we try to get further assurance from the British that the ships of their Navy would not be sunk but would sail for North America or British Empire ports where they would remain afloat and available.

It was agreed that I would call William Allen White, who has recently talked with Willkie on this subject; ask White to come to Washington at once to see Hull, Knox, and Stimson and after that to see me; then returning to see Willkie and seek to get Willkie's approval, the support of Joe Martin [House minority leader] and Charlie McNary [Senate minority leader and Willkie's running mate] for such a plan. It was agreed that if this procedure went through successfully that I would, at once, send a definite request to the Congress for the necessary legislation.

I stressed the point that in all probability the legislation would fail if it had substantially unanimous Republic opposition—and that the crux of the matter lay in the vote of the Republican minority in each House. I stressed the importance of having the issue acted on without regard to party politics in any way.

At 8:30 p.m., I talked with William Allen White, who was in Estes Park, Colorado; explained the above to him and asked him to come East.

He told me he was sure that Willkie's attitude in the matter was the same as mine. I explained to him that was wholly insufficient and that the Republican policy in Congress was the one essential.

White told me he would get in touch with Willkie and let me know at the earliest possible moment.

F.D.R.[21]

Roosevelt personally informed Lothian about the outcome of the cabinet discussion, stressing the importance, if legislation were to be enacted, of giving Congress the "molasses" of British assurances on the fleet and base facilities. A filibuster by fifteen or twenty determined isolationist senators could wreck the project until after election, he warned Lothian. There was no way of enforcing closure, he went on, and the bill's passage would depend on its being unanswerably in America's interest and on the public support that would inevitably flow from that being the case. In London, the war cabinet decided to meet some of America's base requirements and on August 3 approved the concept of an exchange of destroyers for bases. On the same day, Churchill cabled Lothian approving an exchange of destroyers for bases, but the latter "should be on lease indefinitely and not sale. It is understood that this will enable us to secure destroyers and flying-boats at once. . . . We can fit them with Asdics [submarine detectors] in about ten days from the time they are in our hands, all preparations having been made. We should also be prepared to give a number of Asdic sets to the United States Navy and assist in their installation and explain their working. Go ahead on these lines full steam."[22]

The package was coming together, but it might fly apart at any moment. Churchill understandably was unwilling to give assurances on the fleet that might depress British spirits and insisted that the British government be the sole judge of the fleet's movements. He advised Halifax:

The nation would not tolerate any discussion of what we should do if our island were overrun. Such a discussion, perhaps on the eve of an invasion, would be injurious to public morale, now so high. Moreover, we must never get into a position where the United States Government might say: "We think the time has come for you to send your Fleet across the Atlantic in accordance with our understanding or agreement when we gave you the destroyers."

We must refuse any declaration such as is suggested, and confine the deal solely to the colonial leases.[23]

There were difficulties, too, over the island bases. Empire loyalists resisted turning over British possessions to the Americans under terms that might weaken British sovereignty. The first British offer of August 8 severely limited the facilities they were willing to grant in those possessions and, at the same time, grandly expanded the British shopping list to what Welles, in a cable to Kennedy, called "a very ample statement of British desiderata for naval vessels and airplanes far greater both in scope and in kind than it would be possible to consider."[24]

On Roosevelt's side, Republican presidential candidate Willkie, although favoring the exchange, was not easy to pin down to specific undertakings that might embroil him with the isolationist wing of his party, especially as represented in Congress. "It's not as bad as it seems," White telegraphed Roosevelt on August 11 from Estes Park, Colorado, where Willkie was also staying. "I have talked with both of you on this subject during the last ten days. I know there is not two bits difference between you on the issue pending. But I can't guarantee either of you to the other. Which is funny for I admire and respect you both. I realize you in your position don't want statements but Congressional votes. Which by all the rules of the game you should have. But I've not quit and as I said it is not as bad as it looks."[25]

All summer, as a backdrop to the negotiations, the battle for public opinion raged in the United States. The most effective appeal for giving Britain destroyers came from the venerable commander of the American Expeditionary Force in World War I, General John J. Pershing.* "By sending help to the British we can still hope with confidence to keep war on the other side of the Atlantic Ocean, where the enemies of liberty, if possible, should be defeated. . . . Today may be the last time when, by measures short of war, we can still prevent war. . . . We have an immense reservoir of destroyers left over from the other war." The United States should let the British have "at least fifty. . . . If the destroyers help save the British fleet, they may save us from the hardships and dangers of another war."

At almost the same time that Pershing was broadcasting this plea over the radio networks, another American hero, Charles Lindbergh, was addressing a rally of 40,000 in Chicago, organized by the Citizens Committee to Keep America Out of War, and, echoing Hitler's peace offensive, urged the United States to "take the lead in offering a plan for peace. . . . In the past we have dealt with a Europe dominated by England and France. In the future we may have to deal with a Europe dominated by Germany." In Lindbergh's view, cooperation with a victorious Germany was possible.

"The Jewish element and Roosevelt fear the spiritual and, particularly, the moral superiority and purity of this man [i.e., Lindbergh]," the German embassy reported to Berlin. "On Sunday, Lindbergh delivered a blow that will hurt the Jews by declaring that America was not threatened, provided she made due preparations for her own protection; that it was unworthy of the American nation to look to England for its defense, and that the people had been influenced by the idea that England's defeat would destroy American security."

Significantly, however, Lindbergh had criticized the proposal to give

---

* "On August 1," wrote Herbert Agar, "three of us [from the Century Group] went to see the President, asking whether there wasn't something we could do to help him on the 'destroyer deal.' He said, 'Yes.' He said he wanted General Pershing, on a nation-wide radio hook-up, to tell America that the 'destroyer deal' was wise, and well-considered, and necessary. He said he himself could not ask General Pershing because everything a President says leaks, and he would be accused of using a national hero to promote a cause which the Congress would not have approved." Agar went to see Pershing. The general's old friends had been urging him to speak out. "All he needed was a word from the President."

Britain destroyers only obliquely. Roosevelt's judgment that the *quid pro quo* aspects would weaken isolationist attacks was proving correct. Should not the U.S. government be officially warned "against an action which is plainly contrary to the recognized principles of neutrality?" the German foreign office inquired of its chargé in Washington. A warning will enable Roosevelt to "whip up Congress," Thomsen replied. The transfer "would require a legislative act of Congress." Better to rely on that restraint and on the unwillingness of the navy to part with the destroyers, he advised.²⁶

Thomsen was accurate about the difficulties Roosevelt faced in the Senate. Sen. Claude E. Pepper, an administration stalwart, had introduced a resolution to authorize the sale of the destroyers. However, in early August he informed the White House that there was little prospect of its adoption. Thinking reverted to the Ben Cohen memorandum, which had argued that the president could authorize the transaction on his own. Cohen enlisted the support of one of the most brilliant legal minds in Washington, Dean Acheson, not yet back in an administration from which he had resigned in 1934 over the gold-purchase issue. Cohen and Acheson repaired to the law library of the New York City Bar Association and produced a tightly reasoned opinion that upheld the president's right to act and elaborated Cohen's original thesis that "there is no reason for us to put a strained or unnecessary interpretation on our own statutes contrary to our national interests. There is no reason to extend the rules of international law beyond the limits generally accepted by other nations to the detriment of our own country." The opinion was sent to the *New York Times* as a letter to the editor and was signed by several distinguished lawyers headed by C. C. Burlingham, whom Acheson described as "the grand old man of the New York bar." The three-and-a-half-column letter had a profound effect.²⁷

Justice Frankfurter, who had encouraged Cohen to seek out Acheson, called Stimson to indicate his agreement with the argument, "although," recorded Stimson, "just as I did he thought the line was a narrow one. . . . I called up the President. He said he felt very, very much encouraged. He said he would talk it over with the Attorney-General tomorrow morning, and is evidently about ready to push it ahead." Word had reached Roosevelt via Senator Pepper that Charles McNary, Republican leader in the Senate and Willkie's running mate, would not be able, because of past commitments, to support Senate action authorizing the transfer but "would make no objection if plausible grounds were found for proceeding without Senate action." McNary "is going to side with us on this matter," Stimson noted in his diary on August 15.

Two days earlier Roosevelt had asked Stimson, Knox, Welles (Hull was on leave), and Morgenthau to meet with him. In order to escape the vigilant eyes of the press they had come by way of the Treasury entrance to the White House. The meeting discussed what Stimson called the "rather vague" British base offer of August 8. The president had drafted "very hastily, but in admirable shape the papers to constitute a message to Great Britain," recorded

Stimson. "In contrast with the form of the papers which we had received from Great Britain, these went to the very teeth of the matter and put us on the broad principles." The American counterproposal enumerated the assistance the United States was prepared to furnish—at least fifty destroyers, motor torpedo boats, five flying boats, and five flying fortresses, the last two items for "war testing purposes." The message then went on: "Such assistance, as I am sure you will understand, would only be furnished if the American people and the Congress frankly recognized that in return therefor the national defense and security of the United States would be enhanced." Roosevelt then asked for a private, not a public, reiteration of Churchill's June 4 statement in Parliament about the fleet and for air and naval base rights in the form of ninety-nine-year leases in Newfoundland, Bermuda, the Bahamas, Saint Lucia, Trinidad, and British Guiana.[28]

"Isn't it a rather hard bargain for you to drive?" a member of the war cabinet said to Kennedy, who discussed Roosevelt's telegram with Churchill. "Certainly not" was Kennedy's quick reply, and in his telegram to Welles, adverting to the failure of the French to deliver on their promises to Churchill about the French fleet, urged that "for the protection of the President and the State Department" Washington consider a situation in which a successor government to Churchill refused to be bound by his promises.[29]

Churchill was fiercely determined not to permit any bargaining about the future disposition of the British fleet. "Although in my speech of June 4 I thought it well to open up to German eyes the prospects of indefinite oceanic war, this was a suggestion in the making of which we could admit no neutral partner," he advised Lothian on August 7. "Of course, if the United States entered the war and became an ally, we should conduct the war with them in common, and make of our own initiative and in agreement with them whatever were the best dispositions at any period in the struggle for the final effectual defeat of the enemy."[30]

But such tough talk was for Lothian's private guidance. Moreover, Churchill himself, in discussing Roosevelt's message with the war cabinet, advanced the reasons why it was not a one-sided bargain at all. The sale of destroyers to a belligerent power was not a neutral act. The fifty destroyers would be of enormous value, and the news of their sale would make a profound impression on Germany. If the exchange went through, the United States would have taken a long step toward coming into the war. The general view of the war cabinet, the official record stated, "was that the present proposal could not be looked at merely from the point of view of the exchange of destroyers, motor torpedo boats, and flying boats for certain facilities by way of naval and air bases. It might well prove to be the first step in constituting an Anglo-Saxon *bloc* or indeed a decisive point in history."

To Roosevelt, Churchill telegraphed enthusiastically:

> I need not tell you how cheered I am by your message or how grateful I feel for your untiring efforts to give us all possible help. You will, I am sure, send us everything you can, for you know well that the worth of every destroyer that you

can spare to us is measured in rubies. But we also need the motor torpedo-boats which you have mentioned, and as many flying-boats and rifles as you can let us have. We have a million men waiting for rifles.

The moral value of this fresh aid from your Government and people at this critical time will be very great and widely felt.

We can meet both the points you consider necessary to help you with Congress and with others concerned but I am sure that you will not misunderstand me if I say that our willingness to do so must be conditioned on our being assured that there will be no delay in letting us have the ships and flying-boats. As regards an assurance about the British Fleet, I am, of course, ready to reiterate to you what I told Parliament on June 4. We intend to fight this out here to the end, and none of us would ever buy peace by surrendering or scuttling the Fleet. But in any use you may make of this repeated assurance you will please bear in mind the disastrous effect from our point of view, and perhaps also from yours, of allowing any impression to grow that we regard the conquest of the British Islands and its naval bases as any other than an impossible contingency. The spirit of our people is splendid. Never have they been so determined. Their confidence in the issue has been enormously and legitimately strengthened by the severe air fighting in the past week. As regards naval and air bases, I readily agree to your proposals for ninety-nine year leases, which are far easier for us than the method of purchase. I have no doubt that once the principle is agreed between us the details can be adjusted and we can discuss them at leisure.

"I hope that Mr. Churchill's excellent reply of this morning will enable you to proceed on destroyers!!" said Lothian's postscript.[31]

Roosevelt needed no prodding. At his press conference that morning he announced that he was holding conversations with the British for the acquisition of naval and air bases. Was this a *quid pro quo* for destroyers? he was asked. "I do not know what the *quid pro quo* is going to be . . . the emphasis is on the acquisition of the bases . . . that is the main point . . . for the protection of this Hemisphere, and I think that is all there is to say." It was a carefully calculated reply. He knew there was almost universal support in the United States for the acquisition of the bases. He wanted that part of the deal to sink into the public consciousness first. There was, moreover, a very practical reason to defer discussion of the destroyer transfer. "Bob Jackson [the attorney general] has apparently found a legal method by which this transfer can be consummated without legislation," Ickes recorded. But the opinion still had to be drafted by the lawyers of the Justice Department. It would require, as Ickes also noted, "some sort of certification from the chief of Naval Operations"; and though Frank Knox was confident he could get that from Stark, that, too, still had to be arranged. But Lothian was content. "The last week has been engaged with trying to get U.S.A. up to the point of sending us destroyers," he wrote Lady Astor. "I think the trick has been done. Donovan has helped a lot and Knox."[32]

William J. Donovan, a close friend of Knox's, had been enlisted by Knox and Stimson in mid-July to go to England to survey Britain's chances of holding out. When Roosevelt heard of the mission, he insisted that Donovan travel as his personal representative. Republican, war hero, Irish-Catholic, Donovan carried weight with a segment of public and congressional opinion that distrusted Roosevelt, even Stimson and Knox. His trip was enthusiastically promoted by Stephenson, the man called "Intrepid," who saw in Donovan a future collaborator in the intelligence business. Donovan arrived in England with the task, as the head of British intelligence put it, of discovering "if we were in earnest about the war, and if we were worth supporting." He was shown everything and talked to everyone, "from King and Churchill down," the United States military attaché in London, Col. Raymond E. Lee, noted in his journal. On his departure at the beginning of August, Donovan "gives odds of 60–40 that the British will beat off the German attack. I will say a little better, say 2 to 1, barring some magical secret weapon." On the basis of what he had seen, Donovan was able on his return to brief cabinet officers, congressmen, and the president himself. To all he had stressed that Britain was very much worth helping; it was not a case, as many in the military argued, of throwing good money after bad. Minds were being changed. On July 26 William Allen White had advised the policy committee of the Committee to Defend America by Aiding the Allies: "If the President really wants to do it, it can be done. But we must show him that the country will follow him in this matter." On August 17, a public-opinion poll disclosed that 62 per cent of those polled approved of the sale of the destroyers, and the German chargé in Washington alerted Berlin that "the English offer is so attractive . . . that the opposition of Congress may fade."[33]

On August 17, Roosevelt was in upstate New York with Stimson to observe large-scale army maneuvers and to meet with Canadian prime minister Mackenzie King. That was also the day Willkie was to deliver his acceptance speech (and Roosevelt was not unmindful of that event). The United States minister to Ottawa, Jay Pierrepont Moffat, accompanied Mackenzie King to the meetings. They found the president, after several hours of inspecting troops in the field,

tired but exhilarated. We all had long cooling drinks while he talked at random about whatever came into his head. His talk on the whole was brilliant and the charm of the man, a happy blend of Chief of State, man of the world, and host, was never more vivid. He wanted to get the text of the Willkie speech of acceptance, but the only flash that came through was that Willkie had challenged him to a series of joint debates. "If that is true," he declared with emphasis, "Willkie is lost." He chuckled at "stealing half the show" because of the fact of his visit to Ogdensberg and his conference with Mackenzie King—although this was not on purpose—happened on the very day of Willkie's speech.[34]

Moffat did not attend the private talks between Roosevelt and King about the destroyers-for-bases deal, but the prime minister filled him in later:

The President will sell about 50 destroyers to the British. He will do this without submitting the matter to Congress. His lawyers are working on the ways and means of doing it legally. Politically, the President believes that the public will accept it, given the fact that the United States is getting the naval bases it desires. Strategically, the President believes that the Navy will now favor it, since the new naval bases are a greater asset to our defense than 50 old destroyers. . . . The

President told Mr. King that Mr. Churchill had at last given a sufficient pledge that he would under no circumstances surrender the British Fleet to the Germans.

Stimson told Moffat that he thought Willkie's acceptance speech was "able and courageous." In the eyes of some, it fell far short of the endorsement of the destroyers-for-bases deal that White had encouraged his friends in Washington to hope might be forthcoming. Indeed, that endorsement had to be read into Willkie's stress on the importance to the United States of the British fleet and his support of the president's Charlottesville pledge to aid the opponents of force, an expression of approval that was somewhat diluted by his espousal of the standard isolationist attack on the president for having "dabbled in inflammatory statements and manufactured panics," "meddled" in the affairs of Europe, and "unscrupulously encouraged other countries to hope for more help than we are able to give." But the charges could have been harsher, as indeed they were to become. And, for the moment, Willkie's rhetoric counted for less than Senator McNary's willingness to go along, even if silently, and Senator Wheeler's endorsement of at least the base-lease concept, even if he argued for cancellation of Britain's war debts as America's contribution to the deal.[35]

On August 20 Churchill reported to the House of Commons on the progress of the war. It was another of his great speeches that summer, this one made memorable by his tribute to the fighter pilots who were then beating back the intensifying onslaught of the Luftwaffe: "Never in the field of human conflict was so much owed by so many to so few." But the speech was also a response to Roosevelt's press-conference announcement of talks on acquiring British bases. There was a reference to the destroyers. A "great flow" of new naval construction was beginning to make itself felt, and "we hope our friends across the ocean will send us a timely reinforcement to bridge the gap between the peace flotillas of 1939 and the war flotillas of 1941." But Churchill carefully kept that matter separate from the bases. He first discussed the air battle. Then he described how the island now "bristled" with defenses. There was an assault on the "men of Vichy" and praise for "de Gaulle and his gallant band." He explained why a statement of war aims, for which he was constantly pressed, would be premature. Only at the very end of the speech did he advert to the base discussion. There had been a British decision "some months ago . . . spontaneously and without being asked or offered any inducement," to lease naval and air facilities to the United States. "There is, of course, no question of any transference of sovereignty," he assured the House, but of a "99 year leasehold basis." Churchill ended with a characteristic flourish that summed up the feelings of most Englishmen and Americans:

Undoubtedly this process means that those two great organisations of the English-speaking democracies, the British Empire and the United States, will have to be somewhat mixed up together in some of their affairs for mutual and general advantage. For my own part, looking out upon the future, I do not view the process with any misgivings. I could not stop it if I wished; no one can stop it. Like the Mississippi, it just keeps rolling along.[36]

The broad principles of the transfer were agreed upon, but the drafting of the formal letters to be exchanged, when Lothian and Welles sat down to the task, proved troublesome. Roosevelt needed to present the transaction as a trade to justify the transfer of the destroyers, especially if Admiral Stark was to certify that their transfer would enhance, not impair, the total defense of the United States. His willingness to accept leases rather than insist on a transfer of the sovereignty had eased the problem. He did not want to acquire "headaches" in the form of a Caribbean empire, Roosevelt explained to Lothian. But Churchill, supported by the war cabinet, even though from the very beginning it had insisted on "substantial advantages" in exchange for the bases, now thought a formal bargain as proposed in the United States drafts out of the question. "I had not contemplated anything in the nature of a contract, bargain or sale between us," Churchill cabled Roosevelt on August 22. "What we want is that you should feel safe on your Atlantic seaboard so far as any facilities in possessions of ours can make you safe." The British were "quite content to trust entirely to your judgment and to the sentiments of the people of the United States about any aid in munitions, etc., you feel able to give us. But this would be entirely a separate spontaneous act on the part of the United States arising out of their view of the world struggle and how their own interests stand in relation to it and the causes it involves."[37]

Separately, Lothian was instructed to inform the Americans that they could present the matter to Congress as a *quid pro quo* but that the British would not link them. Bases, even on a leased basis, for fifty old destroyers would seem an unfair bargain to the British, especially to Churchill's Tory followers. But Welles informed Lothian that Roosevelt felt an exchange of letters was essential. Roosevelt had again referred to the necessity of giving Congress some "molasses," but the critical point was a legal one—that the chief of naval operations had to certify that the transfer of the destroyers enhanced the security of the United States, and this could only be done if the transfer were specifically linked to the acquisition of base facilities. Roosevelt was portrayed by Welles as much exercised over the hitch in a transaction that he had worked hard to make possible and fearful that unless the deal was concluded swiftly the isolationists would undermine it.

Lothian, who had advised his government against linking the two, was persuaded. "About 5 telegrams from Lothian to say Americans don't like P.M.'s procedure and must stick to their exchange of letters idea," Cadogan recorded. "Lothian rang me up to emphasize that this was the only possible course. Went over about 6:30 with D. Scott and Dean to see P.M. He rather incensed and won't have exchange of letters. Says he doesn't mind if we don't get destroyers. Won't expose himself to wrangle with Americans, having made us a definite gift, haggling over the extent of ours. Dare say he is right. Sent provisional telegram to Lothian, and P.M. will dictate his message in car on way down to Chequers [the official country estate of prime ministers]."

Churchill's message to Roosevelt was submitted to Halifax and the admiralty and dispatched on August 25:

I fully understand the legal and constitutional difficulties which make you wish for a formal contract embodied in letters, but I venture to put before you the difficulties and even dangers which I foresee in this procedure. For the sake of the precise list of instrumentalities mentioned, which in our sore need we greatly desire, we are asked to pay undefined concessions in all the islands and places mentioned from Newfoundland to British Guiana "as may be required in the judgment of the United States." Suppose we could not agree to all your experts asked for, should we not be exposed to a charge of breaking our contract for which we have already received value? Your commitment is definite, ours unlimited. Much though we need the destroyers we should not wish to have them at the risk of a misunderstanding with the United States or indeed any serious argument. If the matter is to be represented as a contract, both sides must be defined with far more precision on our side than has hitherto been possible. But this might easily take some time. . . .

If your law or your Admiral requires that any help you may choose to give us must be presented as a *quid pro quo,* I do not see why the British government have to come into that at all. Could you not say that you do not feel able to accept this fine offer which we make unless the United States matched it in some way and that therefore the Admiral would be able to link the one with the other?

I am so very grateful to you for all the trouble you have been taking and I am sorry to add to your burdens knowing what a good friend you have been to us.[38]

The British cabinet was divided, Kennedy reported. "Halifax wants to do it any way the President wishes it done, believing that the idea of the English–United States tie-up on anything is of more value than bases or destroyers. [But Beaverbrook has persuaded Churchill that] 'If we are going to make a gift, well and good, if we are going to make a bargain, I don't want to make a bad one and this is definitely a bad one.' " The solution came from the State Department's legal adviser Green Hackworth, who suggested dividing the base sites into two groups, those to be traded and those to be given. "The President would have his hardheaded deal and the Prime Minister would have his generous gesture," wrote historian Philip Goodhart. On August 27, Churchill cabled Roosevelt accepting the Hackworth formula and urging speed:

Mr. President, this business has become especially urgent in view of the recent menace which Mussolini is showing to Greece. If our business is put through on big lines and in the highest spirit of goodwill, it might even now save that small historic country from invasion and conquest. Even the next forty-eight hours are important.[39]

But there was still no agreement that the exchange should have the formal character of a contract. Roosevelt's decision to transfer the destroyers without seeking the approval of Congress, Hull explained to Lothian, meant that he and the administration were risking their political existence. Even in the form of an exchange of letters the transaction was of "arguable legality." "He [Hull] said that the Admiral [Stark] has passed sleepless nights in trying to adjust his conscience to his obligations under the law. . . . The Admiral is disturbed at the possibility of being summoned before Congress to explain why he had given his certificate that the destroyers were not necessary for the defence of the United States when he is transferring them at once as against a promise to deliver naval bases and facilities at some time in the future." In the foreign office, meanwhile, Vansittart was minuting: "I trust we won't sign up and part with *our* end of the goods without actually having theirs."

"Cabinet at 12," Cadogan recorded. "Winston agreed to give way to the Americans on procedure."

He had just seen Churchill and Halifax, reported Kennedy to Hull. "England will handle her politics in the manner which she thinks best and the United States will of course handle hers in her own way. . . . I think they are inordinately happy about the result."[40]

With respect to the fleet, Lothian was instructed to inform the Americans that the prime minister proposed to say:

You ask, Mr. President, whether my statement in Parliament on June 4 about Great Britain never surrendering or scuttling her Fleet "represents the settled policy of His Majesty's Government." It certainly does. I must however observe that these hypothetical contingencies seem more likely to concern the German Fleet or what is left of it than our own.

One final matter remained to be settled—how Churchill was to explain the agreement. Hull cautioned Lothian that any mishandling of the matter might affect the presidential election. The agreement would be violently attacked in the United States on two grounds: that Mr. Roosevelt had acted without obtaining the consent of Congress; that the transfer of the destroyers was an act of war calculated to involve the United States in the European war. Hull hoped the prime minister would not say that he intended the transfer of the bases to be a free gesture of good will because Congress would take the line that there was no need to give the destroyers in order to secure the bases. "Tell people in England not to talk about an Anglo-American alliance," Lothian cautioned Nancy Astor. "That always means entanglement in Europe to U.S.A. Strengthening the defence of both is a better line." Churchill instructed Lothian to assure Hull that he would have all possible regard for Mr. Roosevelt's difficulties, but the statement of a free offer had already been made; he also had problems with those who thought that Britain got the worst of the bargain. As Lloyd George later remarked to Soviet ambassador Ivan Maisky: "Uncle Sam has remained Uncle Sam. . . . He hasn't been very generous. . . . For this old iron we have had to pay with several very important bases on our territory. . . . But what could we do? There was no other way out."[41]

Despite Churchill's grumblings over Hull's strictures, he carefully heeded them in reporting the "memorable transactions" to the House on September 5. The House should not "read into the official notes which have passed more than the documents bear on their face. . . . Only very ignorant persons would suggest that the transfer of American destroyers to the British flag constitutes the slightest violation of international law or affects in the smallest degree the non-belligerency of the United States." Hitler will not like the transaction, he predicted, and "will pay the United States out, if he ever gets the chance." And then, unable to resist a teasing, if Delphic, reference to the wider implications, Churchill said: "Perhaps I may, however, very respectfully, offer this counsel to the House: When you have got a thing where you want it, it is a good thing to leave it where it is." As he had argued during the war-cabinet discussions of the transaction, the transfer was a decidedly unneutral act by the United States, bringing it "definitely nearer to us and the war." Churchill did not have to spell this out. Parliament and the people understood. "It would be impossible," the *New York Times* reported from London, "to overstate the jubilation in official and unofficial circles caused today by President Roosevelt's announcement that fifty United States destroyers were coming to help Great Britain in her hour of peril."[42]

The Axis also understood. United States intervention in the war, long discounted by Hitler, had to be regarded "as a possibility to be faced any day now," Mussolini wrote Hitler. The German navy was especially concerned. It predicted that American cooperation "with the British Empire will be closer than ever." It appreciated the point made by Churchill that the acquisition of the bases had advanced the air and naval frontiers of the United States "along a wide arc into the Atlantic Ocean." American entry into the war was a certainty, concluded Grand Admiral Raeder. He urged upon Hitler pre-emptive moves into Gibraltar and the Canaries. Raeder feared that the United States might "occupy the Spanish and Portugese Islands in the Atlantic, possibly even the British West African possessions in an attempt to influence and if necessary take over the French West African colonies."[43]

But all this concern was expressed in private. Publicly, Hitler vented his fury—not against the United States, but against the British people. The air battle, which had been mounting in intensity, now turned against the civilian population and England's great cities, London first of all. England was undergoing "a terrific attack," a worried Hull reported to the cabinet on September 6. "Hitler screamed with rage when the destroyer deal went through and announced he was going to turn everything he had on England with a view to overwhelming it without further delay," Ickes wrote after the cabinet meeting. "It was actually claimed in some quarters that England would be suing for peace before last week came to an end, but the British seem to be fighting on as bravely as ever, although I doubt whether any people have ever had to take such terrific punishment."

With American journalists doing a stunning job of reporting from the scene, the United States in September was caught up in the battle. "We literally held our breath, from the President on down," recalled Hull. "The air *Blitzkrieg* started in earnest yesterday—Saturday—with the first big raids on London," reported Mollie Panter-Downes on September 8, adding a week later, "For Londoners, there are no longer such things as good nights; there are only bad nights, worse nights, and better nights. Hardly anyone has slept at all in the past week." The terror attacks upon the civilian population did not shatter British morale. "We shall get used to it" was the understated British reaction. Meanwhile the crucial battle for mastery of the air was being fought out by the fighters. "Since we unfortunately do not possess supremacy at sea," Hitler explained to Mussolini, "the absolute mastery of the air is the most decisive prerequisite for the success of the [invasion] operation." That mastery was never to be won. Nor did Hitler tell Mussolini that on September 17, the same day on which he was writing to the Duce, he had postponed Operation Sea Lion (the planned invasion of England) indefinitely.[44]

The West, of course, did not know this,* and on September 22 Roosevelt was thought to have flashed a warning to Churchill that he had heard via Berlin that the invasion was to take place at three that afternoon.† "It doesn't say whether it's dep[arting] Calais at three or arr[iving] Dover!" the ever-sardonic Cadogan noted. Hours and days were "meaningless," he added. "The thing must turn on the weather." Invasion was expected again on September 27. After that, tides and weather made a cross-Channel invasion highly unlikely before the spring.[46]

Although the massive effort to devastate England from the air went on, Britain's survival for the moment seemed secure. "It is very interesting," Stimson recorded right after the announcement of the destroyer deal, "to see how the tide of opinion has swung in favor of the eventual victory of Great Britain. The air of pessimism which prevailed two months ago has gone. The reports of our observers on the other side have changed and are quite optimistic." The destroyer deal, which Roosevelt in mid-August had feared might lose him the election or, at the least, provoke a terrible row in Congress, had been almost universally acclaimed in the United States.

The *New York Times* reported Roosevelt's announcement of the terms under eight-column banner headlines:

> ROOSEVELT TRADES DESTROYERS FOR SEA BASES;
> TELLS CONGRESS HE ACTED ON HIS OWN AUTHORITY;
> BRITAIN PLEDGES NEVER TO YIELD OR SINK FLEET

The president's message to Congress described the transaction as "the most important action in the reinforcement of our national defense that has been taken since the Louisiana Purchase." That had been done by Jefferson, the president noted to newsmen, "without any treaty" or vote in the Senate.

Even the *Chicago Tribune,* the most virulently isolationist newspaper in America, commented:

---

* According to Frederick W. Winterbotham, in *The Ultra Secret,* British intelligence on September 17 had decrypted a signal from the German general staff to dismantle paratroop air-landing equipment at Dutch airfields. Churchill and his chiefs of staff read this to mean that Hitler had abandoned his plans to invade in 1940. Churchill, however, continued deliberately to emphasize the dangers of invasion, writes Anthony Cave Brown, "in order to rally his own people to meet the threat and to enlist the support and sympathy of the United States." The British interpretation of the September 17 signal, as we now know, was correct, but could Churchill and his chiefs of staff have been as certain of it at the time as Mr. Brown suggests? [45]

† Informed of Roosevelt's message, Eden, at his weekend home, went to the hill overlooking the Channel and reported back to Churchill it was so rough any German who attempted to cross would be very seasick. Actually, there had been a mix-up in codes, and Roosevelt had warned of a Japanese invasion of Indochina, "which proved true enough and fateful."

Any arrangement which gives the United States naval and air bases in regions which must be brought within the American defense zone is to be accepted as a triumph. If the bases could be obtained in no other way, they are to be taken on the terms offered.

Willkie approved the deal in substance while criticizing Roosevelt's failure "to secure the approval of Congress. . . . Congress has constitutional functions as important and sacred as those of the Chief Executive." But the congressional reaction, even among the Republican isolationists, was mild, and within a week Willkie had dropped even the criticisms of method. To Ben Cohen Willkie would say after the election that the criticism was the one act of his campaign that he regretted. "There is virtually no criticism in this country except from legalists," Roosevelt, after his re-election, wrote to King George, "who think it should have been submitted to the Congress first. If I had done that, the subject would still be in the tender care of the Committees of the Congress."[47]

In early August, Hitler had spoken of unsheathing the Japanese sword against the Americans as a way of limiting U.S. intervention in the war in Europe. The destroyer deal made him more eager than ever to convert the ideological affinities embodied in the Anti-Comintern Pact into a military alliance. Japan, which had been reluctant to move too close to the Axis lest it result in a collision with the United States, was more responsive to a German warning that the bases deal in the Atlantic would be followed by one in the Pacific designed to checkmate Japan's advance. An army-dominated government had taken power in July in Tokyo with the avowed purpose of seizing the "golden opportunity," as U.S. ambassador Joseph C. Grew phrased it, presented by the Nazi successes in Europe to build a "new order"—a euphemism for the expulsion of American, British, French, and Dutch interests from the vast areas of Greater East Asia. America was the biggest obstacle in the new government's path.

In June, the Japanese foreign minister had complained to Grew that the stationing of the United States fleet at Pearl Harbor instead of at its home base on the West Coast constituted "an implied suspicion of the intentions of Japan vis-à-vis the Netherlands East Indies and the South Seas." The foreign minister had categorically denied that Japan entertained any territorial ambitions. But the fleet remained. Washington had made no move to renew the trade treaty when it expired at the end of December, 1939, and aid to China had continued, impeding Japanese efforts to end the China "incident." In July, when Japan had pressed Britain to close down Hong Kong and the Burma Road, the two routes of entry into the areas of China still controlled by Generalissimo Chiang Kai-shek, the hard-pressed British had worried over the effect that yielding to Japan would have upon the United States. "If we give way, Americans will give us up, with hopeless results, not only in the Pacific, but also on this side," Cadogan had argued. But Churchill, backed by the military, said that Britain could not afford to fight Japan as well as Germany and Italy, especially since the United States was unwilling to align itself with Britain in a policy either of sanctions or negotiations. "It's hopeless to do as

Winston suggested," Cadogan wrote in his diary, "try to put U.S. on the spot. They simply won't stand there." The cabinet, led by Churchill, was "bent on surrender," thought Cadogan, adding, "we've been bluffed. But it was Winston who resolutely refused to call it."[48]

But the United States was scarcely in a position to criticize. Its policy was one of firm resistance to Japanese aggression short of going to war. Its leaders were divided over the measures that would deter and not provoke, just as Japanese policy makers groped for moves that would realize Japan's expansionist dreams without bringing on war with the United States. Closing the Burma Road, Stimson told Lothian, was a mistake. "I pointed out that as long as Japan was bogged down, so to speak, in China . . . she was less likely to make excursions further South or to attack Australia, or even the East Indies, or Singapore. I rather had them on the hip with this suggestion." Stimson was a hard-liner in respect to Japan. As Hoover's secretary of state, he had initiated the nonrecognition policy toward the Japanese protectorate of Manchuria. All summer, along with Morgenthau, Ickes, and Knox, he had pressed for a tougher policy toward Japan. On the other side, the State Department, with Hull and Welles in the lead, urged caution, as did Admiral Stark of the navy. The fleet might be needed in the Atlantic; it was not ready for war with Japan. Roosevelt, as was his wont, pragmatically sided with one, then with the other. At the end of July, the president embraced the views of the hard-liners, at least to the extent of embargoing aviation fuel and certain types of scrap iron. But when Morgenthau pressed for a tighter embargo, Roosevelt told him to go off in a corner with Welles and settle the issue.[49]

Limited though the embargo was, the direction of U.S. policy was unmistakable. It made the Japanese more amenable, especially after the destroyer deal, to German arguments that a military alliance was the way to dampen American militancy in both the Atlantic and Pacific. The purpose of the projected Tripartite Pact, Foreign Minister Matsuoka, its chief proponent, explained to an imperial conference, was to discourage U.S. entry into the European war, which Germany feared, and, on the other side, to enable Japan to obtain its Greater East Asia objectives without a war with the United States. "A close cooperation with Japan," Hitler wrote Mussolini on September 17, "is the best way either to keep America entirely out of the picture or to render her entry into the war ineffective." Three days later, Ribbentrop went to Rome to secure Italy's adherence. In regard to the United States, he brought good news, he informed the Duce. "In a few days, if Italy agreed, a military alliance between Italy, Japan, and Germany would be concluded." Mussolini was all for the alliance. It would serve to keep America "peaceful and quiet" because the United States stood in great fear of Japan. "The American Navy, like England's Army," Mussolini went on, is "poorly prepared for battle, since both had been developed on a purely dilettante basis." Ribbentrop interrupted: "In a naval battle between Japan and America the chances of a Japanese victory were in his opinion 2 to 1." Franco's Spain, too, would be urged to adhere and to help establish the new order in Europe and Africa, while Japan would be its creator in Asia. And "if America should then desire to set herself against this order, even after the annihilation of England, she would have to contend with practically the whole world, being opposed by Germany, Italy, Spain, and Japan, while Russia stood aloof."[50]

On September 27, news of the Tripartite Pact broke over London and Washington. The crisply worded alliance recognized Japanese leadership in "Greater East Asia" and German-Italian leadership in establishing "a new order" in Europe. The pact pledged mutual assistance if any of the signatories were attacked "by a power at present not involved in the European war or the Sino-Japanese conflict." "On September 27 [the Americans] awakened for the first time from their boundless conceit," the German embassy cabled from Washington, telling Berlin what it wanted to hear. "With proper propagandist treatment," Ribbentrop had predicted to Mussolini, "the agreement with Japan could become the biggest brake on possible efforts by Roosevelt looking toward entry into the war," a strange misreading of American psychology and power, as events were to show.[51]

American leaders reacted calmly. Hull, after talking with Roosevelt, issued a softly worded statement that the "announcement of the alliance merely makes clear to all a relationship which has existed for several years and to which this Government has repeatedly called attention." Its conclusion, he suggested, had already "been fully taken into account . . . in the determining of this country's policies."

But privately Hull told Lothian that he, along with many others, felt that developments such as the Tripartite Pact "will draw United States into war before long. [Hull] said that if war came, American policy in the early stages would be long-distance blockade which would not, he thought, involve any considerable diversion of munitions from us."

"A very serious proposition," Stimson commented in his diary, but not really worrisome. So long as the British fleet remained afloat, "the Axis in Europe could not help Japan if she got into trouble with us and Japan could not help Germany or Italy if they got into trouble with us." And the pact "will be pretty useful" in awakening the American people to America's isolation. "The United States is isolated except for one great power and that's the British Commonwealth."[52]

Roosevelt was in a "rambunctious" mood the day the pact was announced, Stimson grumbled. Three times the secretary had to go to the White House, "the first one related to what we should do to satisfy the negro politicians who are trying to get the army committed to colored officers and various other things they should not do"; the second time, with Marshall, to go over the "time-worn case of what we can give the British," who were pressing for flying-fortress bombers that somehow had fallen out of the destroyers-for-bases deal; the third time to a cabinet meeting where the Tripartite Treaty was at last discussed, but chiefly in terms of whether the United States should not woo Russia a little. This course was strongly opposed by Hull but favored with equal vehemence by Stimson and Morgenthau. "I felt Russia was just as bad in respect to being trusted as Hull did," Stimson noted in his diary, "nevertheless she had very different interests in the Pacific than she had in

Europe, and . . . in Europe her interests ran parallel with ours." Evidently the administration thought it had more than logic to bolster its hopes about how Russia might be viewing its interests. According to Berle, "we had intercepted the Comintern orders (which undoubtedly resulted from the Japanese-German-Italian treaty) to the Russian propaganda and other organizations. They were to say nothing unpleasant about the United States and generally play up the friendship angle. Of course they had not yet reached the New York Communist crowd." Despite Moscow's instructions to its propaganda agents, American efforts to enlist the Russians via Chiang Kai-shek in a triangular agreement to aid China were unsuccessful.

The State Department had sound reasons for moving cautiously. "It was obvious to everyone," recorded Berle, a participant in the high-level strategy meetings convoked by the secretary, "that the Germans hope to embroil us in the Far East as rapidly as they can, thereby assuring to themselves—as they think—a clearer prospect in the Atlantic. Despite this Hornbeck [Hull's chief political adviser] is for sailing into the Japanese." And at the next cabinet meeting on October 4, Roosevelt informed the group: "Japan has already begun to checkmate." Prince Fumimaro Konoye, the new premier, "had warned us not to fortify any American territory in our half of the Pacific without the consent of Japan." The consensus at the cabinet meeting was that "we should do no talking but do some straight-out acting which will show Japan that we mean business and that we are not in the least afraid of her." Roosevelt converted this consensus into a terse formula that he outlined to a congressional delegation that had come on other business:

> We pick no quarrels with Japan.
> We back down on no issue with her.
> We reserve the right to use economic pressure in the hope of bringing Japan to reason.
> The door, meanwhile, is to be left wide open for discussion and accommodation within the framework of our historic position in the Far East.[53]

Like the Americans, the British war cabinet took the view that "the Pact, which would probably anger the United States, left matters very much as they were." But on October 4, Churchill cabled Roosevelt that on October 8 Halifax and he would inform Parliament of the government's decision to reopen the Burma Road.

I shall say that our hopes for a just settlement being reached between Japan and China have not borne fruit and that the Three Power Pact revives the Anti-Comintern Pact of 1939 and that it has a clear pointer against the United States. I know how difficult it is for you to say anything which would commit the United States to any hypothetical course of action in the Pacific. But I venture to ask whether at this time a simple action might not speak louder than words. Would it not be possible for you to send an American squadron, the bigger the better, to pay a friendly visit to Singapore. There they would be welcome in a perfectly normal and rightful way. If desired occasion might be taken of such a visit for a technical discussion of naval and military problems in those and Philippine waters and the Dutch might be invited to join. Anything in this direction would have a marked deterrent effect upon a Japanese declaration of war upon us over the Burma Road opening. I should be very grateful if you would consider action along these lines as it might play an important part in preventing the spreading of the war.[54]

But what American action would deter the Japanese and what would provoke them? That question would haunt American and British leaders up to Pearl Harbor. At the moment, Roosevelt's problem was how America should respond if the Japanese militarily retaliated against Britain for reopening the Burma Road. The Tripartite Pact had strongly affected thinking in Washington. Stark later told the Pearl Harbor inquiry that its announcement had persuaded him that American entry into the war was inevitable. Moffat, on a visit to Washington from Ottawa, noted the growing fatalism. He found the State Department almost wholly preoccupied with the Far East. Hull was "increasingly worried," but "we did not want . . . to become involved in the Pacific if it could be helped." The war, he felt, will be won or lost in Europe, "and there must be no lessening of supplies to England." Welles "could never lose sight of the fact that Japan's aggression might well be a baited trap" to divert the United States from aiding England. Berle told Moffat that "we were fast moving into war and that he saw nothing to stop the prospect." Norman H. Davis, an old foreign-policy hand and presidential emissary, "considers that the chances are ten to one that we will be at war before the end of November. . . . Of all the people in Washington with whom I talked Norman Davis was the one who would view a war with Japan with the greatest equanimity."

"And so we go," Breckinridge Long, another of Hull's confidants, wrote resignedly, "more and more—farther and farther along the road to war. But we are not ready to fight any war now—to say nothing of a war on two oceans at once—and that is what the Berlin-Rome-Tokyo agreement means. Nor will we be ready to fight any war for eighteen months in the future." The military leaders in particular urged caution in the Pacific, partly because they felt they were not ready and partly because they anticipated German moves in the Atlantic: "In order to safeguard our own security the United States may at any time, even before the collapse of the British fleet, need to occupy preventively Dakar and the Azores," a War Department appreciation of the situation read in late September. When Welles reported to Stark and Marshall Churchill's request to Roosevelt that an American naval squadron be sent to Singapore at the time of the reopening of the Burma Road, they demurred, fearing that such a gesture would precipitate Japanese action against the United States. "Every day that we are able to maintain peace and still support the British is valuable time gained," commented Stark, while Marshall called it "as unfavorable a moment as you could choose" for provoking trouble. Roosevelt wanted to send a National Guard division to Hawaii. It was "untrained," Stimson told the president. "We are opposed to doing this," Marshall reported to his staff, "and the Secretary of War succeeded in stopping it. . . . I saw the Secretary when he returned from the White House and we decided that rather than appearing to disapprove all suggestions made by the President, we might send something." They let Roosevelt have an anti-aircraft regiment. Roosevelt "was much pleased with this latter proposition and told me to go ahead," Stimson noted, "but he is also zealous to get some naval preparations made which will be an indication of our direct refusal to be bullied by Japan."[55]

But the navy, as Roosevelt groped for the appropriate signal to Japan, proved irritatingly resistant, especially the commander in chief of the fleet, Adm. J. I. Richardson, who was in Washington and lunched with Roosevelt on October 8. Adm. William D. Leahy, up from Puerto Rico where he was governor, was also at the luncheon, which later figured very prominently in the Pearl Harbor hearings. Richardson argued, as he had done previously with both Knox and Stark, that instead of a forward strategy in the Pacific, returning the fleet to its base on the West Coast where it could be properly prepared and serviced would be more of a deterrent to Japan than an under-manned and unprepared fleet at Pearl Harbor. "Despite what you believe," Roosevelt replied with some asperity, "I know that the presence of the Fleet in the Hawaiian area has had and is now having a restraining influence on the actions of Japan." According to the memo that Richardson prepared for Stark on his talk with the president, Roosevelt also said: "I can be convinced of the desirability of retaining the battleships on the West Coast if I can be given a good statement which will convince the American people, and the Japanese Government, that in bringing the battleships to the West Coast we are not stepping backward."[56]

In his testimony before the Joint Committee on the Investigation of the Pearl Harbor Attack, Richardson also quoted Roosevelt as saying in reply to his query of whether the United States was going to enter the war that, "if the Japanese attacked Thailand, or the Kra Peninsula, or the Dutch East Indies, we would not enter the war, that if they even attacked the Philippines, he doubted whether we would enter the war, but that they could not always avoid making mistakes and that as the war continued and the area of opera-tions expanded sooner or later they would make a mistake and we would enter the war." Richardson's account of the president's statement was dis-puted by Leahy, who was certain that if Japan had invaded the Philippines, the president would have recommended that Congress declare war. Nor did he remember the president's having made the statements ascribed to him by Richardson. But under Republican questioning, he admitted that on the crucial point of whether the president believed the Japanese would make a "mistake" that would bring the United States into the war, "I think it is not in disaccord with the President's ideas, as I understood them at that time." Leahy also recalled his distress at hearing Richardson say the fleet was not ready. He had himself been chief of naval operations and had repeatedly as-sured Congress of the fleet's battle readiness. Knox, too, was upset. On a visit to the fleet in September he had been astonished at the business-as-usual atti-tude he had found. "A large part of my time was directed to inculcating all the officers and men I met with the imminence of war and the high likelihood that we would be involved before it was over. There was too little appreciation of how near war was in the Fleet as I found it."

Knox was also annoyed with Richardson's swift rejection as impractical of a presidential suggestion that, if Japan should attack Britain, the navy should be prepared to back up an economic blockade of Japanese trade with the Americas by patrol lines of light forces. "I am not a strategist," Knox flung at Richardson. "If you don't like the President's plan, draw up one of your own to accomplish the purpose." Richardson did, but the Japanese did not immediately retaliate against Britain and the Richardson proposals merged with the navy's overall planning which now intensified on how to deal with a warlike act by Japan.[57]

The heads of the navy, Stimson fretted in his diary, "are rather cautious men, and . . . what seems to a good many of the Navy to be an important opportunity for bold, affirmative action is being strenuously opposed by the two men who are in the highest positions—Admiral Stark, the CNO, and Admiral Richardson, the Commander of the Fleet. Coupled with that there is a tremendous reluctance in the State Department somewhere to use the power which we have got now under the recent statute to shut off Japan from the war materials which she is comfortably draining away from us. Consequently I sat down this morning and drafted a letter to the President giving my views." Stimson urged the president to dispatch the fleet to Singapore, a proposal that would have rendered the fleet even more vulnerable to a Japanese attack than it was at Pearl Harbor, where the heavy damage would be a consequence of a lack of vigilance rather than of a lack of the means with which to repel the attack.[58]

On October 9 Stark submitted to Roosevelt a list of steps the navy might take "to impress the Japanese with the seriousness of our preparations" for war. The president approved the first three, calling up naval and marine reserves and laying "nets and booms for drill purposes." He directed, however, that none of the others be put into effect "without speaking to me about them." Although the American public thought that the president "was anxious to get into war," Norman Davis advised Moffat, "he [Davis] had been impressed with the President's caution and hesitancy."[59]

Neither America nor Britain, said Churchill in the House on October 8, in the course of a report on the war situation, "was accustomed to react to the threats of violence by submission, and certainly the reception of this strange, ill-balanced declaration [the Tripartite Pact] in the United States has not been at all encouraging to its authors." U.S. polls in October disclosed that 96 per cent of those expressing an opinion approved the total embargo on scrap iron and 90 per cent favored a complete embargo. And the percentage of those who thought the United States should risk a war with Japan to keep her from controlling China had risen from 12 per cent in July to 29 per cent in October, while those who advocated letting Japan control China rather than risk war had fallen from 47 to 30 per cent.[60]

The Tripartite Pact had been a "mistake." Instead of deterring the

United States, the country had been aroused. The Axis powers would make other mistakes, Roosevelt believed, and would present other challenges to American interests and values so unmistakable as to persuade the American people that there was no alternative to war. Meanwhile, the policy was one of firmness. In a rousing address to the Western Hemisphere that ended with the cry *"Viva la democrazia!"* delivered from his campaign train on Columbus Day, 1940, Roosevelt gave his formal answer to the dictators:

No combination of dictator countries of Europe and Asia will stop the help we are giving to almost the last free people now fighting to hold them at bay. . . . We will continue to pile up our defenses and our armaments. We will continue to help those who resist aggression, and who now hold the oppressors far from our shores. . . . The people of the United States, the people of all the Americas, reject the doctrine of appeasement. They recognize it for what it is—a major weapon of the aggressor nations.[61]

Chapter Thirteen

Lions Become Foxes

L ONDON IS BURNING," the sepulchral voice of Edward R. Murrow intoned almost nightly from BBC House. Continental Europe lay prostrate beneath the jack boot. The Tripartite Pact was signed, and the dictators, flushed with their victories, were planning their next moves against the democracies. In the largest democracy, however, political energies during the last few weeks in October shifted from countering transoceanic perils to the final stages of a bitter presidential contest. The process was necessary and, indeed, provided a critical and glorious contrast to totalitarianism—the U.S. government, even in the midst of the gravest perils, continued to be by consent. The system had its advantages. Public pressure, the press, and parliament had brought Churchill to power even as the Nazi armies were invading France and the Low Countries. Submission to the ordeals and vagaries of an election would legitimize Roosevelt's right to continue to lead the country and press forward with his policy of "no appeasement."

Yet that autumn, the detached observer sensed the truth of the Churchillian view that democracy was the worst system of government except for all the others. The last weeks of an election campaign present democratic politics at their shabbiest. Lions become foxes. A momentum takes hold in which victory becomes the paramount consideration. Men and women no longer reflect; they react, swept along on vast, dimly apprehended public tides. Rumors inundate headquarters. The hostility of Italian-American voters because of Roosevelt's "stab in the back" taunt produced one set of jitters among the Democrats; the alleged coolness of the Negro voter another. The pressures mounted on Roosevelt to emphasize his desire for peace, not his defiance of the aggressors.

In the Willkie camp, recklessness took over as the Gallup and *Fortune* polls in October showed the Republican challenger to be closing the gap with "the Champ." Although in reality as strongly interventionist as Roosevelt, Willkie's campaign utterances steadily became more isolationist. In September he had bravely backed the destroyers-for-bases deal, but "within a few days," wrote Joseph P. Barnes, Willkie's sympathetic biographer, "the pressures had been at work and the language had been sharpened. Willkie was now calling the deal 'the most dictatorial and arbitrary act' of any President in the history of the United States." As Willkie's voice grew hoarser and more urgent, and a Hollywood specialist kept it going at a fee of $250 a day, the charges became more strident and extremist. "The man tended to disappear beneath the candidate, for the professionals could not be denied." By the end of September, Willkie was insisting, as he did at a tumultuous rally at Yonkers Raceway, that, "after having seen millions of Americans and realizing more than I ever did how precious a thing this American way is, I want to say to you that if we do not prevail this fall, this way of life will pass."

If Willkie, in the heat of the campaign, saw the president metamorphosing into a dictator, his opponents gave free rein to comparable hallucinations. "I know that if he is elected," Ickes wrote in his Diary, "he will represent the appeasers. I know that he will give us a dose of fascism." And Sen. Joseph Guffey triumphantly reported to Democratic headquarters that, having sent photographers out to Willkie's birthplace in Indiana to photograph the tombstones of Willkie's grandfather and grandmother, he had made the discovery that the spelling on the tombstones was the Germanic one of "Wilcke."[1]

To some degree Willkie was driven to inflammatory utterance by Roosevelt's campaign tactics. The presidential office is so powerful, so resplendent, so much the cynosure of all political activity, that when a president campaigns for re-election the organizations supporting him, party, precinct workers, independent committees, all tend to be secondary, almost superfluous. This was especially the case in 1940. For almost eight years Roosevelt's magisterial personality had commanded the American scene, his vibrant voice the airwaves, his actions and utterances the headlines. He was the issue—his leadership, his policies—and as the 1940 campaign reached its climax, he, master politician, was not campaigning, or, rather, was not campaigning in the traditional sense. They were not making "an ordinary nomination in an ordinary time," Eleanor Roosevelt had placed the Democratic convention on notice in July. "This year the candidate who is the President of the United States cannot make a campaign in the usual sense of the word. He must be on his job." That was true, but it was also canny politics.

In August and early September, Roosevelt made a few forays into the countryside. We have noted his meeting with Canadian prime minister Mac-Kenzie King in northern New York in August, on the day Willkie delivered his first campaign speech. There were times when it was more effective not to campaign openly. A journey through the Tennessee valley over Labor Day to dedicate the Chickamauga Dam gave Roosevelt a chance to talk "government, not politics," as he put it, about this "demonstration of what a democracy at work can do" and about the importance of the TVA in the nation's current defense program. He did not need to say that this most prominent among the symbols of the New Deal was a program that Willkie, a utility grandee, had fought to the bitter end. And the next day at the dedication of the Great Smoky Mountains National Park, his handsome profile against a background of trees "that stood before our forefathers came to this continent," the president spoke about the unprecedented perils of the present moment and the need for preparedness to meet them. On the journey home, he stopped to inspect an armor-plate plant in Charleston, chatted with the press about his experiences in World War I in curbing collusive bidding, and filled in the correspondents on the destroyers-for-bases deal which was being announced in Washington and London. Thus he presented himself to the American people as seasoned world statesman, commander in chief, and serene and authoritative father figure; Wendell Willkie, whose name he never mentioned, was cast in the role of sweaty, overwrought politician, hungry for office.

The president, noted the perceptive correspondent of the London *Times,* "has thus far avoided making a political issue of foreign affairs, unless at such times as this, the most effective way to 'play politics' is not to play politics." Nonpartisanship was not an option open to the challenger. The tousle-haired Hoosier, whose grin and informality were having their effect, faced the problem at the beginning of October that he had had at the beginning of the campaign—how to knock the statesman–commander-in-chief halo from Roosevelt's head and get the president into the arena with him. "There is every likelihood," the London *Times* correspondent alerted his readers, whose very existence depended on what the United States might or might not do, "that American foreign policy will be discussed with increasing bitterness throughout the closing weeks of the campaign." It proved to be an understatement.[2]

Up to the end of September, Roosevelt's strategy had appeared to be working. The newspapers in mid-September reported that the next *Fortune* poll would show Roosevelt to have over 53 per cent of the vote, Willkie 35 per cent, and the remainder undecided. A week later, the Gallup poll confirmed the *Fortune* figures. Roosevelt led in thirty-eight states with 453 electoral votes and Willkie in ten states with only 78 electoral votes. "It staggered even the President's supporters," recorded Ickes. But the Democrats did not trust the polls. They suspected they were being doctored and manipulated. By the end of September, Ed Flynn, who had originally advised the president to confine himself to running the country and to leave partisan attacks to "surrogates" like himself, began to sense vulnerabilities. Contrary to the polls, Democratic reports showed Willkie to be making an impression. His crowds were increasing in size and enthusiasm. Instead of petering out, like his pre-nomination drive in May and June, his campaign appeared to be approaching a carefully calculated climax in which the race would be won or lost in the last lap. Above all, there was anxiety among the Democrats over the war issue. New York's fusion mayor Fiorello La Guardia, with excellent Republican connections, passed on a warning to the White House that "the anti-third-term propaganda would cease about the middle of October and a concentrated drive [would] be made on anti-war."[3]

Flynn dispatched Franklin Jr., who was heading up youth work in the campaign, to plead with his father to make some political speeches. "What brings you to Washington?" Roosevelt teased his son as they dined alone in the Oval Study. "What is this 'urgent' business you had to see me about?"

"Everybody's worried at headquarters."

The president was amused. "Are they out ringing the doorbells?"

"Yeah, they're working their pants off."

"Good, good," the president beamed. "Then they're not relying upon me."

Young Franklin protested: it was not enough; he had to get into it; Flynn had to know when he intended to start campaigning.

"I'll let him know," the president said amiably.

Confident as Roosevelt was, he also had a nagging feeling that public sentiment was quite volatile, particularly on the interventionist issue, and that anything might happen. The Tripartite Pact clearly was meant to intimidate the American electorate. Roosevelt looked for additional demonstrations by the Axis leaders. On October 4 he took the unusual step of reading to the press Herbert L. Matthews's dispatch from Rome in that morning's *New York Times*:

> As far as the United States is concerned, the Axis is interested primarily in keeping it out of the war and in trying to prevent or minimize its help to Great Britain. The three-power alliance was intended to be one step in this direction. It may well be that another step is to be taken.
>
> The Axis is out to defeat President Roosevelt, not as a measure of interference in the internal policies of the United States but because of the President's foreign policy and because of everything which he stands for in the eyes of the Italians and Germans. The coming United States election is realized to be of vast importance to the Axis. Therefore the normal strategy for the Axis is to do something before Nov. 5, that would somehow have a great effect on the electoral campaign.[4]

But to be effective, Axis moves would have to be indirect, unrelated to the elections on the surface. On the same day that the president had read Matthews's dispatch to the press, an alarmed Thomsen, the German chargé in Washington, had cabled Berlin, insisting that it refrain from publishing documents thought to be compromising to Roosevelt, as the chargé knew the foreign office intended doing with material from the French archives. Such actions only played into Roosevelt's hands, Thomsen said, and the president was already accusing the Republican party of collusion with agents of the *Reich*. Matthews was ostentatiously expelled from Rome.[5]

Axis fears of an American backlash did not prevent spectacular meetings intended to bolster the impression of Axis invulnerability. On the day of the Matthews dispatch, Hitler was conferring with Mussolini at the Brenner Pass; a few weeks later he met with Pétain and Laval and then with Franco. " 'Final encirclement' of England by the Axis Powers," Hearst's Berlin correspondent cabled October 24, "is now in full swing as a result of Chancellor Hitler's conferences with French Vice Premier Laval and Spanish General Franco, authoritative German quarters asserted today."

Hitler also was anxious to announce a visit by Molotov to Berlin before November 5. Had the Russians come to any definite agreement with Germany and Japan? Morgenthau asked Roosevelt a week after the Tripartite Pact was signed. The president thought not. "I think they will continue their mugwump policy of sitting on the fence." And there was a real chance to keep them from getting "any closer with Germany and Japan." But that required a firm policy toward Japan, and when constraining measures were discussed in the cabinet, some word usually leaked to the isolationists.

Vice-President John Nance Garner, whom Roosevelt had summoned back to Washington from Uvalde, Texas, where he had been sulking, listened to a cabinet discussion of how to answer the Tripartite Pact, and hurried back to Capitol Hill. He pulled Senator Wheeler, the leader of the Senate isolationists, into a room off the Senate floor. "Go pour yourself a drink and another for me," he directed.

"I'll bet you a grand," Garner said, "that we're in the war by June first of next year."

"Jack, I won't take you."

"I'll make it April first."

"I still won't take you."

"Well," he said flatly, "we're going to be in the war after the election." Garner added, "Hull is more anxious to go to war with the Japs than the Chief is," and, when asked why, explained, "because he thinks we've got to go to war with them sometime and we might as well do it now."[6]

"I know of no well informed Washington observer," wrote Gen. Hugh Johnson, the widely syndicated Scripps-Howard columnist, "who isn't convinced that if Mr. Roosevelt is elected he will drag us into war at the first opportunity, and that if none presents itself he will make one." "I told [Roosevelt]," Breckinridge Long noted in his diary, "that the Hearst press was starting a campaign in New York today to give the definite impression that Roosevelt was headed for war and Willkie for peace. He said that he was not headed for war and that he was going to call the newspaper correspondents aboard his train and give a direct talk to them and emphasize the fact that we were trying to steer clear of war and doing everything possible to keep away from war and were no nearer war now than we were since the war started."

Roosevelt made no such declaration to the correspondents on the way to Dayton, Ohio, for a Columbus Day "nonpolitical" address beamed to the hemisphere. Instead he used that occasion to give his own reply to the Tripartite Pact. "This country wants no war with any nation. This hemisphere wants no war with any nation. . . . We arm to defend ourselves. The strongest reason for that is that it is the strongest guarantee for peace." But defense of the hemisphere covered not only

the territory of North, Central and South America and the immediately adjacent islands; we include the right to the peaceful use of the Atlantic and Pacific Oceans. No combination of dictator countries of Europe and Asia will halt us in the path we see ahead for ourselves and for democracy.

No combination of dictator countries of Europe and Asia will stop the help we are giving to almost the last free people now fighting to hold them at bay.

Our course is clear. Our decision is made. We will continue to pile up our defense and our armaments. We will continue to help those who resist aggression and who now hold the aggressors far from our shores.

"Mr. Roosevelt's 'No'" was the way the London *Times* headlined its leader on the speech. His "noble" Columbus Day broadcast had shown how completely the Tripartite Pact had failed to intimidate the United States. "Mr. Roosevelt has seldom spoken to greater effect. . . . The main object of his speech, downright and uncompromising from start to finish, was to reaffirm American policy 'lest there should be any doubt about our intention to maintain it.'"[7]

The speech heartened foes of the Axis everywhere, but Democratic politicians wondered anxiously whether it would weaken the president politically. The polls could be read in many ways. A poll that had been concluded October 9 asked, "Which of these two things do you think it is the more important for the United States to try to do, (1) To keep out of war ourselves; (2) To help England win, even at the risk of getting into the war?" It showed that 36 per cent favored keeping out of war while 59 per cent elected to help England even at the risk of war. In July, the percentages had gone the other way. It was a decisive shift, but short of Roosevelt's prediction to King George in June, 1939: "If London was bombed, U.S.A. will come in." A poll published soon after the Columbus Day speech showed that 17 per cent of those polled were for going in and 83 per cent were for staying out. And Gallup, commenting on another poll that showed Roosevelt leading Willkie, said that "In fact many voters say that if there were no war, they would not be planning to vote for Roosevelt."

The polls worried him, Roosevelt had confided to Ickes before his October 12 speech. "He was fearful that the next poll would show Willkie to be gaining. He foresaw the possibility of its giving the impression of a horse race with the second horse closing the gap as it goes down the stretch. In that kind of a situation a great effort would be made to convince the voters that Willkie would pass him before the tape. Then, of course, something unexpected might happen.

Ickes, more of a worrier than the president, shared Roosevelt's apprehension. "A really fine speech on the foreign situation," he said of the Columbus Day address, but "I still wish he would make some political speeches."[8]

Willkie had begun his campaign by attacking Roosevelt for his attitude of appeasement at the time of the Munich crisis and for breaking up the London Economic Conference in 1933. But as Willkie's campaign entered its final stages, he was under heavy pressure from the Republican professionals to sharpen his attack on Roosevelt as a warmonger. He tested different formulas. In Providence, on October 10, he declared: "The philosophy of the New Deal leads to weakness. Weakness lead to war. We are closer to war every day." The Republican crowd loved the last line especially. The next day in Boston he tried another variant: "And we can have peace. But we must know how to preserve it. To begin with, we shall not undertake to fight anybody else's war. Our boys shall stay out of European wars. But by the same token we will appease no one."

That was not pointed enough for the party professionals, who were isolationist both by conviction and faction. "The great issue of this campaign," coached Hugh Johnson from his columnar command post, "is becoming crystal clear. It is peace or war. Mr. Roosevelt and his New Dealers are the war party. Mr. Willkie and the Republicans are the peace party." That was the way the professionals wanted the issue drawn.[9]

A powerful voice entered the lists on Willkie's side. On October 14, the night before registration began for America's first peacetime draft, Colonel Lindbergh, over the Mutual Broadcasting System, called for the election the following month of "leaders whose promises we can trust, who know where they are taking us, and tell us where we are going." Despite the absence of a name, wrote the *New York Times,* "the Lindbergh speech was taken here tonight as an attack on President Roosevelt and his policies and accordingly a call for the election of Mr. Willkie." Under Roosevelt's leadership, Lindbergh asserted without naming the president,

We have alienated the most powerful military nations of both Europe and Asia, at a time when we ourselves are unprepared for action, and while the people of our nation are overwhelmingly opposed to war. . . . We have been led to debt and weakness and now we are being led to war. . . . When a man is drafted to serve in the armed forces of our country, he has the right to know that his government has the independent destiny of America as its objective, and that he will not be sent to fight in the wars of a foreign land. [America's future] hangs upon the action we take and the judgment we show.

"Lindbergh's influence is growing," Thomsen, the German military attaché in Washington, cabled his superiors. Thomsen again urged "at the request of persons worthy of attention . . . that Lindbergh, his speeches and his connections with leading German personages not be mentioned in the press, in speeches and discussions, etc."

Lindbergh, some historians have argued persuasively, did not favor a Nazi system for America. But behind his fervent conviction—shared by millions of Americans—that it was more important for the United States to stay out of war than to help Britain prevent a Hitler victory marched a motley band of Nazi and Fascist sympathizers, a point effectively made by Dorothy Thompson. Although a stellar columnist of the Republican *Herald-Tribune,* in a column which that ardently pro-Willkie paper refused to print Miss Thompson declared that "from Berlin there has been a systematic campaign against Franklin D. Roosevelt in which the Nazis have seized upon every argument in opposition to him."

The Communists, too, were opposing Roosevelt, and he would make that opposition an effective point of attack, calling it an "unholy alliance" and declaring that "something evil is happening in this country when a full page advertisement against this Administration, paid for by Republican supporters, appears—where, of all places? in the *Daily Worker,* the newspaper of the Communist Party."[10]

The Lindbergh speech coincided with a new Gallup poll that showed a distinct trend away from Roosevelt and toward Willkie by as much as 4 and 5 per cent in Illinois, Indiana, and Michigan and by 1 per cent in Ohio. The Democratic leaders began to take fright. They expected John L. Lewis to follow Lindbergh, and no one underestimated Lewis's eloquence or his authority with the workers, the core of Roosevelt's strength. He controls "eight to ten million votes," the German embassy had informed Berlin on July 4.[11]

Will Alexander, the former head of the Farm Security Administration and the New Deal's foremost expert on race relations, a jovial man, a southerner trusted by the black leadership, an ally of Eleanor Roosevelt, and currently an adviser to Sidney Hillman, who was labor's top representative in the National Defense Advisory Commission, was summoned to the White House. There, the ushers rushed him upstairs to the living quarters and into the bedroom that Harry Hopkins was using. A gaunt Hopkins was sitting cross-legged on a canopied bed cradling two telephones in his lap, carrying on two long-distance conversations. "Will, this fellow Willkie is about to beat the Boss," Hopkins said, hanging up on one call and covering the receiver on the other, "and we damn well better do something about it."

He did not know the situation was that worrisome, Alexander commented.

Well, I know things you don't know. I know we always depended on the Cardinal [Mundelein] who died in Chicago last winter, for help with the Catholic vote. . . . We have no contact with the Catholic vote worth a bean. . . . We've always had the support of John L. Lewis and his miners. John Lewis is going to make a speech next week. The speech is already written. We know what's in it. He declares that he won't support the President. It means we may lose labor. The President has done more for the Negroes in the country than anybody ever did since Abraham Lincoln, and you can't get a word out of any of them. It looks as though they are all going to go against him. . . . If you can, tell me what to do.

Alexander knew from Walter White, leader of the National Association for the Advancement of Colored People, what the Negroes wanted. They wanted Col. Benjamin O. Davis, who had been passed over on the promotion lists, made a general and they wanted Judge William Hastie, dean of Howard University's Law School, appointed as civilian aide to Secretary Stimson. Alexander so advised Hopkins, and both were done—but not without resistance. Stimson noted:

It turns out now that the special thing that the Negroes want is to have me appoint a Negro civilian aide and Frankfurter has recommended a Negro who was a student of the Harvard Law School and a very good lawyer and after a varied career is now a professor in the Howard University for colored in this city. I told Patterson [undersecretary of war] that I would be willing to do this and so he is going ahead on that basis. The Negroes are taking advantage of this period just before election to try to get everything they can in the way of recognition from the Army. We had General Marshall [in] and he told us that he had decided to organize a brigade of cavalry of which two of the regiments should be colored, the old Ninth and Tenth Cavalry, and that this ought to be a very good recognition of our intentions toward the Negroes. Of course they have certain agitators, particularly a man by the name of White, who are asking for a good deal more, but the bulk of the Negroes we think will be very well satisfied with what we are doing for them . . . we are training colored pilots for the Air Corps. As to the last I have very grave doubts as to their efficiency. I don't think they will have the initiative to do well in the air.[12]

Willkie was mounting a more effective campaign than Roosevelt had expected. On October 16, the press highlighted Willkie's attack upon Roosevelt's refusal to campaign and debate the issues in the traditional sense. "And all this while—all this anxious while," said Willkie, "the man whom the New Deal party has nominated, the man whose trademark is on the depression, the man whose foreign policies helped disrupt the democratic world—that man is silent! He will not discuss the issues that trouble people. He has placed himself above them. He says: Trust me. I can't explain it all to you. You wouldn't understand. Perhaps ten years from now the archives will explain, but for the present you must trust me. You must believe that I am indispensable." The president owed it to the public to discuss the issues being raised by Willkie, Eleanor Roosevelt advised her husband. "I hope you will make a few more speeches and the people have a right to hear your say in opposition to Willkie between now and election day."

On October 15, Roosevelt still was adhering to his original plan. He would make a speech on October 23, to be paid for by the Democratic National Committee (but he did not know whether it would be political, he told the press) and another "paid for" speech on October 29 or 30. He also announced additional "inspection" trips—through the Connecticut valley, New Jersey, and New York. But this did not satisfy Flynn, who was besieged by party organizations throughout the country asking why the president was not out campaigning. Ickes, having just returned to Washington from the hustings, was persuaded that the president had to campaign. He had wired the president from Buffalo, telling FDR that his (Roosevelt's) friends there felt that Willkie was "now gaining" and that they hoped "that you would make some fighting speeches." On the phone with Steve Early on October 16, Ickes insisted that the president give up the inspection-trip charade and make some outright political speeches. The public did not like the deception. Early agreed emphatically but said he had had no effect on Roosevelt. Ickes talked with Missy LeHand. The president had been thinking of some political speeches, she informed Ickes, "but he didn't like to put himself in a position of making it possible for Willkie to say that he, Willkie, had smoked him out." Ickes reminded Missy that the president had left himself a way out when he had said that he would not campaign except to correct misrepresentations and misstatements. Ickes also talked with "Pa" Watson and Doctor McIntire, other members of the president's official family, telling them that "as of that day, I wouldn't bet a nickel that the President would win, but I insisted that he could win if only he would go out and make a fight." Acting as Ickes's ally,

General Watson arranged for Ickes to see the president the next day. But by then the battle had been won. Ed Flynn, in New York, announced the new plans. "Confronted with a reportedly heavy 'trend' toward Willkie," the Hearst press reported, "Mr. Roosevelt increased his projected political addresses to five." "Democratic leaders throughout the country are in a panic," another story in the paper said.[13]

That evening in Saint Louis, Willkie escalated his isolationist attack on Roosevelt and drew his most tumultuous cheer when he hoarsely shouted, "We do not want to send our boys over there again. If you elect me President, they will not be sent. And by the same token, if you re-elect the third-term candidate, I believe they will be sent."

The Willkie attack in Saint Louis was the more galling to Roosevelt because Willkie quoted Winston Churchill's criticisms, made in 1937 and 1938, of Roosevelt's "ruthless" war on private enterprise and his declaration that the best way the United States could aid Europe's democracies was to "repair and maintain her prosperity." What was the role for which the New Deal considered itself so indispensable? Willkie recklessly went on. "Is it that we should send an expeditionary force over there? Is it that we should join again in a foreign war? Is that the role for which the New Deal thinks itself indispensable? Is that the reason for the provocative statements, the gratuitous insults, the whispers, the rumors that keep coming out of Washington?" Willkie, elated by his reception in Saint Louis, moved on through the Midwest.[14]

The panic buttons began to be pressed in Democratic headquarters. "Sherman Minton [Democratic senator from Indiana] telephoned that he hoped at the first opportunity you will emphasize your desire for peace," Byrnes advised the president. "He says that it is evident that Willkie is now going to do what he intended doing at the outset, namely, to urge that your reelection means war. He is of the opinion that it is more important to talk peace than preparedness, and that you should certainly stress that preparedness is being followed only to insure peace." Oscar Ewing, assistant chairman of the Democratic National Committee, sent a memo to Harry Hopkins suggesting presidential speech topics. It began: "The President must iterate and reiterate again and again that the sole aim of his foreign policy and the defense program is to keep this country out of war." Similar advice came from Justice Hugo Black. Nathan R. Margold, solicitor at the Department of the Interior, sent a memorandum to Ben Cohen: "I am convinced that one of the strongest factors in the recent trend in favor of Willkie is the fear that the President, if reelected, will involve the United States in war by spring." Governor John Stelle of Illinois telephoned the White House and left a message for Hopkins: "Said at luncheon yesterday with [Henry A.] Wallace and a couple of others they all decided the most effective way to answer the 'he is leading us into war' argument would be to arrange for Senator Norris to have a national hook-up and for Norris to say, in his opinion that he thought Roosevelt was much less apt to get us into war than Willkie. They picked Norris because of his consistent peace attitude."

Second only to the "he will lead us into war" theme, Republican orators were stressing the threat of one-man rule. The lengths to which they were prepared to go to validate the latter theme were indicated by former President Herbert Hoover, who, on October 17, made what Chief Justice Hughes's biographer termed "a frantic appeal" to the chief justice. "I am about to make a suggestion that may impress you as fantastic. I would not do it if I did not believe that the whole future of the American people hangs upon the decision of this election." His "fantastic suggestion" was that Hughes resign as chief justice "with a declaration to the country of the complete necessity for a change in administration." Hughes turned him down.

"I am fighting mad," Roosevelt informed Ickes after the president decided to make an old-fashioned barnstorming campaign. But to the world he was all serenity and confidence. Budget director Smith was at the White House on the morning of the president's announcement. All Washington was talking about it. General Watson indicated "that politics was now the order of the day." Even though there was some concern because of the slippage in the polls, when Smith entered the president's office, "he had his usual pleasant disposition. If there was anything wrong in the world of a disagreeable nature, you would not guess it from the President's manner."[15]

There were two phrases much on Roosevelt's lips during the campaign —keeping a man "sweet" or preventing him from getting "off the reservation." He would have to be "sweet" to Farley until after the election, he told Mrs. Roosevelt. He used the same expression about Jesse Jones to Morgenthau. Had Morgenthau "noticed Jones' brother had called on Willkie yesterday?" the president asked in August. Baruch was somebody to be kept from "getting off the reservation," as was Ambassador Joseph Kennedy, who had insisted on returning home. "He disagrees completely with what he says are Roosevelt's policies which are leading us straight into war," the U.S. military attaché in the London embassy wrote to his wife. Roosevelt had not wanted Kennedy to come home. "[Roosevelt] looks upon [Kennedy] as a troublemaker and as a person entirely out of hand and out of sympathy," wrote Breckinridge Long. But Kennedy had told Welles on the transatlantic phone that order or not he was coming home and resigning. Roosevelt sent him a letter to reach him at Lisbon, with copies to Bermuda and New York, directing him to make no public statement until they had talked. The Catholic vote was showing signs of erosion. On October 22, the papers quoted Father Gillis as saying in the forthcoming *Catholic World,* of which he was editor: "We can stay out of war if on November 5 we vote Franklin D. Roosevelt out of office." Kennedy's resignation on the war issue could have been very damaging. He wanted to see Joe as soon as he stepped off the plane, he informed Rose Kennedy, the ambassador's wife.[16]

Then there was John L. Lewis. The labor leader had said harsh, wounding things about the president, but a prince had to be both a fox and a lion, as Machiavelli had written.

"John, sit down here by my side," FDR welcomed Lewis, who had been ushered into his bedroom.

According to Lewis, Roosevelt proceeded directly to the point: "John, I want your support."

What assurance could the president give to the CIO? Lewis demanded. "Haven't I always been a friend of labor, John?"

If he was such a friend of labor, Lewis flung back, "why is the FBI tapping all my phones?"

"That's a damn lie," Roosevelt hotly retorted.

Lewis (still according to Lewis) started to walk out, but the president called, "Come back."

Supreme Court Justice Frank Murphy had told him about the FBI, Lewis said angrily. Murphy, when he was attorney general, had seen Roosevelt's order to the FBI on this matter.* They engaged in some small talk. Lewis thought Roosevelt seemed upset. He left and told associates, "Roosevelt and I are done."

That afternoon, Roosevelt joined Hopkins and Rosenman to work on a forthcoming speech. Berle was there too as part of the speech-writing team. The president "took a few minutes off and did an imitation of John L. Lewis coming to call on him," Berle later wrote. "John Lewis had got the idea that he was being followed by the FBI—which happens not to be true." And Berle was in a position to know. He was the State Department's liaison with J. Edgar Hoover and had carefully briefed Hoover on the kind of information the administration wanted about Communist, Nazi, and Fascist operations within the country.

Directly after Roosevelt's unsuccessful interview with Lewis, the latter announced he would deliver a nationwide political broadcast over the three major networks on Friday night, October 25. The broadcast was given under the auspices of "Democrats for Willkie," a Republican campaign organization. But the money for it, carefully laundered, came from the conspiratorial oilman William Rhodes Davis, who had floated the Göring peace feelers in October, 1939.[17]

What was the president's objective? Lewis asked in his most oracular tone. "It is war. His every act leads to this inescapable conclusion." "You," he said, addressing himself to the nation's prospective draftees, "who may be about to die in a foreign war, created at the whim of an international meddler, should you salute your Caesar? In cold, common sense, I think you should vote for Willkie." And to underscore how strongly he felt, ever the showman, he said that if labor did not follow him and the president were re-elected, he would resign as president of the CIO.

But the speech made little real impact. Democrats relaxed when it be-

---

* "A review of our files for information concerning the questions you raised in your letter of November 19th," Clarence M. Kelley, director of the FBI, wrote the author, "failed to reveal that President Franklin D. Roosevelt ordered a wiretap to be placed on John L. Lewis' telephone." Lewis may have been shadowed by Stephenson's agents. He was keeping a close watch on William Rhodes Davis. It is even hinted in *A Man Called Intrepid* that the death of Davis in 1941 by " a sudden seizure of the heart" was the work of British intelligence under Stephenson.

came evident that it had not let loose an avalanche of labor defections. Furthermore, Roosevelt had begun campaigning, and that lifted their spirits. The president's first speech in Philadelphia began with an attack on Republican "falsehoods" and "misrepresentations." That, after all, was his face-saving pretext for hitting the campaign trail. Republican leaders were spreading it about, he said, that there were secret agreements dangerous to United States security, that the government has

pledged in some way the participation of the United States in some foreign war. I give to you and to the people of this country this most solemn assurance: There is no secret Treaty, no secret understanding in any shape or form, direct or indirect, with any Government, or any other nation in any part of the world, to involve this nation in any war or for any other purpose.[18]

But the main thrust of the speech was domestic, a reminder to Americans of the prostrate nation that he had taken over from the Republicans in 1933 and of the Republican opposition to the many reforms of the intervening years. A cry of delighted appreciation ran through the vast audience as his magnificent voice dwelt caressingly on "the tears, the crocodile tears," that the Republican leaders were now shedding for labor, youth, the unemployed, and the elderly after having opposed all the New Deal measures that he had introduced to help these groups. "In 1940, eight years later, what a different tune is played by them! It is a tune played against a sounding board of election day. It is a tune with overtones that whispered, 'Votes, votes, votes.' "

"It was marvelous," Morgenthau told the president the next day. "I never heard you do it any better. This fellow didn't know he was up against a buzz saw." Roosevelt himself felt it had been a success. He had his bit in his teeth, he told Morgenthau, and he was going to let Willkie have it.

One cabinet member, Henry Stimson, did not like the Philadelphia speech. The Frankfurters were at the Stimsons the night of the speech and the secretary was eager to show the justice a letter he had sent to Roosevelt urging that the U.S. fleet be sent to Singapore. The justice

was very much impressed with it, but our evening was spoiled by his desire to listen over the radio to Mr. Roosevelt's speech in Philadelphia. So we had to sit down for three-quarters of an hour listening to that instead of talking over the many things that I wanted to talk with him and the speech was not on a very high level. It was a good campaign speech and may do good in the campaign, but I don't think it will please thoughtful people or do Mr. Roosevelt much good with them.

Effective as Roosevelt's speech was in Philadelphia, his salvo against the opposition at Madison Square Garden on October 28 devastated Willkie. The Republican had coupled his intensifying attacks on Roosevelt as a warmonger with charges that the president had delayed and mismanaged the preparation of the nation's military defenses. Roosevelt now proceeded to review the congressional record on defense appropriations, asking in each case who had opposed his successive proposals for expansion of the army, navy, and air force.

The crowd, before long, was picking up Roosevelt's cadenced answer: "Martin, Barton, and Fish." "When I heard the President hang the isolationist votes of Martin, Barton and Fish on me and get away with it," Willkie later said, "I knew I was licked."

Yet the Garden speech, when it touched on international affairs, trod warily, was almost defensive. The night before, Mussolini had invaded Greece, much to Hitler's dismay because he rightly feared that it would strengthen Roosevelt's re-election prospects. Roosevelt treated this new aggression with kid gloves. He was aware of the inroads being made in the Italian-American vote because of his "stab in the back" phrase, a phrase that Willkie repeatedly had denounced as a provocation, so he limited himself to the statement "I am quite sure that all of you will feel the same sorrow in your hearts that I feel—sorrow for the Italian people and the Grecian people, that they should have been involved together in conflict." An even unhappier concession to the isolationists was his taking credit for the Neutrality Law, a law that he had publicly denounced as encouraging aggression and that he had several times done his best to circumvent.

Such concessions distressed Robert Sherwood, the playwright who had joined the Roosevelt speech-writing team. Sherwood "was not yet as aware as he might have been," wrote Rosenman, "that in order for Roosevelt to be able to do anything for the United States or for the world, he first had to get elected." On balance, the extraordinary thing is how resolutely Roosevelt adhered to his "no appeasement" policy in the face of the Republican attack on him as a warmonger.[19]

On October 29, Roosevelt was scheduled to preside over the drawing of the first numbers in the draft lottery. Over a million men were to be called up. Mayor La Guardia had begged him to postpone the muster until after the election. But the drawing took place, noted Stimson, "before election . . . a brave deed on the part of the President to let it come now, when there is a very bitter campaign being made against him on account of his support of the Draft."

There were other signs of Roosevelt's stanchness in the final weeks of a campaign in which the Republicans were trying to ignite an isolationist fire storm. The United States fleet remained in Hawaii; indeed, naval reservists were called up and American dependents in the Far East called home. When Churchill, who had left the president scrupulously alone in October, appealed to Roosevelt to warn Vichy not to collaborate with the Germans against Britain, as Laval was urging, Roosevelt sent a note that stunned Vichy officials, who protested that it was "painfully curt." Any agreement between France and Germany directed against Britain would "wreck the traditional friendship between the French and American peoples," Roosevelt declared. "A splendid warning," Churchill cabled gratefully, adding a plea for help in matériel. "I do not think the invasion danger is yet at an end, but we are now augmenting our eastern transferences. The strain is very great in both theatres, and all contributions will be thankfully received."

Yet every such move was grist to the mills of his opponents. "Conscripts Face War Service If New Deal Wins," the Hearst press editorialized the day of the draft call-up. If Roosevelt's present pledges to stay out of war were no better than his 1932 pledges to balance the budget, said Willkie on his campaign train, "the boys had better get ready to get on some troop transport." By evening he sharpened this to not only would the boys be on the transports, but "on the basis of his past performances with pledges to the people, you may expect war by April, 1941, if he is elected." "It will be the Republican tune these last days," the London *Times* correspondent sadly reported.

One Republican-generated rumor threatened to undo the effectiveness of the signals Roosevelt was trying to convey to the Japanese. The Republican campaign manager, Roosevelt charged, had held a press conference and at the end of it said:

Wait a minute boys; wait a minute. I want to tell you something off the record and here it is. You must not attribute this to me. But you can spread it around; in effect, spread it around without putting the responsibility on me. Here it is: "The President of the United States has already started the American Fleet westward from Hawaii in the direction of the Far East. And that, as you know, would be regarded, properly, as a hostile act by Japan, and would lead us into war. And the orders have been issued that the day after Election the whole of the United States Fleet will proceed further westward, out to the Philippines. And that, you know, would be an act of war against Japan."

No part of the fleet "has gone west of Hawaii," asserted Roosevelt, which was only accurate in the sense that Admiral Hart's squadron, long based on Manila, was not considered part of the fleet proper. It was Rep. Joseph Martin who had said all this to the press, adding that he had heard it from a high naval officer. Such rumors, said Roosevelt, were "more dangerous to our peaceful international relations, than anything that has ever been done in Washington by this Government."[20]

As the campaign drew to a close, both *Fortune* and Gallup polls showed Willkie gaining, with the key state of New York slipping into the Willkie column, and Roosevelt's national margin over Willkie, which had hovered at 55 to 45 per cent, dropping in the Gallup poll to between 53 to 47 per cent. Yet Roosevelt was beginning to feel quite optimistic. The crowds were as large and enthusiastic as they had been in 1936. Despite Lewis's speech, neither the leadership nor the rank and file in the CIO showed a disposition to follow. Farley had appeared at the Garden rally, and Kennedy, another leading Catholic layman, had stayed "on the reservation." The ambassador had been met at the airport by his wife, who told him, "The President sent you, a Roman Catholic, as Ambassador to London, which probably no other President would have done. He sent you as a representative to the Pope's coronation. You would write yourself down an ingrate in the view of many people if you resign now." Evidently his wife's remarks made an impression. At the White House, after Kennedy had unburdened himself of his complaints about being bypassed in London, Roosevelt asked him to make a speech on his behalf, and he agreed. "The surprising thing about it," wrote General Lee in London, "is that Kennedy certainly left London all primed for a vindictive and vigorous assault upon Roosevelt."

His electoral vote would be 315, Roosevelt confided to Morgenthau. But he was taking no chances. In Boston, the president again yielded to the pressure of the politicians and, with Bob Sherwood approving, diluted a speech that stressed America's growing military might and aid to Britain with a repetition of the Democratic platform's pledge to stay out of foreign wars, without even the platform's qualification "except in case of attack."

> And while I am talking to you mothers and fathers, I give you one more assurance.
> I have said this before, but I shall say it again and again and again.
> Your boys are not going to be sent into any foreign wars.

The next day, in her syndicated column "My Day," Eleanor Roosevelt expressed reservations about such a pledge. "No one can honestly promise you today peace at home or abroad. All any human being can do is to promise that he will do his utmost to prevent this country being involved in war." The lesson of the interwar, appeasement years, she had written a week earlier, is that "when individuals and nations begin to fool themselves, they are building up a dangerous future. You can fool yourself with high ideals and wishful thinking and refuse to face reality and the hard facts of the world in which you live."[21]

Under the impact of events and Roosevelt's guidance, the American people were thinking more realistically. By a substantial majority, as the campaign ended, they favored aid to England even at the risk of war, and 90 per cent favored a complete embargo on war materials to Japan. But confronted with the naked question of whether they wanted to enter the war, they pulled back by a margin of 83 per cent to 17 per cent. Perhaps they recognized this was wishful thinking, for asked whether they thought the United States would enter the war before it was over, 59 per cent fatalistically replied in the affirmative. Americans would remain conflicted up to Pearl Harbor. Meanwhile it was the president's responsibility to fashion a policy of resistance to the Axis within the limits set by public acceptance. "Dictators have forgotten," Roosevelt said in his final radio speech from Hyde Park on election eve, "or perhaps they never knew—the basis upon which democratic Government is founded: that the opinion of all the people, freely formed and freely expressed, without fear or coercion, is wiser than the opinion of any one man or any small group of men." The coming months would sorely test that axiom of his political thought.

Faction, as we have seen, is a powerful narcotic, dulling men's perceptions to the evidence that would suggest more balanced judgment. In reality, as quickly became clear after Election day, Willkie's approach to foreign affairs differed little from Roosevelt's, yet both men by the end of the campaign had persuaded themselves that the other was evil incarnate, Willkie charging

Roosevelt with being hell-bent on war and dictatorship and Roosevelt suspecting that Willkie had become the front man for forces hell-bent on appeasement, perhaps even a coup. "We seem to have averted a putsch, Joe," was Roosevelt's startling good-night comment to the author when the returns were in. When Mrs. Roosevelt later asked him what he meant by that, he replied that he had received information that persons purporting to speak for Willkie and the German government had come to an agreement to compel Britain to make peace* in return for which the United States would have unchallenged sovereignty in the Western Hemisphere. "I have learned a number of things which make me shudder," Roosevelt wrote Rosenman, in answer to the latter's congratulations, "because there were altogether too many people in high places in the Republican campaign who thought in terms of appeasement of Hitler—honest views most of them, and views based on the materialism in which they view not only themselves but their country." "There is absolutely no question," he wrote King George, "that the appeasement element, the pro-Germans, the communists, and the total isolationists did their best for my defeat." This assertion was true. But there never was any evidence to suggest that Willkie had joined the forces of appeasement, and within a few weeks he and Roosevelt would be working together to promote aid to England.[22]

Ironically, the war issue seems to have played little part in the outcome of the election. Roosevelt's 27,243,466 to Willkie's 22,304,755 represented 55 per cent of the vote. That was remarkably close to what the polls had showed FDR to have in midsummer right after the nominating conventions. Careful analysis of representative precincts after the election showed that economics rather than foreign policy had been the chief determinant in how people voted. "Who Elected Roosevelt?" Sam Lubell asked in an election "Post Mortem." "It was the little fellow . . . It was a class-conscious vote for the first time . . . wards and precincts falling into the same economic strata yield virtually the same results; there are almost no freak reversals. So sharp is the cleavage that the campaign could hardly have changed any appreciable number of votes." A postelection analysis by the Bureau of Applied Social Research of Columbia University came to the same conclusion.

Traveling on the campaign train and watching the crowds that turned out to see the president at the wayside crossings and stations, Sherwood had sensed Roosevelt's hold on the "little fellow." "It was always the factory workers and their women-folk who were most emotional in their enthusiasm. They surged out on the tracks and ran after the train shouting 'God bless you!' "[23]

Although foreign-policy issues did not decide the election, Roosevelt's victory did have significant foreign-policy implications. The voters had had a chance to reject Roosevelt's policy of no appeasement of Germany and Japan,

* Willkie was wholeheartedly in favor of all-out aid to Britain, as the British appear to have seen more clearly than Roosevelt, and the author, who was present when Roosevelt made his remark about a "putsch," has never seen anything to suggest that Willkie lent himself to such a maneuver.

of all-out aid to England short of war but including the destroyers deal, and they had not voted to do so. A week after election, Admiral Stark said to Admiral Richardson, commander of the fleet at Pearl Harbor, "You know that we have no definite commitments. Perhaps none can be made. The direction which things finally take may be forced upon us. . . . But no appeasement."

"No appeasement." That was the signal to the world from America's election. Spain, which Germany had been encouraging to try to get from the United States the grain for its starving people that Germany could not provide, reported that as a result of Roosevelt's re-election, the United States attitude had stiffened. The "pro-American" groups around Chiang Kai-shek, the German embassy cabled from Chungking, were resisting Japanese peace proposals, hoping "for strong support on the part of America owing to the re-election of Roosevelt, which has given these circles a powerful impetus." German diplomatic missions all over the world were instructed that "if you should be addressed concerning Roosevelt's election, please say with cool reserve that the outcome was expected by us and we have reckoned with it for a long time." Visiting foreign statesmen in Berlin were assured that the United States could no longer influence the outcome of the war. Victory was certain. And the German people were told the same thing by Hitler, addressing them from Munich's Bürgerbräukeller. "The purpose of the speech," wrote Ciano in his diary, "is to raise the morale of the German people, who are disappointed at the results of the American election. But did the Fuehrer succeed?"

British pleasure in Roosevelt's re-election was unreserved. "Dear Franklin," wrote David Gray, Roosevelt's minister to Ireland and uncle by marriage. "The gentlemanly announcer on the B.B.C. this morning at eight o'clock began. 'Roosevelt is in!' His voice betrayed relief and some exaltation." Harold Nicolson had in the front of his mind accepted the official view that it did not really matter if Willkie won because he was pledged to aid England. "Yet my heart leapt like a young salmon when I heard that Roosevelt had won so triumphantly, which showed me that underneath I had been hoping for his victory. . . . It is the best thing that has happened to us since the outbreak of the war. I thank God!" "I feel I must take advantage of Lord Lothian's return to Washington," wrote King George, "to send you a personal message saying how glad the Queen and I are to think that you are to be the President of the United States of America for a third term. . . . In these grave and anxious days it is a great relief to feel that your wise and helpful policy will continue without interruption."

As usual, Churchill voiced British feelings best. He had awaited the results with an anxiety unequaled since Dunkirk. He wrote:

I did not think it right for me as a foreigner to express any opinion upon American politics while the election was on, but now I feel you will not mind my saying that I prayed for your success and that I am truly thankful for it. This does not mean that I seek or wish for anything more than the full, fair, and free play of your mind upon the world issues now at stake in which our two nations have to discharge their respective duties. We are entering upon a somber phase of what must evidently be a protracted and broadening war, and I look forward to being able to interchange my thoughts with you in all that confidence and good will which have grown up between us since I went to the Admiralty at the outbreak. Things are afoot which will be remembered as long as the English language is spoken in any quarter of the globe, and in expressing the comfort I feel that the people of the United States have once again cast these great burdens upon you I must avow my sure faith that the lights by which we steer will bring us all safely to anchor.[24]

Churchill never received a reply to this message. This troubled him. "Would you kindly find out for me most discreetly," he asked the Washington embassy, "whether President received my personal telegram congratulating him on reelection. It may have been swept up in electioneering congratulations. If not I wonder whether there was anything in it which could have caused offence or been embarrassing for him to receive, Should welcome your advice." Nevile Butler, the minister, said he had delivered the message personally and, when inquiry was made, was told that it must have been lost or mislaid in the flood of postelection congratulations—an implausible explanation. The real reason may have been Churchill's unwillingness to correct Willkie's misuse of criticisms of Roosevelt that Churchill had voiced in the thirties. "It seems unnecessary to have dragged Mr. Churchill into American party politics at this juncture," Professor Whitehead of the foreign office minuted, "especially since the quotation, taken out of its context, is not a fair rendering of the article as a whole."

"Mr. Willkie has been making use of extracts from your pre-war writings in his campaign against the President," Churchill's private secretary, John Colville, advised the prime minister. "Although you clearly could not allow it to be pointed out publicly that Mr. Willkie has made use of certain passages out of their context, the Foreign Office suggests that you might like to send a personal message to the President explaining that the general tone of the essay to which Mr. Willkie refers was in praise of the President's achievements."

The foreign office did telegraph Nevile Butler, its minister in Washington (Lothian was in London), to convey to the president that, "at times Prime Minister has criticised certain aspects of New Deal always in most friendly tone and recognizing great merits; he has however never criticised Mr. Roosevelt personally for whom he has always entertained lively admiration." Butler gave the message to Hull to transmit to the president; but in the meantime Francis Biddle, the solicitor general,* called to say that the Churchill quotations were being repeated to the detriment of the president. Could their effect not be neutralized by a question and answer in the House of Commons? That did not seem feasible to Butler, who cautioned the foreign office that even an article in the *Times* would appear as intervention in the American election and antagonistic to Mr. Willkie. Churchill now demanded that the

---

* In 1941 Roosevelt appointed Biddle attorney general.

embassy supply the "exact words of Willkie's quotations, and if possible, references to the articles from which they purport to have been taken."

Butler sent off the material the next day but with a cautionary note:

I submit the following with all respect.

Electorate in all probability made up their mind by now which way to vote. Therefore anything done in the sense desired by the Solicitor-General would be too late to do any good but so timed as to be extremely conspicuous. There would be therefore serious danger of queering the pitch with those with whom we may have to be working after November 5th.

Willkie is now considered to have quite a good chance and this finds increasing expression in discussion on those [disturbing?] dangers inherent in lame duck period between now and January.

On November 4, Churchill's private secretary notified the foreign office that the prime minister had seen Butler's telegrams, including the Willkie quotations, and had commented: "It was all too true. Less said soonest mended. Do nothing."[25]

The episode may have momentarily shadowed Roosevelt's feeling for Churchill, but not basically. Too much was at stake. In mid-October, Hopkins had enlisted the help of Robert Sherwood, who was ardently interventionist, in writing Roosevelt's speeches. Sherwood described Roosevelt's attitude at the time: "So far as he is concerned, there is absolutely nothing important in the world today but to beat Hitler."[26] Roosevelt now had his chance. And just as Churchill, elevated to the prime ministership, went to bed contentedly even though the Nazi armies were descending upon western Europe, so Roosevelt happily accepted the responsibility of a third term, even though the hour for democracy seemed at its darkest.

Chapter Fourteen

Hitler Misses the Bus

O N NOVEMBER 7, 1940, two days after Roosevelt's re-election, Hitler issued strict orders to the navy to keep the German pocket battleship *Admiral Scheer* out of the "American security zone." Although Grand Admiral Raeder protested that the "zone" covered so wide an area—half of the Atlantic Ocean between South America and Africa, he asserted—that the *Admiral Scheer*'s capabilities as a commerce raider would be severely limited, Hitler refused to budge. He reaffirmed the order and underscored the word *strict*. All through November and December Hitler assured foreign visitors that the United States was a negligible factor in the outcome of the war; that British hopes for American intervention were wishful thinking; that it would take the United States two to three years to complete its rearmament program and by then the war would long be over; that the American army was of no consequence and its navy pinned down by Japan in the Pacific; indeed, that "it was a matter of complete indifference" to him whether the United States entered the war or not. But the orders to the *Admiral Scheer* suggested something more than indifference.

Hitler knew that his failure to challenge the "security zone" or to respond militarily to the destroyers-for-bases deal had been noted by Roosevelt, and he realized that the president, now that the election was over, would use the United States Navy ever more daringly to sustain the British and to keep him from consolidating his victories and building his "thousand-year *Reich*." "We are on his track" had been Churchill's vivid image of the new situation, "and so are our friends across the Atlantic Ocean."[1]

"The supreme law of [Roosevelt's] actions—and we shall have to adapt ourselves to that during the coming four years," cabled German chargé Hans Thomsen from Washington, "is his irreconcilable hostility to the totalitarian powers. His supreme goal is to play a decisive part in forcing these powers to their knees or, in the event that the last bulwark of democracy in Europe is overrun, to take up the fight and continue it in some form from America."

Hitler's counterstrategy was to try to convert the Tripartite Pact into a world coalition that would include France, Spain, and the Soviet Union, the objective being to keep the "money-grubbing" United States out of Europe, Africa, and Asia. Thus, for the United States to intervene actively in the war, he told Molotov, it would "practically have to declare war on the whole world. This would be difficult even for Roosevelt."

Yet this talk of assembling a world coalition came at the time of a decisive major military setback, Germany's first in the war. Germany's attempt to establish air mastery over England—the Battle of Britain—had been repulsed. "And now, gentlemen," a strutting Göring in "a new white gala uniform" had informed his Luftwaffe commanders at the beginning of August, "the Fuehrer has ordered me to crush Britain with my Luftwaffe. By means of hard blows I plan to have this enemy, who has already suffered a decisive moral defeat, down on his knees in the nearest future, so that an occupation of the island by our troops can proceed without any risk." Operation Sea Lion, as the plans for the cross-Channel invasion of Britain were called, was recognized to be highly hazardous, and Hitler's actual order for invasion awaited the outcome of the air offensive. But the air armadas that Göring committed to the Battle of Britain, 1,400 planes on August 12 and equal numbers on August 15, 18 and at the end of the month, were beaten back by the RAF. Given advance warning of Luftwaffe's targets and numbers by the code-breaking operation known as Ultra, the fighters rose from the airfields in Essex, Sussex, and Kent and inflicted losses of three and two to one. In September, the destruction of London rather than the RAF airfields became the Luftwaffe's primary target. "The Fuehrer regards the great attack on London as possibly decisive of the war," the German navy's war diary noted on September 10, "and a systematic and prolonged bombing of London might bring the enemy to a frame of mind that would make Sea Lion quite unnecessary."[2]

German air losses continued to be prohibitive. Instead of the anticipated disintegration of British morale, Londoners demonstrated they could take it. In the middle of September the Battle of Britain was abandoned, Operation Sea Lion was postponed, and the Luftwaffe shifted to night bombing which, although it was savage and relentless, could have no strategic outcome. On October 12, over the signature of Field Marshal Wilhelm Keitel, Operation Sea Lion was officially shelved, at least until the spring.

(1) The Fuehrer has decided that from now on until Spring, preparation for "Sea Lion" should be continued solely for the purpose of maintaining political and military pressure on England.

Should the invasion be reconsidered in the Spring or early Summer of 1941 orders for renewal of operational readiness will be issued later. Meanwhile military conditions for a later invasion are to be improved.

(2) All measures taken to reduce operational readiness must conform to the following principles—

(a) The British must continue to believe that we are preparing an attack on a broad front.

(b) But at the same time our economy must be relieved of some of the heavy strain placed upon it by our invasion preparations.[3]

By spring, British divisions would be better trained and equipped. American matériel would be pouring into the country in ever-mounting quantities, and the island's defenses would be almost invulnerable to direct assault. Postponement of Operation Sea Lion meant in effect its abandonment, although Churchill at the time could not be certain of that. Hitler began to reshape his strategy for bringing the war to a quick and successful conclusion. Instead of invading England, he shifted to a program of laying siege to it, moving at the same time to cut the Mediterranean lifeline of the British Empire. A turn to the Mediterranean had many attractions. Italy was already engaged there and his friend Mussolini needed help. Italian troops were performing ingloriously in Greece, and on November 11 British naval air forces destroyed half the Italian fleet in the Gulf of Taranto with one swift blow, altering the balance of naval power in the Mediterranean. "I am sure you will be pleased about Taranto," Churchill cabled Roosevelt, adding details a few days later:

Success in such an attack was believed to depend on state of the moon, weather, an undetected approach by the Fleet, and good reconnaissance. The latter was provided by flying boats and a Glenn Martin squadron working from Malta. On the night of November 11/12, all the above conditions were met. Unfavourable weather in the Gulf of Taranto prevented a repetition on 12th/13th.[4]

Mussolini's setbacks made the establishment of a powerful German presence in the Mediterranean a matter of urgency. "My heart and my thoughts have been with you more than ever," Hitler consoled his friend. "Know also, Duce, that I am determined to do everything that may be of relief to you in the present situation." The most imperative military measure, he advised Mussolini, was to seal off the Mediterranean. He would try again to induce Spain to enter the war "in order, first of all, to block the western outlet." He hoped that Italian forces in North Africa would push eastward toward Mersa Matrûh in order to establish an air base there from which dive bombers could drive the British fleet from Alexandria and close the Suez Canal. He intended to commit the Luftwaffe to this battle, Hitler said, adding that "the most important goal in the Mediterranean . . . is first of all to expel the British fleet." After talking with Grand Admiral Raeder, Hitler ordered the preparation of a plan (i.e., Felix) for the seizure of Gibraltar, if Franco would cooperate, and occupation of the Cape Verde Islands and the Canaries, and also, if Vichy was agreeable, the occupation of Dakar to secure northwest Africa against a possible Anglo-American takeover. In September at the time of the de Gaulle–British attack on Dakar, he had been prepared to fly in troops to help the French repel the attack.[5]

A Mediterranean strategy had one principal drawback: it challenged British supremacy at sea, which previously had prevented German seizure of Iceland and an invasion of southern Ireland, two projects considered by Hitler. British sea power rendered an assault on British positions in the Mediterranean highly risky. But Hitler's army and navy commanders favored taking this risk—provided the men and weapons required for it would have first claim on Germany's resources. A program of laying siege to the British Empire required in the first instance heavy, long-range four-engined bombers. Germany did not have them. The Luftwaffe planes had been designed primarily to support the army in the field. The siege-and-strangle plan also necessitated a massive U-boat fleet. Yet at the outbreak of the war Germany had only fifty-seven submarines. Despite Hitler's repeated promises to Raeder to give submarine construction the highest priority, other people and departments, especially Göring and the Luftwaffe, got in first, so that in February, 1941, Admiral Karl Doenitz, head of the U-boat fleet, lamented that "the grand total of our operational boats fell to twenty-two." Even so, the squeeze on British shipping approached the point of suffocation. "North Atlantic transport remains the prime anxiety," Churchill cabled Roosevelt December 13, 1940.

Undoubtedly Hitler will augment his U-boat and air attack on shipping and operate ever farther into the ocean. Now that we are denied the use of Irish ports and airfields our difficulties strain our flotillas to the utmost limit. We have so far only been able to bring a very few of your fifty destroyers into action on account of the many defects which they naturally develop when exposed to Atlantic weather after having been laid up so long.[6]

The siege strategy could be decisive, Hitler's commanders felt, but only if other operations did not compete for Germany's resources—in other words, only if Germany was able to keep on friendly terms with Russia. But Hitler had other thoughts. He had first mentioned in July his plan to attack Russia and thus end British hopes of succor from that quarter. Now with the abandonment of Sea Lion, his thoughts turned more actively than ever to settling accounts with Stalin. Yet Hitler, like Churchill, had graven in his memory the experiences of the first war. For Churchill they meant the avoidance at all costs of positional trench warfare; for Hitler they meant, in addition to not provoking the Americans, avoidance of a two-front war. Hitler loathed and despised the Soviet state, but if Stalin was prepared to accommodate himself to his purposes, settlement with him could be left for a later stage. He hoped to find out from Molotov how far Stalin was prepared to go in building "the new order." Churchill's ambassador in Moscow, Sir Stafford Cripps, who before the war had been the leader of the left-wing Labourites, made Hitler uneasy. He did not realize—and neither, for that matter, did Churchill—that a Beaverbrook or a Halifax would have been heard much more respectfully in Moscow because in Stalin's eyes they represented the class that held the power. Not that either could have changed the situation in Moscow, for Stalin's mind moved in another direction. It suited him to have the Nazi and the bourgeois worlds bleeding each other—to the point of mutual exhaustion, he hoped. Approaches by Britain and the United States only increased his ability to extract more from Hitler for maintaining a posture of benevolent neutrality toward Nazi conquests.

But to sorely beset Great Britain, the Nazi-Soviet partnership, whatever

Stalin's intentions, seemed an uneasy one. Cripps saw Russian-German interests in Romania collide and, anticipating more such clashes in the Balkans, recommended to the foreign office that he be authorized to make a new approach to Stalin and Mototov in an all-out effort to divorce Russia from Germany. The package offer should include a British promise to consult Russia on the postwar settlements, a pledge not to form or enter into any anti-Russian alliance after the war, and immediate *de facto* recognition of Russia's sovereignty over the Baltic States. In addition, Britain should offer to ship Russia generous supplies of goods and also guarantee her against attack via Turkey or Persia. The foreign office approved the lavish offering in return for which Britain would ask only that the Soviet government adopt a position of neutrality "as benevolent as that adopted towards Germany."

Thus armed, Cripps sought an appointment with Molotov, only to be fobbed off on Andrei Vishinsky, the deputy foreign minister, a man of shifty brilliance but not a policy maker. And it no doubt amused Stalin that at almost the same time that Cripps was having his session with Vishinsky, he himself was seeing the German ambassador to tell him that Molotov would soon be visiting Berlin. For three weeks Cripps vainly sought to elicit some response from the Kremlin to Britain's far-ranging proposals. Then, on November 10, he heard to his consternation the official announcement of Molotov's forthcoming visit to Berlin.[7]

The United States ambassador in Moscow, Laurence Steinhardt, strongly disapproved of any placatory approach to the Soviet leaders. He was unhappy over the talks that Sumner Welles had begun to hold in Washington with the Soviet ambassador Constantine A. Oumansky, designed to probe whether there was any movement away from the "marriage of convenience" with Hitler. Steinhardt wrote to his friend Loy Henderson in the State Department:

There is not the slightest doubt in my mind but that the publicity going the rounds that an Anglo-American-Soviet alliance was "in the making" has had a very bad effect in the Kremlin. I do not need to labor the point with you that this is the wrong approach to these people. They are realists, if ever there are any realists in this world. Their fear of the German Army—no longer held by the French Army—is, of course, even greater than before France collapsed. The idea that they would change their policy, and run the risk of a German invasion because the British *wish* them to do so, is childish beyond belief. . . . If I am correct in this interpretation, approaches by Britain or the United States must be interpreted here as signs of weakness and the best policy to pursue is one of aloofness, indicating strength, rather than an approach which can have no prospect of success so long as the German military force remains intact and there is no sign of a weakening of German morale. In the Far East it seems to me that the Soviet objective must be war between the United States and Japan. Nothing would be more to their liking and they have apparently decided that this purpose would be best accomplished by a Soviet-Japanese non-aggression pact, which, in their opinion, would bring about such a conflict. . . .

To make matters worse, the Soviet authorities have been more recalcitrant, uncooperative, and stubborn than usual during the past three or four weeks. This is easy to explain. As long as the attitude in Washington was unfriendly, we were getting results here. . . . As you know, from your own experience, the moment that these people here get it into their heads that we are "appeasing them, making up to them, or need them," they immediately stop being cooperative. With Ouman-sky's vindictive nature, I can just imagine what some of his reports to Molotov must look like. . . . My experience has been that they respond only to force and if force cannot be applied, then to straight oriental bartering or trading methods.[8]

Essentially what Hitler and Ribbentrop offered Molotov when he arrived in Berlin was a share in the division of the "bankrupt estate" of the British Empire, principally in Asia, in return for Russia's adherence to the Tripartite Pact. England was finished, Hitler assured the impassive commissar. As soon as the weather improved, "the great and final blow" would fall. But Molotov, stiffened perhaps by the knowledge that the British and Americans were prepared to deal with the Russians, was not to be diverted eastward toward the Indian Ocean, as Hitler intended. He wanted German troops out of Finland. Nor would he give the assurances requested by Hitler that there would be no renewal of the Finnish-Russian War. He did not apologize for Russia's having grabbed more of Lithuania and Romania than the secret protocols of 1939 had stipulated. And, taking the offensive, Molotov inquired what Germany would say if Russia gave Bulgaria, the country nearest the Bosporus, a guarantee similar to that which Hitler had given Romania? Had Bulgaria asked for such a guarantee? Hitler parried. There was, of course, some discussion of "the problem of America," which, said Hitler, "was now pursuing an imperialistic policy." But the "Anglo-Saxon power" represented no imminent danger—"1970 or 1980, at the earliest. . . . The United States had no business either in Europe, or Africa, or in Asia," he decreed, a proposition to which the generally taciturn Molotov promptly assented.

But the next day, undeterred by Molotov's stubborn stand on Finland and ominous probings about Bulgaria and the Balkans, Ribbentrop, at a final conversation which was conducted in an air-raid shelter because British bombers were overhead, handed Molotov a draft agreement of adherence to the Tripartite Pact. Under its terms, Germany, Japan, Italy, and the USSR undertook "to respect each other's natural spheres of influence," such spheres to be detailed in secret protocols after Molotov had had a chance to discuss matters with Stalin. "[Ribbentrop] could only repeat again and again," he said at the end of the discussions, "that the decisive question was whether the Soviet Union was prepared and in a position to cooperate with us in the great liquidation of the British Empire." The Russian, who was not noted for humor, could not resist a parting gibe: "The Germans were assuming that the war against England had already actually been won. If, therefore [as Hitler had said], Germany was waging a life and death struggle against England, he could only construe this as meaning that Germany was fighting 'for life' and England 'for death.' "[9]

However skeptical Russia was of a speedy German victory over England, Stalin was not disposed to challenge the Axis. Soviet Russia was prepared to join the Fascist world coalition, Molotov informed Ribbentrop two weeks later—at a price. Russia insisted on the withdrawal of all German troops from Finland, a Soviet military base close to the Bosporus, and a mutual-assistance pact with Bulgaria. It also asked for recognition of "the area south of Batum and Baku in the general direction of the Persian Gulf . . . as the center of aspirations of the Soviet Union" and a renunciation by Japan of any rights to the oil and coal of northern Sakhalin. The message did not even mention the Indian Ocean, which Hitler had proposed as "the focal point of the territorial aspirations" of the USSR.

"Stalin is clever and cunning," Hitler told his military commanders. "He demands more and more. He is a cold-blooded blackmailer. A German victory is incompatible with Russian ideology. Decision: Russia must be smashed as soon as possible." As for worries about a two-front war, they were rationalized away with the consoling thought that the Finnish-Russian War had exposed the abysmal weakness of the Red Army. He assumed that the *Wehrmacht* would demolish it as easily as it had the Anglo-French forces in Flanders in May. Thus, Hitler, who in July had concluded that the only reason the British hung on and rebuffed his peace offers was hope of Soviet and/or United States intervention, now proceeded to fulfill half of the British hopes. On December 18, he issued the directive for Operation Barbarossa, as the invasion of Russia was code-named, and committed to it some "120 to 130 divisions"; the objective was "to crush Soviet Russia in a quick campaign." "Britain is sustained in her struggle by hopes placed in U.S.A. and Russia," he told his military chiefs on January 8, 1941. "Britain's aim for some time to come will be to set Russia's strength in motion against us. If the U.S.A. and Russia should enter the war against Germany the situation would become very complicated. Hence any possibility for such a threat to develop must be eliminated at the very outset." He argued further that "if Russia collapsed Japan would be greatly relieved; this in turn would mean increased danger to the U.S.A."

Unable to bring the war with England to a speedy conclusion, Hitler turned on Russia, believing he could crush it in a few months. But what if that also proved to be wishful thinking? Then he would have brought about precisely the denouement he was seeking to avoid—a two-front war, an Anglo-Soviet alliance, and, by freeing Japan in the Far East, Pearl Harbor and United States entry into the war.[10]

But the approach of nemesis was only dimly apprehended by Roosevelt and Churchill. Their overtures to Stalin helped bring it about only in the sense that those overtures fed Hitler's suspicions that a switch in alliance was in the making which could be forestalled only by the destruction of Soviet Russia.

At the time that Hitler reshaped his strategy as a result of the abandonment of Operation Sea Lion, so did Churchill. The latter, of course, had little hope, after the cold-shouldering of Cripps in Moscow, of even a more benevolent neutrality by Russia. Little did the prime minister realize that as a result of Hitler's strategical blunder Soviet Russia would become Britain's ally. Churchill's eye, as it ranged the world at the end of 1940 seeking for partners—belligerent or nonbelligerent—focused on the United States.

Britain's plight no longer was as desperate as it had seemed in the summer when even Churchill was close to despair. ("Normally I wake up buoyant to face the new day," Churchill confessed to Eden in December. "Then I awoke with dread in my heart.") Hitler's failure to invade immediately had turned Churchill's thoughts to how to use Britain's supremacy at sea and to the growth of armored formations to strike at the enemy. Even in August he had approved war-office plans to send armor and men to the Middle East to defend Egypt against the expected Italian drive on Mersa Matrûh. He had done so despite his impatience with General Wavell, the commander in chief in the Middle East, who, he told Eden, would "make a good chairman of a Tory association." But when Eden in early November returned from an inspection tour of the Middle East, bringing news that he had not dared to commit to cable—Wavell's plans for a desert offensive— "[Churchill] purred like six cats." The news ended a dispute over which had first claim on British resources—Libya or Greece. Mussolini's invasion of Greece at the end of October had brought into play the guarantee given by Neville Chamberlain to Greece in April, 1939. There had to be a preemptive move into Crete, Churchill had cabled Eden. "So great a prize is worth the risk, and almost equal to [a] successful offensive in Libya." Eden protested the diversion of forces to Greece, but Churchill insisted Greek needs now were dominant and must be considered lest Turkey be lost through Britain's failure to live up to its guarantees. Eden was not persuaded. "Egypt more important than Greece," he wrote on this telegram, and in his diary disgustedly characterized the decision to give priority to Greece as being "strategic folly." But when Churchill was apprised of the plans for an offensive, his immediate reaction was "Here was something worth doing," and the enterprise should have "first claim upon our strained resources."[11]

The planned offensive in the Middle East did not, however, change the basic strategic outlook—that alone, Britain still was on the defensive, its survival still an open question, dependent on its ability to repel an inevitable German descent upon the Mediterranean and, more immediately to counter the deadly U-boat and raider onslaught on British commerce. In three days in October, thirty-three ships, including twenty ships out of one convoy, were sunk by U-boats in the approaches to Great Britain. "You will have seen what very heavy losses we have suffered in the northwestern approaches to our last two convoys," Churchill had cabled Roosevelt.

This is due to our shortage of destroyers in the gap period I mentioned to you. Thank God your 50 are now coming along, and some will soon be in action. We ought to be much better off by the end of the year, as we have a lot of our own anti-U-boat vessels completing, but naturally we are passing through an anxious and critical period with so little small craft having to guard against invasion in the narrow waters, with the very great naval effort we are making in the Mediterranean and the immense amount of convoy work.

The shipping situation did not improve. The overage destroyers proved unusable without extensive alterations. "Gloomy news about shipping," Cadogan noted on December 2. "U-boats got right into an unprotected convoy." The situation was exacerbated by Irish neutrality, which denied the British the use of the ports and bases in southern Ireland that had been available in the first war and forced the British to route their convoys north of Ireland, through the northwest approaches. "I was even more anxious about this battle [against the U-boats] than I had been about the glorious air fight called the Battle of Britain," Churchill confessed to Roosevelt.

We are so hard pressed at sea that we cannot undertake to carry any longer the 400,000 tons of feeding-stuffs and fertilisers which we have hitherto convoyed to Eire through all the attacks of the enemy. We need this tonnage for our own supply, and we do not need the food which Eire has been sending us. We must now concentrate on essentials and the Cabinet proposes to let [Prime Minister] De Valera know that we cannot go on supplying him under present conditions. He will, of course, have plenty of food for his own people, but they will not have the prosperous trading they are making now. I am sorry about this, but we must think of our own self-preservation, and use for vital purposes our own tonnage brought in through so many perils. Perhaps this may loosen things up and make him more ready to consider common interests. I should like to know quite privately what your reactions would be if and when we are forced to concentrate our own tonnage upon the supply of Great Britain. We also do not feel able in present circumstances to continue the heavy subsidies we have hitherto been paying to the Irish agricultural producers. You will realise also that our merchant seamen, as well as public opinion generally, take it much amiss that we should have to carry Irish supplies through air and U-boat attacks and subsidise them handsomely when De Valera is quite content to sit happy and see us strangle.[12]

Churchill might talk of a strategy of victory—blockade, strategic bombing, risings on the Continent—but this was for the record. The most potent of these weapons, the blockade, was less then lethal for, unlike the first war, Hitler had the resources of a whole Continent to draw upon as well as shipments from Soviet Russia. In the autumn of 1940, Britain had only one hope of survival and of victory, and that lay with the United States.

It was not only the man in the street who expected that, the election over, the United States somehow would enter the war: British leaders had the same expectations. As Admiral Stark wrote Admiral Hart: "The British expected us to be in the war within a few days after the reelection of the President—which is another evidence of their slack ways of thought, and of their nonrealistic views of international political conditions, and of our own political system."[13]

Lord Lothian's presence in England from October 20 to November 11 was the occasion of an exhaustive canvass of what Britain required of the United States, including whether it wanted the United States to enter the war. The president and Hull shared the view, Lothian reported, that United States entry into the war would diminish the supply of munitions to Britain. The British disagreed. Even if the United States came into the war as a result of an attack by Japan, that would be an oceanic war confined to the navy and would not divert from Britain the kind of matériel it required. In addition, American industry was not likely to be fully mobilized for war production as long as the United States remained neutral. Summarizing the discussions with Lothian, Llewellyn Woodward, the official historian of British foreign policy, wrote: "The only way to be sure that America would give us all the help in her power until we achieved victory would be for her to burn her bridges behind her and throw in her lot with us. Hence on the few occasions on which our policy might influence an American decision to enter the war, we should always so act as to influence her towards the more vigorous course."

Lothian met with the British chiefs of staff on November 8, three days after Roosevelt's re-election. The Americans, he told the chiefs, were now fully alive to the dangers to the United States of German control of the oceans, and Roosevelt's operative policy was to "save America by helping Britain." With the president's re-election it was urgent to formulate Britain's requirements comprehensively "and present them, whether or not we expected them to be met at once and *in toto*. . . . We should strike while the iron was hot."[14]

"[Lothian] has produced a very good message from Prime Minister for President putting all our cards on the table (which I think is right)," Cadogan noted on November 11. And five days later Churchill alerted Roosevelt: "I am writing you a very long letter on the outlook for 1941 which Lord Lothian will give you in a few days." But the letter took longer than anticipated. Halifax talked with Churchill about it: "[Churchill] did not like much of Lothian's stuff, which he thought verbose and suffering from an overattempt at being comprehensive. I told him that I thought he must make the paper *his own*. And that what it might lose in logical completeness, or perhaps in particular points of presentment or emphasis, it would gain if he could keep it plainly the work of one mind, and that his own—rather than expose it to all the weakness of a *composite* literary effort. I'm sure this is right. He liked some of Lothian. But nobody except the Prime Minister can give it final shape." The letter was finally approved by the war cabinet on December 6 and sent off the next day. Churchill would later describe it as "one of the most important I ever wrote."

The letter first set forth the strategy for winning the Battle of the Atlantic. Lothian had earlier discussed this series of measures with the naval staff, a talk that in turn had reflected his own familiarity with Roosevelt's outlook, the president from the beginning of the war having considered America's interest to be as vitally engaged in the Battle of the Atlantic as Britain's.

Churchill at the outset stressed the stake that the United States had in the preservation of Anglo-American supremacy at sea. Such control was "indispensable to the security and the trade routes of both our countries—" and here the argument became slightly disingenuous because it advanced an outcome that the British knew the president hoped for, but they did not—"and the surest means of preventing war from reaching the shores of the United

States." Another interest that the United States had in sustaining the British, continued Churchill, was to gain the time that it needed, perhaps two years, to complete its vast program of rearmament. "It is our British duty in the common interest, as also for our own survival, to hold the front and grapple with Nazi power until the preparations of the United States are complete." The British were forming as rapidly as possible "between fifty and sixty divisions"* which, combined with sea and air power, could meet the German armies, especially in regions "where only comparatively small forces can be brought into action." Even if the United States were allied with Britain, "we should not ask for a large American expeditionary army."

The invasion danger had receded, replaced, however, by a "less spectacular, but equally deadly," peril. "This mortal danger is the steady and increasing diminution of sea tonnage." Britain would continue to take the blows from the air, but "the decision for 1941 lies upon the seas." The movement of food to the island and of armies and munitions to the various theaters was essential. "It is therefore in shipping and in the power to transport across the oceans, particularly the Atlantic Ocean, that in 1941 the crunch of the whole war will be found."

Here Churchill's argument recapitulated British shipping losses and noted Britain's vulnerability in the Atlantic compared with the last war: "We have now only one effective route of entry to the British Isles, namely the Northern approaches, against which the enemy is increasingly concentrating, reaching ever farther out by U-boat action and long-distance bombing." Churchill enumerated other dangers: "a fleet action, in which the enemy will have two ships at least as good as our two best and only modern ones"; Vichy's joining Hitler's New Order in Europe and, if supported by the French navy, passage of the control of west Africa into Axis hands; and another "sphere of danger," the drive of Japan in the Far East toward Singapore and the Dutch East Indies.

Against such perils the United States could give "supreme and decisive help." Churchill then reiterated the measures discussed by Lothian with the naval staff: revision of the Neutrality Act to permit American ships to enter belligerent ports; convoying; United States use of bases in Eire for such purposes. Such a policy "would constitute a decisive act of constructive non-belligerency by the United States, and more than any other measure, would make it certain that British resistance could be effectively prolonged for the desired period and victory gained."

In the absence of such a decision, could not the neutrality zone and United States patrols in it be extended eastward and an effort made to persuade Eire to give Britain facilities on its southern and western shores for its flotillas and aircraft? Churchill hoped the United States would expand its shipbuilding capacity in order to supply Britain with an additional three mil-

---

* There were divisions and divisions. A territorial army division fit for home-guard duties was one sort; one fit for field duty was quite another. Although the British army's peak strength would rise to three million men, it was able to field only twenty-four divisions for overseas duty, thirteen of them on the western front.

lion tons. And in order to assure "a massive preponderance" in the air, Churchill placed "an immediate order on joint account for a further 2,000 combat aircraft a month," with an emphasis on heavy bombers, "the weapons on which, above all others, we depend to shatter the foundations of German military power."

Last of all, the prime minister addressed himself to the question of finance: Britain's dollar credits will soon be exhausted. "The moment approaches when we shall no longer be able to pay cash for shipping and other supplies." It would not be in America's postwar economic interest and, moreover, it would be wrong, if, after having saved civilization and bought the United States precious time, "we should stand stripped to the bone."

The letter ended on a note of sober dignity: "If, as I believe you are convinced, Mr. President, that the defeat of the Nazi and Fascist tyranny is a matter of high consequence to the people of the United States and to the Western Hemisphere, you will regard this letter not as an appeal for aid, but as a statement of the minimum action necessary to achieve our common purpose."[15]

Roosevelt, too, was pondering how to use his victory to advance the Allied cause. He returned to Washington from Hyde Park on November 7. Stimson, a lifelong Republican who, in the end, had voted for him, decided to join the reception for the president at Union Station. He did not like the idea "of being photographed in a Democratic victory parade," but the president's re-election "will be very salutary to the cause of stopping Hitler," and that was worth celebrating.

At a press conference before he met with his cabinet, Roosevelt disclosed that he had established a "rule of thumb" for the division of war materials needed both by Britain and the United States: "The Rule is a 50–50 rule. In other words, we take half; they take half." The armed services had agreed only reluctantly, Marshall especially balking. The general had a new mass army to equip and quite properly gave that priority. In September, when Roosevelt had pressed him and Stimson to release some flying fortress bombers to the British and Marshall had protested that outside of Panama and Hawaii the United States had only forty-nine bombers fit for duty, "the President's head went back," recorded Stimson, "as if someone had hit him in the chest." But the president had persisted, and the upshot was the fifty-fifty rule. Later, when the problem arose of how General Marshall could in good faith certify, as the Walsh amendment required him to do, that flying fortresses and other advanced equipment were not needed for the defense of the United States, Roosevelt suggested to Stimson that he take up with Hull the legality of sending such material to the British to have it "tested out under combat conditions in order to find weaknesses or necessary improvements" and whether the law would not permit army and navy personnel to go along on " a leave of absence" with the equipment "if no foreign oath of allegiance taken." Twenty-six flying fortresses were released, but Hull was more hesitant about sending American officers along with the planes.

At the first postelection cabinet meeting, there was considerable discussion, prompted by Frank Knox, of what the United States could do to persuade Eire to permit Britain the use of bases on its southern coast. Knox thought a campaign among Irish-Americans in the United States might have an effect upon Prime Minister de Valera. The Irish government was extraordinarily sensitive to American newspaper criticism, David Gray, the United States minister in Dublin, informed the president. "I have told them that the worst is probably yet to come unless they can make some sort of a case to meet the charge of strong anti-British bias to their neutrality." But Gray was not optimistic "since even if De Valera gets over his fear of [a] German victory he cannot renounce his one sure political issue, antagonism to and suspicion of England."

The most significant issue raised for discussion by Roosevelt at the November 8 cabinet meeting was how to finance British purchases in the United States. The British should first use up the credits they still had here, he said. He and Morgenthau figured the British still had about $2 billion they could use, but "the time would surely come," FDR went on, according to Ickes's account of the meeting, "when Great Britain would need loans or credits. He suggested that one way to meet the situation would be for us to supply whatever we could under leasing arrangements with England. For instance, he thought that we could lease ships or any other property that was loanable, returnable or insurable." To Ickes this seemed to be a very good suggestion.*[16]

Thus, a month before the arrival of Churchill's December 7 letter, telling Roosevelt of Britain's needs, and two weeks before Lothian returned to Washington, American leaders were thinking of how to relieve Britain's dollar problem. There were two major obstacles to a solution: the restrictions of the Neutrality Law, which stipulated that Britain could obtain war materials in the United States only on "a cash and carry" basis; and the Johnson Act, which prohibited United States loans to countries in default of their World War I debts. A direct effort to change those laws would mean a confrontation with the isolationists in Congress over issues—war debts, "perfidious Albion," foreign entanglements, and the like—on which internationalists had lost all through the interwar years, joined in this case by other nationalists who felt priority should be given to equipping Marshall's new army. It was not a battle Roosevelt intended to join unless he was sure of victory, for one defeat would destroy his authority and deal a devastating blow to the whole antiappeasement cause.

There was consternation, therefore, from Roosevelt down when Lothian,

---

* Ickes should have thought well of the idea—he had planted it. On August 2, he had written to Roosevelt in support of the destroyer deal, saying, "It seems to me that we Americans are like the householder who refuses to lend or sell his fire extinguishers to help put out the fire in the house that is right next door although that house is all ablaze and the wind is blowing from that direction." A few days later Roosevelt asked Bullitt, "How do you think the country and the Congress would react if I put aid to the British in the form of lending them my garden hose?" As Prof. Warren F. Kimball wrote of this sequence, an idea would be planted in Roosevelt's mind; it would lie dormant, forgotten even by its originator, but not by its new host, who had a husbandman's gift for bringing it to germination when the season and circumstances seemed propitious.

upon arrival in the United States, not only confirmed that Britain was coming to the end of its financial resources, but jocularly remarked to newsmen that "it's your dollars we want." The "calculated indiscretion" angered Roosevelt, for not only was it leaped upon happily by the isolationists, but it suggested that Lothian and the British thought they understood better than Roosevelt and his associates how to deal with Congress. Besides, Roosevelt did not like to be pushed. Kennedy's advice to Halifax in the summer that the president was a stubborn man who was not subject to "rush aggression" appeared to have been forgotten. Also, Churchill's silence during the election may still have rankled FDR. Roosevelt coldly informed Lothian when he saw him on November 25 that he considered a request for financial help premature, that the British must first liquidate their estimated $9 billion of investment in the Western Hemisphere. Morgenthau added to the rebuke. When the secretary went up to the Hill, he scolded the ambassador, telling him that isolationist senators like Gerald P. Nye would say, "Well, on such and such a date Ambassador Lothian said the English were running short of money. By what authority did you let them place additional orders in this country?"

Churchill cabled Lothian:

We are so closely united in thought and friendship that I feel you will not mind my making a few comments on your recent remarks. I do not think it was wise to touch on very serious matters in a newspaper interview to reporters on the landing stage. It is safer to utter a few heartening generalities and leave the graver matters to be raised with the President and his chief lieutenants. The Chancellor of the Exchequer complains that he was not consulted about your financial statements and Treasury does not like their form. While it is generally understood that you were referring wholly to dollar credits, actual words attributed to you give only too much foundation for German propaganda that we are coming to the end of our resources.

"I have learned from a reliable source," Chargé Thomsen cabled Berlin, "that Roosevelt, in his long conversation with Lothian after the latter's return from England, made no secret of his annoyance over the English propaganda pressure. He did not wish to be put under pressure by the English. He had assured the American people that he would not lead them into the war and he intended to keep his word. America was prepared on the present scale to give England the most extensive assistance." Thomsen described Lothian as "greatly depressed by the conversation." The chargé drew hope from Roosevelt's expression "aid on the present scale," which he interpreted to mean that the granting of American credits to England "is by no means imminent." Wishful thinking tinged Thomsen's dispatches, but in this case Lothian also reported to London that the Americans remained "saturated with illusions . . . that we have vast resources available that we have not yet disclosed."[17]

But even as Lothian was being chastised, Roosevelt, Hopkins, Hull, Morgenthau, Stimson, and other administration leaders were casting about for means by which to deal with the dollar problem. Just before Roosevelt left on a cruise on the U.S.S. *Tuscaloosa,* Morgenthau presented him with the list of additional orders—$2 billion worth—that the British purchasing mission wished to place in the United States. The production facilities that would have to be built to fulfill these orders would cost an added $680 million. That was on top of orders already placed that amounted to $2.6 billion. On this memo, dated November 28, Roosevelt scrawled a note: "use U.S. (R.F.C.) funds for plant capital on *U.S.* orders." Morgenthau should take it up with Stimson, Knox, Hull, and Jesse Jones, the president added. When Morgenthau protested that Roosevelt's instructions were a little vague, the president told him, "Well all of you use your imaginations."

When Jesse Jones, the hardheaded conservative banker who headed the Reconstruction Finance Corporation, was informed by Morgenthau at the meeting with Hull, Stimson, Knox, and Marshall, that the president wanted the RFC to order the matériel and build the plants, he weakly protested, "I will have to get a little lower down in the chair." Knox said he saw "no choice" but "to pay for the war from now on." Stimson did not disagree but felt that the administration had to go to Congress for authority. He could not argue against that, Morgenthau observed, and Jones agreed. The amounts involved "were enormous," Stimson noted in his diary. "I was rather shocked at the depths we are getting into and I told Morgenthau frankly at the meeting that I thought that Congress ought to be taken into the confidence of the Executive—that the Executive should not go ahead on such an enormous project alone. Jesse Jones said he felt the same way."[18]

It was generally agreed that congressional approval would have to be obtained for such an undertaking, and administration leaders felt they would have to establish an airtight case that British dollar resources were in fact exhausted. With Sir Frederick Phillips, the representative of the British treasury, Morgenthau took a very hard line. He wanted a complete list of British holdings in the Western Hemisphere, differentiated according to their liquidity, he said. "It is a matter of convincing the general public of the determination, of just how far the English businessman is ready to go. It is a psychological matter as much as anything else." One influential English businessman resented the American pressures. "It would appear that the United States are demanding our South African gold and proposing to collect it and carry it away," Lord Beaverbrook irately wrote Churchill. The U.S. position is this, he went on. "They have conceded nothing. They have exacted payment to the uttermost for all they have done for us. They have taken our bases without valuable consideration. They have taken our gold. They have been given our secrets and offered us a thoroughly inadequate service in return." The time had come for "a complete understanding with the United States."[19]

Beaverbrook's letter was sent a week after Roosevelt had transformed the whole problem of how to aid the British with his proposal for lend-lease. The *Tuscaloosa* docked at Charleston on December 14. Three days later Morgenthau lunched with the president. "I found him in a very good humor, very quiet and self-possessed, and very proud of the fact that he didn't look at a single report that he had taken with him from Washington." But Roosevelt had read the four-thousand-word letter from Churchill, which had been delivered to the *Tuscaloosa,* had brooded and reflected upon it for two days, and, more daring than his Washington-bound lieutenants, had used his imagination, and now with a magnificent concept and a homely illustration cut through the timidities and divergences that had shackled all-out aid to Britain.

"I have been thinking very hard on this trip about what we should do for England, and it seems to me that the thing to do is to get away from a dollar sign," Roosevelt told Morgenthau. "I don't want to put things in terms of dollars or loans, and I think the thing to do is to say that we will manufacture what we need, and the first thing we will do is to increase our productivity, and then we will say to England, 'We will give you the guns and the ships that you need, provided that when the war is over you will return to us in kind the guns and the ships that we have loaned to you, or you will return to us the ships repaired and pay us, always in kind, to make up for the depreciation.'" Roosevelt paused, looking at the secretary, who had stopped munching at his tray, and asked, "What do you think of it?"

"I think it is the best idea yet," Morgenthau said, adding, "If I followed my own heart, I would say, 'Let's give it to them'; but I think it would be much better for you to be in a position that you are insisting before Congress and the people of the United States to get ship for ship when the war is over, and have Congress say that you are too tough, and say, 'Well, let's give it to them,' than to have the reverse true and have Congress say you are too easy."

That afternoon at his press conference Roosevelt presented his concept. He began on a note of American self-interest:

I go back to the idea that one thing that is necessary for American national defense is additional productive facilities; and the more we increase those facilities—factories, shipbuilding ways, munitions plants, etc., and so on—the stronger American national defense is. Now orders from Great Britain are therefore a tremendous asset to American national defense, because they create, automatically, additional facilities. I am talking selfishly, from the American point of view—nothing else.

Having established his tough-minded concern for the American national interest, Roosevelt moved to the problem of financing Britain's future orders. Generosity was the keynote. "Now what I am trying to do is to eliminate the dollar sign." Then came the illustration that clinched the case with American public opinion:

Suppose my neighbor's home catches fire, and I have got a length of garden hose four or five hundred feet away; but, my heaven, if he can take my garden hose and connect it up with his hydrant, I may help him to put out his fire. . . . I don't say to him before that operation, "Neighbor, my garden hose cost me $15; you have got to pay me $15 for it." . . . I don't want $15—I want my garden hose back after the fire is over.

The United States would take over British orders, he explained, and turn them into American orders and then either lease the materials or mortgage them to Britain "on the general theory that it may still prove true that the best defense of Great Britain is the best defense of the United States, and therefore that they would be more useful to the defense of the United States if they were used in Great Britain than if they were kept in storage here."[20]

The British foreign office and, evidently, Churchill failed to appreciate the significance of the president's proposal. Until prodded by the British minister in Washington, no British government message of thanks went to Washington. There was no ambassador, Lord Lothian having died suddenly and tragically because, as a Christian Scientist, he refused to consult doctors. Later, however, in Parliament, Churchill would praise the legislation fulsomely.[21]

Press and public response was generally favorable, but a bruising fight loomed ahead in Congress, which was not in session. Two powerful isolationist committees had been established: America First, headed by Gen. Robert E. Wood of Sears, Roebuck; and the No Foreign Wars Committee, led by Iowa editor Verne Marshall. They pressed the U.S. leadership to bring about a negotiated peace. In Roosevelt's cabinet there was anxious discussion of "the alarming growth of the appeasement movement headed by General Wood and Lindbergh and various others." "I told the President," noted Stimson, "that the only person that the American people took their information on foreign affairs from was the President of the United States and pretty soon he would have to get into action."

Thomsen, who informed Berlin that "we have good relations with both isolationist committees and support them in various ways," did not, however, encourage Berlin to hope that lend-lease legislation might be defeated.

In evaluating the new plan for increased war aid for England announced by the President yesterday one will have to proceed from the fact that this is not the grandiose whim of the moment, but, as the President himself said, the result of careful thought in which the President was guided very decidedly by American interests. Obviously the President assumes that England, unless she collapses in the next few months, will be able to hold out and that then a war of long duration is in prospect in which England will steadily gain in strength until the United States has reached the maximum level of armaments and there is then a prospect of the victory of England.[22]

Congress would not assemble until January and Roosevelt, in one of his fireside chats, used its absence from Washington to build up public support for lend-lease. His broadcast, he emphasized at its beginning, would not be "on war" but rather "on national security." That security at the moment hinged on the survival of Britain. "If Great Britain goes down, the Axis powers will control the continents of Europe, Asia, Africa, Australia, and the high seas—and they will be in a position to bring enormous military and naval resources against this hemisphere." The speech was wide-ranging—an indirect appeal to the Irish, a warning about the Azores, which, indeed, Hitler envisaged as a base for planes directed against the United States. "Could Ireland hold out" if the Nazis won? he asked. "Would Irish freedom be permitted as an amazing pet exception in an unfree world? Or the Islands of the Azores which still fly the flag of Portugal, after five centuries?"

Roosevelt thrust savagely at the appeasers. "There are also American citizens, many of them in high places, who unwittingly in most cases, are aiding and abetting the work of [Axis] agents." (The State Department wanted

Waving good-by to the king and queen at the Hyde Park Station, June 11, 1939. "We all knew the King and Queen were returning home to face a war," wrote Eleanor Roosevelt. —*Franklin D. Roosevelt Library*

King and president. "Why don't my Ministers talk to me as the President did tonight?" the king later wrote. "I feel exactly as though a father were giving me his most careful and wise advice." —*Wide World Photos*

On way to the admiralty, autumn, 1939. "So it was that I came again to the room I had quitted in pain and sorrow almost a quarter of a century before." —*Radio Times Hulton Picture Library*

The Supreme War Council, February 5, 1940: left to right, French Minister of Marine C. Campinchi, Lord Halifax, Premier Édouard Daladier, Prime Minister Neville Chamberlain, First Lord Winston Churchill. This was the first meeting of the council that Chamberlain invited Churchill to attend. "Aid to Finland" was the agenda. —*Popperfoto*

Roosevelt addresses the American Youth Congress which had marched onto the White House lawn singing "We will not go." He called the Soviet Union "a dictatorship as absolute as any other dictatorship in the world." February 10, 1940. —*Wide World Photos*

Colonel Charles A. Lindbergh speaks to a capacity audience at a rally sponsored by America First. "But I do know that an administration which can throw the country into an undeclared naval war against the will of our people, and without asking the consent of Congress, can by similar methods prevent freedom of speech among us." —*Wide World Photos*

Roosevelt inspects the troops of the First Army during maneuvers, August 18, 1940. In the car with him are Canada's prime minister Mackenzie King and Secretary of War Stimson. That same day Wendell Willkie, Roosevelt's Republican opponent in the election, made his first

Ambassador Joseph Kennedy called on the prime minister at Number 10 Downing Street to say good-by, October 17, 1940. —*The Associated Press Ltd.*

U.S. ambassador John G. Winant and the prime minister shake hands after signing the agreement under which Britain leased certain Atlantic bases to the United States for ninety-nine years. —*The Associated Press Ltd.*

Drawing the first numbers in the draft lottery, October 29, 1940: Roosevelt is behind the podium, Secretary of War Stimson behind the urn. "A brave deed on the part of the President," wrote Stimson, to let it come just before election. —*Franklin D. Roosevelt Library*

FDR, with Fala, en route to the U.S. Capitol for his third inauguration. "Mr. President, would you pick him up?" a reporter asked. "He's not a lap dog," Roosevelt answered. —*UPI*

FDR's third inauguration. "In the face of great perils never before encountered, our strong purpose is to protest and perpetuate the integrity of democracy." January 20, 1941. —*Franklin D. Roosevelt Library*

The president and Mrs. Roosevelt returning to the White House after his third inaugural, January 20, 1941. —*Franklin D. Roosevelt Library*

On the facing page: Churchill in the ruins of the House of Commons. "A mass of twisted girders," wrote Harold Nicolson, ". . . when I turned the corridor, there was the open air and a sort of Tintern Abbey gaping before me." —*Topix Photos*

Churchill's bedroom at the underground headquarters of the war cabinet and the chiefs of staff. One hundred feet below ground, in an underground building designed to hold over 2,000 people, there was a map room, the cabinet room, and radio and power stations. —*Radio Times Hulton Picture Library*

Opposite numbers on H.M.S. *Prince of Wales* at Argentia Bay, Newfoundland, August, 1941. —*Photographs Franklin D. Roosevelt Library*

Above left: Gen. George C. Marshall and Sir John Dill, chief of the Imperial General Staff.

Above right: Left to right, Chief of Naval Operations Adm. Harold R. "Betty" Stark, First Sea Lord Adm. Sir Dudley Pound, Adm. Ernest J. King, commander of the Atlantic fleet.

Below left: Gen. H. H. Arnold, commander of the U.S. Air Force, and Air Vice-Marshal Sir W. R. Freeman.

Below right: Lord Beaverbrook and W. Averell Harriman, who in September, 1941, headed up the Anglo-American supply mission to Moscow. Harriman refused to be "bullied" by Beaverbrook.

Sunday services on board H.M.S. *Prince of Wales,* Argentia Bay. "When I looked upon that densely packed congregation of the fighting men of the same language, of the same faith, of the same ideals and to a large extent, of the same interests and certainly in different degrees facing the same dangers," Churchill later reported to his people, "it swept across me that here was the only hope but also the sure hope of saving the world from merciless degradation." —*Franklin D. Roosevelt Library*

Churchill on H.M.S. *Prince of Wales* watches FDR's departure on the U.S.S. *Augusta.* "Winston was greatly taken by him," King George VI noted in his diary after the prime minister had lunched with him. —*Franklin D. Roosevelt Library*

Prime Minister and Mrs. Churchill in London upon his return from the Atlantic Charter conference, August, 1941. —*Franklin D. Roosevelt Library*

Soviet ambassador Ivan Maisky, third from right, entertains representatives of all the Allied governments, August 29, 1941, just after Churchill's return from the Atlantic conference. The officer in uniform is General Sikorski, the Polish premier. Ambassador Winant is between Churchill and Maisky. —*Radio Times Hulton Picture Library*

Churchill with the Labour members of his coalition cabinet: left to right, Ernest Bevin, minister of labour; Maj. Clement Attlee, lord privy seal; and Arthur Greenwood, minister without portfolio. —*The Associated Press Ltd.*

On the facing page, above: Envoys of friendly Pacific powers wait to confer with Secretary of State Hull about the projected offer of a *modus vivendi* to Japan, November 24, 1941: left to right, Dr. A. Loudon, the Dutch minister; Lord Halifax, the British ambassador; Dr. Hu Shih, the Chinese ambassador; and Richard Casey, the Australian minister. —*Wide World Photos*

Below: A joint press conference in Roosevelt's office. Did he consider U.S. entry into the war one of the war's great "climacterics"? "I sure do!" —*UPI*

Churchill addresses Congress, December 26, 1941. "I cannot help reflecting that if my father had been American and my mother British, instead of the other way round, I might have got here on my own." —*The Associated Press Ltd.*

At Christ Church in Alexandria, Virginia, where Churchill and Roosevelt sat in George Washington's pew. —*Wide World Photos*

him to delete the phrase "many of them in high places." Roosevelt hooted and proceeded to write "many of them in high places, including the State Department," but his speech writers—Hopkins, Rosenman, and Sherwood— wouldn't allow it.) A few days before the president spoke, Senator Wheeler declared that the United States did Great Britain "a great disservice in urging her to go on, and fight until she is exhausted." The president "should insist that a just peace be worked out." A "dictated peace," said Roosevelt, was not "a negotiated peace. Such a dictated peace would be no peace at all. It would be only another armistice, leading to the most gigantic armament race and the most devastating trade wars in all history. And in these contests, the Americas would offer the only real resistance to the Axis powers." There was no de- mand "for sending an American Expeditionary Force outside our own bor- ders," he went on. "The people of Europe who are defending themselves do not ask us to do their fighting. They ask us for the implements of war, the planes, the tanks, the guns, the freighters which will enable them to fight for their liberty and our security."

And then in an inspired sentence that crystallized a policy, Roosevelt ended, "We must be the great arsenal of democracy." The phrase had been coined by Jean Monnet, who, after the collapse of France, had attached him- self to the British purchasing mission and who was being shepherded around Washington by Justice Frankfurter. The latter heard him use it and, struck by its aptness, immediately appropriated it for Roosevelt's use.[23]

In this speech, the sentence that followed the assurance that the British were not demanding an expeditionary force asserted: "There is no intention by any member of your Government to send such a force." Some of Roose- velt's top advisers were no longer sure of this. At a meeting in Morgenthau's office on October 29, Knox had made a powerful impression with his blunt statement "The English are not going to win this war without our . . . mili- tary help. . . . That is what we have got to keep in our minds. We needn't talk about it outdoors, but I think it is true." Two weeks later, Stimson brought up the question "of beginning to think about the future when Great Britain can no longer be saved by 'help less than war.' " And when the presi- dent, on December 27, sent over a draft of his "Arsenal of Democracy" speech, Stimson approved it fully but in his diary observed:

I myself go one step further than the President. I feel confident that we cannot permanently be in a position of toolmaker for other nations which fight and sooner or later I feel certain from what I know of young American men that when once they appreciate this issue between right and wrong they will not be satisfied unless they are offering their own bodies to the flames and are willing to fight as well as make munitions. However, that cannot yet be broached but it will come in time I feel certain and the President went as far as he could at the present time.

A week earlier, the president had even turned aside convoying. During a cabinet discussion of the possible seizure of interned Axis ships and trans- ference of equivalent tonnage to the British, Stimson had proposed that the United States "forcibly stop the German submarines by our intervention.

Well, [Roosevelt] said, he hadn't quite reached that yet." Yet Admiral Stark, who was sensitively attuned to Roosevelt's thinking in naval matters, already had his planners blueprinting a "British Isles detachment" to operate out of Northern Ireland and Scotland. And the day before, in a discussion with Knox, Stark, and Marshall, Stimson to his very great relief

found that they all agreed with me that the eventual big act will have to be to save the lifeline of Great Britain in the North Atlantic. There are a number of things to be done first in the Far East by way of stiffening up the brakes on Japan, but it is very apparent that nothing will save Great Britain from starvation if her supplies [run out], which Stark estimates will necessarily take place in six months except assistance from us by convoy in the Atlantic, and Stark's suggestion that the present lines might be altered by the President—that is the present zones—as to permit access to Ireland which is still neutral—was an ingenious suggestion as to what might be done without legislation.[24]

He was trying to get some "definite pronouncement" from the president, Stark wrote Richardson on November 12, so that he might determine the scope and nature of the effort the navy may be called upon to exert in the various theaters in the event of U.S. entry into the war. He had himself drafted a lengthy appreciation of the world situation and come up with a new plan, Plan Dog, which envisaged a strong offensive in the Atlantic and defensive action in the Pacific, if war with Japan could not be avoided. In this memorandum, Stark went beyond the naval assistance that Britain would require if the United States became its ally. British manpower was insufficient to assure a final victory. "I believe that the United States, in addition to sending naval assistance, would also need to send large air and land forces to Europe or Africa, or both, and to participate strongly in the land offensive." Next to this passage Knox, to whom the memorandum was addressed, wrote "True."

Stark's twenty-four-page document ended with a recommendation for secret staff talks with the British. Lord Lothian had urged such talks in early October before the election and was told that "at the moment, conversations should be confined to exchange of information in London, but the position, it was thought, might alter in two or three weeks time." It did. Stark saw the president in mid-November. Roosevelt withheld approval of the hypothetical strategy outlined in Stark's paper because he did not like to commit himself on "iffy" issues, but he did authorize Anglo-American staff talks to be held in Washington.

To facilitate specific planning, the Stark memorandum was adopted by army planners and became the position the United States military leaders proposed to take in the discussions with the British. On January 16, 1941, Hull, Stimson, Knox, Marshall, and Stark met with the president to review military policy in anticipation of the Anglo-American staff talks. The striking aspect of Roosevelt's directives to the military chiefs, as described by Marshall, was the priority he attached to an undiminished flow of supplies to Britain. He thought there was "one chance out of five" of a concerted attack by Germany and Japan on the United States and cautioned that plans had to be realistic for such an emergency and "we must . . . avoid a state of mind involving plans which could be carried out after the lapse of some months; we must be ready to act with what we had available." He approved the basic concept of Plan Dog—that in the event of a concerted Axis attack "we would stand on the defensive in the Pacific with the fleet based on Hawaii"—but he specifically directed that there be no curtailment of material aid to Britain. "He was strongly of the opinion," General Marshall summarized, "that in the event of hostile action towards us on the part of Germany and Japan we should be able to notify Mr. Churchill immediately that this would not curtail the supply of matériel to England." For the first time Roosevelt indicated—and Marshall's memorandum does not make clear whether this was in the event of war or even before—"that the Navy should be prepared to convoy shipping in the Atlantic to England," but considered it too early to define the offensive mission of the army in case of war. The final paragraph of Marshall's memorandum suggests that at this time the president was far from trying to create an occasion or provoke a war with Germany, but "that we should make every effort to go on the basis of continuing the supply of matériel to Great Britain, primarily in order to disappoint what he thought would be Hitler's principal objective in involving us in a war at this particular time, and also to buck up the English."[25]

Financial exhaustion, calamitous shipping losses, the systematic ravaging of England by the blitz, and the expectation of a German drive through the Balkans toward Egypt were some of the facts that weighed on the spirits of Britain's and America's leaders as the year ended. But there was also good news. Instead of an Italian attack on Mersa Matrûh, General Wavell had launched his armored force of 25,000 men against the Italian positions at Sidi Barrâni, which fell almost overnight along with "acres" of captured officers, including three generals, and thousands of troops. All through December the Italian remnants were in flight through the Western Desert, a retreat that took them to Bardia, Tobruk, and Benghazi. "Winston rang up early in the morning and complained that we were not pursuing enemy and had much to say about missed opportunities," an irate Eden noted December 12. "After an angry riposte from me, it emerged that he had not seen telegram that appeared during night giving details of further plans. But this is all symptomatic of his distrust of local leaders which to my disappointment is not abated at all." "Naturally pursuit will hold the first place in your thoughts," an exultant Churchill signaled Wavell. "It is at this moment when the victor is most exhausted that the greatest forfeit can be exacted from the vanquished. Nothing would shake Mussolini more than a disaster in Libya." Optimism was on the upbeat and it stoked his message to Roosevelt: "I am sure that you will be pleased about our victory in Libya. This, coupled with the Albanian reverses, may go hard with Mussolini if we make good use of our success. The full results of the battle are not yet to hand, but if Italy can be broken, our affairs will be more hopeful than they were four or five months ago."[26]

The stunning British military success—Mussolini likened it to "a thunderbolt"—further dimmed Hitler's hopes of cutting Britain's vital links through the Mediterranean. His naval staff was even gloomier. Admiral

Raeder told Hitler that "the naval staff regards the British fleet as the decisive factor for the outcome of the war; it is no longer possible to drive it from the Mediterranean, as we have so often proposed. Instead a situation is now developing in Africa which is most dangerous both for Germany and Europe."

There were repercussions in both Spain and France. Hitler was aware that Africa, given Anglo-American mastery of the seas, might be Britain's doorway back to Europe. He had exerted enormous pressure on Franco to enter the war on the Axis side and to permit his troops to march through Spain for an assault on Gibraltar, the Canaries, and Cape Verde Islands (Operation Felix). Churchill cabled Roosevelt, November 23, 1940:

Our accounts show that the situation in Spain is deteriorating and that the Peninsula is not far from the starvation point. An offer by you to dole out food month by month so long as they keep out of the war might be decisive. Small things do not count now and this is a time for very plain talk to them. The occupation by Germany of both sides of the Straits would be a very grievous addition to our naval strain, already severe. The Germans would soon have batteries working by radio direction finding which would close the Straits both by night and day. With a major campaign developing in the Eastern Mediterranean and need of reinforcement and supply of our armies there all round the Cape we could not contemplate any military action on the mainland at or near the Straits. The Rock of Gibraltar will stand a long siege but what is the good of that if we cannot use the harbour or pass the Straits? Once in Morocco the Germans will work South, and U-boats and aircraft will soon be operating from Casablanca and Dakar. I need not, Mr. President, enlarge upon the trouble this will cause to us or approach of trouble to the Western Hemisphere. We must gain as much time as possible.

The Americans were being "tiresome," Cadogan had grumbled in his diary a few days earlier, and were insisting on difficult conditions for economic help to Spain—a *public* declaration of non-belligerency." Churchill's cable to Roosevelt was persuasive, and on November 30 Cadogan recorded, "Americans have agreed to be reasonable about Spain. After all it concerns *us* more immediately than them." Subsidized by the United States and given pause by the British military success at Sidi Barrâni, Franco eluded Hitler's embrace. On December 11, the German Führer ordered Operation Felix shelved "as the political conditions no longer obtain."[27]

A combination of United States suasion and British military success also had its effect on France. Hitler in November had warned Mussolini of the "very grave psychological" repercussions from the Duce's ignominious showing in Greece, citing that "even in France the position is undoubtedly being strengthened of those who advocate and affirm that possibly the last word has not after all been spoken in this war." On the eve of the British offensive Hitler had again cautioned Mussolini: "Already the slightest counterstroke could cause North Africa and West Africa to become insecure and—separating themselves from Vichy—they offer England dangerous bases of operation." He was, therefore, temporarily assigning units of the Luftwaffe under the command of Field Marshal Erhard Milch to assist Mussolini.

On December 12, Hitler went further. He ordered preparations for Operation Attila.

Should revolts occur in parts of the French Colonial Empire now under the command of General Weygand, preparations must be made for the speedy occupation of the territories of the French motherland which are still unoccupied. At the same time, it will be necessary for the French Home Fleet and that part of the French Air Force which is on home airfields to be secured, or at least hindered from going over to the side of the enemy.

Preparations must be camouflaged in order to avoid alarming the French.[28]

The anti-Axis potentialities of French North Africa fascinated Roosevelt. In the midst of the election he had spent an hour poring over maps of North Africa with Robert Murphy, who had been United States chargé in Vichy. The president directed Murphy to visit the area and to explore the chances of persuading Weygand to pursue a pro-Allied policy in return for United States economic aid. He had already sensed, Churchill wrote, "the President's interest in Tangiers, Casablanca, and indeed in the whole Atlantic seaboard of Africa, the German occupation of which by U-boat bases was held by American military authorities to endanger the security of the United States." Murphy should report to him directly, Roosevelt ordered. "Don't bother going through the State Department." Roosevelt assumed that Murphy, a Catholic and a conservative, would be able to get along with General Weygand. Similarly, in late November, he appointed as ambassador to Vichy Admiral Leahy, a Catholic, a conservative, and a distinguished military figure, believing that the admiral would be able to gain old Marshal Pétain's confidence. "Ambassador Leahy's task will consist in intervening wherever possible and obstructing cooperation between Germany and France," German ambassador Hans Dieckhoff, who had been stationed in Washington, briefed the foreign office, adding, "the new Ambassador entrusted with this task was not badly chosen." Roosevelt's letter of guidance to Leahy directed that in his talks with Pétain he should stress "our firm conviction that only by defeat of the powers now controlling the destiny of Germany and Italy can the world live in liberty, peace and prosperity; that civilization cannot progress with a return to totalitarianism." Leahy was also to emphasize that "it was United States policy to give Britain all possible assistance short of war."[29]

Churchill, elated by the success of British arms in Libya, also addressed himself to the marshal, more boldly than Roosevelt, but less realistically. His ardor for de Gaulle had cooled after the Dakar fiasco, which was partly caused by de Gaulle's faulty estimate of the degree of support that he commanded inside Dakar. Churchill had received Professor Rougier, an emissary of Vichy, and had discussed with him a *rapprochement* between London and Vichy; and in Madrid, the British ambassador Sir Samuel Hoare was discussing an economic agreement with Pétain's representatives. Now, in secret messages to Pétain and Weygand, Churchill stated that if the French government in the near future decided "to cross to North Africa or resume the war there against Italy and Germany, we should be willing to send a strong and well-equipped expeditionary Force of up to six divisions to aid the defense of Morocco, Algiers, and Tunis." He proposed immediate staff talks and warned that delay was dangerous since at any moment the Germans might strike for Gibraltar. There was no answer to this invitation, Churchill later wrote, "from any quarter."

"I am amazed at the courage of my fellow-countrymen," the flinty Cadogan wrote in his diary as 1940 drew to a close. "Everything-on-paper is against us, but we shall live. I don't frankly see how we are going to win, but I am convinced that we shall not lose. And if you hang on—like a bull-dog— it's funny what things do happen."[30]

And who, in that extraordinary year of 1940, when Britain stood alone, better exemplified or more powerfully evoked the bulldog qualities of the British people than Winston Churchill?

Chapter Fifteen

Two Prima Donnas

My dear Mr. President,

"The interpreter then called for a man servant of his, one Great-heart and bid him take sword, and helmet, and shield."

For me you shall always be "Great-heart" after that speech of last night. Your courage is magnificent and no one ever built a great and useful national policy on any other foundation. God give strength to your arm.

Roosevelt appreciated Frank Knox's little hymn of approval of his "Arsenal of Democracy" speech. He needed praise. The election over, the president had spoken his mind with an unparalleled freedom and urgency in denunciation of appeasers and appeasement and in commitment of the country to the support of Britain and other nations defending themselves against the Axis. "That note of yours makes me glad—and lifted up," Roosevelt wrote Knox the same day, "and I think the response of the country today is all any of us could ask." He had set a course, endorsed not only by the most ardently interventionist members of his cabinet but by the nation.[1]

But in London, Churchill fumed and fretted. His discontent with Roosevelt's policy, primarily because he did not understand it, had boiled over into written protest. Instead of appreciation for the "lending my neighbor a hose" concept, there was a question—how was Britain to pay for the material now in the pipeline—and sharp resistance to U.S. demands that British-owned gold resources in Capetown be transferred to the United States in an American warship. It "may produce embarrassing effects." Instead of plaudits for the "Arsenal of Democracy" speech, there was a new inventory of British needs for raw materials and oils. "Remember, Mr. President, we do not know what you have in mind, exactly what the United States is going to do, and we are fighting for our lives," Churchill admonished the man who in his "Arsenal of Democracy" speech had just made what some historians have called the most extreme commitment ever proposed by an American president. To underscore British feeling that Uncle Sam was behaving like Uncle Shylock,

Churchill wanted to throw in, but was overruled by the foreign office, the admiralty's account, prepared at his order, of the troubles it was having with the overage destroyers, many of which had barely made it across the Atlantic. And, as a reminder of what Britain was contributing to the common cause, Churchill concluded his cable:

They burned a large part of the City of London last night, and the scenes of widespread destruction here and in our provincial centres are shocking; but when I visited the still-burning ruins today, the spirit of the Londoners was as high as in the first days of the indiscriminate bombing in September, four months ago.

"Cabinet at 12," Cadogan wrote in his diary. "Decided to advertise attack on City—quite rightly. This may help us enormously in America at a most critical moment."

The Churchill message ended with heartiest good wishes "in the New Year of storm that is opening upon us,"[2] and was dispatched to the British minister in Washington, Nevile Butler, for delivery to the president. The minister was appalled. Arthur Purvis, the head of the British purchasing mission, had just spent several hours with Roosevelt and Morgenthau discussing British requirements. When Purvis said they were in the range of $15 billion, Roosevelt did not flinch and said he wanted Purvis to meet with the Treasury people who would be drafting the lend-lease legislation. The president was aglow with satisfaction over the reception of his "Arsenal of Democracy" speech. What he wanted, he told Morgenthau, was blanket authority from Congress to order the arms needed by this country and the other nations resisting aggression, and the power to allocate the matériel where it was required. Butler put in a transatlantic telephone call to Anthony Eden, who had replaced Lord Halifax as foreign secretary. Butler, Purvis, and Sir Frederick Phillips, the representative of the Treasury, were all perturbed "at the effect which the delivery of our message #3787 would, in their judgment, have upon the President." Purvis "begged most earnestly" that London should await his account of what the president had in mind, and Butler added that he knew the president would be extremely grateful for a message from the prime minister, which should be "unclouded" in appreciation of Roosevelt's speech. Butler suggested the words "I believe speech will rank among the world's great utterances."[3]

Reluctantly Churchill complied. The complaints about the destroyers were forwarded to the British naval attaché in Washington for transmittal to the Navy Department. The prime minister separated his New Year's greeting from the rest of the message and turned it into a tribute to Roosevelt's speech that fully complied with Butler's wish that it be unqualified. "At this moment when the new year opens in storm," he cabled Roosevelt, "I feel it my duty on behalf of the British Government, and indeed of the whole British Empire, to tell you, Mr. President, how lively is our sense of gratitude and admiration for the memorable declaration which you made to the American people and to the lovers of freedom in all the Continents on Sunday last." As for the gold, the message opened, "I agree with your proposal to stave off our difficulties by sending a warship to Capetown to collect the gold." It went on to speak of his pleasure over Purvis's talk with the president and Morgenthau and his gratitude for the president's "understanding of the problems which will be thrown up in the interval before Congress approves your proposals." The subtle reproach was eliminated. The cable was businesslike in tone.*[4]

Although Roosevelt did not experience the full force of Churchill's discontent, a whole series of episodes—Churchill's failure to disavow Willkie's campaign use of his name; his slowness to appreciate the significance of lend-lease; the suggestion of the aged, appeasement-minded Lloyd George as successor to Lord Lothian (a suggestion that Australian minister Richard Casey recorded as having caused "consternation" at the White House); and the actual naming of Lord Halifax, one of the high priests of appeasement; the unremitting pressure from Churchill to do this and to do that (as if Roosevelt needed prodding), an impatience that reflected Churchill's inability at times to recognize that others might be as determined as he to bring about Hitler's defeat and that Roosevelt was not to be treated as a junior partner—served to revive the suspicions nurtured by Joseph Kennedy and, before him, by Roosevelt's old friend Col. Arthur Murray, the aide of Lord Grey and a pillar of the Liberal establishment, that Churchill was a backward-looking imperialist, anti-American, and anti-Roosevelt.[5]

"You know—a lot of this could be settled if Churchill and I could just sit down together for a while," Roosevelt remarked to Hopkins some time during Christmas week.

"What's stopping you?" Hopkins asked.

"Well—it couldn't be arranged right now. They have no Ambassador here—we have none over there."

Hopkins volunteered, and though Roosevelt at first would not hear of it, Hopkins persisted. By January 3, Butler was cabling the foreign office that Hopkins was coming and that he was "a very useful unofficial channel of communication with the President. . . . He is clearly a person to be cultivated, and I hope therefore that everything will be done to welcome him, and assist him in London." The next day Butler sent a fuller cable on the purpose of the Hopkins mission as explained to him by Sumner Welles. "The President appreciated that the Prime Minister was sending to Washington in person of Lord Halifax one who was thoroughly conversant with his views; in the same spirit he was sending Mr. Hopkins for a short visit." Was there irony in this, a quiet Roosevelt joke, in matching the son of the Sioux City harness maker, social worker, and New Dealer with the fox-hunting British grandee? Hopkins himself had come to see him in the afternoon, Butler's cable continued. "He said idea of his visit was conceived during President's recent holiday in Caribbean after he [Roosevelt] had received the Prime Minister's letter . . . the President wished to have someone who had the in-

---

* Dated January 1, 1941, it will be found in *Foreign Relations of the United States,* State Department Series (Washington, D.C.), 1941, III, pp. 1–2. In his history *The Second World War,* however, Churchill published his original version, dated December 31, 1940, and did not indicate that it never reached Roosevelt.

timate knowledge of his own mind and of the Administration to talk to those who were governing England and to bring back over-all picture. Mr. Hopkins said that one issue that mattered on help was that United States in their own interest should enable Great Britain to beat Hitler. This was the spirit in which he was undertaking his mission and he expected after a stay of three or four weeks to bring back pretty precise ideas on some major aspects, including ships, aeroplanes and specified munitions." He was coming for "business only," Hopkins had emphasized, and did not wish to spend time seeing leaders of governments-in-exile, "nor his own Nationals, nor busybodies. . . . On return to this country, he hoped by knowledge that he had acquired and his access to the President, to be able to override any Departmental attempts to whittle down our orders." He was sending Hopkins to London, Roosevelt wrote a vacationing Ickes "so that he can talk to Churchill like an Iowa farmer."[6]

In preparation for his trip, Hopkins talked with Jean Monnet, and that cool, astute Frenchman advised him to concentrate on Churchill. "Churchill *is* the British War Cabinet, and no one else matters." It was significant of Hopkins's—and Roosevelt's—distrustful mood at the time that Hopkins's response to this advice was a flaring "I suppose Churchill is convinced that he's the greatest man in the world." Another participant in the discussion* said sharply, "Harry—if you're going to London with that chip on your shoulder, like a damned little small-town chauvinist you may as well cancel your passage right now."

"Felix Frankfurter, whom I know well and who is a great friend of Hopkins and close to the President, saw me today," Minister Casey cabled the Australian high commissioner in London.

Hopkins is passionately anti-totalitarian. He has such high regard and affection amounting to almost reverence for the President that he is liable to react against anyone who does not show evidence of similar regard. He has the feeling that Mr. Churchill is not as forthright in his regard for the President as he might be.

Frankfurter believes there is nothing currently more important than that Hopkins' mission should succeed and that Churchill and Roosevelt be brought close together through the medium of Hopkins. Frankfurter therefore urged with great sincerity and conviction that Mr. Churchill go out of his way at an early stage to express to Hopkins his great and cordial admiration for the President as a man and as the leader of this great American nation, and ask that he convey these heartfelt sentiments to the President. . . . He thinks that in the stress of great affairs, Mr. Churchill may take for granted such expressions of regard and that if he does Hopkins may interpret it as indifference.[7]

Churchill accepted the advice. On the day that a bone-weary Hopkins, looking "rather green and ill," landed on the southern coast of England after a five-day clipper flight across the Atlantic, a special train with white-gloved conductors and waiters was waiting at Poole to take him to London. In

---

* Robert Sherwood, chronicler of this event, does not identify this participant, but it may have been Justice Frankfurter, who was Monnet's tireless booster in Washington and who had urged Roosevelt to send Hopkins to London.

London, Churchill used a farewell luncheon in honor of Halifax to say a few matchless words about Roosevelt:

I have always taken the view that the fortunes of mankind in its tremendous journey are principally decided for good or ill—but mainly good, for the path is upward—by its greatest men and its greatest episodes.

I therefore hail it as a most fortunate occurrence that at this awe-striking climax in world affairs there should stand at the head of the American Republic a famous statesman, long versed and experienced in the work of government and administration, in whose heart there burns the fire of resistance to aggression and oppression, and whose sympathies and nature make him the sincere and undoubted champion of justice and of freedom, and of the victims of wrongdoing wherever they may dwell.

And not less—for I may say it now that the party struggle in the United States is over—do I rejoice that this pre-eminent figure should newly have received the unprecedented honor of being called for the third term to lead the American democracies in days of stress and storm.[8]

Hopkins did not go immediately to see the prime minister. Churchill's "man Friday," as Hopkins dubbed Brendan Bracken who had met him at Poole, conveyed Churchill's invitation to dinner, but Hopkins pleaded weariness. He checked in at Claridge's and dined in his room with Herschel Johnson, the American chargé. Then, bidding good night to Johnson, Hopkins for five hours plied Edward R. Murrow, whom he had summoned, with questions about British political personalities and British morale. And when Murrow, in turn, asked him the purpose of his mission, Hopkins, in a cryptic sentence, told Murrow more perhaps than the latter understood: "I suppose you could say that I've come here to try to find a way to be a catalytic agent between two prima donnas."

The next morning Johnson returned, bringing with him Gen. Raymond E. Lee, the U.S. military attaché, and Adm. Robert Lee Ghormley, chief of the U.S. naval group in London. Lee had viewed Hopkins's designation as special presidential envoy rather darkly—a social worker who had had no success at any of the jobs he had undertaken. But the general was quickly won over: "Hopkins is quiet, unassuming and very much to the point." And later, before Churchill carted Hopkins off to a British week end, he noted approvingly Hopkins's comments that the president "is very stubborn about the British and their war effort. We want to help them to the limit, but the President is going to insist that they must prove that they are doing their best before we go all out for them. . . . There is no use blinking the fact that the British are going to look out for themselves primarily and if they can hold out something on us to use after the war, there is no question about it that they will do so."

Before going to see Churchill, Hopkins called on Eden, whom he had met in Washington. In his report to Roosevelt on this meeting, Hopkins highlighted Eden's prognostications about Hitler's next moves—"a 'go' at England," but "unsuccessfully," and a "move through Italy to attack the Greeks," who thus far had more than rebuffed the Italian invaders. Eden's account of the meeting stressed Hopkins's flat prediction that Roosevelt would get the lend-lease bill through Congress. "I told him that everything U.S. could deliver before May was worth double anything after. This seemed rather to depress him."

There was a call on Halifax. "I liked him," Hopkins said. "I think and hope the President will like him. He has no side—has been about—I presume is a hopeless Tory—that isn't too important now if we can get on with our business of licking Hitler. I would not like to see him have much say about a later peace. I should like to have Eden say less."[9]

Then on to lunch with the prime minister. Number 10 Downing Street looked "a bit down at the heels" because of the bombings. There he was greeted by Bracken, who showed him around the famous house, poured him a sherry,and left. "[A] round—smiling—red-faced gentleman appeared—extended a fat but nonetheless convincing hand and welcomed me to England." They were together about three hours, and Churchill's account highlights how he immediately sensed that

here was an envoy from the President of supreme importance to our life. With gleaming eye and quiet, constrained passion he [Hopkins] said:

"The President is determined that we shall win the war together. Make no mistake about it.

"He has sent me here to tell you that at all costs and by all means he will carry you through, no matter what happens to him—there is nothing that he will not do so far as he has human power."

Hopkins's account to Roosevelt of this first talk emphasized other matters. He first reported Churchill's response to Roosevelt's desire to see him:

[Churchill] would bring a small staff—go on a cruiser and by accident meet the President at the appointed place—and discuss our problems at leisure. He talked of remaining as long as two weeks and seemed very anxious to meet the President face to face. We discussed the difficulty of communication with the President at long range—there is no question but that he wants to meet the President—the sooner the better.

I told him there was a feeling in some quarters that he, Churchill, did not like America, Americans or Roosevelt. This set him off on a bitter tho fairly constrained attack on Ambassador Kennedy who he believes is responsible for the impression. He denied it vigorously—sent for a Secretary to show me a telegram which he had sent to the President immediately after his election in which he expressed his warm delight at the President's re-election.

Everything would be open to him, Churchill assured Hopkins in connection with his mission, to find out precisely what the British required to win the war. The prime minister then reviewed the military situation:

[Churchill] thinks the invasion will not come but if they gain a foothold in England with 100,000 men "we shall drive them out." . . . He thinks Greece is lost—altho he is now reinforcing the Greeks—and weakening his African Army. . . . The debacle in Greece will be overcome in part by what he considers to be the sure defeat of the Italians in Africa. . . . He expressed the hope that we would not go too far in feeding any of the dominated countries. He feels that tough as it is that one of Hitler's great weaknesses is to be in control of territory inhabited by a dejected and despairing people. . . . He looks forward with our help to mastery in the air and then Germany with all her armies will be finished. He believes that this war will never see great forces massed against one another.

This last sentence, it should be noted, dovetailed with Roosevelt's own strategic thinking that control of the oceans and the air would enable the democracies to triumph over the Axis—and that no new American expeditionary force would be required.

"I have never had such an enjoyable time," Hopkins remarked to General Lee after this session, "but God, what a force that man has."[10]

The next day, Saturday, Hopkins went with Churchill to Ditchley, a great country house north of Oxford that belonged to Ronald Tree, grandson of Marshall Field and parliamentary private secretary to Bracken. For security reasons, Churchill alternated occasionally between Chequers and Ditchley. After dinner, when the women had left the table, Churchill launched into one of his famous war summaries. This "majestic monologue," said Oliver Lyttelton, president of the Board of Trade, who was present, covered much of the material that later appeared in the first two volumes of Churchill's *The Second World War*. The prime minister finished it off with some unwonted rhetoric about Britain's war aims:

We seek no treasure, we seek no territorial gains, we seek only the right of man to be free; we seek his right to worship his God, to lead his life in his own way, secure from persecution. As the humble labourer returns from his work when the day is done, and sees the smoke curling upwards from his cottage home in the serene evening sky, we wish him to know that no rat-a-tat-tat "here he rapped on table—" of the secret police upon his door will disturb his leisure or interrupt his rest. We seek government with the consent of the people, man's freedom to say what he will, and when he thinks himself injured, to find himself equal in the eyes of the law. But war aims other than these we have none.

Here Churchill paused, said Lyttelton, and asked Hopkins, "What will the President say to all this?" Hopkins thought for a moment and then in his dry, sardonic manner replied, "Well, Mr. Prime Minister, I don't think the President will give a damn for all that." He paused again. "You see, we're only interested in seeing that that goddamn sonofabitch, Hitler, gets licked." Sherwood cast doubt on this story. It showed the adroitness of the able, witty men around Churchill "in developing anecdotes about their gusty chief," he thought.[11]

Yet on Churchill's side, the war-aims peroration quoted by Lyttelton is consistent with the advice he received on how he should treat Hopkins. A longhand memorandum in Churchill's file on Hopkins (the author is not identified) pleads for a statement of war aims. In addition to geopolitical self-interest, the memorandum urged,

there is, I think, another element influencing how much and how quickly they assist us.

Hopkins is the old nonconformist conscience of Victorian liberalism arisen in our midst. He does not believe that a world in which some live in the sun and others in the shadow makes sense. He is sincerely interested to find out if we have similar views and aspirations.

And even if the question of identity of aims did not affect "how quickly and how much America comes in," it would influence something as important.

Every thinking man is beginning to see that the only hope of the world now and *after the war* is some sort of alliance between England and America—and that only two men can bring this about—you and Roosevelt. . . . Surely it will give a great tilt towards such an alliance if the serious minded American is satisfied we are both out to build the same kind of new world both here and in America.

Some echo of this advice had found its way into Churchill's farewell words at the Halifax luncheon, which began, "It is no exaggeration to say that the future of the whole world and the hopes of a broadening civilization founded upon Christian ethics depends upon the relations between the British Empire or Commonwealth of Nations and the United States of America." But these words were not charged with progressivism. Neither, indeed, were Churchill's limp sentences at Ditchley. Britons, in his eyes, were heroes who had stood alone in defiance of Hitler, stoically enduring the destruction of their homes and cities in the blitz. But when J. B. Priestley, the author who had become Britain's favorite broadcaster, said such heroes deserved to be told that out of their bravery and sacrifice would come a new and better world, Churchill equated such talk with "more socialism" and Priestley's broadcasts were stopped. "I had no direct evidence but I soon came to believe—and friends more in the know than I was agreed with me—that it was Churchill who had me taken off the air," Priestley said.[12]

There was a good-humored but sharp and revealing exchange between Ernest Bevin, who was emerging as the strongest Labour man in the cabinet, and Churchill on the subject of war aims. At the end of November, in a luncheon speech on the social implications of the war, Bevin had asserted that probably the largest contributing factor to "the present disaster was the failure to provide an economic basis for the development of resources with a view to securing for humanity a new start." He had summed up his war aims in a sentence: "The motive of our life must be social security." Since Bevin had introduced this avowal with the observation that "you cannot have social security on the basis of the present economic order," the speech caused the Tory press to howl and elicited an admonition from Churchill:

I thought your speech the other day at the Luncheon Club was likely to cause some disturbance in our ranks. Personally, I believe in private enterprise and in private property, so long as these are brought into due harmony with the national interest. I believe that the substitution of the State for the private employer is nearly always attended by waste and loss of efficiency. I am sure that the substitution of one strong State for many weak private employers would be fatal to individual liberty. I am altogether opposed to the National Socialist idea.

I do not think the British nation will ever adopt it. These are, of course, only my own well-known opinions, but I do not think it would be a good thing for me to expatiate upon these in public at this time, because it would upset a lot of your people, and we are all working together, in the full stress of this dire war. There is no question of anyone giving up his private convictions. But this is not the time to emphasize points of difference. We cannot indulge in Party strife at the present time, and it would be disastrous if it broke out.

I am sure you won't mind my giving you this very friendly hint, as I have to try to keep all together till the Hun is beat.

Bevin sent him a copy of the text of his speech, saying, "I am sure you will agree that, compared with those which you and Lloyd George used to make a few years ago, it is extremely mild." But inside the cabinet, the Labour party did not press for a statement of war aims, despite considerable pressure from Parliament and the press. This silence had become more awkward after Roosevelt's annual State of the Union message on January 6, 1941, in which he had said, "Certainly this is no time for any of us to stop thinking about the social and economic problems which are the root cause of the social revolution which is today a supreme factor in the world." The speech ended with a fresh statement of the Four Freedoms:

In the future days, which we seek to make secure, we look forward to a world founded upon four essential freedoms.
The first is freedom of speech and expression—everywhere in the world.
The second is freedom of every person to worship God in his own way—everywhere in the world.
The third is freedom from want—which, translated into world terms, means economic understandings which will secure to every nation a healthy peacetime life for its inhabitants—everywhere in the world.
The fourth is freedom from fear—which, translated into world terms, means a world-wide reduction of armaments to such a point and in such a thorough fashion that no nation will be in a position to commit an act of physical aggression against any neighbor—anywhere in the world.

To the "new order" proclaimed by the totalitarians Roosevelt proposed this "greater order" based on human rights, emphasizing the phrase "everywhere in the world."[13]

Roosevelt undoubtedly would have welcomed Great Britain's associating itself with that statement, but perhaps it was not Hopkins's job to urge the British to do so. When Roosevelt had announced his mission, the press in the United States immediately assumed he was going over to convert Church-illian England to the New Deal faith or, at the very least, to get ideas from the egalitarian democracy that was said to be emerging from England's ruins for the New Deal's next leap forward. But it would have been unseemly for the representative of a country that was not at war, sitting amid those ruins, to offer the British advice. It might, moreover, have interfered with the two objectives that had top priority with Hopkins: to forge a more intimate link between Roosevelt and Churchill and to clear the way for speeding aid to England. Except for Roosevelt there was no one in the United States government who had a surer feeling than Hopkins for "first things first," and it was little wonder that Churchill came to dub him "Lord Root of the Matter."

Roosevelt had gentler, more oblique ways of making his views known. The selection of Hopkins, the nation's leading New Dealer, for this mission spoke for itself. And while Hopkins was in England, Roosevelt decided to send John G. Winant as ambassador. A foreign office minute described Winant, the former head of America's social security system and a liberal Republican, as being "exceedingly shy and very earnest . . . he is difficult in small talk," but he has "a sense of social service which amounts almost to a religious conviction." In sending people like Winant and Ben Cohen to England, Breckinridge Long noted in his diary, Roosevelt "sees the possibility (even probability) of a 'new order' in England. The Country Gentleman type, the landed and industrial aristocracy are being jolted out of position. If Churchill should fall, a new Government would be drafted from a new type." Roosevelt told Wendell Willkie, who was about to make a trip to London with the president's blessing, that he was appointing Gil Winant as ambassador because he anticipated "a social revolution" in England.* Tom Brand, assigned by the British cabinet to serve as Willkie's cicerone during his visit, reported this to the foreign office. Willkie himself gave little comfort to Tories who hoped to come out of the war with Britain's rigid class system intact. A foreign office official reported on a party for Willkie given by Rebecca West and her husband, an official in the Ministry of Economic Warfare. The room was full of "argumentative intelligentsia," he observed. "Mr. Willkie went on to say how greatly he had been impressed by the Prime Minister, and what a grand leader he was for a country to have in times like these. He was not so sure, however, that Mr. Churchill would be so valuable a leader when it came to the postwar period and economic adjustment and reconstruction were necessary." Disdainfully, the foreign office man reported that "these remarks were applauded by his hearers," and added, "it is, in fact, a dreadful lack of stage management to let a man like this fall into hands like these."[14]

There was some discussion in the British cabinet of whether a statement of British war aims should be made in connection with President Roosevelt's inaugural address on January 20, to which the cabinet listened over transatlantic radio. Unlike the president's State of the Union message, however, it sounded no international theme and seemed to require no answer. "There was a good deal to be said," the cabinet minutes reported, "for waiting to see how the position developed in the United States. Would the 'Lend and Lease Bill' pass into law in the United States within, say, the next month, and without substantial modification?" The Churchill position was reaffirmed. Any

---

* In February, when it was disclosed that Benjamin V. Cohen would go to London as Winant's legal adviser, there was again some apprehension that Roosevelt was trying to revolutionize England. A foreign office minute by Professor Whitehead observed tartly: "Mr. Roosevelt is not Lenin and it is highly improbable that he would attempt to interfere with our internal politics." And a cable from Halifax stated reassuringly that although Cohen was a "left wing New Dealer, . . . I am told Mr. Cohen himself is more interested in winning the war."

statement of war aims, if confined to generalities, "would not strike home," while specific proposals "would be bound to give rise to difficulties."

There was another reason why Hopkins did not press Churchill on a statement of war aims. His perception of the doughty leader had altered markedly. After the Ditchley week end, he had accompanied Churchill, who looked very nautical in his blue jacket and peaked cap, and Churchill's wife Clementine, "tall and smart-looking," on an exhausting but instructive tour of fleet bases. On the way home Churchill's train stopped at Glasgow and other areas that had been bombed. There were speeches. Churchill pulled a reluctant Hopkins forward to say something. Hopkins was shy and embarrassed because he thought the British common man should be taking the bows, not he. But he was equal to the occasion. He quoted from the Book of Ruth: "Whither thou goest, I will go . . . even to the end."

One purpose of this little "odyssey," as the Churchill entourage dubbed it, was to bid good-by to the Halifaxes, who were boarding Britain's newest battleship the *King George V* at Scapa Flow for the trip across the Atlantic. Hopkins sent a letter to the president via Colonel Lee, who was returning with Halifax. It reflected Hopkins's new picture of Churchill.

Churchill is the government in every sense of the word—he controls the grand strategy and often the details—labor trusts him—the army, navy, and air force are behind him to a man. The politicians and upper crust pretend to like him. I cannot emphasize too strongly that he is the one and only person over here with whom you need to have a full meeting of minds. . . . I cannot believe that it is true that Churchill dislikes either you or America—it just doesn't make sense.

Churchill's impact on Hopkins was matched by Hopkins's tutelage of Churchill on the subject of Roosevelt. "One can easily see why he is so close to you," Churchill cabled Roosevelt later. "Churchill wants to see you—the sooner the better," Hopkins's letter via Colonel Lee continued, "but I have told him of your problem until the [lend-lease] bill is passed. I am convinced this meeting between you and Churchill is essential—and soon—for the battering continues and Hitler does not wait for Congress." There was another sign of the success of Hopkins's coaching. A telegram from Churchill to Roosevelt invited the president or any of his naval people to board the *King George V* at Annapolis and be shown around. A delighted Roosevelt accepted immediately, said he would be in the harbor to meet Halifax and two rear admirals would board the warship, and "go up the bay on her."

At a party in London that Lord Beaverbrook gave for newspaper proprietors and editors, Hopkins, in informal remarks, returned to the theme of Churchill's hold on the British people irrespective of class. The following foreign office account included some points absent from the version that Sherwood was able to obtain:

[Hopkins] had evidently been profoundly moved by all that he had so far seen during his visit. His tour with the Prime Minister had, in particular, shown him the fine spirit of the country generally and the extraordinary hold which Mr. Churchill exercises over all classes—a point which he said President Roosevelt did not thoroughly realize. Living and moving in the closest contact with the Prime Minister for a period of days had evidently proved for him an exhausting experience and he was full of admiration for the astonishing vigor consistently maintained by the Prime Minister.

President Roosevelt, he said, was determined "to whip Hitler" and to this end would use to the utmost the vast powers he was acquiring by current legislation. . . He felt he was in a position on returning to America to fill in and in many respects to adjust the President's picture of Great Britain. He added that in the future the President and Prime Minister would probably be in regular telephone contact.

Cadogan added a corroborative detail about Churchill's impact on Hopkins that he had heard from Oliver Lyttelton: "At one stage of the Churchill-Hopkins Odyssey the evening finished rather later, at 2 a.m. The Pres. [of the Board of Trade, Lyttelton] crept to bed but was prevented from sleeping by Mr. Hopkins, who slunk into his room and ensconced himself in a chair in front of the fire, muttering at intervals 'Jesus Christ! What a man!' "[15]

One swift consequence of Hopkins's conversations was to dispel Churchill's misconceptions and worries about lend-lease legislation. After his first meeting with Hopkins, Churchill had reported to the war cabinet that "Mr. Hopkins had no doubt that the Loans and Leases Bill would get through Congress, and stressed the importance of the fact that President Roosevelt would have the right of interpretation under the Bill." Roosevelt's discretionary authority, which Churchill, as a result of his briefing by Hopkins, viewed as an advantage for Britain, was the point that the congressional opponents of the bill seized upon as most vulnerable to attack. Some alarm is detectable even in the British minister's telegram from Washington: "Although it was anticipated that the bill would be far-reaching, very wide terms in which it is drawn and very extensive powers which it grants to the President have [come] as rather a surprise and have tended to revive the cry in certain quarters that the President is trying to set himself up as an American dictator." "The wide powers ascribed to the President by the 'Lease-lend bill,' " minuted Professor Whitehead, "are proving something of a stumbling block. The American Constitution does not include provisions for a reasonable Cabinet and so there is no existing body in which to vest whole authority except Congress (which is too big) or the President (who is too small)."[16]

Sen. Burton K. Wheeler, perhaps the most effective isolationist spokesman in the Congress, quickly attacked the "blank check" aspect of a program, which he described as "the New Deal's Triple A foreign policy; it will plow under every fourth American boy." That, said Roosevelt at his press conference, is "the rottenest thing that has been said in public life in my generation." And as for the issue of presidential power, "nobody wants—Lord knows I don't want—the power that is apparently given in this bill, but somebody has to do it—somebody has to have the power in such shape that quick action can be taken . . . if the policy of the Nation is to help the democracies to survive, you have to have methods of speed that are legalized."

In one of his first messages, Hopkins had adjured Roosevelt: "This is-

land needs our help now Mr. President with everything we can give them."
Hopkins promptly had his answer. Hopkins had received a message from
President Roosevelt, Churchill reported to the war cabinet, "requesting him
to cable to America at once a list of our most immediate demands which
could be met during the next few months. The President hoped that the
'Lease-Lend' Bill would be passed into law towards the end of February."

Second only to the dictatorship charge, the opposition to the bill, which
included Colonel Lindbergh, Father Couglin, Herbert Hoover, Joseph Kennedy, General Wood, and Norman Thomas, focused on the accusation that
it was a "war measure." Administration spokesmen carefully qualified their
answer to this line of attack. Passage of the bill was less likely to lead to war
than its nonpassage. Adoption of the bill was the best hope of stopping Hitler
without sending American men to Europe.*[17]

Churchill, with his flair for the telling phrase, gave powerful support to
this line of advocacy in a radio speech, which was written with the assistance
of Hopkins and beamed to the United States. According to a cable from Halifax, it was a broadcast that had been urged by, among others, Walter Lippmann, who was afraid that "Americans might still be frightened into thinking
that their help was too late to be of use. . . . Colonel Lindbergh had cleverly
and successfully touched this weak and cowardly spot in the American character by his testimony before the Foreign Affairs Committee last week." Lippmann thought, continued Halifax, that a broadcast by Churchill was "the best
antidote to this insidious disease for he sincerely believed that at the present

---

* At about this time, Roosevelt is said to have directed the FBI to keep track of
America First. The author requested the FBI, under the Freedom of Information–Privacy
Acts [FOIPA], to make available its files relating to this surveillance. In the end he was
sent 176 pages of Xeroxed material from FBI files that were considerably more volumi-
nous. Hoover's first report to the White House on America First, dated March 1, 1941,
was made in response to a presidential request relayed through Press Secretary Early to
find out who was paying for a leaflet that denounced lend-lease as a "War Dictatorship
Bill." The eight-page report listed the purposes of the committee, its letterhead with
identifying material of the kind that would be found in *Who's Who,* added that "in
connection with the financing of the said Committee attention is respectfully directed
to the financial positions held by . . . ," and then enumerated such wealthy sponsors of
the movement as Gen. Robert E. Wood, Henry Ford, and J. C. Hormel. Hoover's letter
to Early also said that, "if it is the President's wish that a more exhaustive investigation
be made relative to the means by which the America First Committee is being financed,
I hope you will not hesitate to call upon me to conduct such investigation." Evidently no
such investigation was requested. A report to Attorney General Biddle on December 4,
1941, on the America First Committee began: "The Bureau's information on the America First Committee has not resulted from investigation initiated by this Bureau but has
been either voluntarily submitted by outside sources, received as an incident to other
investigation, or extracted from articles which have appeared in the press. Because of
this limitation, a full and complete analysis of the organization cannot be presented."
This particular survey made extensive use of an exposé of America First that had been
published in the Communist *New Masses* after Germany's invasion of Russia had caused
the Communists to switch from isolationism to interventionism. Of course, the reference
in Hoover's memorandum to information voluntarily submitted by "outside sources"
was a significant ambiguity. Among the outside sources was Stephenson's British intelligence operation, which not only monitored but harassed America First's activities.

moment you were [i.e., Churchill was] a more popular figure in the United States than the President himself." Churchill's broadcast of February 9 began with a summary of the war situation. The island had survived the winter, the days were growing longer. But the British air force was stronger, and the Italian army in Libya had been smashed. Churchill referred to the visits of Hopkins and Willkie, both of whom will tell the truth about what they had seen. "The rest we leave with great confidence to the judgment of the President, the Congress and the people of the United States." After predicting that the war was soon going to enter "upon a phase of greater violence," Churchill came to the critical paragraph:

It seems now to be certain that the Government and people of the United States intend to supply us with all that is necessary for victory. In the last war the United States sent two million men across the Atlantic. But this is not a war of vast armies, firing immense masses of shells at one another. We do not need the gallant armies which are forming throughout the American Union. We do not need them this year, nor next year; nor any year that I can foresee. But we do need most urgently an immense and continuous supply of war materials and technical apparatus of all kinds. We need them here and we need to bring them here. We shall need a great mass of shipping in 1942, far more than we can build ourselves, if we are to maintain and augment our war effort in the West and in the East.

At the end of his broadcast the prime minister referred to the letter of introduction that Roosevelt had given Willkie and the inspired inclusion in Roosevelt's own handwriting of some lines from Longfellow which Roosevelt said "applies to you people as it does to us." Churchill proceeded to read the verse:

> Sail on, O Ship of State!
> Sail on, O Union strong and great!
> Humanity with all its fears,
> With all the hopes of future years,
> Is hanging breathless on thy fate!

"What is the answer that I shall give, in your name, to this great man, the thrice-chosen head of a nation of a hundred and thirty million? Give us the tools," Churchill ended the speech, "and we will finish the job."[18]

Did he believe this? Did Roosevelt? Churchill less so than the president. The object of British policy was to bring the United States into the war. As for Roosevelt, he had stated the case candidly in his "Arsenal of Democracy" speech: "If we are to be completely honest with ourselves, we must admit that there is risk in any course we may take. But I deeply believe that the great majority of our people agree that the course that I advocate involves the least risk now and the greatest hope for world peace in the future."[19]

It was the final week end of Hopkins's stay in London. In Washington at a cabinet meeting, the president, according to Ickes, was "handing himself large bouquets for having sent Harry Hopkins to London. . . . He wanted us to know that he had worked it out in his own mind that his friend from Iowa was just the right kind of human being who would make the greatest impression on Winston Churchill, son of a duke, English gentleman, etc. And, according to the President, the deeply laid plot had worked out even better than he had anticipated. Apparently the first thing that Churchill asks for when he gets awake in the morning is Harry Hopkins, and Harry is the last one he sees at night." Maybe so, growled Ickes, but even if the president had sent someone with the bubonic plague as his personal representative, "Churchill would, nevertheless, see a good deal of him."

Hopkins had spent the week end before the Churchill broadcast at Chequers, in part assisting the prime minister in the preparation of his speech and marveling at the difference in style from Roosevelt, for Churchill paced up and down dictating his speech from notes that he had jotted down previously. He acted out his speech as if he were addressing a session of the House. "People are still saying that the Prime Minister's broadcast last Sunday was his best to date," wrote Mollie Panter-Downes in the *New Yorker*. "They always enjoy a chuckle over his deliberate Anglicising of foreign names and the lip-smacking gusto with which he invariably introduces a reference to one or another of 'those wicked men' but what they most like is his great gift for making them forget discomfort, danger, and loss and remember only that they are living history."

On Sunday, Hopkins penned a farewell note:

My dear Mr. Prime Minister—

I shall never forget these days with you—your supreme confidence and will to victory. Britain I have ever liked—I like it the more.

As I leave for America tonight I wish you great and good luck—confusion to your enemies—victory for Britain.

Ever so cordially,
Harry Hopkins

Accompanied again by Bracken and joined by Churchill's aide, Commander Thompson, Hopkins journeyed to Bournemouth to catch the flight to Lisbon. There was another British member in the party who would accompany Hopkins across the Atlantic. As a minute in Churchill's file recorded:

When Mr. Hopkins returned to America he was to take with him some most secret British official documents and he said that he did not like the idea of carrying them himself in case any loss occurred on the way. The Prime Minister therefore gave instructions which were carried out by General Ismay that an officer should be detailed to accompany Mr. Hopkins as a courier to be responsible for the documents in question.

Hopkins reached Washington on the seventeenth. "Arrived safely today," he cabled the prime minister. "Dinner President. He sends you his warmest regards. Remember me cordially to Mrs. Churchill and thanks for many courtesies."

The waves from his visit spread through Washington. "I was very glad to learn a good deal of your latest mind from Hopkins," Halifax cabled Churchill. Stimson, after a meeting at the White House, persuaded Hopkins to return with him to the War Department, where the secretary called in Marshall and his top aides and for several hours listened spellbound. "It was a most interesting—indeed almost thrilling—description that [Hopkins] gave us, because he spent nearly all his time with Winston Churchill and had been admitted freely to meetings of the Cabinet and had seen at close range the defense arrangements—in fact he was able to outline for us the theory of the tactical defense which Britain intends to make." The next day Stimson had second thoughts. "Harry Hopkins has come back loaded down with the British view and I think now, in the light of what our people report, that the British are over-confident and are in for a bad time and it makes another problem that I have got to take up with the President to keep him from being too much influenced by Harry Hopkins' report. It is quite natural for Hopkins, who has been living very close to the heads of the British Army and to Winston Churchill, to imbibe their views but I think they are all living in a state of undue optimism." A week later, however, Stimson concluded that it was "a godsend that he should be at the White House," an opinion to which he stuck.[20]

Hopkins left no record of his discussions with Roosevelt on his return. He communicated to everyone his sense of urgency about getting the "tools" to the British. As to harmonizing Anglo-American views with regard to the larger purposes of the war, he accepted Churchill's approach that this was not the time to discuss them. At least that was what he said to Eleanor Roosevelt when she plied him with questions about the British leader's war aims. Everyone was persuaded that there was no turning back, Hopkins told her, that Hitler must be defeated whatever the cost in privileges. The British did not believe that this must be stated explicitly. It was part of the atmosphere of wartime Britain, a kind of tacit understanding. One of Hopkins's week ends had been spent with Lord Beaverbrook at his country house, Cherkley. Beaverbrook, minister of aircraft production, was a press lord whose capitalist credentials were unimpeachable. Two Labour party leaders, Clement Attlee and Arthur Greenwood, had also been there that week end. They sat at a piano with Beaverbrook, Hopkins reported, and sang a workers' song together. Dozing on the couch in the president's study on the second floor of the White House, Hopkins suddenly opened one eye and said to the president, Mrs. Roosevelt reported with pleasure, "You know, Winston is much more left than you."

British wartime egalitarianism represented no permanent restructuring of British class relationships, as became clear after the war; but Roosevelt as well as Hopkins accepted the view that the party battle had to be subordinated to the grand strategy of the struggle against Hitler. "I'm sick and tired of having to listen to complaints from those goddam New Dealers!" Hopkins exclaimed to Sherwood after he had turned down a request from a former WPA associate to forward a letter to Roosevelt urging the president to keep Congress from abolishing the agency. And the sharp eye of Mr. Justice Frankfurter detected a new note in Roosevelt's reply to a press conference query as to whether Winant was taking over ideas "as to what sort of peace to negotiate after the war is over." "I should say the first thing to do is to win the war, wouldn't you?" Roosevelt had retorted. But to Sherwood, who was depressed by the petulance and vindictiveness of some Roosevelt remarks that the latter had dictated for a speech after the passage of the Lend-Lease Act, Hopkins said sharply, "He has no intention of using all that irritable stuff you say he dictated. He's just getting it off his chest." And then Hopkins continued in words that reflected the fires that burned in his own stomach as well as Roosevelt's:

You and I are for Roosevelt because he's a great spiritual figure, because he's an idealist like Wilson, and he's got the guts to drive through any opposition to realize those ideals. Oh—he sometimes tries to appear tough and cynical and flippant, but that's an act he likes to put on, especially at press conferences. He wants to make the boys think he is hard-boiled. Maybe he fools some of them, now and then—but don't ever let him fool you, or you won't be any use to him. You can see the real Roosevelt when he comes out with something like the Four Freedoms. And don't get the idea that those are any catch phrases. *He believes them!* He believes they can be practically attained.[21]

In London, Churchill's stentorian nationalism had softened. It showed itself in many ways. The negotiation of the terms under which the United States would build and occupy bases in the Caribbean had become difficult. What the foreign office and admiralty were prepared to yield, the colonial office resisted—with powerful backing: "I read a paper of Ld. Lloyd's," the king wrote in his diary,

on the West Indian Islands where the U.S. bases have been leased. I was much disturbed over it, as the U.S.A. is asking for more facilities than were originally agreed to, & wishes to fortify & have garrisons in Bermuda & Trinidad. I told Alex H. [his Private Secretary] that there was no question of my giving my consent to hand over the sovereignty of these B.W.I. as I am the custodian of my subjects.

Churchill, as firm as the king that no West Indian subjects should be driven out of the Empire, was more disposed now to find ways to meet U.S. requirements. When British negotiators gagged at the American formula that obligated the United States to consult the British on the application of the agreements only in the event the United States should become engaged in a war, the prime minister urged the cabinet to accept the United States formula. "The United States had now openly espoused our cause and had virtually promised us financial help of inestimable value. We must do what we could to meet American difficulties."

And two weeks later, on receipt of a telegram from Halifax stating "that it was of the utmost importance that we should without delay hand over to America our remaining financial resources in that country," Churchill advised the war cabinet, "We should have to resign ourselves to meeting American wishes." A few weeks ago he had doubted the wisdom of this course; now, he no longer did so since "it was clear that we should receive from America far more than we could possibly give." He proposed, however, "to send a private telegram to the President asking him to ensure that our securities were not taken over at knock-down prices. . . . Hopkins had telegraphed for full details on British taxation," Churchill continued. "The fact that the Americans were imposing additional taxation made it all the more necessary that we should show that we were willing to make the sacrifice."

Beaverbrook feared that Churchill had turned sentimental about Roosevelt and the Americans. A memorandum that same day recited his bill of grievances against the United States:

We were told that if we agreed to the twelve-mile limit off the American coast, all would be well. We did agree. But all was not well.

We were told that if we stopped the export of drink from the Empire to the United States, there would be a wonderful improvement in our relations with America. There was not.

If we made peace with Ireland, we were to enjoy forever and forever the favour of America. We did as we were told. But it brought us no comfort in Ireland and little credit in America.

If only we settled the war debt, even at five cents in the dollar, we should have the complete approval of the United States. We settled, and earned ruin in England and abuse in America.

We were incited by the Americans to break the alliance with Japan. We did so. And look where it has taken us! The Japanese are our relentless enemies. And the Americans are our unrelenting creditors.

Now we are told by Roosevelt and Willkie that if only we stand up to Germany, all will be well. We are doing so. But we would stand up better if we knew that there would be something left to provide sustenance for our people in the day of hardship.

If we give everything away, we gain little or no advantage over our present situation.

Stand up to the Democrats![22]

On March 8 the lend-lease bill passed, and Hopkins immediately telephoned the news to Churchill, who immediately cabled Hopkins: "The strain has been serious so I thank God for your news."

Roosevelt's speech a few days later to the White House Correspondents' Association stressed speed and urgency. "But, now, *now,* the time element is of supreme importance. Every plane, every other instrument of war, old and new, every instrument that we can spare now, we will send overseas because that is the common sense of strategy." There was a salute to Churchill—"In this historic crisis, Britain is blessed with a great leader in Winston Churchill" —and a softening of the emphasis on the four freedoms—"They are the ultimate stake. They may not be immediately attainable throughout the world but humanity does move toward these glorious ideals through democratic process."

"We, the American people, are writing new history today," Roosevelt climaxed his speech: "The British people and their Grecian allies need ships. From America they will get ships. They need planes. From America they will get planes. They need food. From America they will get food. They need tanks and guns and ammunition and supplies of all kinds. From America they will get tanks and guns and ammunition and supplies of all kinds."[23]

The Germans appreciated the significance of what had happened. Ambassador Dieckhoff told his superiors:

As was to be expected, [Roosevelt's] will prevailed almost entirely. He is receiving essentially all of the powers which he wanted, and the concessions which he had to make to the opposition are slight. On the basis of the large majorities in both Houses of Congress he can with some justice point to the "national unity" regarding aid to England—a fact to which he attached great importance from the start, and which is significant for further developments as the President desires them.

One Briton understood from personal experience the act's importance: "This is a big victory for us!" Lloyd George exulted to Maisky, the Soviet ambassador. "Now all the financial difficulties and worries involved in carrying on the war have been solved for us. . . . Winston has been luckier than I was. . . . My God, what a terrible problem the financing of the last war was for me! But Winston can now concentrate his attention entirely on the purely military side." And Churchill would salute the legislation as "the most unsordid legislative act" in parliamentary history.[24]

As for repayment, Roosevelt himself had resisted pressures to demand transfer of the Caribbean Islands to American sovereignty. "If we can get our naval bases why, for example, should we buy with them two million headaches, consisting of that number of human beings who would be a definite economic drag on this country, and who would stir up questions of racial stocks by virtue of their new status as American citizens?" The negotiation of the "consideration" in lieu of cash repayment that would be required from the British would take months of bargaining between an American team headed by Dean Acheson and a British group led by Lord Keynes in which the principal United States objective, as laid down by Roosevelt, was to gain British acquiescence to certain broad principles relating to world peace and international economic relations—chiefly, the modification of the Ottawa Agreements, which would shut the United States out of postwar dominion markets.

Administration leaders were divided on how hard the British should be pressed on this point. The "two predominant influences" at the White House, Minister Moffat wrote on March 31 on a visit to Washington, were "Harry Hopkins and Mr. Justice Frankfurter. Harry Hopkins is sound in his ideas and, while tremendously impressed with the need for haste in sending aid to Britain, is under no illusions that we can postpone indefinitely obtaining what we want and trusting to ultimate British generosity. Mr. Justice Frankfurter on the other hand has, I am told, virtually become the lawyer for the British case and argues for them on all occasions, even against the State Department which is the guardian of American interests."[25]

Passage of the Lend-Lease Act occasioned renewed discussion within the foreign office on the future of Anglo-American relations. A Halifax cable on the subject precipitated it: "With the passage of the Bill, it can be said that except for a small number of irreconcilable isolationists the whole country is united in its support of the Allies against the totalitarian powers." Roosevelt's position had been greatly enhanced. A Gallup poll showed 72 per cent of those polled supported him. Passage of the bill marked the end of an isolationism that had begun with Congress's refusal to ratify the Treaty of Versailles, Halifax went on, and it was now realized that the United States will have to play "a large if not predominant part" in the postwar settlement. "Thinking people are more and more coming to the view that the United States and British Empire will have to stand very close and share responsibility for keeping peace in the world." There was one untoward consequence: "the scope of our diplomatic action vis-à-vis the United States Government may well be somewhat restricted."

The telegram's "uncritical optimism" disturbed that most thoughtful of America-watchers in the foreign office, Professor Whitehead. He wrote a long comment that was so well thought of that it was printed and circulated to all government officials concerned with American affairs. The Americans were "a mercurial people," he warned, and "until they are finally committed to actual warfare, it would be unwise to assume that, in certain circumstances, the Americans would be incapable of checking their present helpful trend. The Americans are coming on well, but they are not yet in the bag." United States opinion had evolved. "Aid short of war" was no longer the dominant view; aid "at some risk of war" now represented "the most numerous and influential group."

Whitehead doubted that American isolationism was gone for good. It was too deep-rooted and had two facets: an intense dislike of entanglements in any continent, particularly Europe, outside of the Western Hemisphere; and "a disinclination to acknowledge those international responsibilities which result from a given geographical and material position." Both facets reflected the failure to recognize the connection "between privilege and responsibility." Here, Sir David Scott, the head of the American department, noted in the margin, "Yes, indeed. Americans are incapable of 'thinking imperially.'" Vansittart demurred: "I am certain she will be so thinking within a decade."

In analyzing the possibilities of postwar Anglo-American collaboration, Whitehead cautioned against British condescension. "A successful Anglo-American collaboration must presuppose that we shall be as ready to share American views and policies as we are undoubtedly ready to share her strength and labor. Wisdom is not entirely confined to the British, and it will be a poor outlook for the English-speaking world if the Empire nations do not show the same respect for American interests as they do for those of each other."

The final version of this commentary pointed to a large difficulty that should be anticipated from the United States side: "Through lack of practice the American Administration has not developed any procedures for maintaining reasonable continuity of policy in international affairs. This difficulty is greatly enhanced from the fact that public opinion has so great an influence in this field."

"Is it so much a lack of practice?" R. T. E. Latham of the Far Eastern department inquired. "Perhaps, as a constitutional lawyer, I am biased, but my diagnosis would be that the central fault is the power of the Senate and Congress in foreign affairs. It seems to me absolutely hopeless for a democracy to have an effective foreign policy except through the device of responsible government on the British model. Only because the United States of

America is a giant among pygmies in the Americas, and physically isolated from other continents, has she been able to survive at all with this cumbrous system."

"I agree that the United States Constitution does not help matters," riposted Whitehead. "But if there has been sufficient experience in a given task the laws (or Constitution) tend to get reinterpreted or otherwise modified in practice to make the task practicable, I think."

A final grumpy comment by Vansittart: "Many here have an uneasy feeling that, if we study America, she may in her turn yet rat on us. This does not mean that we should despair. At present it appears that the Anglo Saxon (Rhodes) ideal is the finest before us. I feel this deeply yet I intend to approach this ideal realizing that my country is, for the second time, doing America's fighting for her and that my country has more right than wrong on her side."[26]

As usual, Churchill would put in its historic setting what had happened with the enactment of lend-lease. He called it the war's "Third Climacteric." The first two were the fall of France and the Battle of Britain; the fourth would be the attack on Russia; and the fifth, Pearl Harbor.

Chapter Sixteen

The Battle of the Atlantic

ID SHORT of military action "will not probably secure a military victory." Such had been Stimson's "somber" conclusion in January about the situation that would confront Britain even with the passage of lend-lease legislation. He urged consideration of convoys in order to secure "the lifeline of British supplies across the Atlantic and relieve their convoy duty units of her fleet which are sorely needed elsewhere." By February, 1941, British shipping losses threatened the island's survival. "The highest possible priority must be given to the measures necessary to deal with the double menace to our shipping constituted by submarines and Focke Wulf aircraft, acting in combination," Churchill alerted the war cabinet. "Our effort against this renewed danger must, for the moment, be our supreme exertion." Germany knew the toll it was exacting. "Even now," Ribbentrop assured the Japanese ambassador in Berlin, "England was experiencing serious trouble in keeping up her food supply as the result of losses in tonnage. Meat and fats were already in very short supply. The important thing now was to sink enough ships to reduce England's imports to below the absolute minimum necessary for existence."

The Battle of the Atlantic was under way. To win it Germany wanted Japan's help in the form of a Pacific diversion. This was the moment to attack Singapore, Ribbentrop urged the Japanese ambassador. "This would wipe out England's key position in the Far East," and "the creation of such an accomplished fact would also be the best way to keep America out of the conflict." The army and the navy were making their preparations for such an attack, the ambassador replied. "They would be completed by the end of May." Such a war, he pointed out, "had to be prepared not only against England but also against America," which in all likelihood would come in.

The British had gotten wind of these German pressures on Japan. Japan could only be prevented "from taking the plunge," the British chiefs of staff advised Eden, "by a joint declaration to the Japanese by the United States of

America and the British Empire that any attack on the Netherlands East In- dies, or on British possessions in the Far East, will involve Japan in immedi- ate war with both our countries." "The proposals for a joint declaration are, I fear, unrealizable," Eden reported to Churchill.

At the same time it is clearly of the first importance that the United States should independently go as far as they can in making plain their attitude to the Japanese Government. I have spoken in this sense to Mr. Hopkins at luncheon today, and I am sure that he fully appreciates the gravity of the situation. . . . I think that Mr. Hopkins will telegraph to the President, urging at least some steps going be- yond the ordinary execution of maneuvers from Hawaii. He told me that he thought the most effective results would be produced by the President sending for the Japanese Ambassador and making plain the United States interest in Far Eastern affairs in words of one syllable.

In the course of our conversation Mr. Hopkins said that he knew, though I had not said it, that we were conscious of a threat to Hongkong. He was quite clear in his own mind what the President would do if such a threat were to develop, and if the Japanese attacked Hongkong. He did not, however, feel justi- fied in defining this impression further to me. I assured Mr. Hopkins that I did not want him to do so.

Hopkins appears to have believed that Roosevelt would regard seizure of Hong Kong—with which his Delano forbears had ties of sentiment going back to the years that they were in the China trade—as a *casus belli*. Perhaps. The president was much more cautious about what the American people would regard as a *casus belli* in the Far East when he discussed the situation with Lord Halifax that same day. "There were three directions in which the Japanese might take action," Roosevelt, according to Halifax, speculated,

against Netherlands East Indies, against Thailand or directly against Singapore. He had been anxiously considering what action the United States Government could take in any of these eventualities. While the United States Government would declare war on Japan if the latter were to attack American possessions, he did not think that the country would approve of this action if the Japanese only attacked the Netherlands East Indies or British possessions. Moreover, even if the United States were to be involved in war with Japan, he felt that to fight an active war in the Pacific would mean a dangerous diversion of forces and material from the main theatre of operations which in his view was the Atlantic and Great Britain. Therefore should the United States become involved in war, he thought that they would have to fight a "holding war" in the Pacific.[1]

But it was difficult to devise measures to deter Japan that did not divert forces from the looming Battle of the Atlantic. The day after Roosevelt con- ferred with Halifax, he met with Hull, Stimson, Knox, Marshall, and Stark in response to Hopkins's message that "Eden is very anxious that we find a way to emphasize our determination to prevent Japan from making further en- croachments."

"It was the old subject," Stimson noted a little forlornly in his diary, "of what we should do in the Far East to slow down the Japs." Stimson doubted the effectiveness of the steps that Roosevelt authorized. These included the pulling of "a very long face" when he received the new Japanese ambassador, Kichisaburo Nomura; the recall of dependents from the Far East; and the dispatch of some additional ships to the Philippines. Since the latter were over 5,000 statute miles to the west of Pearl Harbor where the Pacific Fleet was based, this last proposal brought a protesting letter from Admiral Stark to whom the thought of further dispersing the fleet gave a sleepless night.

Roosevelt, a consummate performer, was at his best when a few days later Hull brought Admiral Nomura to present his credentials. The president skillfully blended personal warmth toward the ambassador, whom he had known in Wilson's Washington and whom he addressed as "Admiral," with flashes of steely resolve when he discussed Japan's expansionist policies. He recalled their previous association and went on to lament that relations were "deteriorating." The American people, although not yet bitter, were thoroughly concerned by Japanese moves southward toward Indochina. They were equally concerned by Japan's alliance with Germany in the Tripartite Pact. An incident like the *Maine* or the *Panay* could trigger an explosive reaction. He was glad the admiral was here and he hoped his presence would lend itself to some frank talks. There was plenty of room in the Pacific for everybody and neither the United States nor Japan would benefit from a war. Then, putting aside his formal address, the president added a few pungent words about the chauvinist and militarist groups in control of Japanese policy in Tokyo. They were the chief obstacles to improved relations. Throughout, commented Hull, the ambassador bowed. "One would have thought from his demeanor and manifestations that the Ambassador was in entire harmony with each point the President brought out."

The next day a message arrived from Churchill, who did not know the outcome of the session with Nomura, setting forth "the naval consequences," to which he knew Roosevelt would be particularly sensitive, of a Japanese movement against British positions in the Far East:

Many drifting straws seem to indicate Japanese intention to make war on us or do something that would force us to make war on them in the next few weeks or months. I am not myself convinced that this is not a war of nerves designed to cover Japanese encroachments in Siam and Indochina. However, I think I ought to let you know that the weight of the Japanese Navy, if thrown against us, would confront us with situations beyond the scope of our naval resources. I do not myself think that the Japanese would be likely to send the large military expedition necessary to lay siege to Singapore. The Japanese would no doubt occupy whatever strategic points and oilfields in Dutch East Indies and thereabouts that they covet and thus get into a far better position for a full-scale attack on Singapore later on. They would also raid Australia and New Zealand ports and coasts causing deep anxiety in those Dominions which have already sent all their best-trained fighting men to the Middle East. But the attack which I fear the most would be by raiders including possibly battle-cruisers upon our trade routes and communications across the Pacific and Indian Oceans.

We could by courting disaster elsewhere send a few strong ships into these vast waters, but all trade would have to go into convoy and escorts would be few and far between. Not only would this be a most grievous additional restriction and derangement of our whole war economy, but it would bring altogether to an end all reinforcements of the armies we had planned to build up in the Middle East from Australian and Indian resources. Any threat of a major invasion of Australia or New Zealand would of course force us to withdraw our fleet from the Eastern Mediterranean with disastrous military possibilities there, the certainty that Turkey would have to make some accommodation, and reopen German trade and oil supplies from the Black Sea.

You will therefore see, Mr. President, the awful enfeeblement of our war effort that would result merely from the sending out by Japan of her battle-cruisers, and her twelve eight-inch gun cruisers into the Eastern oceans, and still more from any serious invasion threat against the two Australasian democracies in the southern Pacific.

Some believe that Japan in her present mood would not hesitate to court an attempt to wage war both against Great Britain and the United States. Personally, I think the odds are definitely against that, but no one can tell. Everything that you can do to inspire the Japanese with fear of a double war may avert the danger. If however they come in against us and we are alone, the grave character of the consequences cannot easily be overstated.[2]

The British had been tapping Japanese communications. "They were evidently in a high state of excitement, and they chattered to one another with much indiscretion," Churchill wrote of this episode later. Within a week, however, the British breathed more easily. "Have received better news concerning Japan," Churchill reported to Roosevelt. "It seems Jap Foreign Minister is shortly going to Moscow, Berlin and Rome for the purpose of covering the failure of action against us. The fear of the United States appears to have postponed attack which seemed imminent . . . the more these fears can be aroused the better. Appreciation given in my last message to you of naval consequences subsequent to Jap attack against us remains the same in all circumstances."

The United States also was monitoring Japanese communications via Magic, the name given to the process of breaking down Japanese coded messages. "I have just read the purported instructions from Foreign Minister Matsuoka to Ambassador Nomura dated February 14," Roosevelt informed Welles. "Please read them. These instructions seem to me to be the product of a mind which is deeply disturbed and unable to think quietly or logically." Matsuoka wanted United States recognition of Japanese hegemony in the western Pacific as the price of avoiding war and made it clear that Japan's ultimate aim was to incorporate south Asia in the Greater East Asia Co-Prosperity Sphere.

An intricate diplomatic game was getting under way between the United States and Japan. Coinciding with Nomura's arrival in Washington, the Japanese, working through Bishop James E. Walsh, the superior general of the Maryknoll Fathers, and Postmaster General Frank Walker, the leading Catholic layman in Roosevelt's cabinet, arranged to send to Washington two unofficial emissaries empowered to negotiate a settlement of all outstanding issues.

Roosevelt approved their coming. He also favored a visit by Matsuoka, the pro-Axis–minded foreign minister. Of all this the British were not informed. This was a hand the United States felt it should play alone.[3]

He had thus far fended off, Stark wrote Admiral Kimmel, the commander in chief of the Pacific Fleet, "a *visit* [Stark's emphasis] of a detachment of surface forces to the Far East." But Stark feared the time might come when his views would not prevail. "The difficulty is that the entire country is in a dozen minds about the war—to stay out altogether, to go in against Germany in the Atlantic, to concentrate against Japan in the Pacific and the Far East—I simply cannot predict the outcome." If the navy should have to "swing to that tide"—meaning a movement of public opinion for action against Japan—"any reinforcement to the Atlantic might become impossible, and in any case, would be reduced by just so much as we would send to the Asiatic. And that might be a very serious matter for Britain." It would mean, in reality, the shelving of Plan Dog, as the Hitler-first strategy of the United States armed forces was called. The unpredictability of U.S. public opinion threatened that strategy. So did British pressure in the secret staff talks that began in Washington on January 29. Although the British delegates agreed with the Hitler-first strategy, they wanted the United States also to underwrite the defense of Singapore. An old story, Churchill had first proposed it at the time of the fall of France. He had returned to it after the Tripartite Pact was announced at the end of September. He was now pressing for it again via diplomatic channels. And in the staff talks, his military representatives proposed that the United States should immediately dispatch a detachment of four heavy cruisers, one aircraft carrier, planes, and submarines to Singapore, advancing the arguments that Churchill had used in his telegram to Roosevelt of February 15, 1941.

The American chiefs balked. The security of the North Atlantic and the British Isles had top priority in their strategic thinking. In addition, they felt that showing the flag in Singapore was unnecessarily provocative to the Japanese at a moment when United States forces, especially the army that General Marshall was training, were not yet ready. "Every day that we are able to maintain peace and still support the British is valuable time gained," Admiral Stark had said of the Singapore proposal in early October. That was still his and Marshall's view. And there was Mahan's warning against dispersal of the fleet. Dispatch of units to the Philippines was a serious violation of Mahan's central doctrine; dispatch of units to Singapore, an extra 1,500 miles westward, would be even more so. Beyond these considerations, there was the political argument that had been summed up by the army's and navy's Joint Planning Committee: "It is to be expected that proposals of the British representatives will have been drawn up with chief regard for the British Commonwealth. Never absent from British minds are their postwar interests, commercial and military. We should likewise safeguard our eventual interests."[4]

But what were those interests? Japan knew what it wanted—"the Greater East Asia Co-Prosperity Sphere." The British knew what they were defending—an Empire and a Commonwealth, and Singapore was their symbol in the Pacific. But what ordering principle did the United States have in mind in the Pacific? A new Asia animated by the Four Freedoms with its major spokesman a China based on Sun Yat-sen's three principles of nationalism, democracy, and the people's livelihood? That appears to have been the working conception in Roosevelt's mind. In any case, the United States intended to have a major voice in shaping the Pacific's future—the talks with Japan, kept secret from the British, were a manifestation of that. So was Roosevelt's decision to extend lend-lease aid to China at the same time that he continued to exempt it from the prohibitions of the Neutrality Law under the fiction that Japan and China were not at war. Frances Perkins recalled after the war:

I remember plainly the President talking about how promising the future looked in China. They did have hidden resources that had never been exploited, and I remember him saying . . . that the most important thing that we could give to China, at the end of the war, was electrical equipment and know-how. He felt that what Americans had to be prepared to do for China—a backward country that had been deprived of the means of modern civilization—was to move in and erect great telegraph lines and great power-carrying lines—to show them how and where to build a dam and utilize their rivers that flooded every year or two to make a power source, and to distribute that power source and to electrify China. He believed that once China was electrified, the Americans could withdraw from the operation of those things.[5]

The British yielded in the staff talks. "I entirely agree with the point of view of the Prime Minister as expressed in a personal minute to me of the 17th February that 'the first thing to do is to get the United States into the war;' and that in order to do this I am inclined to think it is best to accept the dispositions proposed by the United States Delegates rather than to continue our argument with them over Singapore." So A. V. Alexander, first lord of the admiralty, telegraphed Washington on March 17.

"We finally got the Englishmen talking frankly and fully about the situation," Stimson noted of a talk that he, Knox, Stark, and Marshall had with the British representatives a week later. "They agreed, each one of them, that they could not, with their present naval forces, assume the entire escort duty that is required to protect the convoys of munitions to Great Britain. They also agreed and admitted the food shortage in Great Britain was becoming alarming. . . . I was interested to hear Admiral Stark say that in his opinion the most important part of our work was to get at once into the convoying of these vessels over."

"The basic idea of the United States–British plan," Stark informed his fleet commanders, "is that the United States will draw forces from the Pacific Fleet to reinforce the Atlantic Fleet and that the British will, if necessary, transfer naval forces to the Far East to attempt to hold the Japanese north of the Malay Barrier. The United States Asiatic Fleet (based on Manila) would not be reinforced, but would be supported by offensive operations by the United States Pacific Fleet." The letter ended ominously: "My own personal view is that we may be in the war (possibly undeclared) against Germany and Italy within two months but that there is a reasonable possibility that Japan may remain out altogether. However, we cannot at present act on that possibility."

This was followed by a more personal letter to Admiral Kimmel in which Stark reported that, when he had shown to Roosevelt the letter to his fleet commanders, he had received the president's "general assent to it." He had also given the president a memorandum on the fleet disposition needed for convoy duty, "a picture of what is now being done, what we propose to do if we convoyed, and of our ability to do it. . . . I feel it is only a matter of time before King is directed to convoy, or patrol, or whatever form the protective measures take. The situation is obviously critical in the Atlantic," he emphasized. "In my opinion, it is hopeless except as we take strong measures to save it."[6]

Roosevelt had ordered his military advisers to prepare to convoy back on January 16 when they had met with him to prepare for the secret staff talks. Two weeks later he had promoted Rear Adm. Ernest J. King, commander of the patrol force (as the neutrality patrol had been renamed), to full admiral and his force to full fleet status. And in mid-March, FDR had directed that the Atlantic fleet be brought to wartime readiness.

But the president still hesitated to order the fleet into action. Right after the passage of the lend-lease bill he had gone south on a fishing trip to the Bahamas, taking with him Hopkins, Jackson, Ickes, and members of his White House staff. At dinner on March 24 he remarked that " 'things are coming to a head; Germany will be making a blunder soon.' There could be no doubt," recorded Ickes, "of the President's scarcely concealed desire that there might be an incident which would justify our declaring a state of war against Germany or at least providing convoys to merchantmen carrying supplies to Great Britain." That was at the beginning of the trip. At the end, on March 30, that was still FDR's hope. The United States would probably have to wait for a German "incident," Roosevelt told Ickes, but the latter suspected that "the Germans will avoid at all possible costs any such incident as the President would like to take advantage of." And, indeed, Hitler still prohibited Admiral Raeder from encroaching on the area Roosevelt had designated as the hemispheric neutrality zone and from halting American ships anywhere.[7]

Roosevelt's return to Washington was marked by a new wave of gloom over Britain's prospects. A pro-Allied coup in Yugoslavia had produced a swift and terrible retaliation, a blow ordered by Hitler to be carried out "with unmerciful harshness." When it fell, it left Belgrade in ashes and placed German panzers in Greece. Even more disheartening was the success of Gen. Erwin Rommel's newly established Afrika Korps in driving Britain out of Cyrenaica, except for Tobruk, with a speed almost equal to Britain's earlier victory over Mussolini. And in the Battle of the Atlantic, the German battle cruisers *Scharnhorst* and *Gneisenau* attacked British convoys far to the west of the thirtieth meridian—about five hundred miles southeast of Newfoundland. "It would be a very great help if some American warships and aircraft," Churchill cabled Roosevelt, "could cruise about in this area as they have a perfect right to do without any prejudice to neutrality. Their mere presence might be decisive as the enemy would fear that they might report what they saw and we could then despatch an adequate force to try to engage them. The more ships that go out to cruise and the sooner they go the greater advantage."

Worse shipping news was to come. On the night of April 3–4, a German wolf pack attacked a British convoy south of Iceland and sank ten merchantmen. Roosevelt directed Admiral Stark to transfer three battleships, one carrrier, four light cruisers, and two squadrons of destroyers from the Pacific to the Atlantic. The U.S. destroyer *Niblack* was dispatched to the waters around Iceland on a reconnaissance mission and while there picked up some survivors and dropped a depth charge. As a measure of hemispheric defense, an agreement was signed with the Danish minister in Washington for the American takeover of Greenland, where sites for U.S. airfields had already been surveyed.

The pressures on Roosevelt to convoy were unrelenting. April 10 was "a very long day, mostly spent at the White House," Stimson recorded.

The President has evidently been thinking out things as far as he could to see how far he could go toward the direction [of] protection of the British Transport line. He made up his mind that it was too dangerous to ask the Congress for the power to convoy. He thought that if such a resolution was pressed now it would probably be defeated. On this point I am rather inclined to differ with him, provided that he took the lead vigorously and showed the reasons for it. Nevertheless, he had made a decision and it was an honest one. Therefore he is trying to see how far over in the direction of Great Britain we could get and how would be the best way to do it. We had the Atlas out and by drawing a line midway between the westernmost bulge of Africa and the easternmost bulge of Brazil, we found that the median line between the two continents was at about longitude line 25. . . . His plan is that we shall patrol the high seas west of this median line, all the way down as far as we can furnish the force to do it, and that the British will swing their convoys over westward to the westside of this line, so that they will be within our area. Then by the use of patrol planes and patrol vessels we can patrol and follow the convoys and notify them of any German raiders or submarines that we may see and give them a chance to escape.[8]

"We propose immediately to take the following steps in relation to the security of the Western Hemisphere, which steps will favorably affect your shipping problem," Roosevelt cabled Churchill. "It is important for domestic political reasons, which you will readily understand, that this action be taken by us unilaterally and not after diplomatic conversations between you and us. Therefore before taking this unilateral action I want to tell you about the proposal." Roosevelt then outlined the plan, describing it as an extension of the existing hemispheric security zone.[9]

There was other welcome news for Churchill, who at the time was obsessed with Britain's heavy shipping losses. "You should rub it in all you can," he had advised Halifax in regard to shipping losses after the passage of the Lend-Lease Act. "We have declared Red Sea area no longer a combat zone," Roosevelt went on. "We propose sending all types of goods in unarmed American flagships to Egypt or any other non-belligerent port via Red Sea or Persian Gulf. We think we can work out sending wheat and other goods in American ships to Greenland or Iceland through the next six months. We hope to make available for direct haul to England a large amount of your present shipping which is now utilized for other purposes. We expect to make use of Danish ships very soon and Italian ships in about two months." The United States had recently seized these ships, which had been interned in U.S. ports; Roosevelt's lawyers held that they were exempt from the Neutrality Act's prohibitions against entry into belligerent ports. "Another of his carefully calculated steps towards giving us full assistance," Whitehead minuted.[10]

Roosevelt's cable ended on a cautionary note. "I believe advisable that when this new policy is adopted here no statement be issued at your end. It is not certain I would make specific announcement. I may decide to issue necessary naval operations orders and let time bring out the existence of the new patrol area."

Although the decision to patrol to the twenty-fifth meridian had been made, how publicly and aggressively to present it was still being debated by Roosevelt and his advisers when news from Moscow added to Roosevelt's caution. Matsuoka, after conferring with Hitler in Berlin, where he had promised to do his best to bring about the attack on Singapore, had stopped off again in Moscow on the way home. There he signed a neutrality pact with Stalin. Stalin was so pleased with this accomplishment that he went to the railway station and saw Matsuoka off with a hug. There was also an embrace for the German ambassador and the plea, "We must remain friends and you must do everything to that end." Behind the ardent amenities there were strains and suspicions. Hitler had kept Operation Barbarossa, the planned attack on Russia, secret from Matsuoka, but the West did not know this. What was clear was that the neutrality pact freed Japan for the move southward.

"Now, let's take up the letter we sent you regarding the Detachment coming to the Atlantic," Stark wrote Kimmel,

and without checking up, I believe it was 3 battleships, 1 aircraft carrier, 4 light cruisers and 2 squadrons of destroyers. The entire world set-up was gone into very carefully and this detachment was one of the first means of implementing what we had every reason to anticipate here. It was agreed to, authorized and directed in its detail by the President. It was also canceled by the President, and he gave the specific direction to bring only the 1 aircraft carrier and 1 division of destroyers with which you are now familiar. The reason for the change was that the President did not want, at this particular moment, to give any signs of seriously weakening the forces in the Pacific, and it is my opinion that this will hold until there is some further clarification, incident to Matsuoka's return to Toyko and this further illumination on the Russo-Japanese Treaty.

April 15 was another day of crisis in Washington. Should the extension of the patrol zone be announced by proclamation or kept secret, letting the fact of the new orders to the United States fleet emerge gradually? Morgenthau opposed secrecy, arguing that it could not be maintained. Stimson favored a proclamation in order to bolster British morale and shatter whatever appeasement sentiment still existed in Britain. After the meeting at the White House, Stimson renewed his plea to Hopkins, who came to see him. "It was vital that we should give a lift to British morale . . . that could only be done by naval action and vigorous action at that." He called in Knox, who backed him up, adding, "If the Navy were turned loose they could clean up the North Atlantic situation in thirty days." Hopkins sought the advice of the army planners on whether the United States should risk going to war. They advised that the army was unready and that it was, therefore, "highly desirable that we withhold active participation as long as possible."

Roosevelt's decision after this round of conferences was to stand on the patrolling plan that he had communicated to Churchill on April 11. He summoned Admiral King, commander in chief of the Atlantic fleet, to Hyde Park. "Hemispheric Plan No. 1 goes by the board, and a substitute with no teeth is being prepared today," a disappointed Stark informed Kimmel.[11]

Churchill, however, received the news with satisfaction:

I had intended to cable you more fully on your momentous message about the Atlantic. Admiralty received the news with the greatest relief and satisfaction and have prepared a technical paper. . . . The matter is certainly of highest urgency and consequence. There are about 15 U-boats now operating on the 30th meridian and, of course, United States flying boats working from Greenland would be a most useful immediate measure.

This may have been making a virtue out of necessity except that the satisfaction was widely shared. "Cabinet at 12," Cadogan, the least sentimental of British officials, noted in his diary. "Not v. much news except that Winston told Cabinet of Roosevelt's decision to police the Western half of Atlantic. Which is *very* good." And the king wrote to the same effect in his journal: "The new American patrols, which have just come into force, are going a long way to solve our difficulty of escorting convoys. Public opinion in U.S.A. is coming around to our way of thinking faster than before."[12]

But among the knowledgeable men and women in the United States, anxiety over Britain's ability to survive a new series of disasters in Greece and Libya continued unabated. And with reason. "Evacuation going fairly well," Cadogan wrote of the British withdrawal from Greece to Crete. "That's all that we're really good at! . . . Our soldiers are the most pathetic amateurs, pitted against professionals. . . . Tired, depressed and defeatist!"

This was the period—and it would continue until July, when convoys were ordered—when men who usually had faith in Roosevelt's sense of timing were most discontented with his failure to give a strong lead, when the president's normal tendency to throw up a discursive smoke screen of storytelling and charm to avoid systematic analysis and decision baffled and exasperated his most loyal supporters. W. Averell Harriman, liberal industrialist, close friend of Hopkins, and admirer of Roosevelt, left in March for England as lend-lease expediter. He saw Roosevelt before his departure and came away distressed at the president's reluctance to force the issue on convoys. Roosevelt professed to believe "that our material aid would let Britain do the job," a belief, observed Harriman, that was "without the background of reasoning."

After the Easter recess, when Roosevelt had met with his chief advisers on the convoy issue, Stimson was upset because the session "was mainly consumed with the President's reminiscences. . . . It was an example of the President's weakness as an administrator. He has flashes of genius but when it comes to working out a hard problem in a short time and with the aid of expert advisers, well, he just doesn't quite connect and it doesn't work. However, he has done well enough during this past year to be entitled to the confidence of the world and this is just one of the penalties that those who work with him have to pay."

Halifax was equally baffled at the administrative clutter and muddle he found at the White House. "The President seems to me all out to be helpful," he wrote Churchill, "and I thought it was friendly of him the other night to ring me up himself to tell me that they could take the ships you wanted them to repair. But every day that I am here makes me see more and more how terribly disjointed is the whole machine of government. I don't think the President ties up awfully well; I am quite sure Harry Hopkins doesn't." But then he, too, like Stimson, qualified his criticism. The old Washington hands assured him, he went on, that "while all this is true, it really does work better than you would think on the surface, and that somehow or other things move in the right direction."[13]

"Convoys are the general topic of conversation," Halifax wrote Churchill a month later. "I doubt whether the President will do straight convoying, however, just yet. And I have a feeling that he is, with all his good intentions and desire to help, perhaps ultra respectful of public opinion. He has got to respect it of course, and cannot move without it, but I have the feeling that it is sometimes ahead of him, and he is afraid to acknowledge it, and that he could move it a bit faster than he has done by being too ready to wait for it to move independently."

"I cautioned [the president]," Stimson wrote after a private meeting with Roosevelt on April 22, "on the necessity of his taking the lead and that without a lead on his part it was useless to expect the people would voluntarily take the initiative in letting him know whether or not they would follow him if he did take the lead." The issue was an old one with Roosevelt—when to lead and when to wait until men's minds were better disposed to follow leadership. Had Halifax and Stimson associated more with New Dealers, they would have better understood Roosevelt's methods. The complaint against Roosevelt, Arthur Schlesinger, Jr., observed of the New Deal years, was "his weakness for postponement. Yet his caution was always within an assumption of constant advance."

All through the New Deal years, Roosevelt had observed how often the advocates of good programs assumed that the intensity of their own feelings reflected the public's: they would persuade themselves that if only the president lifted his voice the cause could be won. "Merely shouting from the housetops—you cannot do it that way," he had once explained to a group of impatient youth leaders. It took the "shocks" of events to induce men to listen. Haranguing the country did not help. When he was not ready to show his hand, he could maintain a charade that mystified even his most intimate friends as to his true intentions. In a meeting with Stimson and Knox on April 24, recorded Stimson, Roosevelt "kept reverting to the fact that the force in the Atlantic was merely going to be a patrol to watch for any aggressor and to report that to America. I answered then, with a smile on my face, saying 'But you are not going to report the presence of the German Fleet to the Americans. You are going to report it to the British Fleet.' I wanted him to be honest with himself. To me it seems a clearly hostile act to the Germans, and I am prepared to take the responsibility of it. He seems to be trying to hide it into the character of a purely reconnaissance action which it really is not." "Presidents sometimes don't tell themselves things," Stimson's old friend Felix Frankfurther would later explain. Roosevelt was a great one, Morgenthau noted, for not telling his left hand what his right was doing. Stark, although disappointed by Roosevelt's caution, saw the reason for his bobbing and weaving: "I had hoped that with the passage of the Lend-Lease Bill we could look forward to some unity on Capitol Hill but just at present there seems to be far from that desired unity on vital issues. What will be done about convoy and many other things, and just how much of a part of our Democratic way of life will be handled by Mr. Gallup, is a pure guess. . . . The President has on his hands at the present time about as difficult a situation as ever confronted any man anywhere in public life."[14]

Unlike the destroyer deal and lend-lease legislation, the polls reflected no popular upsurge for convoys. In fact, the Gallup poll in April showed a majority opposed to them. Even more emphatic was congressional sentiment. During the lend-lease debates, the administration, although insisting that the president under his constitutional powers as commander in chief had a right to order convoys, had avoided a confrontation on the issue by acceptance of an amendment that stated that nothing in the Lend-Lease Act authorized convoys. Early in May, through the "courtesy" of J. Edgar Hoover, the administration got an advance look at a poll of congressional opinion which showed 80 per cent opposed to convoys even "if believed necessary to prevent British defeat by Hitler." Another poll showed fifty senators for convoys to forty-five against. By putting on the pressure, radio commentator and journalist Raymond Gram Swing was told, this margin might be increased to fifty-five to forty. "But a vote of fifty-five to forty is not a great enough majority to create the national unity needed to support a war." Sen. Walter F. George of Georgia, chairman of the Senate Foreign Relations Committee, had powerfully aided passage of the lend-lease bill without amendments that might have crippled the president's powers, but he had drawn the line at convoys. When Sen. Charles W. Tobey of New Hampshire, a leading isolationist, introduced a resolution prohibiting convoys and the isolationists in Congress, cast down by their defeat on lend-lease, revived and rallied, Roosevelt passed the word to the interventionist groups "not to wave the red flag of immediate convoy."

The cabinet was divided over the issue of an aggressive Atlantic policy. Hull in particular, preoccupied with the Far East and cautious by temperament, favored wariness and had thought this was also the president's attitude, at least so he told Breckinridge Long early in April. But other presidential moves left him fretful and suspicious. "Having gone this far" in aid of the British, Knox wound up a speech to the American Newspaper Publishers Association, "we can only go on. Hitler cannot allow our war supplies and food to reach England—he will be defeated if they do. We cannot allow our goods to be sunk in the Atlantic—we shall be beaten if they do. We must make our promises good and give aid to the British. We must see the job through." He had wanted to say that the United States intended "to insure the delivery" of lend-lease supplies, but Roosevelt had asked him to soften that. Hull, nevertheless, was furious. "He is quite provoked at the speech Frank Knox made last night," Long noted. "Knox made statements which were rather definite as far as our foreign policy is concerned and were more advanced than any the Secretary felt justified in saying. Knox made the statement that the President had O.K.'d his speech. The Secretary constantly has his feelings hurt that way and every once in a while he unburdens his soul to me." Long concluded this entry with a statement reflective of Hull's as well as his own views on convoying: "My very definite feeling is that as soon as we convoy we are in the war, and it will be assumed by Germany to be an aggressive act. . . . We are not ready now."[15]

Churchill sensed the divisions in the United States government and thought that Knox better represented Roosevelt's intentions than Hull. On April 18, Halifax cabled that Hull "in strict confidence and on his personal responsibility alone" had asked whether the British could find crews to man twenty-five or fifty destroyers "for a period of say two to three months. He begged me to make this enquiry as from myself and therefore his name should *on no account* be disclosed or mentioned to the U.S. Embassy." He had prepared a long answer, Churchill finally replied on May 5, "but it has been superseded by the President's action" (in ordering the patrols). He sent Halifax a copy of what he had written originally, adjuring him to treat it as both secret and obsolete: "Are you sure that Knox is not pressing for still more vigorous action, i.e., convoys, and perhaps Hull with diplomatic caution is not feeling his way to half measures. . . . Such complications are found in many Governments. I should be inclined to go a little slow on this till the reactions following on the reverses in the Middle East are more clear."[16]

There were strategic objections to convoying. It meant dividing the fleet and thus weakening its deterrent effect on Japan. This so troubled Roosevelt that he instructed Stark to find out from the British admiralty whether it considered the transfer of a substantial number of vessels, including three battleships, to the Atlantic "advisable." The admiralty favored a limited shift, but was opposed to the transfer of "almost the whole of the Pacific Fleet into the Atlantic," as Knox was urging. Cadogan thought it "insane" to endorse this suggestion, "but Winston very obstinate that this was the right thing to do."

Churchill had persuaded himself, despite his February 15 plea to Roosevelt to keep the pressure on Japan, that Japan would not enter the war until after a successful invasion of Britain, wrote Cadogan. "And he suffers from the delusion that any cold water thrown on any hare-brained U.S. suggestion will stop U.S. coming into the war!" The British amended their original statement on the advisability of the transfer of a powerful naval detachment to the Atlantic. The United States fleet would not have a deterrent effect upon the Japanese, they carefully specified, unless it "consisted of not less than 6 capital ships and 2 aircraft carriers. Inclusion of the latter is considered of the greatest importance."[17]

At least the U.S. Navy was geared for action and generally supportive of Roosevelt's policy of all possible aid to Britain. The army strenuously resisted moves that might precipitate it into hostilities before its planners thought it was ready, and some influential army strategists violently opposed Roosevelt's interventionist policies. They were defeatist about Britain and contemptuous of Churchill as warlord. Stimson at this time became so fed up with the way G-2 (i.e., army intelligence) overrated German military capabilities that he asked Marshall to put in some men who "have a little broader vision." Col. Truman Smith, who had been military attaché in Berlin in the thirties and had squired Colonel Lindbergh around during his visit there, was the author of the report that had provoked Stimson's wrath. Smith, recorded Stimson,

had volunteered the statement that the decision of the British to send troops to Greece was the worst instance of the political element of the Government interfering with the military strategy that has happened since General Halleck. When later in the morning Colonel Donovan came in and talked over the situation with me, I mentioned that to him and he reminded me that the decision to send British troops to Greece had not been made by the Cabinet or Churchill at all but by Wavell himself and that Donovan had been present when it was made. I told Donovan that when this statement had been brought to me by Smith I told Marshall to call the G-2 men together and tell them that I didn't want any more talk of that sort because I regarded that such talk necessarily might influence people to regard the tenure of Churchill as uncertain and that I regarded our main safety in respect to keeping the British Fleet intact depended on the continuance of the Churchill Government.

Maj. Gen. Stanley D. Embick, who had been called in by Marshall to advise on military strategy, distrusted Churchill's strategic judgment and considered Stimson naïve and the United States Army unready. And as to voluntary intervention into the European war, he thought it wrong militarily and unfair to the American people. Embick's influence, wrote Prof. Forrest Pogue, Marshall's authorized biographer, "was exerted through his own reports and through the views of his son-in-law, Colonel (later General) Albert C. Wedemeyer, a member of the War Plans Division." Wedemeyer, who had been a student at the German War College in 1936–1938, believed that the United States was " 'propagandized into World War I,' a view that made him sympathetic to the aims of the America First organization."

The great and deserved prestige of General Marshall later drew a veil over this whole episode. But an army leadership that in some measure at least was infected with defeatism where the British were concerned was another factor that caused Roosevelt to move cautiously. He was prepared to take tremendous risks. A wrongly timed move, however, meant not only personal repudiation, but repudiation of a policy.[18]

The plans for the patrol, meanwhile were being put into effect. On April 24, Churchill transmitted the admiralty's survey of the Atlantic danger areas where American aerial and sea reconnaissance would be welcome. They included the zone south of Greenland, the stretch of ocean from Freetown up through the Cape Verde Islands to the Azores, and the area off Newfoundland. And later that day, when he received the U.S. "Navy Western Hemisphere Defense Plan No. 2," the prime minister dispatched a follow-up message to the president that it "almost entirely covers the points made in my cable to you. . . . We are deeply impressed by the rapidity with which it is being brought into play." Churchill also applauded "the energetic steps" the United States Navy was taking to prepare bases in Northern Ireland and Iceland. He ended with a request: "We are, of course, observing the strictest secrecy. You will, I am sure, however, realise that if it were possible for you to make any kind of disclosure or declaration on these lines, it might powerfully influence the attitude both of Turkey and Spain at a cardinal moment."

Roosevelt responded to Churchill's plea that he go public. At his news conference the next day, when correspondents pressed him on whether the April 24 speeches by Knox and, ironically, Hull meant convoys, the president disclosed the search-and-patrol system, describing it as an extension of the hemispheric security zone that had been established in 1939 at the war's beginning. In the course of his description, he reinterpreted the function of hemispheric protection to include the protection of merchant convoys by "reconnaissance." When asked what a patrol would do if it spotted "some apparently aggressive ship," Roosevelt evaded an answer with the sally "Let me know." He ended the press conference with a harsh attack on Lindbergh, who had emerged as the most effective spokesman for a negotiated peace. The night before, the colonel had addressed an America First rally in New York City in which 35,000 people had jammed the streets around the hall where he was speaking. His central emphasis was that "we cannot win this war for England, regardless of how much assistance we send." At his news conference, Roosevelt likened Lindbergh to Clement L. Vallandigham of Ohio, leader of the "Copperheads" during the American Civil War:

Well, Vallandigham, as you know, was an appeaser. He wanted to make peace from 1863 on because the North "couldn't win." Once upon a time there was a place called Valley Forge and there were an awful lot of appeasers that pleaded with Washington to quit, because he "couldn't win." Just because he "couldn't win." See what Tom Paine said at that time in favor of Washington keeping on fighting![19]

Jan Ciechanowski, who in mid-March presented his credentials as the representative of the Polish government-in-exile, wrote that Roosevelt was "sounding out public opinion and, simultaneously, helping it to crystallize into a state of alertness and preparedness." Although FDR's mind was probably made up, it was Ciechanowski's belief that the president wanted to create "the impression that his leadership, when he finally assumed it, would be the expression of an already determined American public opinion." The ambassador, who had represented Poland in Washington during the Coolidge era, could not keep from wondering what would have happened if Coolidge instead of Roosevelt were in the White House. "What would have been [Coolidge's] relationship with the Britain of Winston Churchill?"[20]

As unhappy as men like Knox and Stimson were with Roosevelt's circumspection and ambiguities, Churchill brilliantly knitted the "patrol" scheme into a fabric of hope, using it to demonstrate the closeness in relations between the United States and Britain and arguing that that would be the decisive factor in the war. For all of Hitler's victories, present and future, the prime minister said in a radio broadcast, "in order to win this war he must either conquer this island or he must cut the ocean lifeline which joins us to the United States." It was, therefore, "with indescribable relief" that he had learned "of the tremendous decision lately taken by the President and people of the United States." He then described the hemisphere-patrol scheme and went on to predict "the eventual and total defeat of Hitler and Mussolini . . . in view of the respective declared resolves of the British and American democracies." And as emblematic of the deepening relationship between the two countries and symbolic of Britain's further expectations, Churchill quoted the nineteenth-century poet Arthur Hugh Clough:

> For while the tired waves, vainly breaking,
>   Seem here no painful inch to gain,
> Far back through creeks and inlets making,
>   Comes silent, flooding in, the main.
>
> And not, by eastern windows only,
>   When daylight comes, comes in the light;
> In front the sun climbs slow, how slowly,
>   But westward, look, the land is bright.[21]

The headline of the *New York Times* the next day effectively caught that moment of despair and hope:

CHURCHILL SEES VICTORY WITH U.S. SEA AID;

NAZIS HOLD ATHENS, ENTER PELOPONNESUS,

HARRY BRITISH ON SEA; AXIS GAINS IN EGYPT

Chapter Seventeen

A Moment of Gloom

NOT EVERYTHING pleased Roosevelt in Churchill's April 24 messages hailing the extension of the patrol system. His reply to a British proposal for cooperation on the Azores was sharp, almost peremptory. Fearful that the Germans might try to close the western end of the Mediterranean, Churchill was holding in readiness two expeditions for dispatch to the Azores and the Cape Verdes. But, as he informed Roosevelt, "with our other naval burdens we have not the forces to maintain a continuous watch. It would be a very great advantage if you could send an American squadron for a friendly cruise in these regions at the earliest moment. This would probably warn Nazi raiders off, and would keep the place warm for us as well as giving us invaluable information."

British occupation of the Azores might undermine Roosevelt's whole rationale for pushing America's naval frontier far into the Atlantic. That rationale was essentially one of hemispheric protection against aggression. The foundation of United States relations with the other American republics, which feared the northern colossus, was one of nonaggression and nonintervention. With their concurrence, the president had just drawn the line separating Europe from America so that the Azores were included in the Western Hemisphere. British pre-emptive occupation of the Azores would fuel Axis propaganda throughout the hemisphere about Anglo-Saxon imperialism. It would highlight the contradiction between Roosevelt's policy of patrolling to aid the British and a patrol system to protect the hemisphere's neutrality, which had been its original justification.

Portugal, Roosevelt now informed Churchill, had by no means been pleased to have the United States make even a "friendly visit" to the Azores and the Cape Verdes. Then he continued almost sternly:

It is, of course, of utmost importance, in my judgment, that you send no expedition to either place unless Portugal is attacked or you get definite word of an immediate German attack on the islands. Furthermore, I know you will not mind my saying that in the event of a British expeditionary force you make it very clear to the American people that in the case of Azores it is for the purpose of British defense and not for permanent occupation.

The remainder of Roosevelt's message jolted Churchill even more. It obviously contemplated further British defeats in the eastern Mediterranean and appeared to be resigned to the loss of the Middle East. Churchill, in messages on April 25 and 29, had described Britain's bleak prospects of holding Crete, to which the British had withdrawn, warned of a Nazi thrust toward the Suez Canal via Syria, but hoped that the situation in Libya could be stabilized. "Having sent all men and equipment to Greece you could possibly spare," Roosevelt continued in words meant to be encouraging but, to Churchill's ears, sounding defeatist,

you have fought a wholly justified delaying action and will continue to do so in other parts of Eastern Mediterranean, including North Africa and the Near East. Furthermore, . . . if additional withdrawals become necessary, they will all be part of the plan which at this stage of the war shortens British lines, greatly extends the Axis lines, and compels the enemy to expend great quantities of men and equipment. I am satisfied that both here and in Britain public opinion is growing to realize that even if you have to withdraw further in the Eastern Mediterranean, you will not allow any great debacle or surrender, and that in the last analysis the Naval control of the Indian Ocean and the Atlantic Ocean will in time win the war.[1]

Roosevelt's message to Churchill also reflected differences in approach to Vichy. The president did not think there was any chance of persuading Pétain to break with the Germans. He nevertheless felt that the British should permit food shipments to go through the blockade "as a lever," as Stimson put it, "to keep up Pétain's hands and keep up his backbone and enable him to resist the Germans, particularly to enable him to protect North Africa."

Churchill, "tired and depressed," did not take kindly to this message. "He had just returned from Plymouth which was badly battered," reported Ambassador John Winant. "He seemed both sad and discouraged. We talked about your message and I had the impression that he was troubled about it. I told him it was a supporting message. He rather felt it was a message of delay." It took the whole American department of the foreign office, backed up by Foreign Secretary Eden and by Deputy Prime Minister Attlee, to keep him from firing off a reply which all considered unsuitable. At a meeting in Eden's room to appraise Roosevelt's message, the participants agreed that the president was not sufficiently aware of "the dangers to us consequent on a loss of the Mediterranean Theatre." But the group deprecated implications in Churchill's draft reply that loss of the Mediterranean might cause Britain to question the advisability of continuing to fight. The moment had come, the group decided, for a blunt appeal from the prime minister to the president for bolder action. "The President has always shown great skill in making it appear that his public was leading him rather than the reverse; he has not always shown an equal facility for coming out into the open and leading them at a crisis. We appear to be at such a crisis now and if the Prime Minister could put it into the mind of the President to take a bold step forward Americans would probably accept his lead with positive relief." The redrafted message was taken by Eden to Chequers.

The reply as finally dispatched by Churchill was conciliatory in tone but unyielding in content. If Spain and Portugal were given advance warning, that would "make it almost certain that we shall be forestalled." The prime minister was perfectly willing to have the United States guarantee that Britain would restore the islands to Portuguese sovereignty at the end of the war. "We are far from wishing to add to our territory, but only to preserve our life and perhaps yours." He was more than willing that the United States should take the lead with Vichy "and work out how to get the best from them by threats or favors. You alone can forestall the Germans in Morocco."

But the heart of Churchill's message dealt with the larger strategic picture:

We must not be too sure that the consequences of the loss of Egypt and the Middle East would not be grave. It would seriously increase the hazards of the Atlantic and Pacific and could hardly fail to prolong the war with all the suffering and military dangers that this would entail. We shall fight on whatever happens, but please remember that the attitude of Spain, Vichy, Turkey, and Japan may be finally determined by the outcome of the struggle in this theater of war. I cannot take the view that the loss of Egypt and the Middle East would be a mere preliminary to the successful maintenance of a prolonged oceanic war. If all Europe, the greater part of Asia and Africa became, either by conquest or agreement under duress, a part of the Axis system, a war maintained by the British Isles, the United States, Canada, and Australia against this mighty agglomeration would be a hard, long, and bleak proposition. Therefore, if you cannot take more advanced positions now or very soon, the vast balances may be tilted heavily to our disadvantage.

All this was preliminary to the request to which he had been silently awaiting an answer since the desperate days of the collapse of France—that the United States come into the war.

Mr. President, I am sure that you will not misunderstand me if I speak to you exactly what is in my mind. The one decisive counterweight I can see to balance the growing pessimism in Turkey, the Near East, and in Spain would be if the United States were immediately to range herself with us as a belligerent power. If this were possible I have little doubt that we could hold the situation in the Mediterranean until the weight of your munitions gained the day.

Roosevelt realized that his earlier message may have sounded harsh and overly pessimistic. "In my message of May 1, I did not intend to minimize in any degree the gravity of the situation, particularly as regards the Mediterranean. I am well aware of its strategic importance and I share your anxiety in regard to it." Thirty ships would sail with supplies for the Middle East "within the next three weeks." The supplies would continue to flow until there is a final decision in Mediterranean. . . . My previous message merely meant to indicate that should the Mediterranean prove in the last analysis to be an impossible battle ground I do not feel that such fact alone would mean the defeat of our mutual interests. I say this because I believe the outcome of struggle is going to be decided in the Atlantic and unless Hitler can win there he cannot win anywhere in the world in the end.

There was praise for the British military effort in Greece and Africa and an account of Ambassador Leahy's latest news from Vichy that included Marshal Pétain's assurance that French collaboration with Hitler would not go "beyond the requirements of the armistice agreement. . . . Leahy believes that Pétain has the genuine support of all the French people but that they do not share the same confidence in Darlan. He further believes that most of the people are openly or secretly supporting your cause." Roosevelt ended on a personal note: "With this message goes my warm personal regards to you." On the typed draft the president penciled a note to "C.H. & S.W. [Cordell Hull and Sumner Welles]: "This seems better than draft. If ok please send," suggesting it was a substitute for a State Department draft. Perhaps the May 1 message also had been composed there.[2]

Roosevelt had no comment on Churchill's plea that the United States should become a belligerent. Although Roosevelt was pushing America's naval frontier closer and closer toward Europe in order to aid the British, there were steps he would not take. Churchill, in his message of April 29, and Halifax that same day in Washington, had proposed that units of the United States fleet visit Dakar and Casablanca to warn both the Germans and Vichy of its interest in west and North Africa. But, as naval historian Capt. Tracy B. Kittredge has recorded, "the President was not prepared to approve any Naval activities or demonstrations, such as that suggested by Lord Halifax, on 29 April 41, which might involve any immediate armed conflict with the Germans." In January, he had laid down two principles to guide United States military representatives in the secret joint staff talks: (1) "our military course must be very conservative until our strength [has] developed"; and (2) "we must be ready to act with what is available." Those principles still held.

Hitler sensed that the swift, brilliantly executed German victories in Greece and Cyrenaica had triggered a wave of pessimism in the United States and convened the *Reichstag* on May 4 for a victory speech. He jibed and jeered at Churchill, who "as a soldier is a bad politician and as a politician is an equally bad soldier. . . . I prophesied more correctly than Mr. Churchill in my last speech in which I announced that wherever the British might set foot on the Continent they would be attacked by us and driven into the sea." He ridiculed Churchill as "one of the most hopeless dabblers in strategy" who had "managed to lose two theaters of war at a single blow" and ended on a note of invincibility which even if self-proclaimed was, at the moment, not without plausibility: "The German Reich and its allies represent power, military, economic, and above all, in moral respects, which is superior to any possible coalition in the modern world."

The British reply to Hitler's speech took the form of a debate in the House of Commons on the military situation in which critics aired their discontents and which ended with a division in which they could show their lack of confidence in the policies of the government. Churchill made no direct reply to Hitler's address, particularly to the Führer's scurrilous personal attacks, when he rose to close the Commons debate on the government's war policies except to note that England's enemies had high hopes of the government breaking up due to a loss of nerve. "The only way in which those doubts can be removed and these expectations disappointed is by a full debate followed by a Division, and the Government are entitled to ask that such a vote shall express itself in unmistakeable terms." Dressed in the prescriptive black suit that was unrelieved except for a heavy silver watch chain across his paunch, Churchill dealt gently with the critics of the government, the most notable of whom was the venerable Lloyd George. He chided his old ministerial comrade-in-arms for an "unhelpful" speech at a moment that he himself conceded was one of "discouragement and disheartenment." He reviewed the reasons why forces had been diverted from North Africa, where they would probably have brought Rommel up short, to fight a losing battle—as he had predicted would be the case to Hopkins in January—in Greece. "If we had again to tread that stony path, even with the knowledge that we possess today, I for one would do the same thing again"—and so, he appended, would all of his war cabinet colleagues. The only hope he could offer the House of better prospects related to American help. The patrol system "takes a considerable part of the Atlantic to a certain degree off our hands, but we need a good deal more help. I expect we shall get a good deal more help in many ways. In fact, it has been declared we are to have all help necessary, but here I speak with great caution, because it is not for a British Minister to forecast, still less to prescribe, the policy of the United States." He added to the portentousness of this statement a taunt that was the more telling than all of Hitler's personal gibes: "Any one can see Hitler's fear of the United States from the fact he has not long ago declared war on them."

The House had hung upon his every word. And when it divided, only three members voted against the government. As Churchill left the chamber, the House broke into applause. "I am happy about the House today," noted Nicolson. "Members are a bit defeatist. But Winston cheers them up."[3]

Roosevelt's willingness to contemplate the loss of Egypt was particularly galling to Churchill because the latter had had the same argument with some of his own generals. At Chequers the last week end in April, the director of military operations in the war office, Gen. Sir John Kennedy, had suggested it might not be possible to hold Egypt. In such an event, Churchill retorted as if stung, there would be firing parties "to shoot the generals." He upbraided Kennedy with defeatism for even mentioning the possibility. But it was a normal function of staff and command work to prepare for the worst as well as other contingencies, Kennedy protested. Surely the prime minister knew that General Wavell, the commander in the Middle East, had a plan for withdrawal from Egypt should it be forced upon him. "This," exclaimed the prime minister, "comes like a flash of lightning to me. I never heard such ideas. War is a contest of wills. It is pure defeatism to speak as you have done." Wavell had a plan, Kennedy wrote, "for an even worse case, namely for carrying on the war in Africa in the event not merely of Egypt but of the British Isles being lost." Fortunately, "for Mr. Churchill's peace of mind," the war office did not learn of it until later.

In the testing of wills, Churchill was ready to take large risks. Long experience had taught him how much on the battlefield was a matter of hazard, how generals in the absence of sure intelligence tended to overestimate the enemy's prowess and underestimate their own, even when the difficulties and imperfections of the opposition were all too obvious. Even the generals who were most critical of Churchill's meddling and who had to spend hours and days moderating his "unsound and impracticable" directives, as some of them appeared to be, were disarmed by the "splendid spirit of courage, defiance and initiative" that animated those directives. "It appeared in our 'In Trays' at a moment when our fortunes had suffered grievous setbacks," wrote General Kennedy of one particularly offensive directive on "The War in the Mediterranean" that the prime minister had dashed off in mid-April, "and, even as we grumbled at the work it caused us, we could not but delight in its sentiments." Overcautiousness in war was a disease of generals in Churchill's book, related to and only slightly less abhorrent than defeatism. When General Brooke, whom he had placed in charge of Britain's preparations against invasion, reported on some wintertime home-defense exercises, the prime minister was "very flattering about the defensive measures that had been taken" but "considered that the umpires had exaggerated the German threat of invasion. He even implied that this had been done in order to influence him into considering the threat greater than it really was. . . . Nothing that I said had much effect, his suspicious nature had been aroused." In the Commons debate over the conduct of the war, his sharpest reproach to Lloyd George was that the former prime minister, who had been accustomed in the First World War to "brush aside despondency and alarm," had made "the sort of speech with which, I imagine, the illustrious and venerable Marshal Pétain might well have enlivened the closing days of M. Reynaud's Cabinet."[4]

British reverses in May were the more difficult to bear because of the successes that had preceded them. London on May 10 had its worst night in the blitz: almost 1,500 people were killed, 1,800 seriously injured, fires raged everywhere, and Westminster was left, as Nicolson wrote, "a sort of Tintern Abbey gaping before me." As in June, 1940, when France had collapsed and left Britain to fight on alone, Churchill's courage, resilience, and stubborness again set an example for the nation, infected associates, and impressed America anew.

In military affairs, the Churchillian resilience reflected itself in what General Brooke called "a passion for the offensive," and the officers on the receiving end were the commanders in the Middle East, headed by Wavell, who were called upon to contain and repel Rommel in Cyrenaica, to hold Crete against the expected German onslaught by sea and air, to dispatch a mobile column from Palestine to Baghdad where Rashid Ali with German support was marching on the RAF base at Habbaniya, and to support a Free French advance into Vichy-controlled Syria when Nazi penetration began to assume dangerous proportions. It was a case, said Wavell, "of spreading the butter very thin."

War may be a contest of wills. But General Freyberg, the brave New Zealander who uncomplainingly organized Crete's defenses although dubious it could be held, finally had to signal Wavell six days after Germany's airborne troops had gained a lodgment on the island, "I regret to have to report that in my opinion limit of endurance has been reached by troops under my command here at Suda Bay." And Admiral Cunningham, enraged by suggestions from London that his fleet was avoiding risks, fired back, "It is inadvisable to drive men beyond a certain point." Yet that was what Churchill insisted on, as if his eyes could not register or his mind comprehend the signals that flashed defeat. "Victory in Crete is essential at this turning point in the war. Keep hurling in all aid you can," he telegraphed Wavell even as the commanders on the spot had decided on evacuation.[5]

May 26 was one of Churchill's unhappiest days. The German superbattleship *Bismarck,* accompanied by the *Prinz Eugen,* sortied into the North Atlantic to prey on British commerce. Engaged by a powerful British squadron headed by the *Prince of Wales* and the *Hood,* it had sunk the latter and then had been lost in the mists. In the Western Desert, Rommel pushed his forces forward, although Wavell's brigades had been augmented by a convoy of tanks that Churchill, over the protests of most of his advisers, had sent through the hazardous waters of the Mediterranean rather than around the Cape, in order to expedite their delivery. "Poor Winston will recover all right if we get a bit of good news," wrote Cadogan. "Tonight he was almost throwing his hand in. But there is a bit of the histrionic art in that." Eden, too, recorded the day as one of the worst. "A most gloomy day. *Bismarck* appears to have been lost. We face defeat in Crete and make little progress towards Baghdad. The worst Cabinet we have yet had in evening. Winston was nervy and unreasonable and everyone else on edge."

Afterward, Churchill took refuge in the admiralty war room and spent most of the night following the pursuit of the *Bismarck.* By the next morning when the cabinet met again, the *Bismarck* had been located and severely damaged. He dwelt on this news in his report to the House and, with the cabinet's approval, held back on the disaster in Crete except to prepare the way by warning that there had been "heavy losses" to the fleet there because of German air superiority. He then turned to the breakout of the *Bismarck.* "He does it beautifully," recorded Nicolson, building up the story, the discovery of the breakout, the pursuit, the disappearance in the rain and snow, at which point the House, with a "hush of despair," prepared to hear him say that she had escaped. Instead, Churchill went on to report that the Fleet Air Arm, catching up with her at dawn, had fired torpedoes that damaged her steering gear and that she was now making uncontrollable immense circles in the sea. The efforts to finish her off were under way, "as I speak." He went on to deal with conscription in Northern Ireland, Nicolson recorded, "and left the House with a sense of *coitus interruptus.*" A little later, a secretary in the official gallery violently gestured to Brendan Bracken with a small bit of paper. He took it and passed it to the Prime Minister who glanced at it and rose: "I do not know whether I might venture, with great respect, to intervene for one moment. I have just received news that the *Bismarck* is sunk."

The House broke into wild cheers. For the moment the anxiety over Crete was thrust into the background. Later that day, General Brooke, who thought the decision to intervene in Greece was a strategic blunder because it meant a dispersal of forces, attended a tank "parliament," at which Churchill was present, on the design and use of tanks. "P.M. in great form," he wrote afterward, "and on the whole a very successful meeting. It is surprising how he maintains a light-hearted exterior in spite of the vast burden he is bearing. He is quite the most wonderful man I have ever met, and it is a source of never-ending interest, studying him and getting to realize that occasionally such human beings make their appearance on this earth—human beings who stand out head and shoulders above all others."

"The *Bismarck* has been sunk," Ciano wrote in his diary. "This is important especially on account of the repercussion it will have in the United States, where it will prove that the sea is dominated by the Anglo-Saxons."[6]

Roosevelt had followed the *Bismarck*'s menacing career in the Atlantic with the same minute-to-minute intensity that Churchill had shown. Admiralty bulletins on the course of the battle were rushed to him in the Oval Study as soon as they arrived. America's whole neutrality-zone patrol system in the Atlantic was placed on the alert. Patrol Squadron 52, consisting of navy Catalinas (PBYs), was ordered out from Argentia in Newfoundland, where it was based to look for the *Bismarck*. A large part of the first engagement between the *Bismarck* and the *Prinz Eugen* on one side and the *Prince of Wales* and the *Hood* on the other was witnessed by several coast guard cutters engaged in rescuing British survivors from a transatlantic convoy off the southern tip of Greenland. And when the "monster ship," as Sherwood called it, got away in the rain and snow, it was another Catalina PBY, operated by the British Coastal Command but piloted by an American who had been lent to the British, that picked up the trail two days later that led to its destruction. Mr. Roosevelt's navy, in other words, already represented a force in the Atlantic that the Germans could not ignore. And in the tense two days during which the *Bismarck* had been lost from view, Roosevelt had asked Sherwood and others, "Suppose the *Bismarck* showed up in the Caribbean. We have some submarines down there. Suppose we order them to attack her and attempt to sink her? Do you think the people would demand to have me impeached?"

The ties of mutuality between Roosevelt and Churchill were many and various, but one of the most compelling was their fingertip response to any challenge to Anglo-American supremacy in the Atlantic.

Against the background of British disasters in the Balkans, Greece, and the Middle East, Roosevelt grappled with how to give greater aid to Britain without going to war. The debate in the United States centered around convoys, but the real issue was how to ensure Britain's survival and accomplish Hitler's defeat.

By mid-May Britain was gaining the upper hand in the Battle of the Atlantic. To General Smuts Churchill wrote:

Finally, the Battle of the Atlantic is going fairly well. Instead of Hitler reaching a climax of blockade in May as he expected, we have finished the best six weeks of convoys for many months. We shall certainly get increasing American help in the Atlantic, and personally I feel confident our position will be strengthened in all essentials before the year is out. The Americans are making very great provision to replace shipping losses in 1942, and I feel they are being drawn nearer and nearer to their great decision. It is better, however, not to count too much on this.*

Convoys were not the issue. As Roosevelt wrote Sen. Josiah W. Bailey of North Carolina: "[For] purely selfish reasons, [we must] prevent at almost any hazard the Axis domination of the world. . . . Why debate convoys? . . . This whole thing is, of course, a matter of military and naval strategy in its relationship to the defense of the Western Hemisphere, and all that experts can do at the present time is to list a lengthy series of answers to potentialities of the future, if such potentialities were to come to pass." Germinating in Roosevelt's mind were pre-emptive moves into the Azores, into the Cape Verdes, into Iceland, even a declaration that Dakar, at the westernmost tip of Africa, was covered by the Monroe Doctrine.

The issue was how to come to grips with the enemy in a way that would not fatally divide the country. So far, in this delicate balancing act between the nation's desire to stay out of the war and its recognition that Britain's survival served America's interests, Roosevelt had had the nation with him. A current poll showed that 50 per cent of those polled thought the president had gone about the right distance in aiding Great Britain, 23 per cent that he had not gone far enough, and only 19 per cent that he had gone too far. But no such consensus seemed in prospect on convoys.[7]

An article by Raymond Gram Swing in the London *Sunday Express,* May 11, 1941, explaining Roosevelt's approach to the debate over convoys, made a considerable impression on the British foreign office, where it was extensively minuted. It was also read carefully by some of the people around Roosevelt. Speaking of Roosevelt's seeming passivity, Swing wrote:

If he should assume the leadership now, and appear to be "taking" the country into war, the public would turn on him later and reproach him for having brought the country to its dark hours. At such times the only possibility of maintaining unity and morale is that the President shall not have whipped up sentiment for war, that he should appear to have yielded to public insistence, and that war should be an enterprise of partnership rather than something entered at his behest. . . . This being the situation in the United States, the impatience on this [Ameri-

* Churchill's evaluations of how this battle was going, like those of the dangers of invasion, fluctuated violently. The Battle of the Atlantic would not be won decisively until 1943.

ca's] side must rise. But in Britain the patience must rise in the same degree. Both are investments in sound cooperation to come.

The article demonstrated, wrote Sir David Scott, the head of the American department, "why it would be a mistake—apart from the fact that it is always a mistake to beg America to do things for us—to try to hustle the President over convoys—or anything else. He knows what we want and why we want it and the degree of urgency of our need. If he moves cautiously, it is because he deems it best for *the common cause* in the long run; & we must leave to him to judge how the American contribution to that cause can be most effectively made."

Swing's point, summarized Cadogan, is "that Roosevelt must appear to be led or even forced into his policy, but that that must appear to be a 'national movement,' and that in Britain there must be 'patience.' Mr. Swing may be right and his intentions are, I believe, unquestionably good, and therefore we should pay attention to what he says. But I don't know that it would rule out a private direct appeal from the P.M. to the President (though this has been tried quite lately)."

The prime minister, the foreign office, and Lord Halifax in Washington were constantly examining when new proposals to marry the United States to the British cause could be taken up with advantage. Halifax on May 7 suggested that Churchill offer sites for United States naval and air bases in any part of the British Commonwealth "in return for any statement made by the President announcing wholehearted cooperation between the United States and the British Commonwealth in the defeat of Hitler." Eden forwarded the suggestion to Churchill, who commented, "I don't think we ought to press them too much; and certainly this is no time for us to give more." The United States had shown no disposition to use British bases in the Far East, Eden pointed out to Halifax, in contrast to its eagerness for bases in the Caribbean. Is there not a risk that it might be regarded as an attempt on our part to inveigle the United States into underwriting the security of the British Empire? Eden asked. And when Halifax persisted and requested permission to present the idea to the president confidentially, Eden in an interdepartmental minute inquired: "Incidentally do we want to see United States bases established, say, at Auckland & in Fiji, at Takoradi, & Trincomalee? Some of them are a far cry for the United States, and others are not, & I would not happily contemplate a wholesale extension of U.S. bases throughout the British Commonwealth. Singapore U.S. will not use, anyway." Churchill ended the matter: "I think you should deprecate raising the question at the present time."

"I find everyone here from the Prime Minister down deeply appreciative of the increasing aid that you are giving," Harriman wrote Roosevelt. "It is natural that they hope for a belligerent status but I am surprised how understanding all are of the psychology they went through themselves." Whenever the British tended to become impatient with United States isolationism, they reminded themselves of their own peace-at-almost-any-price illusions that had led to Munich.[8]

The British leader most likely to misjudge the psychology of both the American public and its president was Churchill. Even though he was the greatest asset to Anglo-American relations, he was also, on occasion, its greatest menace because of his impetuosity and impatience, because of the fixity with which he held to his ideas, and above all because of his inability to put himself in the other fellow's shoes. Fortunately, there were advisers around strong enough to hold him down. At Chequers one week end in May, a cable was forwarded to Churchill from Wendell Willkie. It expressed concern because friends of Britain not connected with the Roosevelt administration were being told different things as to British needs than were those inside the government. He, Willkie, had returned advocating destroyers for Britain "after talks with you and Alexander." Colonel Donovan had returned urging convoys. Now Forrestal, the undersecretary of the navy, had come back from England saying that "convoys are not necessary and that bombers are sufficient." Was there not some way to keep Britain's friends advised "as to changes of needs"?

Churchill drafted a reply, cabled Ambassador Winant (who fortunately happened to be at Chequers that week end) to the president, but wanted to be sure "that it would not in any way embarrass you." Britain wanted all three, the prime minister's proposed reply stated, "destroyers and long range bombers but far more we want effective convoy to farthest possible point." British protection of shipping in the Atlantic was paid for by losses elsewhere and by reduction in the war effort in the Mediterranean. "I have never said that the British Empire cannot make its way out of this war without American belligerence, but no peace that is of any use to you or which will liberate Europe can be obtained without American belligerence towards which convoy is a decisive step. Every day's delay adds to the length of the war and the difficulties to be encountered."

Roosevelt was both astonished and irritated. Would the ambassador please explain to the prime minister, the president instructed Winant—"entirely off the record"—that he was placed "in a most embarrassing situation" with regard to Willkie's telegram and the suggested answer.

Quite aside from the Logan Act and solely on the formation and maintenance of public opinion here, it would be very serious if it became known publicly that Mr. Willkie, who is giving splendid cooperation to all of us, were communicating directly with the Prime Minister and receiving direct replies, especially in view of the fact that communications go through the Consul General in New York.

Such communications are almost sure to leak out and the revulsion of feeling in the Congress and the Administration would be very bad.

The gratuitous reference to the ambiguities of the Logan Act, which forbids private citizens to carry on diplomatic negotiations with foreign governments, showed how annoyed Roosevelt was. The president suggested to Churchill that he thank Willkie and urge that the latter keep in touch with changing policy through Halifax and the president. "We must not get our wires crossed." Churchill accepted this advice and cabled Willkie: "Most grateful for your telegram and for all you are doing. Please have a talk with Lord Halifax who knows the situation." A copy of Churchill's message was given to Hull by Halifax to transmit to the president. "I did not say to him that I thought you were also familiar with this matter," Hull commented laconically.[9]

Chapter Eighteen

Freedom of the Seas Reasserted

Roosevelt was scheduled to speak on May 14 to a meeting of the Pan-American Union and, as usual, British hopes of another advance in American intervention soared. "The P.M. has given Mr. Hopkins the picture of the shipping situation in his telegram of May 9 and his message to the President earlier in the week went so far as to suggest that the United States should participate in the war. I do not think we can do more at this stage," noted John Balfour of the American department. "The President has the facts and must make the decision."

Roosevelt was considering whether to announce that the Azores and Dakar must not fall into German hands, a suggestion that "rather horrified" Stimson, who, although favoring bolder intervention, feared that making such an announcement before the Atlantic fleet was reinforced might encourage the Germans to seize those areas first. He so told Robert Sherwood, who was working on the May 14 speech with the president and had come to the War Department for a quick lesson in strategy. But the preparations for the speech were suddenly halted by Roosevelt's illness. All that winter and spring he had been plagued with colds. Now Stimson was told that the president "has eaten something that has disagreed with him very seriously." To Stimson, who still was hoping that most of the fleet would be moved to the Atlantic, this was "quite a knockout blow."

The war secretary was a rather elderly gentleman whose keenness tended to flag at times. Under the impression that the greater part of the fleet would be moved to the Atlantic, he failed to read the warning lights that the president and others—Hull, Prime Minister Menzies of Australia (who was in Washington), and Stark—were flashing that the bulk of the fleet had to remain at Pearl Harbor as a background to the negotiations with the Japanese. When, on May 13, Hull reported that "the President was ready now to order the first three capital ships and their accompanying vessels through the Canal," Stimson assumed that that was only a first installment on a full naval force. But when he pressed for a full Atlantic naval force, "Stark, as before, held back and was very weak compared with the position that he had taken before. Knox didn't say much. Hull still thinks he has some chance—he puts it at one to ten—to win something out of negotiations with the Japs. I only hope he may do it."

Behind Stimson's disagreement with Roosevelt and Hull over fleet deployment was a large divergence over the timing and scope of America's participation in the war—whether it should be limited or all-out, whether it should be declared or undeclared, at what stage of America's rearmament should war be waged, on America's initiative or the enemy's, with the nation split or substantially united, against Germany alone or against Japan as well. Different members of the administration answered these questions differently. Roosevelt alone saw the whole picture—insofar as the whole picture was available to anyone in the United States. His associates, moreover, offered their advice in the knowledge that the president was there to say "yes," "no," "not yet." But when Roosevelt made up his mind, there was no one to back-stop him. Stimson and Knox favored participation in the war. So, now, did Morgenthau, who noted in his diary on May 14:

Hopkins wanted to discuss the question of what we were going to do and what the President was going to say in his speech on the 27th [the new date]. He said that following Hull, Stimson and Knox the President had to say something and that most of his friends felt that the next move was to get us into the war. I told Hopkins that during the last week or ten days . . . I had arrived at the conclusion that if we were going to save England we would have to get into this war, and that we needed England, if for no other reason, as a stepping stone to bomb Germany. I told him that we also needed the British Fleet. . . .

I think that both the President and Hopkins are groping as to what to do. They feel that something has to be done but don't know just what. Hopkins said that the President has never said so in so many words, but he thinks the President is loath to get into this war, and he would rather follow public opinion than lead it.[1]

Events in Vichy and the Red Sea area gave Roosevelt his chance to take another step ahead. Admiral Darlan on May 12 held talks with Hitler and Ribbentrop in which—as Churchill had warned—he indicated his readiness to join the war against England. This meant, in effect, use of the French navy. A radio speech by Marshal Pétain that called on the French people to withhold judgment until the facts were known further alarmed Roosevelt and Churchill. At the same time, Hitler declared a blockade of the Red Sea, where American freighters were unloading supplies for the British. Roosevelt promptly issued a statement warning Vichy that collaboration with Germany would be considered by the United States to be a menace to the Western Hemisphere:

The people of the United States can hardly believe that the present Government of France could be brought to lend itself to a plan of voluntary alliance implied or otherwise which would apparently deliver up France and its colonial empire, including French African colonies and their Atlantic coasts with the menace which that involves to the peace and safety of the Western Hemisphere.

The next day Roosevelt sounded a new note at his press conference—freedom of the seas, which, he reminded the newsmen, was "a historic American policy." Referring to Hitler's proclamation of a Red Sea blockade, he noted that "you couldn't simply by a decree create a blockade." The United States had fought two undeclared wars, one against the Barbary pirates in the Mediterranean, another against French privateers in the West Indies, in defense of the long-maintained policy of freedom of the seas. In the case of the French privateers, "without declaring war, we sent the infant Navy down there, and we cleaned up. I think they had something like 101 different actions—engagements—in the general West Indian area, and made it—the whole area—safe for American shipping. The thing last[ed] two and a half years . . . that's just a little lead for you to follow up."[2]

With that declaration, Roosevelt shifted the debate over convoys and moved onto conceptual ground that he found more congenial, easier to explain, better related to the strategic dangers to which he was trying to educate the country. The convoy demand made him uncomfortable. Back in January, fearful that the issue of convoys might prevent the passage of lend-lease, he had, perhaps rashly, told the press that "obviously, when a nation convoys ships, either its own flag or another flag through a hostile zone, just on the doctrine of chance there is apt to be some shooting—pretty sure that there will be shooting—and shooting comes awfully close to war, doesn't it." The words were soon all over Capitol Hill. Senator George, in the final stages of the lend-lease debate, had invoked them in assuring his colleagues that lend-lease did not mean convoys. Isolationist spokesmen subsequently turned the president's statement into a battle cry: "The President has said convoying means shooting and shooting means war." And while public support of convoys increased—as the British situation deteriorated—those opposed to entering the war remained fixed at 85 per cent.

Senator George had added one qualification to his assurance about convoys, and it turned out to be the key to Roosevelt's own thinking: he was not ready, the Georgian said, "to abandon the principle of the freedom of the high seas." Churchill's letter of December 7, 1940, is thought of mainly as the stimulus for lend-lease. But at the outset of that lengthy missive, the prime minister had dealt with the need to reduce British shipping losses, which he said could be accomplished by, among other alternatives,

(1) the reassertion by the United States of the doctrine of the freedom of the seas from illegal and barbarous warfare in accordance with the decisions reached after the late Great War, and as freely accepted and defined by Germany in 1935. From this, the United States ships should be free to trade with countries against which there is not an effective legal blockade. (2) It would . . . follow that protection should be given this lawful trading by United States forces, i.e., escorting battleships, cruisers, destroyers, and air flotillas.[3]

Freedom of the seas was a venerable principle that, according to isolationist analysis, Woodrow Wilson had manipulated in order to entangle the United States in the First World War. In the thirties, this conviction had taken the legislative form of the Neutrality Act's prohibitions on United States ships from entering belligerent ports. Senator Nye, the main mover in the enactment of the Neutrality Act, now reminded the Senate that freedom of the seas was a principle that Britain, with her naval supremacy, had never recognized. When Wilson had included it as point 2 of the Fourteen Points that he had put forward as the basis of a peace settlement, Lloyd George, as historian Winston Churchill had chronicled approvingly in *The World Crisis: The Aftermath,* informed Colonel House that Britain could not accept the clause under any conditions, could not accept that the right of blockade in time of war should be abolished. "Great Britain would spend her last guinea to keep her navy superior to that of the United States or any other Power, and . . . no Cabinet official could continue in the Government of England who took a different position." And, indeed, in the first six months of the Second World War, Roosevelt's neutrality-zone concept, which he considered an aid to the British, had encountered more challenges from London than from Berlin. But freedom of the seas, however wobbly its intellectual claims, *was* a principle of international law and a manner of asserting American rights that was sanctioned by history and tradition. To announce convoying, in the light of his press-conference statement in January, would open FDR to the charge that the United States had fired the first shot, whereas Roosevelt was grimly determined to force Hitler to shoot first. That alone, the president thought, would unite Congress and the public in support of the measures— no longer short of war—that he knew had to be taken to sustain Britain. Having lived through the Wilson experience, he better than any of his associates appreciated how quickly public support for policies that involved genuine hardship and sacrifices—casualty lists, higher taxes, rationing— could erode and dissipate.

Hitler understood Roosevelt's dilemma of trying to lead a country torn between its fear of war and its fear of the Axis. He knew, also, that the solution to Roosevelt's dilemma would be a clear-cut act of aggression against U.S. interests. So he played on American fears of getting into the war in words while ordering his commanders to avoid incidents with the United States. In May, he received the former U.S. ambassador to Belgium, John Cudahy, an isolationist and close friend of Lindbergh, who urged him to warn the United States that convoys meant war, a statement that Cudahy thought "would even at this time establish publicly the responsibility of the American Government for drawing the United States into the war. This clear realization, however, would produce such a reaction among the American people who are against the war that it would defeat the resolution to provide American protection for trans-Atlantic convoys." Hitler gave Cudahy such a statement as part of an interview to be published in *Time* magazine some time in June. Cudahy tried, unsuccessfully, to get the newspapers to publish the interview before Roosevelt's speech, now scheduled for May 27. At the same time, as part of the same campaign, Admiral Raeder gave an exclusive interview to the Japanese news agency Domei, in which he warned, "I can only confirm President Roosevelt's opinion that convoying means 'shooting' and since according to American statements cargoes of convoyed ships must be regarded as contraband the introduction of such a convoy system would be not only an unneutral act under international law but a plain act of war and unprovoked aggression." Simultaneously, in Tokyo, Matsuoka advised Joseph C. Grew, the U.S. ambassador, that convoys would force Hitler to declare war and in such an event Japan would "unfailingly fulfill" her obligations under the Tripartite Pact. Roosevelt considered the commitment of the *Bismarck* to the Battle of the Atlantic as another warning to him. "I was in the White House during the whole career of the *Bismarck*," Robert Sherwood wrote an English friend, "and it was inexpressibly thrilling to hear the repeated bulletins that came from the Admiralty to Roosevelt. The belief is that Hitler sent the *Bismarck* primarily to scare the U.S. with a tremendous display of Nazi might right on our own doorstep. He thus expected to kill the effect of Roosevelt's forthcoming speech." If a strong line were taken, Ribbentrop had lectured Mussolini in mid-May, "and if it were explained that American convoy protection meant war, the Americans would probably hesitate, for the American rearmament was the biggest bluff in history." But in their innermost councils the Germans were less sure of Roosevelt's reactions, and Raeder, after his interview, was reminded that Hitler's orders against attacks on American shipping still held. "The Fuehrer wants to avoid everything that could lead to incidents with the United States."[4]

"When I saw the President at six o'clock this evening," Morgenthau recorded the day after the freedom-of-the-seas news conference, "[he said,] 'I am waiting to be pushed into this situation.' He had previously said that he thought something might happen at any time, and I gathered that he wanted to be pushed into the war rather than lead us into it. This is no doubt what he meant." But waiting "to be pushed" did not mean presidential passivity. In mid-May, the orders had finally been reinstituted to complete the movement of almost a fourth of the Pacific Fleet to the Atlantic. Three battleships, four light cruisers, and fourteen destroyers now followed the aircraft carrier and five destroyers that had gone ahead. The transit took almost a month. As the powerful detachment neared the Panama Canal, Roosevelt, on May 22, ordered Admiral Stark to be prepared within a month to occupy the Azores. Shortly afterward, he directed Stark and Marshall to prepare plans to relieve the British garrison in Iceland. He also was giving thought to a takeover of Dakar.

But presidential orders were one thing, the assembling of a military expedition was quite another. In late May, Marshall "had to admit with considerable embarrassment that the Army could not meet" the timetable. Nor was the general able to gather a force for the Iceland operation—the job would have to be left to the marines.

Like Churchill, Roosevelt was unhappy over the cautiousness of his military advisers. At the meeting of his unofficial war cabinet* on May 22,

---

* Morgenthau listed those present at this meeting as Hull, Stimson, Knox, himself, Marshall, Stark, Richmond Kelly Turner (the head of the Naval War College), several army and navy officers, and Harry Hopkins.

when the president had asked Admiral Stark how long it would take him to get ready to move into the Azores and Cape Verdes and the admiral had answered "three months," Roosevelt had snapped back, "We've got to be ready in one month." When Stark kept telling him how hard the operation would be, the president's questions became so mocking that Morgenthau was embarrassed and also disappointed because he thought Roosevelt had been argued out of the expedition, which was not the case.

By the end of May, the worsening of the British position in the Mediterranean climaxed by the humiliating evacuation in Crete, the approach of the fleet detachment to its new stations in the Atlantic, the weakness of the isolationist attack on the freedom-of-the-seas concept in contrast to the effectiveness of their attack on convoys had prepared the ground for Roosevelt's speech of May 27. The leader was at last prepared to lead, impatient interventionist associates like Stimson, Knox, and Ickes said. But in fact the situation was similar to the destroyers-for-bases deal (and, before that, the third-term nomination): while Roosevelt was being accused of a failure to lead, he had been quietly setting the stage for the final act where he both responded to the public's demand for action and moved the action forward. No man was ever more determined about his objectives or more flexible about his means, said Rexford G. Tugwell, and Hitler now was finding out what Roosevelt's domestic opponents long had known.

"I hope you will like the speech tonight," the president telegraphed Churchill. "It goes further than I thought was possible even two weeks ago and I like to hope that it will receive general approval from the fairly large element which has been confused by details and unable hitherto to see the simpler facts. All of us are made very happy by the fine tracking down of the *Bismarck* and that she is literally gone for good."[5]

Roosevelt's speech again schooled the nation in military strategy. Hemispheric security was dependent on a great strategic arc that ran from Greenland,* through Iceland, Great Britain, the Azores, the Cape Verdes, and Dakar, where even a Nazi foothold would endanger the United States and would be resisted. Moreover, in the days of lightninglike attack, "it is stupid to wait until a probable enemy has gained a foothold from which to attack. Old-fashioned common sense calls for the use of a strategy that will prevent such an enemy from gaining a foothold in the first place." FDR had wanted to quote Confederate general Nathan Bedford Forrest, that strategy consisted in "gitting thar fustest with the mostest," but Stimson had objected, fearing that Hitler was in a position to move faster than the United States. Roosevelt did state, however, that the United States would act to keep "Hitlerism away from any point in the world which could be used or would be used as a basis of attack against the Americas."

* "I remember," said Frances Perkins, "that at the May 1, 1941, cabinet meeting, Roosevelt said that we were going to use Greenland for patrols. I remember being so startled at the thought of Greenland's icy mountains coming to be an air base. . . . All of a sudden the world shrank. Greenland was something you went to and did things with, not just a place where Eskimos lived."

It became clear in his speech how central freedom of the seas had become in Roosevelt's own thinking. The main strategic aim of the Axis, the president declared, was to obtain control of the seas. That was the path to world domination. But to achieve it, "they must capture Great Britain." Alternatively, "if the Axis Powers failed to gain control of the seas, then they are certainly defeated." All of American history was tied up with freedom of the seas, and "we shall certainly resist [Hitler's] every attempt to gain control of the seas." American patrols were helping "to insure the delivery of the needed supplies to Britain." That was the phrase he had not permitted Knox to use a month earlier. Now he went further. "All additional measures necessary to deliver the goods will be taken."

"We reassert the ancient American doctrine of freedom of the seas," he began an almost thunderous summation. He then sounded a nationalistic note that applied as much to Britain as to the dictatorial powers: "We in the Americas will decide for ourselves whether, and when, and where, our American interests are attacked or our security is threatened."

"We are placing our armed forces in strategic military position." And to underline the solemnity of the moment, Roosevelt ended his speech by reading in vibrant tones a proclamation of "unlimited national emergency" that sounded almost like a call to arms.[6]

"At four thirty last Wednesday morning," wrote Mollie Panter-Downes,

lots of Londoners broke off the beauty sleep of yet another uncannily blitz-free night and got up to join the world at President Roosevelt's fireside. His speech had been more eagerly awaited than any other pronouncement since the war began. When the President was through talking, its implications were eagerly discussed. . . . When the full text was published later in the day, the general impression seemed to be one of keen satisfaction over a piece of speaking plain enough to leave no one, friend or enemy, in any possible doubt. The minority which still likes its declarations of war cut and dried in the old, now demoded way, was disappointed that the President had not announced a definite, immediate program involving convoys. The vast majority, however, believed that reassurance on this point could be read into his firm promise to get the goods here by any means and in spite of any intimidation. British admiration is profound for the Roosevelt sense of strategic timing, which people here regard as second to none, not barring Hitler's. Hearing the words of the great proclamation ringing out in the unusual stillness of the London night was a moving experience.

In his broadcast, wrote Professor Whitehead,

the President, in effect, committed the United States to a "shooting war." This is how the American public interpreted the President's speech. We know from other telegrams that the President, in his capacity of C-in-C of armed forces, has already placed some of his forces on their war stations and is preparing other forces for a similar purpose. The Germans are being placed in a position in which they will have to relinquish their hopes of achieving certain objectives of great value to them, or fight Americans. The shooting cannot be long delayed but for understandable reasons, each side is trying to get the other side to fire the first shot.[7]

In Washington, Halifax spoke with the president the day after the speech and inquired what practical steps he had in mind "as regards freedom of the seas in application to merchant vessels. I did not get much out of him, beyond the statement that he did not want to embark on a dog-fight with Congress over amendment of the Neutrality Act, and thought he could get around it in other ways. He particularly mentioned American ships going to Iceland for transshipment." At a press conference that day, Roosevelt denied that his speech was preparatory to a move to repeal the Neutrality Act. A great speech, a disgusted Stimson recorded, has been followed "by a press conference which was one of his worst and almost undid the effect of his speech."

But Halifax, who lunched with Roosevelt and was given a complete picture of what the president had in mind as a follow-up, was more content. "The President said that he was anxious to get to complete understanding with you [i.e., Churchill] in regard to action to be taken about the Azores and Cape Verde Islands in the event of the Germans going into Spain or Portugal. He had for political reasons felt bound to stress the importance of these islands in his speech last night and wished to get common plan agreed with us which could function on the pressing of a button. . . . He was preparing expeditionary force of 25,000 men and was at present engaged in pressing the military authorities to accelerate their arrangements." Halifax asked what was happening about American ships keeping watch around these islands. Roosevelt said "that in deference to Portuguese susceptibilities they were not going into ports or flying their planes over the islands, but they were cruising round them and keeping a look out." A Halifax cable later that day informed Churchill that he had subsequently ascertained "by enquiries from the Navy Department that United States warships are in fact cruising around the islands." "Good news," Professor Whitehead noted on this message.

The practical measure that seemed most to interest Roosevelt, Halifax went on, was an American presence in Iceland.

If it was agreeable to us and could be arranged with Icelandic authorities, he thought he could, as soon as practical arrangements could be made, take over our occupation of Iceland thus relieving our men and equipment. He was preparing another force that would be capable of doing this, if we approved of the idea and thought it could be put into effect in three or four weeks.

From the way in which he approached the question and spoke, I got the impression that he was rather keen after his speech on taking some effective overt action and that this action in Iceland appealed to him. He also thinks Iceland may be of increasing importance for transit purposes. In particular he looks forward to the time when American pilots would take aircraft due for delivery to us as far as Iceland and relieve the strain on our pilots by delivery of them there. He thought so far as American public opinion was concerned he could do it any time.

[As for Dakar,] he said American opinion at present would draw a distinction between action in the Atlantic islands or Iceland as compared with action on the mainland of Africa. But it might well move forward in a week or two, and I have no doubt they are preparing for the possibilities that may develop at Dakar.

Newsmen told Halifax after the latter left the president that messages from London were critical because the speech had not been definite. "That is certainly not the impression here," Halifax cabled Churchill, "and I think it important that the speech should be welcomed and applauded on your side. I hope you may send [the president] suitable message yourself. He looked much better than when I saw him last, was in good heart, and like a man who has taken his decision and is completely at rest with himself."[8]

What Halifax advised, Churchill had already done.

We are uplifted and fortified by your memorable declaration and by the far-reaching executive measures involved in the state of emergency you have proclaimed.* Pray accept, Mr. President, my heartfelt thanks. It was very kind of you to let me know beforehand of the great advance you found it possible to make.

I have now also received your message about the impressive additional output you are sending to the Middle East in United States ships. Winant will tell you what I managed to send out there secretly and the hopes I have of some good news coming to hand before long.†

It seems most important to find the *Prinz Eugen* before she cuts into our convoys. The Admiralty and Ghormley are in the closest touch. But this is a new, very fast and powerful ship, and there is much danger while she is at large for any convoy unprotected by battleship escort.

I will send you later the inside story of the fighting with the *Bismarck*. She was a terrific ship and a masterpiece of naval construction. Her removal eases our battleship situation as we should have had to keep *King George Fifth*, *Prince of Wales* and the two *Nelsons* practically tied to Scapa Flow to guard against sorties of *Bismarck* and *Tirpitz* as they could choose their moment and we should have to allow for one of our ships refitting. Now it is a different story. The effect upon the Japanese will be highly beneficial. I expect they are doing all their sums again.

After Churchill received Halifax's report on what the president intended, he was even more enthusiastic:

We cordially welcome your taking over Iceland at the earliest possible moment, and will hold ourselves and all our resources there at your disposal as may be found convenient. It would liberate a British division for defence against invasion of the Middle East. It would enable us to concentrate our flying boats now there on northwestern approaches. If it could be done in the next three weeks or less, or even begun, it would have a moral effect even beyond its military importance. You have only to say the word and our staffs can get to work at once.

---

* Foreign-office efforts to find out what additional powers to aid Britain the president had obtained by proclaiming an "unlimited" emergency were in vain. Neither the United States embassy in London nor the British embassy in Washington was able to shed any light. Perhaps there was none to be shed. As Oscar Cox [Hopkins's lend-lease assistant] advised Hopkins in advance of Roosevelt's speech, there were no "outstandingly significant" legal advantages to the proclamation of a full emergency, but he thought there might be decided psychological advantages.[9]

† Winant had returned to Washington for consultations. Churchill was referring to the decision to ship tanks to Wavell via the hazardous route of the Mediterranean, an operation that was dubbed Tiger. But the offensive that Wavell launched in mid-June, although stiffened by Tiger's "cubs," was quickly stalled by Rommel.

He was less disposed to yield the leadership to the United States with regard to the Azores and the Cape Verdes:

At any time now Hitler may obtain air bases in southern Spain or in North Africa, Spanish or French, from which he can make Gibraltar harbor unusable by our fleet. The moment this happens or we are sure it is going to happen, we shall send our expeditions which have long been prepared and are waiting besides their ships, to occupy the Grand Canary, the Cape Verde Islands and one of the Azores. The code names for these three expeditions will be cabled in a separate message. . . .

We should welcome collaboration with an American token force, before, during or after occupation of Atlantic Islands and if you wish would turn them over to you as a matter of mutual war convenience.

We should naturally welcome United States occupation of Dakar, and would afford all facilities in our power. We have some rather costly experience and knowledge of this place. Surest method by landing tanks from specially constructed vessels on neighboring beaches. I suggest that immediate consultation between your officers and ours should begin to make a workable plan, and have it ready in case circumstances should require its use.[10]

Again, the gall and wormwood of British disaster were being mitigated by the American connection. At the end of March, Ribbentrop had told Matsuoka that "there was no doubt that the British would long since have abandoned the war if Roosevelt had not always given Churchill new hope." The observation was even truer now. Even patriotic Britons were referring to the BEF as "Back Every Fortnight" after Crete, and in the U.S. State Department its professionals were despondent about Britain's prospects. "And world opinion is that they are licked," wrote Breckinridge Long. "We hear it from South America, from the Far East, from West Africa. Rochat [secretary-general of the French foreign office] in Africa tells Murphy so. Our missions in South Africa report the opinion of responsible statesmen there to that effect. The Turks act that way—so do the Russians—the Finns even are turning; the Swedes are impressed, the Japs are convinced." Berle, searching for historical precedents, thought of the Napoleonic Wars: "I cannot get out of my head that the situation now means either our prompt entry into the war or a Peace of Amiens, or something of the kind, in which case we shall have our work cut out for us." (At Amiens in 1802, Britain and France had made a peace which turned out to be a fourteen-month pause in the fighting.)[11]

Hitler, who summoned Mussolini to Brenner Pass, talked hopefully about Churchill's resignation. British morale had "greatly deteriorated," he claimed, and the blockade was "particularly effective." Things were so bad that Churchill had sent Winant to Washington "with an SOS to Roosevelt, especially because England among other things had been greatly disappointed by Roosevelt's address." Mussolini thought Churchill's last speech in the House of Commons "had been unusually feeble," and Ribbentrop interrupted to say that "Churchill seemed in general to be losing his nerve." The dictators even began to pick his successor. Sir Samuel Hoare, one of the men of Munich and now ambassador to Spain, was mentioned, but Hitler thought it was more likely to be Lloyd George, whom he remembered as "the most intelligent of all the

English visitors" and the most "understanding" of Germany's point of view.

Wishful thinking turned to wariness, however, when they discussed Roosevelt. It was better not to reply to him, they agreed. The speech, which Ciano privately in his diary described as "a very strong document," had enraged Mussolini, who fulminated against Roosevelt, "saying that never in the course of history has a nation been guided by a paralytic." But a reply would only stir up the warmongers in America. The way to rein in Roosevelt was through playing the Japanese card: "Both the Fuehrer and the Duce declared as very satisfactory the statement of the Japanese Foreign Minister who had unmistakably stated Japan's readiness to stand by the Tripartite Pact down to the utmost contingencies. If Japan would continue her firm adherence, America would not enter the war. The Foreign Minister [i.e., Ribbentrop] commented on this that, as he had heard from circles close to Roosevelt, the latter was very much afraid of a two-front war."

Yet after that meeting and despite the glittering Nazi triumphs in Libya, the Balkans, and Crete, Ciano summarized the conversations pessimistically: "The general impression is that for the moment Hitler has no precise plan of action. Russia, Turkey, Spain, are all subsidiary elements: complements or dispersion of forces, but it is not there that one can find the solution of a problem. The greatest German hope is now in the action of its submarine fleet."

It was a sound strategic observation. Without winning the Battle of the Atlantic and forcing England to its knees, the war would not be won. And standing in the way of victory in the Atlantic was a British fleet that had just sunk the *Bismarck* and that was now rapidly being augmented by the American fleet. Morgenthau, who saw the president for his weekly lunch on June 4, noted afterward: "The President's whole interest today is in the Atlantic Fleet and getting first to these various outlying islands (Azores, Cape Verdes and Iceland). He never mentioned any domestic matters to me."

As for Churchill, of whom the dictators spoke as unnerved by Britain's setbacks, he was again pressing his generals to assume the offensive:

Everything must now be centred upon destroying the German forces in the Western Desert. Now, before the enemy has recovered from the violent exertions and heavy losses involved in his onslaught upon Crete, is the time to fight a decisive battle in Libya and go on day after day facing all necessary losses until you have beaten the life out of General Rommel's army. In this way the loss of Crete will be more than repaired and the future of the whole campaign in the Middle East will be opened out.[12]

Chapter Nineteen

Roosevelt Occupies Iceland

C HURCHILL was not the only member of the British war
cabinet to praise Roosevelt's speech. Eden used his first
public speech as foreign secretary to "offer Roosevelt some incense," as he
put it. Eden had a following in the United States second only to Churchill's.
Americans remembered him as that rarity among politicians, a handsome and
young politician with principles, one who had resigned the foreign secretaryship in protest against Chamberlain's policy of appeasement. There was a
closer relationship between Winant, the U.S. ambassador, and Eden than between Winant and Churchill—perhaps because both were a little intimidated
by that audacious figure. When Winant went down to Eden's country house in
Sussex, he helped the foreign secretary weed his garden. "We would put our
dispatch boxes at either end, and when we had completed a row we would do
penance by reading messages and writing the necessary replies. Then we
would start again our menial task. . . . I liked Eden. I found him simple,
truthful, and courageous."

The "keynote" of the president's speech, Eden said at Mansion House,
"lies in his repeated declaration that the national existence of free nations must
ultimately depend upon the freedom of the seas. This freedom has been maintained in the past by the British and American Navies and both countries have
fought on many occasions to preserve it." Eden's main purpose, however, was
to show the similarity between British and American thinking on war aims and
to answer the isolationist charge that Britain's real war aim "was to put the
British Empire back where it was, entirely for the benefit of the investing
classes and Imperialists." (This was the way Eden had described the purpose
of his speech in his introductory note to it in the collection *Freedom and
Order.*)

Roosevelt, on May 27, had once again sounded the theme of the Four
Freedoms, for he considered it essential to tell the country that one of the
American interests to be served by his steadily escalating interventionism

was to ensure a better world. But he limited himself to guiding principles and eschewed specific commitments:

We will not accept a Hitler-dominated world. And we will not accept a world, like the postwar world of the 1920's, in which the seed of Hitlerism can again be planted and allowed to grow.

We will accept only a world consecrated to freedom of speech and expression—freedom of every person to worship God in his own way—freedom from want—and freedom from terror.

During a meeting with Halifax and John Maynard Keynes, Roosevelt had been shown a copy of the speech Eden intended to deliver. Keynes was in the United States working on a draft of the "consideration" the British would ultimately give in return for lend-lease aid. Since Eden's speech was, in fact, based on a memorandum by Keynes, it was natural that the economist should bring it up. For some time now Keynes had thought the British had to make some reply to Hitler's "New Order." Even Hitler understood that visions powered men's loyalties more than fear, and Nazi projection of a Europe of order, jobs, and prosperity had achieved a definite audience. But Roosevelt "did not much like what I had to say," wrote Eden, "because it was too British or too European."

Roosevelt's objections were significant. He was telling the British that peace had to be conceived in global terms and that the United States intended to be at the peace table. His views were described more fully by Keynes's official biographer Prof. R. T. Harrod:

The President felt that any important statement concerning war aims should take the whole world for its province. It was not only in Europe that a great reconstructive effort would be required. Furthermore, he noted that a British policy was being offered for the consideration of the nations as giving better promise of genuine advancement than anything that the Germans could offer. But, as he pointed out, the United States was also standing by. If the British could offer more than the Germans, how much more could the British and Americans together offer. If an alternative was to be presented to the world, let it be not in a British but in a joint British and American initiative.

Since Roosevelt already had in mind that he would soon be meeting with Churchill,* "he may have felt," Professor Harrod thought, "that an important British declaration of aims might spoil the market for what he hoped to bring about on a joint basis."

Eden revised his speech to meet some of Roosevelt's suggestions. As delivered, it did emphasize that the United States and the British Empire alone had the material means and the will to bring about the reconstruction of a starving and bankrupt Europe, a reconstruction based on freedom and national independence. For the first time, the British government formally associated itself with Roosevelt's statement of the Four Freedoms "as the keynote

---

* Roosevelt had summoned Admiral King to Hyde Park on April 18 and told him that he wanted to meet with Churchill in complete privacy and that he thought Argentia, the site of a leased naval base off Newfoundland, was a suitable place.

of our own purposes." This was no projection "of a distant millennium," said Eden. "It is a definite basis for a kind of world attainable in our time and generation." The speech was noted in Washington, where, the foreign office was told, it gave "the greatest pleasure" because of its tribute to the president's broadcast and also because it showed "that the British were thinking of the future in the same general terms as the Americans." But outside official quarters it was little remarked. It would take those master showmen, Roosevelt and Churchill, to launch Anglo-American war aims in a way that would make an impact on men's minds everywhere.

Eden had little to say about the Far East, except to recognize that there would be reconstruction problems in Asia of a magnitude similar to those in Europe "after the unhappy struggle now in progress between Japan and China" was over.[1] However, the Far East was very much on his mind. The British foreign office was at that time in a state of shock over the discovery of the secret talks between the United States and Japan, a discovery made a few weeks after Hull had once again turned down as too provocative a British proposal for a joint *démarche* addressed to Japan by the United States, Great Britain, and the Netherlands warning that country against any major move southward. In light of the secret United States–Japanese talks, Hull's reasons had been less than candid. The talks had been going on since Ambassador Nomura's arrival in Washington. They were kept secret not only from the British and the Chinese but from Roosevelt's unofficial war cabinet (except for Hull, who was handling them for the United States and a few of his associates in the State Department). The Japanese had sent two unofficial emissaries—Col. Hideo Iwakuro, representing the Japanese army, and Tadao Wikawa, a representative of the most influential civilian group in the Japanese government—to handle the talks together with Nomura. By April, they had handed in a working paper, which was carefully analyzed by Hull's chief adviser on Far Eastern affairs, Stanley Hornbeck. The latter's crucial comment related to a Japanese proposal that the United States serve as intermediary in bringing the Sino-Japanese conflict to an end:

It may be said that the suggestions which appear in this draft on the subject of mediation of the China conflict and the manner and terms hereof are by no means without merit. It must be remembered, however, that the Japanese-Chinese conflict cannot be dealt with as an isolated phenomenon and without relation to other parts of the world conflict of which it is a part. . . . It is the belief of the undersigned that so long as and while Japan remains a member of the Tripartite Alliance, it would not be in the interest of the United States or of Great Britain that the Japanese-Chinese hostilities be brought to an end by any process which leaves Japan's military machine undefeated (undiscredited) and intact. Japan has sent her armies into China and is employing a part of her navy and a part of her merchant marine and a great part of her general resources in the supporting of that army there.

Japan now wants to extricate them, Hornbeck went on, to have them available "for possible activities in some other direction, which might be against British interests or Dutch interests or even American interests—or Soviet interests. The world situation being what it is, the world conflicts and problems being what they are, Japan's present involvement in China is to the advantage of the United States and Great Britain."

If the British had known of the Hornbeck memorandum, perhaps they would not have been quite so hostile to the talks when they learned of them. They were told about them inadvertently. Reading over some G-2 messages, Stimson was "horrified to find the terms of the negotiations which have been going on between the State Department and Japan. I can't help being worried lest the State Department get itself into a very equivocal position and will seem to be double-dealing." Since the British were privy to G-2's information under an exchange agreement concluded the previous December, Stimson thought this "particularly dangerous. . . . I fear they will not very much like the terms of the negotiations between this Government and Japan." Hull was furious that the British might have learned of the negotiations via G-2 and thought it prudent to give Ambassador Halifax a general account of the informal talks. "[Hull] was under the mistaken impression that he had told me of them earlier," Halifax cabled London. Hull minimized the importance of the talks, but "if there was one chance in twenty-five of being able to get an understanding with [Nomura's] Government that we could all accept, it would be wrong to miss it." He was, added Hull, simply listening to what Nomura had to say. This, too, was disingenuous, for that very day Hull had submitted a set of "written observations" on a second Japanese draft. "I told Hull that I thought the danger to be avoided was any action that might be plausibly represented in Japan as a successful attempt on the part of the Japanese to divide the United States and ourselves," Halifax went on. The ambassador appended two other items to his dispatch, neither of them likely to reassure London: that the Japanese had approached Wendell Willkie with a suggestion that he visit Japan and that Sumner Welles "was inclined to attach rather more importance to this talk of Japanese Ambassador than he would have a short time ago. . . . Anyhow they would very soon know if there was anything in it because they had put some questions, of which he did not tell me the exact nature but which he said were pretty searching, to the Ambassador, and on the nature of the replies they would be able to judge whether there is anything to be made of it or not. He will keep me informed."[2]

The Halifax telegram set the alarm bells ringing in the foreign office. It was forcefully minuted: "I do not believe that the Japanese can make an offer to the United States which would be acceptable to them," commented Ashley Clarke of the Far Eastern department. "If such an agreement were possible it holds serious dangers for us. It must in any case be disadvantageous to us by giving sanction to Japanese advances which, at this moment, with all our other commitments, we could not contest." John Balfour of the American department saw it as a "bold bid" by the Japanese government "to bamboozle the U.S.A. into thinking that the moment is favorable for a reasonable settlement in the Far East. At a moment when America is drawing nearer to becoming involved in war with Germany the State Department obviously do not wish to let slip any opportunity for such a settlement, however improbable the prospect. . . . It wd certainly be fatal if the wish for security in the Far East were to leave Japan a free hand for expansion there." Clarke drafted a telegram of guidance to Halifax. "This is a good draft and states true position well," minuted Eden. "I am grateful to dept. for a useful piece of work."

Halifax read the main points of the telegram to Welles and left it with him for Hull in the form of an *aide-mémoire*. It pictured Nomura as a "mouthpiece of Mr. Matsuoka in a scheme which the latter has discussed with Ribbentrop." The facts in this respect were quite the reverse of what the British imagined them to be. Matsuoka was a reluctant fellow traveler in these talks with the United States, and the Germans, when they heard of them, considered them potentially as dangerous to their interests as the British did to theirs.

The foreign-office memorandum went on to describe Japanese purposes in these negotiations as:

(a) to divide United States and ourselves
(b) to enable Japan to withdraw from commitments in China with minimum loss of face while retaining Manchukuo and essential advantages acquired during China incident, including her position in Indo-China and Thailand, and
(c) to diminish possibility of U.S. assistance to ourselves, not only in Pacific but also in Atlantic. For this latter purpose, Mr. Matsuoka is trying, simultaneously with offer of settlement, to intimidate U.S. as to consequences likely to follow U.S. involvement in war with Germany, regardless of manner in which that might come about.

The telegram went on to suggest that if Matsuoka could free Japan of the China incubus and of the fear of United States intervention, he would then be in a position to press Britain "to compromise with Germany, thus indulging his ambition to bring about world peace on Axis terms." This was an unwise way to handle the Japanese, the British thought. "We believe that if Japan is to be detached from the Axis and real peace achieved in the Pacific, it will be by a display of resolution and firmness on the part of the United States, the Netherlands and ourselves, and that present Japanese and Japanese-sponsored moves are a trap into which we are confident that the United States Government will not allow themselves to fall, though no doubt every artifice will be used so to work on United States public opinion as to force them into it."[3]

Halifax had preceded handing over the *aide-mémoire* to Welles with the reading of a secret message from Eden to him (Halifax), which the foreign secretary had instructed him to burn after reading to Welles and which was based on British monitoring of German-Japanese communications. This indicated that the German and Italian governments were fully informed about the Nomura-Hull talks, that the United States was prepared for a deal in which a defensive attitude by Japan toward the Tripartite Pact would be matched by a purely defensive approach by the United States to the European war, that the talks were initiated by the United States, and that the reason why he had acted without consulting the Axis envoys in Tokyo, Matsuoka had told them, was to forestall American convoys. In fact, the Germans were doing their best to break up the Hull-Nomura talks. "Political agreements of any sort between Japan and the United States are undesirable at the present time," State Secretary Weizsäcker telegraphed Ribbentrop, who was away from Berlin. "The treaty text, moreover, as it reads now, would mean that Japan is disengaging herself from us. It would leave the field of conflict with England and the United States to us alone."

Hull saw Halifax on May 24 and, as he put it, offered "some rather vigorous comments" on what he had felt was "a lecture," one that he considered full of inaccuracies and offensive in its suggestion that the United States would do anything in the Far East prejudicial to British interests. "Lord Halifax thereupon 'retained' the *aide-mémoire*," Hull's memorandum on the meeting stated.

Hull's rebuff brought an immediate message of mollification from Eden that no criticism of Hull's conduct of the negotiations had been intended. And when Halifax again saw Hull on May 28, the secretary informed the ambassador that he was insisting on three basic points in his talks with Nomura: "a satisfactory Chinese settlement, assurance that the Japanese will not go South for purposes of military conquest, and assurance that they will not fight for Germany in case the United States should be drawn into the war." Hull later described Halifax as "pleased" with their talk, and Halifax summarized that he and Hull had agreed that if there were to be progress on the three points outlined by Hull, "it would mean the disappearance of Matsuoka."[4]

British fears of the talks were only superficially allayed. In mid-June, their ambassador in Tokyo informed the foreign office that his United States colleague had been asked by the State Department to ascertain whether the Japanese government would be likely to implement an American-Japanese agreement of the kind now under discussion, including the immediate withdrawal of all Japanese troops from China, if it could be concluded. The Far Eastern department's comments on this news were scorching. One official wrote: "The State Department's question may have been hypothetical, but one has the uncomfortable feeling that they are playing with fire in continuing these discussions with the Japanese Ambassador." "Yes:—these talks are a menace," agreed Ashley Clarke, drafter of the cable to Halifax, "but we have entered our *caveat* & gotten our heads bitten off for so doing." "But only because the approach was made tactlessly," interposed the head of the American department. "I think we should ask Lord Halifax to make an enquiry as to the present position if he has a suitable opportunity," the Far Eastern department suggested, adding, "Diffidence in dealing with the United States Government is understandable, but the matter is one of considerable importance & we are, I think, entitled to expect more information & greater frankness than we have hitherto been shown." "A tactful enquiry seems indicated," commented Balfour of the American department, and Sir David Scott agreed: "I imagine that the talks do have one advantage . . . they must make the Axis doubtful about Japanese readiness to play." Halifax was instructed to see Welles (Hull was away) and to inquire how the talks were going. Welles was "not communciative," reported Halifax, except to say that Hull had told him "that matters looked hopeful." This irritated the British Far Eastern experts: "The State Department lack of frankness persists. Can it be that Mr. Hull is trying to achieve some coup of historic importance such as detaching Japan from the Axis, and in such a way that he will be able to claim all the credit?" "It is decidedly puzzling and the statement that matters looked hopeful is ominous," minuted Clarke.[5]

Hull and Eden undoubtedly kept their principals, Roosevelt and Churchill, apprised of these differences over the Hull-Nomura talks. Neither Roosevelt nor Churchill, however, considered it desirable to join the argument himself, and Churchill, in his memoirs, wrote of the period up to the end of July that, "for several months the British and American Governments had been acting towards Japan in close accord," which was scarcely in close accord with the facts.

The basic reason the United States was negotiating with Japan was its unreadiness for war—not to speak of a two-front war. "We had in the forefront of our minds," wrote Hull, "the advice repeatedly given us by our highest military officers that they needed time to prepare the defenses vital to ourselves as well as to the countries resisting aggression." United States factories were just beginning to produce war materials in substantial quantities, but much of it was going directly to the British. Some of the draftees in Marshall's armies were training with broomsticks for rifles and sawhorses for anti-tank guns. Planes were being produced at the rate of 1,374 a month by July, 349 of which went to Great Britain, whose own monthly capacity was 1,600 compared with Germany's 2,400. United States front-line fighters and bombers in July, 1941, totaled a meager 2,366 compared with the British Empire's 10,100, Germany's 11,500, and Japan's 2,950. Light (twelve-ton) tanks were being turned out at the rate of 150 a month (as of June 1, 1941), and medium tanks were being redesigned because the old design was so inferior to the German version. A critical statistic, supplied by Myron Taylor, former head of United States Steel, to Roosevelt at the end of May, was the relative steel capacity of the principal powers:

This is the approximate world steel ingot capacity—

COUNTRY	TONS
United States	92 million
England	15 million
Russia	22 million
Japan	7 million
Italy	3 million
Germany, including acquired capacity	45 million *

* Of this total, 15 million tons were acquired in conquering France, Belgium, and Luxembourg.

Time was the key to making this disparity count. The longer Roosevelt could delay American participation in a shooting war, the better prepared the United

States would be. And, in fact, by the end of 1941, American production of planes totaled 19,290, compared with 3,797 in 1940 and 47,873 in 1942; and tank production in 1941 was 3,900, compared with 280 in 1940 and 24,800 in 1942.[6]

In their June, 1941, meeting at the Brenner Pass, Hitler and Mussolini had drawn comfort from United States rearmament figures as their intelligence agencies supplied them. They ridiculed United States reports which stated that by 1942 America would produce 18,000 aircraft, 30,000 by 1943.

The Fuehrer pointed out that in ten months the Americans had delivered only 700 aircraft [to Britain]. Upon closer examination, it was concluded that neither on the basis of American productive capacity, nor on the basis of aluminum supplies or available skilled manpower, was a large production of aircraft to be expected immediately. . . . Just as childish were the statements of the Americans that within a few months they would attain an output of 400 tanks, although so far not even the experimental stage had been concluded. In Germany one knew very well that such matters took much longer. The manufacture of a 38-cm. gun for example took 16 to 18 months.

The situation regarding the training of pilots was similar.

But Ambassador Dieckhoff, who had spent some time in the United States and who was Ribbentrop's chief adviser on American affairs, cautioned against placing too much reliance on American unpreparedness as a guarantee against that country's immediate entry into the war. Roosevelt was deterred, he thought, by

the still unsettled situation in the Pacific (Japan) [and] public opinion in his country, which is still predominantly against entry into the war.

These are the decisive reasons which force upon the President his hesitating and temporizing policy. Without knowing what Japan will do the President cannot dare to enter the war; he cannot bring about an entry into the war, which under the Constitution can be declared only by Congress, in opposition to the predominant public opinion among his people.

The question of military preparedness and the getting under way of war industry are in my opinion of merely secondary nature.

This anaylsis was remarkably perceptive. As Roosevelt patiently explained to Ickes, who in ignorance of the Hull-Nomura talks had, as newly appointed petroleum coordinator, promptly held up a shipment of oil products to Japan:

I think it will interest you to know that the Japs are having a real dragdown and knock-out fight among themselves and have been for the past week—trying to decide which way they are going to jump—attack Russia, attack the South Seas (thus throwing in their lot definitely with Germany), or whether they will sit on the fence and be more friendly with us. No one knows what the decision will be but, as you know, it is terribly important for the control of the Atlantic to help keep peace in the Pacific. I simply have not got enough Navy to go round—and every little episode in the Pacific means fewer ships in the Atlantic.[7]

The Atlantic was the focus of Roosevelt's concern. At a luncheon on June 6, Bill Bullitt, who prided himself on his mastery of foreign affairs, learned that Roosevelt not only had his own views on how and when to come to grips with the Germans, but was convinced that United States intervention would come in time. Bullitt felt that the United States had to get into the war or England would fall:

According to Bill [Ickes wrote of this luncheon], the President knows this too. But also according to Bill, the President will continue to play his luck. He can't bring himself to going in as cold-bloodedly as he would be going in if something were done now. He is waiting for an incident, fully conscious of the fact that none may come before it is too late.

The Australian minister in Washington, Richard Casey, noted on June 15 (and presumably the word went to London): "One of the President's close associates told me lately that Mr. Roosevelt had said to him: 'I appreciate very much the fact that the British are not pressing me. I know their situation and apart from keeping me up-to-date, there is nothing more that they can add. They must be very impatient with me, but their restraint in not seeking to press me to go faster than I can go is admirable.' "[8]

On June 10, Washington began to receive reports from the survivors of the *Robin Moor,* an American freighter that had been torpedoed in the middle of the South Atlantic on May 21, the first American vessel sunk by the Germans and, in view of Hitler's orders, probably a mistake. But the United States did not know that. What it now learned from the survivors, who had finally been picked up by friendly vessels and landed in Brazil, was that a submarine, which had refused to identify itself, had torpedoed the vessel and left the survivors—men, women, and children—in open boats in mid-ocean. Roosevelt's first thought was to seize a German ship somewhere on the "eye for an eye and tooth for a tooth" principle, but at least two of his closest associates hoped he might use this as the occasion to get into the war. Ickes so told the president, and Harry Hopkins, in a memorandum, advised Roosevelt that the episode gave him an excuse to move beyond the observational patrol:

The sinking of the *Robin Moor* violated international law at sea; it violates your policy of freedom of the seas. . . .
    The present observation patrol of the Navy for observing and reporting the movement of ships that are potential aggressors could be changed to a security patrol charged with the duty of providing security for all American flagships travelling on the seas outside of the danger zone.
    It occurred to me that your instruction to the Navy Department could be that the United States Atlantic patrol forces, to be specific, are to, in effect, establish the freedom of the seas, leaving it to the judgment of the Navy as to what measures of security are required to achieve that objective.

"But nothing has been done," Ickes wrote disgustedly in his diary on June 22. "I believe that when it came to the final decision the President did not have the nerve to go through."

Roosevelt's message to Congress on the *Robin Moor* simply stated the facts, placed them in the context of an attempt by Hitler to intimidate the

United States, and did not indicate how he intended to respond. Perhaps he was deterred from seizing a ship by the surfacing at that particular moment of the story that back in April the U.S.S. *Niblack,* picking up survivors off Iceland, had dropped depth charges on a German submarine in the vicinity. That report, in an Alsop-Kintner column, caused a rare display of Roosevveltian anger, for FDR's whole strategy was to force Hitler to fire first. So he did not seize a German ship, for that would, in the circumstances, have seemed too aggressive an action. But he did retaliate by an order that froze German and Italian assets in the United States, followed by another order that directed the German government to close down its consulates and all German agencies on United States territory except for the embassy itself. "I have a distinct feeling in my bones," he cabled Churchill on June 17, "that things are looking up with you and with us. After freezing the German and Italian assets on Saturday, I closed the German consulates and agencies yesterday and the reaction here is, I should say, 90 per cent favorable."

Hitler's response to the news of the *Robin Moor* and of Roosevelt's retaliatory moves against German assets and consulates was to reaffirm his orders to avoid incidents with the United States:

The Fuehrer declares in detail that until operation *Barbarossa* [against Russia] is well under way he wishes to avoid any incident with the United States of America. After a few weeks the situation will become clearer and can be expected to have a favorable effect on the U.S.A. and Japan. America will have less inclination to enter the war, due to the threat from Japan which will then increase. If possible, therefore, in the next few weeks all attacks on naval vessels in the closed areas should cease, especially since in the past few months such attacks have been exceptions in any case.[9]

But Roosevelt did not propose to leave the initiative to Hitler. At the end of the State Department's draft of the message that he had sent to Congress on the *Robin Moor* he had penciled in the defiant sentence "We are not yielding; we do not propose to yield." His next move was to Iceland. This involved not only the preparation of an expeditionary force but a substantial fleet detachment to convoy it. And since the Selective Service Act prohibited the use of selectees outside of continental limits except in areas under United States sovereignty, a marine brigade composed entirely of volunteers was being assembled for the expedition.

"I am much encouraged by Ghormley's letter about your marines taking over that cold place," Churchill telegraphed Roosevelt on June 14, "and I hope that once the first instalment have arrived you will give full publicity to it. People must have hope to face the long haul that lies ahead. It would also produce the best effects in Spain, Vichy France and Turkey." This message, incidentally, since it also included the news that a new and unfortunately ill-starred offensive against Rommel would begin the next day, was accompanied by explicit instructions to Cadogan—for Churchill was a stickler about security—that "this should be sent off so as to reach the President shortly before he retires to rest this Saturday night. The United States time should be studied, also the time taken to cypher and decypher and transmit."

The political aspect of the United States move into Iceland concerned Roosevelt greatly. A major reason for the suspension of the Azores operation had been Portugal's protests to the references to the Azores in Roosevelt's May 27 speech. As late as June 18, the best that the British could report was that "Mr. Churchill apparently feels optimistic with regard to the probability that Dr. Salazar [the Portuguese prime minister] will be willing in the event of imminent German aggression to request Great Britain and the United States to assist in the defense of the Azores. Mr. Churchill feels, however, that plans should now be formulated as to the action to be taken in the event that such a request were not forthcoming at the crucial moment." In the case of Iceland, Roosevelt insisted that the Icelandic government request the United States to establish a protective force and said it was up to the British to secure the invitation. "I emphasized the fact," Welles reported of his conversation with Halifax,

that the President believed that in as much as the whole basis of our relations with the other American Republics was based upon our policy of non-aggression and non-intervention, the occupation by the United States of Iceland without having received from the Icelandic Government a request to do so, would destroy in great measure the confidence which the other American Republics possessed in this Government and would be utilized by Axis propagandists throughout the Western Hemisphere. The President felt, I said, that exactly the same strong argument presented itself in so far as any action which we might later take with regard to the Azores was concerned. It must be clear to the British Government that if the United States occupied through force the territory of Iceland without receiving any request from the Icelandic authorities to take such action, the fears of Portugal with regard to our possible action in the Azores would be materially stimulated and would be exploited to our disadvantage and that of the British by German propaganda in Portugal.

Roosevelt's preoccupation with a proper invitation from Iceland—and the Azores—reflected his need to carry the hemisphere with him in his Atlantic policy. It also represented his sensitivity to the issue of great-power domination that lay at the heart of the rising anticolonialist movement.

On June 24, Halifax read to Stimson, who happened to be with him when the message was decoded, Iceland's "unsatisfying answer." It was, added Stimson, "a stupid one and like one that might be expected from a little Provincial Governor up there in the Arctic who couldn't see the broad repercussions of his actions, but it was not a hopeless one. He evidenced reluctance but indicated he would not oppose it if done. I told Halifax that it was highly important that the report should be improved—that the British envoy should succeed in getting a cordial invitation for us—and he agreed with me." But the British minister in Reykjavík was unable to get Iceland to use the word *invite:*

Despite my every argument and insistence Iceland Government refuses to use word "invite." Their position is that during last session of Parliament there was a large majority in all parties against asking United States for protection. They cannot therefore assume responsibility for "inviting" without consulting Parliament but they are anxious whole plan should not come to naught. Therefore they ask me to send the following reply in hope that it will be sufficient for President's purpose. It will be seen that impression conveyed is that this question has been discussed between the United States and Iceland and that Iceland agrees it is in her interest that United States troops come and therefore non-aggression platform of President is completely defended. It is also not expressly stated which side took the initiative.

For a time, the threat of a German pre-emptive move seemed very real to Allied planners. On June 14, Halifax forwarded to Roosevelt intelligence reports showing a concentration of German forces and ships in northern Norwegian ports. They were probably intended for use against Russia, commented Halifax, but "it would be possible for them to be employed at short notice for an expedition to Iceland instead."

On June 22, American Naval Task Force Nineteen was ordered to proceed to Placentia Bay, Newfoundland, to accompany the first convoy of American forces to Iceland. Yet on July 2, the joint board of the army and navy devoted its meeting to advancing reasons why the United States should not occupy Iceland although, points out naval historian Kittredge, "the Naval Expeditionary Force was already en route for Newfoundland to Iceland." "[Knox] told me," wrote Stimson about a conversation he had had with Knox on June 20, "how he had to fight against the timidity of his own admirals on any aggressive movement including this one; how all their estimates and advice were predicated on the failure of the British and the fear of being left with a garrison up in the air at Iceland, on the Azores, or where you would, and how he always combatted that kind of argument and assumption."

"This bids fair to be an eventful day in history," Stimson noted with some relief on July 1. "First I got a telephone message from Lord Halifax in the morning telling me that the expected cable in regard to Indigo [Iceland] had come and was satisfactory." Later, the president telephoned "that he had given the necessary orders and he expected the thing would ripen on Saturday."

The Icelandic note stated that the British minister had explained that the British forces in Iceland were needed elsewhere and that Roosevelt, as part of his program of ensuring the safety of the Western Hemisphere, was prepared to replace the British forces there, but only on invitation. The government of Iceland, the note continued, "admits that this measure is in accordance with the interest of Iceland, and therefore are ready to entrust the protection of Iceland to the United States." The task force of 4,400 marines landed at Reykjavík on July 7.[10]

Stimson had urged the president to inform Congress of the occupation of Iceland "not by message but face to face and do it with personal and disarming frankness," presenting the move as tantamount to United States entry into the war. But Roosevelt disregarded his advice. He was, in fact, a little disenchanted with the secretary of war, who was constantly pressing him, despite the Japanese danger, to transfer more of the fleet from the Pacific to the Atlantic. When Morgenthau recently had suggested that the overly cautious Hull be put on the Supreme Court and Stimson made secretary of state, "to my surprise, [FDR] said Stimson did not prepare his cases well, that he came in to see the President often unprepared, and that while Hull was slow he prepared his facts very carefully." Roosevelt's written message to Congress, which included the Icelandic note, emphasized that the step was a precautionary move designed to head off enemy control of a strategic outpost from which the enemy could threaten all shipping in the North Atlantic and interfere with the steady flow of the munitions to Great Britain that, he reminded Congress, it had approved in its passage of lend-lease. Then there was a portent of things to come. He informed Congress that "as Commander in Chief I have consequently issued orders to the Navy that all necessary steps be taken to insure the safety of communications in the approaches between Iceland and the United States, as well as the seas between the United States and all other strategic outposts." Two days before the marines disembarked in Iceland, Roosevelt notified Stark and Marshall that the approach of any Axis force within fifty miles of Iceland was to be deemed conclusive evidence of hostile intention and, therefore, would justify an attack by the armed forces of the United States.

The isolationist protest was relatively muted. Someone had tipped off Senator Wheeler, who had denounced the expedition on the Senate floor while it was en route to Reykjavík; but, fortunately, he had "fixed the probable date as two or three weeks later than the actual one." The White House openly rebuked Wheeler for his lack of patriotism, and Churchill expressed concern "at Senator Wheeler's indiscretion or worse. . . . I pray God your men will get there safely." Senator Nye noted with bitterness and some resignation that the Icelandic occupation was being defended in the Senate as part of

the obligation that is upon us to see that the freedom of the seas is maintained. Back in 1914, 1915 and 1916, we were not insisting upon our right to station troops in Iceland or in Ireland or in Scotland. We had not dared go that far, as a nation determined to keep out of war and maintain the strictest neutrality. All we insisted upon then—and our insistence was not too strong—was a right and freedom for American ships to carry supplies to nations engaging in war on the continent of Europe. That insistence ultimately won us a place in the war.

"I was delighted but not surprised at the reception the [Iceland] message got both in and out of Congress," Secretary Knox wrote his wife. "It did surprise the President, I think, who was prepared for a vitriolic outburst. Even Wheeler approved it as a 'defense' measure! but soon caught his breath and became anti—violently." The ineffective isolationist response constrained Stimson to acknowledge that Roosevelt's approach had been right. "I think that the reception which has been given to your Iceland message has fully justified your method of approach as most wise and appropriate. And your frank statement of your purpose to keep the sea lanes from America to Iceland open for all purposes forestalls any valid criticism as to not taking the Congress into your confidence."

"The reaction to the landing of the American naval forces in Iceland shows how skilfully Roosevelt exploits the powers which he has gradually usurped," the German chargé cabled Berlin ruefully. "To this extent the occupation of Iceland is to be regarded as a touchstone of what public opinion and a generally quite amenable Congress will accept." The American people were not yet ready for "blood sacrifices," but "if there should be an incident because of Iceland, then Roosevelt will operate with the argument of defense against an unprovoked attack." At the same time, Gen. Friedrich von Bötticher, the military attaché who had many friends on the American general staff, sharply revised his estimates of United States military readiness. Although only two American army divisions "can be considered as fully equipped, and a total of five as being ready for immediate use," and, acknowledging that in the past he had called attention to the "weaknesses" of the United States rearmament program, "I urgently warned against overestimating the weakness and underestimating American efficiency and the American determination to perform. . . . As I have done for years I repeat in particular my report that the American officers' corps of the Army and the Air Force in general meets high requirements and . . . the influence of the tradition going back to Washington and Steuben, and thereby to Frederick the Great."

At Hitler's field headquarters, the naval command requested

a political decision on whether with regard to naval warfare the occupation of Iceland is to be considered as the entry into the war by the United States of America, or whether it is to be regarded as a provocation which should be ignored.

The Fuehrer stated in this connection that he is most anxious to delay the entry into the war by the United States of America for another month or two, because on the one hand, the entire Luftwaffe is needed for the campaign in the East, and on the other hand, a victorious campaign will have a tremendous effect on the situation as a whole—and presumably also in the U.S.A Therefore, the existing instructions issued to the Navy are not to be changed for the time being; rather, one should continue to avoid all incidents.[11]

In the meantime, new orders had been issued to Admiral King, the commander in chief of the United States Atlantic fleet, that would make it increasingly difficult for the German navy to comply with Hitler's orders to avoid incidents. They were called "Special Instructions Concerning U.S. Navy Western Hemisphere Defense Plan No. 4—(WPL-51)":

1. The President, in his message to the Congress, notified the Congress that:
   (a) communications between the United States and U.S. naval bases on the one side, and Iceland on the other, would be kept open, and
   (b) that such communications by water would be protected against attack or threat of attack. It is obviously impossible to define "threat of attack" by the presence of a German submarine or surface raider a given number of miles away from a convoyed vessel. It is necessary under the conditions of modern sea warfare to recognize that the words "threat of attack" may extend to reasonably longer distances away from a convoy, ship or ships.

2. It thus seems clear that the very presence of a German submarine or raider on or near the line of communications, and near to or approaching United States or Iceland ships, constitutes threat of attack.

3. Therefore, the presence of any German submarine or raider under such circumstances, should be dealt with by action looking to the elimination of such "threat of attack."

4. It should be made clear to your command that:
    (a) The United States and Iceland are in agreement that the United States is engaged in the protection of Iceland against German occupation, for the broad objective of Western Hemisphere defense;
    (b) That in maintaining this protection, sea and air communications between the United States and Iceland must of necessity be fully protected also.

He doubted that Roosevelt wanted a formal declaration of war, the German chargé advised Berlin in connection with reports that Roosevelt had recently told Willkie of his "firm resolution to bring about a state of war with Germany, and as early as possible at that." Roosevelt still believes, cabled Thomsen, "that he will be able to attain his goals, namely the protection of the Western Hemisphere and the destruction of National Socialism without a full war effort of his own." But this did not exclude an intention to wage undeclared war. "The frequent use of the expression 'pirates' with regard to German air and naval forces indicates a tendency toward 'shooting without a declaration of war.' . . . The President on the basis of his powers is at any time in a position to take steps which place America *de facto* in a state of war, and with respect to which Congress has no other choice than to give its subsequent approval if he demands it."

On July 25, Admiral Stark informed the president that "the carrier with planes for Iceland and her escort departs Sunday. We will keep you informed if anything happens." Stark himself was going off on a little holiday. "If I am all clear with the Secretary and also with the State Department, I am going up into our little shanty in the Blue Ridge for a breath of air. I can get away very quickly."[12]

Chapter Twenty

Sauce for the Soviet Gander

THROUGHOUT THE MONTHS that Churchill's England clung tenaciously to an enemy that it did not know how it would defeat and Roosevelt sought to come to grips with that same enemy, the offers from Hitler of a compromise peace never wholly ceased. He had found it hard to believe that England would go to war with him over Poland; nor could he understand why England persisted in waging war after the collapse of France. Some offers of peace were simply exercises in propaganda; some were definite; some were ambiguous.

Falling into this last category was the arrival from Germany of a one-man peace mission in the form of Rudolf Hess, who had landed in Scotland on the evening of May 10 in a Messerschmidt-110. Although it turned out—at least according to Hitler's associates—that the Führer's deputy and close confidant was acting on his own and that the news of his flight had hit Hitler "as though a bomb had struck the Berghof," Hess was unshakably convinced that there were still influential Britons (of whom the Duke of Hamilton, on whose estate he had parachuted, he thought to be one) who recognized that England's true interests would be served by an alliance against Bolshevism and who, therefore, must be prepared to accept the generous peace settlement that Hitler was ready to offer. This conviction was not far from Hitler's own. The terms Hess outlined to his captors were much like those that Hitler had offered to Chamberlain on the eve of the attack on Poland: Germany would have a free hand in Europe in return for which England would have "a completely free hand in the Empire." Hitler had attached one new condition—he would not negotiate with a government headed by Mr. Churchill.

The Hess affair fascinated the world. The British government, after arguing down Churchill, who had wanted to address the House on the subject, maintained absolute silence and let the world speculate. The embarrassed Nazis offered a brief explanation that few believed: "It seemed that Party Comrade Hess lived in a state of hallucination, as a result of which he believed he could bring about an understanding between England and Germany. . . . The National Socialist Party regrets that this idealist fell a victim to his hallucination. This, however, will have no effect on continuance of the war, which has been forced on the German people."

"In my opinion," confided Ciano in his diary, "it is a very serious matter: the first real victory for the English." Ribbentrop made a hurried, uninvited visit to Rome to explain, but his explanations were treated cynically. Stalin was sure there was some deep plot between Hitler and Churchill to switch the war to one in which all ganged up on Russia, and three years later, when Churchill told him the facts, because the episode continued to fascinate the Soviet leader, Stalin did not believe him.

"From this distance," Roosevelt cabled Churchill, "I can assure you that the Hess flight has captured the American imagination and the story should be kept alive for just as many days or even weeks as possible." If Hess was saying anything about Germany's real intentions toward the United States or the Western Hemisphere, "it should be kept separate from other parts and featured by itself." Churchill did send Roosevelt an account of the interviews. "Here we think it best to let the press have a good run for a bit and keep the Germans guessing." As to Hess's references to the United States, "nothing much emerged save incidentally some rather disparaging remarks about your country and the degree of assistance that you will be able to furnish to us. I am afraid, in particular, he is not sufficiently impressed by what he thinks he knows of your aircraft types and production." Churchill's explanation did not wholly satisfy Roosevelt. "I wonder what is *really* behind this story," he exclaimed at dinner with Hopkins, Sherwood, and Welles after the latter had described Hess's "fanatical, mystical devotion" to Hitler.[1]

At the beginning of June, Ambassador Winant returned to the United States to report to Roosevelt. Roosevelt told his press conference on June 6 that he had in his possession German orders to Nazi agents and sympathizers in the United States to spread the story that Winant had come back with British peace proposals. "Can you say definitely that Winant brought no peace proposal of any kind to your consideration?" several reporters wanted to know. "Absolutely nothing like it. . . . Not even a——not even a tenth cousin of a peace offer, or anything like that, or any discussion of peace."

One American who was circulating reports about Hess peace proposals, although, of course, he was neither a German agent nor sympathizer, was ex-President Herbert Hoover. On Sunday, June 22, Lord Halifax called on Sumner Welles, who made a memorandum of the conversation and sent it to the president:

Lord Halifax called to see me this morning at his request.
The Ambassador brought up the subject of information which had reached him to the effect that Mr. Herbert Hoover was busily engaged in spreading the report in many circles in the United States that Hess had brought to Great Britain specific and concrete German peace proposals. The reports emanating from Mr. Hoover further allege that when the leaders of the Conservative Party in England learned of this fact, they called upon Mr. Churchill and demanded that he give

these proposals full consideration, with the threat that, inasmuch as the Conservative Party constituted the chief support of Mr. Churchill in the House of Commons, such support would be withdrawn unless Mr. Churchill agreed to discuss these peace proposals; furthermore, that it was for this reason that Mr. Churchill had urged Ambassador Winant to return to Washington by air immediately in order to lay these facts before the President and obtain the President's acquiescence to consideration by the British Government of these peace proposals. Mr. Hoover further was claiming that Hess was the seventh peace emissary sent to England since the outbreak of the war and that the other emissaries had been sent from Germany to Dublin in a German plane and returned in a British plane. Mr. Hoover was maintaining that he was absolutely positive that these facts were correct as he set them forth since he obtained his information from Hugh Gibson who is now in London and who got them from reliable inside sources.

Lord Halifax said he merely wished me to know of the information he had obtained in this regard in order that the Administration might be able to deal with these reports in any way it saw fit. He said that it was unnecessary for him to say that the reports were entirely untrue and that, of course, this Government was aware of the general nature of the statements that Hess had made upon his arrival in Scotland.[2]

Sunday, June 22, the day that Halifax gave this information to Welles, was also the day that Hitler launched his colossal attack on the Soviet Union. "When *Barbarossa* begins the world will hold its breath," he had told his generals in February. At 3:00 A.M., six thousands guns opened fire and three armies, consisting of 120 divisions, moved forward, one aimed at Leningrad, another at Moscow, and the third at the Ukraine. "You have only to kick in the door," Hitler advised Field Marshal von Rundstedt, "and the whole rotten structure will come crashing down."

It was a measure of Hess's disciplined self-possession that he never discussed Operation Barbarossa or the imminence of invasion. Not that the United States and Britain lacked information on Hitler's plans, information that they had passed on to a Soviet government that had dismissed such intelligence as Western provocations. But Hess's silence on Hitler's military plans lent some confirmation to Beaverbrook's conclusion after he had talked with Hess that Hitler must have known of Hess's mission even if he had not authorized it. Anti-Bolshevism had worked so often before to demoralize and divide his victims, why should it not work with the British, especially when accompanied by an offer to respect the British Empire?

Churchill himself for almost two decades after the Russian Revolution was a prime exemplar of the way class bias influenced *his* political and military judgments. In 1944, Eleanor Roosevelt would send her husband a memorandum with the terse observation, "It is not surprising if Mr. Stalin is slow to forget!" She attached to it excerpts from Churchill's 1929 *The World Crisis: The Aftermath,* in which he describes the support that he, in 1919, as war secretary, gave to the White armies of Admiral Kolchak and General Denikin and his grievance against the Allied leaders for pursuing what a later generation of anti-Communists called a "no win" policy, which, Churchill claimed, was the main reason for the survival of the Bolsheviks. To Churchill, Bolshevism was "foul baboonery," a "plague-bearing" infection. He was not a participant in the original Allied decision, after Russia left the war in 1917, to encourage and call into being White armies sympathetic to the Allied cause and to support them with interventionist troops. But as secretary of state for war, to which he was appointed by Lloyd George in January, 1919, after the "coupon" election,* he passionately embraced the anti-Bolshevik standard. "Winston against Bolshevism," Sir Henry Wilson, chief of the Imperial General Staff, noted on January 20, 1919, "and therefore, in this, against Lloyd George."

Churchill fought to keep the interventionist armies in Russia as long as possible, although the original reason for the interference had disappeared with the war's end. He supported a final offensive by British troops in the Archangel–White Sea area, arguing that Britain could not just slink out of the country. And he supported Henry Wilson's view that such an offensive was necessary for eventual successful withdrawal. Nor was Churchill averse to using the threat of Japan against the United States in order to overcome its resistance to intervention. He told Lloyd George that "he would make a plain proposition to the United States that if they were not prepared to come in and do their share they should have no right to stop the [White Russian] Omsk Government [headed by Admiral Kolchak] from coming to terms with the Japanese. If the Russians could come to terms with the Japanese to send a few effective divisions to strike at the Bolsheviks, he could not see that British interests were affected. He suggested that we should send a few thousand British volunteers so that we were properly represented, and let the Japanese carry on."

When British public opinion rendered direct military intervention impossible, Churchill dispatched massive material aid and "advisers" to General Denikin to help the latter's advance on Moscow. And when that collapsed, Churchill espoused the idea of a "Sanitary Cordon" around Russia that combined all the border states from the Gulf of Finland to the Black Sea. "By the end of 1920," he noted with satisfaction a decade later, "the 'Sanitary Cordon' which protected Europe from the Bolshevik infection was formed by living national organisms in themselves hostile to the disease and immune through experience against its ravages."

He had been hostile to the provisional government headed by Alexander Kerensky, and the root of the matter lay in his sympathies for Imperial Russia. He sentimentalized Nicholas II. In the "coupon" election, the slogan of "Hang the Kaiser" made him uncomfortable. "Churchill would never give his support to anything that savored of regicide," wrote his good friend Beaverbrook. "So far as he was concerned, monarchs were safe from the gallows." His class feelings reached beyond sympathy for empires and monarchs. In the "secret and urgent" circular, not only did Churchill ask for volunteers to fight in Russia, but he also asked for information "on the attitude of the men to orders to help preserve the public peace and for assistance in strike breaking,

* Liberals who did not have Lloyd George's endorsement, "the coupon," were faced with Tory opponents who also had Lloyd George's support.

and of the influence of trade unionism on them." A copy was obtained and published by the *Daily Herald* and the episode did nothing to improve Churchill's relations with the trade union movement," commented Robert Rhodes James. A National Hands Off Russia Committee made Churchill its central target.[3]

Churchill had always been hostile to Lloyd George's program of reconciliation with Russia. He objected to Lloyd George's receiving a Russian trade delegation under Leonid Krassin, asking later, "Did you shake hands with the hairy baboon?" And as late as 1922, when Lloyd George proposed to treat with Russia, Churchill headed the group that strongly opposed recognition. "Since the Armistice," he advised Lloyd George in March, 1920, "my policy would have been 'Peace with the German people, war on the Bolshevik tyranny.' Willingly or unavoidably, you have followed something very near the reverse." In the mid-thirties, when Hitler's policies loomed up as a more immediate and larger threat to British interests than Stalin's, Churchill had altered his views. But class feeling had blinded him to the threat to Britain that General Franco's rebellion constituted. If the Loyalists had won, he would tell Eleanor Roosevelt in 1942, "you and I would have been the first to lose our heads." But he transcended his class bias, especially after Munich, and, in December, 1938, after his son-in-law Duncan Sandys visited Spain, wrote that "the British Empire would run far less risk from the victory of the Spanish Government than from that of General Franco." Similarly, it was in British interests to have Russia as an ally against Hitler, and from 1938 on he was a vigorous advocate of a "Grand Alliance" of Britain, France, and the Soviet Union.

But Churchill's underlying antipathy to Bolshevist Russia reasserted itself during the Finnish-Russian War. He was the principal organizer of the projected Anglo-French expeditionary force, presumably to aid the Finns but in reality to seize the Swedish iron mines. This bit of folly risked adding Soviet Russia to the list of Britain's adversaries. It might also have precipitated a Nazi occupation of Sweden, which the British and French were as ill-prepared to prevent as they were Germany's pre-emptive occupation of Norway a few weeks later, after Finland had made peace with Russia.

In the year that Great Britain stood alone, it was clearly in Britain's interest to try to separate Soviet Russia from Germany as, indeed, it was in Russia's interest that Britain should hold out, a mutuality of interests that to Churchill's great credit he perceived much more clearly than did Stalin. In the fall of 1940, the war cabinet, including Churchill, had permitted Sir Stafford Cripps, as we have seen, to offer far-reaching political and economic concessions to Russia in return for its adopting a position of neutrality "as benevolent as that adopted towards Germany." But after Cripps's humiliating rebuff at the hands of Stalin and Molotov—who had declined even to see him—Cripps, like Ambassador Steinhardt, his American colleague, and with London's support, took the view that efforts to conciliate the Russians produced results diametrically opposite to those expected and that the Soviet government was more responsive to pressure than to concessions. Cripps made no further attempt to see Soviet officials and, like Steinhardt, was persuaded that the key to the Soviet attitude was a determination not to provoke the Germans. Thus we arrive in June at the event that Churchill called the war's "fourth climacteric."[4]

"There is tremendous German pressure on Soviets," Eden noted in his diary on June 5. "I continue to believe that the latter will give way unless their skin is asked of them." A week later the Joint Intelligence Committee reported to Churchill that "fresh evidence is now at hand that Hitler has made up his mind to have done with Soviet obstruction and to attack." Churchill, the anti-Bolshevik, cabled Roosevelt:

From every source at my disposal, . . . including some most trustworthy, it looks as if a vast German onslaught on Russia was imminent. Not only are the German armies deployed from Finland to Roumania, but the final arrivals of air and armored forces are being completed. The pocket battleship "Lutzow" which put her nose out of the Skagerrak yesterday and was promptly torpedoed by our coastal aircraft, was very likely going north to give naval strength on the arctic flank. Should this new war break out, we shall of course, give all encouragement and any help we can spare to the Russians following principle that Hitler is the foe we have to beat. I do not expect any class political reactions here and trust a German-Russian conflict will not cause you any embarrassment.

Roosevelt's reply was delivered by Winant, who was sped by special plane directly to Chequers on his return from the United States, reaching there on June 20. "In the event that the Germans struck at Russia," he reported to Churchill, "the President promised an immediate supporting statement following any announcement the Prime Minister might make welcoming Russia as an ally."[5]

Roosevelt's journey to June 22 and the decision to aid Russia was considerably different from Churchill's. The two leaders ended up with a common policy on June 22, but different perceptions of the Soviet experience in the past would, as the war progressed, produce new divergencies. In the interventionist period, it seems probable that as a Wilsonian, Roosevelt was closer to the viewpoint of Lloyd George than to that of Churchill. The Bolshevik Revolution aroused distaste rather than apprehension among the Wilsonians. *Bolshevik* was a term of reproach and opprobrium in the Roosevelt circle as, indeed, it was with most Wilsonian liberals. But few idealized Imperial Russia, and Wilson resisted the pressures to intervene. He did finally authorize the dispatch of troops to Vladivostok, primarily, however, to offset and neutralize the Japanese, who would have been content to have the Maritime Province to themselves. After the war, Wilson was in the forefront of those who sought a way to make peace with the Bolsheviks—as was Lloyd George.

Roosevelt said little about Soviet Russia up until his campaign for the presidency in 1932. In his campaign for vice-president in 1920, his only reference to Russia was in connection with the League of Nations: "If Senator Harding is elected we play either a lone hand or form an association of our own with Bolshevists, Revolutionists and Turks." In the 1932 campaign, although FDR did not make an issue of the United States policy of non-recognition, even though he disapproved of it, he was in touch, through his wife's friend Esther Lape and others, with groups who wanted to change that policy. One of those who supported his campaign and who had been sent to him by Colonel House was William C. Bullitt. After the Inauguration Roosevelt had used Bullitt to negotiate the preliminaries of recognition and then had sent him to Moscow as ambassador. The choice of Bullitt was charged with meaning. As a young man of twenty-eight and a very junior official in the State Department in Paris in February, 1919, Bullitt had obtained authorization from Secretary of State Robert Lansing to journey to Moscow to find out on what terms the Bolsheviks were prepared to make peace with the interventionist forces. Lloyd George, through his private secretary Philip Kerr (later Lord Lothian), also endorsed his mission. In Russia, Bullitt conferred with Lenin and other Bolshevik leaders and in a few weeks returned to Paris with a peace proposal. "He had returned," George F. Kennan wrote later in his memoirs, "with Soviet proposals which were not ideal but which did offer the most favorable opportunity yet extended, or ever to be extended, to the Western powers for extracting themselves with some measure of good grace from the profitless involvement of the military intervention in Russia and for the creation of an acceptable relationship to the Soviet regime." But on his arrival in Paris, Bullitt was disowned by Wilson and Lloyd George.

The Americans, wrote Winston Churchill of this episode, "with the assent of Mr. Lloyd George sent a certain Mr. Bullitt to Russia on February 22. He returned to Paris in a week or two with proposals for an accommodation from the Soviet Government in his pocket. The moment was unpropitious. Kolchak's armies had just gained notable successes in Siberia. . . . The Soviet proposal to Mr. Bullitt, which were of course in themselves fraudulent, were treated with general disdain, and Mr. Bullitt himself was not without some difficulty disowned by those who had sent him." A hotheaded, emotional man, Bullitt resigned in anger and wrote a letter to Wilson castigating the Versailles Treaty "in prophetic terms," according to Charles Bohlen. He had subsequently testified before the Senate Foreign Relations Committee and had given Republican senator Henry Cabot Lodge, much to Roosevelt's disgust, considerable ammunition in his fight against United States participation in the League of Nations. All of this was known to Roosevelt when he appointed Bullitt his first ambassador to the Soviet Union.

But the man who had married John Reed's widow soon became disenchanted with the realities of Soviet Communism. And the final break came over the Seventh Congress of the Comintern, which, in violation of the 1933 Roosevelt-Litvinov agreement to ban organizations seeking the overthrow of the American government, was held in Moscow in 1935. What exasperated Bullitt was Litvinov's contention that neither he nor Stalin knew the Comintern was going to meet. Bullitt changed from a friend of the Soviet Union into one of its bitterest enemies. "Actually he was accurate in his prognostications and analyses of Soviet misbehavior," wrote Charles Bohlen, a junior secretary in the Moscow embassy. "What he could be faulted for was his reacting with violence, prejudice and unreason."[6]

Roosevelt, at Bullitt's request, sent him to Paris and replaced him in Moscow with Joseph E. Davies, lawyer and wealthy Democratic politician. Davies, wrote Bohlen, "was determined, possibly with Bullitt's failure in mind, to maintain a Pollyanna attitude. He took the Soviet line on everything except issues between the two governments. He never even faintly understood the purges, going far toward accepting the official Soviet version of the existence of a conspiracy against the state. . . . I still blush when I think of some of the telegrams he sent to the State Department about the trial."

Although Roosevelt corresponded personally with Bullitt and Davies, both of whom wrote him fully and freely, he rarely responded to the events they described or disclosed his own views. But he had a strong aversion to Communism and, like his wife, was persuaded that Communism could gain a hearing in the United States only if its social system failed to provide Americans with jobs, security, and justice. He also knew from personal experience that anti-Communism was cynically exploited by the rich and powerful to prevent change. He himself was denounced sometimes as a Kerensky, sometimes as a Lenin. Even Churchill in the mid-thirties had conjured up the figure of Kerensky in writing of Roosevelt.

Roosevelt considered the sixteen-year policy of nonrecognition and noncommunication folly and was proud that he had ended it. Although he saw the New Deal and his leadership of it as the democratic alternative to Hitler's Nazism and Stalin's Communism, he pursued a policy of friendliness toward Moscow in the interests of world peace. This was especially the case in the period of the popular front, when the Soviet Union, in fear of Hitler, embraced a policy of collective security. On the eve of the war, Roosevelt encouraged the Soviet Union to reach a military agreement with Britain and France against aggression. "It would prove to have a decidedly stabilizing effect in the interest of world peace," he advised Oumansky, the Soviet ambassador, "in the maintenance of which, of course, the United States as well as the Soviet Union had a fundamental interest." Prophetically, he warned the ambassador that if war did break out, Russia's position "would be affected more rapidly than the position of the United States."

Roosevelt's attitude toward Russia hardened when the Nazi-Soviet pact, which he understood, although he did not defend, on the basis of *Realpolitik,* was followed by the dismemberment of Poland and the invasion of Finland. Whatever his earlier sympathies with the Soviet experiment and his hopes that it would eventually become "a peace-loving popular government with a free ballot," Roosevelt told an American Youth Congress audience that assembled on the White House lawn on February 11, 1940, it was today "a dictatorship as absolute as any other dictatorship in the world."[7]

Soviet-American relations plummeted. A "moral" embargo was imposed on the Soviet Union, and Roosevelt directed the State Department to intimate to Oumansky that "the President honestly wonders whether the Soviet Gov-

ernment considers it worthwhile to continue diplomatic relations." And when
Ambassador Steinhardt complained that "long distance calls can no longer be
made from the Embassy in Moscow except by personal appearance at the
central telephone station," Roosevelt suggested that Oumansky be told the
United States was thinking of applying the same rule to him. "What is
sauce for the goose might well be sauce for him too!" This was in accord with
Steinhardt's firm view that the Soviets were more amenable to retaliatory action than to customary diplomatic methods and his conviction "that so long
as the German Army remains intact and unengaged there can be little expectation of a basic alteration in Soviet policy towards Germany."

Nevertheless, it was so clearly in the Soviet interest, especially after the
collapse of France, to have Britain continue to fight and, after the conclusion
of the Tripartite Pact, to have the United States restrain Japan, that from the
summer of 1940 on Welles had engaged Oumansky, whom Washington considered as little better than a police agent, in a series of probing conversations
to determine whether there was any chance of weaning away Stalin from his
marriage of convenience with Hitler. In January, 1941, the State Department
lifted the moral embargo, and hopes were held out to Oumansky that the machine tools the Russians had ordered months ago might at last be released for
delivery. The United States had a powerful incentive for such gestures in the
mounting tension with Japan and the need to forestall a Soviet-Japanese
alignment. As Hull explained to a protesting Halifax—for this was a period
when Britain, in its relations with Moscow, had recoiled to a position of aloofness and economic pressure—"Our purpose is to give less occasion for Soviet
officials to feel unkindly toward this Government, especially in the event of
some pivotal development where the slightest influence might tip the scales at
Moscow against us in a most damaging and far-reaching way."

The United States had reliable information that a "pivotal" development was in the making. In January, 1941, it received from Sam E. Woods,
its commercial attaché in Berlin, a copy of Hitler's December 18 directive for
Operation Barbarossa that a highly placed anti-Nazi German had slipped
Woods in the darkness of a movie theater. The information was checked out,
and the president decided that the Kremlin should be warned of Hitler's plan
to attack. Steinhardt was instructed to seek out Molotov to give him the information, but the ambassador balked. It would be viewed cynically by the
Russians as another attempt to drive a wedge between Russia and Germany
and might, as a consequence, hasten a Soviet-Japanese deal, an agreement
with Germany at Turkey's expense, even the occupation of Finland. Steinhardt
was spared the chore, for Welles in the meantime had transmitted the information to Oumansky in Washington, information that was supplemented
on March 20 by other confirmatory data. The Kremlin did, indeed, receive
the reports, Maxim Litvinov, Oumansky's successor, would later acknowledge, but had shrugged them off "because it considered it would have been
madness on [Hitler's] part to undertake a war in the East . . . before
finishing off his war in the West."[8]

Ivan Maisky, the Soviet ambassador to London, later wrote that he, too, had communicated on June 10 an enumeration given to him by Cadogan of German military movements and preparations that signaled an intention to attack. The only response from the Kremlin was an indirect denunciation in Tass of "clumsily cooked up propaganda" by the Western powers. The blame for the failure to treat these warnings seriously was Stalin's, wrote Maisky in the period of de-Stalinization. He cited Red Army general P. A. Korochkin's discussion at a conference of Soviet military historians of "the big blunder made before the war by Stalin in the evaluation of the military situation, its military and political aspects, and also of the designs and potentialities of fascist Germany."

Maisky fully expected the Red Army promptly to eject the Nazi invaders: "In the summer of 1941, like very many others, I did not clearly understand either the cult of Stalin's personality or all the tragic consequences of that cult," he explained. Churchill could write more bluntly and contemptuously. "They had shown a total indifference to the fate of the Western powers although this meant the destruction of that 'Second Front' for which they were soon to clamor. . . . We have hitherto rated them as selfish calculators. In this period they were proved simpletons as well."

As the reports of Nazi preparations accumulated (Russia received more than a hundred such reports, a scholar has estimated), Steinhardt in Moscow was sure a vast new Munich was taking shape. "As I have previously informed the Department I am convinced that in order to avoid war at this time Stalin is prepared to make almost any concessions provided they do not impair the ability of the Soviet Union to defend itself. . . . Some of my colleagues believe that a successful invasion of the Soviet Union would require over three months and that the cost of the campaign in men, materials and in particular in airplanes would be considerable." Steinhardt was confident that no hostile initiative would be taken by Stalin. Hull sent Steinhardt a statement of United States future policy toward the Soviet Union. It can be summed up in a few words: U.S.-Soviet relations should be governed strictly by the principle of reciprocity and *quid pro quo.*

He was "wholeheartedly in accord," Steinhardt telegraphed back. "Their psychology recognizes only firmness, power and force, and reflects primitive instincts and reactions entirely devoid of the restraints of civilization." He had arrived at these grim views independently, Steinhardt said, but the experience of the German ambassador Count von der Schulenburg confirmed them. "On several occasions [Schulenburg] told me quite frankly that more considerate treatment was accorded German interests and the German Government by the Soviet authorities during the period when the violence of the German campaign against the Soviet Union was at its height than at any time prior or subsequent to that period."

On June 21, the State Department's Division of European Affairs prepared a hard-nosed memorandum on "Policy with Regard to the Soviet Union in Case of the Outbreak of War between the Soviet Union and Germany." "We should offer the Soviet Union no suggestions or advice unless the Soviet Union approaches us," it began. The emphasis was on reciprocity. If approached, the United States should relax restrictions on aid and exports consistent with its own requirements and those of Great Britain. Such aid should be given directly "on the basis of mutual advantage and not in co-operation with any third power." Furthermore, the United States "should steadfastly adhere to the line that the fact that the Soviet Union is fighting Germany does not mean that it is defending, struggling for, or adhering to, the principles of international relations which we are supporting." And as a re-flection of the pessimism of the department's experts in regard to Russia's ability to withstand the Nazi onslaught, the memorandum concluded: "In particular we should engage in no undertaking which might make it appear that we have not acted in good faith if later we should refuse to recognize a refugee Soviet Government or cease to recognize the Soviet Ambassador in Washington as the diplomatic representative of Russia in case the Soviet Union should be defeated and the Soviet Government should be obliged to leave the country."

But Roosevelt's position, as we have seen, placed first things first. The defeat of Hitler had primacy with him as it had with Churchill. He would, the president indicated through Ambassador Winant, support any statement Churchill might make welcoming Soviet Russia as an ally.[9]

Chapter Twenty-one

Britain's New and Demanding Ally

C HURCHILL WAS AT Chequers on Sunday, June 22. The Edens and the Winants were with him. At dinner the night before, as recalled by John Colville, the private secretary who was on duty, the talk was about the coming German attack on Russia which Churchill now considered certain. "Hitler was counting on enlisting capitalist and Right Wing sympathizers in this country and the U.S.A.," Churchill thought. "Hitler was, however, wrong and we should go all out to help Russia. Winant said the same would be true of U.S.A." After dinner, Colville asked the prime minister "whether for him, the arch anti-Communist, this was [not] bowing down in the House of Rimmon. Mr. Churchill replied, 'Not at all. I have only one purpose, the destruction of Hitler, and my life is much simplified thereby. If Hitler invaded Hell I would make at least a favorable reference to the Devil in the House of Commons.' "

News of the invasion was flashed to Colville at 4:00 A.M., but since Churchill's standing orders were that he was never to be awakened for anything but the invasion of England, Colville postponed telling the prime minister about it till 8:00 A.M. "Tell the B.B.C. I will broadcast at nine tonight" were his orders to Colville, and Churchill dispatched his valet to Eden's bedroom with the message "The Prime Minister's compliments and the German armies have invaded Russia" along with a large cigar on a silver salver which the valet presented to the foreign secretary.

Churchill spent the day preparing his broadcast. Beaverbrook arrived, as did Sir Stafford Cripps, who was in London for consultations. Cripps had told the war cabinet a week earlier that the prevailing view in Moscow diplomatic circles was that Russia could not hold out against Germany for more than three or four weeks. The chief of the Imperial General Staff, Sir John Dill, believed that Britain would be unwise to count on more than six or seven.

Churchill, the invincible optimist who never was able to abide his associates' pessimism, alone asserted a contrary hope. "Hitler was about to make the identical mistake Napoleon had made; the German leader would be swallowed up in the deep snows of Russia . . . and, whatever General Dill, or Mr. Winant or anybody else present at Chequers that day might assert, he believed Stalin's armies would fight valiantly, and perhaps in the end victoriously, for the soil of Holy Russia." But as we shall see, this reflected buoyancy of temperament. His reasoned judgment, which governed his operational decisions, assumed, as Hopkins would put it a few weeks later (and it was the almost unanimous view in London and Washington), that Hitler's invasion at best gave Britain "a temporary breather."[1]

The conviction that Russia would be knocked out of the war within a few weeks (Ribbentrop assured Ciano that "the Russia of Stalin will be erased from the map within eight weeks") was a powerful shaping influence on British thinking on June 22. British relief at no longer being alone walked hand in hand with British anxiety that Russia would be defeated before the United States came in. "The earliest date upon which they fix the possibility of a German assault on Britain is August 31," General Lee, the U.S. military attaché, recorded on July 5. The hard-won pre–June 22 lessons of reciprocity, of the wisdom of not wooing the Russians, of not offering concessions except on the basis of *quid pro quo* yielded to the larger urgencies of doing what was possible to enable Russia to survive the titanic Nazi onslaught and of not permitting Hitler again to divide his opponents. "No one has been a more consistent opponent of Communism than I have for the last twenty-five years," Churchill began his BBC broadcast. "But all this fades away before the spectacle which is now unfolding. The past, with its crimes, its follies, and its tragedies, flashes away." Churchill conjured up a picture of eternal Mother Russia of ten thousand villages, guarded by her faithful Russian soldiery, where maidens laughed and children played, now being assailed by the brutal Nazi war machine. "I have to declare the decision of His Majesty's Government . . . for we must speak out now at once, without a day's delay. I have to make the declaration, but can you doubt what our policy will be? We have but one aim and one single, irrevocable purpose. We are resolved to destroy Hitler and every vestige of the Nazi regime. From this nothing will turn us— nothing. We will never parley, we will never negotiate with Hitler or any of his gang. . . . Any man or state who fights on against Nazidom will have our aid." He could not speak for the United States, "but this I will say, if Hitler imagines that his attack on Soviet Russia will cause the slightest divergence of aims or slackening of effort in the great democracies who are resolved upon his doom, he is woefully mistaken."

The deepest motive for Hitler's Russian adventure, Churchill continued, was the wish to destroy

the Russian power because he hopes that if he succeeds in this he will be able to bring back the main strength of his army and air force from the East and hurl it upon this island, which he knows he must conquer or suffer the penalty of his crimes. His invasion of Russia is no more than a prelude to an attempted invasion of the British Isles. He hopes, no doubt, that all this may be accomplished before the winter comes, and that he can overwhelm Great Britain before the Fleet and air power of the United States may intervene. He hopes that he may once again repeat, upon a greater scale than ever before, that process of destroying his enemies one by one by which he has so long thrived and prospered, and that then the scene will be clear for the final act, without which all his conquests would be in vain—namely, the subjugation of the Western Hemisphere to his will and to his system.

The Russian danger is, therefore, our danger, and the danger of the United States, just as the cause of any Russian fighting for his hearth and home is the cause of free men and free peoples in every quarter of the globe.[2]

This speech had a marked impact on public opinion in the United States. Both Churchill and Roosevelt feared that America, less endangered and more hostile to Russia and Communism than Britain, might well be susceptible to isolationist and Catholic exhortations to let the Nazis and Communists fight it out. "It's a case of dog eat dog," commented Sen. Bennett Champ Clark of Missouri. Why should the U.S. ally itself with "an Asiatic butcher and his godless crew?" asked the *Chicago Tribune*. Britain had to accept this new ally in order to save itself, but "we can resist the filthy disease." Even the interventionist *New York Times* was dubious about aiding Russia. "Stalin is on our side today. Where will he be tomorrow? In the light of his record no one can say that he will not switch sides again, make a sudden treacherous peace with Germany and become, in effect, Hitler's *Gauleiter* in the East. We should be in a fine state of affairs if we succeeded in landing a hundred bombers on Russian soil just in time for this reconciliation."*

Burton K. Wheeler, the most effective of the Senate isolationists, was, said Ickes, "particularly nasty about it in referring to Churchill and Roosevelt sleeping in the same bed with Stalin." Ickes was grateful for Churchill's speech, which he thought had done "much to direct our own public opinion and policy" while there was "not a word from the President. . . . It would be just like him to wait for some expression of public opinion instead of giving direction to that public opinion." In this period, Ickes was consumed by jealousy of Hopkins, and many of his judgments were flawed. He did not know that Roosevelt and Churchill had exchanged messages before Hitler had attacked, agreeing that Churchill should take the lead in establishing a policy of aid to Russia. A few days later, Ickes had Ambassador Oumansky to dinner and listened sympathetically to his weeping and wailing about the bad treatment he had received at the hands of the State Department.

Roosevelt kept his own counsel, but he authorized Welles, who was acting secretary of state, to declare on June 23 that Hitler's plan for "the ultimate destruction of the remaining democracies" was the primary challenge facing America and that "any defense against Hitlerism, any rallying of the

* I have quoted from the *Chicago Tribune* of August 16, 1941, and the *New York Times* of August 6, 1941. These samples of American attitudes are the more expressive of America's antipathy in that they were written after the initial shock and delight over Stalin's discomfiture had worn off.

forces opposing Hitlerism, from whatever source these forces may spring, will hasten the eventual downfall of the present German leaders and will therefore redound to the benefit of our defense and security." To this lackluster statement, which had been drafted by Welles, Roosevelt added in his own handwriting: "Hitler's armies are today the chief dangers to the Americas." Roosevelt followed this up at his press conference on June 24: "Of course we are going to give all the aid that we possibly can to Russia." But as yet the United States had no list of Soviet requirements. "Absolutely nothing. We have had no request."

Why had Hitler attacked Russia? Roosevelt kept asking himself. "[The president] has not been able to find an explanation that was intellectually satisfying to him," Halifax telegraphed London on July 7. "He was inclined to think that Hitler's main purpose was to rally public opinion throughout the world by an attack on Communism and the result seemed to the President to show Hitler to have made his first big political miscalculation psychologically. Meanwhile the time we had been able to gain had made the President feel much more hopeful than the President did three weeks ago."[3]

Roosevelt's guess was not far from the mark. "Since the Fuehrer hopes," noted the journal of the German naval general staff, "that the imminent collapse of the Soviet Union will have an important effect on the attitude of Great Britain and the United States, it is absolutely essential that all incidents with the United States should be avoided. . . . Germany's attitude to America is therefore to remain as before: not to let herself be provoked, and to avoid all discussion." The scenario that Hitler envisaged was a lightning triumph over Russia, this new display of Nazi invincibility dazzling British Conservatives, who would then bring down Churchill's government as a prelude to seeking peace.

Preliminary peace soundings were already being made. "It appears that there is a Philadelphia Quaker," Welles reported at a cabinet meeting on July 11, "who had been acting as a go-between between Thomsen, the German chargé d'affaires, and Halifax. He had been to see Halifax, after having a talk with Thomsen, to say that when the Germans had defeated Russia, Hitler would make a peace proposal to England. There seems now to be little doubt," commented Ickes, who recorded Welles's report, "that some such proposal would be made. Hitler would say that he did not want to destroy the British Empire but that he wanted to be left free to constitute a United States of Europe." Such a peace offer, Ickes feared, would create "a very difficult domestic situation," and even Churchill would have some difficulty. "His government might be overthrown and a Cabinet formed under Lloyd George or someone else who would come to terms with Hitler." The British minister had called on him, noted Welles a few days later, and had passed on a report from Switzerland that Hitler, after the occupation of Leningrad and Moscow, would conclude his campaign in Russia and put peace proposals to England. Another piece of intelligence that the British minister passed on was that the French ambassador in Washington, Gaston Henry-Haye, had cabled Vichy that if such peace proposals were made, isolationist sentiment in the United States would prevent the president from opposing them.

A relaxed Hitler wrote to Mussolini on the eve of the invasion: "Since I struggled through to this decision, I again feel spiritually free. The partnership with the Soviet Union, in spite of the complete sincerity of our efforts to bring about a final reconciliation, was nevertheless often very irksome to me, for in some way or other it seemed to me to be a break with my whole origin, my concepts and my former obligations. I am happy now to be relieved of these mental agonies." Hitler was relieved. Churchill and Roosevelt rejoiced over the turn of events. The Soviet leaders alone were incredulous and plaintive. "Do you believe we deserved that?" was Molotov's comment after German Ambassador Schulenburg had read him the declaration of war.[4]

Within a few weeks, however, this hitherto benevolently neutral partner of Hitler's war on the democracies began to request things of its new allies, to make conditions, and to assert rights. Alliance against a common enemy did not exclude hard, almost brazen bargaining. On June 22, Eden returned briefly to London to speak with Maisky. The Soviet envoy was certain that Germany's invasion of Russia would be accompanied by a peace offer to Britain. "Could the Soviet Government be assured that our war effort would not slacken?" Maisky inquired anxiously. When Eden assured him that British efforts would increase, the ambassador spoke of his anxieties about the United States. The envoy should talk with Winant, Eden suggested. "Behind the Russian interrogation," wrote Eden, "was the fear that we would stand inactively watching their life-and-death struggle, as they had watched ours. It was almost as much for this reason as because they needed help, that the next six months were filled with Soviet requests, even demands, for a second front, for enormous quantities of material aid, for British troops to fight in Russia and for a political treaty."

The day after the invasion began and following Churchill's speech, Moscow informed London that it was ready to receive the military mission that Eden had suggested on June 13. It reached Moscow on June 27, accompanied, at the suggestion of the war cabinet, by Sir Stafford Cripps. No sooner had Cripps arrived in Moscow than Molotov summoned him. How much cooperation was Britain ready to give? the Russian inquired. Was it ready for a political agreement? Cripps, who in October, 1940, was prepared to offer political as well as economic inducements to the Soviet Union but was refused an audience by the Berlin-bound Molotov, thought it a little early to discuss political agreements. After all, the new relationship between Britain and Russia had existed only for five days. Mutual trust could not be simply declared; it was something that had to be nurtured and that needed time to take root. But at the back of Cripps's mind was an unnerving fear. "It would be frightful," he told his American colleague Steinhardt, "if the Russians should collapse. That would mean an attempt at invasion of Britain in September." The usually impassive Molotov seemed to the British envoy to be "pale, nervous, obviously shaken."

A Beaverbrook indiscretion, in the meantime, started Molotov on a new train of requests. Maisky had informed him, Molotov advised Cripps, that Beaverbrook had said that Britain might be prepared to help Russia by a landing in northern France, by naval activity in the White Sea area, and by increased air activity over France and west Germany. Such matters, Cripps said, would have to be taken up with the British military mission, which had, in fact, been cooling its heels in Moscow. He would see the head of the mission at 3:00 A.M., Molotov said. But when, at the predawn meeting, the mission head asked for detailed information about the Russian front so that the British chiefs of staff in London could make their decisions on how to relieve the Russians on the basis of facts, Molotov was brusque. Time was being wasted. He would take up the question in London. "Mr. Maisky stressed the importance psychologically of our taking some initiative," parliamentary under-undersecretary R. A. Butler reported to his colleagues in the foreign office, "either by a landing on the coast of France or by an expedition in the White Sea area. He was understanding about the difficulties of our sending a large expeditionary force and seemed chiefly interested in some action which would impress his Government with our determination to help the Soviet Union at this time."

British leaders already were distressed and ashamed at the paucity of the aid they could render Russia. 'We are not prepared to take advantage of this Heaven-sent (and short) opportunity of the Germans being heavily engaged in Russia," Cadogan recorded in some despair and disgust. "We shall look awful fools. But there it is."[5]

There was, however, the American connection. "This is, then, the most critical moment of all," Cripps cabled on July 1. "If at this moment, United States could be persuaded to join in it would have most tremendous effect on the morale of all anti-Nazi forces and the wobblers . . . suggest a direct appeal to Roosevelt by Prime Minister. While Russian power and resistance is still on our side we have an enormous advantage which may be forfeited by failure of the United States at the critical moment to that effect." After consulting Churchill, Eden replied that the "Prime Minister sent a personal message to the President yesterday and there is nothing more we can do at present by that means. Winant is being consistently helpful and you may be sure that I shall not forget importance of psychological moment." However, Churchill's message to Roosevelt on July 1 dealt with shipping losses and convoys, not cobelligerency. He had thanked the president for the news about a vast expansion in American merchant shipbuilding to replace British losses and suggested delicately that "any increase in our escorts will produce an immediate saving in losses. Forgive me mentioning this when I know all you are doing." A sentence in this message showed that Churchill was not counting on the Russians holding out long. "I am asking that everything here shall be at concert pitch for invasion from September 1st."

Eden had spent three hours with Churchill, from 11:00 P.M. to 2:00 A.M., canvassing what the British might do to relieve the pressures on the Russians, "but I gather nothing much emerges," recorded Cadogan. Within the week, the foreign office decided that Halifax should put to Roosevelt Cripps's view on this being "the critical moment" for the United States to come in. "I took the occasion," reported Halifax, "to speak to [Roosevelt] in the sense of Sir Stafford Cripps' views in his telegram No. 695, without however suggesting that I thought United States could immediately do more than they already were doing about Iceland. I emphasized, the value, I hoped, Iceland action created for Russian morale. President's comment was that he thought it would mean that as regards United States position that 'whole thing would now boil up very quickly and that there would soon be shooting.' "

The obliqueness of Halifax's presentation of the Cripps view disappointed the foreign office. Should the matter not be put to the president "with greater vigor and with considerably more bluntness than we have been in the habit of employing in our approaches to him on the subject of American intervention?" asked Sir Orme Sargent, the deputy undersecretary. The landing of the marines in Iceland was no substitute for Anglo-American action to take advantage of Germany's momentary vulnerability in the West. "Still less is it in any way a substitute for the actual entry of America into the war which, if it took place now that Russia is a belligerent, would have the effect of presenting Germany with what she has always dreaded, namely a *real* war on two fronts."

Russian resistance was giving Britain "an unlooked for opportunity," Cadogan agreed,

and comparative inaction on our part will have a very bad effect.
But I suspect that the President would not think that the present situation gives *him* a very good opportunity with his public. The German attack on the Soviet Union has, on the whole, fortunately been taken well by the American public. But there were some days of wavering in certain quarters, and not everyone has yet recovered his equilibrium. . . . I should, therefore, most regretfully, guess that this is not a very good moment for further pressure.

But Cadogan wanted the views of Sir David Scott, the head of the American department. There were steps the president might take, Sir David thought, that would not start Americans talking about aiding the Communists.

A declaration of war, is not, of course, in the President's hands, but we have already instructed Lord Halifax to raise with the State Department the possibility of a visit by U.S. warships to Casablanca or Dakar and I suggest that we await the reply to that telegram (or remind if no reply comes in by tomorrow) before doing anything else. I agree that Lord Halifax might have spoken with a little more enthusiasm or fire but the Americans must be fully aware of the situation—Mr. Winant has no doubt reported his conversations with [Eden]—and the President, while desperately keen to do anything possible to help, is very conscious of how far his public opinion will let him go, and I think we should be careful not to seem to be "fussing" him.

This advice evidently prevailed, at least until Churchill's meeting with Roosevelt at Argentia in Newfoundland.[6]

There was another pressure prompting Britain to try, through diplomatic action, to create the second front it was unable to launch militarily: the effect of British inactivity upon world opinion generally and its leadership in a post-war Europe specifically. "It has hitherto been assumed that Germany would gain a rapid victory over Russia," wrote R. A. Leeper, head of foreign office's news department, in a paper called "Political Aspects of a German Defeat by Russia," and "on this assumption the future strategy of the war has been planned." But suppose this time the Nazi blitz is stalled.

The Russian Revolution was the most arresting event of the last war; Russian resistance to Germany may prove the most arresting event in this war. Hitherto the Battle of Britain last autumn has been the epic of this war, but it may well be dimmed by the much greater battle now in progress between Germany and Russia, a battle on which so much depends and in which we are playing no significant part in the eyes of Europe. The Russians may in fact put us completely in the shade. . . . [Stalin] is in fact making a bid for European leadership. If he repels the German attack, this leadership will become a most important factor in Europe. It will be said that Russia alone could defeat Germany. . . . It is not too much to suggest that the relief and consequent enthusiasm felt for a Russian victory will make many people forget the excesses and brutalities of Communism. . . . Our gigantic war effort, when we stood alone at the height of the German triumph last summer, would be largely forgotten. We should be accused of having done nothing during the greatest battle of the war.

He was not competent, Leeper went on, to elucidate the military consequences of this analysis, but among the political implications, he thought, was the desirability of the Allied governments in London making "as rapid progress as possible in defining the kind of new order in Europe for which they stand. Something will be required to fire the imagination of Europe in the way we should desire."

Although Leeper's paper was initialed by the top officials of the foreign office, including Eden, the comments were sparse and perplexed. Perhaps that was because the prospects of a Russian triumph seemed a little academic. And if it did happen, was there not another possibility, asked Cadogan, "a revulsion of fear of Russian domination on the continent, which might have the most perplexing and possibl[y] dangerous results?" The net effect of the Leeper analysis, however, undoubtedly was to accentuate the British search for ways to aid the Russians. Roosevelt, incidentally, did not fear that Russia might become the dominant power in Europe. "Now comes this Russian diversion," he wrote almost breezily to Admiral Leahy in Vichy. "If it is more than just that it will mean the liberation of Europe from Nazi domination— and at the same time I do not think we need worry about any possibility of Russian domination."[7]

Churchill, in this period, was awaiting anxiously for some reaction from Stalin to his June 22 speech. The first response came in Stalin's broadcast to the Soviet people on July 3 in which the Russian leader called for a war of liberation, announced a scorched-earth policy, and assured his undoubtedly stunned and bewildered countrymen that they had allies: "In this connection the historic statement of the British Prime Minister, Mr. Churchill regarding aid to the Soviet Union, and the declaration of the United States Government signifying readiness to render aid to our country, which can only evoke a feeling of gratitude in the hearts of the people of the Soviet Union, are fully comprehensible and symptomatic." This was far from the personal message that Churchill hoped for, and he found Stalin's silence "oppressive." Might it be Soviet "shyness" in view of their policy before the invasion or his own anti-Bolshevik record that was inhibiting communication? Churchill decided it was his "duty to break the ice." A personal message went to Stalin that, among other sentiments, declared, "We shall do everything to help you that time, geography, and our growing resources allow. The longer the war lasts, the more help we can give." The British air force already was carrying out heavy attacks on German towns and the navy was preparing an operation in the Arctic, "after which I hope contact will be established between the British and Russian Navies. . . . We have only got to go on fighting and beat the life out of these fellows." A small squadron of British ships sent to the Archangel Region, Churchill advised the admiralty, would have a psychological effect far beyond its size. "The advantage we should reap if the Russians could keep the field and go on with the war, at any rate until the winter closes in, is measureless."

Cripps remained with Stalin alone for an hour when the former delivered Churchill's message. Stalin made no attempt to conceal the seriousness of the situation at the front, which had not yet been stabilized. He also brought up the proposal for a political agreement between Great Britain and the USSR, just as Molotov had a week earlier. Cripps reminded Stalin that an agreement had been offered in the autumn of 1940, "and [Stalin] pointed out that for the Soviet Government to have done anything then would have been tantamount to attacking Germany." But political agreement was indispensable now if military cooperation was to be effective, Stalin went on. He proposed a treaty with but two provisions: mutual aid and no separate peace. Although the impression in the diplomatic colony had been that Stalin had "a deep-seated hatred" of Britain, especially of its statesmen and diplomats, whom he considered arrogant, he now had pleasant words for the British people, even for Churchill. "He stated," reported Cripps, "in comparing the present Prime Minister's Government with that of his predecessor, that it was because the present Prime Minister understood the needs of the workers that it had been possible for him to form a real government of national unity, and it was this fact which accounted for the determined resistance of the British people."[8]

Britain consulted the United States about the proposed agreement with Russia, which it wanted to sign. Did Washington have any objections? If it contained nothing more than mutual aid and no separate peace, Welles said to Halifax, the United States had no reason to object. "I stated, however, that I felt it would be desirable for Lord Halifax to be authorized to assure me specifically that no secret provisions beyond those I had mentioned were being included in the agreement negotiated, unless this Government were given an opportunity of previously knowing of it." Behind Welles's strictures were not only American memories of secret agreements made before the United States had entered World War I and which had bedeviled peacemaking at Versailles, but a disconcerting talk he had had with Halifax a month earlier, when Halifax had raised the possibility of America extending aid to Russia in the event the USSR was attacked and Britain and Russia became allies. Welles had reacted quite coolly. United States and British requirements would continue to have priority, he had said, and had gone on to caution Halifax against British recognition of Soviet incorporation of the Baltic States on which the Russians had been insisting. "To my surprise," Welles recorded,

Lord Halifax said he felt he was rather cynical with regard to the Baltic States. He said that he did not think the Baltic peoples were peoples who demanded very much respect or consideration and that in the situation in which Great Britain now found herself, concentrating as her sole objective upon the defeat of Hitler, he could conceive of a situation developing in which the British Government, in order to form close relations with the Soviet Union, might desire to take some steps with regard to recognizing the Soviet claims with regard to the Baltic states and the Baltic peoples.

That would undermine one of Britain's greatest assets, Welles cautioned Halifax, "namely, the innate strength of the moral issues involved. What logical distinction, I said, could be drawn between the recognition of the brutal conquest by Russia of the Baltic states and the brutal conquest by Hitler of other independent peoples such as the Dutch and the Belgians . . . ?" Halifax's reply was that "the Baltic states for over a century had been under the domination of Russia." The same might be said of the Finns, retorted Welles. "Lord Halifax replied to this by saying he did not have the same respect and regard for the Baltic peoples that he did for the Finnish people." The talk ended with a word of caution from Welles. The United States would not depart "from its support of the moral issues involved in the present world struggle."[9]

Feeling somewhat guilty over their inability even to harry the Germans in the west, the British were not disposed to make difficulties over Stalin's proposal for a mutual-assistance pact. "I am in favor of giving them all they want—no haggling," recorded Cadogan. "Winston wants to do the same and to send a personal message to Stalin. [Anthony Eden] against that." Eden did not want the prime minister to become involved in the day-to-day business of diplomacy, but Churchill hoped—so he later wrote—on the basis of personal telegrams, to build up "the same kind of happy relations which I had developed with President Roosevelt." This was an interesting statement in view of British postwar criticism of Roosevelt's naïveté in seeking to establish a personal relationship with Stalin.

The war cabinet authorized an "immediate and generous response" to Stalin's proposal, and it also agreed that British acceptance should take the form of a message from Churchill to Stalin. It deleted as unwise from Churchill's draft a reference to the peace conference after the war where territorial settlements should be decided upon the basis of self-determination. The deleted paragraph read:

You will of course understand that at the victorious Peace Conference, in which the United States will certainly be a leading party, our line would be that territorial frontiers will have to be settled in accordance with the wishes of the people who live there and on general ethnographical lines, and secondly, that these units, when established, must be free to choose their own form of government and system of life, so long as they do not interfere with the similar rights of neighboring peoples.

Such a declaration, the war cabinet feared, might cause difficulties for the Poles in their discussions with the Russians. The British, at the time, were trying to bring about a resumption of relations between Russia and the Polish government-in-exile headed by General Sikorski, and to secure the release of Polish soldiers who had been carried off as prisoners at the time of dismemberment. The first Soviet reply was that they would set up national committees of Poles, Czechs, and Yugoslavs in Russia with facilities to form military units. The Poles resisted. Moscow finally agreed to the creation of an independent Polish army on Soviet soil, and diplomatic relations were reestablished. By the common consent of Poland, Great Britain, and the USSR, discussion of frontiers was left aside for the moment.

Churchill wrote in explanation:

In the summer of 1941, less than two weeks after the appearance of Russia on our side in the struggle against Germany, we could not force our new and sorely threatened ally to abandon, even on paper, regions on her frontiers which she had regarded for generations as vital to her security. There was no way out. The issue of the territorial future of Poland must be postponed until easier times. We had the invidious responsibility of recommending General Sikorski to rely on Soviet good faith in the future settlement of Russian-Polish relations and not to insist at this moment on any written guarantees for the future. I sincerely hoped for my part that with the deepening experience of comradeship in arms against Hitler the major Allies would be able to resolve the territorial problems in amicable discussions at the conference table.

In Washington, Polish Ambassador Ciechanowski proposed to Welles that American aid to Russia be made conditional upon restoration of Poland's prewar boundaries. All that Welles would say was that he would keep the matter in mind.[10]

The decision not to argue about frontiers and postwar settlements had Roosevelt's hearty concurrence. The Wilson experience with secret treaties was much on his mind. Preliminary commitments were being made, "chiefly in London," regarding the postwar settlement of Europe, Berle alerted Roosevelt. "You will recall that at Versailles President Wilson was seriously handicapped by commitments made to which he was not a party and of which he was not always informed." Berle listed the commitments that had come to the attention of the State Department. Trieste was to go to a reconstitued Yugoslavia. In the Polish negotiations, Moscow wanted to establish national committees of Polish, Czech, and Yugoslav nationals as the nucleus of a postwar federation. Russia was no doubt insisting on recognition of Russian title to the Baltic States, and the British appeared to be sympathetic. Berle also was disturbed by British plans, to which the European governments-in-exile had agreed, to supply their postwar needs for food and raw materials. "Much of the material and shipping will be, derivatively, American. A plan to regionalize the world (leaving the Western Hemisphere) has already been turned down by our people. The obvious intent is partly humanitarian but may be to channelize the trade and economics of this area through London when the war is over."

Berle's memorandum disturbed Roosevelt, who drafted a message to Churchill and dispatched it after Welles had said that he was in "hearty accord" and urged it be sent "without delay." The message read:

I know you will not mind my mentioning to you a matter which is not in any way serious at this time but which might cause unpleasant repercussions over here later on. I refer to rumors which of course are nothing more nor less than rumors regarding trades or deals which the British Government is alleged to be making with some of the occupied nations. As for example the stupid story that you have promised to set up Yugoslavia again as it formerly existed and the other story that you had promised Trieste to Yugoslavia.

In certain racial groups in this country there is of course enthusiastic approval for such promises in relation to post-war commitments, but on the other hand there is dissension and argument among other groups such as the Czechs and Slovaks and among the Walloons and Flemish.

You will of course remember that back in early 1919 there was serious trouble over actual and alleged promises to the Italians and to others.

It seems to me that it is much too early for any of us to make any commitments for the very good reason that both Britain and the United States want assurance of future peace by disarming all trouble-makers and secondly by considering the possibility of reviving small states in the interest of harmony even if this has to be accomplished through plebiscite methods.

The plebiscite was on the whole one of the few successful outcomes of the Versailles Treaty and it may be possible for us to extend the idea by suggesting in some cases preliminary plebiscites to be followed a good deal later on by second or even third plebiscites.

For example none of us knows at the present time whether it is advisable in the interest of quiet conditions to keep the Croats away from the throats of the Serbs and vice versa.

I am inclined to think that an overall statement on your part would be useful at this time, making it clear that no post-war peace commitments as to territories, populations or economies have been given. I could then back up your statement in very strong terms.

There is no hurry about this but you might think it over.

Roosevelt

Churchill did not reply to Roosevelt's suggestion of public statements by both that no commitments had been made. The explanation may be found in a diary note made by Eden on July 21 after Hopkins, who was on his second visit to England, had been to see him. "Winston was clearly not interested in the peace and H[opkins] therefore had been told to speak urgently to me. I explained our position, and that I was as eager to keep my hands free as anybody, but the spectacle of an American President talking at large on European frontiers chilled me with Wilsonian memories."[11]

In retrospect, the question arises whether Churchill and Roosevelt were wise to postpone the discussion of frontiers, the status of the Baltic States, and similar issues. Granted that the military defeat of Hitler had prior claims on their attention, should the political aims for which the war was being fought have been deferred? Admittedly, it was a moment of mortal danger for Soviet Russia, but as the peril receded, the West's bargaining power with its Soviet ally would also recede. And Stalin soon would demonstrate that he would not hesitate to press his maximum demands. He was a wily as well as a tough bargainer, deftly and delicately raising the specter of a new Nazi-Soviet pact. He was "most pleased" with Churchill's message agreeing to a mutual assistance pact, reported Cripps. Stalin proposed that the declaration be signed in Moscow as soon as possible "because some Communists in Russia were speaking in a pro-German sense and the publication of the agreement would enable him to put a stop to their activities." There were two contingencies that might end Soviet resistance to Hitler, Joseph E. Davies, former ambassador to Moscow, advised Hopkins: "a Trotzkyite Pro-Germany" coup against Stalin or "Stalin himself making a Hitler peace. Stalin is oriental, coldly realistic and getting along in years. It is not impossible that he might even again 'fall' for Hitler's peace as the lesser of two evils." It was "of vital importance that Stalin be impressed with the fact that he is not 'pulling the chestnuts out of the fire' for allies who have no use for him."[12]

Davies's views were taken most seriously at the White House. Roosevelt knew that Davies had been one of the few Western ambassadors to predict the Nazi-Soviet pact. On June 8, 1939, Davies had written Roosevelt from Brussels, where he was stationed after his stay in Moscow, that "Chamberlain will soon have to make up his mind or the old Bear will get tired of being cuffed around and make peace on his own terms possibly with Germany. If that happens, Europe will be in the hollow of Hitler's hand. . . . It is perfectly amazing to me that the power and strength of the Soviet Government and Army is not accepted in spite of the overwhelming evidence that is at hand." Davies was about the only Soviet expert who, when Hitler invaded Russia on June 22, flatly asserted that the resistance of the Red Army would amaze the world.

But it is doubtful that a pro-German faction remained in the Soviet leadership on July 10—as Cripps and Davies feared. Hitler's armies had advanced deep into Russia. His order to his commanders was that "the so-called Commissars should not be considered prisoners-of-war." By mid-July, it was clear to the Soviet leaders that for them at least it was a case of conquer or perish. Stalin's military situation was desperate, but he never ceased to think politically. "The position of the military forces at the front remains tense," he said in his first personal communication to Churchill on July 19, and the full consequences of Hitler's "unexpected breach" of the Nazi-Soviet pact and "the sudden attack" were still to be felt. But imagine what the position of the German forces would have been "had the Soviet troops had to face the attack of the German forces, not in the regions Kishinev, Lwow, Brest, Kaunas, and Viborg, but in the region of Odessa, Kamenets, Podolski, Minsk, and the environs of Leningrad." Having offered this oblique defense of Soviet moves into Poland, Romania, the Baltic States, and Finland, Stalin moved on to the necessity of establishing "a front against Hitler in the West—Northern France, and in the North—the Arctic. A front in Northern France could not only divert Hitler's forces from the East, but at the same time would make it impossible for Hitler to invade Great Britain. The establishment of the front just mentioned would be popular with the British Army, as well as with the whole population of Southern England." Stalin realized "the difficulties," but this was "the propitious moment" to establish such a front while Hitler's forces were diverted to the East and before the Führer had consolidated his position there.

Churchill viewed Stalin's brief exposition of the strategic considerations behind his seizures of his neighbors' territories in the period of the Nazi-Soviet pact as a "sign of compunction." And as a military strategist himself, the prime minister was not unsympathetic to the thesis. "I have never underrated the argument, and could well afford to reply in comprehending terms upon it."

"I fully realize," Churchill replied to Stalin, "the military advantage you have gained by forcing the enemy to deploy and engage on a forward westerly front, thus exhausting some of the force of his initial effort." This was a significant statement of which Stalin no doubt took note, emboldening him within a short time to demand anew British recognition of Soviet absorption of the Baltic States, taking advantage of the British sense of guilt over not being able to create a diversion in France.

The bulk of Churchill's message dealt with the question of a front in France. "Anything sensible and effective that we can do to help will be done. I beg you however to realize the limitations imposed upon us by our resources and geographical position." Britain's resources after a year of fighting alone were strained to the utmost by the Battle of the Atlantic and the requirements of the Middle East. Churchill explained why a landing in France would be repulsed bloodily, "and petty raids would only lead to fiascos doing far more harm than good to both of us." It was in the north that the British could help, and he described several actions the naval staff had under way. "This is the most we can do at the moment."[13]

Chapter Twenty-two

"No talk about war"

T HE GREAT STATESMEN looked at their terrestrial globes and saw that for the first time in history the planet's surface of sea, earth, and air was almost entirely enveloped in war. On the vast Russian front,, the frightful collisions involved millions of men. The Battle of the Atlantic grew in silent fury as the United States Navy joined the fray. In the Pacific, Japan prepared its challenge to the West. The three thunderous themes were merging into one. And one mind on which they converged with a painful intensity was that of the president of the United States as they beat out a remorseless message—that he should lead his people into the war.

On the evening of the day that Hitler invaded Russia, Hopkins dined with the Polish ambassador Jan Ciechanowski. The new war, Hopkins feared, would stoke up appeasement sentiment in the United States and Britain, strengthening the hands of those Americans who asserted that it was the president's duty to arm America rather than England and of those Englishmen who believed that Britain should seek a compromise peace. "Hopkins threw up his hands and said," reported Ciechanowski, "Ah! If only today we could give an answer to Churchill's eternal question: 'When will America finally join us against the common menace?' Of course we must give him the fullest support. There is complete understanding on this subject at the White House, but our public opinion is not yet ripe. The President has to proceed very cautiously and to time his policy step by step."

"Secretary Knox made a rousing speech before a conference of State Governors last night," noted Stimson a week after Russia was invaded, "coming out for immediate use of the Navy to clear the North Atlantic, saying that this was a God-given chance now that Hitler's back was turned in Russia." And from the other side of the administration, Ickes, spokesman for the New Dealers, declared in an address at Hartford that "if America does not go quickly all out for Britain, she may find herself all in without Britain." This echoed advice he had put more bluntly to Roosevelt: "It may be difficult to get into this war the right way, but if we do not do it now, we will be when our turn comes without any ally anywhere in the world." At the War Department, Stimson, Marshall, and the members of the general staff concluded that this was the moment to push ahead vigorously "with an affirmative policy in the Atlantic." The United States and Britain had a period of respite of one to three months in which Germany "will be thoroughly occupied in beating Russia," and during that period "Germany must give up on or slack up on" its pressures on the British, including "any invasion of the British Isles" and "any attempt to attack herself or prevent us from occupying Iceland."

But Roosevelt was not prepared to order the navy to clear the Atlantic. Wary of American public opinion and of Japan, which at the moment was deciding its policy in light of the Nazi invasion, all that he was ready to do was to proceed with the Iceland operation and to direct the navy to protect communications between Iceland and the United States. This, however, did mean the start of convoying, at least to Iceland. Admiral Stark wrote to Capt. Charles M. Cooke on July 31, 1941, sending a copy of the letter to Admiral Kimmel:

Within forty-eight hours after the Russian situation broke, I went to the President with the Secretary's approval, and stated that on the assumption that the Country's decision is not to let England fall, we should immediately seize the psychological opportunity presented by the Russian-German clash and announce and start escorting immediately, and protecting the Western Atlantic on a large scale, that such a declaration, followed by immediate action on our part, would almost certainly involve us in war, and that I considered every day of delay in our getting into the war as dangerous, and that much more delay might be fatal to Britain's survival. I reminded him that I had been asking this for months in the State Department and elsewhere, etc. etc. etc. . . .

The Iceland situation may produce an "incident." . . . Whether or not we will get an "incident" because of the protection we are giving Iceland and the shipping which we must send in support of Iceland and our troops, I do not know. Only Hitler can answer.

If the Russians failed to hold out through the summer, Roosevelt wrote Mackenzie King of Canada, he foresaw "an intensified effort against Britain itself, and especially for the control of the Atlantic. We may be able to help a great deal more than seems apparent today." By the beginning of July, Churchill had received a copy of "Western Hemisphere Defense Plan No. 4," which provided for navy escort of British as well as United States shipping as far as longitude twenty-six degrees west. He had cabled Roosevelt: "Putting such a plan into immediate operation would give timely and needed aid. At present the strain upon our resources is far too great." In the House of Commons, Churchill welcomed American occupation of Iceland "as one of the most important things that have happened since the war began" and underscored its significance for the Battle of the Atlantic:

The position of the United States forces in Iceland will, of course, require their being sustained or reinforced by sea from time to time . . . and, as we have a very large traffic constantly passing through these waters, I daresay it may be found in practice mutually advantageous for the two navies involved to assist each other.[1]

Hopkins was about to make his second trip to London. On the night of July 11, Roosevelt had a long talk with him about those matters he wanted him to take up with Churchill. The president penciled a line on a map torn from *National Geographic* that showed the area the U.S. Navy would patrol. It not only included Iceland, but swung eastward of Iceland some two hundred miles, an area of importance in terms of convoys to Russia. Hopkins's notes indicated also that British convoys could join American flagships under escort to Iceland, but that it "must be an American ship if conflict comes," meaning that U.S. naval vessels could actively protect only American vessels. A week later, at his press conference, Roosevelt indicated what he had in mind about keeping American communications open, omitting, however, Churchill's stress on the cooperation of the two navies:

First, communications between the United States and United States naval bases on the one side—well, that means Bermuda, Newfoundland, and Iceland at the other end of the line—will be kept open, obviously. You can't maintain a garrison in Iceland and not maintain the lines of communication. Just A-B-C stuff, and it can't be distorted.

Secondly, that in the protection of such communications they will be protected against what? attack, or threat of attack. Well, that's about all there is to say. Now there's nobody in this room that can define what 'threat of attack' is. I can't. Threat of attack! And the orders are to keep the communications open against attack, or threat of attack.

Stimson noted in his diary on July 21 that Knox had come in to tell him of his troubles. "He has been getting the final orders off for the convoy of ships both of our own and the British, between the Western Continent and Iceland and it has been the devil for him to do. The President, of course, in his Message to Congress, a week or two ago, said that he was going to make those lanes in the ocean safe but when it came to the job he again jibbed but Knox finally stuck to it and got it through."

Stimson regretted that Roosevelt had refused to make "the frank statement" on the orders that "Knox wanted him to do and I am afraid he is going to get troubles from that." But Stimson had discovered that Roosevelt's "jibbing," his circumspection, and his secrecy had a powerful precedent in American history: "I have been reading the portion about the period between Lincoln's actual inauguration and Fort Sumter and the terrific trouble that they had there in the vacillations and the pulling back and forth, trying to make the Confederates fire the first shot. Well, that is what apparently the President is trying to do here. The difficulty is that the danger now to the country is very much greater even than it was then, though not so palpably apparent, and a great deal depends on our not having this delay and give Hitler a chance to jump us."[2]

Action in the Atlantic in aid of Britain while Germany was busy in Russia had a strong appeal politically to administration leaders. It was a way of avoiding the issue of aid to Russia. This was stated succinctly in a memorandum to Hopkins by Oscar Cox on June 23. Cox by then was functioning not only as Hopkins's alter ego in the supervision of lend-lease, but as his one-man brain trust. During the battle to enact lend-lease, Hopkins, spotting Cox as a problem solver, had snatched him away from Morgenthau. On June 23, Cox prepared several memoranda for Hopkins on the Russian situation, including a list of antireligious quotations from Hitler and a summary of the legislative history of lend-lease vis-à-vis Russia. Although there was "no doubt at all that aid can legally be rendered to Russia under the Lend-Lease Act," Cox wrote, substantial deliveries did not appear feasible as a practical matter. "More action to aid Britain while Hitler is busy with Russia," he concluded, "can be our best reaction to Russia's fighting. Politically it would be wise to take this tack. Practically it would help Russia more than sending it direct aid."

The White House learned with considerable relief that American public opinion on the whole shared its view that Hitler was the main danger to the Americas and that in the clash between the totalitarians 73 per cent of those polled by Gallup preferred to see the Russians win as against the 4 per cent who favored Germany. Nevertheless, the president did not want to run afoul of the politically potent Catholic hierarchy. The best that Msgr. Michael J. Ready, general secretary of the National Catholic Welfare Conference, was able to do for the administration at a meeting of archbishops and bishops on June 24 was to delay the convening of a conference on United States policy toward Russia. Ready was certain that such a conference would go on record against "our Government's giving aid, in any form, to the Soviet Union." Before "confusion becomes more exaggerated," the monsignor advised Welles, who sent his letter on to Roosevelt, "and before the most vocal of our orators do their work, it would be most effective if the President could find an occasion to demand of Russia, as a condition of United States aid, a declaration of adherence to the four freedoms."

Catholic plus isolationist opposition to aid to Russia persuaded Roosevelt that it was more prudent to extend that aid outside of lend-lease. The administration had to go to Congress for a new appropriation and it was afraid that aid to Britain and China might be delayed if it were entangled with the issue of aid to Russia.

Soviet foreign-office officials in the meantime had handed in a list of their requirements. Replacements for its fighter and bomber force, much of which had been destroyed by the Germans at the outset of the fighting, headed the list. But then there was a surprise. The Russians wanted whole factories—rolling mills, cracking plants, machinery to manufacture tires. The State Department construed this as a reassuring sign that Russia's leaders were planning in terms of a long war. That, too, was Ambassador Oumansky's theme at a little dinner that he arranged in a country restaurant outside Washington with Loy Henderson, the assistant chief of the European affairs division. Oumansky was, reported Henderson, in "a cheerful and optimistic mood." He insisted the United States military authorities were badly informed with regard to the ability of the Red Army to put up an effective resistance. The conversation proceeded harmoniously until Oumansky brought up the issue of the Baltic ships that the United States had seized in American harbors when Russia had occupied the Baltic States. Oumansky hoped they would now be released. He should not press the matter, Henderson advised. It was insoluble and academic since it would imply United States recognition of Soviet conquests in eastern Europe. Oumansky insisted. Henderson with equal firmness said, "No use." So the dinner party ended.[3]

Despite the pessimism of Roosevelt's military advisers over Russia's chances of holding out, Roosevelt himself was determined to send as much aid to the Soviets as could reach them before October 1. The July 8 memorandum from Joseph E. Davies to Harry Hopkins was one of the few that supported such a decision. "The resistance of the Russian Army has been more effective than was generally expected," Davies asserted. If the United States wanted to strengthen and encourage such resistance, it was essential to build up Stalin's confidence in Allied intentions: "Word ought to be gotten to Stalin direct that our attitude is 'all out' to beat Hitler and that our historic policy of friendliness to Russia still exists."

Influenced by Davies and by the obvious fact that every additional day the Russians stayed in the war postponed by that much the invasion of Britain, Roosevelt, on July 10, met with Oumansky and told him what the United States was prepared to do. As Welles reported to Halifax:

The President said that we would undertake to supply urgently to the Soviet Union such of the orders which the Soviet Government desired to place in the United States which it might find it possible to ship and that the President had emphasized the fact that whatever was sent of an urgent character should actually reach the Soviet Union before October 1 at the latest. I added that the President had made clear his own opinion that if the Russians could hold the Germans until October 1 that that would be of great value in defeating Hitler since after that date no effective military operations with Russia could be carried on and the consequent tying up of a number of German troops and machines for that period of time would be of great practical value in assuring the ultimate defeat of Hitler. The President had also stressed his belief that the more machines the Germans were forced to use up in the Russian campaign, the more certain would be the rapidity with which Germany would be defeated, since he did not believe that the ability for replacement on the part of Germany was nearly as great as that which had been supposed. Finally, the President . . . had laid particular stress upon the fact that whatever it was decided by this Government to send to Russia would be the subject of consultation between this Government and the British Government, since it was a matter of common concern to all three Governments that the supplies which this country might have available be utilized in those particular places where, from the military standpoint, they might prove to be most useful.

To get the United States armed forces to give priority to British matériel requirements had been difficult. It was doubly so now in the case of Russia. A week after the president's meeting with Oumansky, Welles reported to the cabinet that little had been done about Russian requests which, incidentally, totaled some $1.85 billion in value and included such items as three thousand fighter planes and three thousand bombers. An impatient Roosevelt wrote formal letters to Stimson and Knox requesting them to report within forty-eight hours such items as might be provided and shipped to Russia by October 1. The army's attitude toward this new call upon its resources was reflected in Stimson's diary entry for July 21. The secretary had returned from a brief holiday and had discovered that there were lots of things "which are coming up which will require all my effort again to try to prevent our Army from being disintegrated and our resources in the shape of matériel scattered among various nations. On my desk was lying an appeal for the President to do something about Russia. Also I found that Harry Hopkins, who has gone away to England again, before he left had brought in a new tremendous appeal from the British for some fourteen billions of dollars under the Lease-Loan Act."

Between divided authority in Washington, Soviet mix-ups as to what they wanted and where they wanted it delivered, and deliberate delays, so little was actually shipped to Russia that at the cabinet meeting on August 1, just before Roosevelt left for his meeting with Churchill, he gave the State and War departments what Ickes described as "one of the most complete dressings down that I have witnessed." FDR was "terrific," recorded Morgenthau, who was an old hand at cutting through Washington red tape in order to expedite supplies to Britain and China, but whose authority in this field his rivals had succeeded in emasculating. He "went to town in a way I have never heard him go to town before." He said that he was "sick and tired of hearing that [the Russians] are going to get this and they are going to get that. . . . Whatever we are going to give them, it has to be over by the first of October, and the only answer I want to hear is that it is under way."

Most of Roosevelt's fire was directed at Stimson, who, said Morgenthau, looked "thoroughly miserable." Stimson's account was quite snappish. He described Roosevelt as having "pranced in" and put the blame on the War Department for the run-around the Russians had been getting. "I thought this was highly unfair to the War Department and I said so. Furthermore, I thought it was due largely to the uncorrelated organization which the President had set up that this should happen." Except for the item of planes, the list of Russian wants had never been presented to Stimson or to anyone in the War Department. As for the planes, the difficulty is "that we haven't got the planes to replace them. But in his outburst today the President said that we must get 'em, even if it was necessary to take them from troops and I felt very badly about it. I didn't get half a chance with him. He was really in a hoity-toity humor and wouldn't listen to argument." Stimson was deeply annoyed. And after a week end at Highhold on Long Island, he still was angry.

But this Russian munitions business thus far has shown the President at his worst. He has no system. He goes haphazard and he scatters responsibility among a lot of uncoordinated men and consequently things are never done. This time I got very angry over it for he had no business to talk that way in Cabinet about a run-around and indicate that it was the War Department. I am the only man in the whole Government that is responsible for the difficult decision of whether we can give up planes or other munitions with safety to our defense. All of these other people are just hell-bent to satisfy a passing impulse or emotion to help out some other nation that is fighting on our side and they have no responsibility over whether or not our own army and our own forces are going to be left un-armed or not.

But that was not the way Roosevelt saw it. Morgenthau, he thought, was right when he had said, "The trouble, Mr. President, is that with Harry Hopkins away Oscar Cox tells me that he just hasn't got enough authority to get anywhere . . . and that he does get the run-around all the time." He intended to put one of his best administrators in charge of the Russian order, Roosevelt told Morgenthau, "and his job will be to see that the Russians get what they need." The day after the August 1 cabinet meeting, the president chose management expert Wayne Coy and instructed him to "please get out the list and please, with my full authority, use a heavy hand—act as a burr under the saddle and get things moving! . . . Step on it!" That same day, August 2, an Anglo-American-Soviet committee, set up by the president to handle aid to Russia, met with Monnet representing the British, Oumansky representing the Russians, and Gen. James H. Burns, who was there for Hopkins, representing the United States. "We discussed," recorded the methodical Oscar Cox, "(a) The objectives of the Committee—on which all were agreed: to get Russia as much aid as possible out of stocks on hand and out of production."

Two telephone calls summoned Cox out of that meeting: one from Morgenthau at his home in Beacon, New York, telling Cox how the president had lit into Stimson at the cabinet meeting; the other from John J. McCloy, Stimson's trouble shooter, to assure him that Stimson was all for the Russian-aid program "and was pushing it hard."[4]

Hitler's reasoning, it will be recalled, in plunging his armies into Russia before settling scores with England was that this was also the most expeditious route to ending England's resistance. England lives "only on hopes," he wrote the Duce: "Russia and America. We have no chance of eliminating America. But it does lie in our power to exclude Russia. The elimination of Russia means, at the same time, a tremendous relief for Japan in East Asia, and thereby the possibility of a much stronger threat to American activities through Japanese intervention."

When Matsuoka, the bullet-headed "talking machine," had been in Berlin at the end of March, Hitler had not told him of Operation Barbarossa. At the time, it had seemed to Hitler that the most important contribution Japan could make to an Axis victory was to attack the British bastion in south Asia, Singapore. Its loss, he and Ribbentrop had argued, would go far in bringing Britain to its knees and would also tie down United States forces in the Pacific. And if, as a result, Japan "got into a conflict with the

United States, Germany on her part would take the necessary steps at once."

But within a week after Operation Barbarossa began, Ribbentrop was entreating Matsuoka for help in the battle against Russia. To be sure, he put it in terms of Japanese opportunity: the enemy's best divisions had already been partially demolished, its air force "almost completely smashed," and its resistance "in the entire European area will be broken—perhaps only in a few weeeks." Russia's imminent collapse "offers Japan the unique opportunity to free herself from the Russian threat and give the Japanese empire the security in the north which is a necessary condition for the vitally important expansion in the south. It therefore seems to me that the need of the hour is for the Japanese Army to seize Vladivostok as soon as possible and penetrate as deeply toward the West as possible."[5]

Ribbentrop sent this message to Matsuoka because he knew (as did Roosevelt) that the German invasion of Russia had plunged Tokyo's rulers into a frenzied reappraisal of Japan's position. Although Matsuoka, the most pro-German member of the Japanese hierarchy, suffered a tremendous loss of face because he had not been informed of Operation Barbarossa, he had promptly advised the emperor that Japan should use the opportunity to move north and to refrain from acting in the south. This advice was treated coolly, almost disdainfully. Prince Konoye, the premier, as careful and reticent as Matsuoka was impetuous and verbose, spent a week in conferences with the men who represented the power in his cabinet, chiefly the army and the navy. "Finally, I requested the convening of a council in the presence of the Emperor on July 2nd, where it was decided that for the time being Japan would not undertake action against the Soviets." That was not all that was decided. Everyone, including the emperor, was in uniform, and the fundamental decision was for war if necessary. By July 8, Roosevelt and other United States leaders knew through Magic the "principal points" that had been decided "for coping with the Changing Situation" in the advancement of Japanese "Imperial Policy." As decoded the message read:

The Policy

1. Imperial Japan shall adhere to the policy of contributing to world peace by establishing the Great East Asia Sphere of Co-prosperity, regardless of how the world situation may change.*
2. The Imperial Government shall continue its endeavor to dispose of the China Incident and shall take measures with a view to advancing southward in order to establish firmly a basis for her self-existence and self-protection.†
3. The Imperial Government will carry out the above program no matter what obstacles may be encountered.

---

* The Greater East Asia Co-Prosperity Sphere had been defined in July, 1940, as Japan's main national objective. It included all British, Dutch, French, and Portuguese possessions in the Far East and ultimately the Philippines, India, and Australia.

† Konoye's record of this decision in his Memoirs contains an additional sentence that probably was not sent: "This will involve an advance into the Southern regions and, depending on future developments, a settlement of the Soviet question as well."

The Principal Points

For the purpose of bringing the *Chiang* Regime to submission, increasing pressure shall be added from various points in the south, and by means of both propaganda and fighting, plans for the taking over of concessions shall be carried out.

Diplomatic negotiations shall be continued, and various other plans shall be speeded with regard to the vital points in the south. Concomitantly, preparations for southward advance shall be reinforced and the policy already decided upon with reference to French Indo-China and Thailand shall be executed. As regards the Russo-German war, although the spirit of the Three-Power Axis shall be maintained, every preparation shall be made at the present and the situation shall be dealt with in our own way. In the meantime, diplomatic negotiations shall be carried on with extreme care. Although every means available shall be resorted to in order to prevent the United States from joining the war, if need be, Japan shall act in accordance with the Three-Power Pact and shall decide when and how force will be employed.

Konoye's summary of the principal points was blunter: "In carrying out the plans outlined . . . we will not be deterred by the possibility of being involved in a war with England and America," and "all plans, especially the use of armed forces, will be carried out in such a way as to place no serious obstacles in the path of our basic military preparations for a war with England and America."

Diplomatic negotiations would be continued; the push southward would continue with the seizure of Indochina; and "in case the German-Soviet War should develop to our advantage, we will make use of our military strength, settle the Soviet question and guarantee the safety of our northern borders." This was the Japanese program as both the United States and Britain understood it soon after the imperial conference was held. For almost a year, Roosevelt had hesitated to embargo exports to Japan lest it provoke rather than deter. When Ickes, on June 23, had recommended the immediate cessation of oil shipments to Japan, Roosevelt had retorted coldly: "Please let me know if this would continue to be your judgment if this were to tip the delicate scales and cause Japan to decide either to attack Russia or to attack the Dutch East Indies." But the Magic intercepts now showed that Japan was determined to establish hegemony over Asia, preferably by diplomatic negotiations, if necessary by war.[6]

On July 10, Cadogan reported that Sumner Welles had shown Halifax "a lot of fairly definite stuff suggesting that the Japs had made up their minds to have a go." What would the United States do if Japan occupied the whole of Indochina? Halifax asked Welles. "I stated that the President had authorized me to say that in the event that Japan now took any overt step through force or the exercise of pressure to conquer or to acquire alien territories in the Far East, the Government of the United States would immediately impose various embargoes, both economic and financial, which measures had been under consideration for some time past and which had been held in abeyance for reasons which were well-known to the Ambassador." What if Japan attacked Siberia? The answer was the same, said Welles. Both men were in a somber, reflective mood. It was quite clear, said Halifax, that neither Britain nor the United States wanted war with Japan "if that could possibly be avoided, provided the legitimate rights and interests of both Governments were respected and maintained."

Halifax's report that the United States intended to respond to a Japanese move into Indochina by an embargo on oil, metals, and cotton—everything, in fact, but foodstuffs—upset the British. "Complete economic embargo" would force the issue, the foreign office telegraphed Halifax, and compel Japan either to reverse its policy or to push southward. Was the United States prepared to give the Netherlands East Indies and the British "fullest support in the event of Japan's taking the wrong course?" The British also were perturbed by the president's view, as reported by Halifax, that "neither they nor we could fight a war simultaneously in the Atlantic and the Pacific Ocean and that if that situation developed, we should have to say to Japan that we were busy at the moment with Germany and Europe, but they should make no mistake that when we had finished with the most pressing tasks we should clear up our differences with them later."

Welles sought to allay British fears that an embargo would precipitate Japan into the Netherlands East Indies. There was such a possibility but he "did not rate it very high." Japan had a twelve-month stock of oil. It was bogged down in China. It had to stand guard against Russia in the north. The United States general staff did not think Japan "likely to embark on a major adventure in East Indies." Halifax also saw Roosevelt that day and showed him British intelligence reports of renewed Japanese penetration of Indochina. "About 7 [o'clock] we got Japanese intercepts showing the monkeys have decided to seize bases in Indo-China by the 20th," recorded Cadogan in July. Roosevelt's reaction to this news seemed to the British disconcertingly relaxed. The president thought that the "gaining of time was the principal purpose to which our efforts ought to be directed. He did not believe the Japanese would launch into any large-scale adventure at this moment, although he also agreed with me that by establishing themselves in Indo-China they would be better placed for undertaking any adventure that might seem possible later on." As to this, Roosevelt thought that even if they did get into Indochina, "it would not be a very difficult job for the United States and British Governments acting together, when relieved of their European anxieties, to make it impossible for the Japanese to maintain themselves there."[7]

In mid-July, Konoye reconstituted his cabinet without the discredited Matsuoka. The administrative shift involved no change in basic policy, Japan's ambassadors were informed in a message that was read by the United States. According to Ickes, at the weekly cabinet meeting on July 18 Roosevelt said "that he would not be surprised if Japan should invade Indochina tomorrow.* From Indochina, Japan could strike either at the Dutch East

* Ickes made this entry in his diary on July 20, so "tomorrow" was July 21.

Indies or at Singapore or at Burma. . . . We seem ready to freeze Japanese credits here if Japan should get out of bounds, either tomorrow or in the near future." Roosevelt still moved cautiously. At the next cabinet meeting, after Japan had seized the bases it wanted in southern Indochina, the president was still "unwilling," recorded Ickes, "to draw the noose tight" and state publicly that the freezing of Japanese credits, which had been ordered, also meant an embargo on shipments of oil and gasoline. "He thought it might be better to slip the noose around Japan's neck and give it a jerk now and then."

Since Roosevelt expected at any moment to be involved in a shooting war in the Atlantic, his chief concern in the Pacific was to buy time without appearing to back down. "We note with some concern," Eden, with Churchill's approval, telegraphed Halifax, "that President still cherishes the idea that we can deal with Japan when we are free from our European preoccupations. When you next have an opportunity of mentioning the subject to him it might be well to suggest that even in these days prevention is better than cure and that the best prevention is fear on the part of the Japanese of immediate war with the United States if they go too far." Anglo-American intimacy had its limitations. Hopkins was in London at the time and, in keeping with Churchill's "we have no secrets from you" policy, even attended war-cabinet meetings. "Cabinet at 5," recorded Cadogan. "Lasted till nearly 8. Hopkins there again. This is rather absurd, and we had to get rid of him before the end on the excuse that we were going to discuss home affairs, and then discussed America and the Far East! P.M. digs his toes in against any assurance to the Dutch. He's frightened of nothing but Japan. Long and tiresome discussion. [Eden] fought him and found, of course, no support."[8]

The British refused to give a hard and fast commitment to the Dutch that they would go to war with Japan in the event of a Japanese attack on the East Indies. And Roosevelt was prevented by constitutional limitations from giving such a commitment to either the British or the Dutch; the most that he could do was to hint. On July 24, in the course of a conversation with Admiral Nomura in which Roosevelt proposed the "neutralization" of Indochina and threatened an oil embargo if Japan did not agree, he also cautioned Japan against any attempt to seize oil by force in the Netherlands East Indies. If Japan did so, "the Dutch would, without the shadow of a doubt, resist, the British would immediately come to their assistance, war would then result between Japan, the British and the Dutch, and in view of our policy of assisting Great Britain, an exceedingly serious situation would immediately result."

Roosevelt cabled Hopkins on July 26:

Tell Former Naval Person our concurrent action in regard to Japan is, I think, bearing fruit. I hear their Government much upset and no conclusive future policy has been determined on. Tell him also in great confidence that I have suggested to Nomura that Indochina be neutralized by Britain, Dutch, Chinese, Japan and ourselves, placing Indochina somewhat in status of Switzerland. Japan to get rice and fertilizer but all on condition that Japan withdraw armed forces from Indochina in toto. I have had no answer yet. When it comes in it will probably be unfavorable but we have made at least one more effort to avoid Japanese expansion to South Pacific.

Veiled hints that the United States might go to war were not enough of a guarantee for Britain's dominions, especially Australia and New Zealand. "These stupid Dominions," fumed Cadogan, "of course get cold feet, & don't want to freeze Japanese assets without an assurance of support from U.S. They *must* know that they can't *get* this." It was London's view that "the United States Government, will in fact be compelled to support us if need arises. It is clear that if the Japanese are provoked to extreme measures, it will be a result of the drastic action taken by the United States and not of our cooperation therein. Both by reason of the general war policy of the United States towards us and their special interest in the Far East we do not believe that they would find it possible not to give us their full support."

This was insufficient for Prime Minister Menzies of Australia. "If the Americans feel in their hearts that, in the event of war-like retaliation by Japan, they could not remain aloof from the conflict, surely they can be made to see that a plain indication by them to Japan at this stage would probably avoid war."

The Japanese meanwhile, scarcely pausing to consolidate the bases they had seized in Indochina, began to demand bases from Thailand, bases that would have brought them that much closer to Singapore and the Dutch East Indies. Halifax was instructed to point out to Roosevelt that, in light of the Indochinese experience, "any warning, if it is to be effective, must be given before the Japanese are committed to any forward step" and that the British were prepared to take parallel action. Halifax sought to reassure London. The president and his advisers were alert to the dangers to the British in the Far East. But Roosevelt's constitutional difficulties were "very real and mean that if the President were to give us an assurance of support, he might be in fact unable to implement it owing to Congressional opposition or obstruction." But London should bear in mind that a war with Japan "would be much more readily accepted than a war with Germany, and I have little doubt that if we got into hostilities by reason of pretty clear Japanese aggression, there would be very great popular support here for active intervention."

Additional action to obtain assurances from the United States was postponed pending the meeting between Roosevelt and Churchill off the coast of Newfoundland. This was in line with advice that Winant offered to Eden and Cadogan. It was better not to approach the State Department and Mr. Hull on the subject. The British should wait and allow the prime minister to speak to the president directly: "He thought that the President was more likely to understand the difficulties of our position than others might be."[9]

On July 13, Hopkins had flown to England in a lend-lease bomber, one of twenty-one B-24s, part of the growing stream of planes that was beginning to flow from U.S. production lines to the British Isles. Hopkins made a list of four items that Roosevelt wanted him to take up with Churchill. The one on United States convoys to Iceland has already been dealt with. At the last moment the sentence that authorized the protection of British shipping on the Iceland route was deleted, perhaps because Roosevelt thought its announcement after his meeting with Churchill would answer British hopes of United States belligerency. The second item was "Economic or territorial deals—NO." It underscored Roosevelt's worry that he might be confronted with British postwar commitments on territories, populations, economies. The inclusion on Hopkins's list of "Harriman not policy" reflected the increasingly difficult relationship between Harriman and Winant. Although Harriman was in London as lend-lease expediter, he had also been dealing with political matters, which was Winant's territory. Churchill felt more comfortable with Harriman than with the shy ambassador, and Harriman's close relationship with Roosevelt and Hopkins made it difficult to limit his writ to supply, shipping, and production. Harriman, on his mission to the Middle East that Churchill had persuaded Roosevelt to authorize, carried a letter from the prime minister to General Wavell stating in rather fulsome terms that "Mr. Harriman enjoys my complete confidence and is in the most intimate relations with the President and with Mr. Harry Hopkins. No one can do more for you." Roosevelt wished to strengthen Winant's hand. "I want to say," Hopkins told General Lee, the military attaché, "that I have given Harriman the most strict and explicit instructions not to touch anything which is in any way political. That is the Ambassador's business and his alone. I also told Churchill that we had at the moment in England the best, the finest and most highly qualified man for ambassador that we have had for twenty-five years, and a man who is the most sincere friend of Great Britain, and therefore that he [Churchill] must deal with Winant direct and fully in all matters which had any political aspect whatever." "It is doubtful that this explanation had any appreciable effect on the situation," wrote Sherwood.

The final point that Hopkins was to discuss with Churchill related to the forthcoming Atlantic conference, whose preparation was the main purpose of his journey. It read starkly "No talk about war," and reflected Roosevelt's stubborn determination to go his own gait in the face of the convergence of pressures on him to bring the United States into the war.

Hopkins himself brought up the subject. At one of the meetings of the war cabinet that he attended, Hopkins spoke of American attitudes toward the war and of the country's acceptance of the president's decision to send troops to Iceland: "While it would not be true to say that the American people as a whole were anxious to enter the war, if the President decided that the time had come to make war against Germany, the vast majority of the population of all parties would endorse this action and accord him their full support." The president was the key, and Churchill was confident that at least informally the question of when the United States might come in would inevitably be discussed.

While Hopkins was in London, he and the United States military observers stationed there met with Churchill and the latter's chiefs of staff to discuss grand strategy. Hopkins presented the view of the American chiefs of staff that the British Empire was making "too many sacrifices in trying to maintain an indefensible position in the Middle East." This was also the view of Sir John Dill, chief of the Imperial General Staff, but Hopkins did not know that. "Our Chiefs-of-Staff believe," Hopkins went on, "that the Battle of the Atlantic is the final, decisive battle of the war and everything has got to be concentrated on winning it. Now, the President has a somewhat different attitude. He shares the belief that British chances in the Middle East are not too good. But he realizes that the British have got to fight the enemy wherever they find him. He is, therefore, more inclined to support continuing the campaign in the Middle East." But Hopkins went on to say that Roosevelt himself "has never been given a comprehensive explanation of the broad strategy of the Middle East Campaign."

Churchill left the exposition of further British plans for the Middle East to his chiefs of staff except to assert pugnaciously that, in spite of American objections, Britain would continue to reinforce the Middle East. "The clinching argument with them," summed up General Lee, is "that [the Middle East] is the one place where at present they can kill Germans." Churchill, in his remarks, was hopeful about the Battle of the Atlantic, especially in view of the news that Hopkins had brought about the decision to convoy to Iceland, and he was confident, too, that Britain could beat off any invasion attempt. But he was tremendously concerned about the Far East. He voiced his fear of a Japanese attack on British possessions there and the threat that the Japanese navy would constitute to the eastern trade routes, to Australia and New Zealand, and the consequent necessity for Britain to move naval forces from the Mediterranean to the Far East. "Needless to say," Sherwood paraphrased his concluding remarks on this subject, "the situation would be entirely different if the United States were to enter the war in the Pacific after Japan had attacked Britain." It was an argument that would soon be pressed on Roosevelt with all of Churchill's vigor, eloquence, and pertinacity.[10]

The tremendous battles on the Russian front were much on the minds of Churchill and Hopkins but scarcely figured in the discussion of Anglo-American military strategy, perhaps because the operating assumption of the generals still was that Russia soon would be knocked out of the war. A Churchill telegram of July 25 to Roosevelt outlining Britain's long-range strategy for bringing Germany to its knees did not refer to Russia:

We have been considering here our war plans, not only for the fighting of 1942 but also for 1943. After providing for the security of essential bases it is necessary to plan on the largest scale the forces needed for victory. In broad outline, we must aim first at intensifying the blockade and propaganda. Then, we must subject Germany and Italy to a ceaseless and ever growing air bombardment. These measures may themselves produce an internal convulsion or collapse. But plans ought also to be made for coming to the aid of the conquered populations by landing armies of liberation when opportunity is ripe. For this purpose it will be necessary, not only to have great numbers of tanks but also of vessels capable of carrying them and landing them direct onto beaches. It ought not to be difficult for you to make the necessary adaptation in some of the vast numbers of merchant vessels you are building so as to fit them for tank-landing fast ships.

If you agree with the broad conception of bringing Germany to her knees, we should not lose a moment in:

(A) Framing an agreed estimate as to our joint requirements of the primary weapons of war: e.g. aircraft, tanks, etc.

(B) Therefore, considering how these requirements are to be met by our joint production.

Meanwhile I suggest that our combined staffs in London should set to work as soon as possible on (A) and that thereafter our technical experts should proceed with (B).

This telegram was understandably vague about how Britain intended to close with and destroy the so-far invincible German military machine. Yet even at this stage, United States military planners operated on the assumption that the defeat of Germany required direct confrontation on the European continent with three-hundred and possibly four-hundred German and satellite divisions. The differences were not accidental. One reflected the thinking of an island people brave but whose resources already were strained and who commanded an empire that was on the wane; the other, of a superpower capable of fielding a force of thirteen-million men and women, equipping it and the armies of its allies as well. Here was a difference that could not be offset either by Churchill's eloquence or Roosevelt's good will.[11]

In the meantime, the Russians demanded to be heard. At Chequers, on Saturday, July 19, Ambassador Maisky had suddenly arrived, bringing Stalin's message proposing a second front. After Churchill had explained to the Soviet ambassador why such a request was impracticable, he had led him out to the drawing room and presented him to his thin, gaunt guest. "Let me introduce you: this is Mr. Hopkins." Churchill informed Hopkins of the message Maisky had brought about a second front. "We can't do it at present. . . . We are not strong enough," he said grumpily and moved off. Maisky then told Hopkins the substance of the talk he had had with Churchill (and Maisky's version is the only one we have of this conversation and must be treated with reserve). Hopkins put a few questions to him, and Maisky left soon afterward "carrying away the impression that Hopkins' attitude to this question of aid for the U.S.S.R. was much more sympathetic than Churchill's."

The encounter emboldened Maisky to telephone Winant and propose lunch with Hopkins. Winant was more than willing. At the luncheon, Maisky described the situation on the eastern front more fully and again stressed the importance of a second front. "Hopkins listened to me very attentively, and with obvious sympathy for the Soviet Union," recorded Maisky. "Winant openly declared for a second front." There was nothing that the United States, a nonbelligerent, could do about a second front, said Hopkins, "but as regards supplies things are different . . . what do you require? Couldn't you tell me?" Maisky, in fact, did not know. Why did Hopkins not visit Moscow? Winant immediately endorsed that suggestion, said Maisky, but Hopkins avoided a definite reply except to stress the importance of Roosevelt and Stalin getting to know each other. Five days passed. The following Sunday, Maisky was away from London on an English week end at the home of Dr. Juan Negrin, the exiled Loyalist premier of Spain, where Winant tracked him down. He had to see him. At 10:00 P.M., the American ambassador appeared and plumped on Maisky's desk three passports—for Hopkins and two aides—and asked the Russian to visa them. Maisky wrote the authorizations by hand.

Hopkins was in frail health. He always traveled with a small satchel of medicines. The sympathetic General Lee noted how "frightfully tired" he looked, but Hopkins knew that to hold the Atlantic conference without a detailed knowledge of the situation at the Soviet front and of Soviet requirements would be to operate in the dark. Did the president think it would be useful and important for him to go to Moscow? he cabled on July 25. "I have a feeling that everything possible should be done to make certain the Russians maintain a permanent front even though they be defeated in this immediate battle. If Stalin could in any way be influenced at a critical time I think it would be worth doing by a direct communication from you through a personal envoy. I think the stakes are so great that it should be done. Stalin would then know in an unmistakable way that we mean business on a long term supply job."

That same day, the "former naval person" cabled the president:

Cabinet has approved my leaving. Am arranging, if convenient to you, to sail August 4, meeting you some time 8th–9th–10th. Actual secret rendezvous need not be settled till later. Admiralty will propose details through usual channels. Am bringing First Sea Lord Admiral Pound, C.I.G.S. Dill, and Vice Chief Air Freeman. Am looking forward enormously to our talks, which may be of service to the future.

"Welles and I highly approve Moscow trip," Roosevelt replied immediately to Hopkins, who was at Chequers, "and assume you would go in a few days. Possibly you could get back to North America by August eight. I will send you tonight a message for Stalin."

In Washington, a skeptical Berle, who did not know that Hopkins was on his way to Moscow, sent him a word of warning:

The Russian denouement is unpredictable. There might be a peace of Brest-Litovsk. Or there might be a military coup in Germany with a General appearing as dictator and an immediate Russian-German alliance. Judging by their propaganda, the Russians are apparently playing for something like this now. The Russian hatred of Britain is, if possible, more deeply implanted than the Russian hatred of Germany, though Fate puts them on the same side for the moment. . . . So for God's sake, tell the sentimentalists to watch themselves. I am in favor of giving all the things we can to Russia for her immediate defense. . . . But she ought not to have anything she can sell or turn over to someone else should there be a violent change in party line.

Churchill, wrote Sherwood, was "not enthusiastic about the idea of Hopkins taking so long and hazardous a trip." It may not have been Hopkins's health alone that worried Churchill. Already the danger that American efforts to fill Soviet requirements might cut into the deliveries to his own forces alarmed the prime minister. A situation in which the Russians and Americans, because of the political hazards attending aid to the Soviet Union, remained at arm's length would, moreover, have enabled the British to serve as broker between the two, a role that Britain with its balance-of-power point of view in foreign affairs had often played. In Maisky's memoirs, Eden is described in August and September as offering Britain's good offices in obtaining lend-lease aid from the United States for Russia. An unpleasant business that Hopkins had to investigate while he was in London was the persistent rumor that the British were re-exporting lend-lease materials in commercial trade. Hopkins took these reports seriously enough to request Oscar Cox to draft a formal presidential statement reminding Churchill that the Lend-Lease Act required United States consent for any retransfer of lend-lease articles and that distribution through commercial channels necessarily "involves a re-transfer and my consent."

Of course, once Roosevelt authorized the trip to Russia, Churchill did everything to expedite the arrangements. Having made sure that Hopkins would be back in time to accompany him to his meeting with Roosevelt, he personally ordered a PBY flying boat to be ready to take him from Invergordon in Scotland to Archangel. "Tell him, tell him," Churchill said, after Hopkins had asked the prime minister's permission to inform Stalin of British plans for aid to Russia. "Tell him that Britain has but one ambition today, but one desire—to crush Hitler. Tell him that he can depend on us. . . . Good-by—God bless you, Harry." As the train was pulling out of Euston Station, Winant hurried up and passed the visaed passports to Hopkins through the window. In Hopkins's pocket was the president's message: "I ask you to treat Mr. Hopkins with the identical confidence you would feel if you were talking directly to me." The message concluded with an appropriate expression of "the great admiration all of us in the United States feel for the superb bravery displayed by the Russian people in the defense of their liberty and in their fight for the independence of Russia."[12]

Hopkins, who appraised leaders with a sharp and searching eye, found Stalin to be a man of imposing directness. He talked "straight and hard," wasted little time on pleasantries, knew "what he wanted, knew what Russia wanted, and he assumed that you knew." Stalin's answers to Hopkins's questions "were ready, unequivocal, spoken as if the man had them on his tongue for years." The office they met in was hushed and austere. No telephones rang. No secretaries came in unless summoned. The man himself seemed equally Spartan. He wore no decorations on his fitted blouse. Baggy pants were thrust into polished boots. His shortness—Hopkins estimated him to be five feet six inches in height—and his heaviness, about 190 pounds, added up to a picture of rugged compactness. Hopkins thought him very impressive.

Hopkins began the discussion by telling Stalin, as he had told Churchill at their first meeting, that the president considered Hitler "the enemy of mankind and that he therefore wished to aid the Soviet Union in the fight against

Germany," that Roosevelt believed "the most important thing to be done in the world today was to defeat Hitler and Hitlerism."

Their first talk was devoted to Soviet matériel requirements. Stalin ticked off a list that was headed by antiaircraft guns, 50-caliber machine guns, 30-caliber rifles, short-range bombers, and aluminum for airplanes. He suggested Archangel as the place of delivery. "Give us anti-aircraft guns and the aluminum and we can fight for three or four years," he asserted.

The next day, Hopkins called on Molotov, who was equally squat, direct, and determined but was without Stalin's "quick, managed smile" and occasional sally. Their talk was principally of the Far East, where Japan was still expected to make a lunge north in a grab for Russia's Maritime Province. The United States, said Hopkins, appreciated the friendly, stable relations that had existed between Russia and America in the North Pacific, although the two countries were only some fifty miles apart. America had a stake in continued stability in the region, Hopkins said. Molotov got immediately to the point. One way to keep Japan from making an aggressive move, he said, "would be for the President to find some appropriate means of giving Japan what Mr. Molotov described as a 'warning.'" Hopkins interpreted this to mean that the Russians wanted "a statement that the United States would come to the assistance of the Soviet Union in the event of its being attacked by Japan." The Russians clearly were not constrained by their recent alliance with Hitler against putting forward maximum demands.

That became even more evident at Hopkins's next and final session with Stalin, a three-hour meeting of the two alone except for Maxim Litvinov, who, having disappeared during the period of the Nazi-Soviet pact, suddenly re-emerged to serve as interpreter. At Hopkins's request, Stalin first gave his appreciation and analysis of the war with Germany. The latter had 232 divisions at the front and could mobilize 300; the Russians had 240 at the front, with 20 in reserve, and could mobilize 350. Germany had underestimated the strength of the Russian army and soon would have to go on the defensive. The tank deployment was immense. Stalin thought Germany had some 30,000 tanks, compared to Russia's 24,000. "The tank losses on both sides were very great but that Germany could produce more tanks per month this winter than Russia." The German air force was strong and powerful and German aircraft production was probably 2,500 bombers and fighters per month compared with a monthly production in Russia of 1,800.

As to the future, Stalin did not underrate the German army, but thought that "it would be difficult for the Germans to operate offensively much after the 1st of September, when the heavy rains will begin." The German soldier, moreover, was tired and had no stomach for the offensive. "Mr. Stalin expressed repeatedly his confidence that the Russian lines would hold within 100 kilometers of their present position." After Hopkins conveyed Stalin's review of the military situation to Roosevelt and Churchill, both men were less inclined to credit predictions of an early Russian collapse.

The second part of Hopkins's report related to the desirability of convening a three-power conference to deal with long-range supply problems. "I told him that I knew that our Government, and I believed the British Government, would be unwilling to send any heavy munitions, such as tanks aircraft and anti-aircraft guns, to the Russian front unless and until a conference had been held between our three Governments, at which the relative strategic interests of each front, as well as the interests of our several countries, [were] fully and jointly explored." Stalin indicated he would receive such a proposal sympathetically.

Part Three of Hopkins's report was marked "For the President Only":

Stalin said Hitler's greatest weakness was found in the vast number of oppressed people who hate Hitler and the immoral ways of his Government. He believed these people and countless other millions in nations still unconquered could receive the kind of encouragement and moral strength they needed to resist Hitler from only one source, and that was the United States. He stated that the world influence of the President and the Government of the United States was enormous.

Contrary wise, he believed that the morale of the German army and the German people, which he thinks is already pretty low, would be demoralized by an announcement that the United States is going to join in the war against Hitler.

Stalin said that he believed it was inevitable that we should finally come to grips with Hitler on some battlefield. The might of Germany was so great that, even though Russia might defend herself, it would be very difficult for Britain and Russia combined to crush the German military machine. He said that the one thing that could defeat Hitler, and perhaps without ever firing a shot, would be the announcement that the United States was going to war with Germany. . . .

He repeatedly said that the President of the United States had more influence with the common people of the world today than any other force.[13]

Stalin's argument was logical. It was the reasoning of a man who operated heedless of public opinion. It omitted one large factor—that Roosevelt, unlike himself, was no despot; that in the United States the citizen was king, and that the king was not yet persuaded it was "inevitable," as Stalin had put it, that America "should finally come to grips with Hitler on some battlefield." In fact, even as Roosevelt and Churchill were steaming to their rendezvous at Placentia Bay in Newfoundland, the United States Congress was moving toward a vote on legislation to extend the draft from one year to two, without whose passage General Marshall's armies would melt away. The isolationists were mustering their greatest display of strength since the war began, and in the training camps, selectees, as their year of service drew to an end, were defiantly chalking up on walls "O.H.I.O." meaning "over the hills in October."

What gave new power to the isolationists were British statements that touched the neuralgic nerve in the American body politic. Asked whether the tools appealed for by Churchill in February would insure victory, General Wavell, the retiring commander in the Middle East, replied, "No, undoubtedly we shall need manpower if the war continues long enough, and I have no doubt it will. We shall have to have planes, tanks, munitions, transports and, finally, men. . . . The sooner the better. I suppose you will be able to equip any number of men for anywhere in the world." And General Auchinleck, who had replaced Wavell and whom Churchill described to Roosevelt as a commander who "will infuse a new energy and precision into the defence of the Nile Valley," was no less forthright: "We certainly are going to need American manpower, just as we did in the last war."

"A certain disturbance," Halifax cabled the foreign office,

has been caused here by what Wavell and Auchinleck are alleged to have said about the necessity of AEF to assure victory. Owing to their coincidence with arrival of troops in Iceland and General Marshall's proposals that selective service recruits be allowed to be used outside the Western Hemisphere, these alleged statements have attracted added attention. The difference from the Prime Minister's views as expressed in the tools and the job speech has not, of course, escaped attention and will no doubt be used. I should be glad to know whether there is any change in the view of His Majesty's Government as expressed by Prime Minister. You will appreciate that incautious expression of opinion can still do much mischief here.

"As regards the Enquiry in the last sentence," John Balfour of the American department minuted, "we should presumably reassure the Ambassador that His Majesty's Government abide by the Prime Minister's statement Although we shall require many thousands of American technicians alone if we are to finish the job adequately, I agree that the process of enlightenment must be left to the Americans." Although General Marshall abandoned the effort to lift the restrictions on the use of selectees outside of the Western Hemisphere and warned Congress that failure to extend the draft "might well involve a national tragedy," it survived by only one vote.[14]

Until Pearl Harbor, neither the process of enlightenment nor the march of events would persuade half the nation—perhaps more—to approve entrance into the war, not to mention an American expeditionary force. In the circumstances, what was the president's obligation when he believed the life of the nation to be at stake? Was his duty under the Constitution to defer to Congress in the declaration of war superseded by a higher duty of national self-preservation? He did not, as we have seen, answer this question lightly. Thus far, public opinion had sustained him in all the steps that he had taken, nor had the opposition in Congress been able to muster a vote of repudiation. But severer tests were ahead.

Chapter Twenty-three

"How near is America to war?"

Y OU'D HAVE THOUGHT he was being carried up into the heavens to meet God." So Hopkins described Churchill's state of mind as the *Prince of Wales,* one of Britain's most modern battleships, carried the prime minister and his entourage to his rendezvous with Roosevelt in Placentia Bay. The meeting mattered to Churchill enormously, and he was anxious about how he and the president would hit it off. "He had firmly determined from 1940 onwards that nothing must stand in the way of his friendship for the President on which so much depended," wrote Sir Ian Jacob, a member of the little band of private secretaries and staff around Churchill known as the "secret circle." Churchill had studied Roosevelt's mind, and his lengthy messages to the president had been acts of courtship as well as expressions of policy, so that when Roosevelt began his letters with the salutation "Dear Prime Minister" in reply to his "My dear Mr. President," like some young swain Churchill worried whether it was lack of warmth until assured it was only American usage. "I wonder if he will like me," Churchill said to Harriman before the meeting, a query that changed to the present tense "Does he like me?" during the meetings when he thought he might have pressed Roosevelt too hard.

As the *Prince of Wales,* escorted by a covey of destroyers, progressed across the North Atlantic, the "former naval person" cabled to the president:

Harry returned dead-beat from Russia, but is lively again now. We shall get him in fine trim on the voyage. We are just off. It is twenty-seven years ago today that Huns began their last war. We must make a good job of it this time. Twice ought to be enough. Look forward so much to our meeting. Kindest regards.

He did not believe that the president would have asked for the meeting, Churchill informed the dominion prime ministers, "unless he contemplated some further forward step." The forward step that was always in Churchill's mind was to associate the United States with Britain as a cobelligerent. The meeting itself, expressive as it was of the closeness of the two English-speaking democracies, would have, when it became known, an uplifting effect on the spirits of the English people. But after two years of war, the British were tired. Understandably, they were asking: How will it end? "What they want are facts indicating how we are to beat the Germans," wrote Nicolson after the defeats in North Africa and Greece. What hope was there for victory unless the United States came in? The symbolic value of Argentia, which was the site of the U.S. naval base in Newfoundland where the meeting was to be held, would be quickly deflated unless Churchill was able to answer the question uppermost in British minds: "How near is the United States to war?" Yet that was the one subject, Hopkins had cautioned the prime minister, that the president did *not* want to discuss.[1]

Roosevelt's feelings, as he secretly transferred off Martha's Vineyard from the presidential yacht *Potomac* to the cruiser *Augusta* for the journey to Placentia Bay, are mostly conjecture. There was admiration for Churchill, of course, and gratitude for a policy that dovetailed so well with his own. There was, too, some jealousy, inevitably, of Churchill's powers as orator and writer and perhaps, as a consequence, a readiness to worry over Churchill's "reactionary imperialist attitudes," a disquiet that had been accentuated by the prime minister's failure to answer Roosevelt's July 14 message, repeated by Hopkins personally, that they make parallel statements that there were no secret deals or treaties.

Frances Perkins was one of the few members of Roosevelt's cabinet who had met Churchill. She had, in fact, known him as a young man, and Roosevelt repeatedly would press her to tell him more about what the prime minister was like. "He's pigheaded in his own way," she cautioned Roosevelt. "He's often right and brilliant, but . . ." "Will he keep his word?" the president had asked her during the summer. "Oh, yes, I think he's a man of his word. I have never heard that complaint from any of his friends. As I've said to you before, what they complain about is that he doesn't listen to the advice they give him and that he dashes off and does what he wants to do, what he's determined to do anyhow, that he's not cooperative, that he's a leader rather than a committee man." Roosevelt had laughed. He savored the approaching encounter, to which he had long looked forward.

Not in a long time had Roosevelt had to make his views and personality prevail against so redoubtable a partner. He shared with Churchill the implacable determination to crush Hitler. That, wrote Hopkins, "was the common ground they'd meet on." He also shared with Churchill a sense for the drama of an occasion, especially for the event that moved history forward—on to "a new and better Brenner," he had gaily dubbed their coming meeting, referring to the Alpine pass between Italy and Austria where Hitler and Mussolini so often had met. But he had his own political necessities and purposes to serve by the meeting and, always the realist, knew they were, in detail at least, different from Churchill's. Although he had supreme confidence in his own power to persuade and charm, and that added to the zest and spice of the occasion, Roosevelt knew he was in for some strenuous days of argument.[2]

The divergencies, although slight, already were manifesting themselves. As the *Augusta* and its attendant destroyers journeyed eastward, Roosevelt was informed by Winant that Eden had sent for him to say there had been some leakage and very clever guesswork about Churchill's absence. Eden proposed that a statement be made in Parliament that Churchill was meeting with the president. Roosevelt quickly replied (through Winant) that he considered such a statement "highly inadvisable at this time. The President recommends that it should merely be said that the Prime Minister is on a short vacation. He thinks that any reference to the officers accompanying him would be very bad. He considers it important to avoid giving any hint whatever to the enemy. In short, his view is that 'when in doubt, say nothing.'" "I don't see much harm in leakage," a relaxed Churchill broke radio silence the next day to cable Attlee, who, in Churchill's absence, was serving as head of the war cabinet.

This distressed Roosevelt. He had gone to elaborate lengths to elude the press in order to prevent rumors of a meeting with Churchill, which would inevitably be portrayed as a "war" parley. The presidential yacht *Potomac* was sent through the Cape Cod Canal with four men sitting on the afterdeck impersonating the president and his aides. Previously prepared fake messages were dispatched regularly, such as: "Watson [General 'Pa'] got the big fish today." It was evidently all in vain. The Japanese ambassador in Washington, Admiral Nomura, for example, cabled Tokyo on August 7, two days before Churchill reached Argentia, that "the President accompanied by high army and navy officials is meeting with Churchill."

Roosevelt would be jolted again when he learned that, contrary to their agreement, Churchill was bringing in his entourage two distinguished writers, disguised as Ministry of Information officials, to cover the proceedings. He was furious. The members of the American press corps, to whom he had given the slip, would "tear him to pieces," he thought, for what they would rightly consider discriminatory treatment. He did not like being surprised in this way and presented with *faits accomplis*. Extraordinarily self-controlled himself, he liked to control his environment. He appears to have said nothing to Churchill. But he unburdened himself to his intimates, and the two writers were banned from all American ships at Argentia. He was on guard.[3]

But these jarring notes were minor dissonances in the great harmonies of the occasion. As the sun burned through the morning fog, the mist broke, revealing a hill-rimmed harbor filled with United States ships of all sizes, their decks lined with seamen that were cheering and bands that were playing. Slowly and majestically the *Prince of Wales,* its band playing and a marine detachment standing at present arms, moved to its anchorage. After an exchange of naval courtesies, Churchill in the blue uniform of Warden of the Cinque Ports, attended by his military chiefs, arrived in the admiral's barge for his first meeting with Roosevelt.

As Churchill mounted the gangway of the *Augusta,* its marine band struck up "God Save the King" followed by "The Star-Spangled Banner." He approached Roosevelt, who, in a tan Palm Beach suit, awaited him under an awning on the arm of his son Elliott. The prime minister bowed slightly and presented to the president a letter from King George VI. "My dear President Roosevelt," it read. "This is just a note to bring you my best wishes, and to say how glad I am that you have an opportunity at last of getting to know my Prime Minister. I am sure that you will agree that he is a very remarkable man, and I have no doubt that your meeting will prove of great benefit to our two countries in the pursuit of our common goal." The president was on the level of the king, and what protocol decreed, disparity in national power reinforced. Churchill always remembered, wrote Sir Ian Jacob, "that he had to deal with a man who was not only Chief Executive of the American Government, but also Head of State. He was careful to give due precedence to the President, and he several times referred to himself as the 'President's lieutenant' at their joint meetings." But it was the deference of a great statesman who knew his own power of command, captivation, and persuasion.

Churchill stayed for lunch, and the first meeting of the two men, after an initial gaff, went easily. And even the blunder was veiled by bonhomie. Churchill indicated how happy he was at last to meet the man with whom he had had such a sympathetic correspondence by cable and phone. But they had met before, Roosevelt interjected. Churchill demurred, and Roosevelt recalled the dinner at Gray's Inn in 1918 where he, then assistant secretary of the navy, had spoken and Churchill had been one of the members of the British cabinet in attendance. "The question was raised when they had met, and it was decided conclusively that they *had* met before," Commander Thompson, Churchill's personal assistant and bodyguard, informed the foreign office. Thereafter, Churchill went to great lengths to describe the vivid impression the young American official had made on him. It irked Roosevelt that Churchill had not remembered, even though Roosevelt, in the fulsome letter-diaries that he kept on his 1918 trip, did not find it sufficiently noteworthy to record that he had met Churchill.[4]

The two agreed on an agenda. Opposites should meet with opposites: Welles with Cadogan; Marshall with Dill; Stark with Pound; Arnold with Freeman. At the same time, Churchill and Roosevelt, conferring informally, would get a feeling for each other's minds and personalities, deal with disagreements as they came up from their advisers, and give decisions when required. Roosevelt invited Churchill and his party to return to the *Augusta* for dinner, and Hopkins informed the prime minister that the president was "very anxious" that after dinner Churchill give one of his now-celebrated general appreciations of the war.

"[Roosevelt] certainly has great and natural charm," wrote Cadogan, who sat next to the president at dinner. Afterward, the tables were cleared and additional chairs set up for the officers who came in. The president, seated, made a short speech, and Churchill followed with his *tour d'horizon*. To his British companions, to Hopkins and Harriman, and even to Roosevelt, he covered familiar themes. But to most of the Americans, it was a masterly review of the military situation, invested, as always, with the glow of his personality and the vividness of his phrasing. "This was a mechanized war,"

Churchill started out, according to General Arnold, "not a war of 1917–1918 where the doughboys in the mud and trenches fought it out to a conclusion. This was a mobile war, in the air, on the land, at sea." Consequently, the strategy of victory should include blockade, subversion, strategic bombing, and assaults on the enemy's perimeter where communications were stretched the longest and where the enemy was at an additional disadvantage because of Allied control of the seas. The prime minister argued powerfully for reinforcement of the Near East, to which he knew the American military chiefs were opposed. On the basis of the information Hopkins had brought to him, he projected the importance of the United States Navy's taking over of the North Atlantic convoy route. Turning to the Far East, he pleaded the advantages of Singapore as an Allied strong point and the desirability of a joint warning to Japan backed by a threat of war in order to avert war. Churchill ended with a call for a new League of Nations or similar body to prevent wars in the future.

According to Elliott Roosevelt, not the most reliable of witnesses, the Americans, including his father, who usually dominated every gathering, listened silently, intently. "Pa" Watson was fascinated by Churchill's personality. "He had a big 'frog' mouth typical of so many Irishmen," was very "deliberate" in his reactions and speech, which, however, was "very effective." The prime minister's uniform that evening was a "funny-looking combination of civilian and naval officer garb. He had a collar on him that stood straight up" and reminded "Pa" of portraits of eighteenth-century worthies, and, something that was much discussed among the Americans, "he drank freely but never seemed to show the effects of it." As for his speech that evening, Watson considered it "most interesting." Some of the British were less impressed. "Not his best," commented Cadogan.[5]

The next morning, Sunday, the president and his party boarded the *Prince of Wales,* accompanied by several hundred bluejackets and marines who, together with the ship's complement, formed a square in the hollow of which sat president and prime minister as the leading participants in church services on the quarterdeck conducted by two chaplains, one English and one American.

"We had a church parade on Sunday in our Atlantic Bay," Churchill later reported to the British people:

The sun shone bright and warm while we all sang the old hymns which are our common inheritance and which we learned as children in our homes. We sang the hymn founded on the psalm which John Hampden's soldiers sang when they bore his body to the grave and in which the brief precarious span of human life is contrasted with the immutability of Him to whom a thousand ages are but as yesterday and as a watch that is passed in the night.

We sang the sailors' hymn "For Those in Peril," and there are very many in peril on the sea. We sang "Onward, Christian Soldiers," and indeed I felt that this was no vain presumption, but that we had the right to feel that we were serving a cause for the sake of which a trumpet has sounded from on high.

When I looked upon that densely packed congregation of the fighting men of the same language, of the same faith, of the same ideals and to a large extent, of the same interests and certainly in different degrees facing the same dangers, it swept across me that here was the only hope but also the sure hope of saving the world from merciless degradation.

Even if it was the Protestant Church militant, not ecumenical, the service was emblematic of the gathering of the forces of the English-speaking peoples. "We live by symbols," Frankfurter wrote Roosevelt in a letter that the president later gave to the press without identifying the author. "And you two in that ocean . . . in the setting of that Sunday service, gave meaning to the conflict between civilization and arrogant, brute challenge; and gave promise more powerful and binding than any formal treaty could, that civilization has brains and resources that tyranny will not be able to overcome."

In time, Holy Russia, which, massed behind its own icons, was at that moment giving Hitler's armies their roughest handling since the war began, would have to be represented at the summit, and China, too, whose anguish at not being included in this meeting was a sign that the sleeping giant of the East could no longer be represented by proxies—and white men at that. But that was in the future. For the moment, the symbolic coming together of the English-speaking peoples was an indispensable preliminary toward the wider coalition that would be needed to defeat the Axis.

After the service, Roosevelt, by wheel chair, toured the *Prince of Wales* accompanied by Churchill. Both men were buoyed up by the service, the fine weather, and their pleasure in each other's company. Nothing fascinated Roosevelt more than a fine battleship, and Churchill, in his "brief nautical jacket," as the British described it, and "peaked cap" that was slightly askew, enjoyed showing the battle-marked vessel to him. The menu on the *Prince of Wales* that day was caviar and vodka, presumably in honor of the absent Stalin, and roast grouse and champagne. The latter was good, recorded Watson, but not up to the two cases that he had bought at J. B. Spunds and Company before starting out and which brought from Churchill the declaration that he had never tasted such wonderful champagne.[6]

Welles and Cadogan, meanwhile, and the generals and admirals, had settled down to their business. The discussions among the service chiefs were, in fact, a continuation of the secret staff talks that had been held in Washington in late winter and out of which had come a "Hitler-first" strategy in the event the United States came into the war. These staff talks and the exchanges that followed them, wrote Sherwood, "provided the highest degree of strategic preparedness that the United States or probably any other nonaggressor nation has ever had before entry into war." It did not wholly seem that way at Argentia. The Americans, although inclined to defer somewhat to the battle-seasoned British, resisted aid allocations to Britain and Russia that might be made at the expense of American forces. In the event the United States entered the war, the American people, their military leaders felt, would expect "action, not excuses, and we, the leaders, would be holding the sack." They were especially dismayed to learn that the British were eager to involve American troops in a combined operation in French North Africa and to use American help to reinforce the Middle East. The Americans were against such premature and piecemeal intervention. American military planning already was in terms of coming to grips with the full power of the German military machine, of a massive thrust at the heart of Germany. However, the Americans did not say this to the British, and the latter came away from Argentia believing that the Americans "have so far not formulated any joint strategy for the defeat of Germany in the event of their entry into the war." The British chiefs argued, as Churchill had the previous evening, that Germany could be defeated without Allied landings on the Continent. Perhaps they thought that that was what the Americans wanted to hear. The British, in turn, were shocked by General Marshall's preoccupation with what seemed to them the remote possibility of a Nazi coup in Brazil and with the need to dispatch troops to Colombia and Venezuela as well as to Brazil in order to protect the Panama Canal. However, they thought they had persuaded the Americans of the soundness of British military policy in the Middle East.[7]

In any case, although American professional military planners proposed, the president as commander in chief disposed. "It must be borne in mind," wrote Mark Watson in the official history *Chief of Staff: Prewar Plans and Preparations,* "that President Franklin D. Roosevelt was the real and not merely a nominal Commander in Chief of the armed forces. Every President has possessed the Constitutional authority which the title indicates, but few Presidents have shared Mr. Roosevelt's readiness to exercise it in fact and in detail and with such determination . . . nobody, reading the record, can doubt that the determining influence in the making of military policy in these prewar days was that of the President as Commander in Chief, as is the Constitutional design." Roosevelt had already shown, and would continue to show, his determination to send matériel to Britain and Russia, even at the cost of the immediate rearming of the United States. He insisted on the dispatch of army forces to replace the marines in Iceland, in spite of the pleas of the professionals that the army was not ready. Influenced perhaps by Churchill's view that vast armies of infantry would not be needed, he moved in September, 1941, to reduce the size of the army. But he needed no persuasion by Churchill to regard North Africa as the region where the United States might first come to grips with the enemy. He had been carefully cultivating Marshal Weygand with an eye to that possibility. It was indicative of how he regarded his role as commander in chief that he brought Marshall and Stark to Argentia and left Stimson and Knox at home, showing thereby that he considered the chief of staff and the chief of naval operations to be his immediate advisers rather than the advisers to his appointed secretaries of war and navy.

But Roosevelt's interventions related to matters of political policy. Unlike Churchill, he did not involve himself in day-to-day operations, nor did he communicate directly with his commanders in the field. The British system did not make the prime minister commander in chief; but as minister of defence, Churchill conducted the military side of the war from grand strategy to grubby defensive detail. As he had explained to the House on May 7 when Lloyd George and others had charged him with taking too much onto himself, "the Chiefs of Staff of the three Services sit each day together, and I, as Prime Minister and Minister of Defence, convene with them and preside over them when I think it necessary, inviting, when business requires it, the three Service Ministers." "Mr. Churchill held all the strings of the war effort in his fingers," wrote Professor Butler in the official military history *Grand Strategy,* "and his considerable military knowledge, though his advisers might think it in some respects out-of-date, could not be ignored; apart from his political position his main strength lay in his towering personality . . . even on technical points he pressed [the chiefs of staff] hard and it was not easy to resist his impact."

The exchanges among the chiefs of staff, wrote General Arnold of Argentia, "had given the British staff officers and us a wonderful opportunity to meet and make a personal estimate of one another; it gave us a better understanding of the British problems." And one event during the Argentia meetings gave the British a vivid appreciation of American realities. On August 12, the Americans learned that the bill to extend selective service, without which the army would have disintegrated, had passed the House of Representatives by only one vote. "Coming when it did," wrote official historian Gwyer, "it impressed the British Chiefs of Staff, as nothing else could have done, with the difficulties and hazards of their colleagues' position."

One United States military commitment was finally consummated. Navy Hemisphere Plan No. 4, which on July 25 had directed the United States Navy to escort American and Icelandic ships along the Iceland route, now was amended to include "shipping of any nationality." "United States Navy is effectively taking over USA-Iceland stretch of Atlantic," Churchill cabled Eden, "thus giving us relief equal to over fifty destroyers and corvettes soon to be available in home waters and South Atlantic." The move had an additional and more audacious interventionist significance which Churchill would divulge to the war cabinet only after he had returned from Argentia.[8]

The most immediate result of Argentia, unexpected in its far-reaching impact, was the Atlantic Charter. In genesis little better than a mimeographed press release, it seized men's imaginations and framed their hopes. Churchill had been under considerable pressure to make a public statement of war aims, partly to align British policy with Roosevelt's several statements on the Four Freedoms; partly to answer the isolationist attack on Britain as snob-ridden, caste-ruled, and imperialistic; partly to respond to domestic demands for such a statement. When the president, at their first meeting, suggested a joint declaration of principles, Churchill promptly instructed Cadogan to prepare a draft, which, the next day with some revisions of his own, he handed to Roosevelt. This enabled Churchill later to write in *The Grand Alliance* that, "considering all the tales of my reactionary, Old World outlook, and the pain this is said to have caused the President, I am glad it should be on record that the substance and spirit of what came to be called the 'Atlantic Charter' was in its first draft a British production cast in my own words." This was a strangely defensive assertion of pride of authorship, especially in light of Churchill's subsequent disavowal—as early as September 9 in Parliament—that the charter's promises with respect to self-determination and self-government applied to the Empire.

The charter served a special purpose from Churchill's point of view. It enabled him to argue with Roosevelt that it answered affirmatively his Wilson-haunted obsession with secret treaties, especially his pressure at Argentia for a statement that no secret agreements had been entered into during the course of their meetings there. A flat disavowal of such agreements, Churchill asserted stoutly, would have a demoralizing effect on the people of the occupied countries and his own people, who, he knew, would have one hope above all other on their minds when the meeting at Argentia was announced—that it had brought the United States closer to war.

Roosevelt handed the Cadogan text to Welles to revise. Welles toned it down to eliminate phrases like "resolve and concert" that might justify congressional complaints that the document should have been submitted to Congress under its treaty-making functions. The Cadogan paragraph with respect to postwar economic policies said nothing about the elimination of discriminatory trade barriers, a subject on which Roosevelt and Welles knew they would have to confront the absent Hull. Welles rewrote it to conform with United States policy. Churchill's paragraph on postwar organization also was drastically reshaped. Roosevelt at this time envisaged peacemaking in two stages. In the first, the victors, notably the United States and Britain, which were presumed to be "peace-loving," would police the world essentially to see that the aggressor nations were disarmed and stayed so. This interim stage would gradually yield to general and universal disarmament under international auspices. Roosevelt struck out the reference to an "effective international organization" because he believed it was a negative symbol with the American people and with the Congress.

"Prime Minister to Lord Privy Seal," Churchill reported to the war cabinet. "The President wishes to issue at the moment of general release of meeting story, probably 14th or 15th, a Joint Declaration, signed by him and me on behalf of His Majesty's Government, of the broad principles which animate the United States and Great Britain at this favorable time." Roosevelt's draft, he went on, was not "free from difficulties," especially the fourth paragraph, which would have to be amended to safeguard the Ottawa Agreements "and not prejudice the future of Imperial Preference." He had already suggested amendments to that effect. "The seventh paragraph is remarkable for its realism. The President undoubtedly contemplates the disarmament of the guilty nations, coupled with the maintenance of strong united British and American armaments both by sea and air for a long indefinite period." The prime minister intended to press for a reference to "the establishment of a wider and more permanent system of general security." The president "will not like this very much but he attaches so much importance to the Joint Declaration which he believes will affect the whole movement of United States opinion, that I think he will agree."

Routed from their beds at 1:45 A.M., the members of the war cabinet sent the prime minister "a first indication" of their view that "while the Declaration in certain respects fell short of what the War Cabinet would themselves like to have seen issued, the right course was to accept it in its present form subject to modification on a limited number of points." The cabinet met again at 11:00 A.M., and the main discussion was on imperial preference. The chancellor of the exchequer recalled the pressure that had been exerted on Keynes in Washington to agree to the abolition of trade restrictions as the "consideration" to be paid by Britain for lend-lease aid. The cabinet proposed a substitute paragraph to Churchill, but the prime minister did not press the issue with Roosevelt. The president, at the urging of Hopkins but over the remonstrances of Welles, who could not forget Hull's fanaticism on the subject, had already accepted Churchill's amendment. This qualified the nondiscrimination pledge by the clause "with due respect for their existing obligations." This was one of those small-print subordinate clauses so beloved by diplomats and lawyers that deftly took away with the left hand the trade liberalization that the right hand appeared so generously to proffer. Welles, out of conviction and because he knew that it would not escape Hull's eagle eye, protested, but Roosevelt, because "time was of the essence," overruled him.

Both Churchill and Roosevelt readily accepted the war cabinet's suggestion that a point be added about social security in line with Roosevelt's stress on freedom from want in his enumeration of the Four Freedoms. And on the subject of "international organization," Welles and Hopkins persuaded Roosevelt to accept the more general language suggested by Churchill that measures disarming the aggressor nations would be implemented by the victors "pending the establishment of a wider and permanent system of general security."

Roosevelt would later assert that there was no formally signed, engrossed copy of the Atlantic Charter—indeed, no official text—only a press release that declared some guiding principles. Yet its eight points had as persistent and wide-ranging an appeal as Woodrow Wilson's Fourteen Points in 1918, with the difference, however, that it was not a unilateral declaration. It associated the United States with the postwar settlement and thus carried the unspoken implication of American armed intervention sufficient to ensure the aims laid down in the charter, including "the final destruction of the Nazi tyranny."

Two additional pieces of business were negotiated at the meeting. One was related to the issuance of parallel warnings to Japan; the other was related to the Roosevelt-Churchill message to "dear old Joe" (as Churchill referred to Stalin) on the three-power conference to settle the allocation of war resources to "our common effort." An exuberant Churchill cabled the war cabinet: "Your promptness has enabled me to start home today, 12th. President is sending American destroyers with us, who are not considered escort but will chip in if any trouble occurs."[9]

Like Churchill, Roosevelt was delighted with the outcome of the Argentia meeting. He told his cabinet on his return how much he had liked Churchill personally. Churchill's spell still worked, mused Frances Perkins. "When he was a young man he could cast a spell over people." He had had "a most winning way of winning people's affection and confidence," and she was very glad that Roosevelt had liked the British leader. "It was much safer for the country, as well as for the world, if President Roosevelt liked and was able to make rapprochement with Churchill, able to believe, able to take some leadership from him."

Roosevelt felt that his Yankee Delano forbears would have been pleased with his handling of the British prime minister. He had recognized some of the qualities of a trader in Churchill, he informed his cabinet. "But, of course, you know Granpa's pretty good at trading too." Someone in the cabinet spoke out warningly, "You want to look out, Mr. President. Churchill may be pulling your leg by letting you win the first round." The teasing did not bother Roosevelt. He was doing a better job of handling the British than Woodrow Wilson, he told Harold Smith, his budget director. Churchill was "the orator," FDR told his wife, he was the realist. The duke of Kent, a shy man, was a guest at Hyde Park that week end. There was talk about peace aims. The president, as realist, suggested the idea of an Anglo-American condominium. Military power in the postwar world should be concentrated in U.S. and British hands. The great powers would have to consider themselves "trustees" of the colonial peoples. But the Russians were not to be denied. This is the "tenth week" was the way the president, in a reference to the Red Army's holding up better than the experts had predicted, greeted his guests when he was wheeled into the dining room.[10]

Although Churchill was satisfied with the results of Argentia, the British reaction was tinged, wrote Mollie Panter-Downes in the *New Yorker,* with "the slight flavor of disappointment." The average Londoner wanted to know when the war would end. He now realized that without American entry into the war no end was in sight and that the charter was no substitute for a declaration of war. In higher circles, the same worry received more sophisticated expression: Would the burdens of postwar reconstruction in line with the fine principles of the Atlantic Charter fall on Britain alone? "The U.S.A. had deserted us after the Great War in Europe and might easily do so again if she does not come in and feel the effects," the king told one of his ministers.

Aware of this feeling of letdown, Churchill's report to the war cabinet and to the king on his discussions with Roosevelt centered on the question of how near the United States was to war. Churchill reached London on August 19. He reported to the cabinet at 11:30 A.M. and then lunched with the king. "The President has been overjoyed at the meeting," the cabinet minutes recorded him as saying. "The greatest cordiality had prevailed and the Americans had missed no opportunity of identifying themselves with our cause. The American Naval Officers had not concealed their eagerness to enter the war." As to the president, "Winston was greatly taken by him," the king noted, "and has come back feeling that he knows him." The prime minister gave the king a letter that Roosevelt had written on the *Augusta* that said in reference to his pleasure at meeting Churchill, "I am very confident that our minds travel together, and that our talks are bearing practical fruits for both nations." They had six meals together, five of them on the president's ship. "He was obviously determined that they should come in," Churchill told the cabinet, but "clearly he was skating on pretty thin ice in his relations with Congress, which, however, he did not regard as truly representative of the country. If he were to put the issue of peace or war to Congress, they would debate it for three months. The President had said that he would wage war but not declare it, and that he would become more and more provocative. If the Germans did not like it, they could attack American forces." The United States Navy was taking over the convoy route to Iceland. "The President's orders to these escorts were to attack any U-boat which showed itself, even if it were two hundred or three hundred miles away from the convoy. . . . Everything was to be done to force 'an incident.' " Hitler would be faced with the dilemma of either attacking the convoys and clashing with the United States Navy or holding off, thus "giving us victory in the Battle of the Atlantic. It might suit us in six or eight weeks' time to provoke Hitler by taunting him with this difficult choice."

He had thought it right, Churchill continued, "to give the President a warning. He had told him that he would not answer for the consequences if Russia was compelled to sue for peace and, say, by the Spring of next year, hope died in Britain that the United States were coming into the war. The President had taken this very well, and had made it clear that he would look for an 'incident' which would justify him in opening hostilities." The family influence on the president "was great," Churchill noted in passing. "Both his sons were in uniform and clearly urged him that American assistance in money and matériel was not enough."[11]

Churchill could say little of this to the country except in veiled terms. In his public account of the meeting, he asked the question "How near is the United States to war?" and in reply noted Hitler's technique of dispatching his enemies "one by one." Thankfully, the president of the United States was aware of this design, and it was "indeed by the mercy of God that he began eight years ago that revival of the strength of the American Navy . . . with which the United States still retains the power to marshal her gigantic strength and, in saving itself, render an incomparable service to mankind." But that same day, within the privacy of the war cabinet, the discussion about when the United States might come in was more critical of Roosevelt. Lord Beaverbrook had just returned from Washington and "did not think that there was much chance of the United States coming into the war in the immediate future." The whole administration favored it, but they were waiting on public opinion, and the Republican party was voting against the administration. Halifax, who was at the meeting, agreed. He thought the president "was perhaps unnecessarily prudent about not putting too great a strain on American public opinion. He had, however, handled the situation so well that it would be a mistake to criticize him."

Churchill voiced his "anxieties about the position. The United States public was being called upon to put up with all the inconveniences of war without the stimulus of being at war. He sometimes wondered whether the President realized the risk which the United States were running by keeping out of the war. If Germany beat Russia to a standstill . . . while no doubt we could hope to keep going, this was a very different matter from imposing our will on Nazi Germany." Someone suggested Britain, meaning Churchill, should do more to resolve the impasse. Mackenzie King of Canada considered that highly dangerous. "President Roosevelt had the support both of those who wanted to get America into the war and those who wanted to keep America out. It would therefore be very rash for us to attempt action in order to force American public opinion." Halifax suggested a statement by the prime minister. The cabinet was reminded, a little mischievously, that "American opinion was perhaps apt to attach particular importance to the Prime Minister's statement 'Give us the tools and we will finish the job.' " The prime minister's statements, Halifax chimed in, "had as much, if not more effect in the United States, as those made by the President." The matter "required considerable further reflection," Churchill ended the discussion. He reminded the cabinet of the new convoying arrangements. "This might bring about developments which would affect the position materially." "I think it *is* true that the President lags behind a bit," Cadogan commented after the three-hour meeting, "and the American public wants a jolt and are ready for a jolt. I wonder whether a statement by the P.M. would help—to effect that we are all right and can defend ourselves, but that to get a [quick] victory and to impose the 8-point declaration on the world, America must come in."

Cabinet dissatisfaction with the results of Argentia was reinforced by a telegram from the revered General Smuts: "As regards America the position is clearly far from being satisfactory. . . . We shall not win this war without active American assistance. . . . I fear that we are all relying too much on continued Russian resistance and disillusion may overtake us when America is still out of the war and unprepared and we have to face the storm alone. Our own preparations have to be accelerated but not less so all possible steps to get the United States into the war." The pressures produced a gloomy cable from Churchill to Hopkins. The president's post-Argentia press-conference statement that the United States was "no closer to war" had had a depressing effect on the cabinet and informed circles. "I don't know what will happen if England is fighting alone when 1942 comes." A heavy shipping toll was being exacted by the thirty U-boats between Iceland and Northern Ireland, which was outside the United States patrol route, and Hitler was keeping clear of the twenty-sixth meridian, so there was "little prospect of an 'incident.' " Could Hopkins give him any kind of hope?

"I talked to the President about this cablegram," Hopkins recorded, "and the only thing we can make out of it is that Churchill is pretty depressed and takes it out on us in this fashion. I told the President, however, that not only Churchill but all the members of the Cabinet and all the British people I talked to believed that ultimately we will get into the war on some basis or other and if they ever reached the conclusion that this was not to be the case, that would be a very critical moment in the war and the British appeasers might have some influence on Churchill."[12]

The Axis tried to offset the meeting at Argentia. Mussolini traveled to Hitler's headquarters at Rastenburg in East Prussia. But, for the first time, the initiative was no longer in Hitler's hands. German military intelligence had failed, the Führer confessed. "It had in fact not reported that Russia had a very well armed and equipped army composed for the most part of men imbued with a veritable fanaticism who, despite their racial heterogeneity, were now fighting with blind fury." He believed, nonetheless, "that Red military strength would inevitably collapse not later than October," and he informed the Duce, "in absolute secrecy—that after the completion of the Russian campaign he intended to deal England the final blow by invading the island." There was only a brief reference to the "Potomac meeting." The attitude of the United States, observed the Duce, "was now clear enough and, as matters stood, it was preferable to avoid any useless polemics." Hitler blamed American policy on "the Jewish clique surrounding Roosevelt and exploiting the American people. He would not for anything in the world live in a country like the United States, which had a concept of life inspired by the most vulgar commercialism and had no feeling for any of the most sublime expressions of the human spirit, such as music."

Since the present was proving more refractory than he had anticipated, Hitler's thoughts turned to the future and the war's end at which time he would "come to Italy and spend some time in Florence, the city that he preferred above all others for the harmony of its art and the beauty of its natural surroundings. This project was enthusiastically received by the Duce, who immediately invited the Fuehrer to come to Florence, once the war was over."[13]

Chapter Twenty-four

Warning to Japan

THE NOOSE of the American embargo on Japan was tightening. The British feared that at any moment the Japanese might, as Churchill put it, "run amuck," and high on the list of his objectives at Argentia was to obtain a commitment from Roosevelt that in the event Japan did lash out at British and Dutch possessions in the Pacific, the United States would go to war in the Far East. Cadogan, in his first talk with Welles, asked for a presidential commitment that Roosevelt would go to Congress for the necessary authorization. But Welles demurred. Congress would resent such a pledge as a form of presidential pressure. Nevertheless, the next day Churchill handed Roosevelt suggested drafts for parallel declarations to be delivered to Japan by the United States, Britain, and the Netherlands warning that future encroachments might lead to war and pledging the president to seek congressional authorization to aid the British and Dutch. If the United States was unable to join in such a declaration, Churchill informed Welles, "the prevention of war between Great Britain and Japan appeared to be hopeless." And if Japan were added to the ranks of Britain's enemies, "the blow to the British Government might be almost decisive." But when Roosevelt ruled out any promise on his part to ask Congress for armed support, the discussion quickly moved to a new Japanese proposal that had come to Washington after Roosevelt had left for Argentia, one suggesting a meeting between Premier Konoye and Roosevelt.

The President handed round copies of the annexed two documents received from the Japanese Ambassador in Washington on August 6th. He proposed to inform the Japanese that the United States Government were interested in the suggestion there made, and that the U.S. Government were ready to begin discussions on them, but that it would be a *sine qua non* that during these discussions the Japanese should not extend their occupation of Indochina and should not make it a base of operations against China. When these discussions were opened he would again put forward his proposals for neutralization both of Indochina and Siam. He would add the warning that any further move by Japan would produce a situation in which U.S. Government would be compelled to take certain measures even though this might lead to war between U.S. and Japan.

Continuation of the Japanese-American talks, Roosevelt thought, might result in "a moratorium of say 30 days" during which the embargo against Japan would be maintained in full force and Britain could strengthen its defenses in the Singapore area.

"[Roosevelt] has agreed to end his communication with a very severe warning which I drafted," Churchill cabled the war cabinet, "that further encroachment either in the south or north of the Pacific will be met by counter measures which may lead to war between Japan and U.S.A. With this we should, of course, associate ourselves." The dominions should be informed, he advised Eden, "and made to see that it is a very great advance towards gripping of Japanese aggression by United States."[1]

"We didn't of course get 100% of what we wanted on FE [the Far East]," Cadogan recorded, "but we must remember that it must be read in conjunction with the Joint Declaration, which will give the Japanese a jar." Churchill had succeeded in persuading Roosevelt to communicate with Japan in language that was almost bellicose. But had he gotten an assurance from Roosevelt that the latter would ask Congress for authority to give armed support to the British and Dutch in the event of a Japanese attack? The records available to scholars do not resolve this question conclusively. "We do not yet know whether this particular point was discussed," a foreign-office memorandum written on August 15 stated. The warning to Japan "does not in itself appear to constitute the necessary assurance that we can count on armed United States support in the event of hostilities with Japan arising out of a Japanese attack on British or Dutch possessions in the Far East. It will be necessary, therefore, on the Prime Minister's return to consider what further action, if any, is required on the latter point."

Roosevelt might well have indicated his intention to give armed support to the British during one of the six meals that he had had with Churchill. But intentions are one thing and a formal commitment another. It would have been strange, indeed, if as a result of the United States freezing order and embargo, which Britain and the Dutch were obliged to follow,* Japan attacked Singapore or the Dutch East Indies and the United States did not react. But if and when it did react, it would be doing so because it considered its own vast Pacific interests in jeopardy, not because it had a commitment to Britain.[2]

By the end of August, events in the Pacific were moving to a fateful and sanguinary climax. At the Naval Staff College in Tokyo, Adm. Isoroku Yamamoto was war gaming a hypothetical attack on Pearl Harbor, but the precipi-

---

* Not that the British opposed the freezing order. When Eden thought there were indications that the order might relate to war supplies alone, he told the war cabinet that "it was both dangerous and unwise to follow a bold decision by feeble and ineffective activity. We, at any rate, should enforce the freezing order strictly, and only grant licenses to the exceptional cases where it was in the interest of our war effort to do so."

tating factor in navy and army war planning was the embargo. The principal argument of the advocates of immediate war in Tokyo was "the gradual impoverishment of military supplies and resources" as a result of the embargo and freezing order, Prince Konoye wrote in his memoirs. Yet of all Roosevelt's anti-Axis moves, the embargo was the most widely supported. In 1937, when Japan had first gotten bogged down in China, Roosevelt had wanted to embargo trade with Japan, but public opinion, said Welles, was not ready, Hull was opposed, and so were most of the ranking admirals; moreover, Chamberlain's policy was one of appeasement. But the July 26 embargo and freeze had elicited little protest, even from the isolationist members of Congress. "I think the President did the right thing," Senator Wheeler said of the embargo order. "You may say that I agree with him—for the first time." And for the first time, the Gallup poll showed that a majority of those polled (51 per cent) favored a check on Japan even at the risk of war, with only 31 per cent opposed. Nomura cautioned Tokyo on August 16:

As I have already informed you, the United States has not yet attained sufficient unity of mind with regard to participation in the European war, and the President is himself hesitant. However, the people are unanimous with regard to taking a strong hand in the Far East. According to those well versed in political affairs, this is what Great Britain approves of and both China and Germany desire.

I hardly think the President will go to the extreme, inasmuch as he and the naval leaders realize what a tremendous undertaking a Pacific war would be. I understand that the British believe that if they could only have a Japanese-American war started at the back door, there would be a good prospect of getting the United States to participate in the European war.[3]

The Germans, as Nomura's reference to Germany indicates, were as unhappy as the British over any renewal of the Japanese-American talks. Ribbentrop was pressing Japan to attack the Russian Maritime Province as earlier he had pressed it to attack Singapore. Germany also favored menacing movements by Japan in the Pacific, which, it hoped, would keep Roosevelt quiet in the Atlantic. But the Wilhelmstrasse was warned by Thomsen, its chargé in Washington, that a Japanese attack on Manila "would undoubtedly be answered by an American declaration of war on Japan. In this connection it should be borne in mind that a war on Japan would, in such circumstances, be extremely popular and might at one stroke overcome the reluctance of the American people for war."

It is easy to read, as Nomura did, Britain's insistence on an almost pugnacious confrontation with Japan as motivated by a desire to embroil the United States in a war with Japan. But contemporary documents, including Churchill's, give another reading of what actuated Churchill. Basically, it was the fear that as the noose on Japan tightened, the British might be left to deal with Japan alone. As he began to appreciate "the formidable effect" of the embargoes, Churchill wrote, he became increasingly anxious to confront Japan with the strongest possible deterrent combination. He advised the first sea lord in connection with the formation of an eastern fleet: "I cannot feel that Japan will face the combination now forming against her of the United

States, Great Britain, and Russia, while already preoccupied in China. It is very likely that she will negotiate with the United States for at least three months without making any further aggressive move or joining the Axis actively. Nothing would increase her hesitation more than the appearance of the force I mentioned, and above all a *King George V*. This might indeed be a decisive deterrent."

He did feel, Churchill later wrote, "that if Japan attacked us the United States would come in. If the United States did not come in, we had no means of defending the Dutch East Indies, or indeed our own Empire in the East. If, on the other hand, Japanese aggression drew in America I would be content to have it. On this I rested."*[4]

Welles returned to Washington on Friday, August 15, and handed Hull a copy of the warning to Japan that Churchill had drafted and to which Roosevelt had agreed. Hull, rancorous toward Welles because of Welles's presence at Argentia, scrutinized its results with a gimlet eye. The warning drafted by Churchill "needed toning down," Hull felt. He huddled with his Far Eastern advisers, "and it was decided to suggest to the President upon his return on August 17 that he receive the Japanese Ambassador and deliver to him two communications, one of which would contain a warning and the other, in the nature of an olive branch," would indicate United States readiness to continue the conversations, looking toward a peaceful settlement. The less provocative wording, argued Hull, would give the navy more time to prepare and would not play into the hands of the Japanese extremists.

On Sunday morning, August 17, Hull took the revised texts to the White House, and the president, he wrote, "readily agreed to the changes." As rewritten the warning read:

Such being the case, this Government now finds it necessary to say to the Government of Japan that if the Japanese Government takes any further steps in pursuance of a policy or program of military domination by force or threat of force of neighboring countries, the Government of the United States will be compelled to take immediately any and all steps which it may deem necessary toward safeguarding the legitimate rights and interests of the United States and American nationals and toward insuring the safety and security of the United States.

Roosevelt did not consider it necessary to inform Churchill of the change in advance of his meeting with Nomura. The only agreement with regard to parallel action made by Roosevelt, Welles testified at the Pearl Harbor hearings, was "the promise to Mr. Churchill that the Government of the

---

* Two months after Pearl Harbor, Churchill, speaking to a House of Commons that was distressed by the speed with which the Japanese had overrun British positions in the Pacific, described how careful he had been that Britain "should not be exposed single-handed to their onslaught." On the other hand, "the probability since the Atlantic conference at which I discussed these matters with Mr. Roosevelt that the United States even if not herself attacked would come into the war in the Far East and thus make final victory sure seems to allay some of these anxieties. That expectation has not been falsified by the events." The statement bothered Hopkins, who warned Roosevelt that "some day soon Wheeler and some of his crowd may pick [it] up." They did.

United States, in its own words and in its own way, would issue a warning to the Japanese Government of the character which actually was made by the President on August 17."[5]

But the wording that Welles brought back from Argentia was the wording that Churchill had every right to assume was the one Roosevelt would employ. Was it just another case of Churchill's experiencing what many in the United States had already realized—that friendly and cordial words, as Francis Biddle put it, "meant little more than that F.D.R. found it difficult not to give the appearance of yielding to any friend who asked for something?" Or had Roosevelt prepared Churchill for the changes by indicating in their private talks the indispensability of Hull's concurrence since the secretary carried the responsibility for the discussions with the Japanese and his influence with Congress was considerable. Capitol Hill looked upon Hull, said Biddle, "with something approaching veneration." Without his active support, it might be impossible to persuade the legislators that an attack upon Singapore or the Dutch East Indies was tantamount to an attack upon American interests. Moreover, Roosevelt respected Hull's meticulous effort to weigh all the possible consequences of a course of action, even when in the end he was impatient with Hull's caution and ready to override his counsel.[6]

Roosevelt and Hull met with Nomura on the Sunday following the Argentia meetings. Roosevelt liked Nomura. They shared a love of the sea. Tall and amiable, the Japanese envoy was conciliatory in manner and speech. The president began the talk with a few preliminary remarks about how he had enjoyed life on the water. Then he turned to the business at hand. There were third powers, he suggested, but not Britain or the Soviet Union, he specified, who desired war in the Pacific. This was a veiled reference to German pressure on Japan (which the United States knew of through Magic) to attack the Soviet Union. Since neither the president nor the ambassador, Roosevelt went on, was a diplomat, they could dispense with diplomatic conventions and say what had to be said, which, Nomura reported to Tokyo, Roosevelt proceeded to do "in a clean-cut, spirited manner." The statement, delivered orally, which Roosevelt also handed to Nomura, recalled the president's proposal for the neutralization of Indochina, to which the Japanese had not responded, and ended with the warning against further expansionist moves, whose gravity the president underscored by falling silent.

Roosevelt then shifted to the "olive branch." The United States was ready to resume "informal exploratory conversations," and the president looked forward to a meeting between himself and the premier. But before such a meeting could take place, Nomura reported home, "the United States would like to be advised of the aims of the Japanese Government." Roosevelt already had sufficiently pondered the details of such a meeting to suggest Juneau, Alaska, as a possible site and the middle of October as a date.

Then referring to the United States embargo, Roosevelt said, "It is not that I welcome the 'closed door' such as we have today, but, since we have been forced to it by Japanese actions, there is only one country that can open the door. This time it's Japan's turn." From beginning to end, Nomura reported, the president "maintained an extremely tactful attitude and received me with kindness. (I got the impression that he was undoubtedly thrilled at the reception given by the British people to the joint British-American peace terms which he had succeeded in getting from Churchill in his conversations with him during the past few days. . . . In addition, some 14 or 15 days of life at sea, which he likes so well, have left him in the best of spirits.)"

The Sunday meeting impressed Nomura, as it was intended to do, with the solemnity of the messages conveyed. But the ambassador also concluded that Roosevelt genuinely favored a meeting with Konoye "on certain conditions."[7]

He had spoken to the Japanese Ambassador, Roosevelt informed Halifax the next day, along the lines agreed on with the prime minister. And to Churchill the president cabled that he had given Nomura a statement "no less vigorous than" and "substantially similar" to that discussed at Argentia. But it was not until August 22 that the actual text of the president's warning was turned over to the British. Roosevelt also gave Halifax the gist of the rest of his talk with Nomura—that he was ready to resume discussions and would be glad to meet with Konoye provided the Japanese did nothing to disturb the status quo. "The President did not expect much to come of this proposal as he thought Japanese policy was being mainly influenced by progress of German-Russian battles rather than by regard for the United States. Welles took a rather different view and was disposed to rate somewhat higher the chance of something coming from Konoye démarche."

The British foreign office was less troubled by Roosevelt's departure from the text of the warning drafted by Churchill than by the resumption of negotiations and the projected meeting of Roosevelt and Konoye. "However," one of its Far Eastern experts summed up, "we cannot prevent the negotiations from proceeding or the meeting from taking place and we must put the best face on it that we can." Cadogan agreed with the experts' reservations, "but in all this it is the United States that calls the tune."

"The P.M.'s idea," Cadogan advised the Far Eastern department, "was that he should on his return from the meeting with Pres. Roosevelt, send for the Japanese Chargé d'Affaires and give him a similar warning. (I think he meant to hand him a written *aide-mémoire* as well.) Things have not turned out exactly as we had hoped. The American warning with the omission of the word 'war' and the emphasis on 'ensuring the safety and security of the United States' is rather different from what we originally proposed." On August 24, Churchill's broadcast on the Atlantic conference fell in line with Roosevelt's position on Japan:

Now, they stretch a grasping hand into the southern seas of China. They snatch Indochina from the wretched Vichy French. They menace by their movements Siam, menace Singapore, the British link with Australia, and menace the Philippine Islands, under the protection of the United States.

It is certain that this has got to stop. Every effort will be made to secure a peaceful settlement. The United States are laboring with infinite patience to arrive at a fair and amicable settlement which will give Japan the utmost reassurances for her legitimate interests. We earnestly hope those negotiations will succeed. But this I must say: That if these hopes should fail, we shall, of course, range ourselves unhesitatingly at the side of the United States.

Senator Wheeler, incidentally, who supported a firm line against Japan, ridiculed the British pledge of aid. "We don't need any help from Great Britain or anybody else. We're able to take care of ourselves."[8]

For a few days after Churchill's speech, the foreign office proceeded on the assumption that the prime minister would summon the Japanese chargé and warn him that any further Japanese encroachment in the South Pacific would mean war. "Either of the two formulas suggested," telegraphed General Smuts of South Africa,

uses word war and would clearly mean throwing down gauntlet to Japanese in case of further aggression. United States of America uses strong language without following it up with strong action but British practice has been the opposite.

Question arises whether, if war with Japan does come, we shall not have to bear the brunt of it and this at a time when we may be most heavily committed in both Europe and Africa.

What really is the position of the United States of America? How far is she in fact prepared for war and in particular for first class war in South Pacific? In spite of much propaganda about American production and preparedness we have little definite information to go on. . . .

We should take most serious view of situation in Europe next winter and Spring when Russia may be practically out of war and full blast of German attack may be launched against us alone. Before using provocative language to Japan we should make quite sure of America's fullest active support in war.

"I certainly think we must consult Washington," Cadogan advised, "if (as I think we should) we propose to adhere to the original formula, as Washington *may* think we are getting ahead of them." British minister Sir Ronald Campbell on August 30 did show Hull two alternative drafts of the warning Churchill intended to give Japan. "I went over the situation in the Far East with Sir Ronald," wrote Hull, "particularly the domestic political situation in Japan which I thought in an explosive stage so that his Government could form its own conclusions about presenting its ultimatum at this time." The idea of a warning was gradually abandoned. The Japanese are in "one of their hesitation periods," Admiral Stark wrote Admiral Hart, who was in command in the Philippines.

The new round of talks with the Japanese proceeded throughout September and caused the British, the Chinese, and the Germans almost as much uneasiness as the spring talks had. "It is inevitable that we and the Chinese should feel misgivings about these talks both because they are going on at all and because we are being kept in the dark as to their progress," noted Ashley Clarke of the Far Eastern department in mid-September. When Halifax, after a long talk with Hull at the end of September, got the impression that if the United States could get the Japanese to agree to evacuate China it would not quarrel about Manchukuo, Cadogan cautioned his rebellious aides: "We are committed to letting the Americans conduct these 'exploratory talks.' Mr. Roosevelt obtained the Prime Minister's consent to them, and said at the time—as Mr. Hull says now—that he didn't expect to gain much except time from them. We can always make suggestions or utter warnings, but I agree that we must not take up the point about Manchukuo." Eden concurred: "We must let Americans play this hand, and I would not give them advice about Manchukuo."[9]

In Tokyo, with the departure of Matsuoka from the foreign ministry, the German ambassador Gen. Eugen Ott had found himself kept largely in the dark as to the real intentions of the group surrounding Prince Konoye. Was Japan departing from the policy that had been laid down at the imperial conference in July? Ott wanted to know. That conference had resolved on an advance into the "Southern Regions" and a settlement of "the Soviet Question as well . . . no matter what obstacles may be encountered." There had been no change in policy, Deputy Foreign Minister Eiji Amau assured him. But reminding Ott of Germany's "mild" response to America's hostile actions in the Atlantic, Amau suggested that from the point of view of Japanese interests it might be desirable to "appease [the Americans] and bring about a domestic disintegration, rather than to excite and unify them." Ott asked repeatedly to see a copy of the message that the press reported Konoye had sent Roosevelt at the end of August. That would require Roosevelt's consent, Japanese Foreign Minister Teijiro Toyoda parried. "Could Germany assume then that Roosevelt had not made the text available to Churchill?" To this there was no reply. The major restraint on Roosevelt's getting into the war, Ott argued, "was the American people's fear of a two-ocean war. The American Government was trying to give the American people the impression that there was no danger of a two-ocean war. It was using the present Japanese-American negotiations as an important argument." A week later, Toyoda made a formal request: "The Japanese Government expressed the wish that the Reich Government may trust it to conduct the present negotiations between Japan and America in the spirit of the Tripartite Pact."[10]

In keeping the talks going, Roosevelt and Hull had two purposes: the negotiations bought the West time; and there was always the outside chance of a settlement. Roosevelt placed more emphasis on the first, Hull on the second. The latter complained to Breckinridge Long on August 30 that the "distinct progress" he had made in his talks with Nomura had been imperiled by the decisions reached at the Atlantic conference. If Roosevelt's commitment to Churchill at Argentia had been carried out, it would, in Hull's view, have "upset the whole program." He still had hopes for a Far Eastern settlement, he went on. "It was a hope—distinctly—but real progress had been made on two of the points and the third was having heavy going. . . . I was left with the impression it was the withdrawal from China that was the hardest."

The Japanese had, indeed, indicated a readiness to freeze expansionist troop movements, to make an "independent" interpretation of their obligations under the Tripartite Pact, and to guarantee nondiscriminatory economic treatment. The sticking point was the evacuation of China. "Despite Japan's insistence that she cannot alter her policy towards China," Nomura cabled Tokyo on August 29, "the United States Government is unwilling to seek adjustments in Japanese-American relations at the expense of existing American-Chinese relations."

Konoye was persuaded that the United States now meant what it said and that there would be no further appeasement. Sumner Welles described the prince as a "highly civilized Japanese statesman, weak and vacillating in character" who "must have appreciated far more accurately than any of his colleagues the tremendous odds Japan would face if she gambled on war with the United States." Konoye genuinely wanted a conference with Roosevelt as a way out of a catastrophic Japanese-American war. But the army tied his hands. It would not agree to withdraw from China and, at the beginning of September at a conference in the Imperial presence, gave the premier a dead-line of six weeks in which to get an agreement with Roosevelt during which time Japan would prepare for the opening of hostilities with America. What was "the probable length of hostilities in case of a Japanese-American war?" the emperor asked army chief of staff Gen. Hajime Sugiyama. "The Chief of Staff replied that he believed operations in the South Pacific could be disposed of in three months." The emperor then reminded the general that in 1937 the latter had informed the throne that the China incident "would be disposed of in about one month." In great trepidation, Sugiyama explained that China's vast hinterland had made it difficult to bring the operation in China to a con-clusion. "At this, the Emperor raised his voice and said that if the Chinese hinterland was extensive, the Pacific was boundless." This discussion, which had preceded the imperial conference, was followed by the emperor's futile and cryptic intervention in support of Konoye at the conference itself. He drew from his pocket a piece of paper on which was written a poem of the Emperor Meiji:

> Since all are brothers in this world
> Why is there such constant turmoil?

"Everyone present was struck with awe, and there was silence throughout the hall," recorded Konoye. And the meeting, which had given him until Oc-tober 15 to get an agreement with the United States, "adjourned in an atmo-sphere of unprecedented tenseness."

Konoye tried vainly to get the army to agree at least to "the formalities" that the United States seemed to require in the matter of stationing troops in China.

But the Minister of War [Tojo] said in answer to this, "The problem of the station-ing of troops in itself means the life of the Army and we shall not be able to make any concessions at all." I said, "At this time isn't it all right to forget about the glory but to take the fruits; perform the formalities as America wants, and achieve a result that will in actuality be the same as stationing troops?" To this the Minister of War did not yield and in the end, though the conference lasted from two o'clock till six o'clock, we did not arrive at any conclusion and adjourned.

On October 14, two days later, the army demanded that negotiations with the United States be broken off and that Prince Konoye resign. On the sixteenth, Konoye asked the emperor to relieve him of his responsibilities.

The War Minister insisted that although he greatly appreciated my position and sincerity, it was impossible from the standpoint of preserving military morale for him to agree to the withdrawal of troops; that if we once gave in to America that country would become so arrogant that there would be no end of its depredations; and that even if we should be able to settle the China Affair now, Sino-Japanese relations would again reach a deadlock in a mere two or three years. He pointed out that while there are certain weak points in our position America also has it weak points and that we should therefore grasp the present opportunity and get ready for war at once.[11]

Even before Konoye resigned to be replaced by General Tojo, Roosevelt was highly dubious that the Hull negotiations would produce an agreement. "Very little was going on as regards these talks," the British representative Sir Ronald Campbell was told on October 1, "but [Roosevelt] felt that nevertheless he was gaining useful time. He did not think the present Japanese Government wanted to go to extremes, but it was delicately poised and extremists might gain the upper hand." Such news as he had from Japan, the president advised Halifax ten days later, "was not encouraging," and it was his guess "that the Japanese intention would be to pinch off the Vladivostok peninsula." Halifax also reported that the president had suggested to Stalin that "if things became acute in the West to withdraw troops from Siberia and not mind too much what the Japanese did there since it could be corrected later." This troubled the Far Eastern department of the foreign office, which recalled that Roosevelt had said the same thing in regard to Indochina: "If we could be sure that he, or someone else with his ideas, would be at the helm in Washington for many years to come, and that Anglo-American collaboration would continue to be as close as it is now, we might be able to subscribe to this thesis."[12]

Chapter Twenty-five

Undeclared War in the Atlantic

I N THE PACIFIC, Roosevelt and Churchill were playing for
time. They genuinely believed that a policy of firmness and
unity would hold off hostilities. But in the Atlantic, Roosevelt, with Churchill's concurrence, was looking for an incident ("everything was to be done to
force an incident," he had advised Churchill), one that would permit him to
wage war in the Atlantic without declaring it.

"There is much doing in the Atlantic in the formative stage," Stark reported to Admiral Kimmel on the former's return to Washington. "Thank
God we should have things in full swing before long and with plans fairly
complete. It has been changed so many times—but now I think we at last
have something fairly definite—maybe." A few days later Stark wrote Admiral Hart in the Philippines, "We are starting considerable operations between North America and Iceland and the Good Lord knows if the Germans
want an excuse for war, they have plenty."

But Hitler was seeking to avoid a war with the United States. He had
told his naval commanders at the end of July to avoid incidents with the
United States "while the Eastern Campaign is still in progress. . . . After
the Eastern Campaign [Hitler] reserves the right to take severe action against
the U.S.A. as well." A month later these orders were still in force.

The German blockade was exacting a grim toll. In Churchill's gloomy
August 28 message to Hopkins, he warned that "if 1942 opens with Russia
knocked out and Britain left again alone, all kinds of dangers may arise. I do
not think Hitler will help in any way. Tonight he has 30 U-boats in line from
the eastern part of Iceland to northern tip of Ireland. We have lost 25,000
tons yesterday 27th and today 28th, but he keeps clear of 26th meridian. You
will know best whether anything more can be done."[1]

The Battle of the Atlantic was very much on Roosevelt's mind on his return from Argentia. Among the documents that he studied very carefully was
a brief from the State Department's legal adviser Green Hackworth on the

"Extent to Which the President May Use the Navy in the Protection of American Interests." It asserted that the president, under his powers as commander in chief, "may use the Navy in any manner that seems to him proper. He may act wisely or unwisely in so doing but the only way by which Congress can control his acts is through the withholding of appropriations or by impeachment." Hackworth cited authorities with impeccable Republican credentials in support of this view: Chief Justice Taft, Charles Evans Hughes, and Theodore Roosevelt. He pointed out that when Sen. Henry Cabot Lodge had sought to reserve for Congress not only the sole power to declare war but to "authorize the employment of the military or naval forces" it was Senator Borah, the leader of the isolationist forces in the interwar years, who urged that this reservation be stricken out. The brief cited more than a hundred instances involving the president's use of land and naval forces "for various purposes short of war and without involving us in war."

"Put in middle drawer of the president's desk in the office," Roosevelt instructed Grace Tully.

Roosevelt did not know that Hitler had assured his naval commanders that he intended to take "severe action" against the United States later. But Hitler's one-by-one strategy of disposing of his opponents was by now widely understood. Roosevelt spoke of it in reference to the navy in a Labor Day radio broadcast in which he again affirmed that it was the American purpose to "do everything in our power to crush Hitler and his Nazi forces." Hitler and his allies, said Roosevelt, "all know that we possess a strong Navy—a Navy gaining in strength. They know that that Navy—as long as the navies of the British Empire and the Netherlands and Norway and Russia exist—can together guarantee the freedom of the seas. These enemies know also that if these other navies are destroyed, the American Navy cannot now, or in the future, maintain the freedom of the seas against all the rest of the world." On same day that Roosevelt delivered this speech, Admiral King, commander of the Atlantic fleet, set up a Denmark Strait patrol consisting of two battleships, two heavy cruisers, and a division of destroyers. Its assignment was to close to Axis ships the exit into the Atlantic between Iceland and Greenland while the British home fleet took responsibility for the other exit between Iceland and the Faeroes.

Roosevelt himself wrote the paragraph about the navy in his Labor Day speech, Hopkins noted. But a similar paragraph, drafted by Hopkins, about the growing strength of the army and its interdependence with the armies of Britain and Russia the president toned down to the simple statement "These enemies know that our Army is increasing daily in its all-round strength." Roosevelt was heading toward undeclared war with Hitler as America's contribution to the destruction of Hitlerism, but one that he still hoped could be fought primarily by the navy and the air force.

By the beginning of September, Admiral King's Atlantic fleet was ready to take over from the British the entire job of aggressively patrolling the North Atlantic west of the twenty-sixth meridian. Roosevelt called the area he proposed to deny to the Axis "our side" of the Atlantic. It covered almost three quarters of the ocean.

Roosevelt had told Churchill that he would speak early in September, when the patrol deployments were fully effective, on the reasons for and the meanings of the new convoy policy. He was searching in his mind for the homely metaphor that would enable the public to understand the need for shooting orders, just as his use of the lending-one's-neighbor-a-garden-hose metaphor had been so helpful in winning public support for lend-lease. The week before Labor Day, one of his luncheon guests at Hyde Park was Myron Taylor, formerly head of U.S. Steel and currently the president's special representative to the Vatican. As Eleanor Roosevelt entertained the other guests at the luncheon table, Roosevelt and Taylor sat together at their own little table, discussing how to present the shoot-on-sight orders that were being issued to the Atlantic fleet. Taylor gave the president the down-to-earth analogy he needed: "If I am armed and lawfully in a forest, and suddenly along my path I hear the warning rattle of a rattlesnake, and though it has not yet otherwise disclosed itself, I would feel justified in discharging a shot."[2]

A few days later, the president learned that a German submarine had attacked the American destroyer *Greer* in the vicinity of Iceland. He decided that that was the peg on which to address the country. He lunched with Hull and Hopkins on September 5 and discussed the speech. Hull, Hopkins recorded, was all fire and brimstone and elaborated a possible United States response in language that was "very aggressive and stern" and which Roosevelt asked him to dictate and to send over to the White House. "For your private and very confidential information," FDR cabled Churchill, "I am planning to make radio address Monday night relative to the attack on our destroyer and to make perfectly clear the action we intend to take in the Atlantic."

Roosevelt made the broadcast from a desk in the White House basement. He wore a black mourning band on account of his mother's recent death, was unwontedly stern of visage in keeping with the message he had to deliver, and there was a trace of gauntness in his face (was it the strain of his mother's final illness or a premonition of his own?).

He began with a description of the torpedo attack on the *Greer,* which was based on a memorandum from the navy and which proved to be seriously misleading. Roosevelt called the attack "piracy legally and morally." Together with other German attacks on American shipping, it evidenced a "Nazi design to abolish the freedom of the seas and to acquire absolute control and domination of those seas for themselves." To achieve world mastery,

Hitler knows that he must get control of the seas. He must first destroy the bridge of ships which we are building across the Atlantic and over which we shall continue to roll the implements of war to help destroy him, to destroy all his works in the end. He must wipe out our patrol on sea and in the air if he is to do it. He must silence the British Navy.

I think it must be explained over and over again to people who like to think of the United States Navy as an invincible protection that this can be true only if the British Navy survives. And that, my friends, is simple arithmetic.

The Nazis would not be deterred from their plans "by the use of long-range invective."

But when you see a rattlesnake poised to strike, you do not wait until he has struck before you crush him.

These Nazi submarines and raiders are the rattlesnakes of the Atlantic. They are a menace to the free pathways of the high seas. They are a challenge to our sovereignty. . . .

The time for active defense is now. . . .

In the waters which we deem necessary for our defense, American naval vessels and American planes will no longer wait until Axis submarines lurking under the water, or Axis raiders on the surface of the sea, strike their deadly blow—first.

The Atlantic fleet henceforth

will protect all merchant ships—not only American ships but ships of any flag— engaged in commerce in our defensive waters. . . . From now on, if German or Italian vessels of war enter the waters, the protection of which is necessary for American defense, they do so at their own peril.

The orders which I have given as Commander in Chief of the United States Army and Navy are to carry out that policy—at once.[3]

That same day Roosevelt approved the redefinition of "defensive waters" as proposed by Admirals Stark and King. "The line which has been drawn by the President," Churchill recorded in a war-cabinet minute, "was far more favourable than had been expected." It included some three quarters of the North Atlantic and, commented Churchill, "the dispositions made by the President must almost certainly lead to conflict with German U-boats, and . . . such conflict would result in a rise of tempers." "So far as the Atlantic is concerned, we are all but, if not actually, in it," Stark informed Admiral Hart in Manila.

At a conference with Hitler, Admiral Raeder analyzed the strategic and political implications of Roosevelt's shoot-on-sight orders. "In the future American forces will no longer be employed merely for reconnaissance but also for convoy duty, including escort of British ships. German forces must expect offensive war measures by these U.S. forces in every case of an encounter. There is no longer any difference between British and American ships." Raeder and Admiral Doenitz, who was in command of submarines, wanted Hitler to amend the standing orders to avoid encounters with the Americans. But "on the basis of a detailed discussion of the situation as a whole, in which it appears that the end of September will bring the great decision in the Russian campaign, the *Fuehrer* requests that care should be taken to avoid incidents in the war on merchant shipping before the middle of October. Therefore the C-in-C Navy, and the Admiral, Commanding Submarines withdraw their suggestions."[4]

Within the United States, the isolationist counterattack to the orders to convoy and to shoot on sight was immediate, sharp, and ineffective. Back in June, Senator Wheeler had secured an investigation by the Senate Naval Affairs Committee of charges that the navy already was patrolling aggressively as part of its convoy duties in the North Atlantic. In the committee's "preliminary report," submitted to the Senate on July 29, the examination of Secretary Knox ended with this exchange:

THE CHAIRMAN: And we can assure the American people that there is not an undeclared war, a hidden war, or a naval war as far as we are concerned?
SECRETARY KNOX: That is right.

This was no longer true, but, as Stark had informed Hart, the president had put the matter "squarely before the country."

In one respect, however, the president's presentation had been misleading —his description of what had happened to the *Greer*. On September 11, a few hours before Roosevelt's broadcast, Senator Nye had introduced a resolution "directing that the Committee on Naval Affairs ascertain the facts" with respect to the *Greer* incident. Bennett C. Clark, the Democratic isolationist senator from Missouri, had introduced a resolution calling for the *Greer*'s log for the days involved. The German embassy in Washington, instructed by Ribbentrop, encouraged the isolationists to press for an investigation. "Introduction of the resolution was purposely so timed as to cause embarrassment to Roosevelt and give him no time for any countermove," reported Thomsen.

"Clearly," said Nye in a comment on Roosevelt's speech after it was delivered, "we are going to have convoys irrespective of law and irrespective of President Roosevelt's own promises and assurances. This means definitely that we are nearer to a shooting war by Presidential proclamation. The President declares in effect that we shall defend our rights on such seas as are essential to our security, with the President reserving to himself alone the determination of which waters are thus essential, be they the Caribbean, Red or Black Seas." Eminent constitutional scholars such as Philip Jessup, Edwin S. Corwin, and Edward M. Borchard considered Roosevelt's speech "a great threat to the constitutional powers of Congress and to the democratic principles of majority rule. . . . The President has declared that shooting should begin. . . . It is authorized by no statute and undermines the constitutional provision which gives the war power to Congress alone." Roosevelt was right to protest the sinking of American merchant ships "without adequate protection to the crews," said ex-President Hoover in a nationwide broadcast, "even though they were all carrying contraband. But the President's policy of edging our warships into danger zones, of sending American merchant ships with contraband raises the most critical of all questions. These steps to war are unapproved and undeclared by Congress. That is not in accord with the spirit of representative government, and it should be remembered that these incidents are the consequence of violating the spirit of the Neutrality Act." Gen. Robert E. Wood, the head of America First, was more cutting and emphatic: "The President has initiated an undeclared war in plain violation of the Constitution. . . . The attempt to take the American people into war, in betrayal of the most solemn promises a candidate ever made to his people, will be repudiated."

But the public did not rise in wrath as General Wood urged it to do. Gallup disclosed that 62 per cent of those polled approved of the president's speech. Nor was there a movement in Congress to call the president to account for waging war without its concurrence. This was the more surprising in that events soon showed there was merit to some of the isolationist charges. The *Greer* episode had been misrepresented. It did appear as if Roosevelt had been looking for an incident that would enable him to portray the enemy as having fired the first shot in order to justify convoying. Yet standing in the way of the acceptance of the isolationist indictment was the majority's perception of Hitlerism, inside of Congress as well as out, that differed from that of the isolationist spokesmen. Educated by events—and by Roosevelt—a majority in Congress shared the administration's view that a Hitler victory would constitute mortal danger for American interests and the American way of life and that the United States had a vital stake in supporting the nations fighting Hitler. The majority also shared the administration's conviction that Hitler must be defeated. Although the public and, even more so, Congress willed the ends, they shrank from willing the means. Congress had been content to allow Roosevelt to negotiate the destroyer deal by executive agreement. In that situation, Senate Republican leader McNary's intimation that he preferred not to have the transaction submitted to the Senate for approval had been a critical element in Roosevelt's decision to bypass the Senate. It was Senator McNary again who, after the "shoot on sight" speech, said: "It was a candid statement on the part of the President of his purposes and policies *without any attempt to involve Congress* [author's italics]." In other words, McNary, a key member of the Senate establishment, was happy to have Roosevelt take the responsibility.[5]

It was a replay of the situation that had confronted Roosevelt at his first inauguration in 1933, when Congress, frightened by the nation's drift into general economic paralysis, begged him to concentrate authority into his own hands and lead. The practice of making broad grants of power to the president to meet emergencies, said Francis Biddle, Roosevelt's newly appointed attorney general and a noted constitutionalist, was neither new nor dangerous. The "magnitude of the threatened disaster," he went on, was the measure of the president's "power and duty" to take the steps necessary to avert it. But in his postwar memoir of his incumbency during the war years as attorney general, Biddle acknowledged somewhat ruefully that "the Constitution has never greatly disturbed or bothered any wartime President" and that Roosevelt was "never theoretical about things. What must be done to defend the country must be done."

"Perspective is easily lost in time of crisis," said Senator Fulbright in 1971 after the sobering events in Vietnam. "You do what you think you have to do to meet a threat or seize an opportunity—with little regard for procedure or precedent. Ends give way to means, law is subordinated to policy, in an atmosphere of urgency, real or contrived. In 1940 President Roosevelt usurped the treaty power of the Senate by his 'destroyer deal' with Great Britain, and then, in 1941, he circumvented the war power of the Congress—by engaging in an undeclared naval war in the Atlantic—not because he wished to set himself up as a dictator but because he judged the nation to be endangered by Germany and Japan—as indeed it was—and he needed to act in a hurry." Roosevelt's choice, wrote Arthur Schlesinger in *The Imperial Presidency,* "was to go to Congress and risk the fall of Britain to Hitler or to proceed on his own with measures which, 'whether strictly legal or not, were ventured upon under what appeared to be a popular demand and a public necessity; trusting then as now that Congress would readily ratify them.' "

Yet the *Greer* incident remains troublesome. Roosevelt's account of what had happened—that the *Greer,* "proceeding on a legitimate mission," had been fired upon by a German submarine "without warning and with deliberate design to sink her"—was in accord with the memorandum that the navy had given him reporting what had happened, but it was not a full description of the facts. These were supplied by Admiral Stark on September 20 in response to a written interrogatory from the Senate Naval Affairs Committee and made public October 1. They showed that the *Greer* had been alerted by a British plane about a submarine that lay ten miles ahead. It went to general quarters and caught up with the submerged U-boat, making contact with it through its sound gear. For several hours the *Greer* and the British plane trailed the submarine. The British pilot finally broke off and, ascertaining that the *Greer* did not intend to attack, dumped his depth charges in the vicinity of the U-boat and returned to base. It was only after this that the U-boat turned and launched its first torpedo. The *Greer* then counterattacked with depth charges to which the U-boat responded with a second torpedo. The *Greer* then lost contact and later resumed its course for Iceland.

The disclosures, wrote Arthur Krock with quiet understatement, showed the value of a "legislative check on the Executive in time of war as well as in peace."

Stark's final description of the *Greer* episode was in accord with what we now know—that Hitler, for reasons of his own, at the time was seeking to avoid an incident while Roosevelt was looking for one. History, nonetheless, has vindicated Roosevelt in the sense that his judgment of Hitler's larger plans and purposes was fully borne out by the testimony of the Nazi leaders at Nuremberg and by the German documents seized by the Allies at the end of the war. But after a generation of presidential wars it is possible to see that, in the hands of Roosevelt's successors, the powers that he wielded as commander in chief to deploy the army, navy, and air force as he deemed necessary in the national interest and to portray clashes in distant waters and skies as enemy-initiated led the nation into the Vietnamese quagmire. "The fact that Roosevelt and Truman [in Korea] were substantially right in their assessment of the national interest," said Fulbright, "in no way diminishes the blamefulness of the precedents they set. F.D.R.'s deviousness in a good cause made it much easier for LBJ to practice the same kind of deviousness in a bad cause."[6]

Churchill was "content" with the president's action, he advised General Smuts. "Hitler will have to choose between losing the Battle of the Atlantic or coming into frequent collision with United States ships and warships. . . . American public have accepted the 'shoot at sight' declaration without knowing the vast area to which it is to be applied, and in my opinion they will support the President in fuller and further application of this principle, out of which at any moment war may come."

Halifax saw Roosevelt on October 10 and sent Churchill a lengthy account on Roosevelt's thinking.

> [Roosevelt] told me what indeed we have always known, that his perpetual problem was to steer a course between the two factors represented by:
>
> (1) The wish of 70 percent of Americans to keep out of war;
> (2) The wish of 70 percent of Americans to do everything to break Hitler even if it means war.
>
> He said that if he asked for a declaration of war he wouldn't get it, and opinion would swing against him. He therefore intended to go on doing whatever he best could to help us, and declarations of war were, he said, out of fashion. I told him that it seemed to me that whenever he has told the country straight out what he wanted, they had accepted and approved, and that he surely must have been well satisfied with the way the action he had taken had rallied them. It looked, therefore, as if, provided he put the right label on the bottle, it might not be too difficult to get acceptance of anything he wanted. He assented to all this, but it pretty well confirms my view, which I think is yours, that he is going to move to the undeclared rather than the other, although no doubt things might change overnight if the right things were to happen.

Roosevelt still hoped that America's direct military contribution to the defeat of Hitler might be limited to the waging of air and naval warfare. He was at heart a navalist and a disciple of Mahan. Anglo-American strategy, he felt, should reflect Anglo-American supremacy at sea. German military planners, too, considered this inferiority at sea their greatest vulnerability. The chiefs of Germany's armed forces appraised the "overall strategic position" for Hitler at the end of the summer when they realized that Germany faced a long and exhausting struggle in the East. The biggest danger, they said, was an Anglo-American drive to remove "the German-Italian bridgehead in North Africa" and gain "sea and air mastery in the Mediterranean."* This would open "the way to the Americans for an invited entrance" into French North and west Africa, permit the tightening of the blockade in Central Europe, and lead, the chiefs feared, to the collapse of Italy. There was little Germany could do to counter such a strategy until Russia was defeated, they continued. "One

---

* "Some hope did remain," wrote Rommel, "as long as our submarines were able to maintain their mastery of the Atlantic, for the greatest production of tanks, guns and vehicles would have availed America nothing if she could not have carried them across the seas. But this 'Battle of the Atlantic,' which in all probability decided the whole war, was soon lost by us with frightful casualties among our U-boats. All else was dependent on this fact, and we were now doomed to inevitable defeat at any place which was accessible to the Anglo-American transport fleets."

thing is certain and that is that England, for as long as she continues to struggle, must never be allowed to believe that the danger of an invasion has been removed. Otherwise the strong armies which are now tied down in England could be made available for the struggle on the periphery in so far as shipping space permits or else made available for her war industry, either of which consequences would be only disadvantageous for us."[7]

Shipping space was indeed a problem for the British as they decided to reinforce their Middle Eastern armies. Would the president lend him "twelve United States liners and twenty United States cargo ships manned by American crews from early October till February?" Churchill cabled Roosevelt in words that reinforced the president's hopes that the United States would not have to dispatch large land armies to Europe:

I know, Mr. President, from our talks that this will be difficult to do, but there is a great need for more British troops in the Middle East and it will be an enormous advantage if we can hold Turkey and sustain Russia, and by so doing bar further advance eastward by Hitler. It is quite true that the loan of these liners would hamper any large despatch of United States forces to Europe or Africa, but as you know I have never asked for this in any period we can reasonably foresee in the near future.

He was sure, Roosevelt replied on September 5, that

we can help with your project to reinforce the Middle East Army. At any rate I can now assure you that we can provide transports for 20,000 men. These ships will be U.S. Navy Transports manned by Navy crews. Our Neutrality Act permits public ships of the Navy to go to any port. . . . I am loaning to you our best transport ships. Incidentally I am delighted that you are going to reinforce the Middle East.

Roosevelt welcomed a strategy oriented toward the Mediterranean, as did the navy. But United States Army planners, led by General Marshall, balked. They were already proceeding on the assumption that naval and air attacks alone could not defeat Germany, that only land armies could finally win wars. They tenaciously resisted commitments that dispersed or dissipated forces that in their view would be needed, when the United States entered the war, for the ultimate battle on the continent of Europe, an offensive that army thinking targeted for July, 1943. Listing his disagreements with the navy, Marshall on September 10 noted the

many suggestions that we should arm or help to arm the British, the Russians, the French in North Africa, as well as China, the Netherlands East Indies, and Malaya. While agreeing in general that we should aid where we can I believe that such broad statements [as in the navy proposals] may give the President an erroneous idea of the amount of aid which we can offer and might lead to commitments which would seriously impair the efficiency of our own forces. Furthermore, in this paragraph the suggestion is made that a large proportion of the troops of the Associated Powers employed in North and West Africa should be supplied from the United States. This statement seems rather premature.

Troubled by the Army's resistance to what a military historian has called "the early projection of American military power into French Africa" and concerned even more lest the army's long-range requirements deprive Russia and Britain of the matériel their armies needed now, Roosevelt began to press Stimson and Marshall to reduce the army's strength. The president "was afraid," Stimson noted, "of any assumption of the position that we must invade Germany and crush Germany." Stimson, on the other hand, favored what he called "the direct line of our strategical route towards victory"—that is, to the northeast through Iceland and Ireland.

Marshall's opposition to Roosevelt's preoccupation with what the chief of staff considered diversionary projects did not wear him out or result in his replacement, as did the resistance of Sir John Dill, the chief of the Imperial General Staff, to "the many madcap projects put to him [by Churchill], during a period when it was our duty to hold our own and to husband our slowly growing resources." In November, Churchill summoned to Chequers General Brooke, commander of the home forces, to inform him that he would succeed Dill. "I had seen enough of [Churchill] to realize his impetuous nature," wrote Brooke in his diary, "his gambler's spirit, and his determination to follow his own selected path at all costs, to realize fully what I was faced with."

"When I was talking to [Roosevelt] yesterday," Halifax noted in his letter of October 10 to Churchill,

he said that he had told Stimson and Marshall to make a study of the possibility of sending an AEF to West Africa. This had greatly excited Stimson and Marshall, who thought he was going off the deep end and embarking on a dispersal of effort that they thought unwise. He had explained to them, however, that he did not contemplate anything immediate, but nonetheless wanted the question studied. Pétain might die, and Weygand might feel himself released from his personal pledge of loyalty and things might move. . . .

Stimson told me that he was inclined to hold the President off schemes that would dissipate United States effort, the possibilities of which were still severely limited, but went on to discuss the possibility of the situation arising in which the Americans could put a force of two or three divisions into Southern Ireland![8]

Roosevelt's fascination with North Africa as the next area for the projection of American power emerged again in a talk with another navalist, Lord Mountbatten. He gave Mountbatten, who was slated to head up British commando forces, a longhand letter for the prime minister:

Oct. 15, 1941

Dear Winston:

Mountbatten has been really useful to our Navy people and he will tell you of his visit to the Fleet in Hawaii. The Jap situation is definitely worse and I think they are headed North—however in spite of this you and I have two months of respite in the Far East.

Dicky will tell you of a possibility for your people to study—to be used only if Pétain goes and Weygand plays with us.

I wish I could see you again!

As ever yours,
Franklin D. Roosevelt

Churchill wrote to General Ismay:

I have received advices from America that our friends there are much attracted by the idea of American intervention in Morocco, and Colonel Knox talked to Lord Halifax about 150,000 United States troops being landed there. We must be ready if possible with a simultaneous offer, or anyhow a British offer, to General Weygand at any moment which seems timely after a success in *Crusader* [code name for the British offensive in the Western Desert whose beginning Churchill was anxiously and impatiently awaiting]. This might turn the scales in our favour. The offer should therefore be couched in the most effective terms. I will not myself address the President on the subject until after the results of *Crusader* are apparent.

I have had a letter from him by Lord Mountbatten in which he expresses lively interest in Tangier. This should also be examined, but it evidently raises very great complication with the Spaniards and the French, and it would be wrong to sacrifice the chances of French cooperation for the sake of it. . . .

Churchill was holding a large task force in readiness in Britain to move into Morocco, he informed Roosevelt, "or otherwise help to exploit in the Mediterranean a victory in Libya." He was also planning a "descent upon the Norwegian coast" in order to mask the operations in Libya as well as to relieve the Russians around Murmansk. These moves might take as many as four or five divisions out of the United Kingdom. Churchill had taken note of Halifax's report of Stimson's interest in the dispatch of American troops to Ireland. He was less interested in Stimson's inconsistencies than in getting U.S. forces closer to the battle front. Disregarding what he had said to Roosevelt himself on September 1 about not envisaging any large dispatch of U.S. forces to Europe in the near future, Churchill now felt that

it would be a very great reassurance and a military advantage of the highest order if you were able to place a United States Army Corps and Armored Division, with all the air force possible, in the North of Ireland (of course at the invitation of that Government as well as of His Majesty's Government), thus enabling us to withdraw the three divisions we now have for the defence of Great Britain, besides the troops in Iceland, which are now being relieved. . . . [The] arrival of American troops in Northern Ireland would exercise a powerful effect upon the whole of Eire, with favorable consequences that cannot be measured. It would also be a deterrent upon German invasion schemes."

He was again racing far ahead of Roosevelt, who in the meantime had felt it prudent to modify his offer of navy transports to take British troops to the Middle East:

I have determined to send a message to Congress in the immediate future recommending sweeping amendments to our Neutrality Act. I am convinced that the Act is seriously crippling our means of helping you. I want not only to arm all of our ships but I want to get authority from Congress to send American Flagships directly into British ports. After long conferences with congressional leaders, I have reached the conclusion that it would be disastrous to this legislation if one of our transports proceeding to or from Britain and in British waters or British port, were to be sunk, when manned by U.S. Navy officers and men. Such an event might jeopardize our Lend Lease and other aid.

Roosevelt suggested two alternatives: he could transfer the six transports to the British to be manned by British crews, or the United States could continue to man the transports but British troops would have to be sent to Halifax in Nova Scotia to board them. "We would then transport the expedition through Western Hemisphere waters and thence to the Near East destination. . . . Of the two alternatives offered, I prefer the first, namely using your crews to man the transports." But Churchill, who was always pushing and prodding the United States closer to the edge of danger, preferred to have the U.S. Navy transport his troops. "We definitely prefer your second alternative of sending our troops to Halifax for transshipment and onward passage to Near East in United States escorts so far as needful. This plan lessens greatly dislocation of complex escort programs and delay in subsequent convoys. Furthermore, your valuable fast ships would not run any appreciable risk from U-boat attack by having to run in and out of danger zones."[9]

In considering whether to press ahead with revision of the Neutrality Act, the Roosevelt administration also had to consider "the advantages and disadvantages that would occur should Hitler declare war on the United States." A memorandum from Stark to Hull, dated October 8, 1941, indicated the admiral's readiness for all-out war:

It has long been my opinion that Germany cannot be defeated unless the United States is wholeheartedly in the war and makes a strong military and naval effort wherever strategy dictates. It would be very desirable to enter the war under circumstances in which Germany were the aggressor and in which case Japan might then be able to remain neutral. However, on the whole, it is my opinion that the United States should enter the war against Germany as soon as possible, even if hostilities with Japan must be accepted. . . .

I might finally add that I have assumed for the past two years that our country would not let Great Britain fall; that ultimately in order to prevent this we would have to enter the war and as noted above I have long felt and have stated that the sooner we get in the better.

Then Stark added a postscript:

I did not set down in the attached notes what I have mentioned to you before, namely, that I do not believe Germany will declare war on us until she is good and ready; that it will be a cold-blooded decision on Hitler's part if and when he thinks it will pay, and not until then.

He has every excuse in the world to declare war on us now, if he were of a mind to.

He had no legitimate excuse in the world (except to serve his own ends) to invade the countries he has.

When he is ready, he will strike, and not before.

Roosevelt had broached the subject of Neutrality Act revision in early July, but Senators Connally and George, the Senate's most influential spokesmen on foreign affairs, advised that "while in their judgment there would be an undoubted majority in both Houses in favor of a revision of the Act, they feel that the debate would be prolonged and that the isolationist group would filibuster on the issue." Roosevelt had decided against action at that time. But now, after the nation's acceptance of the "shoot on sight" policy, he moved swiftly to secure abrogation of the Neutrality Act's chief limitations on aid to Britain and Russia—its ban on the arming of U.S. merchantmen and its exclusion of American shipping from proclaimed combat areas. In April, 61 per cent of those polled had opposed the use of United States ships to carry war materials to Britain. Now, in October, 46 per cent favored such use, and the percentage of those opposed had fallen to 40. As to arming American merchant ships, 72 per cent of those polled approved, and only 21 per cent opposed.

Churchill, in one of his periodic reviews of the war in the House of Commons, scoffed at leaders who paid too much attention to Gallup polls. His remarks specifically were directed at the mounting public clamor for a second front, but they also could be read as impatience with his American friend's deliberateness of movement into the war:

Nothing is more dangerous in wartime than to live in a temperamental atmosphere of Gallup polls or of feeling one's pulse or asking one's temperature. I see that a speaker at the weekend said that this was the time when leaders should keep their ears to the ground. All I can say is that the British nation will find it very hard to look up to leaders who were detected in that somewhat ungainly posture. If today I am very kindly treated by the mass of people of this country it is certainly because I have not followed public opinion in recent years. There is only one duty, only one safe course, and that is to be right and not to fear to do or say what you believe to be right.

Roosevelt was a careful student of public opinion. His whole policy from 1937 on had been to educate his nation to the necessities of an internationalist policy. He had described his philosophy of leadership in a speech to the Commonwealth Club in September, 1932: "Government includes the art of formulating a policy and using the political technique to attain so much of that policy as will receive general support, persuading, leading, sacrificing, teaching always, because the greatest duty of a statesman is to educate." In 1941, as he confronted a Congress in which many key committees were controlled by isolationists and in which procedures made it vulnerable to minority obstruction, Roosevelt's ability to mobilize public support for his policy had been his chief lever for persuading that Congress to act. And when the urgency of action obliged him to bypass Congress, public support gave a semblance of legitimacy to such assertion of presidential prerogative. His relationship with the public was almost symbiotic in its intimacy, and what even to his closest associates often appeared as vacillating was simply waiting for the moment when the people—as well as their president—were prepared to move together. Ten years earlier, Felix Frankfurter had cautioned Walter Lippmann, who had criticized Roosevelt for his slowness in declaring himself against a soldiers' bonus:

He has his own sense of timing and timeliness, as I have experienced on other matters. Had I been in his place, I would have disposed of the bonus business long ago—at least I think I would have, though God only knows what a candidature would do to a man. And so he may well be subject to criticism for biding his time in the way he does. But it has nothing to do with lack of decision or conviction. In fact, it is one form that his decisiveness takes. And what has struck me in the limited knowledge I have had of some of his campaign decisions is that he makes his own. . . . I was interested in the independence of his judgment and the confidence that he has in it, alongside of the eager accessibility of his mind.

Churchill would pay a heavy price for his unwillingness to keep "his ear to the ground." Germany defeated, he would be voted out of office, much to his own astonishment.[10]

During the course of the congressional debate over revision of the Neutrality Act, German submarines attacked two American destroyers. The torpedoing of the U.S.S. *Kearny* 350 miles southwest of Iceland, resulted in the deaths of eleven members of the crew. The *Kearny* was attacked while escorting a convoy. Roosevelt promptly went on the air. "We have wished to avoid shooting," he said. "But the shooting has started. And history has recorded who fired the first shot." At his press conference, however, Roosevelt's answers indicated that it was only technically correct to say that the Germans had fired first since the *Kearny,* as the president himself said, "was hunting submarines, in the midst of quite a number of ships that were scattered—or had scattered all over the ocean." "The purpose of Hitler's attack," Roosevelt said in his speech, "was to frighten the American people off the high seas—to force us to make a trembling retreat." This was undoubtedly correct. The timing of the attack in the middle of the debate over revision of the Neutrality Act was meant to influence that debate. "If our national policy were to be dominated by the fear of shooting, then all of our ships and those of our sister Republics would have to be tied up in home harbors. Our Navy would have to remain respectfully—abjectly—behind any line which Hitler might decree on any ocean as his own dictated version of his own war zone." The speech ended with a line that Judge Rosenman, who edited the president's public papers, singled out to convey the thrust of the speech, "We Americans have cleared our decks and taken our battle stations." And in his footnote to the speech, Judge Rosenman observed that "by the time the President delivered the foregoing address on Navy and Total Defense Day at the Mayflower Hotel in Washington, D.C., he was convinced that American entry into the war was almost unavoidable."

A few days later, another destroyer, the *Reuben James,* was torpedoed and 115 members of the crew lost. In the Senate, isolationist leaders, fighting a rear-guard battle, taxed with inconsistency Senator George, who in March had agreed with them that convoys meant shooting and that shooting meant war. "If we are convoying half way across the Atlantic we have a right to convoy," Senator George replied. "Wherever an American merchantman may rightfully go on the high seas, there may go the whole Navy. The doctrine of freedom of the seas would be meaningless if that were not true. I take it that we would have the right to convoy our merchant vessels to Iceland." That surprised Senator Taft, who pointed out that "the Senator's remarks are entirely inconsistent with what he said only six months ago in the Senate."

"But at that time the free right to sail on the high seas had not been challenged by Germany," protested George. Yet, said Taft "the same war zones had been declared [by Germany] in the Atlantic."

On November 7, the Senate voted 50 to 37 to revise the Neutrality Act in line with the administration's wishes. Roosevelt knew the road he was treading. In the early months of 1917, he had been in constant conflict with his chief, Secretary of the Navy Josephus Daniels, over the same issues. For Daniels, who resisted every move that might carry the United States into the war, those four months of 1917 were "the agony of Gethsemane." He opposed convoying. He opposed the arming of merchant ships. Roosevelt favored both. And when a filibuster prevented congressional authorization of the arming of merchantmen, Roosevelt was impatient with Wilson for not immediately using his executive power to arm. He dined at the Metropolitan Club with a group of Republican "warhawks," to use a phrase of later coinage. It included Theodore Roosevelt, General Wood, J. P. Morgan, Elihu Root. The primary topic of discussion was, according to Roosevelt's diary, "how to make Administration steer clear course to uphold rights." This was a euphemism for an aggressive policy on the high seas that would result in incidents and involve the United States in the war. War was probable anyway. Germany had already declared unrestricted submarine warfare, and Wilson had broken relations as a consequence. But the policy advocated by young Roosevelt and his friends was meant to make the probable inevitable. In revising the Neutrality Act in 1941, he could not have been unmindful of the 1917 precedent.

By November 7, Admiral Stark would later testify, the navy was "in the war." The Battle of the Atlantic was now an American undertaking.[11]

Hitler still ordered his naval commanders to avoid incidents with American vessels outside of the combat zones. But "in reply to a question from the Commander in Chief Navy, regarding the Fuehrer's intention in case Congress repeals the Neutrality Law, the Fuehrer stated that he would let the order stand that all merchant ships, including the American ones, may be torpedoed without warning in the old blockade area. Further orders will depend on how the situation develops." The Germans understood the implications of neutrality revision. Their missions all over the world were told to expect an increased number of incidents. They drew comfort from the close vote in the House of Representatives—212 to 194—which showed "that there is no united public opinion in these foreign policy questions" and that the president had suffered "a rather embarrassing set-back."

In London, King George's evaluation of what had happened was roughly similar. He recorded in his diary on November 14, 1941:

Yesterday came the news that the House of Representatives in U.S.A. had passed by 18 votes the Bill to amend the Neutrality Act so as [to] allow U.S. merchantmen to sail to war zones. This is a very great help to us, though it appears the President had to send a special message to Congress to have it passed. America is not really ready for war. But she will wake up when the enemy sinks armed U.S. merchantmen.

But the venerable General Smuts was impatient with Roosevelt's deliberateness. In a "most secret and personal message" to Churchill, dated November 4, 1941, he urged the prime minister to press more vigorously for American entry:

I am struck by the growth of the impression here and elsewhere that the war is going to end in stalemate and thus fatally for us.

This is mainly due to two causes—the steady wearing down of Russia which we can do little to prevent and the growing belief that Roosevelt means to keep America out of war, in spite of his brave words. His strong speeches over many months are beginning to be discounted. If Germany has further successes against Russia and Roosevelt continues Hamlet-like to hesitate, this decline in public morale may seriously affect our cause.

In particular, America's entry into the war may decisively warn off Japan and do more than anything else in keeping Russia in the war.

Your influence with Roosevelt is so great that a personal approach by you may prove a decisive factor in moving him to action. He has let slip so many opportunities for action including the sinking of American warships that I fail to see what stronger provocation is likely to be effective.

The message ended with a reminder of how decisive Lloyd George's frank message to Wilson had been in 1917.

Another personal appeal would be futile, Churchill replied.

I entirely agree with all you wish but I do not think it would be any use for me to make a personal appeal to Roosevelt at this juncture to enter the war. At the Atlantic Meeting I told his circle that I would rather have an American declaration of war now and no supplies for six months than double the supplies and no declaration. When this was repeated to him he thought it a hard saying. We must not underrate his Constitutional difficulties. He may take action as Chief Executive but only Congress can declare war. He went so far as to say to me, "I shall never declare war. I shall make war. If I were to ask Congress to declare war they might argue about it for three months." The draft Bill without which the American Army would have gone to pieces passed by only one vote. He has now carried through the Senate by a small majority the virtual repeal of the Neutrality Act. This must mean if endorsed by the House constant fighting in the Atlantic between German and American ships. Public opinion in the United States has advanced lately but with Congress it is all a matter of counting heads. Naturally if I saw any way of helping to lift this situation on to a higher plane I would do so. In the meanwhile we must have patience and trust to the tide which is flowing our way and to events.[12]

Chapter Twenty-six

No Strings on Russian Aid

ONE DAY IN OCTOBER, Churchill summoned General Kennedy, the British army's chief planner, to Number 10 Downing Street. Kennedy held a somewhat mordant view of Churchill as master strategist. The prime minister wanted once again to review the plans for the impending offensive against Rommel's Afrika Korps—i.e., Operation Crusader. In zippered coveralls, cigar in mouth, he held forth on how the battle should go.

"There will be actions at Tobruk, at Bardia and at Benghazi," he said. Bardia and Benghazi should be left to wither on the vine. "We need not assault them, but we must be able to hold them. Let them starve—those animals. Now, there is Tobruk," he continued. "It has held out successfully for four months. And yet, when it was decided to stand there, I was told it was a mistake."

Here Kennedy interrupted. "One thing, and one thing only has saved Tobruk."

"What?" Churchill asked.

"Russia," replied Kennedy.

"At this," recorded Kennedy, "he got up and walked about the room."

Anglo-American planners still had not fully digested the degree to which the vast collisions on the eastern front were altering the strategic requirements of the war. Britain and the United States were fighting one war in the Atlantic and North Africa, the Soviet Union another in the East. There was neither a combined strategy, nor a common political objective.

Churchill and Roosevelt, however, had drawn one major conclusion in regard to the overall military outlook. The enormous casualties the Nazis were suffering bolstered their hopes that Germany could be defeated without the landing of vast armies on the Continent.*

* Churchill told the House on September 9, 1941, that "already in three months he has lost more German blood than was shed in any single year of the last war." A mathematically minded House member estimated that this meant two million casualties.

Even United States Army planners who considered a mass invasion of the Continent inevitable in order to defeat Hitler emphasized the dependence of such a strategy on the continuance of Russian resistance:

The maintenance of an active front in Russia offers by far the best opportunity for a successful land offensive against Germany, because only Russia possesses adequate manpower, situated in favorable proximity to the center of German military power. For Russia, ground and aviation forces are most important. Predictions as to the result of the present conflict in Russia are premature. However, were the Soviet forces to be driven even beyond the Ural Mountains, and were they there to continue an organized resistance, there would always remain the hope of a final and complete defeat of Germany by land operations. The effective arming of Russian forces, both by the supply of munitions from the outside and by providing industrial capacity in the Volga Basin, or to the east of the Ural Mountains, would be one of the most important moves that could be made by the associated Powers.

Both Churchill and Roosevelt were predisposed by their memories of World War I to a basic strategy that would not necessitate a mass invasion of the Continent. An entire generation was missing from English life because of the million men who had fallen in France in that war. "It's no use—you are arguing against the casualties on the Somme," Lord Cherwell* would later advise General Marshall when the latter was contending for prompt and direct invasion of the Continent. The memory of those casualties, as well as Churchill's conviction that the Dardanelles strategy would have resulted in the defeat of Germany had it been fully supported and properly executed, powerfully inclined his mind to the strategy that he had outlined to Roosevelt at Argentia —blockade, intensive air bombing, armored thrusts around the periphery, risings on the Continent, all culminating in an armored strike at Germany's heart when Germany was on the point of collapse.

Such a strategy had indeed been made more feasible by Russia's engagement of better than 300 German divisions on the eastern front. Nevertheless, it still gravely underestimated what would be required to defeat Germany, even if Russia remained in the war. It was little short of derisory should Russia be knocked out. In September, 1941, more than a year after Dunkirk, there were only twenty-six divisions in all of the British Isles. And in the United States, General Marshall was scarcely able to muster the handful of divisions capable of taking the Azores and occupying Iceland.

It is no wonder that Churchill and Roosevelt considered a godsend the addition of the Red Army's 280 divisions to the forces resisting the *Wehrmacht*. The more strongly the two men hoped that Germany might be defeated without an Allied invasion, the more eager they were to provide Russia with the weapons with which to chew up the Nazi armies. With Roosevelt, there was an additional factor powering his hopes that no new American expeditionary forces would be needed: his 1940 campaign pledge to the American people to that effect.

---

* Prof. F. A. Lindemann, "the Prof.," was Churchill's scientific adviser and a member of the prime minister's inner circle.

"Roosevelt was very much affected by World War I, which he had, of course, seen at close range," wrote Harriman, who was slated to go to Moscow with Lord Beaverbrook to work out a tripartite agreement on war supplies:

He had a horror of American troops landing again on the continent and becoming involved in the kind of warfare he had seen before—trench warfare with all its appalling losses. I believe he had in mind that if the great armies of Russia could be kept in being this might well make it possible for us to limit our participation largely to naval and air power. The overriding motivation of President Roosevelt in giving every bit of help that was possible was that he wanted to do everything possible to help keep the Russians in the war. He wanted to err on the side of generosity, rather than skimping the aid we sent, even when some of us felt that particular Russian requests were not necessary or had not been justified.

The reader will also recall in this connection Churchill's message to Roosevelt of September 1, reminding the president that he had "never asked for any large dispatch of United States forces to Europe or Africa in the near and foreseeable future," and Roosevelt's pressure on Stimson and Marshall at about this time to reduce the size of the army so that more matériel would be available for the Soviet Union and Britain.[1]

From Argentia, Roosevelt and Churchill had cabled Stalin that short-term supplies were on their way and that the three-power conference in Moscow on "the apportionment of our joint resources" would deal with his long-term requirements. To head this mission, Roosevelt had selected W. Averell Harriman, a confidant and protégé of Harry Hopkins, and Churchill had picked his old crony and war-cabinet colleague Lord Beaverbrook. Both Harriman and Beaverbrook had impeccable capitalist credentials. Both were seasoned, astute negotiators. Both fulfilled their assignment with spectacular success, even though in light of what is now known a better bargain from the point of view of Western interests appears to have been possible.

Since scholars still are denied access to Soviet archives, the process from the Soviet side can only be surmised. However, the Soviet ambassador in London, Ivan Maisky, in his memoirs, written in the moment of frankness that attended de-Stalinization, has given some clues.

It was Britain's duty and in her interest to give all possible aid to Russia, Churchill's instructions to Beaverbrook read, but Beaverbrook should "make sure we are not bled white in the process." And thinking of Beaverbrook's current zeal for all-out aid to Russia, Churchill added the admonition, "even if you find yourself affected by the Russian atmosphere I shall be quite stiff about it here."

Russia, however, was demanding much more from its new ally than tanks and planes—or so it appeared from a cable that Stalin sent to Churchill on September 3, renewing his plea for a second front somewhere in the West. This cable had, in fact, been inspired by Maisky. Without instructions, Maisky had met with Eden on August 26 and had bitterly upbraided the British government for not giving Russia greater aid. To his surprise his verbal assault had upset rather than offended the British foreign secretary. The next day,

Eden, evidently seeking to placate Maisky, reported that he had talked with Churchill, who had decided to send immediately as a "present to the Red Army" two hundred Hurricanes, one of Britain's best fighter planes.

The episode made a considerable impression on Maisky. Eden and his associates were so embarrassed by Britain's inability to open a second front in France, he concluded, that they were the more disposed to make amends in the field of supplies and matériel. He, therefore, suggested to Stalin, who unexpectedly had congratulated him on his *démarche* to Eden, that the Soviet leader address a message to Churchill "raising two points: one on the opening of a second front in France; the other on supplying the Red Army with arms and war materials. I warned Stalin that on the first question there would be no practical results, but it was important constantly to remind the British of the need for a second front. But on the second question, I wrote, judging from [the] mood prevalent in London, there were chances to get something real."

On September 3, Stalin sent Maisky the message for Churchill along the lines the ambassador had recommended. Churchill received Maisky at ten that evening. The prime minister was in a dinner jacket, "the inevitable cigar between his teeth." They sat at a long table covered with green cloth, Eden at the prime minister's side. Churchill began reading Stalin's message. "I express thanks for promise to *sell* the Soviet Union a further two hundred fighters," the message began. Maisky noted that Churchill's right eyebrow rose in surprise at the word *sell*. Churchill went on reading. It was a grim chronicle. The "relative stabilization" that had been achieved at the front had broken down because the Germans were able to transfer to the East thirty to thirty-four fresh infantry divisions and enormous quantities of tanks and aircraft. They had done so "with impunity, being convinced that no second front exists in the West, and that none will exist. Germans consider it quite possible to smash their enemies singly: first Russia, then the English."

Stalin saw only one way out, and that was

to establish in the present year a second front somewhere in the Balkans or France, capable of drawing away from the Eastern front thirty to forty divisions, and at the same time of ensuring the Soviet Union thirty thousand tons of aluminum by the beginning of October next and a monthly minimum of aid amounting to four hundred aircraft and five hundred tanks (of small or medium size). Without these two forms of help the Soviet Union will either suffer defeat or be weakened to such an extent that it will lose for a long period any capacity to render assistance to its allies by its actual operations on the fronts of the struggle against Hitlerism.

Churchill, in reply, reviewed again the reasons why Britain was unable to open a second front in France or the Balkans. To this Maisky hotly protested that Russia was bearing almost alone the weight of an unprecedented onslaught. If Hitler triumphed in the East, "there would descend on humanity a black night of the most monstrous reaction and who could know how long it might continue? And if Hitler was victorious, what would be the fate of Britain? It was not difficult to imagine." Here Churchill, sensing menace in Maisky's words, began to bristle: "Don't forget that only four months ago we stood alone against Germany, and didn't know whose side you would be on." According to Maisky, he interrupted Churchill to say, "Thank Chamberlain for that," but Churchill does not mention this. He may not even have heard the comment for his anger was mounting as his words flowed: "We never thought our survival was dependent on your action either way. Whatever happens, and whatever you do, you of all people have no right to make reproaches to us."

Maisky beat a retreat: "Less warmth, dear Mr. Churchill, more calm! After all, we must come to some practical result."[2]

Maisky had achieved the practical result he intended. Churchill immediately convened his cabinet and chiefs of staff to consider how aid to Russia might be expedited. That night he cabled Stalin:

For our part we are now prepared to send you *from British production,* one-half of the monthly total for which you ask in aircraft and tanks. We hope the United States will supply the other half of your requirements. . . . In your first paragraph you used the word "sell." We had not viewed the matter in such terms and have never thought of payment. Any assistance we can give you would better be upon the same basis of comradeship as the American Lend-Lease Bill, of which no formal account is kept in money.

An alarmed cable went from Churchill to Roosevelt:

The Soviet Ambassador brought the subjoined message to me and Eden last night, and used language of vague import about the gravity of the occasion and the turning-point character which would attach to our reply. Although nothing in his language warranted the assumption, we could not exclude the impression that they might be thinking of separate terms. The Cabinet have thought it right to send the attached reply. Hope you will not object to our references to possible American aid. I feel that the moment may be decisive. We can but do our best.

After the war, Maisky read this cable in Churchill's memoirs and he added this footnote to his own account of the episode:

Of course in the conversation of 4 September I had no idea whatever of the possibility of a separate peace with Germany. This was an obvious illusion on Churchill's part, because his conscience on the question of a second front was not quite clear. Looking back on the events of those days, I think that the impression which Churchill formed of my words at the time was perhaps almost useful for us. It obliged the wheels of the British political and military machine to begin turning more rapidly, and in particular to the granting to us of Lend-Lease."[3]

It had a more serious consequence. The Beaverbrook-Harriman mission would go to Moscow and lavish supplies on the Russians with no thought of exacting political and economic concessions in return. Fearful lest Stalin or a successor government might again switch alliances even if the cost was humiliation and subordination to Hitler, the West approached the Moscow meeting as suppliants. The touchstone for appraising the wartime policies of Britain and the United States toward the Soviet Union, wrote George Kennan, "will be found . . . in the soundness and accuracy of their fears with relation to the possibility of a separate German-Soviet peace." And though Kennan had primary reference to a later period in the war, the mechanism already was at work.

Stalin evidently was delighted with the effectiveness of the Maisky formula. On September 15, he sent another message to Churchill. If a second front in France was impossible, "Great Britain could without risk land in Archangel twenty-five to thirty divisions, or transport them across Iran to the southern regions of the U.S.S.R. In this way there could be established military collaboration between the Soviet and British troops on the territory of the U.S.S.R." He then proceeded to thank Churchill for the latter's promise of monthly deliveries of aluminum, tanks, and aircraft "not on the usual commercial basis [but] of comradeship and collaboration."

The twenty-five-division proposal seemed to Churchill a physical impossibility—absurdly so. "It seemed hopeless to argue with a man thinking in terms of utter unreality." He never replied directly to this part of Stalin's message, but explained to Sir Stafford Cripps that it was with the greatest difficulty that he had recently managed to send the Fiftieth Division to the Middle East and that he was now using "extraordinary measures" to reinforce General Auchinleck with another division in preparation for the general's offensive in the Western Desert. But to judge by Maisky, Stalin never expected the British to send him twenty-five divisions. Perhaps, too, he was twitting Churchill, for the suggestion of Archangel, the Caucasus, and the Caspian was a way of reminding Churchill of his ingenuity in 1919 in landing interventionist forces in those very regions.[4]

Cripps, the British ambassador in Moscow, aware of Churchill's resourcefulness in finding divisions and transports to reinforce Auchinleck in the Middle East, felt that Churchill should be making a comparable "superhuman" effort to aid the Russians militarily:

We have unfortunately considered the war here as no direct responsibility of ours, but merely as a war which we desired to assist in any way that we could without unduly endangering our own position. I have tried to emphasize how vital it was that we should do our utmost if we wanted to keep this front effectively in being but I fear it is now almost too late unless we are prepared to throw everything in, in an effort to save this front.

Churchill had kept his chiefs of staff busy exploring the possibilities of a serious diversionary operation only to conclude that they would all result in "costly fiascoes." "When you speak . . . of a 'superhuman effort,' " he replied to Cripps, "you mean I presume an effort rising superior to space, time and geography. Unfortunately, such attributes are denied us." He himself had called for superhuman efforts in the battles for Greece and Crete, but he had learned his lesson. "I wonder that the losses sustained by our shipping and the Fleet in the evacuations of Greece and Crete have been forgotten. The conditions are far more adverse now than then, and our naval strength is reduced."

Churchill's warning to Roosevelt that Russia "might be thinking of separate terms" accelerated American preparations for the tripartite conference in

Moscow. Of all "the hungry guests," as Churchill called the competitors for United States supplies, the most recent arrival was the most demanding. This led General Marshall at the end of August to warn Stimson that "the President should have it clearly pointed out to him that Mr. Oumansky will take everything we own if we submit to his criticisms." Roosevelt's response to such pressures took the shape of a formal notification to Stimson and Knox that he considered aid to Russia of paramount importance for the safety and security of the United States. He had directed them to prepare by September 10 a schedule of allocations among the three powers of the "expected United States production of munitions of war," so as to be in a position to advise the Harriman mission "as to the aid which will be supplied by this country." He was at Hyde Park when Churchill's cable warning that Stalin might be thinking of a separate peace arrived. It was Hopkins who replied, sending a copy of Roosevelt's instructions to Stimson and Knox and proposing that the Harriman group rendezvous with Beaverbrook and his aides in London on September 15. It seemed to Hopkins that "in the light of the Prime Minister's recent cable the sooner this mission gets to Moscow the better."

Britain's willingness to extend aid to Russia on a lend-lease basis, Maisky thought, paved the way for the United States to do the same: "Very powerful groups in the ranks of the American ruling class were strongly objecting, and demanding that the U.S.S.R. should pay for American supplies in gold, foreign currency and natural resources, or in extreme necessity should make economic concessions, particularly by abolishing the State monopoly of foreign trade. The granting to us of British Lend-Lease was a most significant precedent which enabled Roosevelt to extend the Lend-Lease to the U.S.S.R."

Roosevelt met with Oumansky on September 11 to deal with the ambassador's request that Russia be included under lend-lease. Hull and Hopkins were also present. It was very difficult, Roosevelt explained, to obtain the necessary authority from Congress in view of Russia's unpopularity with large groups of Americans "who exercise great political power in Congress." A good deal of the opposition was Catholic in origin. Roosevelt suggested to Oumansky that, since the Soviet constitution of 1936 permitted religious worship, some publicity back to this country indicating that freedom of religion was respected in deed as well as in word and that churches were open would influence the debate in Congress. This was a typical Rooseveltian gambit— using the argument of political expediency on behalf of a human right about which he felt deeply. But the Russians were adept at the game of lip-service concessions. "The Ambassador agreed that he would attend to this matter." Oumansky then turned to items that seemed to him more pressing. Moscow, he said, was "bitter about the credit situation. The Soviet Government needs 140 million dollars whereas the Amtorg Trading Corporation [the Soviet trading agency in the United States] has only $160,000." Roosevelt said he would try to do something through the Reconstruction Finance Corporation.

The hope that the war might induce a more hospitable Soviet attitude toward religious freedom was also reflected in the letter Roosevelt sent Pope Pius XII via Myron Taylor, which delicately argued the case for aid to Russia:

In so far as I am informed, churches in Russia are open. I believe there is a real possibility that Russia may as a result of the present conflict recognize freedom of religion in Russia, although, of course, without recognition of any official intervention on the part of any church in education or political matters within Russia. I feel that if this can be accomplished it will put the possibility of the restoration of real religious liberty in Russia on a much better footing than religious freedom is in Germany.

Roosevelt urged the pope to distinguish between Communism and Nazism, not as systems of government, but because of the latter's resort to force in its dealings with other nations:

There are in the United States many people in *all* churches who have the feeling that Russia is governed completely by a communistic form of society. In my opinion, the fact is that Russia is governed by a dictatorship, as rigid in its manner of being as is the dictatorship in Germany. I believe, however, that this Russian dictatorship is less dangerous to the safety of other nations than is the German form of dictatorship.

The message had an influence. The *Denver Catholic Register* published a pastoral sermon by Archbishop John T. McNichols of Cincinnati, which recalled the letter of Piux XI on the horrors visited upon the Church by Nazism. It noted that the same pontiff's condemnation of "atheistic communism" in the twenties, which the opponents of aid to Russia were using to good effect, had not kept him from sending a relief mission to Soviet Russia. Nor did his condemnation constitute a "moral direction to governments regarding aid or refusal of aid to Russia in case of a war of defense."

The clarification of the Vatican's attitude had a marked effect in diminishing resistance to the inclusion of Russia as a lend-lease recipient. The new $5-billion appropriation was approved by Congress after an amendment prohibiting lend-lease aid to Russia was voted down.[5]

While Taylor discussed these matters at the Vatican, Harriman was instructed to raise the issue of a more favorable attitude toward religious freedom in Moscow. It was one of the few issues not related to supply that he was directed to discuss with Russia's leaders.

The chief British anxiety as Harriman and his group arrived in London was that American promises of aid to Russia would come out of supplies previously promised to Britain. But before Beaverbrook could even discuss the British view that allocations already promised Britain should remain intact and be fulfilled, he discovered fierce American resistance on another point. Beaverbrook was proceeding on the assumption that America and Britain were allies, preparing a joint offer to the Russians. "We were now brusquely reminded that the Americans did not regard themselves as our allies. They took the view that their country occupied a more isolated and more important position, that of a general dispenser of supplies to a number of recipients, including the United Kingdom, Russia, China and certain South American states." Beaverbrook's proposed procedure "was firmly and even roughly rejected by Mr. Harriman."

American versions of this first session were more graphic. They portrayed Beaverbrook as seeking to take command of the American as well as the British group and to make himself agent for both, empowering him to tell Stalin what both Western nations were prepared to give the Soviets, a procedure that would have redounded to the greater glory of Beaverbrook and Britain and relegated the United States to the role of a junior partner. "Beaverbrook had led off by proposing that all the aid the United States was prepared to give to Russia should be turned over to him, the British Minister of Supply, and then he in turn would turn it over to the Russians." So General Lee, the United States military attaché in London, recorded the reaction of the shocked Americans. When Beaverbrook insisted that the meeting begin with the Americans listing what the United States was prepared to offer and then Britain would know how much it would have to add, Harriman, a man not to be bullied by war lords or press lords, stopped him: "If this is your attitude, we might as well go home." There was no need for the United States group to go to Moscow at all. Beaverbrook retreated. "Oh, no, no, no. We must go together." When Churchill heard about the unpropitious beginning, he quickly invited Harriman to dinner. "I know you and Max had a fight. I know how difficult he can be. But it's a vital matter. I depend on you." Beaverbrook was inclined to be a "ruffian," wrote Harriman's daughter, who was at the dinner. Harriman in the end prevailed. The American delegation, he said, would state the total quantity of supplies which was available for export over the next nine months; and the sole question before the meeting was what proportion of this total should be allocated to Russia. The British had no recourse but to accept. By the end of the London meetings, states the British official history, "we had reached almost exactly the position which Lord Beaverbrook and the Chiefs of Staff had feared: American allocations to Russia were being carved out of allocations already promised to Britain, so that the sacrifices fell almost entirely on us and not on the American armed forces."

The issue was not simply a matter of personalities—a phlegmatic and stubborn Harriman against a buccaneering Beaverbrook. The clash foreshadowed future difficulties for the Roosevelt-Churchill conception of an intimate Anglo-American partnership presiding over the postwar world. It was a warning, too, of the great obstacles in the way of cooperation with the Soviet Union. If Britain and the United States, linked by language, blood ties, and culture, found themselves so easily prey to suspicion and misunderstanding, what would happen in the encounter with Russia, where a traditional distrust of foreigners had fed a paranoia endemic to Leninism? "The new men," wrote Dean Acheson of Oumansky and other Soviet diplomats, "cultivated boorishness as a method of showing their contempt for the capitalist world with which they wished minimum contact." Even the sophisticated Maisky, on his way to present Churchill with Stalin's demand for a second front, thought of himself as the representative "of two opposite worlds, which by the wheel of history have found themselves in the same camp." This belief was never far from the consciousness of all Soviet negotiators. Grief would come to the West when their representatives failed to recognize that this was rooted in the Leninist view of the world.⁶

Tanks were a critical item in short supply. The Russians were losing enormous quantities in great tank battles in the East. The British needed them for their new offensive against Rommel. The United States Army was clamoring for them in the training camps. "We are both making to Russia necessary and worthwhile offers," Churchill cabled Hopkins. "They make grievous inroads, however, into what is required by you for expanding your forces and by us for intensifying our war effort and there is no disguising this fact. In the next nine months you know where the shoe will pinch most." The only solution, said Churchill, was for the United States to raise its production sights. Hopkins agreed. He was spending all his time backstopping the efforts of the Moscow mission. "There is still an amazing number of people here who do not want to help Russia and who don't seem to be able to pound into their thick heads the strategic importance of that front."

Harriman's journey from Washington to London to Moscow was punctuated by a flow of cables from Roosevelt on what the United States would be able to do to meet the demands of the various fronts for tanks. He was doing his best to expedite production, Roosevelt cabled Churchill on September 17, in order to reach a monthly rate of 1,400 by May, 1942. He was also working on a program that will "get our full tank capacity up to a minimum of 2,500 a month and a maximum of 3,000 a month." This was welcome news to Churchill. "Your cheering cable about tanks arrived when we were feeling very blue about all we have to give up to Russia. The prospect of nearly doubling the previous figures encouraged everyone. The missions have started in great goodwill and friendship." At a White House conference with his production chiefs, the president, when he came to the schedule calling for 1,400 tanks a month, "paused, placed a cigarette in his famous long holder, lit it, and then calmly issued this short directive: 'Double it!' "

Stimson, who sometimes expressed doubts about Roosevelt's intellectual and administrative pertinacity, went in to see him about the tank situation: "He is making a study of that production and is going over the figures with great penetration and great shrewdness. It is marvelous how he can give so much attention to a detail and to do it so well as he has done this and it is an instance I am bound to say, of what I have seen carried out in many other ways. He has spread himself out extremely thin but nevertheless he does carry a wonderful memory and a great amount of administrative shrewdness into each of these activities."

"We are keeping only a very modest number for ourselves," Roosevelt informed Harriman just before the latter left for Moscow. The quality of the new American tanks, moreover, agreeably surprised the British. "There is no doubt that they are excellent machines, very handy and really maneuverable and fast," General Auchinleck reported in a message that Churchill forwarded to Roosevelt. "Our officers are delighted with their reliability and endurance when compared with our own tanks, and are frankly amazed at the length of time they can be kept in work without having to go into the shops to be overhauled."[7]

The London preliminaries had gone well, Churchill reported. "The Harriman-Beaverbrook combination are firmly knit together. I hope for a successful agreement with Stalin. On the whole the last week on the Russian front has been better than was feared. Kindest regards." It was a measure of the importance of the Churchill-Roosevelt relationship and the growing confidence each had in the other's purposes that minor differences were not permitted to interrupt the steady movement toward an Anglo-American fighting partnership. The two missions were not as closely knit as Churchill professed. Harriman, in his memoirs, speaks of the two groups starting out for Moscow "with their disagreements intact." As it turned out, the United States and Britain were harder and more obdurate in their negotiations with each other than with the Russians.

"Although their pride will not permit the Soviet authorities to give expression to any foreigner of their innermost feelings," Ambassador Steinhardt cabled Washington on the eve of Harriman's arrival, "I am convinced that they are counting heavily on the impending three-power conference to furnish them with the war matériel necessary to stabilize the eastern front." Steinhardt was an experienced observer of the Moscow scene as well as a good negotiator, and Roosevelt had directed Harriman to keep the ambassador "fully and promptly informed." But Steinhardt as well as Cripps were excluded from the talks with Stalin. This primarily was Beaverbrook's doing. He could not abide Cripps either politically (Cripps had been a leader of the Labour party's left) or personally. Cripps was a teetotaler, without humor or small talk, while Beaverbrook was jolly, full of stories and gossip, a great companion over the bottle. Moreover, Beaverbrook hoped to capture the leadership of the British working classes by making himself the champion of all-out aid to Russia, an arena in which he regarded Cripps as a rival. He was determined to keep the ambassador out of the talks with Stalin. Harriman fell in with his plans because Cripps had irritated him by protesting the inclusion of Quentin Reynolds, a U.S. journalist, in the American delegation, a matter that Harriman considered none of Cripps's business. Moreover, Hopkins had a low opinion of Steinhardt. "Both Beaverbrook and I felt that Stalin would be franker with us if we didn't take the ambassadors along," Harriman later wrote. Hopkins had cautioned him that Steinhardt was disliked by Stalin and the rest of the Soviet leadership. "We knew that Stalin had no very high regard for either of them, so there was nothing to be gained by taking them." Both the United States and Great Britain, Harriman told Steinhardt, desired "to start negotiations 'with a clean slate.' "

As a consequence, the talks with Stalin were conducted by two men who had little experience in dealing with the Russians and who had denied themselves the help of those who were most knowledgeable in Stalin's ways. Cripps, in particular, who had arrived with illusions about the Soviet system and about Stalin's readiness to deal frankly and loyally with a left-wing Labourite, had learned his lesson. Both he and Steinhardt appreciated that in negotiations with Stalin the emphasis had to be on reciprocity. "The embassy people were concerned," wrote Charles Thayer, then a young third secretary in the U.S. embassy, "lest too much be promised with not enough strings attached." However, Beaverbrook, the canny trader who was always pressing Churchill to insist on a *quid pro quo* from the Americans, had decided that that was the wrong approach to Stalin. "They were not going to Moscow to bargain but to give. . . . The Mission must not only offer supplies. It must offer them in such measure that the Russian leaders would be satisfied and encouraged. The great danger of the enterprise . . . was that the Russians might be disappointed and cast down and even destroyed by neglect to give ample assurances of help and support. In which case the mission would have done better to stay away altogether." Cripps strongly disagreed. Here was a chance to chip away at the Soviet obsession with secrecy by some hard bargaining, by "trading supplies against detailed information about Russian production and resources." Beaverbrook rejected this advice:

The one way to break down the suspicious attitude which had given rise to Russian secrecy was to make clear beyond a doubt the British and American intention to satisfy Russian needs to the utmost in their power, whether the Russians gave anything or not. It was to be a Christmas-tree party, and there must be no excuse for the Russians thinking they were not getting a fair share of the gifts on the tree.

To win people's trust by trusting them is the saint's way in human relations. The sentiments came a little surprisingly from the lips of Beaverbrook, a power-oriented man. They have limited applicability in international relations and seemed particularly inappropriate when applied to Stalin, who divided the world ideologically into two camps and who did not have an iota of sentiment in his make-up. But, then, Beaverbrook saw Stalin as "a kindly man."

There were "eight important differences" between Cripps and himself, Beaverbrook alerted Churchill after the meetings, just in case Cripps returned to London and opened up a public attack on Churchill and himself. "He wanted me to force the Russians to come clean. . . . He pressed strongly for discussions on Strategy. . . . Sir Stafford wished to trade goods for information, and to insist on performance by the Russians." He also wanted Beaverbrook to take up equipping the Polish Free Army that was being recruited from among the Poles who had been packed off to prison after the Nazi-Soviet partition of Poland. "It would be right to say that I refused to be caught up in the Polish negotiations at any time."

When Harriman returned to Washington, the Polish ambassador Jan Ciechanowski asked him why he had not more forcefully presented the Polish case in the talks with Stalin. Harriman agreed that a more definite show of interest might have affected Soviet attitudes. But in view of Stalin's suspicions that Britain wanted to see Russia and Germany fight each other to the point of mutual exhaustion, he had felt obliged, according to Ciechanowski's account, "to concentrate exclusively on finding arguments which might satisfactorily prove to Stalin that British and American help was not going to be doled with any such ridiculous idea in view, but wholeheartedly and to the fullest extent. He went to Moscow to encourage Russia to resist, and all other matters had to be subordinated to this one aim. In fact, he could not afford to give the impression that there were any strings attached to American support of the Soviet war effort."

Harriman's concern was to keep the Russians fighting, wrote Adm. William H. Standley, a member of the United States delegation. "In Mr. Harriman's words, 'Give and give and give, with no expectation of any return, with no thought of a *quid pro quo.*' "[8]

In this, Harriman closely reflected the policy of Roosevelt and Hopkins, who, in turn, were deeply influenced by the viewpoint of Joseph E. Davies, former United States ambassador to Moscow and one of the few men in the Western world who on the day of Hitler's invasion of Russia had boldly predicted that Russia's resistance would "amaze" the world. Davies also was extraordinarily naïve about the workings of the Soviet system. He had accepted at face value the Soviet claim that the purges had exposed and broken a vast conspiracy against the state, an analysis that, as his predictions of the Red Army's staying power were borne out, he offered more emphatically than ever. "There were no Fifth Columnists in Russia in 1941—they had shot them. The purge had cleansed the country and rid it of treason." So his book *Mission to Moscow,* rushed to press and published in December, 1941, summarized his dispatches about the trials. He even spoke of Stalin as a man of "kindness and gentle simplicity."

Roosevelt's connections with Davies went back to the Wilson administration, in which both had served as young progressives. FDR had noted Davies's prediction on June 22 and had invited him to the White House. "Immediately after the attack I was in constant touch with the White House, with Harry Hopkins and the President," Davies later asserted. All summer, Davies had been warning high and low of the dangers of a new deal between Stalin and Hitler. When asked at the Dutch Treat Club "Will Stalin make a separate peace with Hitler?" he reproached the questioner. The very question "indicated to me how utterly people of this country misjudge the Russian situation. The real question which is vital now is, 'Will we force Stalin to make peace with Hitler again?' We, or rather the European democracies, forced Stalin into Hitler's arms in August of 1939. We—that is to say, England and America— could force Stalin into Hitler's arms again if Stalin were to believe that we were ready to let him down, use the Soviet army merely as a cat's paw and double-cross him in the way Chamberlain and Daladier did before and after Munich and up to the eve of Armageddon." There was enough truth in Davies's assertions about Chamberlain to give added force to his warnings about the possibility of Stalin again switching alliances. "I always thought," wrote "Chip" Bohlen, "that the primary reason for the overcommitments to the Soviets was the fear that the Soviet armies might collapse, that the Bolshevik regime might surrender or make a deal with Hitler." In the flyleaf of Roosevelt's copy of Davies's book, Roosevelt wrote, "This book will last."

Ironically, the few who were right about the Red Army's power of resistance did not understand the nature of Stalinist totalitarianism, while Soviet experts like Loy Henderson and William Bullitt, who viewed the Soviet system more critically and were counseling wariness in dealing with Stalin, were totally wrong about Russia's staying power. "I know no man in Washington who believes that the Soviet Army can defeat the German Army," Bullitt told the American Legion in mid-August. "The probability is that after severe [Red Army] losses Hitler will seize the vast resources of the Soviet Union and will then prepare an overwhelming force for the conquest of Great Britain, then of South America and the United States. The grim truth is that sooner or later we face war."

Bullitt agreed, however, that it was in the Western interest to help Russia with supplies. "At the moment Stalin is sapping Hitler's strength. In spite of himself he is helping the forces of civilization. We are right to hope that he will be able to continue for a long time to sap Hitler's strength. We ought to rejoice that Satan and Lucifer are fighting each other. But we ought not to be so blindly sentimental as to believe that Satan will ever help to establish a peace of Christian freedom."

The wrongness of Bullitt's predictions about Russia's power of resistance impeached his political advice. It was symptomatic of the relative standings of Bullitt and Davies at the White House at the time of the Harriman mission that Roosevelt had Davies as a guest at his press conference on October 3 when the Beaverbrook-Harriman missions had concluded their work, a sure sign of presidential confidence. There was one other Soviet expert who shared Davies's confidence in the Red Army. Colonel Phillip R. Faymonville had been on the embassy staff during the thirties as military attaché. Bohlen described him as "a slender, pink-faced man with a fringe of white hair who had a definite pro-Russian bias." But Faymonville's analyses of military developments on the eastern front were so much sounder than that of the other military experts, including the U.S. military attaché then in Moscow, that Hopkins attached him to the Harriman mission.[9]

Six tripartite committees went to work in Moscow to deal with specific areas of supply, but these groups were a waste of time because no Soviet general dared make a decision or venture an opinion. The sessions with Stalin alone mattered. There were three—the first, at which Stalin reviewed the situation at the front and outlined Soviet requirements, much along the lines that he had discussed with Hopkins; the second, at which Stalin turned restless and rude, ostentatiously leaving unread a letter that Beaverbrook had given him from Churchill and expressing dissatisfaction with the list of supplies that Beaverbrook and Harriman had handed to him, suggesting even that Britain and America were prepared to see the Soviet regime defeated; and the final session, when Stalin became cordial again and Maxim Litvinov, the interpreter, "bounded out of his seat and said with passion, 'Now we shall win the war,' " as Beaverbrook had read off the final list of materials the United States and Britain were prepared to send. "It was sunshine after rain," Beaverbrook's account of this episode ended.

At the time, Beaverbrook and Harriman were inclined to explain Stalin's refractory mood at the second session by the bad news that he might have received from the front—and the news was bad. But Allied negotiators would conclude, as the war went on and there were more meetings with Stalin, Molotov, and other Soviet leaders, that the abrupt, patterned alternation in moods was, in fact, a Soviet negotiating technique. General Ismay, whom Churchill had sent with Beaverbrook to Moscow in the hope that Stalin would want to discuss overall strategy, wrote:

I wondered then, and I have often wondered since, whether we were right when confronted with that kind of behavior to turn the other cheek as we persistently did throughout the war. No one will deny that it was in our own interests to give the Russians the wherewithal to fight our common enemy; nor will anyone deny that the Red Army was making splendid use of what we gave them. But it was surely unnecessary, and even unwise, to allow them to bully us in the way that they did. Should we not have said something like this: "Do not imagine for a moment that you are conferring a favor upon us by accepting our generous help. The boot is on the other leg. If you persist in your attitude of taking everything and conceding nothing in return, we will leave you to deal with your recent friend, Hitler, as best you can." The argument that has always put forward against this tougher approach was that it involved the risk that Russia would come to terms with Germany. But what sort of terms would they have been offered by the man whose consuming passion was the annihilation of Communism? Stalin was a realist, and knew perfectly well that the only alternatives open to the Russians were either to keep on fighting for their lives or to become slaves of Hitler.

There was little political discussion at the meetings. Although Beaverbrook was a law unto himself and, in preparation for political talks with Stalin, had obtained Churchill's permission to interview Rudolf Hess, the Nazi prisoner who continued to fascinate Stalin, foreign affairs were Eden's domain. And political talks were certainly not part of Harriman's writ. It was firm United States policy, moreover, to concentrate on winning the war and to postpone issues of frontiers and territories until after the war was won. Roosevelt had obtained Churchill's assurance at Argentia that there were no secret commitments that would tie Britain's hands in the postwar territorial settlement. Stalin, nevertheless, probed. The Leninist view, which Stalin fully shared, was that military strategy could not be separated from political strategy. They not only influenced each other but they were of a different order of importance: primacy always belonged to politics. And his highest political priority on the assumption of victory was to obtain Anglo-American recognition of his 1941 frontiers. He asked Beaverbrook about peace objectives. Beaverbrook spoke about the eight points of the Atlantic Charter. Would the eight points satisfy him? Stalin asked. Beaverbrook reacted noncommittally. What did he have in mind? inquired Harriman. "What about getting the Germans to pay for the damage?" Beaverbrook evaded a direct reply, Harriman recorded, "with some generality about 'We must win the war first.' " Later, Stalin returned to the subject of peace aims, asking Beaverbrook whether the Anglo-Soviet military alliance "should not be extended to a treaty, an alliance not only for war but for post-war as well." He personally favored it, and thought the time was opportune to conclude such a treaty, Beaverbrook replied. The matter was dropped with Stalin's observation that "all the Soviet Government officials favored the proposal."

According to A. J. P. Taylor, Beaverbrook's official biographer, Beaverbrook also "listened sympathetically to Stalin's demand that Great Britain should recognize Russia's frontiers as they existed in 1941—incorporating, that is, the Baltic states and the territory of former Poland which Russia occupied in 1939." Even if the issue of frontiers was not directly raised, it was implicit in Stalin's proposal for a political agreement. And Beaverbrook's lack of interest in the Polish question spoke volumes. Harriman, by contrast, not only met with General Władysław Anders, the Polish leader who had been released from Lubianka prison after the Nazi invasion, but argued with Molotov on behalf of equipping and provisioning the Free Polish divisions that Anders was raising.[10]

The Moscow negotiations ended with a banquet in the Kremlin in the ornate Catherine the Great Hall. Stalin, in a well-cut blouse of dove gray without medals or decorations, sat between Beaverbrook and Harriman. If his costume was austere, the banquet was lavish. It began with caviar and ended with fresh fruits flown from the Crimea. The contrast between the tables groaning with delectables and the hunger in the streets and countryside, between the rigor with which Churchill conformed with Britain's rations and the privileged self-indulgence of Russia's rulers, disgusted Harriman. Stalin's remarks during the dinner were at times equally gross. "What is the good of having an army if it doesn't fight?" he taunted Beaverbrook, speaking of the army which had stood alone from Dunkirk until Hitler's invasion of Russia. "An army which does not fight will lose its spirit," he went on. Harriman thought Stalin's gibe was tasteless, but neither he nor Beaverbrook considered it the moment to get into an argument with Russia's leader. General Ismay did his best to explain to Stalin why an invasion of France was out of the question, but Stalin shrugged him off.

Harriman, at the first talk with Stalin, had raised the religious question, as instructed by Roosevelt. But when the Soviet leader failed to react, Harriman pressed him no further, although he did take it up with Molotov and others. The day after Harriman left Moscow, the Soviet government announced its agreement with a statement that Roosevelt had made at a press conference that Article 124 of the Soviet constitution did assure freedom of religious worship as well as freedom of antireligious propaganda. Harriman doubted, however, that the Soviets would ever give the principle more than lip service, nor was Roosevelt satisfied with the assurances that he had obtained: "He made me feel that it was not enough and took me to task on my return."

If Roosevelt is to be praised for the soundness of political instinct that caused him to press for religious freedom at the moment of Russia's most desperate need for Western help, what is to be said, even if in hindsight, of his reluctance to face up to Russia's territorial demands promptly? William C. Bullitt wrote after the war that he had urged Roosevelt to make lend-lease aid to Russia conditional on a promise to respect Europe's eastern boundaries as they existed in 1939. Although there is no contemporary record, letter or otherwise, to confirm that Bullitt said this to Roosevelt in 1941, there were diplomats, notably Sir Stafford Cripps, who were warning of the consequences of postponement. By the end of the Moscow conference, Harriman had revised his judgment of the British envoy. He perceived Cripps to be a man of high intelligence. Among the notes that Harriman made of a long talk with Cripps at an embassy party after an evening at the ballet was the following:

Russia would unquestionably want a Russian-dominated Balkans [after the war]. On what terms? What boundaries?

[Cripps] thought at the present time the Russians would be quite reasonable in their demands; but when victory came particularly if [Russia's] part was important in the ultimate success, the demand would be much greater and hard to meet.

[Cripps] commented that Winston was not interested in the peace and contended that he would resign, and let someone else make it, which was quite impossible.

But to have confronted Russia's territorial aspirations in the fall of 1941 would have involved insuperable difficulties for Roosevelt. It would have been awkward for American policy makers to deal with the concrete aims of a war in which the United States was not yet a full participant. America was opposed to Russia's incorporation of the Baltic States and its appropriation of parts of Poland. But the British, including Cripps, fearful that they might be left again to stand alone against the full might of the Nazis, were less so. Powerful ethnic minorities strongly represented in Congress and the Democratic party were opposed to any territorial concessions to the Russians. It was, moreover, Roosevelt's hope that territorial issues could be settled by self-determination through plebiscites. And a free vote would only be possible after the war was over.*[11]

---

* Roosevelt was similarly reluctant to place pressure upon the British in regard to India and other colonial possessions. The Atlantic Charter's affirmation of the principle of self-determination had had extraordinary repercussions in England's Empire. It read, "Third, they [the United States and United Kingdom] respect the right of all peoples to choose the form of government under which they will live; and they wish to see sovereign rights and self-government restored to those who have been forcibly deprived of them." The alacrity with which the Congress party in India and the Tory imperialists in Britain seized upon this pledge, the former with hope, the latter with indignation, had obliged Churchill to make a clarifying statement in the House. Winant begged him not to do so, arguing with him up to a few minutes before he actually had to appear in Parliament, but Churchill said it was a matter of internal British politics. In his speech to the House, Churchill specifically excluded India, Burma, and other parts of the Empire from the charter's pledges with respect to self-government: "At the Atlantic meeting, we had in mind, primarily, the restoration of the sovereignty, self-government and national life of the States and nations of Europe under the Nazi yoke." The statement accentuated the

In line with their purpose of maintaining Russian resistance for as long as possible, Beaverbrook and Harriman were content with the outcome of their talks with Stalin. Beaverbrook felt that he had had a tonic effect on the Soviet leader, an impression confirmed by Harriman, who concluded his report on the Moscow conference with a posy for the man whom at first he had considered something of a bully: "Beaverbrook has been a great salesman. His personal sincerity was convincing. His genius never worked more effectively." Harriman also thought that if Britain and America "came through as had been promised and if personal relations were retained with Stalin, the suspicion that has existed between the Soviet Government and our two governments might well be eradicated." "The effect of this agreement has been an immense strengthening of the morale of Moscow," Beaverbrook cabled Churchill. "The maintenance of the morale will depend on delivery." Stalin appeared to be equally satisfied. "The arrival of the British and American Missions in Moscow and particularly the fact that they were led by Lord Beaverbrook and Mr. Harriman had a most favorable effect," he cabled Churchill. "As for Lord Beaverbrook, he did his utmost to expedite consideration and, possibly solution of the most pressing problems discussed at the Moscow Tripartite Conference and to make them fruitful. I can say the same for Mr. Harriman."

Churchill, too, was delighted. "No one could have done it but you," he cabled Beaverbrook. "Now come home and make the stuff. Impossible to restrain the feeling of optimism here." He was equally cheery to Roosevelt: "Max and Averell seem to have had great success at Moscow, and now the vital thing is to act up to our bargain in early deliveries. Hitler evidently feels the draught." Roosevelt replied in kind: "I am delighted with the outcome of the Moscow conference. The important thing now is to get the goods to them." But the interlude of good feeling was short-lived.[12]

As Russia's battlefield prospects improved, Stalin's demands, on Britain particularly, revived. A superstitious Hitler, remembering the fate of Napoleon, had, against the advice of his generals, hitherto avoided an all-out attack on Moscow, diverting huge forces toward Kiev and Kharkov in the south and toward the investment of Leningrad in the north. "He has an instinctive aversion to treading the same path as Napoleon," General Jodl had explained to the protesting generals. "Moscow gives him a sinister feeling. He

desperation of India's nationalists. With most of the Congress party leaders in jail, Gandhi expressed the hope that Great Britain and Germany would exhaust each other and the war end in stalemate. The United States should not aid Britain without guarantees. "She should ask what will happen to India, Asia and African possessions. She should withdraw any help unless there are guarantees of human liberties. . . . America would lose nothing by making stipulations concerning her war help." But Roosevelt hesitated to put too much pressure on the British. They were fighting for their lives in a war in which the United States was not a participant. He favored self-government, perhaps, if that was what the four hundred million people of India wanted, eventual independence. Self-determination was his guiding principle, but timing was the essence of his approach. He awaited the propitious moment. In the autumn of 1941, his primary objective was to forge the widest possible alliance against Hitler.

fears that there might be a life-and-death struggle with Bolshevism." But on October 2, Hitler announced "the last great decisive battle of the year," and the German armies began to drive along the road which Napoleon had taken to Moscow. Under the shock of Hitler's thrust, the Red Army reeled backward. In vast battles between Vyazma and Bryansk, large Soviet forces were encircled and destroyed. By mid-October, German units were so close to Moscow that foreign embassies and many government ministries were evacuated to Kuibyshev, five hundred miles to the east. An eerie silence fell on the capital, reported Thayer, which, for the first time in memory, was empty of police, all of whom had been sent to the front. In the south, Odessa and Kharkov fell. But the autumn rains had begun and German armor bogged down in mud. The Red Army fought tenaciously. "And now, when Moscow was already almost in sight," wrote German General Blumentritt, "the mood both of commanders and troops began to change. Enemy resistance stiffened and the fighting became more bitter. . . . Many of our companies were reduced to a mere sixty or seventy men. . . . Winter was about to begin, but there was no sign of winter clothing. . . . Far behind the front the first partisan units were beginning to make their presence felt in the vast forests and swamps. Supply columns were frequently ambushed." In late October, there were snow flurries and by early November the temperature had fallen to below the freezing point. Machine guns were unable to fire because of the cold, and regiments were decimated by frostbite. "The result," wrote Gen. Heinz Guderian, "was a panic which reached as far back as Bogorodsk. This was the first time that such a thing had occurred during the Russian campaign, and it was a warning that the combat ability of our infantry was at an end."

There was little direct exchange of messages between Stalin, Churchill, and Roosevelt in this period, but there was continuing pressure through diplomatic channels for the dispatch of British troops to aid the Russian armies either via Archangel or Iran. Within Britain, Beaverbrook, abetted by Britain's Communists and by left-wing Labourites, championed aid to Russia and a second front. A sharp Beaverbrook memorandum addressed to the war cabinet, a copy of which he sent to Hopkins, charged that "since the start of the German campaign against Russia, our military leaders have shown themselves consistently averse to taking any offensive action."

From Moscow, Cripps warned that the Russians were obsessed with the view that the British were "sitting back and watching them." The pressure on Churchill was unremitting. His own wife told him she could not understand Britain's failure to come to the help of the Russians with a second front. His hopes were on Operation Crusader, and when General Auchinleck, the commander in the Middle East, informed him that the offensive had to be postponed from November 1 to November 15, the prime minister flared back in a telegram: "It is impossible to explain to Parliament and the nation how it is our Middle East armies have had to stand for 4-½ months without engaging the enemy while all the time Russia is being battered to pieces."

The offensive in Libya, which Churchill hoped would pave the way for the invasion of Sicily (Operation Whipcord), was Churchill's answer to Soviet demands for helpful action in the West. "These dispositions," he wrote Roosevelt, "as I have set them out, do not allow us *in the next six months* to make any serious contribution to the Russian defence of the Caucasus and Caspian Basin." As for the twenty-five divisions Britain had at home, "we must expect that as soon as Hitler stabilizes the Russian front he will begin to gather perhaps fifty or sixty divisions in the west for the invasion of the British Isles. . . . One may well suppose his program to be: 1939, Poland; 1940 France; 1941, Russia; 1942, England; 1943, ? I feel that we must be prepared to meet a supreme onslaught from March onwards." The defence committee, when it considered Beaverbrook's memorandum, was unanimously against it. It again reviewed, at Beaverbrook's request, the possibilities of a diversionary attack via Norway and again dismissed them. All agreed that greater results would be achieved from the impending offensive in Libya. To Cripps Churchill sent an indignant telegram that was indicative of the strength of feeling that lay at the basis of his resistance to Soviet pressures:

[The Russians] certainly have no right to reproach us. They brought their own fate upon themselves when, by their pact with Ribbentrop, they let Hitler loose upon Poland and so started the war. They cut themselves off from an effective second front when they let the French Army be destroyed. If prior to June 22 they had consulted with us beforehand, many arrangements could have been made to bring earlier the great help we are now sending them in munitions. We did not however know until Hitler attacked them whether they would fight, or what side they would be on. We were left alone for a whole year while every Communist in England under orders from Moscow did his best to hamper our war effort. If we had been invaded or destroyed in July or August, 1941, or starved out this year in the Battle of the Atlantic, they would have remained utterly indifferent. If they had moved when the Balkans were attacked, much might have been done, but they left it all to Hitler to choose his moment and his foes. That a Government with this record should accuse us of trying to make conquests in Africa or gain advantages in Persia at their expense or being willing to "fight to the last Russian soldier" leaves me quite cold. If they harbor suspicions of us, it is only because of the guilt and self-reproach in their own hearts.

2. We have acted with absolute honesty. We have done our very best to help them at the cost of deranging all our plans for rearmament and exposing ourselves to heavy risks when the spring invasion season comes. We will do anything more in our power that is sensible, but it would be silly to send two or three British or British-Indian divisions into the heart of Russia to be surrounded and cut to pieces as a symbolic sacrifice. Russia has never been short of man-power, and has now millions of trained soldiers for whom modern equipment is required. That modern equipment we are sending, and shall send to the utmost limit of the parts and communications.

3. Meanwhile we shall presently be fighting ourselves as the result of long-prepared plans, which it would be madness to upset. We have offered to relieve the five Russian divisions in Northern Persia which can be done with Indian troops fitted to maintain internal order but not equipped to face Germans. I am sorry that Molotov rejects the idea of our sending modest forces to the Caucasus. We are doing all we can to keep Turkey a friendly neutral and prevent her being tempted by German promises of territorial gain at Russia's expense. Naturally we

do not expect gratitude from men undergoing such frightful bludgeonings and fighting so bravely, but neither need we be disturbed by their reproaches. There is of course no need for you to rub all these salt truths into the Russian wounds, but I count upon you to do your utmost to convince Russians of the loyalty, integrity, and courage of the British nation.[13]

At the beginning of November, Cripps first learned that Stalin in his talks with Beaverbrook had suggested an extension of the Anglo-Russian military alliance to cover postwar questions. The British envoy thought that Britain's failure to follow this up might very well be the key to the deterioration in Anglo-Soviet relations since the Moscow conference. Harriman, on his way back to Washington, had informed Eden privately that "Stalin had spoken of an alliance after the war and proposed it to Max. He thought Stalin would be offended if we did not return some reply." Cripps strongly urged upon the foreign office the desirability of reaching an immediate agreement with the Soviet Union on the broad lines of a European settlement.

Churchill soon discovered that Cripps's diagnosis of what was troubling Anglo-Soviet relations was correct. At the beginning of November, he told Stalin that Generals Wavell and Paget, top British commanders, were prepared to go to Moscow in order to "clear things up and plan for the future." Eden suggested that it might be useful if he also went to Moscow. Churchill agreed but "thought it better after results of *Crusader* were visible." Churchill's message to Stalin also dealt with the Russian's repeated requests that Britain declare war on Finland, Hungary, and Romania, which were at war with Russia. Britain was willing to do so, said Churchill, but was it really "good business?" The prime minister was particularly worried over Finland, "which has many friends in the United States and it is prudent to take account of this fact." As to the delivery of the supplies that had been promised, they were moving in a swelling flood through Archangel and Persia. But Churchill hoped Stalin would see to it they were received by personnel competent to handle their transfer and preparation for use. This veiled reproach was accompanied by a playful thrust at Soviet secretiveness: "I cannot tell you about our immediate military plans, any more than you can tell me about yours, but rest assured we are not going to be idle."

Although Churchill complained about Soviet secretiveness, he was not wholly without information. At about this time, "Jock" Whitney, Donovan's representative in London, spent three days with the prime minister in the country and on the train and sent back notes on Churchill's attitudes on various matters. On Russia, reported Whitney, "putting together all the reports from the Eastern front, [Churchill's] intuition tells him that there is real chance that the Nazis are stopped before Moscow. Recently his Moscow odds were five to four on the Germans, he confided in the War Cabinet, but now he has reversed those odds. . . . [Gen. A. I.] Denikin got to Tula in 1919 and was stopped by the hero [Marshal S. M.] Budënny. Batum-Baku line excellent defensive position, if Germans get that far."

Stalin, emboldened perhaps by the knowledge that the German offensive was grinding to a halt, replied in terms that Churchill called "chilling" and that even worried Maisky, who delivered the message to the prime minister with the plea, "I very much ask you, Mr. Churchill, to treat this with the greatest possible calm." Churchill looked at him suspiciously. As he began to read, his face reddened and his hand clenched and unclenched:

I agree with you that we need clarity, which at the moment is lacking in relations between the USSR and Great Britain. The unclarity is due to two circumstances; first, there is no definite understanding between our two countries concerning war aims and plans for the post-war organization of peace; secondly, there is no treaty between the USSR and Great Britain on mutual military aid in Europe against Hitler. Until understanding is reached on these two main points, not only will there be no clarity in Anglo-Soviet relations, but, if we are to speak frankly, there will be no mutual trust. To be sure, the agreement on military supplies to the Soviet Union is of great positive significance, but that does not settle the issue, nor does it fully cover the question of relations between the two countries.

If General Wavell and General Paget, whom you mention in your message, come to Moscow to conclude agreements on the main points stated above, I shall be willing, naturally, to meet them and consider these points. If, however, the mission of the two Generals is to be restricted to information and examination of secondary issues, then I see no need for keeping them from their duties, nor can I engage myself to go out of my way to engage in talks of that nature.

The British position on Finland, Romania and Hungary, the telegram curtly continued, was "intolerable." Stalin was incensed over the leakage into the press of rumors on the subject and asked whether "the purpose is to demonstrate that there is disagreement between the USSR and Great Britain." As to Churchill's admonition about the handling of supplies, "I must add, however, even though it is a trifling matter, that the tanks, guns and aircraft are badly packed, some parts of the guns come in different ships and the aircraft are so badly crated that we get them in a damaged state."

"I can't understand what Stalin wants," Churchill growled at the hapless Maisky. "Bad relations? A rupture? . . . Whom will that benefit?"

Eden, who was present, urged Churchill to postpone any reply. The next day, Beaverbrook, in distress, came to Maisky. "An unpleasant thing has happened. . . . There's been a misunderstanding between Winston and Uncle Joe. . . . That's no good at all. . . . They should be reconciled." Eden that same day told Maisky that the cabinet had been surprised and pained at the tone and contents of the message. Could he speak off the record? asked Maisky. The ambassador agreed that Stalin's tone was not the happiest although his proposals were not unreasonable. Eden should bear in mind the great strain Stalin was under. Eden also went "off the record" and seized the occasion to tell Maisky of British displeasure with Soviet efforts by means of the political influence it exerted in Great Britain through the Communists to influence British policy. Nor had the cabinet liked Stalin's linking of the visit of the two generals to demands for a discussion of postwar policy, which the generals obviously were not qualified to discuss. Ah, said Maisky, intent on Russia's main goal, why limit the discussion to generals? He had better get word to Molotov, Eden continued, that a message was needed "which would enable me to build a bridge again." Eden then went to see Churchill, who "was impressed with the strength of our hand in dealing with Stalin. His need of us is greater than our need of him. I need not go to Moscow except that the red carpet is out, etc. There is much force in all this."

A few days later, Maisky did receive instruction to backtrack. He informed Eden that Stalin had not intended to offend any member of the British government, least of all the prime minister; that he was scarcely able to think of anything but affairs at the front; and that the problems he had raised were too important to be complicated by personal feelings. The upshot of the exchange was that the British government decided to send Eden to Moscow to discuss peace objectives and postwar collaboration.

Churchill responded to Maisky's communication in words of conciliation:

Many thanks for your message, just received. At the very beginning of the war I began a personal correspondence with President Roosevelt, which has led to a very solid understanding being established between us and has often helped in getting things done quickly. My only hope is to work on equal terms of comradeship and confidence with you.

About Finland, Britain was not responsible for the leakage, and if the Finns do not halt hostilities in a fortnight "and you still wish us to declare war on them, we will certainly do so." He was sending Eden to Moscow.

He would be accompanied by high military and other experts, and will be able to discuss every question relating to war. . . . I notice that you wish also to discuss the post-war organization of peace. Our intention is to fight the war in alliance with you and in constant consultation with you to the utmost of our strength, and however long it lasts, and when the war is won, as I am sure it will be, we expect that Soviet Russia, Great Britain, and the United States will meet at the council table of the victors as the three principal partners and agencies by which Nazism will have been destroyed. Naturally, the first object will be to prevent Germany and particularly Prussia, breaking out upon us for the third time. The fact that Russia is a Communist State and Britain and the United States are not, and do not intend to be, is not any obstacle to our making a good plan for our mutual safety and rightful interests. The Foreign Secretary will be able to discuss this whole field with you.

To the Americans, Churchill was more specific about his attitude toward Germany after the war. As "Jock" Whitney reported it on November 12: "German and Prussian militarism must be destroyed—presumably division of Germany into at least two States."

Churchill ended his cable to Stalin with congratulations on the way Moscow and Leningrad were being defended as well as on Russia's "splended resistance to the invader along the whole Russian front."

Stalin was equally conciliatory. He could afford to be. He had pushed Britain into discussions of a postwar settlement.

I fully support your proposal for sending Mr. Eden your Foreign Secretary to the USSR in the near future. . . . It is quite true that the discussion and adoption of a plan for the post-war organization of peace should be designated to keep Germany, above all, Prussia, from again breaking the peace and plunging the nations into a new bloodbath.

I also agree that difference of political system in the USSR, on the one hand, and of Great Britain and the U.S.A. on the other, should not and cannot be an obstacle to a favorable solution of the fundamental problems of safeguarding our mutual security and rightful interests. I hope that reticence or doubts on this score, if any, will be dispelled by the talks with Mr. Eden.

Discussion of the postwar settlement meant inevitably discussion of Russia's frontiers. The British would resist Stalin's demands, already well known to London and Washington, for recognition of Russia's incorporation of the Baltic States, of Bessarabia, and of a substantial part of Poland. But Stalin also knew from Cripps's offer in October, 1940, and from the Russian's talks with Beaverbrook, that there were powerful forces within the British government ready to recognize Russia's frontiers as they existed on the eve of the Nazi invasion. He also perceived that obtaining the agreement of Britain, a European power, to his 1941 frontiers, was the key to breaking down the categorical and unyielding opposition of the Americans.

"The conflict between Churchill and Stalin was settled," Maisky wrote in his memoirs. "The next thing was to be Eden's visit to Moscow."[14]

In Washington, Roosevelt, on October 30, cabled Stalin that he had approved the schedule of items agreed to in the Moscow protocol and provided for their financing under lend-lease, which the Soviet government would repay by installments that would "begin five years after the war and continue over a period of ten years thereafter." There would be no interest.

Hopkins had originally prepared a memorandum on the financing of Russian lend-lease that would have required the Russians to repay either in gold or raw materials and 1.8-per-cent interest. He showed the memorandum to Morgenthau.

I [i.e., Morgenthau] told him that I didn't like the memorandum and he asked me what my objections were. I said, "This is not the way to do the thing. I think it is a mistake at this time to bother Stalin with any financial arrangements and take his mind off the war. It would make him think we are nothing but a bunch of Yankee traders trying to squeeze the last drop out of him." I said, "Do you feel or does the President feel that because the English paid down so much cash that we have to get so much gold from the Russians?" Hopkins said, "No."

I told Hopkins that I would simply send word to Stalin that we are going to let him have so much material; that the matter has been turned over to the State Department to draft some kind of an arrangement (which means it will take them a couple of years); that the material will come to him, and he should not worry. Hopkins said, "I absolutely agree with you. I am going to put on my hat and go over to see Hull and try to sell the idea. Then Hull, you and I should see the President." In other words, I got Hopkins to completely reverse himself. What will happen, I don't know.

The Morgenthau formula was adopted. Faymonville, promoted to general, was sent to Moscow to head up the United States supply mission there.

He had instructions from the president, wrote Gen. John R. Deane (later chief of the U.S. mission to Moscow), "that no strings were to be attached to our aid to Russia and that the program was not to be used as a lever to obtain information about and from the Russians."[15]

Chapter Twenty-seven

"Not enough Navy to go round" *

THE NEWS that the Konoye cabinet had fallen reached Washington on October 16. Roosevelt canceled a cabinet meeting and instead spent the afternoon with his war council.† This consisted of Hull, Stimson, Knox, Hopkins, Marshall, and Stark. The grimness with which these men viewed the development was reflected in Stark's warning to his fleet commanders immediately after the meeting to "take due precautions including such preparatory deployments as will not disclose strategic intention nor constitute provocative action against Japan." The purport of the caution against "provocative action" was explained in Stimson's diary: "and so we face the delicate question of the diplomatic fencing to be done so as to be sure that Japan was put into the wrong and made the first bad move—overt move."

The news the next day that Konoye's war minister Gen. Hideki Tojo had become prime minister confirmed Washington's worst fears that Tokyo was turning from diplomacy to war in its drive toward hegemony in the Pacific. "[Tojo] has been called the father of modern Japanese Army strategy," G-2 advised Marshall, "and is known to be anti-foreign, with a particular dislike for the Russians, and an open admiration for German methods. He created a sensation in 1938 when, as Vice Minister of War, he predicted that Japan would have to fight Russia as well as China. He also warned that America would have to be watched. When the Axis Alliance was signed September 1940 he said that the road Japan would follow had been 'definitely decided' and there was no turning back."

---

* "I simply have not got enough Navy to go round—and every little episode in the Pacific means fewer ships in the Atlantic" (letter from Roosevelt to Ickes, July 1, 1941, explaining why the president had not yet embargoed exports to Japan).

† In Stimson's diary, it is also called the war cabinet. The group had no formal status but consisted of the officials who, by Roosevelt's invitation, counseled him on matters of grand strategy.

The British agreed that "extremist hands" had taken over in Japan and feared it meant an imminent move southward against Thailand, which would bring it within striking distance of Singapore, or northward against Siberia. Halifax was directed to find out what the United States would do in either event. "We have been well content to leave the handling of the Japanese problem to the United States," Eden cabled Halifax, "and to follow the United States in their policy of maximum economic pressure. . . . Naturally, we should still prefer if possible to keep Japan out of the world conflict and to detach her from the Axis by some means short of war. If there is anything else the United States Government thinks we can do to deter Japan from war we should be glad to give it immediate consideration."[1]

Hull, Halifax discovered, still hoped to delay the collision through negotiations. The United States military wanted time. The army said it needed until mid-December to reinforce the Philippines, especially with the new four-engined bomber, which "bids fair," Stimson advised Roosevelt, "to stop Japan's march to the south and secure the safety of Singapore." Stark said he needed until February, partly because the Battle of the Atlantic had first call on destroyers and cruisers, and partly in order to complete training exercises. Moreover, said Hull to Halifax, it might be worth testing whether any forces for moderation still survived in Tokyo. He proposed to offer a small barter exchange of United States cotton for Japanese silk on condition that the Japanese agreed to respect the *status quo*. Halifax, an inveterate conciliator, forwarded Hull's suggestion to London with his approval: "If however any limited action that could be taken was clearly limited in scope, and treated as an isolated transaction it might be that the advantages to be gained by the encouragement of peaceful elements in Japan would outweigh objections."

"Foreign Secretary," Churchill minuted, and the words, although on paper, fairly bristled, "this is the thin edge of the appeasement wedge."

Hull did not press his suggestion in the light of London's negative attitude, but with Roosevelt's support, his search went on for ways to postpone hostilities. "We shall continue to strive to maintain the *status quo* in the Pacific," Stark wrote Admiral Kimmel. "How long it can be kept going I don't know, but the President and Mr. Hull are working on it. . . . The stumbling block, of course, is the China incident and personally . . . I hardly see any way around it." Nomura, writing to congratulate the new foreign minister, Shigenori Togo, shared Stark's assessment that the China issue was critical in Japanese-American relations. Nomura "had expected the United States to take a more or less conciliatory attitude toward us as soon as the situation was favorable, but, contrary to my surmises, so far all America has done is to stick to her own national policy. . . . I think that probably in the last analysis this is due to the fact that the United States has too many interests in China."

Confrontation began to appear inevitable. Magic intercepts of messages to Nomura increasingly stressed a deadline. Continue the talks, Togo instructed his ambassador. Even though the new cabinet was formulating its policy, Nomura should "let it be known to the United States by indirection that our country is not in a position to spend much more time discussing this matter." The embassy's minister-counselor Kaname Wakasugi, who had just returned from a visit to Japan, sent back his appraisal of American policy for the guidance of the new cabinet. America's basic policy was to crush "Hitlerism," he cabled, and, "working from this principle . . . Britain and China have been set up as the first line of national defense." Tokyo should not expect concessions or "any further counter-proposals from them. They have decided on a course of economic pressure plus watchful waiting."[2]

Wakasugi was wrong about counterproposals. Hull held a long talk with Stimson, one of the cabinet's most hawkish members. "[Hull] wanted to know whether I favored immediate declaration of war against Japan," Stimson recorded. "I said NO—that my purpose was to take advantage of this wonderful opportunity of strengthening our position in the Philippines by air and to use it as a means of strengthening his diplomatic arm in forcing the Japanese to keep away from Singapore and perhaps, if we are in good luck, to shake the Japanese out of the Axis. . . . The announcement has gone out [said Hull] that the [new] Cabinet will resume the negotiations of the old Cabinet. Hull thinks he has the Emperor on his side." Hopkins, who spent the afternoon of October 30 smoothing the feathers of Stimson and Marshall, was told the War Department's "full strategic plans," which Stimson and Marshall delivered "at great length, including the techniques to keep Japan out of the war."

But between Japan's determination to seize "the opportunity of a thousand years" and the equal determination of the West to pry it loose from the Axis and to force it to evacuate China and Indochina, there was little room for compromise—only for delay. The men who knew what was going on took that as their starting point. There were hopes on the part of Britain and the United States that Japan's ties with the Axis might be loosened and that it might be deterred from a new expansionist surge, and on the part of the Japanese that through diplomacy they might obtain an easing of the embargo. But neither side was prepared to yield what it considered basic. In Tokyo, where the Tojo cabinet, under the pressure of the embargo, felt it had to force events, there was a "tight, tense and trapped feeling" as the final interrelated diplomatic and military moves were being mapped for submission to an imperial conference on November 5.

While the West waited to see how the Tojo cabinet would move, the alarm bells suddenly went off in Chungking, the inland city to which Generalissimo Chiang Kai-shek had withdrawn. Worried messages poured in on Washington and London of an impending attack through Yunnan province in the south of China aimed at taking Kunming and cutting the Burma Road and other Chinese lines of communication with Britain and the United States. Chiang wanted Roosevelt to warn Japan against such an attack and asked Churchill to supply air support.

Churchill was in the process of strengthening Britain's defenses in south Asia. He was sending the *Prince of Wales* into the Indian Ocean, he informed Roosevelt, "as part of the squadron we are forming there. This ought to serve as a deterrent on Japan. There is nothing like having something that can catch and kill anything. . . . The firmer your attitude and ours, the less chance of their taking the plunge." But firmness stopped short of sending British air power to Chungking. Churchill was

prepared to send pilots and even some planes if they could arrive in time.

What we need now is a deterrent of the most general and formidable character. The Japanese have as yet taken no final decision, and the Emperor appears to be exercising restraint. When we talked about this at Placentia you spoke of gaining time, and this policy has been brilliantly successful so far. But our joint embargo is steadily forcing the Japanese to decisions for peace or war. . . .

No independent action by ourselves will deter Japan, because we are so much tied up elsewhere. But of course we will stand with you and do our utmost to back you in whatever course you choose. I think myself that Japan is more likely to drift into war than to plunge in. Please let me know what you think.

In Roosevelt's reply to Churchill, the president minimized the threat to Yunnan in the immediate future and promised to expedite lend-lease aid to China and build up the American volunteer air force:

We feel that measures such as the foregoing and those which you have in mind along the lines we are taking, together with continuing efforts to strengthen our defenses in the Philippine Islands, paralleled by similar efforts by you in the Singapore area will tend to increase Japan's hesitation, whereas in Japan's present mood new formalized verbal warning or remonstrances might have, with at least even chance, an opposite effect.[3]

America's top military people disapproved of the dispatch of United States forces to China. The nation's primary military objective, their report to Roosevelt stated, was the defeat of Germany. To wage offensive war in the Pacific would require withdrawals from the Atlantic that "might well cause the United Kingdom to lose the Battle of the Atlantic." War with Japan should be avoided unless Japan attacked or directly threatened

territories whose security to the United States is of very great importance. Military action against Japan should be undertaken only in one or more of the following contingencies:

(1) A direct act of war by Japanese armed forces against the territory or mandated territory of the United States, the British Commonwealth, or the Netherlands East Indies;

(2) The movement of Japanese forces into Thailand to the West of 100° North; or into Portuguese Timor, New Caledonia, or the Loyalty Islands.

This document is essential to an understanding of Roosevelt's policy in the months between his meeting with Churchill and Pearl Harbor. The Battle of the Atlantic had primacy, but there was a line beyond which the United States would not permit Japan to move. And if Japan did breach that line, it was essential—and this Roosevelt stressed in all his meetings with his top advisers—that Japan should be seen clearly to have been the aggressor. All of Roosevelt's political subtlety (his opponents called it deviousness) was committed to these objectives in the final weeks before Pearl Harbor.

For several days, Magic intercepts had indicated that the Tojo cabinet together with imperial headquarters were reaching the point of decision. Nomura had been advised to expect new orders on November 5. "This will be our Government's last effort to improve diplomatic relations." Two days later he was told that relations "between Japan and the United States have reached the edge." A counterproposal was being sent to him. "Both in name and spirit this counterproposal of ours is, indeed, the last." If it did not produce a quick accord, "the talks will certainly be ruptured."

The counterproposal was in two parts. Proposal A would be presented first. In the two respects of greatest importance to the United States, it was bound to be unsatisfactory. It was evasive and ambiguous (as the Japanese proposals had been all along) on Japan's obligations under the Tripartite Pact and, as the foreign minister himself conceded, made only qualified concessions on the withdrawal of Japanese troops from China. "I think that in all probability the question of evacuation will be the hardest . . . our purpose is to shift the regions of occupation and our officials, thus attempting to dispel their suspicions. . . . How hard, indeed, have we fought in China for four years! What tremendous sacrifices have we made. They must know this, so their demands in this connection must have been only 'wishful thinking.' "

If the United States did not respond quickly and affirmatively to proposal A, proposal B should be presented. The foreign minister knew that proposal B had even less chance of acceptance since not only would it have kept Japanese troops in China and Indochina, but it would have prohibited the United States from engaging in any "activity which might put an obstacle in the way of Japan in her efforts to make peace with China."

The next intercept indicated that special envoy Saburo Kurusu was being sent to assist Nomura "to show our Empire's sincerity in the negotiations." And then the most ominous sentence of all. "Because of various circumstances, it is absolutely necessary that all arrangements for the signing of this agreement be completed by the 25th of this month."[4]

Nomura was also informed that the foreign minister would himself approach the British and American ambassadors in Tokyo to impress upon them that this was the last chance for peace. Both envoys, Sir Robert Craigie and Joseph C. Grew, neither of whom, for reasons of security, knew the intentions of the Japanese government as revealed by Magic, sent impassioned cables home after their meetings with Togo emphasizing the moment's gravity.

The British ambassador objected to leaving the critical negotiations in the hands of the United States alone. British and American interests in the Far East "have never been identical." Washington paid too little attention, he feared, "to Japanese psychology and the facts of the international situation here, which forbid so sudden and drastic a change in policy as the United States Government appears to demand. . . . What we presumably want is the United States in the war on our side, and Japan *really* neutral—and it is premature to abandon hope as yet of bringing this off."

"We have realized," a foreign-office minute on this and other Craigie telegrams along similar lines pointed out, "ever since it was decided to impose a virtual British-American-Netherlands embargo on Japanese trade that the result would probably be to force Japan to decide whether to try to obtain what she wants by war or to come to terms with the United States and ourselves. . . . There is undoubtedly an increase of tension, of which Sir Robert Craigie is naturally acutely aware, but it is what we expected. There is absolutely no indication, however, that Japan is any more inclined now than she has been at any time during the past five or ten years to mend her ways, and indeed the tone of the Japanese press is more uncompromising and more menacing than ever. This is surely the fundamental fact, which makes it highly questionable whether there is any hope at all of keeping Japan *really* neutral." British and American interests in China were not identical, the writer agreed. "We have had disputes with them in the past and may have others in the future, but they will not involve the risk of war, nor endanger the Empire's territories in the Far East. If, however, we adopt a policy which will lead to Japan becoming all powerful in the Far East, we can say good-bye to our position there forever."

As usual, Cadogan put the matter most pointedly:

The Japanese announcement of Mr. Kurusu's mission to Washington must bring things to a head soon. That mission must either secure terms acceptable to Japan, or there must be confessed failure of the negotiations. The former is, to me, inconceivable. That means that the process of "gaining time" is nearing its limit. And this would not be a good moment to come into the negotiations.[5]

In Washington, Roosevelt, without telling the members of his cabinet (a majority of whom were not privy to Magic) that a deadline had been set by the Japanese on the negotiations, polled it on the question of whether the country "would back us up in case we struck at Japan down there and what the tactics should be," Stimson recorded. "He went around the table—first Hull and then myself, and then around and through the whole number and it was unanimous in feeling that the country would support us. . . . The thing would have been much stronger if the Cabinet had known—and they did not know except in the case of Hull and the President—what the Army is doing with the big bombers and how ready we are to pitch in." Secretary of Labor Frances Perkins remembered that she had been very firm at that meeting. "Certainly almost everybody said that they thought we should go to the relief of Britain if attacked at Singapore. That's what I said, I remember. Not everybody said that. Not everybody said it as strongly or as clearly as that."

Perkins remembered something else about that cabinet meeting:

One thing that kept coming through was that we must be extraordinarily careful that nothing that we did was provocative. There must be no action on our part. The President turned to Mr. Hull and said, "We must strain every nerve to satisfy and keep on good relations with this group of Japanese negotiators. Don't let it deteriorate and break up if you can possibly help it. Let us make no move of ill will. Let us do nothing to precipitate a crisis. The hazard is terribly difficult. The hazard in the Pacific seems to be greater than that in the Atlantic at the moment. But it may pass."

Both in Washington and Tokyo, policy makers now moved on two levels, the diplomatic and the military. The significant difference was the attitude of the armed forces. Marshall and Stark wanted to avoid a two-front war and concentrate on the defeat of Hitler. They pressed Roosevelt and Hull for more time in which to prepare American defenses in the Pacific. Roosevelt, moreover, wanted to see whether Soviet resistance would survive the winter and the effect a German failure would have on the Japanese. In Tokyo, however, the armed forces considered this to be the golden moment in which to expel the West from Asia and the Pacific and to make Japan self-sufficient in oil, minerals, and food. And the armed forces were now in control of the government. "Two irreconcilable policies cannot go on forever—particularly if one party can not live with the set-up," Stark wrote Kimmel after the November 7 cabinet meeting. "It doesn't look good." The objectors to war with the United States, Tojo later stated in his deposition to the Far Eastern military tribunal, were answered that "rather than await extinction it were better to face death by breaking through the encircling ring to find a way for existence." On November 3, Admiral Yamamoto, commander in chief of the combined fleet, approved Order Number 1: "The Japanese Empire will declare war on the United States, Great Britain and the Netherlands. War will be declared on X-day. This order will become effective on Y-day." The order detailed the strike south, including the attack on Pearl Harbor. On November 10, Vice Admiral Nagumo designated Hitokappu Bay in the Kuril Islands as the rendezvous place for his Pearl Harbor task force. Battle preparations were to be completed by November 20. For planning purposes, "X-day" was set at zero hours, December 8, Tokyo time (December 7, Hawaii).[6]

Roosevelt was still playing for time, still probing for an opening by which the United States might avoid or at least postpone involvement in a two-front war. "We talked about the Far Eastern situation and the approaching conference with the messenger who is coming from Japan," Stimson recorded on November 6:

The President outlined what he thought we might say. He was trying to think of something which would give us further time. He suggested he might propose a truce in which there would be no movement or armament for six months, and then if the Japanese and Chinese had not settled their arrangement in that meanwhile, we could go on on the same basis. I told him I frankly saw two great objections to that: first, that it tied up our hands just at a time when it was vitally important that we should go on completing our reenforcement of the Philippines; and second that the Chinese would feel that any such arrangement was a desertion of them. I reminded him that it has always been our historic policy since the Washington conference not to leave the Chinese and Japanese alone together, because the Japanese were always able to [overawe?] the Chinese and the Chinese know it. I told him that I thought the Chinese would refuse to go into such an arrangement.

Roosevelt put the six-months truce formula aside. It would surface again two weeks later. In advance of Kurusu's arrival, Nomura presented proposal A to Roosevelt and Hull. Both already knew its contents. Both agreed that it was unacceptable. That, however, was not said to Nomura. Instead, Roosevelt directed himself to the ambassador's soft reproaches that for six months "the conversations dragged on and on" and to his oblique warning that in certain circles in Japan "some skepticism has arisen as to the true intentions of the United States Government." After all, commented Roosevelt, it had taken three years to dispose of the Shantung problem after World War I, while he and Hull "had only consumed some six months . . . patience was necessary." Then, reported Nomura to Tokyo, "the President said he is leaving on the 15th and will be away for one week, as he must attend, as is his custom, a children's party at Warm Springs during the Thanksgiving week (the 20th) and that he wondered whether he should have the opportunity of meeting Ambassador Kurusu before he leaves."

An impatient Tokyo fired back: "Judging from the progress of the conversations, there seem to be indications that the United States is still not fully aware of the exceeding criticalness of the situation here. The fact remains that the date [November 25] set forth in my message #736 is absolutely immovable under present conditions. It is a definite deadline and therefore it is essential that a settlement be reached by about that time." The United States was not to be stampeded, Nomura cautioned his superiors. He had sent an American, Frederick Moore, the legal adviser to the Japanese embassy, to speak to Hull and to Sen. Elbert D. Thomas of the Senate Foreign Relations Committee, and Moore's report, Nomura cabled Tokyo, was that "the United States is not bluffing. If Japan invades again, the United States will fight with Japan. Psychologically the American people are ready. The Navy is prepared and ready for action." Nomura had also met with Postmaster General Frank C. Walker, the cabinet member who had been instrumental in setting up the Japanese-American talks. Walker had not split hairs: "You are indeed a dear friend of mine and I tell this to you alone. The American Government is receiving a number of reliable reports that Japan will be on the move soon. The American Government does not believe that your visit on Monday to the President or the coming of Mr. Kurusu will have any effect on the general situation."

On November 14, Hull gave Nomura the United States formal reply to proposal A. It was a restatement of American questions and objections to earlier variants of the Japanese proposal. Tokyo instructed Nomura to prepare to present proposal B. Another cautionary cable went to Tokyo. The United States was prepared to stop "any further moves on our part either southward or northward." It was prepared "to fight us" rather than go through a "Munich conference." A substantial number of Americans still opposed war with Germany, "but there is not the slightest opposition to war in the Pacific." And it will be a long war in which "this little victory or that little victory, or this little defeat and that little defeat" would not count for much. "I feel that should the situation in Japan permit, I would like to caution patience for one or two months in order to get a clear view of the world situation. This, I believe, would be the best plan."

He was grateful for all of Nomura's efforts, the foreign minister replied, "but the fate of our Empire hangs by the thread of a few days, so please fight harder than you ever did before." He had considered Nomura's plea for delay. "In your opinion we ought to wait and see what turn the war takes and remain patient. However, I am awfully sorry to say that the situation renders this out of the question." He again reminded him of the November 25 deadline. He did not say, but in fact, fleets were gathering at various rendezvous points, armies were on the move. A cable the day before gave detailed instructions for the destruction of code machines "in the event of an emergency."[7]

An illuminating précis of how Churchill regarded a Japanese-American war reached Roosevelt at about this time. It was part of Whitney's report to Donovan. On "U.S. intervention," cabled Whitney, "two assumptions by Churchill. (1) every week sooner we come in will reduce war by one month; (2) order of choice—(a) United States without Japan; (b) U.S. and Japan both in war; (c) neither at war; (d) Japan without America (this possibility unthinkable)."

Churchill's order of choices was not far from Roosevelt's: the United States in the war against Germany, at least with its navy and air force, but not at war with Japan. That order of choices influenced Roosevelt's approach to his first meeting with Kurusu on the seventeenth. He postponed his departure for Warm Springs in order to talk with the special envoy.

He liked Nomura but did not trust Kurusu, who had been the Japanese envoy in Berlin at the time the Tripartite Pact was sealed and signed. But Roosevelt was cordial, recalling at one point that "a long time ago, Secretary of State Bryan once said, 'There is no last word between friends.' " The situation all across the Pacific, Kurusu said, "was like a powder keg," and some way must be found to bring about a settlement. Both Roosevelt and Hull seemed particularly concerned with Japan's obligations under the Tripartite Pact, Kurusu noted, and this is what his cable home emphasized. He had told the president that "Japan alone will determine" Japan's obligations under the pact. "The United States apparently interprets this to mean that Japan will wait until the United States is deeply involved in the battle in the Atlantic and then stab the United States in the back." Kurusu had assured Roosevelt that "this is not the case." He thought that the president was "very much in earnest in regard to effecting an understanding between Japan and the United States," and Tokyo should not jump to conclusions that diplomacy was finished. It seemed both to him and to Nomura that, with the revision of the Neutrality Act, "the attention of the United States has turned more and more than ever toward the Atlantic of late . . . there seems to be a desire to be reassured as to their rear by negotiations with our country. Herein seems to be the chief reason why both the conference with the President on the 17th and in the one with Secretary Hull on the 18th the point of emphasis was on the Three Power Pact, and there was more insistence than heretofore on this."

So impressed were the Japanese envoys by this new emphasis on the American side and its reflection, as they thought, of American preoccupation with the Atlantic, that they went so far as to say to Tokyo that "it seems very clear that they are of a mind to bring about a compromise after making sure of our peaceful intentions." They asked permission to withhold proposal B and to continue discussions on the basis of proposal A. Evidently Tokyo did not agree, but Nomura, presumably speaking also for Kurusu, stuck to his guns. "The displeasure felt by the Government is beyond my powers of comprehension, but as I view it, the present after exhausting our strength by four years of the China incident, following right upon the Manchuria incident, is hardly an opportune time for venturing upon another long drawn out warfare on a large scale. I think it would be better to fix up a temporary 'truce' now in the spirit of give and take and make this the prelude to greater achievements to come later."

Very much for the reasons that Nomura and Kurusu had surmised, Roosevelt and Hull were indeed probing for a truce formula. The Battle of the Atlantic was not proving to be the easy routs of the U-boat and surface raider that Knox and Stimson had predicted. With the revision of the Neutrality Act, the United States Navy would be escorting convoys to the British Isles. Reinforcement of Admiral King's Atlantic fleet meant stripping Kimmel's fleet dangerously. "We *just* haven't *any* destroyers or cruisers to give you at the moment, nor is the prospect bright for your getting any in the near future," Stark advised Kimmel on November 7. "I will not burden you with a recital of King's troubles, but he is up against it for DDs [destroyers] for escort—and defense against raiders." No doubt the cruisers and destroyers were needed in the Atlantic, Kimmel replied. "But I must insist that more consideration be given to the needs of the Pacific Fleet." The realities decreed otherwise. "We have sweat blood," Stark replied to Kimmel, "in this endeavor to divide adequately our forces for a two-ocean war; but you cannot take inadequate forces and divide them into two or three parts and get adequate forces anywhere. . . . We are at our wit's end in the Atlantic with the butter spread extremely thin and the job continuously increasing in toughness." When Clement Attlee and Harold Balfour saw Roosevelt on November 9 to ask for more heavy bombers, they were told that Britain would have to wait until the Far Eastern position clarified. "His present Japanese policy in one of stalling and holding off. If during the next few weeks, this policy looks likely to succeed for some months ahead, or alternately if the President can sign up for peace with Japan so as to ensure no sudden hostilities then he will feel able at once to direct a further diversion of heavy bombers to U.K."[8]

Henry Morgenthau, Jr., was not a member of the war council, but Roosevelt valued his advice. On November 17, the treasury secretary transmitted to Roosevelt and Hull a powerful plea for a bold new approach to the Japanese. Entitled "An Approach to the Problem of Eliminating Tension with Japan and Insuring Defeat of Germany," it was drafted by one of Morgenthau's brainiest aides, Harry Dexter White. It argued that, through diplomacy, the United States could turn Japan from a "powerful enemy into a peaceful and prosperous neighbor." The most immediately important advantage that would flow from such a switch in alliances, White contended, would be to enable the United States "to concentrate as soon as possible her naval forces in the

Atlantic so as to be prepared for any emergency against a potential enemy with whom there is no current basis for friendship." The memorandum proposed a comprehensive settlement with Japan, whose terms would include a twenty-year nonaggression pact, withdrawal of the bulk of the American fleet from the Pacific, the neutralization of Indochina under a five-power condominium, lifting of the embargo, withdrawal of Japanese forces from China and Indochina, the thinning out of Japanese forces along the Manchurian-Soviet frontier, the expulsion of German technicians and propagandists.

Hull, old and ailing, had exhausted himself in the protracted discussions with the Japanese, which, in turn, had had to be prepared in endless huddles with his advisers. But he was gamely prepared for a wholly new approach, especially when one of his top Far Eastern advisers called the Morgenthau proposal "the most constructive one which I have yet seen."

It dovetailed with the search of Roosevelt and Hull for some formula by which to try to avoid a two-front war. What gave it an almost electrifying relevance, however, were the hints that Kurusu had dropped of an interest in a temporary truce or *modus vivendi* that seemed to offer a genuine *quid pro quo*. So impressed had Hull been that he had promptly discussed it with the British. Sir Ronald Campbell, the British minister in Washington, cabled London:

Mr. Hull said that Mr. Kurusu had been "in a great state" over the breakdown on all these three points [relations with the Axis, withdrawal from China, Japanese commercial policy] and had asked whether there was not some way round the difficulty. Could not some means be found of giving the Japanese Government time to educate public opinion away from its present state of mind towards one in which the basis of negotiations with the United States would be possible? For instance, if the Japanese were now to withdraw their troops from Indochina, could the United States ease their economic pressure to the point of sending small quantities of rice and oil far below the full requirements of Japan, Japan guaranteeing that nothing would find its way to Japanese forces? Mr. Hull replied that he was ready to think whether this suggestion was attractive enough to warrant its being tried at least.

Hull said he was also informing the Chinese of the Kurusu overture in case London and Chungking desired to make any comments. The embargo had been imposed in the first place because of Japan's movement of troops into Indochina. If they were now to be withdrawn, thus lifting the threat to Singapore, that would be a significant concession. The British reaction to the Kurusu suggestion was favorable. "If the Japanese were first to take some definite step such as a substantial withdrawal of troops from Indochina," Cadogan minuted, "I shd not close my mind against the possibility of some relaxation of our measures, subject to suitable safeguards. But I find it difficult to believe that the Japanese Government will find it possible to do anything of the sort."

If this was a genuine offer, the foreign office instructed Halifax, it would be worthwhile to respond, provided this could be done in such a way that there was no semblance of abandoning China.[9]

In the meantime there had been two developments in Washington: Roosevelt had revived his own formula for a six-month truce, and Nomura and Kurusu had been instructed by Tokyo to drop their compromise proposal and to present proposal B. However, it was not clear to Washington from the intercepts that Tokyo had rejected the Kurusu-Nomura formula. Testifying at the Pearl Harbor hearings, Hull said of the American decision to press for a *modus vivendi* despite the presentation of proposal B:

Our policy was not to say "No" to the Japanese ultimatum of November 20. It was not to remain silent even, it was to grab every straw in sight, in an effort to keep up the conversation and to give time to our armies and navies here, and among our future Allies to make further preparations, and also to show our continuing interest in peace.

So this *modus vivendi* was given every possible consideration and attention. On November 21, 22, 23, 24, and 25, we made a desperate effort to get something worked out that might stop the hand of the Japanese armies and navies for a few days or a few weeks at any rate, by some possibility. I am sure—I was making every possible effort to get some delay.

Did the State Department and Roosevelt regard the presentation of proposal B as an "ultimatum," as indeed it was, or was this a retrospective judgment? Ickes, who saw Roosevelt on November 21, recorded in his diary that "the President remarked to me that he wished he knew whether Japan was playing poker or not. He was not sure whether or not Japan had a gun up its sleeve. . . . It seemed to me that the President had not yet reached the state of mind where he is willing to be aggressive as to Japan." The contemporary evidence indicates that Roosevelt, Hull, Stimson, and the British considered proposal B a basis for negotiations. And the next few days were spent in seeking to marry Roosevelt's proposal for a six-month truce, which he had revived, to proposal B. Roosevelt's memorandum to Hull read:

6 months

1. U.S. to resume economic relations—some oil and rice now—more later.
2. Japan to send no more troops to Indochina or Manchurian border or any place South (Dutch, Brit. or Siam).
3. Japan to agree not to invoke tripartite pact even if U.S. gets into European war.
4. U.S. to introduce Japs to Chinese to talk things over but U.S. to take no part in their conversations.

Later on Pacific agreements.

Roosevelt wanted to keep Japan from further aggression north and south and to pry it loose from the Axis. In return, he was prepared to ease the economic embargo. The Chinese would not be happy, but they would be no worse off in terms of military realities than they had been.[10]

Nevertheless, this was a marked shift from America's earlier emphasis in its talks with the Japanese, which had placed as much stress on the evacuation of China and Indochina as on the Tripartite Pact. One is tempted to speculate what might have happened had Roosevelt met with Konoye before his fall and presented him with a proposal such as the six-months formula embodied. Would it have postponed the showdown with Japan, and would the breathing spell thus gained have led to the "Pacific agreements" mentioned at the tail end of Roosevelt's memorandum and which had been spelled out in statesmanlike amplitude in Harry Dexter White's proposal? The question is unanswerable. It is tempting to believe that a course was open to Roosevelt that might have kept the United States from its disastrous postwar involvement in Asia, but, as Churchill remarked in the course of defending his policy at Gallipoli in World War I: "It is no good coming along afterwards and applying to these events the light of after-knowledge and the assumption of plenary powers. The future was unknown. No one possessed plenary powers."

Hull showed a preliminary version of the *modus vivendi* to Stark and Gen. Leonard T. Gerow (General Marshall was out of town), both of whom said "the document was satisfactory from a military viewpoint." In the army's more detailed comment, General Gerow added, "War Plans Division wishes to emphasize it is of grave importance to the success of our war effort in Europe that we should reach a *modus vivendi* with Japan."

The new formula was sent by Roosevelt to Churchill. Before it was received, Churchill, in a minute to Eden, had approved American efforts to modify Japan's proposal B:

Our major interest is: no further encroachments and no war, as we have already enough of this latter. The United States will not throw over the Chinese cause, and we may safely follow them on this part of the subject. We could not of course agree to an arrangement whereby Japan was free to attack Russia in Siberia. I doubt myself whether this is likely at the present time. I remember that President Roosevelt at the Atlantic Conference himself wrote in, "There must be no further encroachment in the North." I should think that this could be agreed [with the Americans]. The formal denunciation of the Axis Pact by Japan is not, in my opinion, necessary. Their stopping out of the war is in itself a great disappointment and injury to the Germans. We ought not to agree to any veto on American or British help to China. But we shall not be asked to by the United States.

Subject to the above, it would be worthwhile to ease up upon Japan economically sufficiently for them to live from hand to mouth—even if we only got another three months. These, however, are only first impressions.

I must say I should feel pleased if I read that an American-Japanese agreement had been made by which we were able to be no worse off three months hence in the Far East than we are now.

On November 24, Roosevelt sent Churchill a description of the exact terms the United States was prepared to offer in the way of a *modus vivendi*. These were described as a counterproposal to Japan's offer of November 20:

This Government proposes to inform the Japanese Government that in the opinion of this Government the Japanese proposals contain features not in harmony with the fundamental principles which underlie the proposed general settlement and to which each Government has declared that it is committed. It is also proposed to offer to the Japanese Government an alternatitve proposal for a *modus vivendi* which will contain mutual pledges of peaceful intent, a recriprocal undertaking not to make an armed advancement into areas which would include northeastern Asia and the northern Pacific area, southeast Asia and the southern Pacific area, an undertaking by Japan to withdraw its forces from southern French Indochina, not to replace those forces, to limit those in northern Indochina to the number there on July 26, 1941, which number shall not be subject to replacement and shall not in any case exceed 25,000 and not to send additional forces to Indochina. This Government would undertake to modify its freezing orders to the extent to permit exports from the United States to Japan of bunkers and ship supplies, food products and pharmaceuticals with certain qualifications, raw cotton up to $600,000 monthly, petroleum on a monthly basis for civilian needs, the proportionate amount to be exported from this country to be determined after consultation with the British and Dutch Governments. The United States would permit imports in general provided that raw silk constitute at least two-thirds in value of such imports. The proceeds of such imports would be available for the purchase of the designated exports from the United States and for the payment of interest and principal of Japanese obligations within the United States. This Government would undertake to approach the British, Dutch and Australian Governments on the question of their taking similar economic measures. Provision is made that the *modus vivendi* shall remain in force for three months with the understanding that at the instance of either party the two parties shall confer to determine whether the prospects of reaching a peaceful settlement covering the entire Pacific area warrant extension of the *modus vivendi*.

This part of the message was drafted in the State Department. On it was scrawled "OK. See addition. FDR." Roosevelt's postscript said: "This seems to me a fair proposition for the Japanese but its acceptance or rejection is really a matter of internal Japanese politics. I am not very hopeful and we must all be prepared for real trouble, possibly soon."[11]

What had triggered the president's skeptical addition were Magic intercepts. One, dated November 22, extended the deadline for the signing of an agreement from November 25 to November 29. "After that things are automatically going to happen." The second, dated November 24, not only ruled out any departures from proposal B but stated flatly that "our demand for a cessation of aid to Chiang (the acquisitions of Netherlands East Indian goods and at the same time the supply of American petroleum to Japan as well) is a most essential condition." Hull shared Roosevelt's doubts. He had a long talk with Stark on November 24, as a result of which Stark sent a warning signal to all naval commands:

Chances of favorable outcome with Japan very doubtful. This situation coupled with statements of Japanese government and movements of their naval and military forces indicate in our opinion that a surprise aggressive movement in any direction including attack on Philippines or Guam is a possibility. Chief of Staff has seen this dispatch concurs and requests action addressees to inform senior army officers their areas. Utmost secrecy necessary in order not to complicate an already tense situation or precipitate Japanese action.

The intricate game went forward in Washington of preparing to present the U.S. version of a *modus vivendi* with one hand, while the other was alerting America's military forces in the Pacific to the danger of a surprise attack. On the twenty-fifth, the U.S. version of the *modus vivendi* was being considered in London and Chungking. That morning, Hull showed it to Stimson and Knox, among the least appeasement-minded members of Roosevelt's cabinet. "It adequately safeguarded all our interests, I thought as we read it," wrote Stimson, "but I don't think there is any chance of the Japanese accepting it because it was so drastic. In return for the propositions which they were to do; namely, to at once evacuate and at once to stop all preparations or threats of action, and to take no aggressive action against any of her neighbors, etc., we were to give them open trade in sufficient quantities only for their civilian population. This restriction was particularly applicable to oil."

A few hours after Stimson had indicated approval of the *modus vivendi,*

we (viz., General Marshall and I) went to the White House, where we were until nearly half past one. At the meeting were Hull, Knox, Marshall, Stark, and myself. There the President, instead of bringing up the Victory Parade ["this was an office nickname," Stimson noted, "for the General Staff strategic plan of national action in case of war in Europe"], brought up entirely the relations with the Japanese. He brought up the event that we were likely to be attacked perhaps [as soon as] next Monday, for the Japanese are notorious for making an attack without warning, and the question was what we should do. The question was how we should maneuver them into the position of firing the first shot without allowing too much danger to ourselves. It was a difficult proposition. Hull laid out his general broad propositions on which the thing should be rested—the freedom of the seas and the fact that Japan was in alliance with Hitler and was carrying out his policy of world aggression. The others brought out the fact that any such expedition to the South as the Japanese were likely to take would be an encirclement of our interests in the Philippines and cutting into our vital supplies of rubber from Malaysia. I pointed out to the President that he had already taken the first steps towards an ultimatum in notifying Japan way back last summer that if she crossed the border into Thailand she was violating our safety and that therefore he had only to point out (to Japan) that to follow any such expedition was a violation of a warning we had already given. So Hull is to go to work on preparing that.

Stark again communicated his concern over a sudden Japanese thrust southward. Neither the president nor Hull, he wrote to Kimmel, "would be surprised over a Japanese surprise attack. From many angles an attack on the Philippines would be the most embarrassing thing that could happen to us. . . . I won't go into the pros and cons of what the United States may do. I will be damned if I know. I wish I did. The only thing I do know is that we may do most anything and that's the only thing I know to be prepared for; or we may do nothing—I think it is more likely to be 'anything.' "

Meanwhile, the proposed *modus vivendi,* which had not yet been presented to the Japanese, was meeting stiff resistance from America's allies. The most violent protests came from China. Chiang Kai-shek mobilized all his partisans in Washington and London against it. Professor Owen Lattimore, who was serving as Chiang's adviser, cabled Lauchlin Currie, one of Roosevelt's aides, that he should "urgently advise the President of the Generalissimo's very strong reaction. I have never seen him really agitated before. . . . A relaxation of American pressure while Japan has its forces in China would dismay the Chinese." Chiang also cabled directly to Morgenthau, Stimson, and Knox, warning that any concession to Japan would be disastrous for Chinese morale. The United States should "announce that if the withdrawal of the Japanese Armies from China is not settled, the question of relaxation of the embargo or freezing could not be considered." Morgenthau, on the basis of what Chiang's brother-in-law T. V. Soong told him about the terms of the *modus vivendi,* thought the Chinese had every reason to be disturbed. The proposed arrangement "is lovely for us, but it leaves the poor Chinese holding the bag with twenty five thousand troops right at their back door."

Morgenthau went into the president's bedroom the next morning, the twenty-sixth, to see him at breakfast. He felt sorry for the president. "He had not touched his coffee. He had some kippered herring which he had just begun to eat when Cordell Hull called up. He was talking to Hull and trying to eat his food at the same time, but by the time he finished his conversation his food was cold and he didn't touch it." He heard Roosevelt say to Hull that he would see Soong and the Chinese ambassador Hu Shih: "I will quiet them down."

Morgenthau was so upset himself that he drafted a letter to the president that he did not send because the *modus vivendi* was abandoned, imploring him "that the need is for iron firmness. No settlement with Japan that in any way seems to the American people, or to the rest of the world, to be a retreat, no matter how temporary, from our increasingly clear policy of opposition to aggressors, will be viewed as inconsistent with the position of our Government or with the leadership that you have established." When Ickes, after the event, learned of the proposed *modus vivendi,* he asserted in his diary that if it had not been dropped he would have resigned from the cabinet "with a ringing statement attacking the arrangement and raising hell generally with the State Department and its policy of appeasement. . . . The country would have reacted violently."[12]

Some time between the evening of the twenty-fifth and the morning of the twenty-sixth Hull renounced the effort to achieve a temporary truce. He was furious with the Chinese—and the British. He resented the way Chiang had "sent numerous hysterical cable messages to different cabinet officers and high officials in the Government other than the State Department and sometimes even ignoring the President, intruding into a delicate and serious situation with no real idea of what the facts are." The British had angered him because "it would have been better if, when Churchill received Chiang Kai-shek's loud protest about our negotiations here with Japan, instead of passing the protest on to us without objection on his part, thereby qualifying and virtually killing what we knew were the individual views of the British Government toward these negotiations, he had sent a strong cable back to Chiang Kai-shek telling him to brace up and fight with the same zeal as the Japanese and Germans are displaying instead of weakening and telling the Chinese people that all of the friendly countries were now striving primarily to protect themselves and to force an agreement between China and Japan."

Churchill's cable to Roosevelt had said that "of course, it is for you to handle this business and we certainly do not want an additional war. There is only one point that disquiets us. What about Chiang Kai-shek? Is he not having a very thin diet? Our anxiety is about China. If they collapse our joint dangers would enormously increase. We are sure that the regard of the United States for the Chinese will govern your action. We feel that the Japanese are most unsure of themselves."

Churchill's view of the Japanese as vacillating and uncertain was shared by Hull's chief political adviser Stanley K. Hornbeck, who discounted the strength of the Japanese threat. And when Hull argued against putting aside the truce, stating that the navy wanted another three months, Hornbeck retorted that the navy "had asked for six months last February and that the Secretary, through his negotiations had got them that six months. Now they wanted three more. Hornbeck's idea was that the President ought to stop asking the Navy and tell it." A Hornbeck memorandum on November 27 offered to wager 5 to 1 that the United States and Japan would not be at war before December 15; 3 to 1 that they would not be at war before January 15; and even money on no war by March. 1.

But Churchill and Hornbeck were mistaken about Japanese hesitations. On November 26, the Pearl Harbor Task Force weighed anchor and, shrouded in fog and radio silence, began to sail toward its target. This movement was undetected by the United States, but American intelligence did spot substantial troop movements southward. "When I got back to the Department," Stimson recorded on the twenty-fifth, referring to the afternoon after the war cabinet's meeting, "I found news from G-2 that an expedition had started. Five divisions have come down from Shantung and Shansi to Shanghai and there they had embarked on ships—20, 40 or 50 ships—and have been sighted south of Formosa. I at once called up Hull and told him about it and sent copies to him and the President of the message from G-2."

For some reason the message did not reach Roosevelt. But the next morning, when Stimson mentioned it to FDR over the phone, "he fairly blew up—jumped up into the air so to speak, and said that he hadn't seen it and that that changed the whole situation because it was evidence of bad faith on the part of the Japanese that while they were negotiating for an entire truce—an entire withdrawal—they should be sending this expedition down there to Indochina." With Roosevelt's approval, Hull broke off serious negotiations with Nomura and Kurusu, handing them a bulky ten-point declaration that restated America's long-standing. principles and positions and that caused Kurusu to remark that "his Government would be likely to throw up its hands" on receiving it. By then, the Pearl Harbor Task Force, although it still could be ordered to return, had been under way for twenty-four hours. "I have washed my hands of it and it is now in the hands of you and Knox—the Army and the Navy," Hull informed Stimson on November 27 when the war secretary inquired about the status of the negotiations.[13]

America's military commands in the Pacific were again alerted. Marshall cabled his generals:

Negotiations with Japan appear to be terminated to all practical purposes with only the barest possibilities that the Japanese Government might come back and offer to continue. Japanese future action unpredictable but hostile action possible at any moment. If hostilities cannot comma repeat cannot comma be avoided the United States desires that Japan commit the first overt act. This policy should not comma repeat not comma be construed as restricting you to a course of action that might jeopardize your defense.

Stark's radiogram was even more final:

This dispatch is to be considered a war warning. Negotiations with Japan looking toward stabilization of conditions in the Pacific have ceased and an aggressive move is expected by Japan within the next few days. The number and equipment of Japanese troops and the organization of naval task forces indicates an amphibious expedition against either the Philippines, Thai or Kra Peninsula or possibly Borneo. Execute an appropriate defensive deployment preparatory to carrying out the tasks assigned in WPL46. Inform district and Army authorities. A similar warning is being sent by the War Department.

Roosevelt sent his son Capt. James Roosevelt to William Stephenson, the head of British intelligence in the United States, to inform the British government. "Japanese negotiations off," Stephenson cabled London on November 27. "Services expect action within two weeks." An agitated foreign office cabled Halifax for confirmation, but the ambassador was off hunting in Virginia.

How much the United States knew was even clearer in Roosevelt's cable to the high commissioner in the Philippines, Francis Sayre: "Preparations are becoming apparent in China, Formosa and Indochina for an early aggressive movement of some character, although as yet there are no clear indications as to its strength, or whether it will be directed against the Burma Road, Thailand, Malay Peninsula, Netherlands East Indies or the Philippines. Advance against Thailand seems the most probable. I consider it possible that this next Japanese aggression might cause an outbreak of hostilities between the United States and Japan." Intercepts confirmed that war was imminent. Kurusu was instructed in a special voice code over the phone after he and the foreign office agreed that the crisis was at hand. "Regarding negotiations, don't break them off." This was reiterated in a telegram later in the day stating that a *de facto* rupture of negotiations within two or three days was inevitable. "However I do not wish you to give the impressions that negotiations are broken off. . . . From now on do the best you can." And the

United States knew that after November 29 things were to happen "automatically"[14]

Roosevelt, nevertheless, just before departing for Warm Springs on Friday, November 28, met with Nomura and Kurusu and said that, despite recent moves and utterances by Japan that had had the effect of "a cold bath" on American opinion, the United States was prepared "to continue to be patient if Japan's courses of action permit continuance of such an attitude on our part." But there could be no "substantial relaxation in its economic restrictions unless Japan gives this country some clear manifestation of peaceful intent. If that occurs, we can also take some steps of a concrete character designed to improve the general situation." But neither Roosevelt nor Hull was spending time any longer on devising formulas for a truce. The Roosevelt declaration was for the record. In the war cabinet that day, the members focused on where the Japanese expeditionary force that had left Shanghai and was headed south might strike.

It was now the opinion of everyone that if this expedition was allowed to get around the southern point of Indochina and to go off and land in the Gulf of Siam, either at Bangkok or further West, it would be a terrific blow at all of the three Powers, Britain at Singapore, the Netherlands, and ourselves in the Philippines. It was the consensus of everybody that this must not be allowed. Then we discussed how to prevent it. It was agreed that if the Japanese got into the Isthmus of Kra, the British would fight. It was also agreed that if the British fought, we would have to fight. And it now seems clear that if this expedition was allowed to round the southern point of Indochina, this whole chain of disastrous events would be set on foot of going.

The president favored a final warning in the form of a letter to the emperor when the expeditionary force approached the critical line. Stimson preferred embodying the warning in a message to Congress. The president compromised. He would send a letter to the emperor but keep it secret and also speak to Congress. He asked Hull, Knox, and Stimson to prepare drafts. He was off to Warm Springs, he said determinedly, "to keep his engagement . . . to have Thanksgiving with the children." Stimson regretted his departure "but nobody spoke out and warned him." It was extraordinary that he should have left Washington at that moment. But the Pacific commands had been alerted. He had told the Japanese envoys that a *quid pro quo* was still possible. He had ruled out a pre-emptive strike because it had to be clear to the nation that Japan was the aggressor. If the Japanese did strike on the twenty-ninth or soon thereafter, his absence from the capital would bolster the image of the peacemaker betrayed.

By Monday, however, Roosevelt was back in Washington. Hull had called him at Warm Springs and asked him to return. A Japanese attack on Thailand was imminent, including a sea-borne landing on the Kra Isthmus, the British had reported. Moreover, the Japanese prime minister, General Tojo, was stirring up Japanese public opinion with what Berle described as "a cutthroat statement saying that the time had come to end American and British exploitation in the Far East forever."

Among the Magic intercepts that awaited Roosevelt at the White House were messages between Japanese Ambassador Oshima in Berlin and the foreign office in Tokyo. "Say very secretly to them," Oshima was instructed to inform Hitler and Ribbentrop, "that there is extreme danger that the war may suddenly break out between the Anglo-Saxon nations and Japan through some clash of arms and add that the time of the breaking out of this war may come quicker than anyone desires." At the same time, Oshima had cabled Tokyo that Ribbentrop had pledged flatly, "Should Japan become engaged in a war against the United States, Germany, of course, would join the war immediately. There is absolutely no possibility of Germany's entering into separate peace with the United States. The Fuehrer is determined on that point."

Again Churchill pressed for a flat-out warning to Japan:

It seems to me that one important method remains unused in averting war between Japan and our two countries, namely a plain declaration, secret or public as may be thought best, that any further act of aggression by Japan will lead immediately to the gravest consequence. I realize your constitutional difficulties but it would be tragic if Japan drifted into war by encroachment without having before her fairly and squarely the dire character of a further aggressive step. I beg you to consider whether, at the moment which you judge right which may be very near, you should not say that "any further Japanese aggression would compel you to place the gravest issues before Congress" or words to that effect. We would, of course, make a similar declaration or share in a joint declaration, and in any case arrangements are being made to synchronize our actions with yours. Forgive me, my dear friend, for presuming to press such a course upon you, but I am convinced that it might make all the difference and prevent a melancholy extension of the war.[15]

But Roosevelt no longer believed in the possibility of deterring the Japanese. His concern now was for the unity of the nation when the blow was struck. A warning that would have to be ultimative in character was not the way to bring the nation together, especially not a joint warning with Britain when the blow might fall on the British and Dutch rather than on the Americans and he would have to ask Congress to declare war nonetheless.

Chapter Twenty-eight

All in the Same Boat

T HE DAY AFTER Roosevelt returned to the White House from Warm Springs, he had a fateful luncheon with Halifax. He was now prepared to say what he would do in the event Japan attacked British or Dutch possessions in Asia. Hopkins, who had been in the hospital and whose absence had caused a worried Stimson to fear that the appeasers were getting to the president, was also present. "[Roosevelt's] information was that the Japanese Government was a good deal disturbed by his return," Halifax reported to London. The Japanese envoys had seen Hull and had returned to the subject of an interim agreement. What basis was there for such an arrangement, Hull had replied, when the Japanese "were continuing to move troops all the time?" Britain and the United States, the president went on, should continue their "air patrol," and he had also ordered three submarines to conduct reconnaissance in "likely waters for the sake of information. They would not take offensive action but would act if attacked." Roosevelt dwelt particularly on the flow of Japanese troops to Indochina and said he had considered "some concerted parallel statement" with Britain, but had decided the wiser course was to have Welles on his behalf inquire of the Japanese the intention and purpose of the troop movements.

Hopkins broke in to stress the danger of giving the Japanese the impression that while they acted "we only sent notes and talked." Roosevelt agreed. America and Britain should be clear as to what they would do in the event of an unsatisfactory reply about Indochina or in the event of Japanese pressure or attack on Thailand. "I should be glad to have replies to these questions as early as possible," Halifax said, "and I think that whatever action in these respective cases His Majesty's Government are prepared to take, [Roosevelt] would be disposed to support." The whole tenor of the president's remarks, commented Halifax, was "that we should both recognize any of these hypothetical actions to be clear prelude to some further action and threat to our common interests, against which we ought to react together at once." The kind of actions he had in mind, Roosevelt indicated, was the use of the four-engined bombers in the Philippines and a long-distance naval blockade, which, he added, "of course means shooting. At one point [Roosevelt] threw in an aside that in the case of any direct attack on ourselves or the Dutch, we *should obviously* [Halifax's emphasis] all be together, but he wished to clear up the matters that were less plain." Roosevelt was particularly concerned with a Japanese attack on the Kra Isthmus, with the responses of the United States and Britain, and in what sequence those responses should be made. He was also contemplating a letter to the emperor. "Such communication would be friendly but would make plain that if the present Japanese attitude continued war must result. He is however suspending this for the present." The ambassador's cable ended with a bow to Hopkins, who "was most helpful."

The most important point in this telegram, commented the Far Eastern department of the foreign office, was the president's "aside" about what the United States would do in the event of a direct attack on the British or the Dutch. "The President's attitude, as shown in Washington telegram No. 5519," Eden advised the war cabinet in a printed paper on Far Eastern policy, "is forthcoming and helpful and it is important that we should respond without delay. I have already telegraphed Lord Halifax to ascertain whether the President would prefer that his enquiry to the Japanese should be made by the United States Government alone or whether it would be agreeable to him that we should make a simultaneous enquiry."

Another clarifying report about American intentions came via the Australian minister to Washington:

Friendly American newspaperman tells me that Sumner Welles spoke "off the record" to a group of senior American journalists today of which he was one. Gist was as follows:

There is no basis for optimism regarding our negotiations with Japanese. Japanese troops are continuing to move into Southern Indochina. Line beyond which we cannot allow Japanese to pass has been reached for three reasons (a) we cannot allow ourselves to be cut off from essential defense needs [meaning, Halifax thought, tin and rubber], (b) we cannot be put in the position of asking Japanese permission to trade in the Pacific and (c) we cannot allow the Burma Road, our last remaining means of sending aid to China, to be cut. Japan may seek to enter Thailand by force or by an agreement negotiated under duress. We cannot allow one any more than the other. The British cannot allow the Japanese to occupy Thailand. It is too close to Singapore, Burma and India. The British will fight and we will move in behind.[1]

Roosevelt was prepared to support the British and the Dutch, but the country, he knew, was divided. Neutrality Act revision had passed in the House of Representatives by the slim vote of 212 to 194. Lend-lease, selective service, and revision of the Neutrality Act had all been enacted by the Congress, but only after ferocious struggles. Though the opposition to Roosevelt's policies had diminished in numbers, the desperation, almost recklessness, of isolationist attacks had intensified. "How much longer free speech will be possible in the United States I do not know," declared Lindbergh before a packed audience of 4,000 in Fort Wayne, Indiana, the heartland of isolationism.

But I do know that an administration which can throw the country into an undeclared naval war against the will of our people, and without asking the consent of Congress, can by similar methods prevent freedom of speech among us. There are many signs that such action may be taken in the near future, with as little warning as the occupation of Iceland.

Those of us who oppose war do not know from one week to the next what censorship we will be subjected to. Pressure of every sort is brought to bear on us.

Roosevelt was drawing more and more dictatorial power into his own hands, Lindbergh asserted, and the next step might well be the suspension of the 1942 congressional elections.

Roosevelt responded with equal harshness. He asked Attorney General Francis Biddle, "Will you speak to me about the possibility of a Grand Jury investigation of the America First Committee? It certainly ought to be looked into and I cannot get any action out of Congress." Biddle did look into the matter but decided that "there were no grounds to warrant a grand jury investigation, which, the President believed, would show that much of America First's financial support came directly or indirectly from Germany." This would not be the last occasion on which a president would be persuaded that the opposition to his foreign policy was foreign-inspired and financed.

There *was* a certain amount of underground German support for America First. This is clear from German chargé Thomsen's cable to Berlin on November 13:

Roosevelt is ruthlessly continuing to press the drive against the opposition and its leaders with all available means. Roosevelt's chief antagonist and obstruction to his foreign policy of intervening is the America First Committee, now numbering over 15 million members. Secretary of the Interior Ickes declared open war on it in his speech of October 20, by calling for an investigation of the methods of financing the organization, allegedly supplied by subversive Nazi funds. Following Lindbergh's attack on the Jews, Baruch was given the job of undermining the America First Committee from within by the use of Jewish money. At the same time the Federal Bureau of Investigation and the propaganda squads of the Justice Department are proceeding against the publishers of the well-known magazines *Scribner's Commentator* and *Herald* as the two principal publicity media of the America First Committee.

The danger exists that many leading members of the Committee will be so intimidated by these methods that they will resign. In order that this useful organization not disintegrate, the press officer, through his confidential agents, is endeavoring to ensure that should General Wood, who is the present chairman, resign, Lindbergh would take over the leadership. Despite all attacks and calumnies on the part of the interventionists, Lindbergh's prestige and popularity are on the increase. The negotiations are conducted in such a way that the Embassy's part in them cannot be discerned.

Yet in spite of the German embassy's involvement, the opposition to Roosevelt's policies that America First expressed was indigenous. The isolationists were as passionately persuaded of the rightness of their view of the national interest and how to protect it as were the president and the interventionists.

Their depth of feeling was demonstrated on December 4, when the *Chicago Tribune* and the *Washington Times-Herald,* leading isolationist newspapers, published under the banner headline "F.D.R.'s War Plans" the general staff's blueprint of the strategy it would pursue in the event of war.* "What would you think of an American General Staff," an outraged Stimson asked at his press conference, "which in the present condition of the world did not investigate and study every conceivable type of emergency which may confront this country and every possible method of meeting that emergency?" And, he continued, "What do you think of the patriotism of a man or a newspaper which would take these confidential studies and make them public to the enemies of this country?"

When he reported what he had said to the cabinet, "Harold Ickes grunted that it was entirely too defensive." Ickes believed that "an example ought to be made . . . the charge of treason should have been thrown at McCormick [editor and publisher of the *Chicago Tribune*] immediately after his newspaper was off the press." The attorney general thought the offense "would come within the Statutes of the Espionage Act," but Stimson advised Roosevelt "to also bring in the Conspiracy Statute and to paint the full broad picture instead of trying to prosecute a more substantive crime. On talking it over afterwards with the boys in my own Department, I think it is vitally important to make that a great State prosecution to get rid of this infernal disloyalty which we now have working in the America First and in these McCormick family papers." The revelations of America's war plans was a boon for Germany's intelligence agencies, and most of America by then considered Germany the enemy.[2]

For Roosevelt, the episode underscored once again the depth and fury of the opposition and the peril of going into war with the nation divided as rancorously as it was on the eve of the Civil War, when Lincoln had to cope not only with the secessionist armies but with the Copperhead opposition in

---

* According to William Stevenson in *A Man Called Intrepid,* the alleged war plans turned over by Senator Wheeler to the *Chicago Tribune* were planted on him by British intelligence. "The Political-Warfare Division of BSC [Intrepid's organization] concocted the *Victory Program* out of material already known to have reached the enemy in dribs and drabs, and added some misleading information." The purpose of the leak was "to use isolationist channels as a means of revealing to Hitler a 'secret plan' calculated to provoke him into a declaration of war" on the United States The author finds this difficult to credit. If the leaked war plans were a "concoction," why were America's top war leaders, including General Marshall and Colonel Wedemeyer, the drafter of the plan, taken in by it? Colonel Wedemeyer, because of his America First sympathies, was searchingly examined and exonerated by the FBI. He certainly considered the published account an authentic version of what he had drafted. It is extraordinary that British intelligence should claim "credit" for the leaking of a "concoction," which, had it taken place, would have constituted the grossest interference in the political affairs of its closest ally.

the North. "One problem troubled us very much," Stimson, after the war, told the congressional committee that investigated Pearl Harbor. "If you know that your enemy is going to strike you, it is not usually wise to wait until he gets the jump on you by taking the initiative. In spite of the risk involved, however, in letting the Japanese fire the first shot, we realized that in order to have the full support of the American people it was desirable to make sure the Japanese be the ones to do this so that there should remain no doubt in anyone's mind as to who were the aggressors." As Stimson recorded at the time: "The question was how we should maneuver them into the position of firing the first shot without allowing too much danger to ourselves."

Critics of Roosevelt's policies after the war seized upon the first part of this Stimson entry—about "maneuvering" the Japanese—interpreting it to mean a calculated policy to provoke a war with Japan rather than, as Stimson contended, a deliberate decision to leave the initiative in the hands of the Japanese so that the nation would clearly see which one was the aggressor. But for Roosevelt, who was commander in chief of the country's armed forces, the second part of Stimson's entry—"without allowing too much danger to ourselves"—weighed with equal heaviness. At luncheon with Ickes in mid-November, that pugnacious liberal was sure "that sooner or later, depending upon the progress of Germany, Japan would be at our throats; as for me, when I knew that I was going to be attacked, I preferred to choose my own time and occasion." The pre-emptive strike that recommended itself to Ickes as a matter of temperament and ideology had been carefully considered by the war cabinet as a matter of military necessity on November 28. The group was studying the progress of the Japanese expeditionary force that was heading south, and the consensus was·

that rather than strike at the Force as it went by without any warning on the one hand, which we didn't think we could do; or sitting still and allowing it to go on the other, which we didn't think we could do,—that the only thing for us to do was to address it a warning that if it reached a certain place, or a certain line, or a certain point, we should have to fight. The President's mind evidently was running towards a special telegram from himself to the Emperor of Japan. This he had done with good results at the time of the Panay incident, but for many reasons this did not seem to me to be the right thing now and I pointed them out to the President. In the first place, a letter to the Emperor of Japan could not be couched in terms which contained an explicit warning. One does not warn an Emperor.

The pressure abated somewhat on Monday, December 1, when it appeared as if the expeditionary force was halting in Indochina. "This gives us a little bit of respite," wrote Stimson. The danger remained, however, of allowing Japan to hold the strategic initiative, especially as neither Roosevelt nor the men around him any longer thought that war in the Far East could be avoided. The British offensive in Libya, although "going slowly," and the surprising Russian counterattack at Rostov did ,seem to Stimson to be giving "the Japanese pause. But they have evidently made up their minds to attack as soon as they get what they deem a favorable opportunity." And Welles, who in November had rated the chances of maintaining peace as low as 1 in 1,000, now in December felt the odds had fallen to "about one chance in a million."[3]

On December 1, an imperial conference in Tokyo confirmed the decision to go to war since diplomacy had clearly failed to get Japan what it wanted. In a final comment summing up the conference, Premier Tojo said: "At the moment our Empire stands at the threshold of glory or oblivion. We tremble with fear in the presence of His Majesty. We subjects are keenly aware of the great responsibility we must assume from this point on. Once His Majesty reaches a decision to commence hostilities, we will all strive to repay our obligations to him, bring the Government and the military ever closer together, resolve that the nation united will go on to victory, make an all-out effort to achieve our war aims, and set His Majesty's mind at ease." The transcriber of these notes, Army Chief of Staff Sugiyama, ended his minutes on a note of reverence: "During today's Conference, His Majesty nodded in agreement with the statements being made, and displayed no signs of uneasiness. He seemed to be in an excellent mood, and we were filled with awe." On December 2, Japanese army and navy chiefs reported jointly to the throne and requested imperial sanction for orders that confirmed December 8 (December 7 in Hawaii) as "X-day." The emperor said yes, and the order flashed to the Pearl Harbor task force more than a thousand miles on its way hooded in silence. "Climb Mount Niitaka 1208." Niitaka on Formosa was the highest peak in the Japanese Empire, and deciphered the message read, "December 8 has been fixed as the day hostilities will commence. Attack as planned!"

This message was not deciphered by United States intelligence, but American commands throughout the Pacific were alerted that Japanese diplomatic and consular posts had been instructed to destroy most of their codes and ciphers and to burn important documents.* [4]

Anglo-American strategists spent much of these last days before Pearl

---

* The question was repeatedly asked in the various Pearl Harbor inquiries why intelligence had not picked up the Pearl Harbor Task Force. In fact, Admiral Kimmel, uneasy because of loss of radio contact with the Japanese aircraft carriers, had asked his fleet intelligence officer, Commander Layton, to give him a location report on them. They had been lost since November 16, proceeding in radio silence to their Pearl Harbor rendezvous. But the conclusion that naval intelligence drew from the lack of radio traffic was that the carriers were in home waters where they were using low-power radio direct with shore stations. When Kimmel had reviewed the location sheet on December 2, he said jokingly to Layton: "What, you don't know where the carriers are? Do you mean to say they could be rounding Diamond Head and you wouldn't know it?" Layton's preconceptions kept him from taking this badinage seriously. As he told the Pearl Harbor Investigating Committee: "I did not at any time suggest that the Japanese carriers were under radio silence approaching Oahu. I wish I had. . . . My own personal opinion, and that is what we work on when making estimates to ourselves, was that the carriers were remaining in home waters, preparing for operations so that they would be in a covering position in case we moved against Japan after she attacked, if she did, in southeast Asia."

Harbor trying to determine when and where the Japanese would strike and how the West should respond. The last was of particular importance to Roosevelt because of the special burden he carried of obtaining Congressional approval for any military response to a Japanese attack on the British, the Dutch, or the Thais. Official British historians have described United States diplomatic moves during this week as "surprisingly leisurely." But that judgment fails to give full weight to Roosevelt's domestic problem. Roosevelt had not agreed to Churchill's proposal on November 30 for a final joint warning. Instead, he had Welles (Hull was ill) inquire of Nomura and Kurusu on his behalf the reasons for the Japanese troop movements to southern Indochina. "The President would prefer that this should remain United States initiative for the present. He has in mind largely domestic considerations," Halifax advised Eden.

Nomura and Kurusu were unable to tell Welles what the purpose of the troop movements were. The December 1 imperial conference had instructed the foreign minister to keep his ambassadors uninformed but to keep them talking. Nomura said he would refer Welles's inquiry, which was, in fact, a warning, to Tokyo. Churchill was not wholly satisfied with Roosevelt's reluctance to issue a joint warning or his pledges of support in the event of a Japanese attack. Suppose there was an attack on Thailand, or Singapore, or the Dutch East Indies—would Congress support the president in a decision to go to war? The Germans, who attached more importance to the isolationist opposition than did the Japanese, had counseled their ally to avoid an attack on American territories. "Apparently a surprise occupation of Thailand extending about to the Isthmus of Kra is planned," the German ambassador in Tokyo had cabled Berlin after a talk with the Japanese minister of war. "Simultaneously, possession is to be taken of the oil fields of northern and eastern Borneo. It seems that no decision has been taken as yet on what is to be done about the Philippines. On the basis of previous instructions I said that if adequate armed forces were in readiness an attitude of waiting might be possible and advisable considering the weakness of the Americans, so that the United States may be saddled with the decision of entering the war which is a difficult one on grounds of domestic policy."

"Our settled policy," Churchill notified the foreign secretary,

is not to take forward action in advance of the United States. Except in the case of a Japanese attempt to seize the Kra Isthmus, there will be time for the United States to be squarely confronted with a new act of Japanese aggression. If they move, we will move immediately in support. If they do not move, we must consider our position afresh. . . .

A Japanese attack on the Dutch possessions may be made at any time. This would be a direct affront to the United States, following upon their negotiations with Japan. We should tell the Dutch that we should do nothing to prevent the full impact of this Japanese aggression presenting itself to the United States as a direct issue between them and Japan. If the United States declares war on Japan, we follow within the hour. If, after a reasonable interval, the United States is found to be incapable of taking any decisive action, even with our immediate support we will nevertheless, although alone, make common cause with the Dutch.

Any attack on British possessions carries with it war with Great Britain as a matter of course.[5]

The case of the Kra Isthmus illustrated the complexity of a defense strategy that left the initiative to Japan. It extruded taillike from southern Thailand and controlled access to Malaya and Singapore, the Netherlands East Indies, and Burma. The British wanted to move troops into the Kra Isthmus, but the Thai government, with a long experience of balancing between more powerful neighbors, hesitated, uncertain which side would prevail. When a pre-emptive occupation was under consideration, Roosevelt, as in the case of Iceland and the Azores, wanted the British to get an invitation from the Thais. This was not simply a matter of diplomatic etiquette; it was closely related to his awareness of the rising tide of nationalism.

During his Monday luncheon with Halifax, Roosevelt had passed on information about Japanese intentions in the Kra Isthmus that the United States had obtained through Magic. His information was that the Japanese embassy in Bangkok had advised Tokyo to aim its attack on the isthmus first against British territory just south of the Malaya-Thailand boundary, since this would oblige Britain to occupy the Kra Isthmus and make it appear to be the aggressor against Thailand. It would be desirable, therefore, Roosevelt urged Halifax, for the British to get a Thai invitation. But, he added, "we must clearly do what strategical necessity dictated anyhow."

The difficulty with getting such an invitation, replied the foreign office, "is that we are not militarily in a position to give direct assistance to the Thai Government in the protection of the rest of their territory. . . . The Thai Prime Minister has forcibly represented to us that the only way to save Thailand (Siam) is by a public warning to Japan by the United States and ourselves that if she went to war with Thailand she would find herself at war with us both as well."

What did Roosevelt have in mind when he had said the British could count on America's support in the event of a Japanese attack? Halifax inquired on December 4. He meant "armed" support, the president said, and included support of a British operation in the Kra Isthmus. But his information that day was that the Japanese were headed for the Netherlands East Indies. "He made comment on this that any action of this kind would prove more easy of presentation to United States public opinion on the ground of threat to the Philippines by encirclement."

All week, the British and Americans had been discussing the scope and sequence that parallel warnings to Japan should take. The warnings should include Thailand, Malaya, the Dutch East Indies, but not the Burma Road, Roosevelt now told Halifax. The "Road" had been shut down in the summer of 1940, Roosevelt recalled, without "serious protest in the United States." He was too polite to say that the British themselves had yielded to Japanese pressures and closed down the Burma Road at that time. On the timing of the warnings, "[Roosevelt] would prefer the United States to get in first. On account of political considerations here, it was important that this action should be based on independent necessities of United States defence and not appear to follow ourselves. He assumed that you would be concerting with the Dutch."[6]

Suddenly the *modus vivendi* reappeared. Through various intermediaries, Kurusu had sought to get word to Roosevelt that only an appeal to the emperor could now prevent a final rupture. Baruch had passed on such a message to the White House after having been told that it was all right for him to meet with the Japanese envoy. Another intermediary was Dr. E. Stanley Jones, a prominent Methodist missionary with considerable experience in Japan. "Will you answer [Jones]," Roosevelt instructed his appointments secretary Marvin McIntyre, "and say I was very grateful to him for his letter and that it is a coincidence that two days before, I had taken up the procedure he suggested and may still use it?" Dr. Jones urgently telephoned the White House, and McIntyre told him to be at the White House gate in twenty minutes where he would be brought to the president without reporters seeing him. "I think," Roosevelt commented on these moves to Morgenthau, "the Japanese are doing everything they can to stall until they are ready." The message that Kurusu was so anxious to get to him, Roosevelt informed Halifax on the fourth, Thursday, was "that matters were not yet hopeless and that direct approach to the Emperor might produce results." Kurusu had suggested an arrangement that included "a truce, withdrawal of the bulk of the Japanese there from Indochina, and withdrawal of Japanese troops from North China on a timetable to be agreed between the Japanese and the Chinese military with an American assessor or arbitrator (he was not clear which). The President said the Japanese would obviously want some economic relief."

Roosevelt "did not attach too much importance to the appeal," Halifax went on, "but was naturally reluctant to miss any chance and thought communication with Emperor would strengthen his general case if things went wrong." Halifax was uneasy. Suppose Kurusu's suggestion was worthless? Was there not a danger in delaying the parallel warnings? "Could he make his communication to Emperor if he made it serve as a definite warning?" Roosevelt said he would and he also agreed with Halifax's admonition not to put "a foot wrong with the Chinese after last week's experience." The reply to Roosevelt's inquiry through Welles concerning Japanese intentions in Indochina was expected the next day, Friday. "He will decide whether he does or does not communicate with the Emperor tomorrow Friday morning, and meanwhile wishes us to suspend delivery of warning while making all preparations for it with the Dutch. If he does approach the Emperor, he would hope that three-power warning might be deferred till he had the Emperor's reply for which he would ask urgently."

The Japanese reply brought to Hull by Nomura and Kurusu on Friday was patently evasive. As Hull read its justification of the reinforcements that were pouring into Indochina, he asked whether Japan seriously considered that the Chinese were about to attack them in Indochina. "This is the first time I've known that Japan is on the defensive in Indochina," he commented acidly.[7]

Friday's cabinet meeting was mainly occupied with what to do about the *Chicago Tribune*'s publication of the general staff's war plans. Frances Perkins, after the war, thought that Knox, more tense and high-strung than usual, had told them that the Japanese fleet was out. Perhaps it was out on maneuvers, someone had suggested. And Knox, she remembered, laughed hollowly, "a 'how ridiculous' sort of laugh."

The reports now began to pour in to London and to Washington of three Japanese naval convoys rounding Cambodia, the southernmost point in Indochina. "All may be now in melting-pot if monkeys are going for Kra Isthmus," Cadogan recorded. Stimson had hoped to go back to Long Island to join his wife, "but as the morning went on, the news got worse and worse and the atmosphere indicated that something was going to happen." All day he conferred with Marshall, General Miles of G-2, and General Gerow of war plans. A G-2 estimate of the situation, dated December 5, after enumerating the possibilities open to the Japanese, stated, "The most probable line of action for Japan is the occupation of Thailand." Stimson became urgently concerned with some army supplies en route to the Philippines, especially some big bombers, which were supposed to start that day. Naval operations directed Kimmel at Pearl Harbor, at a moment of his own choosing, to order the destruction of secret and confidential documents "in outlying Pacific islands." Yet so uncertain were Anglo-American strategists about where the Japanese might strike and in what strength that the British chiefs of staff, who spent the day studying the reports that were coming in, could not come to any conclusion: "We examined the situation carefully but from the position of the transports it was not possible to tell whether they were going to Bangkok, to the Kra Peninsula, or whether they were just running around as a bluff."

In Washington, there was less disposition to consider the movement of the transports to be a bluff. A Magic intercept indicated that the Japanese embassy had burned its codes. An intercept earlier in the week about the destruction of codes delivered to the president by his naval aide Capt. John R. Beardall had brought from the president the question: "Well, when do you think it will happen?" Beardall understood the president to mean when was war going to break out, and had replied, "Most any time."* When Budget

* In the postwar period, critics of the administration's pre–Pearl Harbor actions and policies made much of the so-called "winds" messages, which, it was argued, should have told the administration before December 7 that war with the United States was imminent. The "winds" messages were sent by Tokyo to its embassy in Washington on November 19 and intercepted by Magic. They set up a code to be incorporated as part of a Tokyo weather forecast, in which the words "east-wind rain" would signify that United States–Japanese relations were in danger and that all remaining code papers should be destroyed. Witnesses after the war disagreed whether an "execute" message was ever intercepted by the United States before December 7. In any case, as Captain Beardall's delivery to the president indicates, much more explicit code-destruction orders from Tokyo were intercepted on December 2 and deciphered on December 3. A winds-

Director Smith and his assistant came in to discuss budgetary matters with Roosevelt just before noon on December 6, "the President told us, after a telephone call from Secretary of the Navy Knox, of large Japanese convoys and ship movements of their Navy. He added the comment that we might be at war with Japan, although no one knew." Roosevelt also mentioned that he was sending a message to the emperor. At three o'clock, December 6, army intelligence delivered an intercept sent by Tokyo to Nomura which advised him that the Japanese reply to Hull's proposals of November 26 would arrive shortly in fourteen parts, and, more significantly, it informed him that a later dispatch would tell him the exact time the reply was to be delivered to Hull.[8]

The time had come, Roosevelt judged, to send his message to the emperor. It had been drafted at the end of November but held up largely on Hull's insistence that the Japanese might construe it as a sign of weakness. Furthermore, the secretary argued, the emperor was a figurehead, and the Tojo cabinet might be angered because Roosevelt had gone over its head. But Hull abandoned his resistance on Saturday. Late that afternoon, Roosevelt informed the Australian minister Richard Casey that he was sending his message to the emperor that evening, that if the emperor did not reply by Monday evening, the United States would issue its warning on Tuesday, and that the warning by Britain and the others "will not follow until Wednesday morning."

The message to the emperor was not an inspired state paper. Few documents that survived the vettings given to them by Hull and his associates were. He was addressing the emperor, Roosevelt wrote, because of the "deep and far-reaching emergency which appears to be in formation," a situation that was freighted with "tragic possibilities." The continuing troop movements into Indochina had turned southeast Asia into a powder keg. A withdrawal from Indochina was the key to peace. He hoped that the emperor would join him in an effort to restore the traditional amity that had existed between the United States and Japan. "Shoot this to Grew," his memorandum to Hull directed. "I think can go in grey code—saves time—I don't mind if it gets picked up." He was eager to have its contents known. His wife, who had been working in her sitting room on civilian-defense matters with Judge Justine Wise Polier and Paul Kellogg, took them in to the president's study to say good night. "Well, Justine," he greeted them, "this son of man has just sent his final message to the Son of God." He had played his last card for peace in the Pacific, he went on to explain to the startled trio, in a personal message to the Japanese emperor.

---

code execute, if it was intercepted, added nothing new to the information the United States government already had. Nor can an order to destroy codes be construed as tantamount to a declaration of war, as some have contended. In this connection, Roberta Wohlstetter in her study of why United States government agencies, with Magic at their command, failed to anticipate an attack on Pearl Harbor, wrote, "During the first week of December the United States ordered all American consulates in the Far East to destroy all American codes, yet no one has attempted to prove that the order was equivalent to an American declaration of war against Japan."

The message went off at about 9:00 P.M. Half an hour later Lt. L. L. Schulz, assistant to Captain Beardall, delivered to the president the first thirteen parts of the fourteen-part Japanese message. Roosevelt, who was seated at his desk, was expecting it. While Harry Hopkins, who was with him, paced slowly back and forth a few feet away from the desk, the president read through the sheaf of papers. Hopkins then read through them quickly. As he handed them back to Roosevelt, FDR said, "This means war." Hopkins agreed and commented that since war was undoubtedly going to come and at a moment the Japanese considered most opportune from their point of view, it was too bad that the United States could not strike the first blow and prevent any sort of surprise. Roosevelt nodded, but then said, as if arguing with himself as well as with advisers like Stimson and Ickes, who had in the past urged him to seize the strategical initiative. "No, we can't do that. We are a democracy and a peaceful people." His voice rose. "But we have a good record." It was much on his mind that he had permitted Japan to take the military initiative.[9]

At 10:30 the next morning, Hull, Stimson, and Knox met at Hull's office to discuss the draft of a presidential message to Congress. Stimson had wanted Roosevelt to send such a message at the end of November in lieu of an appeal to the emperor, but the careful Hull had objected to that also, fearing it had too much of an air of finality about it and would be used by the Japanese militarists to stoke up popular anger. "Today is the day," Stimson recorded on Sunday morning, "that the Japanese are going to bring their answer to Hull and everything in Magic indicated they had been keeping the time back until now in order to accomplish something hanging in the air." Hull was certain, he went on, that "the Japs are planning some deviltry and we are all wondering where the blow will strike." The most probable target was Thailand. The British thought so, and believed also that they would have to fight. Hull, Stimson, and Knox had agreed a week earlier "that we must fight if the British fought." Their concern Sunday morning was with how to persuade Congress of this necessity.

Stimson returned home. At about two o'clock, "while I [i.e., Stimson] was sitting at lunch, the President called me up on the telephone and in a rather excited voice to ask me, 'Have you heard the news?' I said, 'Well, I have heard the telegrams which have been coming in about the Japanese advances in the Gulf of Siam.' He said, 'Oh, no. I don't mean that. They have attacked Hawaii. They are now bombing Hawaii.' Well, that was an excitement indeed." And recalling how earlier that day he, Hull, and Knox had worried over how to rally the country to the defense of Siam, a relieved Stimson wrote, "But now the Japs have solved the whole thing by attacking us directly in Hawaii."

Knox had telephoned the news to Roosevelt. Navy communications had picked up a Honolulu message advising all posts that Hawaii was under attack and emphasizing that this was "no drill." If the message was true, Roosevelt remarked to Hopkins, and he thought it was, the Japanese "had made the decision" for him. "He always realized," Hopkins wrote a few weeks later, "that Japan would jump on us at an opportune moment and they would merely use the 'one by one' technique of Germany. Hence his great relief at the method that Japan used. In spite of the disaster at Pearl Harbor and the blitz-warfare with the Japanese during the first few weeks, it completely solidified the American people and made the war upon Japan inevitable."

Although Roosevelt's basic feeling was one of relief, as soon as contact with Hawaii was established and the enormity of the military disaster the United States had suffered began to emerge, relief was shadowed by anguish. "The news coming from Hawaii is very bad," recorded Stimson. "They seem to have sprung a complete surprise upon our Fleet and have caught the battleships inside the harbor and bombed them severely with losses. They have also hit our airfields there and have destroyed a great many of our planes, evidently before they got off the ground. It has been staggering to see our people there, who have been warned long ago and were standing on the alert, should have been so caught by surprise." How could it have happened? Senator Connally, chairman of the Foreign Relations Committee, demanded to know when the congressional leadership and the cabinet met with the president at the end of the day. How did it happen, Ickes recorded Connally as saying, that "our warships were caught like tame ducks in Pearl Harbor and why, apparently, [had we] no air patrol?" "It is just unexplainable," Morgenthau recorded. "And they caught us just as unprepared as the others—just the same. . . . They will never be able to explain it."

Frances Perkins was among the many cabinet members who rushed back to town at the request of the White House and who were ushered up to the Oval Room to find it, she wrote, a clutter of communications equipment, maps pinned to the walls, chairs that had been brought in from the other rooms, and Steve Early "tearing around." The president was at his desk, very pale, very calm, completely concentrating on the papers that were being brought to him, talking quietly with the people who brought or took messages. Normally outgoing, he only looked up when, at nine o'clock, "we all sat down." He could hardly bring himself to tell the story, Perkins's account continued.

His pride in the Navy was so terrific that he was having actual physical difficulty in getting out the words that put him on record as knowing that the Navy was caught unawares, that bombs dropped on ships that were not in fighting shape and not prepared to move, but were just tied up. I remember that he said twice to Knox, "Find out, for God's sake, why those ships were tied up in rows."

Knox said, "That's the way they berth them."

It was obvious to me that Roosevelt was having a dreadful time just accepting the idea that the Navy could be caught unawares.

Something else struck Frances Perkins that evening about the president. It left her so uneasy that as soon as she left the White House she jotted down her impression on a White House memo pad. She was troubled by the puckered, sort of "pursed-in" expression on the president's face all evening.

Sometimes I've seen it on his face when he was carrying through a plan which not everybody in the room approved of and about which he didn't intend to tell too

much. I've seen it on his face at times when I thought he was not making everything quite clear and open personally, when he was not exposing the total situation.
It was the sort of expression that he sometimes used when people were making
recommendations to him and he was saying, "Oh yes, oh yes, oh yes," without the
slightest intention of doing anything about it. . . . In other words, there have
been times when I associated that expression with a kind of evasiveness.

Something was wrong, she felt. "This situation was not all it appeared to be.
. . . His surprise was not as great as the surprise of the rest of us." The president seemed to be relieved.

The long tension of wondering what they would do and when they would do it,
and would we have to go to the defense of Singapore without an apparent attack
upon ourselves, and should we go to the relief of Singapore, all these conflicts
which had so harrassed him for so many weeks or months, were ended. You didn't
have to think about that any more. That very wave of relief might have produced
in him that psychological atmosphere, reflected partially in his facial expression
of tenseness and calmness, and yet a sense that something was wrong, that there
was a slight evasion here.

Perhaps, although Perkins did not say so, the expression that troubled her was
a product of the sense of relief Roosevelt felt commingled with his anguish
over what had happened to his navy.[10]

His insistence that the Japanese must be seen to have committed the first
overt move had meant that the strategic initiative was left in the enemy's
hands. He had rejected the forestalling move that Stimson had suggested on
November 28, the move that as a long-time student of military strategy he
knew should have been the answer to the Japanese deployment and movement if the situation were to be viewed simply in military terms. But he could
not view the Japanese moves solely as a problem in military strategy. Under
the Constitution, Congress alone had the power to declare war, and if Congress and the country were to be united in such a declaration, Japan had to
be seen clearly as the aggressor.

As it was, the isolationists, although voting for the declaration of war,
would, when the Pearl Harbor investigation disclosed Roosevelt's concern with
maneuvering Japan into firing the first shot, attempt to twist that piece of information into an admission that Roosevelt had sought war with Japan. Not
Tojo, nor the emperor, nor the militarists, nor Japan's commitments under
the Tripartite Pact, nor the decisions for war indelibly recorded in the minutes
of the imperial conferences of July 2, September 6, November 5, and December 1 were responsible for Pearl Harbor; Roosevelt and his associates were.

The vast majority of the country, however, rejected this view and learned
the more sober lesson that it was only through the exercise of inspired and
strong presidential leadership that the advantages the totalitarian powers had
over the democracies had not proven fatal.

In England, Churchill was at Chequers during the Pearl Harbor attack.
Harriman and his daughter Kathie were with him. Winant had planned to
spend Saturday with Eden, who was scheduled to leave for Moscow on De-

cember 7 but had stayed on in London in order to forward British intelligence dispatches on the sighting of the Japanese convoys. He only reached Eden's house in Sussex at midnight and then stayed up until dawn discussing with the foreign secretary his (i.e., Eden's) trip to Moscow, a journey that had upset the State Department and had brought from Hull, with Roosevelt's "OK," a message that Winant was directed to read to Eden, warning against secret commitments that might affect the postwar settlements. Eden left Sunday morning for Invergordon, and Winant went on to Chequers, arriving there during lunch. He found Churchill pacing up and down outside of the entrance door. Did Winant think there was going to be war with Japan? he greeted the ambassador. "Yes," was Winant's succinct reply. The other guests left after lunch, but Winant and Harriman stayed on. All assembled at dinner, and at nine the fifteen-dollar portable radio that Hopkins had sent Churchill from the United States was switched on. A voice was announcing that the Japanese had attacked the United States fleet at Pearl Harbor. Churchill jumped to his feet. "We shall declare war on Japan," he exclaimed, hastening from the room. Winant followed him, objecting, "Good God, you can't declare war on a radio announcement." The ambassador proposed to put in a call to the president to find out the facts. He was quickly put through. He listened quietly to the president's taut recital and then said he was putting someone else on: "You will know who it is as soon as you hear his voice."

"We are all in the same boat now," Roosevelt greeted Churchill. He was going to Congress the next day. Churchill said that he, too, was going to the House of Commons in the morning and added, "This certainly simplifies things." Later, Churchill put in a call to Eden at Invergordon. The prime minister was "in a high state of excitement," Eden wrote. He (Churchill) must go to the United States, Churchill said, but he wanted Eden to proceed to Moscow. Even though it meant that both of them would be away from London, the intentions of the United States and the USSR were now what mattered.

For a moment, in the elation over America's at last being ranged on Britain's side and in the privacy of his official family, Churchill expressed himself with less than his usual magnanimity. At a meeting with his chiefs of staff on December 8, "someone continued to advocate the same cautious approach to America that had seemed politic when her intervention was in doubt. [Churchill] answered with a wicked leer in his eye: 'Oh! That is the way we talked to her while we were wooing her; now that she is in the harem, we talk to her quite differently.'"

The note of craft and stratagem was eliminated when Churchill, the historian, came to write of his feelings when he heard the news of Pearl Harbor: "So we had won after all! . . . England would live; the Commonwealth of Nations and the Empire would live. How long the war would last or in what fashion it would end, no man could tell, nor did I at this moment care." But, as in Roosevelt's case, joy was soon overtaken by profound distress over the news that the Japanese had sunk the *Prince of Wales* and the *Repulse.* "In all the war I never received a more profound shock. . . . As I turned over and twisted in bed the full horror of the news sank in upon me. There were no British or American capital ships in the Indian Ocean or the Pacific."

On December 8, Roosevelt went before Congress and asked that it declare that "since the unprovoked and dastardly attack by Japan on Sunday, December 7, 1941, a state of war has existed between the United States and the Japanese Empire." "I went to hear the President address both Houses this morning," Halifax telegraphed London. "He was received with prolonged applause on entry, spoke with quiet force and so far as could be seen there was complete unanimity among crowded House and galleries. Particularly significant demonstration was when all present rose and applauded his statement that however long it might take United States would ensure that this kind of treachery should not be possible again."

"A night telephone call from Ribbentrop," Ciano recorded December 8. "He is joyful over the Japanese attack on the United States." Mussolini also was happy. "For a long time now [Mussolini] has been in favor of clarifying the position between America and the Axis." In Berlin, Ribbentrop assured the Japanese ambassador that "immediate participation in the war by Germany and Italy was a matter of course."

The Japanese ambassador in Berlin cabled Tokyo in a message that was intercepted by Magic:

At 1:00 p.m. today (8th), I called on Foreign Minister Ribbentrop and told him our wish was to have Germany and Italy issue formal declarations of war on America at once. Ribbentrop replied that Hitler was then in the midst of a conference at general headquarters discussing how the formalities of declaring war could be carried out so as to make a good impression on the German people, and that he would transmit your wish to him at once and do whatever he was able to have it carried out promptly. At that time Ribbentrop told me that on the morning of the 8th Hitler issued orders to the entire German Navy to attack American ships whenever and wherever they meet them.

In a Fireside Chat on December 9, Roosevelt informed the nation that "Your Government knows that for weeks Germany has been telling Japan that if Japan did not attack the United States, Japan would not share in dividing the spoils with Germany when peace came." Hitler's desire to have Japan attack the United States and divert U.S. interest and power from the Atlantic to the Pacific was rational. But his decision to declare war on the United States was an act of folly comparable to his attack on Russia six months earlier. His repeated orders to his naval commanders to avoid incidents with the United States indicated an underlying respect for American power that belied his propagandistic declarations to the contrary. Why, then, did he not evade fulfillment of his pledges under the Tripartite Pact, as he was perfectly capable of doing?

The answer would appear to be that much as he feared American intervention, the more such intervention seemed inevitable, the greater his fear that Japan, despite its commitment under the Tripartite Pact, might reach an agreement with the United States and leave Germany to confront America,

Britain, and Russia alone. So he and Ribbentrop had egged on the Japanese, and when the attack on Pearl Harbor came, their feeling was one of vast relief. The Japanese attack, Hitler would tell his dinner companions in May, 1942, came at a moment "when the surprises of the Russian winter were pressing most heavily on the morale of our people, and when everybody in Germany was oppressed by the certainty that, sooner or later, the United States would come into the conflict. Japanese intervention, therefore, was, from our point of view, most opportune." Roosevelt could not be certain Germany would declare war on the United States. His December 9 Fireside Chat warned, therefore, "We know also that Germany and Japan are conducting their military and naval operations in accordance with a joint plan." The only way to confound the "grand strategy" of the Axis was to oppose it "with a similar grand strategy" directed against Germany as much as against Japan.

On December 11, the news was received in Washington that Germany and Italy had declared war on the United States. "Resolutions recognizing a state of war with Germany and Italy have been passed unanimously by both Houses of Congress," Halifax cabled London.

"The dictator powers have presented us with a united America," minuted Professor Whitehead.[11]

A message went from King George VI to President Roosevelt. It was drafted by Churchill. On June 4, 1940, with France fallen, Russia locked in its pact with the Nazis, and the United States aloof, Churchill had pledged to "go on to the end . . . until, in God's good time, the New World, with all its power and might steps forth to the rescue and liberation of the Old." Now it had happened. The king's message to the president read:

My thoughts and prayers go out to you and to the great people of the United States at this solemn moment in your history when you have been treacherously attacked by Japan. We are proud indeed to be fighting at your side against the common enemy. We share your inflexible determination and your confidence that, with God's help, the powers of darkness will be overcome and the four freedoms established throughout a world purged of tyranny.

And Roosevelt, who since 1937 had been cajoling, coaxing, educating his reluctant countrymen to the peril that Hitlerism constituted to the United States, could now give the king an adequate answer:

Thank you deeply for your message. Our two nations are now full comrades-in-arms. The courage which your people have shown in two long years of war inspires us as we join the struggle. The forces which have plunged the world in war, however strong, cannot prevail against the indomitable strength of free peoples fighting in a just cause. May God guide us through whatever trials are yet to come to speed the day of victory.

At last Roosevelt and Churchill were free to take the measures they deemed necessary to win the war and establish a just peace. On the night of December 12, Churchill left London for his first wartime trip to Washington.[12]

Bibliographical Note
References
Index

Bibliographical Note

The following abbreviations are used in the References

BTTS	Roger Parkinson, *Blood, Toil, Tears and Sweat* (New York, 1973).
Cadogan	Alexander Cadogan, *The Diaries of Sir Alexander Cadogan*, ed. David Dilks (London, 1971).
Ciano	Galeazzo Ciano, *The Ciano Diaries* (New York, 1946).
DGFP	*Documents on German Foreign Policy, 1918–1945*, Series D (Washington, D.C., 1949–1962).
Eden	Anthony Eden, *The Reckoning* (London, 1965).
FCNA	*Fuehrer Conferences on Naval Affairs* (mimeographed), in *Brassey's Naval Annual* (London, 1948).
FDRL	Franklin D. Roosevelt Library, Hyde Park, New York.
FRUS	*Foreign Relations of the United States*, State Department Series (Washington, D.C.), cited by year and volume.
Hull	Cordell Hull, *The Memoirs of Cordell Hull*, 2 vols. (New York, 1948).
Ickes, III	Harold L. Ickes, *The Lowering Clouds, 1939–1941*, vol. III of *The Secret Diary of Harold L. Ickes*, 3 vols. (New York, 1954).
LC	Library of Congress, Washington, D.C.
Maisky	Ivan Maisky, *Memoirs of a Soviet Ambassador* (New York, 1968).
MPD	Henry Morgenthau, Jr., The Presidential Diary, in the Franklin D. Roosevelt Library, Hyde Park, New York.
M. Watson	Mark Watson, *Chief of Staff: Prewar Plans and Preparations* (Washington, D.C., 1950).
NA	National Archives, Washington, D.C.
NYT	*New York Times.*
OHP	Oral History Project, Columbia University, New York.
PFOT	Roger Parkinson, *Peace for Our Time* (New York, 1971).
PHA	*Pearl Harbor Attack: Hearing before the Joint Committee on the Investigation of the Pearl Harbor Attack*, 39 vols. (Washington, D.C., 1946).
PL	Franklin D. Roosevelt, *F.D.R.: His Personal Letters*, ed. Elliott Roosevelt, 4 vols. (New York, 1947, 1948, 1950), cited by volume and page numbers.
PPA	Franklin D. Roosevelt, *The Public Papers and Addresses of Franklin D. Roosevelt*, ed. Samuel I. Rosenman, 13 vols. (New York, 1938–1950), cited by year volume covers.
PRO	Public Records Office, London, papers from the archives of the foreign office and cabinet office.
R-C FDRL	Correspondence between Franklin D. Roosevelt and Winston S. Churchill on file at the Franklin D. Roosevelt Library, Hyde Park, New York, cited by date.
RPPC	Franklin D. Roosevelt, *Complete Presidential Press Conferences of Franklin D. Roosevelt* (New York, 1972), cited by number and date.
Sherwood	Robert E. Sherwood, *Roosevelt and Hopkins: An Intimate History* (New York, 1948).
Shirer	William L. Shirer, *The Rise and Fall of the Third Reich* (New York, 1959).
Stimson	Henry L. Stimson, Diary, in Yale University Library, New Haven, Connecticut.
TFH	Winston S. Churchill, *Their Finest Hour*, vol. II of *The Second World War*, 6 vols. (Boston, 1949).
TGA	Winston S. Churchill, *The Grand Alliance*, vol. III of *The Second World War*, 6 vols. (Boston, 1950).
TGS	Winston S. Churchill, *The Gathering Storm*, vol. I of *The Second World War*, 6 vols. (Boston, 1948).
Woodward	Llewellyn Woodward, *British Foreign Policy in World War II*, 2 vols. (London, 1962), cited by volume and page number.

Where letters and documents appear in readily available books,
the reference is to the book

References

1. HOW THE CORRESPONDENCE BEGAN

1. *RPPC*, no. 575, Sept. 1, 1939.
2. Walter Warlimont, *Inside Hitler's Headquarters 1939–1945* (London, 1964), pp. 32, 36; Erich von Manstein, *Lost Victories* (Chicago, 1958), pp. 13 ff.; Shirer, pp. 871, 840.
3. Telegram from Joseph Kennedy to Franklin D. Roosevelt, Sept. 11, 1939, in *FRUS*, 1939, I, pp. 421–424.
4. Jay Pierrepont Moffat, *The Moffat Papers* (Cambridge, 1952), p. 253.
5. Telegram from Joseph Kennedy to Franklin D. Roosevelt, Aug. 30, 1939, in *FRUS*, 1939, I, p. 392.
6. Telegram from Cordell Hull to Joseph Kennedy, Aug. 30, 1939, in *FRUS*, 1939, I, pp. 421–424.
7. Letter from Franklin D. Roosevelt to Neville Chamberlain, Sept. 11, 1939, in *FRUS*, 1939, I, p. 671.
8. Letter from Franklin D. Roosevelt to Winston S. Churchill, Sept. 11, 1939, R-C FDRL.
9. Charles A. Beard, *President Roosevelt and the Coming of the War—1941* (New Haven, 1948), pp. 295–296; Winston S. Churchill, *Triumph and Tragedy*, vol. VI of *The Second World War* (Boston, 1955), p. 473.
10. For Hull's account of this episode see Hull, pp. 546–549, 572–581; also see Sumner Welles, *The Time for Decision* (New York, 1944), pp. 64–69; Viscount Templewood (Sir Samuel Hoare), *Nine Troubled Years* (London, 1954), pp. 262–274; *TGS*, p. 255; William L. Langer and S. Everett Gleason, *The Challenge to Isolation* (New York, 1952), pp. 19–30.
11. Arthur Willert, *Washington and Other Memories* (New York, 1972), p. 217.
12. Telegram from Ronald Lindsay to Lord Halifax, Sept. 20, 1938, in Llewellyn Woodward, ed., *Documents on British Foreign Policy, 1919–1939*, 7 vols. (London, 1954), VII, pp. 627–629.
13. Telegram from Lord Halifax to Ronald Lindsay, Sept. 23, 1938, in Woodward, *Documents, op. cit.*, p. 630.
14. Willert, *op. cit.*, p. 210.
15. Templewood, *op. cit.*, pp. 98–99.
16. Winston S. Churchill, *Step by Step* (New York, 1939), p. 166.
17. Winston S. Churchill, speech to the House of Commons, Oct. 5, 1938, in *TGS*, p. 328; letter from Winston S. Churchill to Anthony Eden, Sept. 20, 1937, in *TGS*, p. 247; Franklin D. Roosevelt, Constitution Day address in *PPA*, 1937, pp. 359–367; Margaret L. Coit, *Mr. Baruch* (Boston, 1957), p. 467.
18. *Ibid.*, p. 468.
19. Winston S. Churchill, radio broadcast, London, Oct. 16, 1938.
20. John McVicker Haight, Jr., *American Aid to France, 1938–1940* (New York, 1970), p. 16.
21. Arthur C. Murray, *Master and Brother: Murray of Elibank* (London, 1945), p. 183; id., *At Close Quarters* (London, 1946), pp. 19, 47; id., *Reflections on Some Aspects of British Foreign Policy between the Two World Wars* (London, 1946).
22. Letter from Arthur C. Murray to Franklin D. Roosevelt, Dec. 15, 1938, in FDRL.
23. Langer and Gleason, *op. cit.*, p. 59.
24. Willert, p. 217.
25. Adolf A. Berle, *Navigating the Rapids, 1918–1971* (New York, 1973), p. 212.
26. *TGS*, p. 353.
27. MPD, April 14, 1939.
28. *RPPC*, no. 540, April 18, 1939.
29. Stimson, April 5, 1939.
30. Telegram from Hans Thomsen to Berlin, Sept. 12, 1939, in *DGFP*, VIII, no. 54, pp. 51–52.

2. AN ESSENTIALLY SIMILAR PROBLEM

1. Tracy B. Kittredge, "United States–British Naval Cooperation, 1940–1945," ms. study on microfilm at the New York Public Library, p. 6.
2. *Ibid.*
3. *Ibid.*, pp. 7–11.
4. Winston S. Churchill, *The Great Contemporaries* (New York, 1937), p. 219.
5. Letter from Henry Cabot Lodge to John Hay, April 21, 1898, in John A. Garraty, *Henry Cabot Lodge* (New York, 1953), p. 198.
6. Lionel M. Gelber, *The Rise of Anglo-American Friendship* (London, 1938), p. 24.
7. *Ibid.*, p. 166.
8. *Ibid.*, pp. 131–135.
9. Sara D. Roosevelt, *My Boy Franklin* (New York, 1933), pp. 7, 30; Harlan Miller, in *Washington Post*, Oct. 31, 1939; Frank Freidel, *The Apprenticeship*, vol. I of *Franklin D. Roosevelt*, 4 vols. (Boston, 1952), pp. 27, 48; William L. Neumann, "Franklin D. Roosevelt: A Disciple of Admiral Mahan," *U.S. Naval Institute Proceedings* (July, 1952).
10. Letter from Franklin D. Roosevelt to James and Sara D. Roosevelt, Jan., 1898, in *PL*, I, pp. 156, 160–164.
11. Forrest Davis, *The Atlantic System* (New York, 1941), p. 135.
12. Letter from Franklin D. Roosevelt to Sara D. Roosevelt, Sept. 7, 1905, in *PL*, II, p. 84.
13. Memorandum from Franklin D. Roosevelt to Stephen T. Early, Oct. 19, 1939, in FDRL.
14. Gelber, *op. cit.*, p. 208; Charles A. Beard and Mary R. Beard, *The Rise of American Civilization*, 2 vols. (New York, 1927–1942), II, pp. 611, 614.
15. Garraty, *op. cit.*, p. 152.
16. Letter from Franklin D. Roosevelt to Sara D. Roosevelt, April 22, 1912, in *PL*, II, p. 187.
17. Letter from Franklin D. Roosevelt to Eleanor Roosevelt, Oct. 5, 1915.
18. Freidel, *op. cit.*, p. 165.

19. Bradley A. Fiske, *From Midshipman to Rear Admiral* (New York, 1919), pp. 528, 530.
20. Letter from Theodore Roosevelt to Franklin D. Roosevelt, May 10, 1913, in FDRL.
21. Neumann, *op. cit.*
22. Freidel, p. 223.
23. U.S. Senate Naval Affairs Subcommittee Hearings, *Naval Investigation*, Sixty-sixth Congress, Second Session (Washington, D.C., 1920), p. 808.
24. Letter from Franklin D. Roosevelt to Alfred T. Mahan, May 28, 1914; letter from Alfred T. Mahan to Franklin D. Roosevelt, July 31, 1914, in FDRL.
25. Letter from Alfred T. Mahan to Franklin D. Roosevelt, June 26, 1914, in FDRL.
26. Letters from Alfred T. Mahan to Franklin D. Roosevelt, Aug. 4, 15, and 18, 1914, in FDRL.
27. Letter from C. C. Burlingham to Franklin D. Roosevelt, April 1, 1913, in FDRL; Joseph Coady, "F.D.R.'s Early Washington Years, 1913–1920" (Ph.D. diss., St. John's University, 1968); *Milwaukee Sentinel*, April 27, 1914; Freidel, p. 227.
28. Jonathan Daniels, *The End of Innocence* (New York, 1954), p. 29; Josephus Daniels, *The Wilson Era* (Chapel Hill, 1944), p. 124; letter from Henry Cabot Lodge to Franklin D. Roosevelt, Aug. 1, 1913; letter from Franklin D. Roosevelt to Henry Cabot Lodge, Aug. 2, 1913, in FDRL.
29. U.S. Senate Naval Affairs Subcommittee Hearings, *op. cit.*, pp. 758–766.
30. Josephus Daniels, *op. cit.*, pp. 172, 182; Jonathan Daniels, *op. cit.*, pp. 91–93.
31. Freidel, p. 232; Garraty, p. 305.
32. Freidel, p. 274.
33. Letter from Franklin D. Roosevelt to Eleanor Roosevelt, Aug. 2, 1914, in *PL*, II, pp. 238–239; letter from Franklin D. Roosevelt to Livingston Davis, Aug. 12, 1914, in FDRL.
34. Letter from Alfred T. Mahan to Franklin D. Roosevelt, Aug. 13, 1914, in FDRL; Davis, *op. cit.*, pp. 219–220; press interview, Aug. 4, 1914.

35. C. Carlisle Taylor, *The Life of Admiral Mahan* (New York, 1920), pp. 146–147.
36. Beard and Beard, *op. cit.*, II, p. 611; Walter Millis, *Road to War* (New York, 1935), p. 58; statement by Woodrow Wilson, Aug. 19, 1914.
37. Letters from Franklin D. Roosevelt to Eleanor Roosevelt, Aug. 7 and 10, 1914, in *PL*, II, pp. 245, 248.
38. Millis, *op. cit.*, p. 86; Ernest R. May, *The World War and American Isolation* (Cambridge, 1959), p. 23.
39. May, *op. cit.*, p. 14.
40. *Ibid.*, p. 137.
41. Letter from Franklin D. Roosevelt to Eleanor Roosevelt, Oct., 1914, in *PL*, II, p. 258; Jonathan Daniels, p. 149.
42. Letter from Franklin D. Roosevelt to Eleanor Roosevelt, June 10, 1915, in *PL*, II, p. 270; letter from Franklin D. Roosevelt to Woodrow Wilson, June 9, 1915, in FDRL; Josephus Daniels, p. 428; Freidel, p. 252.
43. Letter from Franklin D. Roosevelt to Eleanor Roosevelt, n.d., in *PL*, II, p. 267; letters from Franklin D. Roosevelt to Eleanor Roosevelt, Aug. 18 and 21, 1915, in *PL*, II, pp. 280, 283.
44. Freidel, p. 267.
45. Franklin D. Roosevelt, log of trip to Haiti, Jan., 1917, in FDRL.
46. Franklin K. Lane, *The Letters of Franklin K. Lane* (Boston, 1922), pp. 239–240; Franklin D. Roosevelt, Diary kept from March 5 to March 12, 1917, in FDRL; Freidel, p. 289.
47. Jonathan Daniels, p. 215.
48. Eleanor Roosevelt, *This Is My Story* (New York, 1937), p. 245.
49. Letter from Eleanor Roosevelt to Sara D. Roosevelt, May 10, 1917, quoted in Joseph P. Lash, *Eleanor and Franklin* (New York, 1971), pp. 208–209.
50. Freidel, p. 305.
51. *Ibid.*, p. 337.
52. Franklin D. Roosevelt, speech given to American Society of Newspaper Editors, in *RPPC*, no. 540-A, April 20, 1939.

3. CHURCHILL AT THE ADMIRALTY: 1914 AND 1939

1. Ronald Hyams, *Elgin and Churchill at the Colonial Office* (New York, 1968), pp. 16, 43; Beatrice Webb, *Our Partnership* (London, 1948), pp. 269–270.
2. Hyams, *op. cit.*, pp. 489, 494, 115–116, 149.
3. Randolph S. Churchill, *Winston S. Churchill: Young Statesman, 1901–1914* (Boston, 1967), pp. 159–160; Winston S. Churchill, speech, London, Feb. 28, 1906.
4. Randolph S. Churchill, *op. cit.*, p. 236; Hyams, p. 489.
5. Jack Fishman, *My Darling Clementine* (New York, 1963), p. 25.
6. Ray Jenkins, *Asquith* (New York, 1964), pp. 194–195.
7. *Ibid.*, p. 339.
8. Randolph S. Churchill, pp. 584, 589.
9. *Ibid.*, pp. 528, 531.
10. Winston S. Churchill, speech, Glasgow, Feb. 9, 1912, in Randolph S. Churchill, p. 545.
11. Winston S. Churchill, *The World Crisis: The Aftermath* (New York, 1929), p. 93, also cited in Randolph S. Churchill, pp. 526, 563.
12. Lord Riddell, Diary, Dec. 18, 1913, cited in Randolph S. Churchill, pp. 640, 641; letter from Lady Wimborne to Winston S. Churchill, Dec. 18, 1913, in Randolph S. Churchill, p. 645; Violet Bonham Carter, *Winston Churchill: An Intimate Portrait* (New York, 1965), p. 158.
13. Letter from Henry Asquith to Winston S. Churchill, Feb. 1, 1914; letter from Winston S. Churchill to Henry Asquith, Feb. 2, 1914; Randolph S. Churchill, pp. 659–661.
14. Randolph S. Churchill, p. 662; Winston S. Churchill, speech, London, March 17, 1914, in Randolph S. Churchill, p. 669.

15. Letter from Winston S. Churchill to Clementine Churchill, June, 1914, in Randolph S. Churchill, p. 700.
16. Jenkins, *op. cit.*, p. 327; Bonham Carter, *op. cit.*, p. 248.
17. A. J. Taylor *et al.*, *Churchill Revised: A Critical Assessment* (New York, 1969), p. 183.
18. Bonham Carter, p. 254.
19. Martin Gilbert, *Winston S. Churchill: The Challenge of War, 1914–1916* (Boston, 1971), p. 31.
20. *Ibid.*, pp. 166, 167; letters from Henry Asquith to Venetia Stanley, Dec. 4 and 20, 1914.
21. Gilbert, *op. cit.*, p. 107; letter from Henry Asquith to Venetia Stanley, Oct. 3, 1914.
22. Gilbert, p. 113; letter from Henry Asquith to Venetia Stanley, Oct. 5, 1915.
23. Bonham Carter, p. 274.
24. Gilbert, p. 180; Margot Asquith, Diary, Nov. 30, 1914.
25. Gilbert, p. 223; letter from Henry Asquith to Venetia Stanley, Dec. 5, 1914.
26. Millis, *Road to War*, cited (ch. 2), p. 133; May, *The World War and American Isolation*, cited (ch. 2), p. 307.
27. Gilbert, p. 309; comment by Henry Asquith to Margot Asquith, March 7, 1915.
28. Taylor *et al.*, *op. cit.*, p. 185.
29. Gilbert, p. 684; letter from Clementine Churchill to Winston S. Churchill, Jan., 1916; Gilbert, p. 798; letter from Winston S. Churchill to Violet Bonham Carter, Aug., 1916.
30. *TGS*, pp. 200–201.
31. *Ibid.*, p. 220.
32. *Ibid.*, pp. 410, 412; letter from Lord Halifax to Winston S. Churchill, in PRO, A8146/9127/5992/51.

4. THE UNSPOKEN NAVAL ALLIANCE

1. Kittredge, "United States–British Naval Co-operation, 1940–1945," cited (ch. 2), pp. 37–58.

2. Letter from Franklin D. Roosevelt to Cordell Hull, Jan. 4, 1938, in *PL*, IV, p. 742.
3. John Wheeler-Bennett, *King George VI* (Lon-

don, 1958), pp. 391–392; foreign-office minute, "The Panama Maritime Security Zone," March 4, 1940, in PRO, A1880/1/51.
4. Hull, p. 690.
5. *DGFP*, VIII, no. 306, Oct. 27, 1939.
6. Letter from Winston S. Churchill to Franklin D. Roosevelt, Oct. 5, 1939, R-C FDRL.
7. Letter from Franklin D. Roosevelt to Charles Edison, Oct. 9, 1939, in *PL*, IV, p. 936.
8. Kittredge, *op. cit.*, p. 77.
9. Minutes by foreign office, Nov. 21 and 22, 1939, in PRO, A8146/5992/51.
10. Letter from Lord Halifax to Lord Lothian, Oct. 3, 1939, in PRO, A6635/6.
11. Letter from Joseph Kennedy to Franklin D. Roosevelt, Oct. 2, 1939, in *FRUS*, 1939, I, pp. 499–500.
12. Letter from Winston S. Churchill to Franklin D. Roosevelt, Oct. 16, 1939, R-C FDRL; *TGS*, p. 493; Templewood, *Nine Troubled Years*, cited (ch. 1), p. 407; Arthur Marder, "Winston Is Back: Churchill at the Admiralty, 1939–1940," *English Historical Review*, suppl. 5 (1972), 19.
13. Letter from Winston S. Churchill to Franklin D. Roosevelt, Dec. 25, 1939, R-C FDRL.
14. Letter from Winston S. Churchill to Lord Halifax, Jan. 12, 1940, in PRO, A434(1940); letter from Lord Halifax to Winston S. Churchill, Jan. 19, 1940, in PRO, A434(1940).
15. Letter from Lord Lothian to Lady Astor, Dec. 20, 1939, quoted in J. R. M. Butler, *Lord Lothian* (London, 1960), p. 275; letter from Franklin D. Roosevelt to Capt. Callaghan, Dec. 5, 1939; letter from Capt. Callaghan to

Franklin D. Roosevelt, Dec. 6, 1939, in *PL*, IV, p. 963; letter from Franklin D. Roosevelt to Mrs. J. Borden Harriman, Sept. 9, 1940, in *PL*, IV, p. 986.
16. Letter from Winston S. Churchill to Franklin D. Roosevelt, Jan. 7, 1940, R-C FDRL; letter from Lord Lothian to Samuel Hoare, Feb. 1, 1940, in Templewood, *op. cit.*, p. 416.
17. Letter from Lord Lothian to Lady Astor, Jan. 22, 1940, in Butler, *op. cit.*, p. 271.
18. Letter from Lord Lothian to Lord Halifax, Jan. 27, 1940, in PRO.
19. Telegrams from Winston S. Churchill to Franklin D. Roosevelt, Jan. 29 and 30, 1940, R-C FDRL.
20. Letter from Franklin D. Roosevelt to Winston S. Churchill, Feb. 1, 1940, R-C FDRL.
21. Letter from Winston S. Churchill to Franklin D. Roosevelt, Feb. 28, 1940, R-C FDRL.
22. Memorandum from Adolf Berle to Franklin D. Roosevelt, March 5, 1940, in FDRL.
23. Moffat, *The Moffat Papers*, cited (ch. 1), pp. 276, 287.
24. Minute by foreign office, Feb. 20, 1940, in PRO, A434/434/45.
25. Stimson, March 12, 1940.
26. Record of conversation among Welles, Churchill, and Chamberlain in *FRUS*, 1940, I, pp. 90–91.
27. Letter from Lord Lothian to Samuel Hoare, Feb. 1, 1940, in Templewood, p. 417; letter from Lord Halifax to Lord Lothian, Jan. 30, 1940, in PRO, A772/301/45; letter from Lord Lothian to Lord Halifax, March 1, 1940, in PRO, A2314/301/45; Butler, p. 278.

5. THE PHONY WAR

1. Telegram from Alan G. Kirk to Navy Department, Dec. 13, 1939, in Library of the Navy Department, Washington, D.C.
2. *Ibid.*, Nov. 3, 1939.
3. *PFOT*, p. 249 (this account of British policy is based on British cabinet minutes).
4. Telegram from Joseph Kennedy to Franklin D. Roosevelt, Oct. 4, 1939, in *FRUS*, 1939, I, pp. 499–502.
5. MPD, Oct. 3, 1939.
6. Letter from William C. Bullitt to Franklin D. Roosevelt, Oct. 4, 1939, in Orville H. Bullitt, ed., *For the President—Personal and Secret: Correspondence between Franklin D. Roosevelt and William C. Bullitt* (Boston, 1972), p. 345.
7. Letter from Neville Chamberlain to Franklin D. Roosevelt, Oct. 4, 1939, in *FRUS*, 1939, I, p. 674.
8. Telegram from Joseph Kennedy to Franklin D. Roosevelt, Oct. 2, 1939, in *FRUS*, 1939, I, pp. 499–500.
9. *DGFP*, VIII, pp. 227–230; Shirer, pp. 882–883; *PFOT*, pp. 255–256.
10. Shirer, pp. 850–853; *PFOT*, p. 258.
11. Shirer, p. 856.
12. Telegram from Winston S. Churchill to Franklin D. Roosevelt, Oct. 16, 1939, R-C FDRL.
13. Letter from William C. Bullitt to Franklin D. Roosevelt, Nov. 1, 1939, in Bullitt, *op. cit.*, p. 381; Stimson, XX, pp. 28–29.
14. Memorandum from Stephen T. Early to Franklin D. Roosevelt, Sept. 7, 1939, in FDRL.
15. Berle, *Navigating the Rapids*, cited (ch. 1), pp. 256–257; Adolf A. Berle, Diary, Oct. 12, 1939, in FDRL.
16. Letter from King Leopold to Franklin D. Roosevelt, Oct. 7, 1939, in *FRUS*, 1939, I, p. 508; letter from Franklin D. Roosevelt to King Leopold, Oct. 19, 1939, in *FRUS*, 1939, I, p. 517; *DGFP*, VIII, no. 326, Nov. 3, 1939.
17. Letter from Neville Chamberlain to Franklin D. Roosevelt, Nov. 8, 1939, in FDRL.
18. Winston S. Churchill, "Ten Weeks of War," radio broadcast, London, Nov. 12, 1939, reprinted in Winston S. Churchill, *Blood, Sweat and Tears* (New York, 1941), pp. 189–193.
19. Turkish reaction to Churchill's speech in *DGFP*, VIII, no. 366, Nov. 17, 1939; letter from Lord Lothian to Franklin D. Roosevelt and Cordell Hull, Nov. 13, 1939, in FDRL;

comment by Richard A. Butler to Ambassador Bastianini, Nov. 20, 1939, in *DGFP*, VIII, p. 426.
20. Adolf Hitler, speech, Berlin, Nov. 23, 1939, in *DGFP*, VIII, no. 384, pp. 439–446.
21. Letter from Samuel Hoare to Lord Lothian, Sept. 25, 1939, in Templewood, *Nine Troubled Years*, cited (ch. 1), p. 403.
22. Telegram from William C. Bullitt to Franklin D. Roosevelt, Oct. 18, 1939, in Bullitt, p. 346.
23. Ickes, III, pp. 84–85, Dec. 10, 1939.
24. Letter from Arthur Purvis to Jean Monnet, in Haight, *American Aid to France*, cited (ch. 1), pp. 170–171.
25. Haight, *op. cit.*, pp. 189, 204, 224; see also John Morton Blum, *Years of Urgency*, vol. II of *From the Morgenthau Diaries*, 3 vols. (Boston, 1965), pp. 119–120.
26. Advice from Winston S. Churchill to Neville Chamberlain, Sept. 10, 1939, in *PFOT*, p. 237; directive from Adolf Hitler to armed forces, Oct. 9, 1939, in Shirer, pp. 852–853; directive from Adolf Hitler to military chiefs, Nov. 23, 1939, in *DGFP*, VIII, no. 384, pp. 439–446.
27. Announcement by Samuel Hoare, Sept. 25, 1939, in Templewood, p. 404.
28. *PFOT*, p. 273; Marder, "Winston Is Back," cited (ch. 4), 333.
29. *Ibid.*, p. 276; letter from Franklin D. Roosevelt to Frederick A. Stirling, April 10, 1939, in *PL*, IV, p. 878.
30. *PFOT*, p. 268.
31. *Ibid.*, p. 277.
32. *Ibid.*, pp. 278–280.
33. Winston S. Churchill, "A House of Many Mansions," radio broadcast, London, Jan. 20, 1940, in Churchill, *Blood, Sweat and Tears*, *op. cit.*, p. 213–216; comment by Halvdan Koht to German minister, Jan. 24, 1940, in *DGFP*, VIII, no. 565, pp. 695–696.
34. Letter from Franklin D. Roosevelt to William Allen White, Dec. 14, 1939, in *PL*, IV, pp. 967–968.
35. Franklin D. Roosevelt, annual message to Congress, Washington, D.C., Jan. 3, 1940, in *PPA*, 1940, p. 2.
36. Telegram from Lord Lothian to foreign office, Feb. 1, 1940, in PRO, A1309/131/45.
37. Minute by David Scott on Ditchley conversation, Feb. 7, 1940, in PRO, A1309/131/45.
38. Harold Stark, estimate of the foreign situation, March 9, 1940, in FDRL.

39. Telegrams from Neville Chamberlain to Lord Lothian for Franklin D. Roosevelt, n.d., in FDRL, but filed under "Welles, 1940."
40. MPD, March 3, 1940.
41. Reports from Sumner Welles to Franklin D. Roosevelt, in *FRUS*, 1940, I, pp. 4–115.
42. Letter from Winston S. Churchill to Maurice Gamelin, March 16, 1940, in Marder, *op. cit.*, p. 27; Hull, p. 739.
43. Bullitt, pp. 403, 410.
44. Welles, *The Time for Decision*, cited (ch. 1), p. 77.

6. "FORMER NAVAL PERSON"

1. Cadogan, p. 263; *PFOT*, p. 312.
2. *TGS*, p. 560; *PFOT*, p. 311.
3. Shirer, p. 917.
4. Cadogan, p. 255; *TGS*, pp. 532, 578, 585; *PFOT*, p. 316; Winston S. Churchill, "A Sterner War," radio broadcast, March 30, 1940, in Churchill, *Blood, Sweat and Tears,* cited (ch. 5), pp. 243–246; J. R. M. Butler, *Grand Strategy*, vol. II of *The Official History of the Second World War*, 6 vols. (London, 1957), p. 123.
5. *PFOT*, p. 318; Butler, *op. cit.*, p. 126; T. K. Derry, *The Campaign in Norway* (London, 1952), p. 26.
6. Liddell Hart, *History of the Second World War* (New York, 1971), p. 59.
7. H. L. Ismay, *The Memoirs of General Lord Ismay* (New York, 1960), p. 120; *TGS*, p. 596.
8. Comment by U.S. naval attaché in Berlin, April 9, 1940, in FDRL; telegram from Alan G. Kirk, April 9, 1940, in FDRL; MPD, April 10, 1940; Harold Nicolson, *The War Years* (New York, 1967), p. 69.
9. Nicolson, *op. cit.*, p. 70.
10. Winston S. Churchill, speech, London, April 11, 1940, in Churchill, *Blood, Sweat and Tears, op. cit.*, pp. 253–260; *TGS*, p. 602.
11. *Hansard*, 359, House of Commons Debates, 753–754.
12. *PFOT*, p. 326; Cadogan, pp. 270, 272; William Edmund Baron Ironside, *The Ironside Diaries,* ed. R. Macleod and D. Kelly (London, 1962), p. 257.
13. Ironside, *Diaries, op. cit.*, p. 278.
14. Cadogan, pp. 273–274; Keith Feiling, *The Life of Neville Chamberlain* (London, 1946), pp. 437–438.
15. Nicolson, p. 74, April 30, 1940.
16. Marder, "Winston Is Back," cited (ch. 4), 51; *Hansard*, 360—1128, 1130.
17. Telegram from Joseph Kennedy to Franklin D. Roosevelt and Cordell Hull, April 26, 1940, in FDRL; letter from Franklin D. Roosevelt to Arthur Murray, April 30, 1940, in FDRL.
18. Nicolson, p. 74.
19. Ironside, pp. 84, 260.
20. Nicolson, p. 73.
21. Edward Spears, *Prelude to Dunkirk*, vol. I of *Assignment to Catastrophe*, 2 vols. (New York, 1954), p. 88; Cadogan, p. 252.
22. Ismay, *op. cit.*, p. 106.
23. *TGS*, p. 577, 582.
24. Eric Seal quoted by Marder, *op. cit.*, 23; Spears, *op. cit.*, p. 82.
25. Nicolson, p. 76.
26. *Hansard*, 360—1085, 1088, 1093, 1101.
27. Telegram from Joseph Kennedy to Franklin D. Roosevelt and Cordell Hull, May 7, 1940, in FDRL; *Hansard*, 360—1130; Nicolson, pp. 76, 77.
28. *Hansard*, 360—1143–1150; Nicolson, p. 77.
29. *Hansard*, 360—1266, 1283; letter from Adolf Hitler to Benito Mussolini, May 3, 1940, in *DGFP*, IX, no. 192, pp. 275–277.
30. *Hansard*, 360—1354–1362; dispatch from Alan G. Kirk, May 6, 1940, in FDRL; Marder, *op. cit.*, 54–55.
31. Nicolson, p. 79.
32. Telegram from Joseph Kennedy to Cordell Hull, May 9, 1940, in NA.
33. Eden, pp. 110–111.
34. Hugh Dalton, *The Fateful Years* (London, 1957), p. 308.
35. Frederick Edwin Smith Lord Birkenhead, *The Life of Lord Halifax* (London, 1965), p. 454; Spears, pp. 130–131.
36. Edward Lord Halifax, *Fullness of Days* (London, 1957), pp. 223–224; Cadogan, p. 280; L. S. Amery, *My Political Life*, 3 vols. (London, 1955), III, p. 371.
37. Francis Williams, *A Prime Minister Remembers* (London, 1961), p. 33.
38. Eden, pp. 110–111.
39. Letter from Neville Chamberlain to Lord Beaverbrook, May 10, 1940, in A. J. P. Taylor, *Beaverbrook* (London, 1972), p. 410; letter from Joseph Kennedy to Cordell Hull, May 10, 1940, in NA; Eden, p. 112; Birkenhead, *op. cit.*, p. 455.
40. Wheeler-Bennett, *King George VI*, cited (ch. 4), p. 443.
41. Birkenhead, p. 457.
42. *Ibid.*, p. 454.
43. *TGS*, p. 667.

7. THE THIRD TERM

1. MPD, May 11, 1940; Ickes, III, p. 176.
2. Berle, *Navigating the Rapids*, cited (ch. 1), p. 310.
3. Taylor, *Beaverbrook*, cited (ch. 6), p. 408; Amery, *My Political Life*, cited (ch. 6), p. 368.
4. Ickes, III, p. 146; Bullitt, *For the President*, cited (ch. 5), p. 411, April 28, 1940.
5. Forrest Davis and Ernest K. Lindley, *How War Came* (New York, 1942), p. 28; Franklin D. Roosevelt, annual message to Congress, Washington, D.C., Jan. 3, 1940, in *PPA*, 1940, p. 2; MPD, May 10 and 13, 1940.
6. MPD, May 16 and Sept. 1, 1939.
7. *Ibid.*, April 18, 1940.
8. Letter from Franklin D. Roosevelt to the Arthur Murrays, April 17, 1940, in FDRL; Berle, *op. cit.*, p. 224.
9. Sherwood, pp. 117–118.
10. Ickes, III, p. 102.
11. Letter from Lord Lothian to Lord Halifax, Dec. 28, 1939, in PRO, A384/39/45; comment by Lord Halifax, Jan. 7, 1940, in PRO, A384/39/45; letter from Neville Butler to foreign office, March 5, 1940, in PRO, A2257/39/45; comment by Alexander Cadogan, April 2, 1940, in PRO, A2257/39/45.
12. MPD, Jan. 24, 1940; Ickes, III, p. 107; Bullitt, *op. cit.*, p. 376.
13. MPD, Jan. 24, 1940.
14. Memorandum from Robert G. Vansittart, March 18, 1940, in Bullitt, p. 376.
15. *DGFP*, VIII, no. 490, p. 579, Dec. 27, 1939.
16. *Ibid.*, VIII, pp. 910–913, March 13, 1940; Shirer, pp. 902–903.
17. *Congressional Record*, pp. 9509–9510, July 11, 1940; Saul Friedlaender, *Prelude to Downfall* (New York, 1967), p. 76.
18. *DGFP*, VIII, no. 665, p. 884, March 10, 1940.
19. *Ibid.*, IX, no. 24, p. 45, March 29 and 30 and May 4, 1940; *Congressional Record*, vol. 186, pp. 1821, 3747; Breckinridge Long. *The War Diary of Breckinridge Long*, ed. Fred L. Israel (Lincoln, 1966), p. 74; *DGFP*, IX, no. 80, pp. 118–119, April 10, 1940.
20. Ickes, III, p. 121; O. John Rogge, *The Official German Report* (New York, 1961), pp. 242–255, 92.
21. *RPPC*, no. 634, April 9, 1940.
22. Minute by T. North Whitehead, April 5, 1940, in PRO, A2387/39/45; minute by member of foreign office, April 7, 1940, in PRO, A2387/39/45.
23. *RPPC*, no. 635, April 12, 1940; *ibid.*, no. 636-A, April 18, 1940.
24. Franklin D. Roosevelt, speech, annual meeting of American Society of Newspaper Editors, Feb. 19, 1940, in *RPPC*, no. 625.
25. Dispatch from Alan G. Kirk to Franklin D. Roosevelt, May 1, 1940, in FDRL.
26. MPD, April 29, 1940; Berle, p. 308.
27. Woodward, I, pp. 172–173.
28. *RPPC*, no. 649-A, June 5, 1940.
29. Berle, p. 311.

30. MPD, May 3, 1940.
31. Hull, p. 855; Long, *op. cit.*, p. 68.
32. Harry Hopkins, Papers, in FDRL.
33. MPD, May 13, 1940; Hull, p. 767; Harold D. Smtih, Diary, May 16, 1940, in FDRL.
34. For Sumner Welles's views on Roosevelt's grasp of geopolitics see Sumner Welles, *Seven*

Decisions That Shaped History (New York, 1950), p. 66; memorandum from "Betty" Stark to Franklin D. Roosevelt, in FDRL; Ickes, III, pp. 178–179; Long, *op. cit.*, p. 94.
35. *RPPC*, no. 649-A, June 5, 1940.
36. MPD, Jan. 24, 1940; Berle, p. 314, May 15, 1940.

8. ACTS OF "FAITH AND LEADERSHIP"

1. Nicolson, *The War Years*, cited (ch. 6), p. 85; Wheeler-Bennett, *King George VI*, cited (ch. 4), p. 450.
2. On Churchill's distrust of Kennedy see Woodward, I, p. 334; telegram from Joseph Kennedy to Franklin D. Roosevelt, May 15, 1940, in *FRUS*, 1940, III, pp. 29–30.
3. Letter from Ronald Campbell to Winston S. Churchill, May 15, 1940, in PRO, A3258/1/51.
4. Telegram from Winston S. Churchill to Franklin D. Roosevelt, May 15, 1940, R-C FDRL.
5. Telegram from Franklin D. Roosevelt to Winston S. Churchill, May 15, 1940, R-C FDRL.
6. Butler, *Lord Lothian*, cited (ch. 4), p. 287, May 20, 1940.
7. Cadogan, p. 284, May 16, 1940.
8. *TFH*, pp. 43, 47; Liddell Hart, in Taylor *et al., Churchill Revised*, cited (ch. 3), p. 264; Manstein, *Lost Victories*, cited (ch. 1), p. 104.
9. Berle, *Navigating the Rapids*, cited (ch. 1), p. 314.
10. Cadogan, pp. 284–285.
11. Paul Baudouin, *The Private Papers of Paul Baudouin*, ed. Sir C. Petrie (London, 1943), pp. 32–33.
12. Cadogan, p. 285.
13. Letter from Winston S. Churchill to Franklin D. Roosevelt, May 18, 1940, R-C FDRL.
14. MPD, May 16–18, 1940.
15. Bullitt, *For the President*, cited (ch. 5), pp. 190–191, May 16, 1940.
16. Comment by Hugh Dowding to Lord Halifax quoted in Taylor, *Beaverbrook*, cited (ch. 6), p. 417; report by Lord Lothian on conversation with Franklin D. Roosevelt in Woodward, I, pp. 338–339.
17. Telegram from Lord Lothian to London, May 20, 1940, in PRO, A3261/1/51; comment by American department, May 20, 1940, in PRO, A3261/1/51.
18. *PFOT*, p. 356; Feiling, *The Life of Neville Chamberlain*, cited (ch. 6), p. 444; Winston S. Churchill, speech, May 19, 1940, in Churchill, *Blood, Sweat and Tears*, cited (ch. 5), pp. 279–282.
19. Cadogan, p. 287; Ickes, III, p. 185.
20. Telegram from Winston S. Churchill to Franklin D. Roosevelt, May 20, 1940, R-C FDRL.
21. Long, *The War Diary*, cited (ch. 7), pp. 97, 113–114, May 22 and June 22, 1940.
22. Bullitt, *op. cit.*, pp. 398–399.
23. Comments on transmission of messages from Churchill through Kennedy to Roosevelt, June, 1940, in PRO, A3261/1/51.
24. *RPPC*, no. 647-A, May 30, 1940.
25. MPD, May 20, 1940.
26. Memorandum from Franklin D. Roosevelt to Robert Jackson, May 21, 1940, in FDRL.
27. Memorandum from J. Edgar Hoover to Edwin M. Watson, June 3, 1940, in FDRL; William Stevenson, *A Man Called Intrepid* (New York, 1976), pp. 80, 127; Stevenson, *op. cit.*, pp. 77–79; H. Montgomery Hyde, *Room 3603*, (New York, 1962), pp. 24–28; *RPPC*, no. 507, Dec. 9, 1938.
28. Winston S. Churchill, speech, June 4, 1940, in Churchill, *Blood, Sweat and Tears*, op. cit., pp. 289–297.
29. MPD, May 20, 1940.
30. *PFOT*, pp. 359–360; Arthur Bryant, *The Turn of the Tide* (London, 1957), p. 117; dispatch

from naval attaché to White House, May 23, 1940, in FDRL.
31. Memorandum from Sumner Welles on talk with Lord Lothian, May 23, 1940, in *FRUS*, 1940, III, pp. 28–30; Blum, *Years of Urgency*, cited (ch. 5), p. 150; telegram from Lord Lothian to London, in Woodward I, p. 340.
32. Taylor, *op. cit.*, p. 417; letter from Winston S. Churchill to Mackenzie King, June 5, 1940, in *TFH*, pp. 145–146.
33. Moffat, *The Moffat Papers*, cited (ch. 1), p. 305; Berle, *op. cit.*, p. 308; *DGFP*, IX, no. 185, p. 262, May 1, 1940; Ciano, p. 242.
34. Berle, pp. 313, 314.
35. *DGFP*, IX, no. 266, pp. 366–367; Ciano, pp. 251–252, May 10, 1940; telegram from Joseph Kennedy, May 20, 1940, in *FRUS*, 1940, III, p. 51.
36. Woodward, I, pp. 198–200, 236–237; Feiling, *op. cit.*, p. 444; *PFOT*, p. 365.
37. *PFOT*, p. 368.
38. Birkenhead, *The Life of Lord Halifax*, cited (ch. 6), p. 458; Cadogan, p. 291; Woodward, I, p. 205.
39. Ciano, p. 255, May 27, 1940.
40. Telegram from Joseph Kennedy to Franklin D. Roosevelt, May 27, 1940, in *FRUS*, 1940, III, p. 233.
41. Letter from Frank Knox to Franklin D. Roosevelt, May 28, 1940, in FDRL.
42. Manfred Jonas, *Isolationism in America* (Ithaca, N.Y., 1966), p. 214; *Public Opinion Quarterly*, IV (Jan., July, and Oct., 1940); *Fortune* (July, 1940); memorandum from Franklin D. Roosevelt to Harold Stark, April 30, 1940, in FDRL.
43. *RPPC*, no. 647-A, May 30, 1940.
44. Warlimont, *Inside Hitler's Headquarters*, cited (ch. 1), p. 95; Manstein, *op. cit.*, p. 124.
45. Baudouin, *op. cit.*, p. 69; minute by member of foreign office, May 31, 1940, in PRO, A3312/26/45.
46. *PFOT*, pp. 370–372; Nicolson, *op. cit.*, p. 91.
47. Comment by T. North Whitehead, May 28, 1940, in PRO, A3310/1/51.
48. Woodward, I, p. 211.
49. Winston S. Churchill, "Dunkirk," speech, London, June 4, 1940, in Churchill, *Blood, Sweat and Tears*, pp. 289–297.
50. Ickes, III, p. 202.
51. Moffat, *op. cit.*, p. 310; Hull, p. 775; comment by Lord Lothian, June 7, 1940, in PRO, A3316/1/51.
52. Telegram from Frank Knox to Franklin D. Roosevelt, June 7, 1940, in FDRL; Langer and Gleason, *The Challenge to Isolation*, cited (ch. 1), pp. 487, 512.
53. Letter from Lewis Douglas to Franklin D. Roosevelt, June 5, 1940, in FDRL; letter from Franklin D. Roosevelt to Lewis Douglas, June 7, 1940, in FDRL; Ickes, III, p. 202.
54. MPD, June 8 and 9, 1940.
55. Ickes, III, p. 200; comment by John Balfour, June 12, 1940, in PRO, A3242/131/45.
56. Butler, *op. cit.*, p. 288.
57. Memorandum from Walter Bedell Smith to White House, June 11, 1940, in Forrest Pogue, *George C. Marshall*, 3 vols. (New York, 1966), II, pp. 52–53.
58. *TFH*, p. 132; Franklin D. Roosevelt, commencement address, University of Virginia, June 10, 1940, in *PPA*, 1940, pp. 263–264.
59. Telegram from Winston S. Churchill to Franklin D. Roosevelt, June 10, 1940, R-C FDRL.

9. FRANCE LEAVES THE WAR

1. Bullitt, *For the President*, cited (ch. 5), pp. 411–412.
2. *FRUS*, 1940, I, p. 241, June 5, 1940.

3. *BTTS*, p. 22; *TFH*, pp. 146–147.
4. *PPA*, 1940, pp. 265–266.
5. Edward Spears, *Fall of France*, vol. II of *As-*

signment to Catastrophe, 2 vols. (New York, 1955), p. 38.

6. *Ibid.,* pp. 149, 152, 169; *TFH,* pp. 152-160; Woodward, I, p. 252; *BTTS,* p. 29; Eden, pp. 135-136.

7. Telegram from Winston S. Churchill to Franklin D. Roosevelt, June 12, 1940, R-C FDRL.

8. Message from Joseph Kennedy to Franklin D. Roosevelt and Cordell Hull, June 12, 1940, in *FRUS,* 1940, II, p. 37.

9. Telegram from Winston S. Churchill to Franklin D. Roosevelt, June 13, 1940, R-C FDRL; Woodward, I, p. 258.

10. Welles, *The Time for Decision,* cited (ch. 1), pp. 150, 155; Berle, *Navigating the Rapids,* cited (ch. 1), pp. 323-324; message from Franklin D. Roosevelt to Winston S. Churchill, June 13, 1940, R-C FDRL.

11. Woodward, I, pp. 259-262; telegram from Winston S. Churchill to Franklin D. Roosevelt, June 14, 1940, R-C FDRL.

12. Message from Joseph Kennedy to Franklin D. Roosevelt and Cordell Hull, June 14, 1940, in *FRUS,* 1940, I, pp. 248-249.

13. Berle, *op. cit.,* p. 324; telegram from Franklin D. Roosevelt to Winston S. Churchill, June 14, 1940, R-C FDRL.

14. *TFH,* p. 187; letter from Winston S. Churchill to Franklin D. Roosevelt, June 15, 1940, R-C FDRL.

15. Letter from Winston Churchill to Franklin D. Roosevelt, June 15, 1940, R-C FDRL.

16. Report by Lord Lothian of his talk with Roosevelt and Hull in Woodward, I, pp. 270-271; Cadogan, p. 299.

17. Letter from Lothian to Lady Astor, June 12, 1940, in Butler, *Lord Lothian,* cited (ch. 4),

p. 288; note from Charles Edison to Franklin D. Roosevelt, June 14, 1940, in FDRL; *NYT,* June 19, 20, and 25, 1940; Langer and Gleason, *The Challenge to Isolation,* cited (ch. 1), pp. 521-522.

18. *DGFP,* X, no. 253, pp. 350-351, May 16, 1940; Rogge, *The Official German Report,* cited (ch. 7), pp. 233-236.

19. *RPPC,* no. 652-A, June 14, 1940.

20. *FRUS,* 1940, II, p. 455, June 17, 1940; Woodward, I, p. 295.

21. Ciano, pp. 265-266; partial record of conversation between Hitler and Mussolini, June 18, 1940, in *DGFP,* IX, no. 479, pp. 608-611.

22. Winston S. Churchill, speech, London, June 18, 1940, in Churchill, *Blood, Sweat and Tears,* cited (ch. 5), p. 314.

23. Nicolson, *The War Years,* cited (ch. 6), pp. 96-97; Wheeler-Bennett, *King George VI,* cited (ch. 4), pp. 460, 462.

24. Charles Eade, ed., *Winston Churchill's Secret Session Speeches* (New York, 1946), pp. 10-11.

25. *BTTS,* pp. 55, 59; note from Lord Lothian to Franklin D. Roosevelt, July 4, 1940, in FDRL; Cadogan, p. 306; Ciano, p. 273, July 4, 1940.

26. Bullitt, *op. cit.,* p. 441, July 1, 1940.

27. Maurice Matloff and Edwin M. Snell, *Strategic Planning for Coalition Warfare, 1941-1942* (Washington, D.C., 1953), p. 191; M. Watson, pp. 109-113.

28. Woodward, I, p. 353; dispatch from Winston S. Churchill to Lord Lothian, June 28, 1940, in *TFH,* pp. 228-229.

29. Donald M. Nelson, *Arsenal of Democracy* (New York, 1946), p. 85.

10. "TODAY ALL PRIVATE PLANS ... HAVE BEEN ... REPEALED"

1. MPD, June 28, 1940; *TFH,* p. 132; Berle, *Navigating the Rapids,* cited (ch. 1), p. 322.

2. Ickes, III, pp. 195, 208-209; Smith, Diary, cited (ch. 7), May 19 and 23, 1940; *RPPC,* no. 647-A, May 31, 1940.

3. Memorandum from Harry H. Woodring to Franklin D. Roosevelt, Sept., 1937, in FDRL.

4. MPD, April 18 and 30, 1940.

5. Bennett Clark, in *Kansas City Times,* June 22 and Aug. 3, 1940; letter from Franklin D. Roosevelt to Harry H. Woodring, June 25, 1940, in FDRL; Langer and Gleason, *The Challenge to Isolation,* cited (ch. 1), p. 511; minutes by foreign office, June 21, 1940, in PRO, A3460/39/45.

6. Letter from Nevile Butler to John Balfour, June 29, 1940, in PRO; Ickes, III, p. 221; letter from William O. Douglas to Franklin D. Roosevelt, July 2, 1940, in FDRL.

7. Max Freedman, ed., *Roosevelt and Frankfurter* (Boston, 1967), p. 533.

8. James F. Byrnes, *All in One Lifetime* (New York, 1958), p. 117-118.

9. Samuel I. Rosenman, *Working with Roosevelt* (New York, 1952), p. 210; Ickes, III, p. 251.

10. Rosenman, *op. cit.,* p. 213; Lash, *Eleanor and Franklin,* cited (ch. 2), p. 623.

11. Rosenman, pp. 215-218.

12. *RPPC,* no. 658, July 5, 1940.

13. *DGFP,* X, no. 91, p. 101, July 3, 1940; Smith, *op. cit.,* July 8-10, 1940; *PPA,* 1940, p. 289.

14. Long, *The War Diary,* cited (ch. 7), p. 121; Byrnes, *op. cit.,* p. 132; Hull, p. 862; telegram from Lord Lothian to London, July 21, 1940, in PRO, A3223/39/45.

15. *PPA,* 1940, pp. 293-303, July 19, 1940.

16. Mollie Panter-Downes, *London War Notes* (New York, 1971), p. 78.

17. Memorandum by Hans Dieckhoff, in *DGFP,* X, no. 199, pp. 259-260, July 21, 1940.

11. THE TWO MEN COMPARED

1. Panter-Downes, *London War Notes,* cited (ch. 10), p. 75; Emmet John Hughes, *The Living Presidency* (New York, 1972), p. 352.

2. E. W. Starling, *Starling of the White House* (New York, 1946), pp. 306-307; Lash, *Eleanor and Franklin,* cited (ch. 2), p. 371.

3. John Wheeler-Bennett, ed., *Action This Day* (New York. 1969), pp. 47 ff.; "Go to It," *Economist* (June 29, 1940), 1100.

4. Birkenhead, *The Life of Lord Halifax,* cited (ch. 6), pp. 456-457; Cadogan, pp. 312, 281.

5. Wheeler-Bennett, *Action This Day, op. cit.,* pp. 164. 170.

6. Berle, *Navigating the Rapids,* cited (ch. 1), p. 151; Roosevelt's inspection of State Department, reported in Smith, Diary, cited (ch. 7), July 25, 1939; Marriner S. Eccles, *Beckoning Frontiers* (New York, 1951), pp. 335-336.

7. Wheeler-Bennett, *Action This Day,* pp. 78, 173, 162; *TFH,* p. 32.

8. Ickes, III, p. 84.

9. Ciano, p. 267; comment by Abe Fortas in Hughes, *op. cit.* p. 332; Winston S. Churchill, speech in Westminster Hall, in *NYT,* Dec. 1, 1954.

10. Cadogan, p. 301; Bryant, *The Turn of the Tide,* cited (ch. 8), pp. 135-137.

11. MPD, May 13, 1940; Kent Roberts Greenfield,

American Strategy in World War II (Baltimore, 1963), pp. 49 ff.

12. MPD, June 3, 1940; interview with Paul Freund; Stimson, Nov. 11, 1940.

13. Harold J. Laski, *The American Presidency* (New York, 1940), p. 32; Stimson, Jan. 4, 1941.

14. "American Debates," *Economist* (June 8, 1940), 1002; comment by Alexander Cadogan, April 2, 1940, in PRO, A2286/39/45.

15. Maurice Hankey, quoted in Taylor, *Beaverbrook,* cited (ch. 6), p. 411; Templewood, *Nine Troubled Years,* cited (ch. 1), p. 337; *TFH,* p. 238; Ismay, *The Memoirs,* cited (ch. 6), p. 154.

16. *TFH,* pp. 18, 15.

17. Winston S. Churchill, *Savrola* (London, 1900), pp. 31, 104-108, 84-85; comment by Lord Esher to Douglas Haig, May 30, 1917, in Martin Gilbert, *The Stricken World, 1916-1922,* vol. IV of *Winston S. Churchill* (Boston, 1975), pp. 21-22; *PL,* II, pp. 135, 544-545; John Maynard Keynes, *The Collected Writings,* 16 vols. (New York, 1972), X, p. 57.

18. Spears, *Fall of France,* cited (ch. 9), p. 128; Spears, *Prelude to Dunkirk,* cited (ch. 6), pp. 313-314.

19. Freedman, *Roosevelt and Frankfurter,* cited (ch. 10), p. 535.
20. *TFH,* p. 17; Robert Rhodes James, *Churchill: A Study in Failure, 1900–1939* (London, 1970), p. 159; Marder, "Winston Is Back," cited (ch. 4), p. 2.
21. "Unofficial Observer," *The New Dealers* (New York, 1934), p. 25.
22. Comment by J. H. Plumb, in *Spectator* (July 1, 1966), quoted by James, *op. cit.,* p. 311; comment by David Lloyd George in Thomas Jones, *A Diary with Letters* (Oxford, 1954), p. 465.
23. Robert J. Lifton, "Psychohistory," *Partisan Review,* vol. 38, no. 1 (1970), 11–32.
24. "Unofficial Observer," *op. cit.,* p. 25; Winston

S. Churchill, *The Great Contemporaries,* cited (ch. 2), p. 126; James, p. 277; Maisky, p. 73.
25. Winston S. Churchill, *Liberalism and the Social Problem* (New York, 1909), pp. 76, 83; James, p. 299; Churchill, *The Great Contemporaries, op. cit.,* pp. 372, 376, 381; Frances Stevenson, *Lloyd George, a Diary* (New York, 1971), p. 278.
26. Letter from Franklin D. Roosevelt to Sara D. Roosevelt and Eleanor Roosevelt, July 30, 1918, in *PL,* II, pp. 392–393.
27. Churchill, *The Great Contemporaries,* p. 163.
28. Winston S. Churchill, *A Roving Commission* (New York, 1930), pp. 45, 62.
29. Churchill, *The Great Contemporaries,* p. 382.

12. GETTING A LITTLE MORE MIXED UP TOGETHER

1. Butler, *Lord Lothian,* cited (ch. 4), p. 290; *Economist* (July 20, 1940); Maisky, p. 100.
2. Dispatch from Winston S. Churchill to Franklin D. Roosevelt, June 15, 1940, R-C FDRL; MPD, June 18, 1940.
3. Pogue, *George C. Marshall,* cited (ch. 8), II, p. 52; *NYT,* June 26, 1940; statement from Navy Department, June 7, 1940, in FDRL; *Congressional Record,* vol. 86, pp. 8777, 8828–8831, June 21, 1940.
4. Basil Rauch, *From Munich to Pearl Harbor* (New York, 1950), p. 229.
5. Memorandum from Benjamin V. Cohen, July 19, 1940, in FDRL; memorandum from Franklin D. Roosevelt to Frank Knox, July 22, 1940, in FDRL.
6. Comment by Günther Blumentritt, May 24, 1940, in Shirer, p. 967; Ciano, p. 265.
7. Dispatch from Donald R. Heath to Cordell Hull, June 27, 1940, in *FRUS,* 1940, III, p. 39; dispatch from William Phillips to Cordell Hull, June 29, 1940, in *FRUS,* 1940, III, p. 39; dispatch from Alexander W. Weddell to Cordell Hull, July 2, 1941, in *FRUS,* 1940, III, p. 41; *DGFP,* X, no. 48, pp. 49–50; Cadogan, p. 309; Feiling, *The Life of Neville Chamberlain,* cited (ch. 6), p. 449; Ernst von Weizsäcker, *Memoir of Ernest von Weizsäcker* (London, 1951), p. 238; *DGFP,* X, no. 73, pp. 79–83, July 1, 1940.
8. Ciano, p. 227, July 19, 1940; *DGFP,* X, no. 201, pp. 262–263, July 22, 1940; telegram from Hans Thomsen to Berlin, July 20, 1940, in *DGFP,* X, no. 195, pp. 254–256.
9. Nicolson, *The War Years,* cited (ch. 6), p. 104; Weizsäcker, *op. cit.,* p. 238; note from Winston S. Churchill to foreign office, July 20, 1940, in *TFH,* p. 260; *DGFP,* X, no. 220, p. 287, July 24, 1940.
10. Extracts from Churchill's July, 1940, minutes and directives in *TFH,* pp. 264–272; Bryant, *The Turn of the Tide,* cited (ch. 8), p. 154.
11. Letter from Donald R. Heath to Sumner Welles, June 6, 1940, in FDRL; *NYT,* Aug. 1, 1940.
12. Franz Halder, Diary, July 31, 1940, in *DGFP,* X, pp. 370–374.
13. Memorandum from Franklin D. Roosevelt, June 13, 1940, in Matloff and Snell, *Strategic Planning for Coalition Warfare,* cited (ch. 9), p. 14.
14. Dispatch from Lord Lothian to foreign office, May 24, 1940, in PRO, A3297/2961/45; war-cabinet discussion, May 27, 1940, in PRO, WP(40)41; dispatch from war cabinet to Lord Lothian, May 29, 1940, in PRO, WP(40)174.
15. Dispatch from Lord Lothian to foreign office, June 17, 1940, in PRO, A3582/131/45; comments by Winston S. Churchill and Lord Halifax, June 24 and 28, 1940, in PRO, A3582/131/45; telegram from Lord Halifax to Lord Lothian, June 30, 1940, in PRO, A3582/131/45; telegrams from Lord Lothian to foreign office, July 2 and 4, 1940, in PRO, A3582/131/45.
16. Kittredge, "United States-British Naval Co-operation," cited (ch. 2), pp. 213–214, 229.
17. Dispatch from Joseph Kennedy to Cordell Hull, July 5, 1940, in *FRUS,* 1940, III, p. 55.
18. Dispatch from Lord Lothian to foreign office, July 10, 1940, in PRO, A3582/131/45; comment by Robert G. Vansittart, July 12, 1940, in PRO, A3582/131/45; comment by T. North

Whitehead, July 14, 1940, in PRO, A3582/131/45; comment by David Scott, July 15, 1940, in PRO, A3582/131/45; comment by Robert G. Vansittart, July 13, 1940, in PRO, A3582/131/45.
19. Herbert Agar, *The Darkest Year, Britain Alone* (New York, 1973), p. 55.
20. Dispatch from Lord Lothian to foreign office, July 21, 1940; dispatch from Lord Lothian to Winston S. Churchill, July 30, 1940; telegram from Winston S. Churchill to Franklin D. Roosevelt, July 31, 1940, R-C FDRL.
21. Ickes, III, p. 283; Stimson, Aug. 2, 1940; Roosevelt's record of cabinet meeting, Aug. 2, 1940, in *PL,* IV, pp. 1050–1051.
22. Dispatch from Lord Lothian to foreign office, Aug. 3, 1940, in Woodward, I, p. 365; telegram from Winston S. Churchill to Lord Lothian, Aug. 3, 1940, in *TFH,* pp. 402–403.
23. Dispatch from Winston S. Churchill to Lord Halifax, Aug. 7, 1940, in *TFH,* pp. 404–405.
24. Telegram from Sumner Welles to Joseph Kennedy, Aug. 14, 1940, in Philip Goodhart, *Fifty Ships That Saved the World* (London, 1965), p. 158.
25. Telegram from William Allen White to Franklin D. Roosevelt, Aug. 11, 1940, in FDRL.
26. John Pershing, speech, in *NYT,* Aug. 4, 1940; Agar, *op. cit.,* p. 147; Charles Lindbergh, speech, Aug. 3, 1940, in *NYT,* Aug. 4, 1940; *DGFP,* X, nos. 312, 322, pp. 441–442, 456–457, Aug. 8 and 10, 1940.
27. Memorandum from Benjamin V. Cohen, in Hughes, *The Living Presidency,* cited (ch. 11), p. 324.
28. Stimson, Aug. 13 and 15, 1940; dispatch from Franklin D. Roosevelt to Winston S. Churchill, Aug. 13, 1940, quoted in Langer and Gleason, *The Challenge to Isolation,* cited (ch. 1), pp. 758–759; Goodhart, *op. cit.,* pp. 164–165.
29. Telegram from Joseph Kennedy to Sumner Welles, Aug. 15, 1940, in *FRUS,* 1940, III, pp. 67–68.
30. Dispatch from Winston S. Churchill to Lord Lothian, Aug. 7, 1940, in *TFH,* pp. 405–406.
31. Record of war-cabinet meeting, Aug. 14, 1940, in PRO, A3793/131/45; Woodward, I, pp. 368–369; telegram from Winston S. Churchill to Franklin D. Roosevelt, Aug. 15, 1940, R-C FDRL; postscript from Lord Lothian, in FDRL.
32. *RPPC,* no. 671, Aug. 16, 1940; Ickes, III, p. 304; letter from Lord Lothian to Lady Astor, Aug. 6, 1940, in Butler, *op. cit.,* p. 299.
33. Hyde, *Room 3603,* cited (ch. 8), pp. 34–41; Raymond E. Lee, *The London Journals of General Raymond E. Lee,* ed. James Leutze (Boston, 1971), pp. 27–28; Walter Johnson, *William Allen White's America* (New York, 1947), p. 532.
34. Moffat, *The Moffat Papers,* cited (ch. 1), pp. 325, 328–329.
35. *NYT,* Aug. 18, 1940; Ickes, III, p. 304.
36. Winston S. Churchill, speech, London, Aug. 20, 1940, in Churchill, *Blood, Sweat and Tears,* cited (ch. 5), p. 84.
37. Davis and Lindley, *How War Came,* cited (ch. 7), p. 84; telegram from Winston S. Churchill to Franklin D. Roosevelt, Aug. 22, 1940, R-C FDRL.
38. Dispatch from foreign office to Lord Lothian, in PRO, A3917/3742/45; Cadogan, pp. 322–

323; dispatch from Winston S. Churchill to Franklin D. Roosevelt, Aug. 25, 1940, R-C FDRL.

39. Dispatch from Joseph Kennedy to Cordell Hull, Aug. 29, 1940, in *FRUS*, 1940, III, pp. 72–73; Hull, p. 837; Goodhart, p. 173; telegram from Winston S. Churchill to Franklin D. Roosevelt, Aug. 27, 1940, R-C FDRL.

40. Dispatch from Lord Lothian to foreign office, Aug. 28, 1940, in Woodward, I, p. 379; minute by Robert G. Vansittart, Aug. 26, 1940, in PRO, A3917/3742/45; Cadogan, p. 324; dispatch from Joseph Kennedy to Cordell Hull, Aug. 29, 1940, in *FRUS*, 1940, III, pp. 72–73.

41. Dispatch from foreign office to Lord Lothian, Aug. 27, 1940, in *TFH*, pp. 413–414; letter from Lord Lothian to Lady Astor, Sept. 1, 1940, in Butler, p. 298; Maisky, p. 101.

42. Winston S. Churchill, speech, London, Sept. 5, 1940, in Churchill, *Blood, Sweat and Tears*, *op. cit.*, pp. 355–356; *NYT*, Sept. 5, 1940.

43. Letter from Benito Mussolini to Adolf Hitler, Aug. 27, 1940, in Friedlaender, *Prelude to Downfall*, cited (ch. 7), p. 24; comment by Erich Raeder, in *FCNA*, pp. 134–135.

44. Ickes, III, p. 314; Hull, p. 844; Panter-Downes, *London War Notes*, cited (ch. 10), pp. 90, 95, 98; dispatch from Adolf Hitler to Benito Mussolini, Sept. 17, 1940, in *DGFP*, XI, no. 68, p. 103; *FCNA*, pp. 137–140.

45. Frederick W. Winterbotham, *The Ultra Secret* (New York, 1974), p. 59; Anthony Cave Brown, *The Bodyguard of Lies* (New York, 1975), p. 38.

46. Cadogan, p. 328; Eden, p. 160.

47. Stimson, Sept. 7, 1940; Grace Tully, *F.D.R. My Boss* (New York, 1949), p. 244; *NYT*, Sept. 4, 1940; *RPPC*, no. 677, Sept. 3, 1940; *Chicago Tribune*, Sept. 4, 1940; Wilkie's reaction quoted in *NYT*, Sept. 4, 1940; letter from Franklin D. Roosevelt to George VI, Nov. 22, 1940, in *PL*, IV, pp. 1083–1084.

48. Joseph C. Grew, *The Turbulent Era* (Boston, 1952), p. 1222; Cadogan, pp. 310–311, 313.

49. Stimson, July 18, 1940; MPD, July 23, 1940; conversation between Joachim von Ribbentrop and Benito Mussolini, Sept. 20, 1940, in *DGFP*, XI, no. 73, pp. 113–123.

50. Letter from Adolf Hitler to Benito Mussolini, Sept. 17, 1940, in *DGFP*, XI, no. 68, pp. 102–105.

51. Telegram from German embassy in Washington, D.C., to foreign ministry in Berlin, Sept. 28, 1940, in *DGFP*, XI, no. 123, pp. 209–211.

52. Hull, p. 909; bulletin from British intelligence to ambassadors, Sept. 29, 1940, in PRO, A4581/4581/45; Stimson, Sept. 27, 1940.

53. Stimson, Sept. 27, 1940; Berle, *Navigating the Rapids*, cited (ch. 1), p. 339, Sept. 28, 1940; John Morton Blum, *Roosevelt and Morgenthau* (New York, 1970), p. 400; cabinet meeting described in Stimson, Oct. 4, 1940, and in Ickes, III, p. 346; Davis and Lindley, *op. cit.*, pp. 157–158.

54. Telegram from Winston S. Churchill to Franklin D. Roosevelt, Oct. 4, 1940, R-C FDRL.

55. Comment by Harold Stark, in *PHA*, pt. 5, pp. 2205–2206; Moffat, *op. cit.*, pp. 330–333, Oct. 6–10, 1940; Long, *The War Diary*, cited (ch. 7), p. 132; memorandum from War Department, Sept. 25, 1940, in M. Watson, pp. 115–117; Stimson, Oct. 8, 1940.

56. *PHA*, pt. 14, exhibit no. 9, p. 342.

57. *Ibid.*, pt. 1, pp. 263–266, 293–325, 356; comment by Frank Knox to Robert L. Ghormley, Nov. 16, 1940, in Kittredge, *op. cit.*, p. 241.

58. Stimson, Oct. 12, 1940.

59. Directive from Franklin D. Roosevelt to Frank Knox, Oct. 10, 1940, in FDRL; Moffat, p. 333, Oct. 10, 1940.

60. Winston S. Churchill, speech, London, Oct. 8, 1940, in Churchill, *Blood, Sweat and Tears*, p. 390; Hadley Cantril, "America Faces the War," *Public Opinion Quarterly* (Dec., 1940), 387.

61. *PPA*, 1940, p. 466, Oct. 12, 1940.

13. LIONS BECOME FOXES

1. Joseph P. Barnes, *Willkie* (New York, 1952), pp. 203, 209; Ickes, III, pp. 316, 321.

2. London *Times*, Oct. 3, 1940.

3. Ickes, III, pp. 324, 330, Sept. 15 and 20, 1940; La Guardia's warning in a memorandum from Edwin M. Watson to Franklin D. Roosevelt, Oct. 1, 1940, in FDRL.

4. Interview with Franklin D. Roosevelt, Jr.; *RPPC*, no. 686, Oct. 4, 1940.

5. Friedlaender, *Prelude to Downfall*, cited (ch. 7), p. 153.

6. MPD, Oct. 3, 1940; Burton K. Wheeler, *Yankee from the West* (New York, 1962), p. 25.

7. Hugh Johnson, in *New York World-Telegram*, Oct. 5, 1940; Long, *The War Diary*, cited (ch. 7), p. 142, Oct. 11, 1940; Franklin D. Roosevelt, Columbus Day speech, Oct. 12, 1940, in *PPA*, 1940, pp. 460–467; London *Times*, Oct. 13, 1940.

8. Wheeler-Bennett, *King George VI*, cited (ch. 4), p. 391; Cantril, "America Faces the War," cited (ch. 12), 387; *Public Opinion Quarterly* (March, 1941), 158 ff.; *NYT*, Oct. 11, 1940; Ickes, III, pp. 344–345, 349, Oct. 7 and 15, 1940.

9. *New York World-Telegram*, Oct. 10, 1940.

10. *NYT*, Oct. 15, 1940; telegram from Hans Thomsen to Berlin, Oct. 16, 1940, in *DGFP*, XI, no. 180, pp. 307–309; Wayne S. Cole, *Charles Lindbergh and the Battle against American Intervention in World War II* (New York, 1974); Marion K. Sanders, *Dorothy Thompson* (Boston, 1973), p. 260; *PPA*, 1940, pp. 531, 532, Nov. 1, 1940.

11. Rogge, *The Official German Report*, cited (ch. 7), p. 254.

12. Will Alexander, OHP; Stimson, Oct. 22, 1940.

13. Editorial in *New York Journal-American*, Oct. 16, 1940; letter from Eleanor Roosevelt to Franklin D. Roosevelt, Oct. 14, 1940, in FDRL; Ickes, III, pp. 349–350, Oct. 19, 1940; *New York Journal-American*, Oct. 17, 1940.

14. *NYT*, Oct. 17 and 18, 1940.

15. Letter from James F. Byrnes to Franklin D. Roosevelt, Oct. 18, 1940, in FDRL; memorandum from Oscar Ewing to Harry Hopkins, Oct. 19, 1940, in Hopkins, Papers, cited (ch. 7); memorandum from Nathan R. Margold to Benjamin V. Cohen, Oct. 31, 1940, in Hopkins, Papers, *op. cit.*, message from John Stelle to Harry Hopkins, Oct. 24, 1940, in Hopkins, Papers; Merlo J. Pusey, *Charles Evans Hughes* (New York, 1951), pp. 785–786; Smith, Diary, cited (ch. 7), Oct. 18, 1940.

16. MPD, Aug. 6 and 14, 1940; Lee, *The London Journals*, cited (ch. 12), p. 81; Long, *op. cit.*, pp. 141–142.

17. Saul Alinsky, *John L. Lewis* (New York, 1949), pp. 186–187; Berle, *Navigating the Rapids*, cited (ch. 1), p. 346; letter from Clarence M. Kelley to Joseph P. Lash, Dec. 2, 1974.

18. Franklin D. Roosevelt, speech, Philadelphia, Oct. 23, 1940, in *PPA*, 1940, pp. 485–495; MPD, Oct. 24, 1940; Stimson, Oct. 12 and 23, 1940.

19. Franklin D. Roosevelt, speech, Madison Square Garden, New York, Oct. 28, 1940, in *PPA*, 1940, pp. 499–510; Barnes, *op. cit.*, p. 224; Rosenman, *Working with Roosevelt*, cited (ch. 10), p. 32.

20. Stimson, Oct. 28, 1940; telegram from Winston S. Churchill to Franklin D. Roosevelt, Oct. 21, 1940, R-C FDRL; note from Franklin D. Roosevelt to French government (copy to Churchill), Oct. 24, 1940, R-C FDRL; telegram from Winston S. Churchill to Franklin D. Roosevelt, Oct. 26, 1940, R-C FDRL; *New York Journal-American*, Oct. 31, 1940; *New York World-Telegram*, Oct. 29, 1940; *NYT*, Oct. 30, 1940; London *Times*, Nov. 1, 1940; extemporaneous remarks by Franklin D. Roosevelt, Nov. 2, 1940, in *PPA*, 1940, p. 543; note from Charles Michelson to Stephen T. Early, Oct. 24, 1940, in FDRL.

21. Arthur Krock, *Memoirs: Sixty Years on the Firing Line* (New York, 1968), p. 336; Lee, *op. cit.*, p. 115; MPD, Oct. 28, 1940; Franklin D. Roosevelt, speech, Boston, Oct. 30, 1940,

in *PPA*, 1940, pp. 515–525; Eleanor Roosevelt, "My Day," syndicated column, Oct. 31 and 23, 1940.
22. Franklin D. Roosevelt, speech, Hyde Park, Nov. 4, 1940, in *PPA*, 1940, pp. 554–557; Joseph P. Lash, *A Friend's Memoir* (New York, 1964), p. 194; letter from Franklin D. Roosevelt to Samuel I. Rosenman, Nov. 13, 1940, in Rosenman, *op. cit.*, p. 236; letter from Franklin D. Roosevelt to George VI, Nov. 24, 1940, in *PL*, IV, pp. 1083–1084.
23. Samuel Lubell, *Saturday Evening Post* (Jan. 25, 1941); Paul F. Lazarsfeld *et al., The People's Choice: How the Voter Makes Up His Mind in a Presidential Election* (New York, 1948); Sherwood, p. 196.
24. Letter from Harold Stark to J. I. Richardson, Nov. 12, 1940, in *PHA*, pt. 14, p. 971; dispatch from German embassy in Spain to Berlin, Nov. 14, 1940, in *DGFP*, XI, no. 335, pp. 574–576; telegram from German embassy in Chungking to Berlin, Nov. 15, 1940, in *DGFP*, XI, no. 336, pp. 576–577; circular from Ernst

von Weizsäcker to German embassies, Nov. 8, 1940, in *DGFP*, XI, no. 305, p. 504; Ciano, p. 318; letter from David Gray to Franklin D. Roosevelt, Nov. 6, 1940, in FDRL; Nicolson, *The War Years*, cited (ch. 6), pp. 125–126; letter from George VI to Franklin D. Roosevelt, Nov. 11, 1940, in FDRL; message from Winston S. Churchill to Franklin D. Roosevelt, Nov. 6, 1940 (the original of this letter is not in R-C FDRL, but appears in *TFH*, pp. 553–554).
25. Minute by T. North Whitehead, Oct. 3, 1940, in PRO, A4279/39/45; minute by John Colville, Oct. 18, 1940, in PRO, A4279/39/45; telegram from foreign office to Nevile Butler, Oct. 23, 1940, in PRO, A4279/39/45; dispatches from Nevile Butler to foreign office, Oct. 29 and 31, 1940, in PRO, A4279/39/45; comment by Winston S. Churchill, Nov. 4, 1940, in PRO, A4279/39/45; dispatch from Winston S. Churchill to Lord Lothian, Nov. 27, 1940, in PRO, A4935/434/45.
26. Sherwood, p. 183.

14. HITLER MISSES THE BUS

1. Memorandum and minute by Ambassador Ritter on Hitler's order to German navy on *Admiral Scheer*, Nov. 9 and 11, 1940, in *DGFP*, XI, no. 307, p. 505; conversation between Joachim von Ribbentrop and Ramón Serrano-Suñer, Nov. 19, 1940, in *DGFP*, XI, no. 357, pp. 619–623; Winston S. Churchill, radio broadcast, Oct. 21, 1940, in Churchill, *Blood, Sweat and Tears*, cited (ch. 5), p. 402.
2. Telegram from Hans Thomsen to Berlin, Nov. 6, 1940, in *DGFP*, XI, no. 292, pp. 476–477; memorandum of conversation between Adolf Hitler and Vyacheslav M. Molotov (held Nov. 12, 1940), Nov. 16, 1940, in *DGFP*, XI, no. 326, pp. 541–549; Telford Taylor, *The Breaking Wave* (New York, 1967), pp. 130, 182; Winterbotham, *The Ultra Secret*, cited (ch. 12), pp. 50–55.
3. Taylor, *op. cit.*, p. 282.
4. Telegram from Winston S. Churchill to Franklin D. Roosevelt, Nov. 16, 1940, R-C FDRL.
5. Letter from Adolf Hitler to Benito Mussolini, Nov. 20, 1940, in *DGFP*, XI, no. 369, pp. 639–643; Baudouin, *The Private Papers*, cited (ch. 8), p. 252.
6. Taylor, p. 23; telegram from Winston S. Churchill to Franklin D. Roosevelt, Dec. 13, 1940, R-C FDRL.
7. Woodward, I, pp. 488–490; *BTTS*, pp. 138–139, 143.
8. Letter from Laurence Steinhardt to Loy Henderson, Oct. 20, 1940, in *FRUS*, 1940, III.
9. Conversation between Adolf Hitler and Vyacheslav M. Molotov, Nov. 16, 1940, in *DGFP*, XI, no. 326, pp. 541–549; *ibid.*, Nov. 15, 1940, in *DGFP*, XI, no. 328, pp. 550–562; *ibid.*, Nov. 18, 1940, in *DGFP*, XI, no. 329, pp. 562–570; conversation between Vyacheslav M. Molotov and Joachim von Ribbentrop, Nov. 26, 1940, in *DGFP*, XI, no. 404, pp. 714–715.
10. Halder, *Diary*, cited (ch. 12), Jan. 16, 1941; *FCNA*, pp. 169–173, Jan. 8 and 9, 1941; Shirer, p. 1062; F. H. Hinsley, *Hitler's Strategy* (Cambridge, 1951), p. 139.
11. Eden, pp. 211, 151, 153, 194–195; *TFH*, pp. 543, 534.
12. Telegram from Winston S. Churchill to Franklin D. Roosevelt, Oct. 21, 1940, R-C FDRL; *TFH*, p. 598; Cadogan, p. 338; telegram from Winston S. Churchill to Franklin D. Roosevelt, Dec. 13, 1940, R-C FDRL.
13. Letter from Harold Stark to Thomas C. Hart, Nov. 12, 1940, in *PHA*, pt. 12, p. 2448.
14. Woodward, I, pp. 385–386; Butler, *Grand Strategy*, cited (ch. 6), p. 418.
15. Cadogan, p. 335; comment by Lord Halifax, in PRO, A4891/131/45; letter from Winston S. Churchill to Franklin D. Roosevelt, Dec. 7, 1940, R-C FDRL.
16. Stimson, Nov. 6, 1940; *RPPC*, no. 694, Nov. 8, 1940; Roosevelt's reaction to low number

of bombers, in Stimson, Nov. 12, 1940; dispatch from David Gray to Franklin D. Roosevelt, Nov. 13, 1940, in FDRL; Ickes, III, p. 367; Warren F. Kimball, *The Most Unsordid Act* (Baltimore, 1969), p. 77.
17. Blum, *Roosevelt and Morgenthau,* cited (ch. 12), pp. 341–342; telegram from Winston S. Churchill to Lord Lothian, Nov. 27, 1940, in PRO, A4935/434/45; telegram from Hans Thomsen to Berlin, Nov. 30, 1940, in *DGFP*, XI, no. 427, pp. 751–752; Blum, *op. cit.,* p. 341.
18. Blum, pp. 343–344; Stimson, Dec. 3, 1940.
19. Blum, *Years of Urgency,* cited (ch. 5), p. 204; letter from Lord Beaverbrook to Winston S. Churchill, Dec. 26, 1940, in Taylor, *Beaverbrook,* cited (ch. 6), pp. 439–440.
20. MPD, Dec. 17, 1940; *RPPC*, no. 702, Dec. 17, 1940.
21. Woodward, I, p. 396.
22. Stimson, Dec. 19, 1940; dispatch from Hans Thomsen to Berlin, Dec. 19, 1940, in *DGFP*, XI, no. 534, pp. 905–906; *ibid.,* Dec. 25, 1940, in *DGFP*, XI, no. 563, pp. 949–950.
23. Franklin D. Roosevelt, radio broadcast, Dec. 29, 1940, in *PPA*, 1940, pp. 633–644; Rosenman, *Working with Roosevelt,* cited (ch. 10), pp. 261–262.
24. Blum, *Years of Urgency, op. cit.,* p. 193; Stimson, Nov. 25, Dec. 27, 19, and 16, 1940.
25. Letter from Harold Stark to J. I. Richardson, Nov. 12, 1940, in *PHA*, pt. 14, p. 971; memorandum from Harold Stark to Frank Knox, Nov. 4, 1940, in FDRL; Kittredge, "United States–British Naval Cooperation," cited (ch. 2), p. 305; Matloff and Snell, *Strategic Planning for Coalition Warfare,* cited (ch. 9), pp. 28–29; M. Watson, pp. 124–125.
26. Eden, p. 209; *TFH*, p. 613; dispatch from Winston S. Churchill to Franklin D. Roosevelt, Dec. 13, 1940, R-C FDRL.
27. Warlimont, *Inside Hitler's Headquarters,* cited (ch. 1), p. 128; telegram from Winston S. Churchill to Franklin D. Roosevelt, Nov. 23, 1940, R-C FDRL; Cadogan, pp. 336, 338.
28. Letter from Adolf Hitler to Benito Mussolini, Nov. 20, 1940, in *DGFP*, XI, no. 369, pp. 639–643; *ibid.,* Dec. 5, 1940, in *DGFP*, XI, no. 452, pp. 789–791.
29. Robert Murphy, *Diplomat among Warriors* (New York, 1964), pp. 67–73; memorandum from Hans Dieckhoff to foreign office, Nov. 24, 1940, in *DGFP*, XI, no. 394, pp. 698–701; letter from Franklin D. Roosevelt to William Leahy, Dec. 20, 1940, in *FRUS*, 1940, II, p. 425.
30. Baudouin, *op. cit.,* p. 274; messages from Winston S. Churchill to Henri Philippe Pétain and Maxime Weygand, Dec. 28, 1940, in *FRUS*, 1940, II, p. 432; Cadogan, p. 346.

15. TWO PRIMA DONNAS

1. Letter from Frank Knox to Franklin D. Roosevelt, Dec. 30, 1940, in FDRL; letter from

Franklin D. Roosevelt to Frank Knox, Dec. 31, 1940, in FDRL.

2. Kimball, *The Most Unsordid Act,* cited (ch. 14), p. 130; telegram from Winston S. Churchill to Franklin D. Roosevelt, Dec. 30, 1940, R-C FDRL; Cadogan, p. 344, Dec. 30, 1940.
3. Dispatch from Nevile Butler to foreign office, Dec. 31, 1940, in PRO, A11/11/45.
4. Telegram from Winston S. Churchill to Franklin D. Roosevelt, Jan. 1, 1941, R-C FDRL.
5. Richard Casey, *Personal Experiences, 1939–1945* (London, 1962), p. 67.
6. Sherwood, p. 230; telegram from Nevile Butler to foreign office, Jan. 4, 1941, in PRO, A101/101/45; letter from Franklin D. Roosevelt to Harold Ickes, Jan. 4, 1941, in *PL,* IV, p. 1100.
7. Sherwood, p. 232; Casey, *op. cit.,* pp. 51–52.
8. Winston S. Churchill, speech at Pilgrims' Luncheon, London, Jan. 9, 1941, in Churchill, *Blood, Sweat and Tears,* cited (ch. 5), pp. 447–448.
9. Lee, *The London Journals,* cited (ch. 12), pp. 201, 220, 222; Eden, p. 294; Sherwood, p. 237.
10. Sherwood, pp. 238–239; Lee, *op. cit.,* p. 220.
11. Oliver Lyttelton, *The Memoirs of Lord Chandos* (London, 1962), pp. 165–166; Sherwood, p. 242.
12. Memorandum on Hopkins, in PRO, PREM/4 25/3; J. B. Priestley, *All England Listened* (New York, 1967), p. xx; Alexander Kendrick, *Prime Time* (Boston, 1969), pp. 22–23.
13. Letter from Winston S. Churchill to Ernest Bevin, Nov. 25, 1940, in PRO, PREM/4 83/1A; letter from Ernest Bevin to Winston S. Churchill, Nov. 26, 1940, in PRO, PREM/4 83/1A; Franklin D. Roosevelt, State of the Union message, Jan. 6, 1941, in *PPA,* 1940, p. 672.
14. Minute by foreign office on John G. Winant, Jan. 22, 1941, in PRO, A716/252/45; Long, *The War Diary,* cited (ch. 7), p. 181, Feb. 15, 1941; minute by T. North Whitehead on Benjamin V. Cohen, Feb. 24, 1941, in PRO, A1054/409/45; accounts of party for Wendell Willkie, Feb., 1941, in PRO, A716/252/45, A743/252/45.
15. Sherwood, p. 243; telegram from Winston S. Churchill to Franklin D. Roosevelt, Jan. 28, 1941, in *TGA,* pp. 25–26; *ibid.,* Jan. 21, 1941, R-C FDRL; telegram from Franklin D. Roosevelt to Winston S. Churchill, Jan. 22, 1941, R-C FDRL; remarks by Harry Hopkins at

press luncheon and comment by Alexander Cadogan, Jan. 25, 1941, in PRO, A101/101/45.
16. Telegram from Nevile Butler to foreign office, Jan. 14, 1941, in PRO, A3/3/45; minute by T. North Whitehead, Jan. 17, 1941, in PRO, A3/3/45.
17. *RPPC,* no. 709, Jan. 10, 1941; *ibid.,* no. 710, Jan. 14, 1941; PRO, CAB 65/17, WM10(41) 127; Kimball, *op. cit.,* p. 177; memorandum from Franklin D. Roosevelt to Stephen T. Early, February 21, 1941, in FBI files; letter from J. Edgar Hoover to Stephen T. Early, March 1, 1941, in FBI files; "Memorandum for the Attorney General, Re: America First Committee," Dec. 4, 1941, in FBI files; Hyde, *Room 3603,* cited (ch. 8), p. 73.
18. Telegram from Lord Halifax to foreign office, Jan. 30, 1941, in PRO, A582/44/45; Winston S. Churchill, radio broadcast, Feb. 9, 1941, in Churchill, *Blood, Sweat and Tears, op. cit.,* pp. 453–462.
19. *PPA,* 1940, p. 640.
20. Ickes, III, p. 429, Feb. 8, 1941; Panter-Downes, *London War Notes,* cited (ch. 10), pp. 136–137; PRO, PREM/4 25/3; telegram from Lord Halifax to Winston S. Churchill, Feb. 21, 1941, in PRO, PREM/4 27/9; Stimson, Feb. 26 and March 5, 1941.
21. Lash, *A Friend's Memoir,* cited (ch. 13), p. 208; Sherwood, p. 280; *RPPC,* no. 721, Feb. 25, 1941; Freedman, *Roosevelt and Frankfurter,* cited (ch. 10), p. 582; Sherwood, p. 266.
22. Wheeler-Bennett, *King George VI,* cited (ch. 4), p. 514; remark by Winston S. Churchill to war cabinet, Feb. 20, 1941, in PRO, CAB 65/17, WMI9(41); memorandum from Lord Beaverbrook, Feb. 20, 1941, in Taylor, *Beaverbrook,* cited (ch. 6), p. 440.
23. Franklin D. Roosevelt, speech to White House Correspondents' Association, March 15, 1941, in *PPA,* 1941, pp. 60–69.
24. *DGFP,* XII, no. 146, pp. 258–259, March 10, 1941; Maisky, p. 133.
25. Memorandum from Franklin D. Roosevelt to Cordell Hull, Jan. 11, 1941, in FDRL; Moffat, *The Moffat Papers,* cited (ch. 1), p. 354.
26. Telegram from Lord Halifax to foreign office, March 18, 1941, in PRO, A893/18/45; comment by T. North Whitehead, March 20, 1941, in PRO, A893/18/45.

16. THE BATTLE OF THE ATLANTIC

1. Comment by Henry Stimson, quoted in *PHA,* pt. 20, exhibit no. 179, pp. 4275–4280; comment by Winston S. Churchill to war cabinet, Feb. 27, 1941, in PRO, WM21(41); record of conversation between Joachim von Ribbentrop and Hiroshi Oshima, Feb. 23, 1941, in *DGFP,* XII, no. 78, pp. 139–151; advice of British chiefs of staff to Anthony Eden and Eden's reaction, Feb. 8 and 9, 1941, in PRO, F677/17/23; Sherwood, pp. 258–259.
2. Sherwood, p. 259; Stimson, Feb. 10, 1941; *FRUS,* Japan, 1931–1941, II, pp. 387–388, Feb. 14, 1941; message from Winston S. Churchill to Franklin D. Roosevelt, Feb. 15, 1941, R-C FDRL.
3. *TGA,* p. 177; dispatch from Winston S. Churchill to Franklin D. Roosevelt, Feb. 20, 1941, text in *PHA,* pt. 19, p. 3454 (a slightly different version is printed in *TGA,* p. 179); memoranda from Franklin D. Roosevelt to Sumner Welles, Feb. 19 and 20, 1941, in *PL,* IV, pp. 1125–1126; on Magic, see Roberta Wohlstetter, *Pearl Harbor: Warning and Decision* (Stanford, 1962), pp. 170 ff., also see David Kahn, *The Codebreakers: The Story of Secret Writing* (New York, 1967).
4. Letter from Harold Stark to H. E. Kimmel, Feb. 25, 1941, in *PHA,* pt. 16, exhibit no. 106, p. 2149; Matloff and Snell, *Strategic Planning for Coalition Warfare,* cited (ch. 9), pp. 30, 34; M. Watson, p. 118.
5. Perkins, OHP, vol. 8, pt. 3.
6. Telegram from A. V. Alexander to Washington, D.C., March 17, 1941, in PRO, A1925/384/45; Stimson, March 25, 1941; directive from Harold Stark to fleet commanders, April 3, 1941, in *PHA,* pt. 17, exhibit no. 112, p.

2462; letter from Harold Stark to H. E. Kimmel, April 4, 1941, in *PHA,* pt. 16, exhibit no. 106, p. 2160.
7. Ernest J. King and Walter M. Whitehill, *Fleet Admiral King* (New York, 1952), pp. 318–319; Samuel E. Morison, *The Battle of the Atlantic, 1939–1943* (Boston, 1947), pp. 45, 51; Ickes, III, pp. 466, 470; Friedlaender, *Prelude to Downfall,* cited (ch. 7), pp. 203–205.
8. Telegram from Winston S. Churchill to Franklin D. Roosevelt, March 20, 1941, R-C FDRL; Stimson, April 10, 1941.
9. Telegram from Franklin D. Roosevelt to Winston S. Churchill, April 11, 1941, R-C FDRL.
10. Dispatch from Winston S. Churchill to Lord Halifax, March 9, 1941, in PRO, PREM/4 27/9; minute by T. North Whitehead, April 2, 1941, in PRO, A2320/3/45.
11. Letter from Harold Stark to H. E. Kimmel, April 19, 1941, in *PHA,* pt. 16, exhibit no. 106, pp. 2164–2165; Stimson, April 15, 1941; M. Watson, pp. 388–389.
12. Telegram from Winston S. Churchill to Franklin D. Roosevelt, April 16, 1941, R-C FDRL; Cadogan, p. 375, April 24, 1941; Wheeler-Bennett, *King George VI,* cited (ch. 4), p. 524; George VI, Journal, April 25, 1941.
13. Cadogan, p. 374, April 29, 1941; W. Averell Harriman and Elie Abel, *Special Envoy to Churchill and Stalin, 1941–1946* (New York, 1975), p. 19; Stimson, April 2, 1941; letter from Lord Halifax to Winston S. Churchill, March 13, 1941, in PRO, PREM/4 27/9.
14. Letter from Lord Halifax to Winston S. Churchill, April 10, 1941, in PRO, PREM/4 27/9; Stimson, April 22 and 24, 1941; Lash,

A Friend's Memoir, cited (ch. 13), p. 43; letter from Harold Stark to H. E. Kimmel, April 19, 1941, in *PHA*, pt. 16, exhibit no. 106, p. 2164.

15. Gallup poll on convoys in *NYT*, April 24, 1941; memorandum from J. Edgar Hoover, May, 1941, in FDRL; Walter F. George in *Congressional Record*, vol. 87. p. 1891, March 6, 1941; letter from Thomas Lamont to Clark Eichelberger, April 8, 1941, in Mark L. Chadwin, *The Warhawks* (New York, 1968), p. 234; Long, *The War Diary*, cited (ch. 7), pp. 195–196, 198–199, April 17 and 25, 1941; Raymond Gram Swing, article in *Sunday Express*, May 11, 1941 (copy in Hopkins, Papers, cited [ch. 7]).

16. Telegram from Lord Halifax to Winston S. Churchill, April 18, 1941, in PRO, A3496/11/45; dispatch from Winston S. Churchill to

Lord Halifax, May 5, 1941, in PRO, A3496/11/45.

17. Cadogan, p. 375, May 1, 1941; exchange between Britain and United States regarding transfer of U.S. fleet in *PHA*, pt. 19, pp. 3456–3461.

18. Stimson, April 17, 1941; Pogue, *George C. Marshall*, cited (ch. 8), II, pp. 131 ff.; M. Watson, pp. 389–390.

19. Telegram from Winston S. Churchill to Franklin D. Roosevelt, March 24, 1941, R-C FDRL; *RPPC*, no. 738, April 25, 1941; Charles A. Lindbergh, speech, New York, April 24, 1941, in *NYT*, April 25, 1941.

20. Jan Ciechanowski, *Defeat in Victory* (New York, 1947), pp. 8, 17.

21. Winston S. Churchill, radio broadcast, May 3, 1941, in *NYT*, May 4, 1941.

17. A MOMENT OF GLOOM

1. Message from Winston S. Churchill to Franklin D. Roosevelt, April 24, 1941, in *TGA*, pp. 143–145; message from Franklin D. Roosevelt to Winston S. Churchill, May 1, 1941, R-C FDRL.

2. Stimson, April 30, 1941; dispatch from John G. Winant to Franklin D. Roosevelt, May 6, 1941, in FDRL; minute by T. North Whitehead, May 3, 1941, in PRO, vol. 35147; message from Winston S. Churchill to Franklin D. Roosevelt, May 3, 1941, R-C FDRL; message from Franklin D. Roosevelt to Winston S. Churchill, May 3, 1941, R-C FDRL.

3. Kittredge, "United States–British Naval Cooperation," cited (ch. 2), p. 439; Greenfield, *American Strategy in World War II*, cited (ch. 11), p. 75; Adolf Hitler, speech, Berlin, May 4, 1941, in *NYT*, May 5, 1941; debate in House of Commons, in *Hansard*, col. 928, May 7, 1941; *NYT*, May 8, 1941; Nicolson, *The War Years*, cited (ch. 6), pp. 164–165.

4. Sir John Kennedy, *The Business of War* (New York, 1958), pp. 94, 104–107; Bryant, *The Turn of Tide*, cited (ch. 8), pp. 193, 203.

5. Nicolson, *op. cit.*, p. 166; John Connell, *Wavell, Soldier and Scholar* (London, 1964), pp. 470–471; *TGA*, pp. 294, 295.

6. Cadogan, p. 381; Eden, p. 283; Nicolson, pp. 168–169; *Hansard*, cols. 1716–1718, May 26 and 27, 1941; Bryant, *op. cit.*, pp. 198, 202; Ciano, p. 357; Sherwood, pp. 204–205; Morison, *The Battle of the Atlantic*, cited (ch. 16),

pp. 64, 69; Malcolm F. Willoughby, *The U.S. Coast Guard in World War II*, (Annapolis, 1957), pp. 20–32; Stevenson, *A Man Called Intrepid*, cited (ch. 8), pp. 239–240.

7. Letter from Winston S. Churchill to Jan Christiaan Smuts, May 16, 1941, in *TGA*, p. 283; letter from Franklin D. Roosevelt to Josiah W. Bailey, May 13, 1941, in *PL*, IV, pp. 1154–1155; memorandum from Anna M. Rosenberg to Edwin M. Watson, May 16, 1941, in FDRL.

8. Minute by David Scott, May 7, 1941, in PRO, A3642/11/45; comment by William Cadogan, May 13, 1941, in PRO, A3642/11/45; dispatch from Lord Halifax to foreign office, May 7, 1941, in PRO, A3642/11/45; message from Winston S. Churchill to Anthony Eden, May 10, 1941, in PRO, A3866/11/45; message from Anthony Eden to Lord Halifax, May 15, 1941, in PRO, A3866/11/45; interdepartmental minute from Anthony Eden, May 21, 1941, in PRO, A3866/11/45; comment by Winston S. Churchill, May 28, 1941, in PRO, A3866/11/45; letter from W. Averell Harriman to Franklin D. Roosevelt, May 7, 1941, in FDRL.

9. Telegram from Winston S. Churchill to Franklin D. Roosevelt, May 19, 1941, R-C FDRL; dispatch from Franklin D. Roosevelt to John G. Winant for Winston S. Churchill, May 19, 1941, R-C FDRL; comment by Cordell Hull, May 22, 1941, in FDRL.

18. FREEDOM OF THE SEAS REASSERTED

1. Comment by John Balfour, May 11, 1941, in PRO, A3642/11/45; Stimson, May 8 and 13, 1941; MPD, vol. 397, pp. 310A, 310B, May 14, 1941.

2. Conversation between Jean Louis Darlan and Joachim von Ribbentrop, May 12, 1941, in *DGFP*, XII, no. 499, pp. 781–782; statement by Franklin D. Roosevelt, May 15, 1941, in *PPA*, 1941, pp. 158–159; *RPPC*, no. 741, May 16, 1941.

3. *RPPC*, no. 712, Jan. 21, 1941; statement by Walter F. George, March 6, 1941, in *Congressional Record*, vol. 87, p. 1891; letter from Winston S. Churchill to Franklin D. Roosevelt, Dec. 7, 1940, R-C FDRL.

4. Winston S. Churchill, *The World Crisis*, cited (ch. 3), pp. 104–108; conversation between Adolf Hitler and John Cudahy, May 5, 1941, in *DGFP*, XII, no. 451, pp. 704–710; *ibid.*, May 23, 1941, in *DGFP*, XII, no. 542, pp. 854–861; interview of Erich Raeder, in *NYT*, May 25, 1941 (also in *DGFP*, XII, no. 608, pp. 987–988, footnote); warning from Yosuke Matsuoka to Joseph C. Grew, May 15, 1941, in *DGFP*, XII, no. 516, pp. 818–819; dispatch from Joseph C. Grew to Cordell Hull, May 14, 1941, in *FRUS*, Japan, 1931–1941, II, p. 189; letter from Robert Sherwood to an English friend, June 4, 1941, in PRO, British foreign office file, vol. 26148; orders from Adolf Hitler against attacks on American shipping, June 9, 1941, in *DGFP*, XII, no. 608, pp. 987–988; record of conversation between Joachim von Ribbentrop and Benito

Mussolini, May 14, 1941, in *DGFP*, XII, no. 511, pp. 797–806.

5. MPD, May 17, 1941; dispatch from Harold Stark to fleet commanders, May, 1941, in *PHA*, pt. 16. exhibit no. 106, pp. 2167–2168; Pogue, *George C. Marshall*, cited (ch. 8), II, pp. 137–138; MPD, May 22, 1941; telegram from Franklin D. Roosevelt to Winston S. Churchill, May 27, 1941, R-C FDRL.

6. Perkins, OHP, vol. 8, p. 1; Franklin D. Roosevelt, speech, May 27, 1941, in *PPA*, 1941, pp. 181–195; Berle, Diary, cited (ch. 5), May 29, 1941.

7. Panter-Downes, *London War Notes*, cited (ch. 10), pp. 150–151; minute by T. North Whitehead, May 30, 1941, in PRO, A4702/3/45.

8. Dispatch from Lord Halifax to foreign office, May 29, 1941, in PRO, A4069/18/45; telegram from Lord Halifax to Winston S. Churchill, May 30, 1941, in PRO, A4071/3/45; Stimson, May 29, 1941.

9. Minute by T. North Whitehead, June 12, 1941, in PRO, A4400/4093/45; memorandum from Oscar Cox to Harry Hopkins, May 22, 1941, in Hopkins, Papers, cited (ch. 7).

10. Telegram from Winston S. Churchill to Franklin D. Roosevelt, May 29, 1941, R-C FDRL.

11. Comment by Joachim von Ribbentrop to Yosuke Matsuoka in record of conversation between Adolf Hitler and Benito Mussolini, June 3, 1941, in *DGFP*, XII, no. 584, pp. 940–951; Long, *The War Diary*, cited (ch. 7), p. 201; Berle, Diary, *op. cit.*, June 5, 1941.

12. Conversation between Adolf Hitler and Benito

Mussolini, June 3, 1941; dispatch from Winston S. Churchill to Archibald P. Wavell, May 28, 1941, in Connell, *Wavell,* cited (ch. 17), p. 48.

19. ROOSEVELT OCCUPIES ICELAND

1. John G. Winant, *Letter from Grosvenor Square* (Boston, 1947), pp. 95-96; Anthony Eden, *Freedom and Order* (London, 1947), pp. 103, 107, 108; Franklin D. Roosevelt, speech, May 27, 1941 in *PPA,* 1941, p. 192; Eden, p. 301; R. T. Harrod, *John Maynard Keynes* (New York, 1951), p. 503; King and Whitehill, *Fleet Admiral King,* cited (ch. 16), p. 329; comment by T. North Whitehead, May 30, 1941, in PRO, A4072/3/45.
2. Hull, pp. 996-997; memorandum by Stanley Hornbeck, April 7, 1941, in *FRUS,* 1941, IV, pp. 124-125; Stimson, May 15, 1941; telegram from Lord Halifax to foreign office, May 17, 1941, in PRO, F4187/12/23; Hull, p. 1003.
3. Comment by Ashley Clarke, May 17, 1941, in PRO, F4187/12/23; comment by John Balfour, May 20, 1941, in PRO, F4187/12/23; minute by Anthony Eden, May 21, 1941, in PRO, F4187/12/23; telegram from foreign office to Lord Halifax, May 21, 1941, in PRO, F4187/12/23.
4. Dispatch from Eugen Ott to Joachim von Ribbentrop, May 10, 1941, in *DGFP,* XII, no. 483, pp. 749-750; telegram from Ernst von Weizsäcker to Joachim von Ribbentrop, May 15, 1941, in *DGFP,* XII, no. 517, p. 819; memorandum from Cordell Hull on meeting with Lord Halifax, May 24, 1941, in *FRUS,* 1941, IV, pp. 210-212; dispatch from Lord Halifax to foreign office, May 28, 1941, in PRO, F4570/86/23; *PHA,* pt. 20, exhibit no. 174, p. 4077.
5. Dispatch from Robert L. Craigie to foreign office, June 11, 1941, in PRO, F5147/86/23; comment by L. H. Foulds, June 14, 1941, in PRO, F5147/86/23; comment by Ashley Clarke, June 16, 1941, in PRO, F5147/86/23; comment by John Balfour, June 21, 1941, in PRO, F5147/86/23; minute by Ashley Clarke, July 2, 1941, in PRO, F5147/86/23.
6. *TGA,* p. 426; Hull, p. 986; report on plane production from division of naval intelligence to Franklin D. Roosevelt, Aug. 25, 1941, in FDRL; report from Myron Taylor to Franklin D. Roosevelt, May, 1941, in FDRL; military production figures at end of 1941 from Samuel I. Rosenman, in speech-material folder, March, 1944, in FDRL.
7. Meeting between Adolf Hitler and Benito Mussolini, June 3, 1941, in *DGFP,* XII, no.

584, pp. 940-951; memorandum from Hans Dieckhoff, June 6, 1941, in *DGFP,* XII, no. 600, pp. 973-974; Ickes, III, p. 567, July 1, 1941.
8. Ickes, III, p. 538; Casey, *Personal Experiences,* cited (ch. 15), p. 66.
9. Memorandum from Harry Hopkins to Franklin D. Roosevelt, June 14, 1941, in FDRL; Ickes, III, p. 552; telegram from Franklin D. Roosevelt to Winston S. Churchill, June 17, 1941, R-C FDRL; *FCNA,* pp. 219 ff., June 24, 1941.
10. Telegram from Winston S. Churchill to Franklin D. Roosevelt, June 14, 1941, R-C FDRL; dispatch from Winston S. Churchill to Alexander Cadogan, June 14, 1941, in PRO, A4604/553/6; memorandum from Sumner Welles to Franklin D. Roosevelt, June 18, 1941, in FDRL; memorandum from Sumner Welles to Franklin D. Roosevelt on Welles's conversation with Lord Halifax, June 22, 1941, in *FRUS,* 1941, III, p. 779; Stimson, June 24, 1941; account by British minister of Iceland's views on *invite,* June 27, 1941, in *FRUS,* 1941, III, p. 779; reports from Lord Halifax to Sumner Welles for Franklin D. Roosevelt, June 14, 1941, in FDRL; Kittredge, "United States-British Naval Cooperation," cited (ch. 2), p. 479; Stimson, June 20 and July 1, 1941.
11. On Roosevelt's feelings about Stimson see MPD, June 4, 1941; message from Franklin D. Roosevelt to Congress, July 7, 1941, in *PPA,* 1941, pp. 255-264; dispatch from Winston S. Churchill to Franklin D. Roosevelt, July 7, 1941, R-C FDRL; comment by Gerald P. Nye in *Congressional Record,* vol. 87, p. 5932, July 10, 1941; letter from Frank Knox to Mrs. Knox, July 31, 1941, in Frank Knox, Papers, LC; memorandum from Henry L. Stimson to Franklin D. Roosevelt, July 9, 1941, in FDRL; telegram from Hans Thomsen to Berlin, July 9, 1941, in *DGFP,* XIII, no. 83, pp. 101-103; dispatch from Friedrich von Bötticher to Berlin, July 12, 1941, in *DGFP,* XIII, no. 99, pp. 125-126; reaction of Adolf Hitler, July 16, 1941, in *DGFP,* XIII, no. 83, pp. 101-103, footnote.
12. WPL-51 in FDRL; dispatch from Hans Thomsen to Berlin, July 13, 1941, in *DGFP,* XIII, no. 104, pp. 130-131; dispatch from Harold Stark to Franklin D. Roosevelt, July 25, 1941, in FDRL.

20. SAUCE FOR THE SOVIET GANDER

1. On the Hess affair see *DGFP,* XII, no. 500, p. 783, May 12, 1941; Ciano, p. 350; *TGA,* p. 55; telegram from Franklin D. Roosevelt to Winston S. Churchill, May 14, 1941, R-C FDRL; dispatch from Winston S. Churchill to Franklin D. Roosevelt, May 17, 1941, in *TGA,* p. 12.
2. *RPPC,* no. 747, June 6, 1941; memorandum from Sumner Welles to Franklin D. Roosevelt, June 22, 1941, in FDRL.
3. Alan Clark, *Barbarossa* (New York, 1965), pp. xix, 43; dispatch from Lord Beaverbrook to foreign office, Nov. 2, 1941, in PRO, H6312/3/31; memorandum from Eleanor Roosevelt to Franklin D. Roosevelt, Aug. 21, 1944, in FDRL; Churchill, *The World Crisis,* cited (ch. 3), pp. 164, 274, 288; James, *Churchill: A Study in Failure,* cited (ch. 11), pp. 105, 117, 108, 120; Lord Beaverbrook, *Men and Power, 1917-1918* (London. 1956), p. 306.
4. Beaverbrook, *op. cit.,* pp. 291-292; James, *op. cit.,* p. 321; dispatch from Laurence Steinhardt to Cordell Hull, Feb. 8, 1941, in *FRUS,* 1941, I, p. 161.
5. Eden, p. 310; *TGA,* p. 356; telegram from Winston S. Churchill to Franklin D. Roosevelt, June 15, 1941, in PRO, A4604/553/G; Winant, *Letter from Grosvenor Square,* cited (ch. 19), p. 203.
6. Franklin D. Roosevelt, speech, Oct. 8, 1920, in FDRL; on Bullitt see Beatrice Farnsworth, *William C. Bullitt and the Soviet Union*

(Bloomington, 1967), chs. 1, 2, 5; George F. Kennan, *Memoirs, 1925-1950* (Boston, 1967), p. 80; Churchill, *The World Crisis, op. cit.,* p. 179; Charles E. Bohlen, *Witness to History, 1929-1969* (New York, 1973), p. 36.
7. Bohlen, *op. cit.,* pp. 44-45, 51; Churchill, *The Great Contemporaries,* cited (ch. 2), p. 381; dispatch from Sumner Welles to Laurence Steinhardt on Roosevelt-Oumansky conversation, Aug. 4, 1939, in *FRUS,* 1939, I, pp. 293-294; Franklin D. Roosevelt, speech to American Youth Congress, Washington, D.C., Feb. 11, 1940, in *PPA,* 1940, pp. 85-94.
8. Memorandum from Franklin D. Roosevelt to Cordell Hull, Dec. 12, 1939, in *PL,* IV, p. 974; *ibid.,* Jan. 10, 1940, in *PL,* IV, pp. 986-987; dispatches from Laurence Steinhardt to Cordell Hull, Nov. 10 and 27, 1940, in *FRUS,* 1940, I, pp. 574, 632; Hull, p. 971; dispatch from Cordell Hull to Laurence Steinhardt, March 1. 1941, in *FRUS,* 1941, I, p. 732; dispatch from Laurence Steinhardt to Cordell Hull, March 3, 1941, in *FRUS,* 1941, I, p. 732; dispatch from Cordell Hull to Laurence Steinhardt, March 4, 1941, in *FRUS,* 1941, I, p. 732; Soviet embassy, *Information Bulletin,* Dec. 15, 1941, quoted in William L. Langer and S. Everett Gleason. *The Undeclared War,* (New York, 1953), p. 342.
9. Maisky, pp. 150, 157; *TGA,* pp. 352-353; dispatch from Laurence Steinhardt to Cordell Hull, June 12, 1941, in FRUS, 1941, I, pp.

764–765; memorandum from Cordell Hull to Laurence Steinhardt, June 14, 1941, in *FRUS*, 1941, I, pp. 764–765; telegram from Laurence Steinhardt to Cordell Hull, June 17, 1941, in

FRUS, 1941, I, pp. 764–765; memorandum from State Department on "Policy with Regard to the Soviet Union . . . ," June 21, 1941, I, pp. 766–767.

21. BRITAIN'S NEW AND DEMANDING ALLY

1. Wheeler-Bennett, *Action This Day*, cited (ch. 11), p. 89; *TGA*, pp. 370–371; Eden, p. 312.
2. Ribbentrop's prediction to Ciano quoted in Sherwood, p. 305; Lee, *The London Journals*, cited (ch. 12), p. 331; Winston S. Churchill, radio broadcast, June 22, 1941, in *TGA*, pp. 371–373.
3. Ickes, III, p. 549; Welles, *The Time for Decision*, cited (ch. 1), p. 171; statement by Sumner Welles, June 23, 1941, in *Documents on American Foreign Relations* (Boston, 1941), III, pp. 364–365; *RPPC*, no. 750, June 24, 1941; telegram from Lord Halifax to foreign office, July 7, 1941, in PRO, N3540/78/38.
4. *FCNA*, pp. 219 ff., June 21, 1941; Clark, *Barbarossa*, cited (ch. 20), p. 58; Halder, *Diary*, June 22 and 30 and July 3, 1941, quoted in Langer and Gleason, *The Undeclared War*, cited (ch. 20), p. 533; Ickes, III, pp. 573, 574; memorandum from Sumner Welles, July 16, 1941, in *FRUS*, 1941, I, p. 184; Shirer, p. 1111.
5. Eden, p. 313; on Stafford Cripps's return to Moscow see Woodward, II, pp. 6–7; dispatch from Laurence Steinhardt to Cordell Hull, June 28, 1941, in *FRUS*, 1941, I, p. 176; memorandum from R. A. Butler to foreign office, July 2, 1941, in PRO, N3502/78/38; Cadogan, pp. 390–391, July 1, 1941.
6. Telegram from Stafford Cripps to foreign office, July 1, 1941, in PRO, A5102/11/45; dispatch from Winston S. Churchill to Franklin D. Roosevelt, July 1, 1941, R-C FDRL; Cadogan, p. 390, July 1, 1941; dispatch from Lord Halifax to foreign office, July 7, 1941, in PRO, N3540/3/38; comment by Orme Sargent, July 9, 1941, in PRO, N3540/3/38; comment by Alexander Cadogan, July 10, 1941, in PRO, N3540/3/38; comment by David Scott, July 10, 1941, in PRO, N3540/3/38.
7. R. A. Leeper, "Political Aspects of a German Defeat by Russia," July 7, 1941; comment by Alexander Cadogan, July 8, 1941, in PRO, N3718; letter from Franklin D. Roosevelt to William D. Leahy, June 26, 1941, in *PL*, IV, p. 1177.
8. *TGA*, pp. 380–381; message from Winston S. Churchill to Joseph Stalin, July 7, 1941, in *TGA*, pp. 380–381; dispatch from Winston S. Churchill to first lord and first sea lord, July 10, 1941, in *TGA*, pp. 381–382; dispatch from Stafford Cripps to foreign office, July 8, 1941, in PRO, N3603/3/38; on Stalin's hatred of the British see dispatch from Laurence Steinhardt to Cordell Hull, May 26, 1941, in *FRUS*, 1941, I, pp. 166–167.
9. Memorandum from Sumner Welles on talk with Lord Halifax, July 10, 1941, in *FRUS*, 1941, I, p. 182; *ibid.*, June 15, 1941, in *FRUS*, 1941, I, pp. 759–761.
10. Cadogan, p. 392, July 9, 1941; on Churchill's hopes with respect to Stalin see *TGA*, p. 388; on war cabinet's action on message to Stalin see Woodward, II, p. 12; on postponement of Polish territorial issue by Churchill see *TGA*, p. 391; Ciechanowski, *Defeat in Victory*, cited (ch. 16), pp. 29 ff.
11. Memorandum from Adolf A. Berle to Franklin D. Roosevelt, July 9, 1941, in Berle, *Navigating the Rapids*, cited (ch. 1), pp. 372–373; message from Franklin D. Roosevelt to Winston S. Churchill, July 14, 1941, R-C FDRL; Eden, p. 316.
12. Dispatch from Stafford Cripps to foreign office, July 10, 1941, paraphrased in Woodward, II, p. 14; letter from Joseph E. Davies to Harry Hopkins, July 8, 1941, in Joseph E. Davies, *Mission to Moscow* (New York, 1941), pp. 493–495.
13. Letter from Joseph E. Davies to Franklin D. Roosevelt, June 8, 1939, in FDRL; on German order not to take "commissars" as prisoners see *TGA*, p. 368; dispatch from Joseph Stalin to Winston S. Churchill, July 19, 1941, in Joseph Stalin, *Correspondence with Churchill, Attlee, Roosevelt, and Truman*, ed. Ministry of Foreign Affairs (Moscow, 1957), pp. 12, 13; on Churchill's reaction see *TGA*, p. 384; telegram from Winston S. Churchill to Joseph Stalin, July 20, 1941, in *TGA*, pp. 384–386.

22. "NO TALK ABOUT WAR"

1. Ciechanowski, *Defeat in Victory*, cited (ch. 16), pp. 26–27; Stimson, July 1, 1941; Harold L. Ickes, speech, Hartford, June 26, 1941, quoted in Langer and Gleason, *The Undeclared War*, cited (ch. 20), p. 538; message from Harold L. Ickes to Franklin D. Roosevelt, June 23, 1941, in FDRL; message from Henry L. Stimson to Franklin D. Roosevelt, June 23, 1941, in FDRL; dispatch from Harold Stark to Charles M. Cooke, July 31, 1941, in *PHA*, pt. 16, p. 2176; letter from Franklin D. Roosevelt to Mackenzie King, July 1, 1941, in *PL*, IV, p. 1179; telegram from Winston S. Churchill to Franklin D. Roosevelt, July 7, 1941, quoted in Langer and Gleason, *The Undeclared War*, *op. cit.*, Ii, p. 578; Winston S. Churchill, speech, London, July 9, 1941, in Winston S. Churchill, *The Unrelenting Struggle* (Boston, 1942), pp. 176–177.
2. Sherwood, pp. 310–313; *RPPC*, no. 756, July 18, 1941; Stimson, July 21, 1941.
3. Oscar Cox, Diary, June 23, 1941, in FDRL; letter from Michael J. Ready to Sumner Welles, July 2, 1941, in FDRL; memorandum from Loy Henderson of conversation with Oumansky, July 2, 1941, in *FRUS*, 1941, I, p. 786.
4. Memorandum from Joseph E. Davies to Harry Hopkins, July 8, 1941, in Sherwood, pp. 306–308; memorandum from Sumner Welles of conversation with Lord Halifax, July 10, 1941, in *FRUS*, 1941, I, pp. 788–789; Stimson, July 21, 1941; Ickes, III, pp. 592–593, Aug. 3, 1941; Blum, *Years of Urgency*, cited (ch. 5), pp. 263–265; Stimson, Aug. 1 and 4, 1941; memorandum from Franklin D. Roosevelt to Wayne

Coy, Aug. 2, 1941, in FDRL; Cox, *op. cit.*, Aug. 2, 1941.
5. Letter from Adolf Hitler to Benito Mussolini, June 21, 1941, in *DGFP*, XII, no. 600, pp. 1006–1009; Shirer, p. 1146; message from Joachim von Ribbentrop to Eugen Ott, July 1, 1941, in *DGFP*, XIII, no. 53, pp. 61–63 (see also nos. 35 and 36, pp. 40, 41).
6. Accounts of Japanese imperial council meeting, July 2, 1941, in Fumimaro Konoye, *Memoirs of Prince Konoye* (March, 1942), in *PHA*, pt. 20, exhibit no. 173, pp. 3985–4029); message from Franklin D. Roosevelt to Harold L. Ickes, June 23, 1941, in Ickes, III, p. 558.
7. Cadogan, p. 392; memorandum from Sumner Welles on conversation with Lord Halifax, July 10, 1941, in *FRUS*, 1941, IV, pp. 300–303; report from Lord Halifax to foreign office, July 8, 1941, in PRO, F5957/9/61; telegram from foreign office to Lord Halifax, July 13, 1941, in PRO, F6101/12/23; report from Lord Halifax to foreign office, July 15, 1941, in PRO, F6272/12/23; Cadogan, p. 392, July 14, 1941.
8. Ickes, III, p. 583, July 20, 1941; *ibid.*, p. 588, July 27, 1941; memorandum from Anthony Eden to Winston S. Churchill, July 21, 1941, in PRO, F6273/9/61; dispatch from Anthony Eden to Lord Halifax, July 22, 1941, in PRO, F6273/9/61; Cadogan, p. 393, July 21, 1941.
9. Record of conversation between Franklin D. Roosevelt and Kichisaburo Nomura, July 24, 1941, in *FRUS*, Japan, 1931–1941, II, pp. 527–530; telegram from Franklin D. Roosevelt to Harry Hopkins, July 26, 1941, in Sherwood, pp. 318–319; Cadogan, p. 394, July 24, 1941;

comment by Robert Gordon Menzies, July 30, 1941, in PRO, F7170/1290/23; dispatch from foreign office to Lord Halifax, Aug. 1, 1941, in PRO, F7169/1299/23; advice from John G. Winant to Anthony Eden and Alexander Cadogan, July 31, 1941, in PRO, F7244/54/61.

10. Sherwood, pp. 308–311; Lee, *The London Journals,* cited (ch. 12), p. 313; report of British cabinet meeting in which Hopkins took part, July 17, 1941, in PRO, CAB 65/19, WM(41)71; Sherwood, pp. 314–315; for John Dill's view see *TGA,* pp. 420–423; Lee, *op. cit.,* p. 351; Sherwood, p. 316.

11. Telegram from Winston S. Churchill to Franklin D. Roosevelt, July 25, 1941; M. Watson, pp. 353–355.

12. Maisky, pp. 177 ff.; Lee, p. 353; telegram from Harry Hopkins to Franklin D. Roosevelt, July 25, 1941, in Sherwood, p. 318; tele-

gram from Winston S. Churchill to Franklin D. Roosevelt, July 25, 1941, R-C FDRL; memorandum from Adolf A. Berle to Harry Hopkins, July 30, 1941, in Berle, Diary, cited (ch. 5); Sherwood, p. 317; Maisky, pp. 184 ff.; Cox, *op. cit.,* Aug. 20, 1941; dispatch from Harry Hopkins to Franklin D. Roosevelt, July 26, 1941, in Hopkins, Papers, cited (ch. 7); Sherwood, pp. 321, 332.

13. Sherwood, pp. 327 ff.

14. Dispatch from Winston S. Churchill to Franklin D. Roosevelt, July 4, 1941, in *TGA,* p. 350, Harold Denny, in *NYT,* July 5 and 7, 1941; Langer and Gleason, *The Undeclared War,* p. 511; telegram from Lord Halifax to foreign office, July 10, 1941, in PRO, A5350/3469/45; minute by John Balfour, July 11, 1941, in PRO, A5350/3469/45.

23. "HOW NEAR IS AMERICA TO WAR?"

1. Sherwood, p. 351; note by Ian Jacob, quoted in Wheeler-Bennett, *Action This Day,* cited (ch. 11), p. 189; Casey, *Personal Experiences,* cited (ch. 15), p. 71; Harriman and Abel, *Special Envoy,* cited (ch. 16), p. 75; telegram from Winston S. Churchill to Franklin D. Roosevelt, Aug. 4, 1941, R-C FDRL; dispatch from Winston S. Churchill to dominion prime ministers, n.d., in PRO, A6944/18/45; Nicolson, *The War Years,* cited (ch. 6), p. 162.

2. Theodore A. Wilson, *The First Summit* (Boston, 1969), p. 65; *FRUS,* 1941, I, pp. 341–343; Perkins, OHP, vol. 8, pp. 18–19; dispatch from Franklin D. Roosevelt to Winston S. Churchill, July 25, 1941, in PRO, A6654/18/45.

3. Telephone message from John G. Winant to Anthony Eden, Aug. 6, 1941, in PRO, A6942/18/45; telegram from Winston S. Churchill to Clement Attlee, Aug. 7, 1941, in *TGA,* p. 430; Edwin M. Watson, "Supplementary Notes to Roosevelt-Churchill Meeting," Sept. 8, 1941, in University of Virginia Library; telegram from Kichisaburo Nomura to Tokyo (Magic trans.), Aug. 7, 1941, in *PHA,* pt. 12, pp. 13–14.

4. Ian Jacob, quoted in Wheeler-Bennett, *Action This Day, op. cit.,* p. 207; dispatch from Commander Thompson to foreign office, Sept. 8, 1941, in PRO, PREM/4 71/1; Sherwood, pp. 350–351; Churchill's description of impression young Roosevelt made on him in *TGS,* p. 440.

5. Cadogan, p. 397; H. H. Arnold, *Global Mission* (New York, 1949), p. 252; Edwin Watson, "Supplementary Notes," *op. cit.*

6. Winston S. Churchill, speech, Aug. 24, 1941, in *NYT,* Aug. 25, 1941; *RPPC* no. 762, Aug. 19, 1941; Edwin Watson, "Supplementary Notes."

7. Sherwood, p. 273; Arnold, *op. cit.,* p. 249; J. M. Gwyer, *Grand Strategy,* 6 vols. (London, 1964), III, pp. 127, 130; Matloff and Snell, *Strategic Planning for Coalition Warfare,* cited (ch. 9), p. 55; Samuel Morison, *American Contributions to the Strategy of*

World War II (London, 1958), pp. 14–17; Pogue, *George C. Marshall,* cited (ch. 8), II, p. 144.

8. M. Watson, pp. 5–7; Matloff and Snell, *op. cit.,* p. 53; *Hansard,* 371, cols. 67–69; Butler, *Grand Strategy,* cited (ch. 6), p. 561; Arnold, p. 256; Gwyer, *op. cit.,* p. 129; Navy Hemisphere Plan No. 4 in *PHA,* pt. 5, p. 2295; telegram from Winston S. Churchill to Anthony Eden, Aug. 11, 1941, Tudor no. 33, in PRO, WP(41)203.

9. *TGA,* p. 434; Winston S. Churchill, statement in House of Commons, London, Sept. 9, 1941, in *Hansard,* 324, cols. 67–69; Sumner Welles, *Where Are We Heading?* (New York, 1946), pp. 1–19; message from Winston S. Churchill to war cabinet, Aug. 11, 1941, in *TGA,* pp. 441–442; telegrams from war cabinet to Winston S. Churchill, Aug. 11 and 12, 1941, Tudor nos. 15 and 23 and Abbey nos. 31 and 35, in PRO, WP(41)203; Woodward, II, pp. 198 ff.; telegram from Winston S. Churchill to Clement Attlee, Aug. 12, 1941, in *TGA,* p. 447.

10. Perkins, OHP, vol. 8, pp. 22, 25; Smith, Diary, cited (ch. 7), Sept. 26, 1941; Lash, *A Friend's Memoir,* cited (ch. 13), pp. 256–257.

11. Panter-Downes, *London War Notes,* cited (ch. 10), p. 167; Wheeler-Bennett, *King George VI,* cited (ch. 4), p. 529; letter from Franklin D. Roosevelt to George VI, Aug. 11, 1941, in *PL,* IV, p. 1198; minutes of meeting between Churchill and war cabinet, Aug. 19, 1941, in PRO, CAB 65 WM(41)84.

12. Winston S. Churchill, speech, Aug. 24, 1941, in *NYT,* Aug. 25, 1941; minutes of meeting of war cabinet, Aug. 25, 1941, in PRO, Annex to WM(41), minute 2; Cadogan, p. 402, Aug. 25, 1941; telegram from Jan Christiaan Smuts to war cabinet, Aug. 29, 1941, in PRO, PREM/3 476/3; telegram from Winston S. Churchill to Harry Hopkins, Aug. 29, 1941, in Sherwood, pp. 373–374; note by Harry Hopkins, Sept. 6, 1941, in Sherwood, pp. 373–374.

13. *DGFP,* XIII, no. 242, Aug. 25, 1941.

24. WARNING TO JAPAN

1. *FRUS,* 1941, I, pp. 354–356; Woodward, II, p. 145; extracts from record of meeting between Churchill and Roosevelt, Aug. 11, 1941, in PRO, Tudor nos. 19 and 15, F7995/86/23, WP(41)203.

2. Cadogan, p. 399, Aug. 11, 1941; British foreign office, "Collaboration with the United States in the Far East," Aug. 15, 1941, in PRO, F7812/86/23; comment by Anthony Eden to war cabinet, July 31, 1941, in PRO, WM(41) 76.

3. Konoye, *Memoirs,* cited (ch. 22), p. 4012; on Roosevelt's moves in 1937 see Welles, *Seven Decisions That Shaped History,* cited (ch. 7), p. 72; comment by Burton K. Wheeler in *NYT,* July 27, 1941; Gallup poll in *NYT,* Aug. 3, 1941; dispatch from Kichisaburo Nomura to Tokyo (Magic trans.), Aug. 16, 1941, in *PHA,* pt. 12, I, p. 17.

4. Dispatch from Hans Thomsen to Berlin, Aug. 27, 1941, in *DGFP,* XIII, no. 249, p. 399; *TGA,* pp. 587, 588, 589; Winston S. Churchill,

speech, London, Jan. 27, 1942, in *NYT,* Jan. 28, 1942; message from Harry Hopkins to Franklin D. Roosevelt, Feb. 21, 1942, in Hopkins, Papers, cited (ch. 7).

5. On Hull's feelings about Welles see Stimson, Aug. 19, 1941; revision of Roosevelt's warning to Japan in *FRUS,* 1941, IV, pp. 370–376; Hull, p. 1019; *PHA,* pt. 2, p. 541.

6. Francis Biddle, *In Brief Authority* (New York, 1962), pp. 164, 180; Welles, *Seven Decisions That Shaped History, op. cit.,* pp. 88–89; on Roosevelt's feelings about Hull see Sherwood, p. 428.

7. *PHA,* pt. 17, p. 1682; *ibid.,* pt. 17, exhibit no. 87, pp. 2749–2756; dispatches from Kichisaburo Nomura to Tokyo (Magic trans.), Aug. 18 and 19, 1941, in *PHA,* pt. 17, exhibit no. 124, pp. 2749–2759.

8. Dispatch from Lord Halifax to foreign office, Aug. 18, 1941, in PRO, F8621/86/23; comment by Alexander Cadogan, Aug. 25, 1941, in PRO, F8218/86/23; message from Franklin

D. Roosevelt through John G. Winant to Winston S. Churchill, Aug. 19, 1941, in *FRUS* 1941, IV, p. 580; Winston S. Churchill, radio broadcast, Aug. 24, 1941, in *FRUS*, 1941, IV, p. 394; comment by Burton K. Wheeler in *NYT*, Aug. 25, 1941.

9. Telegram from Jan Christiaan Smuts, Aug. 29, 1941, in PRO, F8261/86/23; comment by Alexander Cadogan, Aug. 25, 1941, in PRO, F8218/86/23; record of discussion between Campbell and Hull, Aug. 30, 1941, in Hull, p. 1023; dispatch from Harold Stark to Thomas Hart, Aug. 28, 1941, in *PHA*, pt. 16, p. 2451; minute by Ashley Clarke, Sept. 17, 1941, in PRO, F8621/86/23; comment by Alexander Cadogan, Oct. 7, 1941, in PRO, F8261/86/23; comment by Anthony Eden, Oct. 8, 1941, in PRO, F8621/86/23.

10. Dispatches from Eugen Ott to Berlin, Aug. 29 and 30, 1941, in *DGFP*, XIII, nos. 256 and 259, pp. 410–411, 414–415; dispatch from Eugen Ott to Berlin, Sept. 13, 1941, in *DGFP*, XIII, no. 310, pp. 490–493; *ibid.*, Sept. 20, 1941, in *DGFP*, XIII, no. 342, pp. 537–538.

11. Long, *The War Diary*, cited (ch. 7), pp. 214–215, Aug. 31, 1941; telegram from Kichisaburo Nomura to Tokyo (Magic trans.), Aug. 29, 1941, in *PHA*, pt. 12, I, pp. 20–21; Welles, *The Time for Decision*, cited (ch. 1), p. 294; Konoye, *op. cit.*, pp. 4005, 4009, 4026.

12. Dispatch from Ronald Campbell to foreign office, Oct. 6, 1941, in PRO, F10455/86/23; dispatch from Lord Halifax to foreign office, Oct. 11, 1941, in PRO, F10639/86/23; dispatch from Anthony Eden to Lord Halifax, Oct. 18, 1941, in PRO, F10885/86/23.

25. UNDECLARED WAR IN THE ATLANTIC

1. Dispatch from Winston S. Churchill to war cabinet, Aug. 19, 1941, in PRO, WM(41)84, quoted in *TGA*, p. 447; letter from Harold Stark to H. E. Kimmel, Aug. 22, 1941, in *PHA*, pt. 16, p. 2181; letter from Harold Stark to Thomas Hart, Aug. 28, 1941, in *PHA*, pt. 16, p. 2451; *FCNA*, pp. 222, 225, July 25 and Aug. 22, 1941; message from Winston S. Churchill to Harry Hopkins, Aug. 28, 1941, in PRO, WM(41)88.

2. Green Hackworth, "Extent to Which the President May Use the Navy in the Protection of American Interests," in FDRL; Franklin D. Roosevelt, radio broadcast, Sept. 1, 1941, in *PPA*, 1941, pp. 365–369; Morison, *The Battle of the Atlantic*, cited (ch. 16), pp. 81–82; Sherwood, pp. 367, 370; memorandum from Myron Taylor to Grace Tully, Sept. 2, 1941, in FDRL.

3. Telegram from Franklin D. Roosevelt to Winston S. Churchill, Sept. 5, 1941, R-C FDRL; Franklin D. Roosevelt, radio broadcast, Sept. 11, 1941, in *PPA*, 1941, pp. 384–392.

4. Memoranda from Harold Stark to Franklin D. Roosevelt, Sept. 9 and 12, 1941, in FDRL; minute from Winston S. Churchill to war cabinet, Sept. 11, 1941, in PRO, WM(41)92; letter from Harold Stark to Thomas Hart, Sept. 22, 1941, in *PHA*, pt. 16, pp. 2211–2212; *FCNA*, p. 231, Sept. 17, 1941, cited in *DGFP*, XIII, no. 304, p. 481.

5. Senate Naval Affairs Committee, *Documents on American Foreign Relations in World War II*, cited (ch. 21), IV, pp. 89–93; dispatches from Hans Thomsen to Berlin, Sept. 6, 9, and 11, 1941, in *DGFP*, XIII, nos. 282, 292, 299, pp. 454, 468, 474; comment by Gerald Nye in *NYT*, Sept. 12, 1941; Herbert Hoover, radio broadcast, in *NYT*, Sept. 17, 1941; comment by Charles McNary in *NYT*, Sept. 12, 1941; comment by Robert Wood in *NYT*, Sept. 12, 1941.

6. Comment by Francis Biddle in *NYT*, Sept. 19, 1941, and quoted in Biddle, *In Brief Authority*, cited (ch. 24), p. 219; comment by J. William Fulbright, April 14, 1971, in *Congressional Record*, p. 10355; Arthur M. Schlesinger, Jr., *The Imperial Presidency* (Boston, 1973), p. 112; Morison, *The Battle of the Atlantic, op. cit.*, pp. 79–80; U.S. Navy, "Suggested Statement on the *Greer* Incident for Use by the President," Sept. 9, 1941, in FDRL; comment by Arthur Krock in *NYT*, Oct. 16, 1941; comment by J. William Fulbright, April 14, 1971, in *Congressional Record*, p. 10355.

7. Letter from Winston S. Churchill to Jan Christiaan Smuts, Sept. 14, 1941, in *TGA*, p.

517; dispatch from Lord Halifax to Winston S. Churchill, Oct. 11, 1941, in PRO, PREM/4 27/9; memorandum from German high command to Adolf Hitler, Aug. 27, 1941, in *DGFP*, XIII, no. 265, p. 422; comment by Erwin Rommel, quoted in Agar, *The Darkest Year, Britain Alone*, cited (ch. 12), p. 82.

8. Telegram from Winston S. Churchill to Franklin D. Roosevelt, Sept. 1, 1941, R-C FDRL; telegram from Franklin D. Roosevelt to Winston S. Churchill, Sept. 5, 1941, R-C FDRL; memorandum from George C. Marshall to Harold Stark, Sept. 10, 1941, in M. Watson, p. 350; Stimson, Sept. 29 and Oct. 3, 6, 9, and 10, 1941; Kennedy, *The Business of War*, cited (ch. 17), p. 179; Bryant, *The Turn of the Tide*, cited (ch. 8), p. 213; letter from Lord Halifax to Winston S. Churchill, Oct. 11, 1941, in PRO, PREM/4 27/9.

9. Letter from Franklin D. Roosevelt to Winston S. Churchill, Oct. 15, 1941, in *PL*, IV, p. 1223; minute from Winston S. Churchill to Lord Ismay, Oct. 28, 1941, in PRO, PREM/3 439/1; dispatch from Winston S. Churchill to Franklin D. Roosevelt, Oct. 20, 1941, in *TGA*, pp. 544–548; dispatch from Franklin D. Roosevelt to Winston S. Churchill, Oct. 7, 1941, R-C FDRL; dispatch from Winston S. Churchill to Franklin D. Roosevelt, Oct. 9, 1941, R-C FDRL.

10. Memorandum from Harold Stark to Cordell Hull, Oct. 8, 1941, in *PHA*, pt. 16, pp. 2216–2219; report from Sumner Welles to Franklin D. Roosevelt, July 9, 1941, in FDRL; poll on Neutrality Act revision in *NYT*, Oct. 19, 1941; remarks by Winston S. Churchill to House in *NYT*, Sept. 30, 1941; Franklin D. Roosevelt, speech to Commonwealth Club, Sept. 23, 1932, in *PPA*, 1932, pp. 742–756; letter from Felix Frankfurter to Walter Lippmann, Oct. 13, 1932, in Freedman, *Roosevelt and Frankfurter*, cited (ch. 10), p. 89.

11. Franklin D. Roosevelt, radio broadcast, Oct. 27, 1941, in *PPA*, 1941, pp. 438–445; *RPPC*, no. 779, Oct. 28, 1941; comment by William H. Taft, Nov. 3, 1941, in *Congressional Record*, vol. 87, pp. 8430–8433; *PHA*, pt. 5, p. 2292.

12. *FCNA*, p. 239, Nov. 13, 1941; telegram from from German foreign office, Nov. 21, 1941, in *DGFP*, XIII, no. 470, p. 782, footnote 7; Wheeler-Bennett, *King George VI*, cited (ch. 4), p. 531; message from Jan Christiaan Smuts to Winston S. Churchill, Nov. 4, 1941, in PRO, PREM/3 476/3; letter from Winston S. Churchill to Jan Christiaan Smuts, Nov. 8, 1941, in PRO, PREM/3 476/3.

26. NO STRINGS ON RUSSIAN AID

1. Kennedy, *The Business of War*, cited (ch. 17), pp. 171–172, Oct. 4, 1941; George C. Marshall and Harold Stark, "Joint Board Estimate," Sept. 11, 1941, in Sherwood, p. 417; Winston S. Churchill, statement in House, in *Hansard*, 374, col. 77; Harriman and Abel, *Special Envoy*, cited (ch. 16), p. 74.

2. Message from Franklin D. Roosevelt and Winston S. Churchill to Joseph Stalin, Aug. 12, 1941, in *TGA*, pp. 444–445; Instructions from Winston S. Churchill to Lord Beaverbrook,

Aug. 30, 1941, in *TGA*, p. 413; Maisky, pp. 185–188; telegram from Joseph Stalin to Winston S. Churchill, Sept. 3, 1941, in Stalin, *Correspondence*, cited (ch. 21), pp. 20–22; Maisky, pp. 189–194; *TGA*, pp. 455–458.

3. Telegram from Winston S. Churchill to Joseph Stalin, Sept. 4, 1941, in *TGA*, pp. 458–460; telegram from Winston S. Churchill to Franklin D. Roosevelt, Sept. 5, 1941, in *TGA*, p. 460; Maisky, p. 191.

4. George Kennan, *Russia and the West under*

Lenin and Stalin (Boston, 1960), pp. 362–363; message from Joseph Stalin to Winston S. Churchill, Sept. 13, 1941, in Stalin, *op. cit.*, pp. 24–25; comment by Winston S. Churchill in *TGA*, p. 463.

5. Dispatch from Stafford Cripps to Winston S. Churchill, Sept. 3, 1941, in Gwyer, *Grand Strategy*, cited (ch. 23), III, p. 199; telegram from Winston S. Churchill to Joseph Stalin, Sept. 4, 1941, in *TGA*, pp. 458–460; dispatch from Winston S. Churchill to Stafford Cripps, Sept. 5, 1941, in *TGA*, pp. 460–462; warning from George C. Marshall to Henry Stimson, in M. Watson, pp. 329, 330; dispatch from Harry Hopkins to John G. Winant, Sept. 9, 1941, in *FRUS*, 1941, I, pp. 827–830; Maisky, p. 194; conference between Constantine Oumansky and Franklin D. Roosevelt in *FRUS*, 1941, I, pp. 832–834; letter from Franklin D. Roosevelt to Pius XII, Sept. 3, 1941, in *PL*, IV, pp. 1204–1205; statement by John T. McNichols in *Congressional Record*, 1941, p. A5049.

6. On preliminary discussions between the Harriman and Beaverbrook groups in London see Gwyer, *op. cit.*, III, pp. 151–153; Lee, *The London Journals*, cited (ch. 12), p. 400, Sept. 15, 1941; Harriman and Abel, *op. cit.*, pp. 78–79; Dean Acheson, *Present at the Creation* (New York, 1969), p. 34; Maisky, p. 188.

7. Telegram from Winston S. Churchill to Harry Hopkins, Sept. 25, 1941, in Hopkins, Papers, cited (ch. 7); telegram from Harry Hopkins to Winston S. Churchill, Sept. 29, 1941, in Hopkins, Papers, *op. cit.*; telegram from Franklin D. Roosevelt to Winston S. Churchill, Sept. 17, 1941, R-C FDRL; telegram from Winston S. Churchill to Franklin D. Roosevelt, Sept. 22, 1941, R-C FDRL; Harry C. Thompson and Linda Mayo, *The Ordnance Department—Procurement and Supply* (Washington, D.C., 1960), p. 232; Stimson, Sept. 17, 1941; message from Claude Auchinleck, n.d., in Churchill folder, FDRL.

8. Harriman and Abel, pp. 84–85; telegram from Laurence Steinhardt to Cordell Hull, Sept. 25, 1941, in *FRUS*, 1941, I, p. 834; *FRUS*, 1941, I, pp. 836–837; statement by Charles Thayer quoted in Harriman and Abel, p. 85; Taylor, *Beaverbrook*, cited (ch. 6), p. 487; on Beaverbrook's view of Stalin see Sherwood, p. 391; telegram from Lord Beaverbrook to Winston S. Churchill, Oct. 8, 1941, in Taylor, *op. cit.*, p. 491; Ciechanowski, *Defeat in Victory*, cited (ch. 16), pp. 30, 62; William H. Standley and Arthur A. Ageton, *Admiral Ambassador to Russia* (Chicago, 1955), p. 63.

9. Davies, *Mission to Moscow*, cited (ch. 21), pp. 280, 356–357, 509–510; Richard Ullmann, "The Davies Mission and United States–Soviet Relations, 1937–1941," *World Politics*, IX (1956); Bohlen, *Witness to History*, cited (ch.

20), p. 124; Roosevelt's copy of *Mission to Moscow* in FDRL; comment by William C. Bullitt in *NYT*, Aug. 15, 1941.

10. Beaverbrook's account of final meeting with Stalin in Sherwood, p. 389; Ismay, *The Memoirs*, cited (ch. 6), pp. 231–232; Harriman and Abel, pp. 90–91; Taylor, p. 488; PRO, N6312/3/38.

11. On the Kremlin banquet see Harriman and Abel, pp. 98–101; on Roosevelt's dissatisfaction with Soviet concessions on religious question see Harriman and Abel, pp. 103–104; William C. Bullitt, "How We Won the War and Lost the Peace," *Life*, XXV (Sept. 6, 1948), 83–97; on Cripps's views see Harriman and Abel, p. 95; dispatch from John G. Winant to Cordell Hull, Sept. 9, 1941; Winston S. Churchill, address to the House of Commons, London, Sept. 9, 1941, quoted in Hull, p. 1484; statement by Mahatma Gandhi in *NYT*, Oct. 12, 1941.

12. On Harriman's views on Beaverbrook see Taylor, p. 490; telegram from Lord Beaverbrook to Winston S. Churchill, Oct. 4, 1941, in *TGA*, p. 470; telegram from Joseph Stalin to Winston S. Churchill, Oct. 3, 1941, in Stalin, p. 29; telegram from Winston S. Churchill to Lord Beaverbrook, Oct. 3, 1941, in *TGA*, pp. 470–471; telegram from Winston S. Churchill to Franklin D. Roosevelt, Oct. 5, 1941, R-C FDRL; telegram from Franklin D. Roosevelt to Winston S. Churchill, Oct. 8, 1941, R-C FDRL.

13. Warlimont, *Inside Hitler's Headquarters*, cited (ch. 1), p. 189; Shirer, pp. 1126–1128; memorandum from Lord Beaverbrook to war cabinet, Oct. 19, 1941, in Taylor, p. 495; telegram from Stafford Cripps to foreign office, Oct. 25, 1941, in Woodward, II, p. 42; on Mrs. Churchill's views on aiding the Russians see *TGA*, p. 474; telegram from Winston S. Churchill to Claude Auchinleck, Oct. 18, 1941, in *TGA*, p. 543; letter from Winston S. Churchill to Franklin D. Roosevelt, Oct. 20, 1941, in *TGA*, pp. 544–548; telegram from Winston S. Churchill to Stafford Cripps, Oct. 28, 1941, in *TGA*, pp. 472–474.

14. Eden, p. 321, Oct. 10, 1941; Woodward, II, pp. 45–46; message from Winston S. Churchill to Joseph Stalin, Nov. 4, 1941, in *TGA*, pp. 527–528; Eden, p. 324, Nov. 4, 1941; Maisky, pp. 201–202; message from Joseph Stalin to Winston S. Churchill, Nov. 8, 1941, in Stalin, pp. 33–34; report from "Jock" Whitney to William J. Donovan, Nov. 12, 1941, in FDRL; Eden, p. 326, Nov. 14, 1941; message from Winston S. Churchill to Joseph Stalin, Nov. 21, 1941, in *TGA*, pp. 531–532; message from Joseph Stalin to Winston S. Churchill, Nov. 23, 1941, in Stalin, pp. 35–36; Maisky, p. 204.

15. MPD, Oct. 28, 1941; John R. Deane, *The Strange Alliance* (New York, 1947), p. 91.

27. "NOT ENOUGH NAVY TO GO ROUND"

1. Dispatch from Harold Stark to fleet commanders, Oct. 16, 1941, in *PHA*, pt. 14, exhibit no. 37, p. 1402; Stimson, Oct. 16, 1941; message from G-2 to George C. Marshall, Oct. 17, 1941, in *PHA*, pt. 14, exhibit no. 33, p. 1359; telegram from Anthony Eden to Lord Halifax, Oct. 18, 1941, in PRO, F10885/86/23.

2. Stimson, Oct. 21, 1941; dispatch from Lord Halifax to foreign office, Oct. 18, 1941, in PRO, F10960/86/23; minute by Winston S. Churchill, Oct. 19, 1941, in PRO, F10960/86/23; letter from Harold Stark to H. E. Kimmel, Oct. 17, 1941, in *PHA*, pt. 16, p. 2214; cable from Kichisaburo Nomura to Shigenori Togo (Magic trans.), Oct. 20, 1941, in *PHA*, pt. 12, I, p. 80; message from Shigenori Togo to Kichisaburo Nomura (Magic trans.), Oct. 21, 1941, in *PHA*, pt. 12, I, no. 698, p. 81; dispatch from Kaname Wakasugi to Tokyo (Magic trans.), Oct. 28, 1941, in *PHA*, pt. 12, I, no. 1008. pp. 86–88.

3. Stimson, Oct. 28, 1941; memorandum from Harry Hopkins, Oct. 30, 1941, in Hopkins, Papers, cited (ch. 7); Shigenori Togo, *The Cause of Japan* (New York, 1956), p. 52; Herbert Feis, *The Road to Pearl Harbor* (Princeton, 1950), p. 293; message from

Chiang Kai-shek to Franklin D. Roosevelt, Nov. 2, 1941, in *FRUS*, 1941, V, p. 570; message from Winston S. Churchill to Franklin D. Roosevelt, Nov. 2, 1941, R-C FDRL; message from Franklin D. Roosevelt to Winston S. Churchill, Nov. 7, 1941, R-C FDRL.

4. Memorandum from George C. Marshall and Harold Stark to Franklin D. Roosevelt, Nov. 5, 1941, in PHA, pt. 2, pp. 648–649; dispatches from Tokyo to Kichisaburo Nomura (Magic trans.), Nov. 2, 4, and 5, 1941, in *PHA*, pt. 12, I, nos. 722, 725, 726, 736, pp. 90, 92, 94, 100.

5. Telegram from Robert Craigie to foreign office, Nov. 2, 1941, in PRO, F11672/86/23; minute by foreign office, Nov. 3, 1941, in PRO, F11672/86/23; comment by Alexander Cadogan, Nov. 6, 1941, in PRO, F11672/86/23.

6. Stimson, Nov. 7, 1941; Perkins, OHP, vol. 8, pp. 42, 46 (Perkins, who was interviewed for the OHP after the war, remembered the president as having polled the cabinet on Dec. 5, but Stimson, who made his entries at the time, placed it on Nov. 7, 1941); letter from Harold Stark to H. E. Kimmel, Nov. 7, 1941, in *PHA*, pt. 16, exhibit no. 106, p. 2219; Tojo's testimony before the Far Eastern military tribunal

in Feis, *op. cit.*, pp. 293, 296; Robert J. C. Butow, *Tojo and the Coming of the War* (Princeton, 1961), p. 333.

7. Stimson, Nov. 6, 1941; on Roosevelt's meeting with Nomura see *FRUS*, Japan, 1931–1941, II, p. 717; dispatch from Kichisaburo Nomura to Tokyo (Magic trans.), Nov. 10, 1941, in *PHA*, pt. 12, I, no. 1070, p. 115; dispatch from Tokyo to Kichisaburo Nomura (Magic trans.), Nov. 11, 1941, in *PHA*, pt. 12, I, no. 762, p. 116; dispatch from Kichisaburo Nomura to Tokyo (Magic trans.), Nov. 10, 1941, in *PHA*, pt. 12, I, no. 1066, p. 111; *ibid.*, Nov. 14, 1941, in *PHA*, pt. 12, I, no. 1090, p. 127; dispatch from Tokyo to Kichisaburo Nomura (Magic trans.), Nov. 16, 1941, in *PHA*, pt. 12, I, no. 775, p. 130; *ibid.*, Nov. 15, 1941, in *PHA*, pt. 12, circular no. 2330, p. 137.

8. Cable from "Jock" Whitney to William J. Donovan, Nov. 13, 1941, in FDRL; on the meeting between Roosevelt and Kurusu see dispatches from Kichisaburo Nomura to Tokyo (Magic trans.), Nov. 18 and 19, 1941, in *PHA*, pt. 12, nos. 1133, 1134, pp. 150, 152; dispatch from Harold Stark to H. E. Kimmel, Nov. 7, 1941, in *PHA*, pt. 16, no. 106, p. 2219; dispatch from H. E. Kimmel to Harold Stark, Nov. 15, 1941, in *PHA*, pt. 16, exhibit no. 106, p. 2252; dispatch from Harold Stark to H. E. Kimmel, Nov. 25, 1941, in *PHA*, pt. 5, p. 2104; Sherwood, p. 420.

9. Harry Dexter White, "An Approach to the Problems of Eliminating Tension with Japan and Insuring Defeat of Germany," Nov. 17, 1941, transmitted by Morgenthau to Hull with statement that it was also being sent to Roosevelt, Nov. 18, 1941, in *FRUS*, 1941, IV, pp. 606–613; telegram from Ronald Campbell to foreign office, Nov. 18, 1941, in PRO, F12475/86/23; minute by Alexander Cadogan, Nov. 20, 1941, in PRO, F12475/86/23; dispatch from foreign office to Lord Halifax, Nov. 21, 1941, in PRO, F14304/86/23.

10. Instructions from Tokyo to Saburo Kurusu and Kichisaburo Nomura (Magic trans.), Nov. 20, 1941, in *PHA*, pt. 12, I, no. 806, p. 160; testimony of Cordell Hull in *PHA*, pt. 2, p. 554; Ickes, III, pp. 649–650, Nov. 23, 1941; memorandum from Franklin D. Roosevelt to Cordell Hull, n.d., in *FRUS*, 1941, IV, p. 626.

11. Martin Gilbert, *Winston S. Churchill, 1916–1922* (Boston, 1975), IV, p. 6; minute from Winston S. Churchill to Anthony Eden, Nov.

23, 1941, in PRO, F12813/86/23; message from Franklin D. Roosevelt to Winston S. Churchill, Nov. 24, 1941, R-C FDRL; reaction of Harold Stark and Leonard T. Gerow to *modus vivendi* proposal in *PHA*, pt. 9, p. 1103.

12. Dispatches from Tokyo to Kichisaburo Nomura (Magic trans.), Nov. 22 and 24, 1941, in *PHA*, pt. 12, I, nos. 812, 821, pp. 165, 172; dispatch from Harold Stark to fleet commanders, Nov. 24, 1941, in *PHA*, pt. 15, p. 1328; Stimson, Nov. 25, 1941; letter from Harold Stark to H. E. Kimmel, Nov. 25, 1941, in *PHA*, pt. 16, no. 106, p. 2223; telegram from Owen Lattimore to Lauchlin Currie, Nov. 25, 1941, in *FRUS*, 1941, IV, p. 652; Blum, *Roosevelt and Morgenthau*, cited (ch. 14), pp. 415–416; Ickes, III, p. 655, Nov. 30, 1941.

13. Comments by Cordell Hull, in *PHA*, pt. 14, pp. 1494 ff.; telegram from Winston S. Churchill to Franklin D. Roosevelt, Nov. 26, 1941, R-C FDRL; on Hornbeck's views on the Japanese see Berle, *Navigating the Rapids*, cited (ch. 1), pp. 338, 379; memorandum from Stanley Hornbeck, Nov. 27, 1941, in *PHA*, pt. 5, p. 2089; Stimson, Nov. 25 and 26, 1941; dispatch from Cordell Hull to Joseph C. Grew, Nov. 27, 1941, in *PHA*, pt. 4, p. 1708.

14. Dispatch from George C. Marshall to theater commanders, Nov. 27, 1941, in *PHA*, pt. 15, exhibit no. 52, p. 1328; dispatch from Harold Stark to fleet commanders, Nov. 27, 1941, in *PHA*, pt. 15, exhibit no. 52, p. 1328; Stevenson, *A Man Called Intrepid*, cited (ch. 8), p. 299; telegram from Franklin D. Roosevelt to Francis Sayre, Nov. 26, 1941, in *PHA*, pt. 11, p. 5214; telephone conversation between Tokyo and Kichisaburo Nomura and Saburo Kurusu (Magic trans.), Nov. 27, 1941, in *PHA*, pt. 12, I, pp. 188–189; telegram from Tokyo to Kichisaburo Nomura (Magic trans.), Nov. 28, 1941, in *PHA*, pt. 12, no. 844, p. 195.

15. On Roosevelt's meeting with Nomura and Kurusu, Nov. 28, 1941, see *FRUS*, Japan, 1931–1941, II, pp. 770–772; on war-cabinet meeting see Stimson, Nov. 28, 1941; exchanges between Hiroshi Oshima and Tokyo (Magic trans.), Nov. 29 and 30, 1941, in *PHA*, pt. 12, nos. 985, 1393, pp. 204, 200; dispatch from Winston S. Churchill to Franklin D. Roosevelt, Nov. 30, 1941, R-C FDRL.

28. ALL IN THE SAME BOAT

1. Telegram from Lord Halifax to foreign office, Dec. 1, 1941, in PRO, F13114/86/23; comment by Anthony Eden to war cabinet, Dec. 2, 1941, in PRO, WP(41)296; Welles's off-the-record talk reported in dispatch from Lord Halifax to foreign office, Dec. 1, 1941, in PRO, F13115/86/23.

2. Charles A. Lindbergh, speech, Fort Wayne, Ind., in *NYT*, Oct. 4, 1941; Biddle, *In Brief Authority*, cited (ch. 24), p. 189; telegram from Hans Thomsen to Berlin, Nov. 13, 1941, in *DGFP*, XIII, no. 465, p. 772; Stevenson, *A Man Called Intrepid*, cited (ch. 8), pp. 298–300; Albert C. Wedemeyer, *Wedemeyer Reports* (New York, 1958), chs. 2, 3, pp. 15 ff.; Stimson, Dec. 5, 1941; Ickes, III, p. 660.

3. Comment by Henry Stimson in *PHA*, pt. 11, pp. 5415 ff.; Stimson, Nov. 25, 1941; Ickes, III, p. 649, Nov. 23, 1941; Stimson, Nov. 28 and Dec. 1, 1941; comment by Sumner Welles in *PHA*, pt. 2, p. 541.

4. Nobutaka Ike, ed., *Japan's Decision for War* (Stanford, 1967), pp. 262 ff.; Butow, *Tojo and the Coming of the War*, cited (ch. 27), p. 370; *PHA*, pt. 10, p. 4840, cited in Wohlstetter, *Pearl Harbor: Warning and Decision*, cited (ch. 16), pp. 41–45; message from U.S. naval operations, Dec. 3, 1941, in *PHA*, pt. 14, exhibit no. 37, p. 1408.

5. Gwyer, *Grand Strategy*, cited (ch. 23), III, pp. 291, 293; dispatch from Lord Halifax to Anthony Eden, Dec. 2, 1941, in PRO, F13136/86/23; memorandum by Sumner Welles, Dec. 2, 1941, in *FRUS*, Japan, 1931–1941, II, pp. 778–779; telegram from Eugen Ott to Berlin,

Nov. 23, 1941, in *DGFP*, XIII, no. 492, p. 813; dispatch from Winston S. Churchill to Anthony Eden, Dec. 2, 1941, in *TGA*, p. 601.

6. Dispatch from Lord Halifax to foreign office, Dec. 1, 1941, in PRO, F13114/86/23; dispatch from foreign office to Lord Halifax, Dec. 3, 1941, in PRO, F13114/86/23; dispatch from Lord Halifax to foreign office, Dec. 4, 1941, in PRO, F13114/86/23.

7. Message from Franklin D. Roosevelt to Marvin McIntyre, Dec. 2, 1941, in *PL*, IV, p. 1248; John Toland, *The Rising Sun* (New York, 1970), pp. 186–187; comment by Franklin D. Roosevelt to Henry Morgenthau, Dec. 3, 1941, in Blum, *Roosevelt and Morgenthau*, cited (ch. 14), p. 421; Coit, *Mr. Baruch*, cited (ch. 1), p. 489; dispatch from Lord Halifax to foreign office, Dec. 5, 1941, in PRO, F13280/86/23; Hull, p. 1093.

8. Perkins, OHP, vol. 8, p. 49; Cadogan, p. 416, Dec. 6, 1941; Stimson, Dec. 6, 1941; G-2, "Estimate of the Situation," Dec. 5, 1941, in *PHA*, pt. 14, exhibit no. 33, p. 1377; dispatch from Harold Stark to H. E. Kimmel, Dec. 6, 1941, in *PHA*, pt. 4, exhibit no. 37, p. 1408; Wohlstetter, *op. cit.*, p. 388; Bryant, *The Turn of the Tide*, cited (ch. 8), p. 225; comment by John Beardall in *PHA*, pt. 11, p. 5284; Smith, Diary, cited (ch. 7), Dec. 6, 1941.

9. Message from Franklin D. Roosevelt to Hirohito, Dec. 6, 1941, in *PPA*, 1941, pp. 511–513; *PHA*, pt. 11, p. 5166; Lash, *Eleanor and Franklin*, cited (ch. 2), p. 646; testimony by L. L. Schulz on his delivery of final Japanese message to White House on Dec. 6, 1941, in *PHA*, pt. 10, pp. 4662–4663.

10. Stimson, Dec. 7 and Nov. 28, 1941; Sherwood, p. 428; Ickes, III, p. 664; Blum, *op. cit.*, p. 425; Perkins, OHP, vol. 8, pp. 70, 87–88.

11. Dispatch from Cordell Hull to John G. Winant, Dec. 5, 1941, in *PHA*, pt. 19, exhibit no. 166, pp. 3648–3651; Winant, *Letter from Grosvenor Square*, cited (ch. 19), pp. 274 ff.; Gerald Pawle, *The War and Colonel Warden* (New York, 1963), p. 134; Eden, p. 331; Bryant, *op. cit.*, p. 282; *TGA*, pp. 606–607, 620; Franklin D. Roosevelt, speech to Congress, Washington, D.C., Dec. 8, 1941, in *PPA*, 1941, p. 515; telegram from Lord Halifax to foreign office, Dec. 8, 1941, in PRO, A9985/18/45; Ciano, p. 416; conversation between Joachim von Ribbentrop and Hiroshi Oshima, Dec. 8, 1941, in *DGFP*, XIII, no. 567, p. 991; telegram from Hiroshi Oshima to Tokyo (Magic trans.), Dec. 8, 1941, *ibid.;* telegram from Lord Halifax to foreign office, Dec. 11, 1941, in PRO, A10104/10055/45; minute by T. North Whitehead, Dec. 12, 1941, in PRO, A10104/10055/45; *PPA*, 1941, Fireside Chat, Dec. 9, 1941, pp. 522–530; *Hitler's Secret Conversations, 1941–1944* (New York, 1953), p. 396, May 17, 1942.

12. Message from George VI to Franklin D. Roosevelt, Dec. 8, 1941, in PRO, A10242/101/45; message from Franklin D. Roosevelt to George VI, Dec. 11, 1941.

Index